# THOMAS HARDY IN CONTEXT

This collection covers the range of Thomas Hardy's works and their social and intellectual contexts, providing a comprehensive introduction to Hardy's life and times. Featuring short, lively contributions from forty-four international scholars, the volume explores the processes by which Hardy the man became Hardy the published writer; the changing critical responses to his work; his response to the social and political challenges of his time; his engagement with contemporary intellectual debate; and his legacy in the twentieth century and after. Emphasizing the subtle and ongoing interaction between Hardy's life, his creative achievement, and the unique historical moment, the collection also examines Hardy's relationship to such issues as class, education, folklore, archaeology and anthropology, evolution, marriage and masculinity, empire, and the arts. A valuable contextual reference for scholars of Victorian and modernist literature, the collection will also prove accessible for the general reader of Hardy.

Phillip Mallett is Senior Lecturer in English at the University of St Andrews. He has edited a number of collections of essays, including *Satire, Kipling Considered, Thomas Hardy: Texts and Contexts*, and *The Achievement of Thomas Hardy*, as well as critical editions of both *The Return of the Native* and *The Mayor of Casterbridge*. His book, *Rudyard Kipling: A Literary Life*, was published in 2003.

# THOMAS HARDY IN CONTEXT

Edited by

## Phillip Mallett
*University of St Andrews, Scotland*

CAMBRIDGE
UNIVERSITY PRESS

# CAMBRIDGE
## UNIVERSITY PRESS

University Printing House, Cambridge CB2 8BS, United Kingdom

Cambridge University Press is part of the University of Cambridge.

It furthers the University's mission by disseminating knowledge in the pursuit of education, learning and research at the highest international levels of excellence.

www.cambridge.org
Information on this title: www.cambridge.org/9781107454217

© Cambridge University Press 2013

First published 2013
First paperback edition 2015

A catalogue record for this publication is available from the British Library

Library of Congress Cataloguing in Publication data
Thomas Hardy in context / [edited by] Phillip Mallett.
p.  cm.
Includes bibliographical references and index.
ISBN 978-0-521-19648-2 (hardback)
1.  Hardy, Thomas, 1840–1928 – Criticism and interpretation.
I.  Mallett, Phillip, 1946–
PR4754.T494   2012
823'.8–dc23       2012012500

ISBN 978-0-521-19648-2 Hardback
ISBN 978-1-107-45421-7 Paperback

# CONTENTS

# LIST OF ILLUSTRATIONS

# NOTES ON CONTRIBUTORS

DAVID AMIGONI is Professor of Victorian Literature at the University of Keele. He is the author of *Colonies, Cults and Evolution: Literature, Science and Culture in Nineteenth-Century Writing*, and coeditor of *Life-Writing and Victorian Culture*.

MARK ASQUITH teaches at Trinity School, Croydon. In addition to articles and chapters on Hardy and on Wagner, he is the author of *Thomas Hardy, Metaphysics and Music*, and most recently of *Annie Proulx's 'Brokeback Mountain' and 'Postcards'*.

JANE BOWNAS is Head of Science at a College of Further Education. Her work on Hardy includes articles on '"The Very End of the World": The Colonisations of Casterbridge' and 'Exploration and Post-Darwinian Anxiety in Thomas Hardy's *Two on a Tower*'; her current research is on the colonisers and the colonised in Hardy's work.

ADELENE BUCKLAND is Lecturer in Literature at the University of East Anglia. Her work includes *Pictures in the Fire: The Dickensian Hearth and the Concepts of History*, and *Novel Science: Fiction and the Geological Imagination* (forthcoming).

CAROLYN BURDETT is Senior Lecturer in English at Birkbeck, University of London. Her publications include *Olive Schreiner and the Progress of Feminism: Evolution, Gender, Empire*, and two coedited collections: 'Eugenics Old and New' for the journal *New Formations* (with Angelique Richardson) and *The Victorian Supernatural* (with Nicola Brown and Pamela Thurschwel). Her current research focuses on the emergence of the term 'empathy' at the beginning of the twentieth century.

PAMELA DALZIEL is Distinguished University Scholar at the University of British Columbia. She is the editor of *Thomas Hardy: The Excluded and Collaborative Stories* and the Penguin edition of *A Pair of Blue Eyes*, and (with Michael Millgate) of *Thomas Hardy's 'Studies, Specimens &c.'* and *Thomas Hardy's 'Poetical Matter' Notebook*. Her current work is a study of *Visual Hardy: Representing Gender and Genre in the Illustrated Novel*.

CHRISTINE DEVINE is Assistant Professor of English at the University of Louisiana at Lafayette. In addition to articles and chapters on Gissing, Henry James, and George Eliot, she is the author of *Class in Turn-of-the-Century Novels of Gissing, James, Hardy and Wells*. She is currently writing on Victorian travellers to the United States.

TIM DOLIN is Associate Professor in the School of Media, Culture and Creative Arts at Curtin University of Technology in Perth, Western Australia. He is the author of *Thomas Hardy* and *George Eliot*, and the editor of three of Hardy's novels for Penguin, including *Tess of the d'Urbervilles*, and with Peter Widdowson is coeditor of *Thomas Hardy and Contemporary Literary Studies*.

ROGER EBBATSON is Emeritus Professor at the University of Worcester. His many publications include *The Evolutionary Self: Hardy, Forster, Lawrence*; *Hardy: The Margin of the Unexpressed*; *An Imaginary England: Nation, Landscape and Literature, 1840–1920*; and *Heidegger's Bicycle: Interfering with Victorian Texts*.

TRISH FERGUSON is Lecturer in English at Liverpool Hope University. She has written a number of articles on Hardy, the law, and popular culture and a monograph, *Thomas Hardy's Legal Fictions* (forthcoming).

SHANYN FISKE is Assistant Professor of English at Rutgers University Camden. As well as writing articles on Dickens, Charlotte Brontë, and Jane Harrison, she is the author of *Heretical Hellenism: Women Writers, Ancient Greece, and the Victorian Popular Imagination*. Her current project is a study of literary relations between England and China in the late nineteenth and early twentieth centuries.

SIMON GATRELL is Professor of English at the University of Georgia. His work on Hardy includes *Hardy the Creator: A Textual Biography*, *Thomas Hardy and the Proper Study of Mankind*, and *Thomas Hardy's Vision of Wessex*. He coedited the Clarendon Press edition of *Tess of the d'Urbervilles* (with Juliet Grindle) and is General Editor of the Oxford World's Classics edition of Hardy's novels.

SOPHIE GILMARTIN is Reader in Nineteenth-Century Literature at Royal Holloway College, University of London. She is the author of *Ancestry and Narrative in Nineteenth-Century British Literature: Blood Relations from Edgeworth to Hardy*, and with Rod Mengham of *Thomas Hardy's Shorter Fiction: A Critical Study*. Her most recent work is *Letters from the Sea: Literature, Navigation and Identity in the Writings of Nineteenth Century Maritime Women*.

WILLIAM GREENSLADE is Professor of English at the University of the West of England. He is the author of *Degeneration, Culture and the Novel 1880–1940* and editor of *Thomas Hardy's 'Facts' Notebook: A Critical Edition*, as well as coeditor (with Terence Rogers) of *Grant Allen: Literature and Cultural Politics at the Fin de Siècle*.

ANN HEILMANN is Professor of English at the School of English, Communication and Philosophy at the University of Cardiff. Her many publications include monographs on *New Woman Fiction: Women Writing First-Wave Feminism*; *New Woman Strategies: Sarah Grand, Olive Schreiner, Mona Caird*; and with Mark Llewellyn *Neo-Victorianism: The Victorians in the Twenty-First Century, 1999–2009*. Her current work focuses on the poetry and prose of George Moore.

MICHAEL HERBERT is Senior Lecturer in English at the University of St Andrews. His various publications include studies of P. N. Furbank and T. S. Eliot, as well as scholarly editions of Lawrence's *The Virgin and the Gipsy and Other Stories* and Woolf's

*The Waves* (with Susan Sellers), and of *D. H. Lawrence: Selected Critical Writings* for Oxford World's Classics.

JOHN HUGHES is Reader in Nineteenth-Century English Literature at the University of Gloucestershire. His publications include *Lines of Flight* and *'Ecstatic Sound': Music and Individuality in the Work of Thomas Hardy*, as well as articles and chapters on nineteenth- and twentieth-century writers and philosophers.

RENA JACKSON is a freelance copy editor and proofreader, whose research and publications have concentrated on hybridity and migrancy in Hardy and Naipaul.

ELIZABETH LANGLAND is University Vice-President and Dean at Arizona State University. Her many publications include a coedited collection of essays, *Out of Bounds: Male Writers and Gender(ed) Criticism* (with Laura Claridge), *Nobody's Angels: Middle-Class Women and Domestic Ideology in Victorian Culture*, and *Telling Tales: Gender and Narrative Form in Victorian Literature and Culture*.

SARAH E. MAIER is Associate Professor of English and Comparative Literature in the Department of Humanities and Languages at the University of New Brunswick Saint John. Her published work includes an edition of *Tess of the d'Urbervilles* for Broadview Press, and most recently Bram Stoker's *The Lady of the Shroud*.

PHILLIP MALLETT is Senior Lecturer in English at the University of St Andrews and editor of the *Thomas Hardy Journal*. His publications include *Rudyard Kipling: A Literary Life*; a number of edited collections of essays, including *Palgrave Advances in Thomas Hardy Studies*; and critical editions of *The Return of the Native* and *The Mayor of Casterbridge*. He is currently working on a study of Anglo-Indian women novelists in the period 1880–1935.

FRANCESCO MARRONI is Professor of English at the Gabriele d'Annunzio University of Pescara-Chieti and Director of the Centre for Victorian and Edwardian Studies. He has published widely on Hardy and on other Victorian writers, including a monograph, *La Poesia di Thomas Hardy*, and an edited collection of essays (with Norman Page), *Thomas Hardy*. His most recent book is *Victorian Disharmonies: A Reconsideration of Nineteenth-Century English Fiction*.

JANE MATTISSON teaches in Sweden. She is the author of *Knowledge and Survival in the Novels of Thomas Hardy*, published by Lund Studies in English in 2000.

ANDREW NASH is Senior Lecturer in English at the University of Reading, where his main interests are in book and publishing history, and in Scottish literature. He is the author of *Kailyard and Scottish Literature*, coeditor with Simon Eliot and Ian Willison of *Literary Cultures and the Material Book*, and editor of *The Culture of Collected Editions*.

K. M. NEWTON is Emeritus Professor of English at the University of Dundee. His major publications include *George Eliot: Romantic Humanist*; *Interpreting the Text: A Critical Introduction to the Theory and Practice of Literary Interpretation*; *George Eliot, Judaism and the Novels: Jewish Myth and Mysticism* (with Saleel Nurbhai); and *Modern Literature and the Tragic*.

FRANCIS O'GORMAN is Professor of English Literature at the University of Leeds. Among his many books are *John Ruskin*, *Late Ruskin: New Contexts*, *Ruskin and Gender* (edited with Dinah Birch), *Blackwell's Critical Guide to the Victorian Novel*, *The Victorians and the Eighteenth Century: Reassessing the Tradition* (edited with Katherine Turner), and an edited collection on *Victorian Literature and Finance*.

JOHN OSBORNE is Director of American Studies in the University of Hull. He is the editor of *Hull Poets*, was for ten years the editor of *Bête Noire* magazine, and has written extensively on twentieth-century poetry, including a monograph on *Larkin, Ideology and Critical Violence: A Case of Wrongful Conviction*.

PATRICK PARRINDER is Emeritus Professor of English at the University of Reading and General Editor of the *Oxford History of the Novel in English*. His books include *Authors and Authority: English and American Criticism 1750–1990*; *Shadows of the Future: H. G. Wells, Science Fiction and Prophecy*; and *Nation and Novel: The English Novel from Its Origins to the Present Day*.

ANDREW RADFORD lectures in English Literature at the University of Glasgow. His publications include *Thomas Hardy and the Survivals of Time* and *Mapping the Wessex Novel: Landscape, History and the Parochial in British Literature, 1870–1940*.

FRED REID was formerly Reader in History at the University of Warwick. His books include *Keir Hardie: The Making of a Socialist* and *In Search of Willie Patterson: A Scottish Soldier in the Age of Imperialism*. He is currently writing a study of the unknown Hardy.

ANGELIQUE RICHARDSON is Senior Lecturer in English at the University of Exeter. Her books include *Love and Eugenics in the Late Nineteenth Century: Rational Reproduction and the New Woman* and, as coeditor, *Victorian Literature: A Sourcebook* and *After Darwin: Animals, Emotions, and the Mind*. She is now writing a book on Hardy and biology.

MARY RIMMER is Professor of English at the University of New Brunswick. She is the editor of a critical edition of Hardy's *Desperate Remedies* and has collaborated on editions of four early Trinidad novels. She is currently working on a book on Hardy's allusions.

PETER ROBINSON is the author of more than twenty volumes of verse and verse translations, including *This Other Life*, winner of the Cheltenham Prize, and *The Great Friend and Other Translated Poems*. His critical work includes *In the Circumstances: About Poetry and Poets*; *Poetry, Poets, Readers: Making Things Happen*; and *Poetry & Translation: The Art of the Impossible*. His *English Nettles and Other Poems* was published in 2010.

DENNIS TAYLOR is Professor of English at Boston College. In addition to numerous articles and chapters, his work on Hardy includes *Hardy's Poetry, 1860–1928*, *Hardy's Metres and Victorian Prosody*, and *Hardy's Literary Language and Victorian Philology*.

JENNY BOURNE TAYLOR is Professor of English at the University of Sussex. She is the author of *In the Secret Theatre of Home: Wilkie Collins, Sensation Narrative and Nineteenth-Century Psychology*; co-editor with Sally Shuttleworth of *Embodied Selves: An Anthology of Psychological Texts*; and author of *The Cambridge Companion to Wilkie Collins*. She is currently working on a study of motivation and fiction in the nineteenth century.

JANE THOMAS is Senior Lecturer in English at the University of Hull. In additions to numerous articles and chapters, her publications include *Thomas Hardy: Femininity and Dissent, Reassessing the Minor Novels*, and editions of *The Well-Beloved* and *Life's Little Ironies*. She is currently completing a study of *Thomas Hardy and Desire*.

HERBERT F. TUCKER is John C. Coleman Professor of Nineteenth Century Literature at the University of Virginia. His many books include *Epic: Britain's Heroic Muse, 1790–1910*; *Tennyson and the Doom of Romanticism*; and *Browning's Beginnings: The Art of Disclosure*, and a number of edited collections, including *A Companion to Victorian Literature and Culture* and *Victorian Literature 1830–1900*.

NORMAN VANCE is Professor of English at the University of Sussex and a Fellow of the Royal Historical Society. He is the author of *The Sinews of the Spirit: The Ideal of Christian Manliness in Victorian Literature and Religious Thought*, *The Victorians and Ancient Rome*, *Irish Literature since 1800*, and numerous articles on religion and society, Victorian and Irish literature, and classical influences on English literature.

ROGER WEBSTER is Dean of the Faculty of Media, Arts and Social Sciences at Liverpool John Moores University. He is the author of *Studying Literary Theory: An Introduction* and *Expanding Suburbia: Reviewing Suburban Narratives* and is currently working on film depictions of Conrad's London.

REBECCA WELSHMAN is coeditor with Hugoe Matthews of *Richard Jefferies: An Anthology*, and coauthor with Patrick Tolfree of *Thomas Hardy and the Jurassic Coast*. She is currently completing her doctoral thesis on 'Imagining Archaeology'.

GLEN WICKENS is Professor of English at Bishop's University, where he teaches film studies as well as Victorian and modern British literature. He is the author of *Thomas Hardy, Monism and the Carnival Tradition: The One and the Many in 'The Dynasts'*, as well as articles on Hardy, Tennyson, and various aspects of Victorian thought.

MELANIE WILLIAMS is Professor of Law at the University of Exeter School of Law in Cornwall. She has written numerous articles on law and the humanities, as well as the monographs *Empty Justice: One Hundred Years of Law, Literature and Philosophy: Existential, Feminist and Normative Perspectives in Literary Jurisprudence*, and *Secrets and Laws: Essays in Law, Life and Literature*.

KEITH WILSON is Professor of English at the University of Ottawa. His Hardy-related publications include *Thomas Hardy and the Stage*, editions of *The Mayor of Casterbridge* and *The Fiddler of the Reels and Other Stories* (with Kristin Brady), the edited collection *Thomas Hardy Reappraised: Essays in Honour of Michael Millgate*, and the Blackwell *Companion to Thomas Hardy*.

T. R. WRIGHT recently retired as Professor of English at Newcastle University. He has written extensively on Hardy, including *Hardy and the Erotic* and *Hardy and His Readers*, and edited the collection *Thomas Hardy on Screen*. He is also the author of *The Religion of Humanity, Theology and Literature* and *D. H. Lawrence and the Bible*.

# PREFACE

In a Preface written for the Osgood, McIlvaine edition of *Far from the Madding Crowd*, Thomas Hardy recalled that it was in the pages of this novel, in 1874, that he had first 'disinterred' the ancient name of Wessex, in order to give 'territorial definition' to the region of southwest England that was to preoccupy him throughout his long writing career, and thanked the press and public that had willingly joined him in 'the anachronism of imagining a Wessex population living under Queen Victoria; – a modern Wessex of railways, the penny post, mowing and reaping machines, union workhouses, lucifer matches, labourers who could read and write, and National school children'. In 1912, in the General Preface to the Macmillan Wessex Edition of his work, he went further, insisting that his novels provided 'a fairly true record of a vanishing life'. When writing them, he had 'instituted inquiries to correct tricks of memory' and 'striven against temptations to exaggerate': 'At the dates represented in the various narrations things were like that in Wessex: the inhabitants lived in certain ways, engaged in certain occupations, kept alive certain customs, just as they are shown doing in these pages.'

But by 1912, Hardy's Wessex was no longer 'modern'. The railway had first arrived in Dorchester in 1847, though as one of the two main routes from London to the southwest passed to the north of the city, and the other to the south, the effect initially had been to make Dorchester a backwater. The union workhouses, set up under the Poor Law Amendment Act of 1834, were still in existence in 1912 – some 600 of them, with more than 200,000 inmates – but in 1929, the year after Hardy's death, they were abolished by the Local Government Act. Friction matches had been invented by John Walker in 1826–7; his discovery was copied and patented by Samuel Jones, and the first 'lucifer matches' were sold under that name around 1829. Rowland Hill's Penny Post, introduced in 1840, the year of Hardy's birth, provided for letters to be carried at uniform rates based on weight, with the cost paid by the sender rather than the recipient. It was an almost immediate success – in 1840 the average adult received about four letters a year; by the 1890s, when Hardy closed his career as a novelist, the average had risen to around sixty – and letters lost, hidden, misdelivered, stolen, read by the wrong person or at the wrong time feature throughout his fiction. The National Society for Promoting the Education of the Poor in the Principles of the Established Church in England and Wales began work in 1811, and by the 1840s offered education to around one million children, including the young Thomas Hardy. It continues in existence, but by the time Hardy's sister Kate entered the Salisbury Diocesan Training College for Schoolmistresses, in the years following Forster's Elementary Education Act of 1870, there had evolved a dual system of Church and State, with the latter now accepting responsibility for the compulsory schooling of all children.

*Thomas Hardy in Context* is largely concerned with how 'things were like that' in Wessex, and how they changed over the span of Hardy's long life, and there are essays here on class, education, and the conditions of the rural labourer. But in the mid-1860s Hardy began a habit of reading and notetaking that was never to leave him. He considered himself one of the 'earliest acclaimers' of Darwin's *The Origin of Species*, listed Mill's essay *On Liberty* among his 'Cures for despair', read and was unpersuaded by Newman's *Apologia pro vita sua*, read and gave at least partial assent to Auguste Comte's *A General View of Positivism*, and discussed the impact of science upon theology with Leslie Stephen. At his London clubs, the Savile and the Athenaeum, he met and talked with scientists, philosophers, artists, medical men, folklorists, and anthropologists, as well as with soldiers, politicians, and imperialists. The time has long gone when Hardy could be patronised as 'self-educated' (as if there were any other kind of education), and the range and depth of his engagement in the wider intellectual life of late Victorian, Edwardian, and Georgian England is also reflected on in these essays.

The volume is divided into five sections, with the first three closely linked. *Life and Works* explores issues of biography, and the processes by which Thomas Hardy the man became Thomas

Hardy the published writer. *Critical Fortunes* examines changing responses to his work as both novelist and poet. The third section, *The Literary Scene*, considers the kinds of expectations, about genre, and about the nature of both prose fiction and poetry, that Hardy encountered, and that continue to shape our understanding of his work. The larger part of the volume then addresses *The Historical and Cultural Context*: If this is a portmanteau designation, Hardy's development as a writer and a public figure itself suggests the inter-penetration of many nominally discrete 'contexts'. The fifth and final section, *Legacies*, looks at what D. H. Lawrence, Philip Larkin, and the twentieth-century film industry have made of Hardy, and how in turn he may be said to have helped make them.

The suggestions for Further Reading consist mainly of book-length studies, selected both for their own merits and in order to represent the widest possible range of views and approaches. For the most part, chapters and periodical articles have been included where they themselves serve as take-off points for further study.

The photographs of the illustrations to Hardy's work, which accompany the essay on 'Illustration' by Pamela Dalziel, have been prepared by Bayne Stanley, to whom, as to the patient and generous-spirited contributors to this volume, I offer my thanks. I owe lasting debts of gratitude and friendship to Pamela Dalziel, Angelique Richardson, Mary Rimmer, Jane Thomas, and Keith Wilson. The deepest and warmest thanks of all go to Mollie Craven-Mallett.

# A NOTE ON THE EDITIONS

Except where otherwise indicated, references in this volume to Hardy's novels and short stories are to the twenty-four-volume Macmillan Wessex Edition of 1912–31. His poems are cited either from *The Complete Poems of Thomas Hardy*, edited by James Gibson for Macmillan (London: 1976), or from *The Complete Poetical Works of Thomas Hardy*, edited by Samuel Hynes, 5 volumes (Oxford: Clarendon Press, 1982–95). References to *The Dynasts* are to volumes 4 and 5 of Hynes's edition.

Gibson took as his copy text Hardy's *Collected Poems* of 1928 and 1930, the former overseen by Hardy himself, the latter differing from it in the correction of some obvious errors, and the inclusion of a few revisions found in Hardy's *Chosen Poems*, prepared just before his death but not published until 1929.[1] Hynes used as his copy text the first editions of Hardy's first seven volumes of verse and the holograph of the posthumously published *Winter Words*, incorporating corrections made to reprints of the separate editions, and where there exists more than one revision taking that which appears to be the latest (and where the evidence as to date is uncertain, relying on his own critical judgement).[2] Hynes excludes revisions found in the printed edition of *Winter Words* and from the third edition of *Collected Poems*, both published after Hardy's death and so not overseen by him, and those in *Chosen Poems*, where the printer's copy suggests that Florence Hardy and an unknown editor made decisions contrary to Hardy's own. The textual differences between the two editions are real and interesting, but they are also relatively small: Hardy was a lifelong reviser of his texts, but the changes made to the poems rarely extend beyond the rewriting of a line or a word. Both editions are regularly cited, and the choice of which to use has been left to individual authors.

The textual differences between various editions of the fiction, however, are another matter. In the General Preface to the Wessex

Edition, Hardy described this as the 'definite edition'. Most readers, following Richard Little Purdy's foundational *Thomas Hardy: A Bibliographical Study* (Oxford: Oxford University Press, 1954), have taken this to mean definitive, and definitive has been taken to mean authoritative – authoritative enough to provide the copy text for most of the editions currently available. But as Andrew Nash explains in his essay in this volume, all of Hardy's novels had a complicated publishing history, allowing for significant changes to be made at a number of stages and over a number of years. These stages typically include a serial version (the exceptions are *Desperate Remedies* and *Under the Greenwood Tree*), often substantially revised from the manuscript to comply with the demands of editors, or Hardy's attempts to anticipate what those demands might be; a first volume edition, in which the text was revised back towards its pre-serial form, or more precisely – since Hardy's manuscripts show frequent evidence of false starts, or at least of a wish to keep open several possible lines of development – back towards some parts of the pre-serial form; and then the two collected editions, the 'Wessex Novels' edition from Osgood, McIlvaine in 1895–6, and the 'Wessex Edition' from Macmillan in 1912, each marked by extensive revisions, some local and some substantial.

This is complex enough, even if one sets aside the numerous alterations made at the manuscript stage, but in broad terms, one can distinguish three orders of change in the complicated textual history of the novels, overlapping but analytically distinct. There are, first, those made by Hardy's own decision, most of them for the 1895–6 and 1912 editions, in an effort to impose, retrospectively, a unified idea of 'Wessex', which had in fact developed in piecemeal fashion, or in response to criticism of his prose style, occasional solecisms, or handling of dialect. Second, there are those that reflect the need to avoid offending the more prudish readers of the serial versions, represented by their guardians, the magazine editors (Leslie Stephen's anxiety over the treatment of Fanny's maternity in *Far from the Madding Crowd* provides a familiar example). This was a pressure Hardy came increasingly to resent, and one that contributed to his decision to abandon novel writing after the hostile reception given in some quarters to *Jude the Obscure*: the chapter of the *Life* that deals with *Jude* is titled 'Another Novel Finished, Mutilated, and Restored'. Third, and most fascinating, are those changes that reflect a refuelling of Hardy's creative energies as he worked on the texts, and felt compelled to reimagine and rewrite characters and situations.

*The Return of the Native*, first published in 1878, provides examples of all three kinds of change. When Hardy began work on the novel, he had no reason to think that for the next twenty years he would restrict his focus to the southwestern counties of England. But 'Wessex' soon became an expected as well as a marketable feature of his fiction, and in the process of revising the *Return* for the Osgood, McIlvaine edition of 1895, he incorporated a number of place names that had over the years become familiar to his readers – Anglebury (Wareham), Casterbridge (Dorchester), and Weatherbury (Puddletown) – which played no part in the novel in 1878. These serve to locate Egdon Heath, the arena of the novel's action, more precisely in relation to other parts of Wessex; they also qualify the sense of its size, age, and remoteness, and not all readers have welcomed the change.

Other and larger changes affected plot and characterisation, most notably in the relation between Wildeve and Eustacia towards the close of the novel. Wildeve's conduct during their final interview, in Book Fifth, Chapter V, is more scrupulous in 1878 than in the 1895–6 edition, and Eustacia is correspondingly more alive to his continued sexual interest in her in the later text. In 1878 she tells him that she needs time to consider:

'I will think of this,' she said hurriedly. 'Whether I can honestly make use of you as a friend – that is what I must ask myself.'

In 1895 this becomes:

'I will think of this,' she said hurriedly. 'Whether I can honestly make use of you as a friend, or must close with you as a lover – that is what I must ask myself.'

In effect, in the 1878 edition Eustacia is beaten down by the thought of leaving Egdon and England alone, and without money, for an uncertain future; in 1895, what defeats her is the recognition that if she leaves she will do so as Wildeve's mistress.

Whether the later version presents what Hardy had always intended but in 1878 had not dared offer to the public, or whether it reflects a change in his view of Eustacia, or of the dynamics of the novel, must remain an open question. The mere fact of such a question, however, makes it difficult to consider any text as 'definite', or fixed. The Wessex Edition, rather than being definitive, can be seen as the last-produced layer in a record or palimpsest of Hardy's creative moods and decisions at different phases of his working life: in the 1870s and 1880s as a relative newcomer to novel writing, still, as he acknowledged, unsure of his way and constrained by the need to write nothing that might alarm the publishers and reviewers; later, as an experienced hand at the form, grown impatient with the demands of his audience, and emboldened by the sexual radicalism of the 1890s; and finally as the Grand Old Man of Letters, recipient of the Order of Merit and the author of three volumes of poetry as well as a verse-epic, *The Dynasts*, who had long since turned his back on prose fiction.

This might suggest an argument for citing the first volume edition: free from the constraints of serial publication, but free too from later accretions. This is the principle behind the recent Penguin editions of the novels (several of them edited by contributors to this volume), and clearly it can be argued that the Hardy who revised *The Return of the Native* in 1912 was not the same man who wrote it in 1878, and that we should turn to the earlier version for the 'real' novel, just as we might go by choice to the 1805 rather than the 1850 text of Wordsworth's *The Prelude*. There are, however, countervailing arguments, not least that Hardy did not always return to his original conception so soon as the first volume edition. In the serial version of the *Mayor*, for example, Henchard and Lucetta marry on the mistaken assumption that Henchard is a widower; in the first book version, they have a nonsexual relationship; and it was not until the Osgood, McIlvaine edition of 1895 that they have the irregular sexual liaison Hardy seems initially to have intended.

Fortunately, unlike the architectural restorations that Hardy had a hand in but later came to regret, revisions to the text of a novel do not entail the destruction of its previous forms, and those who wish to consult earlier or later versions of Hardy's novels are able to do so. The forthcoming Cambridge edition of the novels will go a long way to resolve these problems, but in the meantime the decision has been taken here to use the Wessex Edition: not on the assumption that it is 'definitive', but because it is the text usually cited in contemporary critical discussion, and the form in which the novels and stories have most often been encountered, read, adapted, loved, and hated for the past century. For ease of reference, citations are to the chapter in which a quoted passage occurs, or, following the layout of the Wessex Edition, to the chapter and section (*Desperate Remedies*), to the Book and chapter (*The Return of the Native*), or Part and chapter (*Under the Greenwood Tree, Jude the Obscure, The Well-Beloved*). Page references to the Wessex Edition are used for quotations from the short stories.

David Amigoni's essay in this volume discusses the two volumes that appeared over the name of Florence Emily Hardy in 1928 and 1930 as *The Early Life of Thomas Hardy, 1840–1891* and *The Later Years of Thomas Hardy, 1892–1928* and that were merged into a one-volume edition in 1962. The subterfuge of Florence's authorship was successfully maintained until 1940, three years after her death (and it would be an unkind reader who grudged her this small satisfaction), but in fact the work was very largely Hardy's own. Since then Michael Millgate has sought to get behind the various post mortem omissions and additions made by Florence (generally on the advice of Sir James Barrie), and to restore the text as closely as possible to what seem to have been Hardy's intentions. Millgate's edition was published under the title *The Life and Work of Thomas Hardy*, with Hardy identified as the author (London: Macmillan, 1984). While some scholars have expressed reservations about this edition, it is the form in which the *Life* is now generally read, and unless otherwise indicated it is the one cited here, abbreviated as *LW*.

### NOTES

1 Gibson's editorial policy is set out in the 'Introduction' to his *The Variorum Edition of the Complete Poems of Thomas Hardy* (Macmillan: London, 1979), pp. xix–xxxii.
2 See Hynes's 'Note on the Present Edition', pp. xxiv–xxviii in Volume I of *CPW*.

# LIST OF ABBREVIATIONS

| | |
|---|---|
| *PPP* | *Poems of the Past and the Present* |
| *PWB* | *The Pursuit of the Well-Beloved* |
| *RN* | *The Return of the Native* |
| *SC* | *Satires of Circumstance* |
| *Tess* | *Tess of the d'Urbervilles* |
| *THPV* | *Thomas Hardy's Public Voice: The Essays, Speeches, and Miscellaneous Prose*, ed. Michael Millgate (Oxford: Clarendon Press, 2001) |
| *THPW* | *Thomas Hardy's Personal Writings*, ed. Harold Orel (London: Macmillan, 1967) |
| *TL* | *Time's Laughingstocks* |
| *TM* | *The Trumpet-Major* |
| *TT* | *Two on a Tower* |
| *UGT* | *Under the Greenwood Tree* |
| *W* | *The Woodlanders* |
| *WB* | *The Well-Beloved* |
| *WP* | *Wessex Poems* |
| *WT* | *Wessex Tales* |
| *WW* | *Winter Words* |

# CHRONOLOGY

### 1840

2 June

Thomas Hardy is born at Higher Bockhampton, near Dorchester, the first of four children of Thomas Hardy, mason, and his wife Jemima, née Hand. Three other children follow: Mary (1841–1915), Henry (1851–1928), and Katharine, usually called Kate (1856–1940). None of the three marry.

Rowland Hill's *Penny Post* (January) revolutionises communication within Britain. Queen Victoria marries Prince Albert.

### 1842

The Chartists' 'People's Petition' is submitted to and rejected by Parliament; widespread strikes and numerous arrests follow.

The *Illustrated London News* begins publication. Charles Mudie opens his circulating library; it expands rapidly and dominates the market for fiction until the late 1880s.

### 1846

May

The repeal of the Corn Laws helps reduce the cost of bread on the mainland. Potato blight in Ireland exacerbates an ongoing famine; between 1845 and 1849 around 800,000 die of starvation, and 1.5 million emigrate.

### 1847

The railway reaches Dorchester; however, the two main routes from London to the southwest run to the north and south of the city, leaving it a backwater.

[Charlotte Brontë, *Jane Eyre*; Emily Brontë, *Wuthering Heights*; Thackeray, *Vanity Fair*]

**1848**

Hardy (TH) enters the newly established National (Church of England) School in Lower Bockhampton; one of the founders of the school, and lady of the manor, Mrs Julia Augusta Martin, takes a special interest in him.

Queen's College, London, offers higher education to women.

Following an outbreak of cholera, the first Public Health Act sets up a Central Board of Health, charged with improving sanitation.

Holman Hunt, Dante Gabriel Rossetti, and John Everett Millais form the Pre-Raphaelite Brotherhood. W. H. Smith opens the first railway station bookstall at Euston.

Nationalist and democratic uprisings take place in a number of European countries, including France, Italy, Denmark, the German states, and much of the Habsburg empire, in the short term with little success.

[Dickens, *Dombey & Son*; Mrs Gaskell, *Mary Barton*]

**1849**

TH passes through London, while travelling with his mother to stay with her sister at Hatfield in Hertfordshire.

**1850**

September   TH enters the British School in Dorchester, run on Nonconformist lines by Isaac Last. He excels in arithmetic and geography; begins to learn Latin.

The restoration of the Roman Catholic hierarchy in England and Wales prompts anti-Catholic demonstrations in Dorchester as elsewhere.

[Dickens, *David Copperfield*; Tennyson, *In Memoriam*]

**1851**

May   The Great Exhibition opens in Hyde Park (1 May–15 October), attracting six million visitors.

William Thomson (later Lord Kelvin) publishes the first and second laws of thermodynamics.

**1853**

Isaac Last opens an independent academy in Dorchester; TH continues to study with him until 1856.

[John Ruskin, *The Stones of Venice*, vols. II and III (vol. I, 1851)]

**1854**

Cholera breaks out in Dorchester; at least thirty people die in September alone.

Work begins on the construction of the London underground. The Working Men's College opens in London.

Britain declares war against Russia in March; hostilities in the Crimea continue until the Treaty of Paris in March 1856. The military and logistical inefficiency of the campaign leads to calls for the reform of the army and civil service.

[Dickens, *Hard Times*; Coventry Patmore, *The Angel in the House* (completed 1856)]

**1856**

May     TH joins the crowd outside Dorchester gaol to witness the execution by hanging of Martha Browne.

July     TH is articled to the Dorchester office of the architect John Hicks. About this time he forms a friendship with Horace Moule, son of the Rev. Henry Moule, Vicar of Fordington. Moule guides his studies but later advises him to give up Greek (and his dreams of university entrance) and concentrate on architecture.

**1857**

January     Death of TH's grandmother Mary Hardy, subject of his poem 'One We Knew'.

May     The 'Indian Mutiny' (or 'Great Rebellion') begins in Meerut. Press, pulpit, and popular opinion demand and rejoice in violent retribution before peace is declared in July 1858.

The Divorce and Matrimonial Causes Act allows men to divorce their wives for adultery; women have to prove adultery combined with further aggravating causes, such as bigamy, cruelty, incest, or desertion without cause for more than two years.

The Obscene Publications Act criminalises works written 'for the single purpose of corrupting the morals of youth'.

[George Eliot, *Scenes of Clerical Life*; Thomas Hughes, *Tom Brown's Schooldays*]

**1858**

TH's earliest surviving poem, 'Domicilium', written about this time.

Lionel de Rothschild becomes the first Member of Parliament to take his seat without being required to affirm 'the true faith of a Christian'.

*English Woman's Journal* begins publication.

**1859**

November    Darwin publishes *On the Origin of Species*. Also published this year is John Stuart Mill's *On Liberty*, which TH listed among his 'Cures for despair'. *Macmillan's Magazine* begins publication.

[George Eliot, *Adam Bede*; Samuel Smiles, *Self-Help*; Tennyson, *Idylls of the King* ('Enid', 'Vivien', 'Elaine', 'Guinevere')]

**1860**

TH completes his pupillage but stays on in Dorchester as Hicks's assistant. Mary Hardy enters the Diocesan Training College for Schoolmistresses in Salisbury, graduating at Christmas 1862.

The publication of *Essays and Reviews* in March 1860 provokes passionate debate on the interpretation of scripture.

The *Cornhill Magazine* begins publication.

[Wilkie Collins, *The Woman in White*; Eliot, *The Mill on the Floss*]

**1861**

Prince Albert dies of typhoid.

Hostilities begin in the American Civil War, after eleven southern states secede from the Union; it ends with the surrender of Confederate forces in April 1865.

[Dickens, *Great Expectations*; Francis Palgrave, *The Golden Treasury*; *Hymns Ancient and Modern*]

**1862**

April

TH moves to London, where he works in the office of Arthur (later Sir Arthur) Blomfield, an architect specialising in church restoration and design. He makes regular visits to the National Gallery, and soon begins his 'Schools of Painting' notebook.

[Mary Braddon, *Lady Audley's Secret*; George Meredith, *Modern Love*; Christina Rossetti, *Goblin Market and Other Poems*; Ruskin, *Unto This Last*]

**1863**

TH forms a close relationship with Eliza Bright Nicholls, its course possibly reflected in the 'She, to Him' sonnets. The relationship founders around 1867.

TH is awarded the silver medal of the Royal Institute of British Architects.

[Thomas Huxley, *Man's Place in Nature*; Charles Lyell, *The Antiquity of Man*; John Stuart Mill, *Utilitarianism*]

**1864**

Introduction of the Contagious Diseases Acts, giving police power to arrest suspected prostitutes in naval and garrison areas; extended in 1866 and 1869, before repeal in 1886, after a long and sometimes violent campaign.

[Robert Browning, *Dramatis Personae*; Newman, *Apologia pro vita sua*; Swinburne, *Atalanta in Calydon*; Trollope, *Can You Forgive Her?*]

**1865**

March

TH's sketch 'How I Built Myself a House' appears in *Chambers's Journal*. He begins to keep his '*Studies, Specimens, &c*' notebook, and writes some of his earliest known poems.

An uprising in Morant Bay, Jamaica, is brutally suppressed by Governor Eyre, dividing public opinion in Britain.

**1867**

July      In poor health, TH leaves London to resume work with Hicks in Dorchester. It is likely that for a time he courted his cousin Tryphena Sparks (1851–90), but there is no clear evidence of a serious attachment.

TH begins his first (unpublished) novel, 'The Poor Man and the Lady'.

The Second Reform Act enfranchises the urban male working class, roughly doubling the number of those entitled to vote.

[Thomas Carlyle, *Shooting Niagara*; Trollope, *The Last Chronicle of Barset*]

**1868**

TH submits manuscript of a novel, 'The Poor Man and the Lady', to Alexander Macmillan in July, to Chapman & Hall in December, but without success.

The Trades Union Congress is established.

Public hanging is abolished.

[Robert Browning, *The Ring and the Book*; Wilkie Collins, *The Moonstone*]

**1869**

March      TH meets George Meredith in the London office of Chapman & Hall, and is encouraged by him to continue writing.

May      TH takes lodgings in Weymouth, to work with the architectural practice of G. R. Crickmay.

Further efforts to place 'The Poor Man and the Lady' are unsuccessful; TH begins work on *Desperate Remedies*.

The Suez Canal opens.

Emily Davies founds Girton College, Cambridge.

[Matthew Arnold, *Culture and Anarchy*; Francis Galton, *Hereditary Genius*; John Stuart Mill, *On the Subjection of Women*]

**1870**

March   TH is sent to examine the church at St Juliot, Cornwall, where he meets and falls in love with Emma Lavinia Gifford.

The Elementary Education Act sets the framework for schooling of children aged 5 to 12 in England and Wales.

The first Married Women's Property Act grants married women control of their earnings after marriage.

Dickens dies on 9 June.

The Franco-Prussian war (July 1870–May 1871) marks the defeat of the Second French Empire under Napoleon III, and the unification of Prussia.

The First Vatican Council defines the doctrine of Papal Infallibility.

**1871**

March   *Desperate Remedies* published by Tinsley Brothers, at TH's expense, to mixed reviews; he works on *Under the Greenwood Tree*, completed by the summer.

Religious tests for matriculation and graduation at Oxford, Cambridge, and Durham universities are abandoned.

H. M. Stanley meets Dr Livingstone at Lake Tanganyika.

[Darwin, *The Descent of Man*; George Eliot, *Middlemarch* (in part-form, from December); Benjamin Jowett, *The Dialogues of Plato* (translation)]

**1872**

June    *Under the Greenwood Tree* is published by Tinsley (to whom TH has sold the copyright) and is moderately successful. TH spends part of the year in London, working for T. Roger Smith on designs for the new Board Schools.

August   *A Pair of Blue Eyes* begins publication in *Tinsleys' Magazine*, in eleven monthly instalments; it appears in volume form in May 1873.

Joseph Arch founds the National Agricultural Labourers' Union.

[Darwin, *The Expression of the Emotions in Man and Animals*; George MacDonald, *The Princess and the Goblin*]

## 1873

TH works on *Far from the Madding Crowd*; most of it is written at his parents' home in Bockhampton. TH goes to hear Joseph Arch speak in Fordington. Horace Moule commits suicide in September.

Beginning of the 'Long Depression', which in the UK lasts until about 1896.

John Stuart Mill dies in May.

[Mill, *Autobiography*; Walter Pater, *Studies in the Renaissance*]

## 1874

January Serialisation of *Far from the Madding Crowd* begins in the *Cornhill Magazine*, under the editorship of Leslie Stephen. The volume publication, in November, brings TH his first major success.

September TH and Emma Gifford marry at St Peter's, Paddington. After a honeymoon in France, they live for some months in the suburbs before moving to the Notting Hill district of London.

[Mill, *Three Essays on Religion*; James Thomson, *City of Dreadful Night*]

## 1875

The Hardys move to Swanage in Dorset. TH works on *The Hand of Ethelberta*, which begins serial publication in the *Cornhill* in July. TH is asked to witness Leslie Stephen's renunciation of holy orders. TH's first poem to be published, 'The Fire at Tranter Sweatley's', appears in the November issue of the *Gentleman's Magazine*.

[Swinburne, *Essays and Studies*; Trollope, *The Way We Live Now*]

**1876**

*The Hand of Ethelberta* appears in volume form in April. The Hardys move first to Yeovil, then in July to Sturminster Newton, before visiting Holland and Germany in May. TH begins an extensive period of reading and note taking; he later describes this as the happiest period in the marriage.

Queen Victoria is declared Empress of India.

[George Eliot, *Daniel Deronda*; Henry James, *Roderick Hudson*; Herbert Spencer, *The Principles of Sociology*, vol. 1]

**1877**

TH works on *The Return of the Native*. Kate Hardy enters the Salisbury teacher training college, having completed a five-year pupil-teaching programme and gained a Queen's Scholarship.

The Grosvenor Gallery opens in London and regularly displays work by artists such as Burne-Jones, Walter Crane, and James Whistler. The Society for the Protection of Ancient Buildings is set up.

Britain annexes the Transvaal.

**1878**

January    *The Return of the Native* begins serialisation in *Belgravia*, after being rejected by both Leslie Stephen and John Blackwood as unsuitable for family reading.

March    The Hardys move back to London; TH begins work on *The Trumpet-Major*. He is elected to the Savile Club.

[Max Müller, *The Origin and Growth of Religion*; Swinburne, *Poems and Ballads, Series II*; James Whistler, *Whistler vs. Ruskin*]

**1879**

Hardy reviews William Barnes's *Poems of Rural Life* in the *New Quarterly Magazine*.

Despite the loss of 1,300 men in the battle at Isandhlwana (January), British forces finally overcome the Zulu people under Cetshwayo.

[Eliot, *The Impressions of Theophrastus Such*; James, *The Europeans*; G. H. Lewes, *The Study of Psychology*; George Meredith, *The Egoist*]

**1880**

January

Serialisation begins of *The Trumpet-Major*, published in volume form in October.

October

TH falls ill and is unable to leave the house until April the following year. Much of *A Laodicean*, serialised in *Harper's New Monthly Magazine*, is dictated to Emma from his bed.

George Eliot dies in December.

[Gissing, *Workers in the Dawn*; Tennyson, *Ballads and Other Poems*]

**1881**

June

The Hardys leave London for Wimborne in Dorset. *A Laodicean* appears in volume form in November.

British forces are heavily defeated by the Boers at the battle of Majuba Hill in February; in October Britain concedes self-government to the Transvaal.

Thomas Carlyle dies in February.

[Carlyle, *Reminiscences*; James, *The Portrait of a Lady*; D. G. Rossetti, *Ballads and Sonnets*]

**1882**

Serialisation begins of *Two on a Tower* in the *Atlantic Monthly*, with volume publication in October.

The second Married Women's Property Act concedes to married women the same rights over their property and earnings as single women.

The Society for Psychical Research is founded.

Britain begins the military occupation of Egypt.

TH attends the funeral in Westminster Abbey of Charles Darwin. Anthony Trollope dies; Virginia Woolf (née Stephen) and James Joyce are born.

[Leslie Stephen, *The Science of Ethics*; R. L. Stevenson, *Treasure Island*]

**1883**

The Hardys move to Dorchester in June; construction of Max Gate begins in November. TH's essay on 'The Dorsetshire Labourer' appears in July in *Longman's Magazine*.

[Richard Jefferies, *The Story of My Heart*; Olive Schreiner, *The Story of an African Farm*; Sir John Seeley, *The Expansion of England*; John Addington Symonds, *A Problem in Greek Ethics*]

**1884**

February     The first 'fascicle' of the *New* (later *Oxford*) *English Dictionary* appears, covering *A–Ant*.

The Third Reform Bill extends the franchise to all male householders. The Fabian Society is founded.

**1885**

*The Mayor of Casterbridge* is completed in April, ready for publication in 1886. In June the Hardys move into Max Gate: their final move.

The Criminal Law Amendment Act raises the age of consent to 16; the Labouchère Amendment to the Act criminalises male homosexuality.

The *Dictionary of National Biography* begins publication (completed 1900).

General Gordon dies at Khartoum in January. D. H. Lawrence is born.

[Richard Burton, *Arabian Nights*; Rider Haggard, *King Solomon's Mines*; Walter Pater, *Marius the Epicurean*]

**1886**

*The Mayor of Casterbridge* appears in serial and volume form.

[Gissing, *Demos*; Stevenson, *Dr Jekyll and Mr Hyde*]

**1887**

*The Woodlanders*, serially published in *Macmillan's Magazine*, appears in volume form in March, when the Hardys take a holiday in Italy.

On 13 November ('Bloody Sunday') a mass demonstration in Trafalgar Square, organised by the Social Democratic Federation, is broken up by 2,000 police and 400 troops; several demonstrators die of their injuries.

[Arthur Conan Doyle, *A Study in Scarlet*; Rider Haggard, *She*; Jefferies, *Amaryllis at the Fair*; Pater, *Imaginary Portraits*; Emile Zola, *La Terre*]

**1888**

*Wessex Tales* is published, as is TH's essay on 'The Profitable Reading of Fiction' (in the New York *Forum*). The Hardys visit Paris.

A selection from 27,000 letters to the *Daily Telegraph* on modern marriage is published as *Is Marriage a Failure?*

Matthew Arnold dies; T. S. Eliot is born.

[Kipling, *Plain Tales from the Hills*; William Morris, *A Dream of John Ball*; Mrs Humphrey Ward, *Robert Elsmere*]

**1889**

TH works on *Tess* (at this stage called 'Too Late, Beloved!'). During the year he meets and is briefly infatuated with Rosamond Tonson.

The London Dock Strike, when 30,000 men strike for five weeks, proves the first major success for organised labour.

Robert Browning, Wilkie Collins, and Gerard Manley Hopkins die.

[Gissing, *The Nether World*; John Ruskin, *Praeterita*; W. B. Yeats, *The Wanderings of Oisin*]

**1890**

*A Group of Noble Dames* begins serialisation in the *Graphic* in December, with volume publication in May 1891. Hardy contributes to a forum in the *New Review* on 'Candour in English Fiction'.

London's first underground railway opens.

[William Booth, *In Darkest England and the Way Out*;
James Frazer, *The Golden Bough*; William Morris, *News
from Nowhere*; H. M. Stanley, *In Darkest Africa*]

**1891**

*Tess of the d'Urbervilles* begins serial publication in July;
it appears in book form in December, with a revised
second edition the following year.

TH is elected to the Athenaeum.

From 1 July, the Chace Act provides conditional
copyright protection to British authors publishing in
the United States; TH is among those who benefit.

[James Barrie, *The Little Minister*; Gissing, *New Grub
Street*; Kipling, *The Light that Failed*; Oscar Wilde, *The
Picture of Dorian Gray* and *Intentions*]

**1892**

July            Death of Hardy's father Thomas (born 1811).

October         Serial publication of *The Pursuit of the Well-Beloved*
begins in the *Illustrated London News*.

Tennyson dies on 6 October.

[W. E. Henley, *Song of the Sword*; Kipling, *Barrack-
Room Ballads*; Israel Zangwill, *Children of the Ghetto*]

**1893**

In May, on a visit to Dublin with Emma, TH meets
Mrs Florence Henniker and forms a deep attachment
to her. They begin an intense correspondence, which
continues for almost thirty years.

The Independent Labour Party is formed.

[Conan Doyle, *The Memoirs of Sherlock Holmes*; Gissing,
*The Odd Women*; Sarah Grand, *The Heavenly Twins*;
George Egerton, *Keynotes*; Pater, *Plato and Platonism*]

**1894**

*Life's Little Ironies* is published in February. Serial
publication of *Jude the Obscure* begins in *Harper's New
Monthly Magazine* in December. TH is sworn in as
Justice of the Peace for the Borough of Dorchester.

Mudie's and W. H. Smith's agree to refuse three-volume novels.

Robert Louis Stevenson dies in Samoa.

[George Du Maurier, *Trilby*; George Moore, *Esther Waters*; Wilde, *Salomé*, with illustrations by Beardsley]

**1895**

*Jude* comes out in volume form in November. The first collected edition of TH's novels, published by Osgood, McIlvaine, begins to appear.

Oscar Wilde is convicted of gross indecency in May and sentenced to two years imprisonment with hard labour.

The National Trust for Places of Historic Interest or Natural Beauty is set up; it continues to have in its care both TH's birthplace and his home at Max Gate.

[Grant Allen, *The Woman Who Did*; Joseph Conrad, *Almayer's Folly*; Marie Corelli, *The Sorrows of Satan*; Sigmund Freud and Josef Breuer, *Studien über Hysterie*; Max Nordau, *Degeneration*; H. G. Wells, *The Time Machine*]

**1896**

The Hardys visit the site of the Battle of Waterloo.

The *Daily Mail* begins publication, followed by the *Daily Express* (1900) and *Daily Mirror* (1903), marking a new era in popular journalism. Cinema begins at the Empire Theatre.

[Edward Carpenter, *Love's Coming of Age*; A. E. Housman, *A Shropshire Lad*; Wells, *The Island of Dr Moreau*]

**1897**

*The Well-Beloved* published in volume form in March. The Hardys holiday in Switzerland.

Queen Victoria's Diamond Jubilee attracts visitors from across the empire.

The National Portrait Gallery opens in London.

[Havelock Ellis, *Studies in the Psychology of Sex*, vol. 1; James, *What Maisie Knew*; Flora Steel, *On the Face of the Waters*; Bram Stoker, *Dracula*]

**1898**

December    Hardy publishes his first poetry collection, *Wessex Poems*, to mixed reviews.

Emile Zola publishes *J'accuse*, charging the French government with anti-semitism and the unlawful imprisonment in 1894 of Alfred Dreyfus.

[G. B. Shaw, *Plays Pleasant and Unpleasant*; Wilde, *Ballad of Reading Gaol*]

**1899**

October    TH responds to the outbreak of the South African war with a number of poems published in the press, including 'Drummer Hodge'. The war, which deeply divides public opinion, continues until May 1902. Both sides ignore many of the terms of the Hague Convention, signed this year.

[Conrad, *Heart of Darkness*; Kipling, *Stalky & Co.*]

**1901**

TH publishes *Poems of the Past and Present* in November. The opening poem 'V.R. 1819–1901. A Reverie', marks the death of Queen Victoria on 21 January 1901.

[Kipling, *Kim*; Yeats, *Poems*]

**1902**

April    TH signs the agreement making Macmillan & Co. his sole publishers, who begin reissuing the volumes taken over from Osgood, McIlvaine. Work on *The Dynasts* occupies him for much of this and the following year.

**1904**

Part First of *The Dynasts* is published; sales are poor.

TH's mother Jemima (born 1813) dies in April. Leslie Stephen, TH's first editor, dies in February.

[Conrad, *Nostromo*; William Hudson, *Green Mansions*; Kipling, *Traffics and Discoveries*]

**1905**

April    TH receives his first honorary degree, from Aberdeen University.

In August Florence Dugdale calls at Max Gate with Florence Henniker. She and TH exchange letters; later she looks up references for him in the British Museum.

Einstein publishes the special theory of relativity.

Revolution breaks out in Russia.

[E. M. Forster, *Where Angels Fear to Tread*; James, *The Golden Bowl*]

**1906**

Part Second of *The Dynasts* is published, and more favourably received.

In November TH tells Millicent Fawcett that he supports female suffrage because it will help 'break up' the 'pernicious conventions' of society, including the 'stereotyped household' as 'the unit of society'.

Britain launches HMS *Dreadnought*; the German Imperial Navy deploys its first submarine.

[Walter de la Mare, *Poems*; John Galsworthy, *The Man of Property*]

**1907**

Rudyard Kipling becomes the first British writer to win the Nobel prize for literature. W. H. Auden is born.

[Conrad, *The Secret Agent*; Edmund Gosse, *Father and Son*]

**1908**

Part Third of *The Dynasts* is published in February, to general acclaim.

[Arnold Bennett, *The Old Wives' Tale*; Forster, *A Room with a View*]

**1909**

*Time's Laughingstocks* is published in December. TH becomes President of the Society of Authors.

Lloyd George introduces the People's Budget, designed to promote welfare and wage war on 'poverty and squalidness'. Its provisions for a land tax lead to a prolonged stand-off between the Commons and the House of Lords.

Louis Bleriot becomes the first man to cross the Channel in a heavier-than-air craft.

Swinburne dies in April; Meredith dies in May.

[Ezra Pound, *Personae and Exultations*; Wells, *Tono-Bungay*]

## 1910
July

TH is awarded the Order of Merit by the new King, George V; Florence Dugdale accompanies him to the investiture. TH receives the Freedom of Dorchester in November.

Roger Fry organises an exhibition at the Grafton Gallery of 'Manet and the Post-Impressionists'.

[Forster, *Howards End*]

## 1911

Emma Hardy completes her autobiographical *Some Recollections*; TH quotes part of it in the *Life*, but it is not published in full until 1961.

Macmillan begin work on the twenty-four-volume Wessex Edition. In June Hardy receives the Gold Medal of the Royal Society of Literature from Henry Newbolt and W. B. Yeats.

[Conrad, *Under Western Eyes*; D. H. Lawrence, *The White Peacock*]

## 1912
November

Emma Hardy dies on 27 November; Hardy begins the sequence of 'Poems of 1912–13'.

The explorer Robert Falcon Scott dies in the Antarctic, in late March. The *Titanic* sinks in April, with the loss of more than 1,500 lives.

## 1913
March

TH visits scenes of his courtship of Emma in Cornwall. During the spring Florence Dugdale moves in to Max Gate; in July TH accepts an honorary fellowship at Magdalene College, Cambridge.

*A Changed Man* is published in October.

The 'Cat and Mouse Act' is introduced, by which suffragette hunger strikers are released and then rearrested.

[Lawrence, *Sons and Lovers*]

## 1914

February   TH marries Florence Dugdale (10 February).

*Satires of Circumstance*, including the 'Poems of 1912–13', is published in November.

D. H. Lawrence writes his 'Study of Thomas Hardy', first published in 1936.

August   On 4 August Germany invades Belgium; Britain declares war on Germany. TH puts his name to a statement of British war aims published in September in *The Times* and *The New York Times* and gives Granville Barker permission to mount a stage version of *The Dynasts* at London's Kingsway Theatre.

[James Joyce, *Dubliners*; Yeats, *Responsibilities*]

## 1915

Death of Hardy's sister Mary from emphysema (24 November).

[Ford Madox Ford, *The Good Soldier*, Lawrence, *The Rainbow*; Virginia Woolf, *The Voyage Out*]

## 1916

TH's *Selected Poems of Thomas Hardy* is published in October. It contains 120 poems, including a section entitled 'War Poems, and lyrics from "The Dynasts"', and is soon reprinted.

The Easter Rising in Dublin leaves almost 500 dead, most of them civilians; fifteen of those arrested are executed within the next few weeks.

Henry James dies.

## 1917

TH continues sifting (and often destroying) papers in preparation for his autobiography, to be published after his death over the name of Florence Hardy. *Moments of Vision*, with 159 poems, appears in November.

The 'Bolshevik Revolution' begins in Russia (October).

The Balfour Declaration proclaims British support for the establishment of a Jewish homeland in Palestine.

[T. S. Eliot, *Prufrock and Other Observations*; Yeats, *The Wild Swans at Coole*]

**1918**

The Great War ends on 11 November, with the signing of the Armistice.

Women older than 30 are given the vote.

**1919**

TH's *Collected Poems* is published. In October TH receives a 'Poet's Tribute', a bound volume of holograph poems by forty-three contemporary poets.

The Irish Republic declares independence from British rule; the Irish Free State comes into being in 1922.

**1920**

TH receives a message of congratulation on his eightieth birthday from King George V.

[Lawrence, *Women in Love*; Katherine Mansfield, *Bliss, and Other Stories*; Wilfred Owen, *Poems*]

**1922**

TH receives an honorary degree from the University of St Andrews and is made an honorary Fellow of Queen's College, Oxford. *Late Lyrics and Earlier* is published in May.

[Eliot, *The Waste Land*; Joyce, *Ulysses*; Yeats, *Later Poems*]

**1923**

The Prince of Wales (later Edward VIII) visits Hardy at Max Gate. T. E. Lawrence, now serving as 'Private Shaw', also visits, and becomes a friend.

*The Famous Tragedy of the Queen of Cornwall* is performed by the Hardy Players (28 December).

The 1857 Divorce Law is revised, making the grounds for divorce the same for men and women.

**1924**

A stage adaptation of *Tess* is performed in Dorchester, with Gertrude Bugler in the title role.

Ramsay MacDonald forms the first Labour Government.

[Forster, *A Passage to India*; Shaw, *St Joan*; Mary Webb, *Precious Bane*]

**1925**

*Human Shows* is published in November.

[Edmund Blunden, *English Poems*; Woolf, *Mrs Dalloway*]

**1926**

The General Strike called in May lasts for nine days, in an unsuccessful attempt to protect the pay and conditions of miners.

**1928**

11 January  Hardy, having been ill since mid December, dies in the evening of 11 January. On 16 January, in a double ceremony, his ashes are interred in Westminster Abbey, and his heart in the churchyard at Stinsford.

October  *Winter Words* is published. The first volume of TH's autobiography, *The Early Life of Thomas Hardy*, appears over his widow's name in this year; the second volume, *The Later Years of Thomas Hardy*, follows in 1930.

# PART I

# Life and Works

I

# *Life* and Life

DAVID AMIGONI

The two volumes of biography published after Hardy's death as *The Early Life of Thomas Hardy 1840–1891* and *The Later Years of Thomas Hardy 1892–1928* (in 1928 and 1930, respectively) were late arrivals in the tradition of the Victorian biographical monument. Hardy was the last of the really eminent Victorian writers to die; his life was recorded, seemingly, in a way befitting the family-managed tradition of the 'life and letters' tribute that marked the Victorian literary celebrity. Both works were authored by Florence Emily Hardy, Hardy's second wife, 'Compiled', as the subtitle ran, 'largely from contemporary notes, letters, diaries, and biographical memoranda, as well as from oral information in conversations extending over many years'. To this extent, Hardy's monument and its ostensible architect followed in the tradition set down for other canonical Victorian authors and intellectuals: George Eliot's life, edited from her letters and journals by her husband of late life, J. W. Cross (1885); Tennyson's biography, compiled by his son, Hallam (1897); Charles Darwin's life, written by his son, Francis (1887). Francis Darwin cast the net wide in an effort to recover the letters, papers, and notebooks that would reveal his father 'the man', as he emphatically put it in correspondence with the publisher John Murray.[1]

As is so often the case with Hardy, though he appeared to follow and be bound by a Victorian convention and aspiration, something much more complex was at work in the two-volume *Life*. Hardy was concealing tracks rather than assembling a paper chase that would definitively reveal him. Reflecting on the materials from which the 'life' was compiled, the 'Prefatory Note' reminded readers that 'the opinions quoted from these fugitive papers are often to be understood as his passing thoughts only ... not as permanent conclusions' (*LW*: 3). Seldom had a Victorian life and letters monument claimed so openly to be founded on 'fugitive papers'; though the 'fugitive' documents comprising Thomas Carlyle's posthumous 'life' similarly strayed beyond the Victorian life-writing pale – an example that is, I shall argue, instructive.

The *Life* that Hardy scholars recognise now is a significantly different text from the two volumes that appeared in 1928 and 1930, and which were merged into a one-volume edition as late as 1962.[2] The *Life* we read now has been 'restored' by the eminent Hardy scholar, Michael Millgate, under the title *The Life and Work of Thomas Hardy*, and attributed to the authorship of Thomas Hardy. Though the *Life* was written in the third person, in the impersonal voice of the biographer, Millgate's edition confirmed what had long been suspected: that Hardy wrote it substantially by himself, in the third person, and that it was typed up by Florence and then corrected by Hardy.

Millgate suggests that the idea for the work perhaps came during 1912–13, following the introspective turn Hardy's mind took after the death of his first wife, Emma Lavinia Hardy, and the discovery of her memoirs and diaries, 'often hostile to himself' (*LW*: xi). There was thus a doubly defensive motive. Hardy was alarmed at the prospect of an unauthorised life; one such, F. A. Hedgcock's *Thomas Hardy: penseur et artiste*, had appeared in French in 1911, generating warnings (in the 'Prefatory Note') against the 'erroneous and grotesque statements' seeping into the public sphere (*LW*: 3). This prompted Hardy into a mechanically complex 'autobiographical impulse', to borrow James Olney's idea, which was anything but impulsive, and included an absolute proscription on the term 'autobiography'.[3] In order to recover his childhood and formative life experiences, he related stories to Florence, who took notes. Referring to papers, correspondence, notebooks, and press cuttings, Hardy himself came gradually to compose a holograph manuscript. The pages comprising this manuscript were typed up by Florence and corrected by Hardy, usually on the 'rough' copy so that Florence would enter the changes on the top copy destined for the printer. Hardy sought to ensure that his holograph did not appear in this copy; where it did, he disguised his customary handwriting (*LW*: xii–xiv). In short, Hardy did everything possible to conceal his role as an author, including burning many primary materials and the holograph manuscript. Hardy's home at Max Gate staged some of the more extensive bonfires of personal papers that lit the skies of late Victorian and Edwardian England.

However, after Hardy's death and prior to publication, Florence, assisted by J. M. Barrie, radically edited the manuscript to produce an image of Hardy that was significantly altered from the one that he had, with her assistance, finalised. Using the only material available, an inconsistently edited first carbon copy of the typescript (*LW*: xxx), Millgate has restored much of what Florence and Barrie erased. However, readers have been left feeling that even though the image has been restored, the result is paradoxically reduced. Millgate's Hardy, who was to all intents and purposes Hardy's Hardy, seems rather too enamoured of the high social connections that he acquired in later life, and somewhat too inclined to enter into acrimonious dialogue with his numerous critics.

How should present-day readers evaluate Hardy's life-writing subterfuge, and the restored yet curiously unsatisfying image of the writer, in context? In part, they need to see it in the context of a 'life-writing industry' in the late nineteenth century and early twentieth century, which was a particular manifestation of a fast moving Victorian publishing industry, greedy for disclosures about authors' lives. This is a field that Trev Lynn Broughton has surveyed authoritatively in *Men of Letters, Writing Lives* (1999). The 'men of letters' of Broughton's title took professional charge of projects such as the *Dictionary of National Biography* (*DNB*), published from 1886, and a whole range of biographical projects that 'mapped' the literary past, such as the 'English Men of Letters' series, edited by John Morley.[4] In one sense, this context attested to the power of the life as a key to literature. It also produced a sense of indirection, defensiveness, and caution among those who might write their own lives in the later nineteenth century, or indeed have their lives written for them.

Broughton's book opens with Leslie Stephen, first editor of the *DNB*. She focuses on one of Stephen's less 'public' biographical duties, his *Mausoleum Book*, a 'private' letter addressed to his children, in which he wrote his recollected 'life' of their mother, his deceased wife Julia Stephen. However, as Broughton shows, Stephen's letter was tortuous, convoluted, and contradictory in its explanation of its purpose to its addressees (one of whom was Virginia Stephen, later Woolf). The letter also proclaimed the impossibility of any attempt among the unqualified to write a life of Leslie Stephen: the biographer's own inner life, such as it was, should go unrecorded.[5] Stephen's writing enacted a defensiveness that would parallel Hardy's wary approach to the business of life writing.

Stephen, a professional biographer and man of letters, was a key figure in Hardy's life. Hardy contributed an anecdote about him in *The Life and Letters of Leslie Stephen*, the 'qualified' biographer eventually being F. W. Maitland (1906). As editor of the *Cornhill Magazine*, Stephen had approached Hardy in 1872, asking him to write a tale for the magazine, *Far from the Madding Crowd* being the eventual publication (*LW*: 97–100). Hardy was later invited to witness an important moment in Stephen's inner, intellectual life: his renunciation of Anglican orders in 1875, conducted 'with due formality', so that even the consequences of inner life have a measured, semipublic solemnity. This story reappeared later in Hardy's own *Life*. Hardy's image of Stephen pacing his domestic library late at night in a 'heath-coloured dressing-gown' ends with Hardy's signature, and the turn of the conversation to 'theologies decayed and defunct, the origin of things, the constitution of matter, the unreality of time' (*LW*: 108–9).

There is a sense here in which the *Life* writes Hardy himself into an authorial elite: one among the men of letters who could concern themselves with the ultimate questions of evolution, matter, faith, time – and candour. Hardy's affectionate account of the episode marked the two men as homosocially bonded and 'apart' from the mainstream of the middle-brow literary culture through which Hardy's reputation was being made, in organs such as *Cornhill Magazine*. This episode of the *Life* includes stories about the fraught business of serialisation for writer and editor (*LW*: 100–2). Hardy's literary career was conducted amidst a publishing industry that had rapidly developed since the early nineteenth century, generating images and commodities associated with modern literary celebrity. Under Florence's posthumous management, Hardy's *Life* would become deeply embedded in this process: six extracts from the first volume appeared in successive issues of *The Times* (22–27 October 1928), just prior to volume publication.

The written *Life* itself is alert to these circuits of commerce. It records the rediscovery in 1918 of the '*revenant*' manuscript of *Far from the Madding Crowd*, which Hardy believed had been 'pulped' after use by the *Cornhill* in the 1870s (*LW*: 416). The rediscovery of manuscripts could prove something of a headache for Victorian biographers and their families as they sought to establish a 'canonical' identity for a major author in a culture of publicity. In December 1892, W. T. Stead, editor of the *Review of Reviews*, wrote to the widowed Lady Tennyson asking her to authenticate an unpublished poem that had come into his possession; the letter goes so far as to cite inside 'information' on the location of the original manuscript in Tennyson's desk at Farringford. Stead added that, if authenticated, he would publish it in the next number of the *Review*. Writing to the publisher Macmillan, Hallam Tennyson, with the embryonic biography of his father on his mind, opined that Stead's behaviour was 'scandalous'. Macmillan wrote to Stead asserting copyright on behalf of the Tennyson estate. The resurfacing of *revenant* manuscripts could lead to both panic and aggression among biographers and publishers.[6]

In Hardy's case, the situation was handled with greater equanimity; *Far from the Madding Crowd* was, after all, published, and part of his *oeuvre*. However, there are legacy issues that the *Life* strives to contest. The commercial value of the rediscovery is noted: the narrative notes how the manuscript was sold initially as part of Christie's Red Cross Sale (charitably assisting the war effort), then routed via a New York dealer to a wealthy American collector. Playing with questions of value, Hardy is made 'whimsically' to regret 'that he had not written it on better paper' (*LW*: 416). The situation of this moment is striking: it occurs in a chapter entitled 'Reflections on Poetry' in which the *Life* is keen to assert a continuous and lasting *poetical* identity for Hardy the writer. These claims are juxtaposed with 'voices' from contemporary criticism, such as the extract from a U.S. periodical, which styles Hardy as '"a realistic novelist who ... has a grim determination to go down to posterity wearing the laurels of a poet"' (*LW*: 415). In this context, the *revenant* manuscript of the early novel comes to have something of an ironic identity, directing 'posterity' one way, whereas the *Life* clearly wishes it to be pushed in another. Millgate's edition has restored reference to 'an excellent article [in the *Edinburgh Review*] on Hardy's lyrics from the experienced pen of Mr Edmund Gosse', which acts as an immediate prelude to the anecdote about the discovery of the *revenant* manuscript. This comment on Gosse's favourable review of Hardy's poetry was edited out of the version published by Florence.

Hardy's insistence on the source of Gosse's article – the *Edinburgh Review*, one of the great heavy-weight quarterlies from the first decades of the nineteenth-century – harks back to earlier, more exclusive monuments of nineteenth century literary culture. The *Life* records the passing of that culture through the deaths of many of his great Victorian literary predecessors. Hardy recounts that 'Crossing Hyde Park one morning in June [1870] he saw the announcement of Dickens's death' (*LW*: 79). In 1880, he records that 'George Eliot died during the winter in which he lay ill, and this set him thinking about Positivism' (*LW*: 150). Eliot's death was rapidly followed by that of Thomas Carlyle; Hardy reflects that 'both he & George Eliot have vanished into nescience while I have been lying here' (*LW*: 152). The emptying out of Carlyle's life force was an unsettling anxiety, reminding Hardy, in the throes of illness, of his own mortality. And yet, there is a sense in which Carlyle's 'living' presence and significance is an ambiguous, contradictory one in the *Life*, which generates complex insight into the composition of Hardy's identity as a writer.

Carlyle's presence seems to haunt Hardy's ostensibly enjoyable social networking in the literary world of London as he established himself as a writer. Thus in 1880, Hardy's pleasant excursion to the Tennysons (on a visit to London during the season), and his record of meetings with T. H. Huxley, Thomas Woolner, and George du Maurier, are followed by a note on '"Hints for Reviewers – adapted from Carlyle"'. The dictum urges the reviewer to '"Observe what is true, not what is false; what is to be loved and held fast, and earnestly laid to heart"' (*LW*: 141). Carlyle, seldom viewed as an apostle of critical balance, sweetness, and light, becomes here a beacon of fortitude for Hardy in the face of persistent adverse criticism. However, the sentiments that are promised give way to Carlylean combativeness, and the note develops into a rant against 'hopeless' critics who 'prove nothing by their probings except their own incompetence for their business' (*LW*: 141). Florence preserved the noble sentiments of the 'Hints' but edited out the rant.[7]

This connects with an earlier significance attached to Carlyle, an actual sighting of the man of letters in 1869, forty years after the publication of the seminal 'Signs of the Times' in the *Edinburgh Review*, in the offices of Carlyle's publisher Chapman and Hall. Poised between a career in literature and architecture, Hardy was invited to a meeting with Frederick Chapman, who

said with nonchalance, ignoring Hardy's business, "You see that old man talking to my clerk. He's Thomas Carlyle.... Have a good look at him ... You'll be glad I pointed him out to you some day." Hardy was rather surprised that Chapman did not think enough of Thomas Carlyle to attend to his wants in person; but said nothing. (*LW*: 62)

This can be read as a striking moment of realisation and recognition in which, at some level, class and social origins play a role: the younger man from rural southwest England, son of a stonemason, aspirant to the office of writer yet hardly born to be one, sees in the heart of London the elderly man from rural lowland Scotland, son of a stonemason, an unlikely entrant to literature. The aged prophet of the heroism of letters is being dealt with by a clerk. Quite what 'gladness' Chapman expected Hardy to derive from seeing the elderly Carlyle in this situation is hard to specify; Hardy certainly observes but is, at the time, publicly silenced by the lesson.

It would be difficult to overestimate the centrality of the life of Thomas Carlyle – professional and domestic – to all aspects of Victorian life writing. He had struggled, in the best traditions of 'self-help', from a humble background to achieve independence through authorship. Carlyle was the writer who in the 1830s and 1840s declared that history was comprised of innumerable biographies; who legislated on the value of biography through his essay on 'Biography' (1832) and commentary on Boswell's *Life of Johnson*; and who articulated the heroism of the man of letters in the context of a culture of print through his lectures *On Heroes, Hero-Worship, and the Heroic in History* (1841).[8]

Yet that culture of print would turn decisively against his legacy after his own death in 1881. Life writings about Carlyle were the source of this downturn, for as Broughton has demonstrated in *Men of Letters, Writing Lives*, the revelation of the deeply unhappy, indeed cruel, domestic life endured by Jane Welsh Carlyle generated an almighty controversy. J. A. Froude, his injudicious literary executor, published Carlyle's indiscreet *Reminiscences* in 1881, in which Carlyle drew less than flattering portraits of those who had helped him into a literary career while revealing something of his wife's unhappiness. Later, Froude published his four-volume life of Carlyle, *Thomas Carlyle: A History of the First Forty Years of His Life* (1882), and *Thomas Carlyle: A History of His Life in London* (1884), together with the *Letters and Memorials of Jane Welsh Carlyle* (1883); texts that had been partially edited and annotated by Carlyle himself, and which revealed much more about Jane's misery. As Broughton's anatomy of the controversy reveals, it erupted in the 1880s and was still being debated publicly in 1903. It raised questions not only about the ethics of life writing and publication but also about middle-class marriage and the place of literary masculinity in domestic relations.[9] For Thomas and Florence Hardy, writing a literary life in the early years of the twentieth century, Carlyle's influence was probably beyond evasion, particularly for complex reasons relating to their own emotional lives. The controversy also possibly affected the tone of the letter writing adopted by Emma Lavinia Hardy during the 1890s as she reflected on her marital and domestic alienation to a range of correspondents.[10]

There are striking parallels between the life writings that traced the married life of the Carlyles and the Hardys. Froude's biography of Carlyle had divided Carlyle's life into two parts: the first forty years of his life, followed by his life in London. Hardy's *Life* also originally appeared in two parts, covering an early and a later life. However, whereas the Carlyles moved from Scottish rustic isolation in part one to a life in London in part two, the Hardys moved from a life in suburban London back to Dorset. And whereas Carlyle was lonely in introspective mourning after 1866, Hardy's *Life* recorded in February 1914 that 'the subject of this memoir married the present writer, who had been for several years the friend of the first Mrs Hardy' (*LW*: 392). Emma Hardy having died in 1912 (*LW*: 387), the *Life* minimally records Hardy's marriage to Florence, formerly a companion to Emma.

There is a sense in which Hardy's *Life* can be read as a managed public response to the disclosure of marital unhappiness and the potential for scandal, a response that seems silently aware of the legacy of and controversy around Carlyle's *Reminiscences*, his atoning response to the death of the wife he had made deeply unhappy. They were a curious, unsettling performance, and it is hard to say whether they are about Carlyle's subjectivity, or the subjectivities of those whose lives had become enmeshed in his own. This is acutely evident in his reminiscence of Jane Welsh Carlyle; reading her letters becomes, for Carlyle, the occasion for his own, candid, self-disclosing (and self-incriminating) memory work. As we have seen, Hardy's *Life* may have been prompted initially by his discovery and reading of Emma's sometimes hostile letters and recollections. The strategy of the *Life*, accordingly, is to incorporate aspects of these writings into the impersonal narrative voice of the 'biography' so that chapter V, 'A Journal, a Supplement, and Literary Vicissitudes', includes verbatim material in Emma's voice, entitled 'Some Recollections'. This is clearly a response to potentially difficult material, and the published extract produces a narrative of romantic encounter ('"My life now began ..."') between the sister-in-law of a clergyman and a young architect from London on a church restoration mission on the isolated North Cornish coast (*LW*: 71). Hardy's *Life*, by enacting the entangling of lives while simultaneously managing the relationship between the impersonal voice of the biographer and the voice of Emma, only succeeded in generating a vibrant contrast, and thus a space prompting further questions.

If the *Life* was designed to manage 'grotesque' speculation, it signally failed. A good example of the life-writing legacy that it produced is Robert Gittings's influential *Young Thomas Hardy* (1975). Gittings views the *Life* perniciously 'as a barrier against biography', a 'deliberate deception' built upon the destruction of the manuscript and its primary sources.[11] He reads it precisely for the questions that it raises yet fails to provide definitive answers to: what, he asks, were Hardy's experiences with women before he met his first wife at the age of twenty-nine? Moreover, the attitudes to social status and class that we have seen reflected in the *Life*'s uses of Carlyle prompt questions about the way in which representations of family genealogy are selectively managed by the work. Considering the effects of Victorian social stratification, Gittings 'can only guess what violence this did to [Hardy's] own nature'.[12] Perhaps, however, we do not have to see Hardy's *Life* as a pernicious barrier to the truth, and we can look instead for guidance to his fictions as read by the critic John Goode.[13] For Goode, Hardy's fictions critically reveal the seams of ideology constructing Victorian thought. For all its strategic evasions, Hardy's 'fugitive'

*Life* was equally sensitive to the criticism and publication practices that helped produce the image of the Victorian writer.

NOTES

1　J. W. Cross, *George Eliot's Life as Related in Her Letters and Journals*, 3 vols. (Edinburgh and London: Blackwood, 1885); Hallam Tennyson, *Alfred Lord Tennyson: A Memoir, by His Son*, 2 vols. (London: Macmillan, 1897); Francis Darwin, *The Life and Letters of Charles Darwin, Including an Autobiographical Chapter, edited by His Son, Francis Darwin* (London: John Murray, 1887); Francis Darwin Correspondence, letter to John Murray III (1884); MS. 40310; John Murray Archive, National Library of Scotland.

2　In this chapter, the title *Life* refers to both Millgate's edition and the work attributed to Florence Hardy.

3　See James Olney, *Metaphors of the Self: The Meaning of Autobiography* (Princeton: Princeton University Press, 1972).

4　See David Amigoni, *Victorian Biography: Intellectuals and the Ordering of Discourse* (Hemel Hempstead: Harvester Wheatsheaf, 1993), ch. 5.

5　Trev Lynn Broughton, *Men of Letters, Writing Lives: Masculinity and Literary Auto/biography in the Late Victorian Period* (London: Routledge, 1999), pp. 5–6.

6　See letters of 13 December 1892 and 4 January 1893; letter from Stead to Lady Tennyson, letters from Hallam Tennyson to Macmillan, and G. L. Craik to Stead; Macmillan Archive, Add. 54981 CXCVI 1891–1893, British Library.

7　Florence Hardy, *The Early Life of Thomas Hardy, 1840–1891* (London: Macmillan, 1928), p. 179.

8　'Biography' and 'Boswell's Life of Johnson', in H. D. Traill, ed. *The Works of Thomas Carlyle*, 30 vols. (London: Chapman and Hall, 1896–9), 28: 44–61 and 28: 62–135.

9　Broughton, *Men of Letters, Writing Lives*, p. 80.

10　See Michael Millgate, ed., *Letters of Emma and Florence Hardy* (Oxford: Clarendon Press, 1996), in particular the letter (1899) of scarcely comforting marital advice to Elspeth Grahame, the new wife of Kenneth Grahame; pp. 15–16.

11　Robert Gittings, *Young Thomas Hardy* (London: Heinemann, 1975), pp. ix, 2.

12　Gittings, *Young Thomas Hardy*, pp. 3–4.

13　John Goode, *Thomas Hardy: The Offensive Truth* (Oxford: Blackwell, 1988).

# 2

# Memoirs and Recollections

TRISH FERGUSON

Given his status as the Great Man of Victorian Letters, honoured by Cambridge and Oxford, awarded the Order of Merit and considered for Poet Laureate, it is curious to find that Hardy was not well known as a public figure. At London clubs and crushes, he remained unrecognized by some other leading literary figures, such as H. G. Wells, who responded with surprise on seeing Hardy, whom he described as 'that grey little man'.[1] But even those who knew him well, such as Edmund Gosse, found him 'sphinx-like' and 'unrevealed'.[2] Hardy's reserve seems to have provoked those interested in him to seek out his acquaintance, and to forestall intrusive biographers he wrote a highly selective autobiography to be published over Florence Hardy's name after his death. To interrogate the image of Hardy thus constructed, it is useful to study accounts by those who knew or who met him. As Hardy and Sir Henry Newbolt once concurred: 'To make a live historical study, breath and blood should be moving, a proportion of the material should be overheard as it were coming down by oral tradition, or picked out of private letters of the time. Better still, if it could be dug for by cross-examination of ancestral ghosts.'[3] While biographies may be written with critical distance from their subject, memoirs may recall honest first hand impressions; their value lies in their closeness to the subject. They allow us to reassess the image variously presented by biographers of Hardy as class-conscious, overly sensitive, morbidly imaginative, pessimistic, and romantically drawn to a series of young women.

The carefully cultivated persona of the Man of Letters, who spoke 'like any educated Englishman with no trace of dialect', can be traced back to class-based attitudes Hardy experienced from his earliest days.[4] The memoirs we have of this time tend to corroborate the image of the young Hardy presented in the *Life* as bookish and shy. Ernest Harding recalled that 'he never played games, and was a quiet, studious child of a retiring disposition', but also that 'the Hardings regarded the Hardys as socially inferior'.[5] Hardy was attracted to Louisa Harding and would have been conscious early in life of the class issues that later permeate his fiction.

Even when fully established at the forefront of the literary world and meeting the celebrated literati of the day, Hardy was unable to escape class issues. His invited guests frequently recorded their impressions with reference to their class prejudices. Gissing read and enjoyed many of Hardy's novels, but on meeting him he concluded: 'Born a peasant, he yet retains much of the peasant's views of life … sadly he needs a larger outlook on upon life – a wider culture.'[6] Even Leonard and Virginia Woolf's favourable impressions of Hardy are corrections to their preconceptions. Leonard Woolf records: 'At first sight, and when he began to talk to you, you might have thought that he was merely one of many men born in English villages. But he is one of the few people who have left upon me the personal impression of greatness.'[7] Contrary to expectation, Virginia Woolf saw 'no trace … of the simple peasant' but found him to be 'very "Great"'.[8] Four years earlier, however, in 1922, she had considered him 'a very vain, conventional, uninteresting old gentleman … His great pride is that the county families ask him to tea.'[9] This seems unfair and unlikely, given that Hardy had gained such accolades as the Order of Merit and the gold medal of the Royal Society of Literature. However, this observation is echoed by his parlour-maid, Ellen Titterington, who recalled that 'Whenever he was called for tea in the afternoon, he invariably asked who was there. If they were titled folk he would come down at once, but if ordinary folk he would take his time, and come later when he was ready.'[10] Sydney Cockerell recollects that Hardy was complaining in his seventies that there were still people in Dorchester who thought themselves too grand to speak to him, and that he exclaimed: 'Ours was also a county family if they only knew!'[11] Such class consciousness affected his posthumous reputation, as evidenced in St John Ervine's 1955 article in *Listener* magazine and W. M. Parker's response, which still debated Hardy's 'peasant' status.[12]

J. M. Barrie, who was a close friend of Hardy in his later years, complained with some justice of the tendency of the *Life* to emphasize his aristocratic and literary connections.[13] But with regard to literary connections Hardy could name a number of authors and publishers, including Alexander Macmillan, John Morley and Henry Holt, among his close friends. Even when he returned to settle in Dorchester, he stayed in touch with the London literary scene and greatly valued his membership of the Savile Club, the Rabelais, and the Athenaeum. Hardy owned the clubs' publications, *The Savile Club: Rules and List of Members* and *Recreations of the Rabelais Club* and a number of books on etiquette, perhaps indicating some insecurity about his ability to mix socially and a conscientiousness to do so correctly.

Socially, Hardy erred on the side of caution, reluctant to speak publicly and acting with a quiet formality. Although Newbolt refers to Hardy as 'a kind of Socrates in the dialogues of the Savile Club', this probably exaggerates his presence there.[14] As the historian of the club records, 'considering his eminence, Hardy seems to have made … small impact at the Savile'.[15] Hardy's private conversations there were often of a nature to support the popular opinion of his philosophical beliefs and temperament. Kipling was grateful to Hardy for putting him at his ease when he went to the Savile for the first time,[16] but while recalling that he 'dined with no less than Hardy', he also referred to his 'grave and bitter humour'.[17] William H. Rideing recalled, 'I took away with me from conversation at a dinner he gave me at the Savile Club the idea of a doomed universe with its population succumbing to the apathy of progressive and sterilizing melancholia.'[18]

Hardy's social reputation as a brooding pessimist seems often to have been based on the tenor of his fiction. Early reviewers criticised him for his 'gloomy fatalism',[19] and G. K. Chesterton famously described him as 'a sort of village atheist brooding and blaspheming over the village idiot'.[20] Hardy admitted to Gosse that he 'suffered terribly' from reviews, but he was particularly sensitive to criticism from those who knew him (*CL* 1: 154). He attached great importance to his literary friendships at the Savile and in the *Life* plaintively rebukes Andrew Lang, a fellow Savilian, for a harsh review of *Tess*, which included an accusation of plagiarism: 'Why should one's club-acquaintance bring such charges?' (*LW*: 261) His famous renunciation of fiction was witnessed in the Savile Club by Rider Haggard, who recalled that Hardy read a review of *Jude the Obscure* in one of the leading papers and pointed to a certain passage, stating 'There's a nice thing to say about a man! ... Well, I'll never write another novel.'[21] At the difficult time of transition from novelist to poet, one of Hardy's greatest resentments was that his image as a pessimist was consolidated by his Savilian colleagues.

*Jude the Obscure* seems to have consolidated the enduring impression of Hardy as unrelenting pessimist, a reputation reflected in visual representations of him by his contemporaries. A sketch of Edmund Gosse's seventieth birthday party depicts Hardy among some of the leading literary figures of the day.[22] A small, bent figure is set apart from the others, appearing to scowl directly at the viewer. This is how Hardy appeared to Max Beerbohm, who told Virginia Woolf 'he couldn't bear *Jude the Obscure*, thought it falsified life, for there is really more happiness than sorrow in life, & Hardy tries to prove the opposite'.[23] Portraits typically give us a sombre, reflective side-profile, but many of his contemporaries thought that they did not give an accurate representation of Hardy. Rosamund Tomson thought it was a pity that the nervous strain of sitting for fashionable photographers brought to his usually mobile face 'an expression of almost harsh austerity which those who have the privilege of his intimate acquaintanceship feel to be a complete misrepresentation of the real man'.[24]

The disparity between Hardy's public image as a gloomy pessimist and his capacity to be jovial and sociable is brought out forcibly in many recollections by those who knew him well. Arthur Compton Rickett recalls that 'He was more often than not, when I saw him, in excellent spirits, full of amusing stories ... and quicker than the majority to see the humorous side of anything.'[25] Hardy's humour is not of an uproarious nature, but rather charming and self-deprecating, as when he viewed a photograph of Augustus John's painting of him and remarked: 'Well, if I look like that the sooner I am underground the better.'[26] Of his visits with Barrie to Stinsford churchyard, where Hardy wished to be buried, Lady Cynthia Asquith recorded: 'Usually he says he is to be buried exactly between his two wives; but sometimes he is to be so many inches nearer to the first; sometimes so many inches nearer to the second'[27] – a joke (if somewhat macabre) with a close and trusted friend.

Hardy's doctor testified to his 'pessimism and depression', and described Emma as contributing to it.[28] This is unprofessional and gossipy, but it also reflects contemporary public opinion. Gertrude Atherton, who saw them in London in the 1890s, records a snide joke with T. P. O'Connor: 'Mrs Hardy,' said T. P. 'Now you may understand the pessimistic nature of the poor devil's work.'[29] Much of what we learn about Hardy from his visitors reflects their opinions of Emma. Visitors tended to side with Hardy, depicting him as patient and reticent. Christine Wood Homer recollects that he 'would look at [Emma] in a rather quizzical but kindly way when she said something particularly childish'.[30] Benson, seemingly aiming to be fair, records 'he is not quite agreeable to her either, but his patience must be incredibly tried'.[31] The recollections of visitors at Max Gate indicate the increasing strain on the relationship. Hardy's acceptance of the Royal Society of Literature's gold medal was low-key with no witnesses, to the surprise of Henry Newbolt and W. B. Yeats, who journeyed to Max Gate to present it to him. Newbolt's recollection of this ceremony illustrates the *Life* at its most deceptive. Whereas the *Life* records a 'pleasant week-end visit from Henry Newbolt and W. B. Yeats', Newbolt recalled this dinner as 'beyond all others unusual and anxious'. Following Hardy's indecorous hint to Emma to leave the room for the presentation, Newbolt records: 'She at once remonstrated, and Yeats and I begged that she should not be asked to leave us. But Hardy insisted and she made no further appeal but gathered up her cats and her train with perfect simplicity and left the room.' Yeats did not record the event, and Newbolt concludes the recollection with Victorian reticence: 'This was the kind of scene which the Academic Committee could not often expect to take part in.'[32]

Although many visitors noted tension in the Hardys' marriage, most seem implicitly to concur with Rebekah Owen's avowal: 'I believe his fidelity to her to have been *perfect*,'[33] although this assertion implies the need to counter gossip. But Hardy's flirtations with Florence Henniker, Gertrude Bugler, Agnes Thornycroft, Elspeth Grahame, and Rosamund Tomson seem to have been conducted so discreetly that they generally evaded public notice. That some rumours circulated is confirmed by Mabel Robinson, who recorded: 'Then came great success and the adulation of women, some lovely and rich, others just lovely, others influential. Hardy became the fashion. May-be the admiration of many accomplished women of the world turned his head a bit, and he came to see

Emma as others saw her – rather plain, very countrified and scatterbrained.'[34] But there is very little evidence in memoirs of public awareness of his flirtations with society women, although it is evident from his correspondence and poetry. If there were rumours about Hardy's fidelity it appears that no one wished to express them and either defended him or deflected obvious inferences. Ellen Titterington, for example, stated that 'Mr. Hardy seemed to come out of his shell when talking to younger women as if a light was suddenly breaking through and he could see them in one of his books. Myself, I do not think he thought of them as women, but just shadowy figures fitting into a space like a jig-saw.'[35] George Douglas defends Hardy's treatment of Emma, noting 'his unfailing desire, as far as possible, to "take her with him" in his pursuits – whether it was a question of reading books together, cycling, or sight-seeing or of associating her with his literary labours'.[36] The memoirs do reveal, unsurprisingly, that social propriety was very important to Hardy; he maintained it throughout their marriage, although apparently with a cool reserve.

Towards the end of his life, Hardy's mind turned toward the subjects of animal cruelty and warfare. Although always reluctant to speak publicly, in his later years he made a number of public statements denouncing cruelty to animals, and on account of his campaigning against blood sports, he was not generally popular with the 'county people'.[37] Those who knew him well, however, attested to his compassion. Christine Wood Homer described him as 'a very humane man [who] always felt keenly the man-inflicted sufferings of animals', and Ellen Titterington noted that he was 'very sensitive to every form of cruelty. He was a man of very great compassion.'[38] Florence recorded that on a visit to German prisoners of war, 'T. H.'s kind heart melted at the sight of the wounded and he expressed his sympathy with them.'[39] War upset him greatly, but he often expressed his hope that mankind would give up warfare, prompting his close friend T. E. Lawrence to remark, 'They used to call this man a pessimist. While really he is full of fancy expectations.'[40] Such recollections of the elderly Hardy by his close friends confirm his own description of himself as a meliorist rather than a pessimist.

'A biographer,' Ralph Pite notes, 'writes in a genre that imposes pattern on a life, giving it shape and meaning.'[41] Although the memoirs may reflect certain individual biases, they can also provide useful correctives to attempts by biographers to present a coherent interpretation of Hardy. Biographers have frequently noted his sensitivity and obfuscations regarding his family origins and social status; however, reading the memoirs engages our sympathy for Hardy in this regard, as they are permeated with class snobbery. They also present a corrective to the image often presented of him as a gloomy pessimist, prone to depression. S. M. Ellis believes that 'the mask he wore to the outer world was an artificial protection of his inner self. To bores and intrusive journalists seeking "copy" he presented his "pessimism" they inspired and desired to find; and these people, who could only see in the "tired eyes" infinite sadness and depression, little knew that the same eyes could twinkle with fun as he told or heard some amusing story.'[42] Many of the memoirs judge Hardy as a pessimist through his fiction, but, interestingly, those in Max Gate who lived closest to him remembered him for those other aspects of his personality that prevail in his fiction: his compassion, his hatred of all types of human cruelty, and advocacy of 'loving-kindness'. They support his own response to charges of pessimism: 'my pessimism, if pessimism it be, does not involve the assumption that the world is going to the dogs ... What are my books but one long plea against "man's inhumanity to man" – to woman – and to the lower animals?'[43] The memoirs and recollections thus allow for a reassessment of Hardy's public image: if they deny us a single coherent profile, they provide us with a more comprehensive perspective from which to approach his literature.

#### NOTES

1 Joshua Harris, 'Writers of Today. – X. Thomas Hardy', *T.P's Weekly* 12 (1908), p. 471.
2 Edmund Gosse, *Portraits from Life*, ed. Ann Thwaite (Aldershot: Scolar, 1991), p. 106 (*IR*: 109).
3 Lady Newbolt, *The Later Life and Letters of Sir Henry Newbolt* (London: Faber and Faber, 1942), pp. 185–6.
4 Harold Lionel Voss, *Motoring with Thomas Hardy* (Monograph No. 7, in J. Stevens Cox, ed., *Monographs on the Life of Thomas Hardy* (Beaminster: The Toucan Press), p. 12); see also J. Vera Mardon, *Thomas Hardy as a Musician* (Monograph No. 15 in Cox, ed., *Monographs*, p. 16).

5 Ernest Oswald Harding, interviewed by J. Stevens Cox, in 'Louisa Harding', *Thomas Hardy: His Secretary Remembers* (Monograph No. 8 in Cox, ed., *Monographs*, p. 50.)

6 *The Letters of George Gissing to Eduard Bertz, 1887–1903*, ed. Arthur C. Young (London: Constable, 1961), pp. 205–6.

7 Leonard Woolf, 'Thomas Hardy', *Athenaeum*, 21 January 1928, pp. 597–8 (*IR*: 121–2).

8 Virginia Woolf, *A Writer's Diary*, ed. Anne Olivier Bell (London: Hogarth Press, 1954), pp. 89–94 (*IR*: 222–6).

9 *The Letters of Virginia Woolf, Volume II: 1912–1922*, ed. Nigel Nicolson (London: Hogarth Press, 1976), p. 559.

10 Ellen Titterington, *Miss E.E.T. (Hardy's Parlour-Maid)* (Monograph No. 4 in Cox, ed., *Monographs*, p. 14).

11 Sidney Cockerell, cited by Michael Millgate, *Thomas Hardy: A Biography Revisited* (Oxford University Press, 2004), p. 8.

12 St John Erving, 'Portrait of Thomas Hardy', *Listener* 54 (1955), pp. 371–72; W. M. Parker, 'Portrait of Thomas Hardy', *Listener* 54 (1955), p. 473.

13 J. M. Barrie to Florence Hardy, 29 January 1928, *Letters of J. M. Barrie*, ed. Viola Meynell (London: P. Davies, 1942), p. 152.

14 Lady Newbolt, *Later Life and Letters*, p. 121.

15 Garrett Anderson, *Hang Your Halo in the Hall: A History of the Savile Club* (London: Savile Club, 1993), p. 52.

16 Rudyard Kipling to Florence Hardy, *The Letters of Rudyard Kipling, Volume V: 1920–30*, ed. Thomas Pinney (Basingstoke: Palgrave Macmillan, 2003), p. 426.

17 Rudyard Kipling, *Something of Myself and Other Autobiographical Writings*, ed. Thomas Pinney (Cambridge: Cambridge University Press, 1990), pp. 50–51.

18 William H. Rideing, 'Lady Helier and Thomas Hardy', *Many Celebrities and a Few Others: a Bundle of Reminiscences* (London: Eveleigh Nash, 1912), p. 287.

19 Unsigned Review, *Spectator*, 8 February 1879, pp. 181–2 (*CH*: 57).

20 G. K. Chesterton, *The Victorian Age in Literature* (London: Williams and Norgate, 1925), p. 143.

21 H. Rider Haggard, *The Days of My Life: An Autobiography*, 2 vols., ed. C. J. Longman (London: Longmans, Green, 1926), I: 273.

22 N. John Hall, *Max Beerbohm Caricatures* (London: Yale University Press, 1997), pp. 60–61.

23 *The Diary of Virginia Woolf*, ed. Anne Oliver Bell (London: The Hogarth Press, 1975–1984), III. 213.

24 Rosamund Tomson, 'TH. I', quoted by Millgate in *A Biography Revisited*, p. 296.

25 Arthur Compton Rickett, *I Look Back: Memory of Fifty Years* (London: Jenkins, 1933), pp. 176–6 (*IR*: 88).

26 Millgate, *A Biography Revisited*, p. 510.

27 Lady Cynthia Asquith, 'Thomas Hardy at Max Gate' (Monograph No. 63 in Cox, ed., *Monographs*, p. 384).

28 F. B. Fisher to Lady Hoare, cited by Millgate, *A Biography Revisited*, p. 286.

29 Gertrude Atherton, *Adventures of a Novelist* (London: Jonathan Cape, 1932), p. 259.

30 Christine Wood Homer, *Thomas Hardy and His Two Wives* (Monograph No. 18 in Cox, ed., *Monographs*, p. 12).

31 Arthur Benson, Diary account of a visit to Max Gate in September 1912 (*IR*: 105).

32 Lady Newbolt, *Later Life and Letters*, pp. 166–8 (*IR*: 98–100).

33 Rebekah Owen to Mrs Fauty, in Carl Weber, *Thomas Hardy and the Lady from Madison Square* (Waterville: Colby College Press, 1952), pp. 162–4.

34 Mabel Robinson to Irene Cooper Willis, December 1937 (*IR*: 24).

35 Ellen E. Titterington, *Afterthoughts of Max Gate* (Monograph No. 59 in Cox, ed., *Monographs*, p. 342).

36 Sir George Douglas, 'Some Recollections and Reflections', *Hibbert Journal*, April 1928, pp. 385–98 (*IR*: 33).

37 Mrs A. I. Priedeaux of Weymouth (Wife of Secretary to Dorset Field Club), 'Hardy Memories', *Hardyana III* (Monograph No. 71 in Cox, ed., *Monographs*, p. 495).

38 Wood Homer, *Thomas Hardy and His Two Wives*, p. 14; Titterington, *Miss E.E.T.*, p. 16.

39 Florence Hardy to Sydney Cockerell, 10 November 1916, in Michael Millgate, ed., *Letters of Emma and Florence Hardy* (Oxford: Clarendon Press, 1996), p. 126.

40 T. E. Lawrence to Robert Graves, *The Letters of T. E. Lawrence of Arabia*, ed. David Garnett (London: Spring Books, 1964), p. 429 (*IR*: 182–4).

41 Ralph Pite, *Thomas Hardy: The Guarded Life* (London: Picador, 2006), p. 8.

42 Stewart M. Ellis, 'T.H.: Some Personal Recollections', *Fortnightly Review*, March 1928, p. 404.

43 William Archer, *Real Conversations (With Twelve Portraits)* (London: William Heinemann, 1904), pp. 46–7 (*IR*: 70).

# 3

# Thomas Hardy and Friendship

WILLIAM GREENSLADE

Have friends. – It is the second existence. Every friend is
good & wise for his friend, & among them all [one] gets well
managed. (*LN* I: 93)

A writer's experience of friendship is likely to contribute significantly – even though in sublimated forms – to the development of
creative imagination and commitment to the aesthetic vocation.
The friendships the young Thomas Hardy enjoyed in his formative
years, first with Henry Bastow and then with Horace (Horatio)
Moule, spoke of the seriousness with which he applied himself
to the business of self-improvement. Bastow, his fellow-pupil at
Hicks's Dorchester architectural firm, was a gifted man, a Baptist
with an interest in doctrinal questions and classical literature; he
and Hardy read together, with Hardy taking up Greek which he
hadn't read at school (*LW*: 32). But his meeting, at seventeen,
with Horace Moule, eight years his senior, was to be the decisive encounter of his young adulthood. This talented teacher and
scholar, consumed by a lack of self-worth, resulting in his suicide
at the age of forty-one, was a figure of indisputable significance to
Hardy's intellectual development and sense of identity.

Moule introduced Hardy, at a crucial time in his life, to a wider
intellectual culture, which took in the shaping ideas of the moment.
He instilled in him a sense of independence, and in the wake of
revisionary writings on the scriptures and the Darwinian revolution, a confidence in rational enquiry and the exercising of individual judgement, particularly in theological matters. He introduced
Hardy to the recently founded *Saturday Review* – 'largely devoted
to comment on current politics and literature'[1] – and to *Essays
and Reviews* (1860), which cast doubt on a literal reading of the
scriptures: one of the essays argued that 'matters of clear and positive fact ... are properly matters of knowledge, not of faith'.[2] The

two shared an enthusiasm for modern sceptical thought, though Hardy had yet to question Christian orthodoxy. But Hardy also had to deal with Moule's own prejudice, as a man of his class, when he discouraged him from the further pursuit of Greek drama, which Hardy viewed as a stepping-stone to University entrance (*LW*: 37–8).

Significantly it was Moule who prompted in Hardy rare reference in his own writing to the experience of friendship. In 'A Confession to a Friend in Trouble', dated 1866, he expresses both empathy for Moule's 'troubles', which included bouts of depression and alcoholism, and a recognition of his alienation from them: '*I will not show zeal again to learn, / Your griefs, and sharing them, renew my pain*' (*CP*: 11–12). In a much later poem, 'An Experience', he probably has Moule in mind when referring to 'the subtlest one, / My friend' (*CP*: 615–16).[3] Moule allowed Hardy to be as open as he could about the importance of male friendship. Whereas Hardy had several close friends during his lifetime, he never again entered into a male relationship of such intellectual intimacy and intensity: his unwillingness to do so perhaps expressed a subconscious wish to preserve his friendship with Moule as powerfully intact.

The world of culture that Moule represented was increasingly to become both necessary and accessible to Hardy. He had, of course, lived in London as single man from 1862 to 1867, and with Emma from 1878 to 1881. Following his return to Dorchester, his visits to the capital became annual ones, 'built into the total economy of his life', as Millgate puts it, 'as periods specifically given over to social engagements and obligations, the maintenance of friendships and professional contacts, and the pacification of Emma'.[4] Residence in London for all or part of the period April to July enabled friendships with rich, titled, and handsome society hostesses such as Lady Portsmouth and Lady Mary Jeune, and important opportunities to meet men and women from a wide range of occupations. Through Mary Jeune, he was introduced to leading figures in the theatre world – Henry Irving, Ellen Terry, George Alexander, and Ada Rehan – and to sculptors and painters like Hamo Thornycroft and Lawrence Alma-Tadema; he also enjoyed access to 'prominent journalists and editors such as William Moy Thomas, Edmund Yates, Clement Shorter, and James Milne' (*THPV*: xxv).

Such contacts could be more easily maintained through attendance at informal dining clubs and membership of two clubs, in particular the Savile and, later, the Athenaeum. Hardy joined the Savile Club in 1879, on his return to London with Emma, following their years in Sturminster Newton. Membership of the Athenaeum followed in the wake of the critical triumph of *Tess of the d'Urbervilles*. Hardy had achieved sufficient status to be elected, in 1891, under 'Rule 2', reserved for men of 'distinguished eminence in Science, Literature, or the Arts, or for Public Service' (*CL* I: 235). By this measure alone his status as a leading figure in his field was assured. Club membership helped him to meet leading figures from the arts, science, and medicine: among them, scientific figures such as E. R. Lankester, whose membership of the Savile dated from 1869, George Romanes (1879), Henry Maudsley (1871), Herbert Spencer (1883), the inebriety expert T. W. Rolleston (1888), and the physician Clifford Allbutt (1891), together with writers like Walter Besant and Edmund Gosse. Members of the more conservative Athenaeum included, again, Lankester (1889), Spencer (1868), and Allbutt (1880), as well as Francis Galton (1855).[5] Whereas few of these became close friends, from the evidence of his letters and *Life and Work* it appears that Hardy found it relatively easy to make the most of such scientific contacts, as when in 1891 he accepted an invitation from Allbutt, a Commissioner of Lunacy, to visit a lunatic asylum, or in 1893 to a *converzazione* at the Royal Society attended by Allbutt, Lankester, and the physician Sir James Crichton-Browne.[6] Such breadth of contact was made possible by Hardy's own eclectic interests and an openness to current ideas which helped ease his conversations with scientists, artists, historians, and politicians.

The conditions of cultural and knowledge production in the late nineteenth century allowed for conversation across disciplines, even as the barriers of specialisation were gradually going up: informal associations between thinkers working in different fields were still possible at a time when disciplinary boundaries were becoming defined and hardened, 'driven by the increasing "professionalization" of intellectual activities within the newly expanding universities'.[7] From the middle of the century, according to Stefan Collini, the 'growing homogeneity of the intellectual élite' formed a contrast both with the more sectarian divisions of the early nineteenth century and with the developing culture of specialisation now gathering pace at the century's end. The growth of periodicals of 'general culture' in the 1860s and 1870s was central to the formation of such an interactive elite: The *Fortnightly Review* (founded in 1865), the *Contemporary Review* (1866), and the *Nineteenth Century* (1877) all aimed to 'sustain a more seriously intellectual level',[8] and many of the scientific debates of the 1880s and 1890s were played out in their pages. Romanes and Spencer engaged in a lengthy exchange on the merits of August Weismann's challenge to the Lamarckian theory of heredity, published in 1889 and debated over the next four years in the *Contemporary Review*, which also published Allbutt's essay on 'Nervous Diseases and Modern Life' in 1895.

Spurred by the prestige attached to Darwinian biology, late nineteenth-century intellectual activity was increasingly mediated through 'scientific paradigms', with scientific enquiry providing 'a model for the acquisition and cultural functions of knowledge'.[9] The confident materialism of contemporary science held out for Hardy a radical, even subversive appeal: He was keenly attracted both to knowledgeable scientific practitioners and to generalists, some of whom had a radical turn of mind, such as Edward Clodd or the novelist and journalist Grant Allen, and with varying degrees of subtlety could marshal popular science, literature, political thought and philosophy to evolutionary theory, and who appeared equally at home in each of these fields. Clodd's interests were broad, ranging from folklore studies to rationalist and positivist thought and literature, and intersected with Hardy's. He was co founder in 1892 of a dining club, the Omar Khayyám, of which Hardy was a member,[10] and which pledged to uphold values that in their pagan/rationalist colouring faced in quite another direction from the established church or nonconformism; it was at one such dinner, held in honour of George Meredith, that Hardy met Gissing.[11] Then there was its predecessor, the Rabelais Club, founded by Walter Besant in 1879 'as a declaration for virility in literature' (*LW*: 136). Hardy had attended its dinners since 1883; he was on good terms with Besant and met, among others, Meredith, James and Henry Irving. Like Hardy, Gissing and Allen were drawn into a circle of literary acquaintances centred on Clodd's annual Whitsun gathering at Aldeburgh, which Hardy first joined, at Clodd's invitation, in June 1891. For a time Hardy had access to a congenial circle of predominantly freethinking, sceptical, antiimperialist progressives.

Hardy was becoming skilled in separating his private preoccupations from his public persona as a writer in demand. With the development of his writing career through the 1870s and 1880s, the literary friendships that inevitably followed were, as Ralph Pite suggests, 'rarely intimate'; he welcomed the 'impersonality' of relationships forged within the London literary world, while not seeing them 'as places where sincerity was possible'.[12] But with women it was different. The question of friendship could easily become confused with romantic and sexual longing. As his relationship with Emma cooled in his mid-forties, Hardy became intensely drawn to younger and more attractive women. He was particularly susceptible to women writers who held more or less unconventional views that might find expression in their work. This helps to explain the interest he took in the careers of up-and-coming 'New Woman' authors – Mona Caird, George Egerton, and Sarah Grand – discussing their work, and making notes from the latest Egerton and Grand as they appeared (*LN* II: 57, 60–1). It was the talented young poet and essayist, Rosamund Tomson, who appeared to fulfil his 'ideal of an emancipated woman', a composite Shellyean fantasy in which an attraction to free thinking and free love were entangled.[13] Imagining her as 'an enfranchised woman', he assumed a level of emotional and intellectual affinity with him and thus an implicit loyalty to his needs that unfortunately missed the point, for Tomson appears to have been self-servingly interested only in parading him 'as one of a long train of admirers'.[14] Some four years later, in the ninth of the twenty-four letters he wrote to Florence Henniker between June and December 1893, he cited 'Epipsychidion' directly, to register his disappointment that 'one whom one would have expected to be an ardent disciple of his school and views – should have allowed herself to be enfeebled to a belief in ritualistic ecclesiasticism' (*CL* II: 23). In his intense romantic feeling for her, Hardy was, of course, guilty of idealising, and so misreading her as a fearless, free-thinker. As a happily married woman and convinced Christian, Henniker had failed to live up to expectations, prompting an impasse between them, which he did not fully work out in the conflicted figure of Sue Florence

Bridehead in *Jude the Obscure*, the novel he was composing at this time.

Until his verbal advances failed to be reciprocated, his relationship with Henniker was dangerously all-consuming. It may be a measure of the emotional trust he placed in her that she was, as far as we know, the sole recipient of his views about friendship and the value he derived from it: 'I have been thinking,' he wrote to her in January 1894, 'that the sort of friend one wants most is a friend with whom mutual confessions can be made of weaknesses without fear of reproach or contempt. What an indescribable luxury! Do you want such an one for yourself? – I wonder if I shall ever find one' (*CL* II: 48). Here emotional self-interest is mixed in with uncontroversial terms of reference: Hardy, as a man of his time, could have only made such a self-conscious pronouncement to a woman. Both the frankness and the evasiveness of these highly coded remarks are characteristic of much of the Hardy–Henniker correspondence. Conducted over nearly thirty years, this relationship stands as a kind of corroboration of Hardy's unusual claim to her. For his feelings of romantic infatuation evidently evolved into something which, if not conferring on him the spontaneously offered endorsement he sought, nonetheless gave him a degree of the support he craved and which he felt himself denied, in the last two decades of his marriage to Emma.

For a hard-working literary practitioner, friends in the trade might be depended upon to demonstrate a sympathetic understanding of the blows to the ego attendant on the grind of a professional working life. In the case of fellow writers, there is habitually little time both to lay the ground of a complaint and to compose a response to a maligned comrade-in-arms. Perhaps unfairly, writers rely on their fellow-practitioners to produce tactful responses to the appearance of another's work and to be equally timely in their expression of solidarity with a fellow-author backed into a corner by an evidently wounding notice. Such support was the more necessary for Hardy, given how consistently he would offend conventional attitudes in his novels and short stories, and so be on the receiving end of painful hostile reviews, even as he must have anticipated such controversy.

It was Edmund Gosse, 'the most nearly intimate of his London friends',[15] on whom Hardy relied most heavily for these all-important gestures of support and affirmation. When, in 1886, Hardy had been reportedly belittled as 'small and unassuming in appearance – does not look like the genius of tradition' by the American writer James Russell Lowell, Gosse defended Hardy energetically to his American correspondents.[16] When Gosse himself ran into trouble over the attack in the *Quarterly Review* by John Churton Collins on his *From Shakespeare to Pope* (1885), Hardy immediately offered him words of comfort, sharing with him his own bruising experiences 'from reviews', particularly the anonymous variety with its 'impersonal means of attack' (*CL* I: 154).

Gosse was one of several friends to whom Hardy turned for support when *Tess* was savaged as 'an unpleasant story' told ' in a very unpleasant way' in an unsigned notice in the *Saturday Review* (*CL* I: 253).[17] The fact that its editor, Walter Pollock, was also a member of the Savile Club clearly added to his distress: 'Now whenever I go to the Savile,' he told Besant, 'I meet a number of S. Reviewers – one of whom is probably my libeller – Pollock I always meet. So that how can I go there again?' (*CL* I: 252). Hardy believed the reviewer was Pollock's assistant editor, George Saintsbury; Gosse suggested, rather clubbishly, in an attempt to reassure him, that it was 'one of those horrid women who live about the Albany' (*CL* I: 255).

Hardy's sensitivity to criticism was well-developed, but when Gosse told him to his face that *Jude the Obscure* 'was the most indecent novel ever written'[18] Hardy was particularly hurt: the terms of this literary comradeship, which assumed unqualified support on both sides, were, for a time, ruptured. Gosse would ensure no subsequent error when he rushed to produce a favourable review of *The Well-Beloved* in the *Saturday Review* (*CL* II: 153) and a further offer of support for Hardy, following a critical notice of the novel in *The World* (*CL* II: 154–9). Hardy confessed to Mary Jeune that he had been 'surprised and distressed' by this 'ferocious attack' (*CL* II: 156) and again sought support from a select number of close friends – including Florence Henniker, George Douglas, and Gosse himself – to solicit, albeit unostentatiously, their approbation for his work. Both Douglas and Gosse had earlier stood by Hardy when they had each written early approving reviews of *Jude* (*CL* II: 104–5). And it was Mary Jeune who in May 1894, at Hardy's request, replied the same day to a letter published in the *Daily Chronicle* by William Archer, which, in protesting at the boycotting of George Moore's *Esther Waters* by W. H. Smith & Son on the grounds of its sexual frankness, suggested that, by the same token, Hardy's own recently published collection, *Life's Little Ironies*, should certainly be suppressed (*CL* II: 56). Not 'one story' of Hardy's, thought Jeune, could 'offend the most sensitive morality' (*CL* II: 56). In such ways were these literary friendships nurtured and confirmed.

The notorious *Blackwood's Magazine* attack on *Jude the Obscure*, Margaret Oliphant's 'The Anti-Marriage League' (January 1896), prompted an example of how writers, if not quite friends, could nonetheless administer friendly support in the form of timely acts of professional solidarity. Hardy received an evidently sympathetic response to the novel from Grant Allen, which then offered Hardy the chance to express, as one writer to another, his annoyance with the 'shameless' Oliphant, who while trying to 'write down rival novelists' had herself 'for the last 30 years flooded the magazines & starved out scores of better workers' (*CL* II: 106). What particularly stuck in Hardy's craw was the fact that the 'better workers', with whom he associated Allen and himself, were now selling well, even outdoing Oliphant herself. Whether Allen, as something of a pot-boiling practitioner, truly counted for Hardy as one of the maligned elect, is not altogether clear. A writer who certainly did, though, was George Gissing, with whom Hardy had first corresponded back in 1886, when he had stated his support for Gissing's declaration of 'high artistic aims': Hardy had clearly identified a fellow-novelist who was 'not merely striving for circulating-library popularity' (*CL* I: 149).

Hardy's later friendships with Dorset and specifically Dorchester residents cannot be overlooked, but their extent is not easy to gauge since the greater likelihood of 'face-to-face meetings' delivered 'a meagre record in terms of correspondence'.[19] But the evidence of his correspondence and notebooks suggests that Hardy was drawn to figures who shared his own concern for the resources of local culture, and was at ease with those who were likewise captured by his curiosity for the history, customs and values of the locality, including the people and places associated with the Dorset that Hardy had been deliberately rediscovering when in the late 1870s he began his researches into the Napoleonic years for what would emerge *as The Trumpet-Major*. These figures included men like Henry Joseph Moule (the eldest of the Moule brothers), George Douglas, Hermann Lea, Frederick Treves – the author, in his retirement from medicine, of *Highways and Byways in Dorset* (1914) – Hardy's solicitor Arthur Lock, his son H. O. Lock, and Alfred Pope.[20] Neither Douglas nor Moule would have chimed with Hardy on all matters, but such was their mutual appreciation of the local past that other differences could be left to one side.

Moule's appointment as first curator of the Dorset County Museum, which opened in new Dorchester premises in January 1884, less than six months after Hardy and Emma had taken up residence in the town, was particularly fortunate. The museum quickly became for Hardy a centre for the study of the historical and archaeological life of Dorchester and the larger county, so important to his developing sense of the local culture at this period. The move to Wimborne, to the rented house in Dorchester and thence to Max Gate, represented, in every sense, a new settlement. Hardy could establish himself in Dorchester precisely because he had sufficiently established himself in the society of London.

It was singularly appropriate that Hardy's first guest, on his arriving at Shire Hall Place in the summer of 1883, was Edmund Gosse, the representative of that world for which he had most affection, and that they should together pay a visit to the ageing poet William Barnes, as the embodied antithesis of the urbane, cosmopolitan world inhabited by Gosse, and a man for whom Hardy nurtured feelings of almost filial devotion. The encounter embodied the creative settlement that Hardy sought, poised between the social and professional compulsions of London and the altogether different lure of Dorset with its imaginative appeal founded in local culture, past and present. Such a carefully arranged, Janus-faced life was fundamental for Hardy in enabling him to gain access to his full, creative resources. The 'good & wise' of Hardy's acquaintances implicitly recognised the terms of that settlement, and its critical importance for him both as a man and a writer.

NOTES

1 Stefan Collini, *Public Moralists: Political Thought and Intellectual Life in Britain 1850–1930* (Oxford: Clarendon Press, 1991; reprinted 2006), p. 53.

2  T. W. Heyck, *The Transformation of Intellectual Life in Victorian England* (London: Croom Helm, 1982), p. 86.
3  'Horace Moule', in Norman Page, ed., *The Oxford Reader's Companion to Hardy* (Oxford University Press, 2000), p. 280.
4  Michael Millgate, *Thomas Hardy: A Biography Revisited* (Oxford: Oxford University Press, 2004), pp. 246–7.
5  *The Savile Club 1868–1923* [Privately Printed for the Committee of the Club] (1923), pp. 99–186; *The Athenaeum. Rules and List of Members (1891)*.
6  William Greenslade, *Degeneration, Culture and the Novel 1880–1940* (Cambridge: Cambridge University Press, 1994; 2010), p. 171.
7  Collini, *Public Moralists*, p. 21.
8  Ibid., p. 54.
9  Heyck, *Transformation of Intellectual Life*, p. 82.
10  Philip Waller, *Writers, Readers and Reputations: Literary Life in Britain 1870–1918* (Oxford University Press, 2006; reprinted 2008), p. 509.
11  Millgate, *A Biography Revisited*, p. 337.
12  Ralph Pite, *Thomas Hardy: The Guarded Life* (Basingstoke: Pan Macmillan, 2006), pp. 389–90.
13  Millgate, *A Biography Revisited*, p. 274.
14  Ibid., p. 275; *CL* II: 24.
15  Millgate, *A Biography Revisited*, p. 252.
16  Martin Ray, *Thomas Hardy Remembered* (Aldershot: Ashgate, 2007), p. 74.
17  *Saturday Review* (16 January 1892), pp. 73–4 (*CH*: 190).
18  Hardy reminded Gosse of the comment in a letter of 1909; see *CL* IV: 33.
19  Millgate, *A Biography Revisited*, p. 422.
20  Pite, *Thomas Hardy*, p. 390; Millgate, *A Biography Revisited*, p. 422.

# 4

# The Public Hardy

SIMON GATRELL

In *British Literary Culture and Publishing Practice 1880–1914*, Peter McDonald usefully adapts Pierre Bourdieu's notion of the 'literary field' to the period and location of his subject.[1] The field McDonald describes is densely complex, and there is no space here to consider in detail the shifting place of Hardy and his work within it. My particular concern is to explore the contexts within which Hardy wrote the most significant of his nonfictional prose, conveniently collected in Michael Millgate's *Thomas Hardy's Public Voice* (Oxford: Clarendon Press, 2001), concentrating, for two reasons, on the years between 1883 and 1896: first, by 1896, with the publication of both *Jude the Obscure* and the first full collected edition of his work, Hardy had completed his primary negotiation with the disseminators and readers of fiction, and though his turn to poetry initially caused some disquiet, it did not affect so substantially his position in the field; second, his relevant work after 1896 does not engage with general debates about literature, but either responds to local concerns in his own work or lays out memories and recollections.[2]

Walter Besant's 1884 lecture 'The Art of Fiction' is well known as the opening move in an era of theoretical analysis of the novel in Britain. Within the year the stakes were raised by Henry James, Andrew Lang, Robert Louis Stevenson, and George Moore.[3] Hardy did not immediately plunge into this free-flowing discussion; his attention was directed around this time instead to the establishment of a proprietorial interest in what he clearly recognised as his most marketable literary asset, the people, culture and geography of Wessex.[4] This is why he agreed to write 'The Dorsetshire Labourer' for *Longman's Magazine*. The invitation came because the Liberal administration planned to extend the franchise to include most male agricultural workers, and Hardy was understood to be a novelist familiar with rural working class life. The essay, published in

1883, enlarged and elevated his position in the literary field, identifying him as an expert whose views on a subject of current sociopolitical interest should be consulted, and was a first step in providing for his fiction the historical and cultural authority subsequently claimed for it by James Barrie's 1889 article in the *Contemporary Review*, 'Thomas Hardy: The Historian of Wessex', and by Hardy himself in the mid 1890s through his revisions and prefaces for the first collected edition of his work. The title also confirms for readers (though too narrowly) the geographical district with which his readers might associate his Wessex construct.

The text of the essay attempts to reinforce the status of the author implied by its title and publication. Hardy selected his linguistic register carefully, establishing the narrative voice as that of a member of the educated and leisured class acting for his peers as guide to a relatively unfamiliar sociological arena; indeed, his primary strategy is to envisage the reader as a middle-class urban Livingstone, an explorer into darkest Dorset, who, to his surprise, will find after several months' enforced and perhaps uncomfortable residence with a Dorset labouring family, that their language and life become comprehensible, rational, and even in some small ways preferable to his own. It is a powerfully effective approach, drawing the reader in, flattering him, making him complicit, interesting him in the detail that follows. It was evidently thought successful at the time too, for Hardy was asked to follow it up with an essay on the implications of enfranchising the people whose culture he had described so effectively; but this commission would have shifted his position from that of a novelist with a professional interest in the cultural realities from which part of his art derived, towards that of a novelist-commentator on political issues. It might only have been a slight shift; nevertheless, he refused and, with the exception of issues raised by the First World War, continued to do so throughout his life.

It was a request from the editor of the American journal *Forum* that prodded Hardy into discussing the art of fiction. The topic offered was 'The Profitable Reading of Fiction' (1888), and his consideration of the collaborative role of the reader in producing meaning is the most interesting element of his account, for it brought something fresh into the literary debate. It was, presumably, for earlier writers too obvious a truth that without readers there would be no books, and the author's art would remain his secret; but Hardy moves at least one step beyond that axiom, in arguing that the generous and imaginative reader is prepared to 'find in a tale not only all that was put there by the author, put he it never so awkwardly', but also to 'find there what was never inserted by him, never foreseen, never contemplated' (*THPV*: 76); or again, that he will 'by affording full scope to his own insight, catch the vision which the writer has in his eye, and is endeavoring to project upon the paper, even while it half eludes him' (*THPV*: 80). He forcibly contrasts this reader with 'the mentally and morally warped ones of both sexes, who will, when practicable, so twist plain and obvious meanings as to see in an honest picture of human nature an attack on religion, morals, or institutions' (*THPV*: 88).

It is uncertain what influence this essay had on literary thought in Britain, and what kind of circulation *Forum* had across the Atlantic, but his next substantial public piece, 'Candour in English Fiction' (1890), addressed an issue on everyone's lips. The anxiety of middle-class society over the proper reading matter for boys, girls, and unmarried women, marked by the vitality of Mrs Grundy and Dr Bowdler, was strong throughout the nineteenth century, but in 1889 the issue reached a point of crisis, triggered by the conviction and imprisonment of Henry Vizetelly for publishing Zola's novels in English translation – novels freely available in England in their original language.[5] Four years earlier, George Moore had attacked a slightly less direct form of censorship of fiction, imposed through the means of distribution, in a pamphlet called *Literature at Nurse, or Circulating Morals*, which had been stimulated by the rejection of his novel *A Modern Lover* by the circulating libraries of Mudie and Smith. By the end of 1889 Hardy was keen to have his say on this issue, since only weeks before *Tess of the d'Urbervilles* had been rejected a third time by a magazine editor, on the grounds of improper explicitness in sexual relations and their consequences.

'Candour' is not Hardy's term, for his essay is one of three appearing together in the *New Review* in January 1890 under that heading. The other participants were Walter Besant and Eliza Lynn Linton. Besant had by this time established his place in the British literary field as the author's advocate with editors and publishers, so he was a natural choice – a writer with an opinion on everything literary, and unafraid to express it. In this instance he proved to be the representative family-values man, arguing that marriage and the family are the basis of civilised society, that free love would destroy both, and that therefore we ought not to advocate or even discuss it in published fiction. While he admits that divorce court reports show that there is free loving going on in Britain, and that anyone may read of it, he still claims that those who wish to uphold a 'standard of purity' are not hypocritical, and adds with pride that British society stands almost alone in the desire to uphold such a standard. It would be hard to find a more compact expression of characteristic gender and class assumptions than the sentences that follow:

Certainly, there is a chapter in the lives of many men which they would not willingly publish. But in almost every such case the chapter is closed and is never reopened after the man has contracted the responsibilities of marriage. And as for the women – those above a certain level – there is never any closed chapter at all in their lives. (*New Review* 2, p. 8)

Anyone who wishes to write directly and sympathetically of extra marital sex, he concludes, had better write in French or keep his work hidden in his study.

Linton has a more complex place in the field; it would have been hard to predict from her writing over the previous thirty years what position she would take on this issue. She is generally thought of as essentially conservative because of her stridently reactionary stance on the changing status of women; but in fact she is as caustic as Hardy in describing the effect on the British novel of Podsnappery exercised through the means of distribution:

we have the queer anomaly of a strong-headed and masculine nation cherishing a feeble, futile, milk-and-water literature – of a truthful and straightforward race accepting the most transparent humbug as pictures of human life. (*New Review* 2, p. 14)

The heart of her discussion is a series of scornful observations with which Hardy would have concurred, some of which indeed he makes in his own contribution:

But would any sane person propose to banish Fielding and Swift and Smollett and Richardson from our libraries, and Bowdlerise all our editions of Shakespeare, and purify the Bible from passages which once were simple everyday facts, that no one was ashamed to discuss, and now are nameless indecencies impossible to be even alluded to, because these are not the fit kind of reading for boys and girls in their teens? With this excessive scrupulosity in fiction we publish the most revolting details in the daily Press; and we let our boys and girls read every paper that comes into the house. If even we debar them from these, with the large amount of uncompanioned liberty they have at the present day, and a penny or even a halfpenny in their pockets, they may sup full of horrors and improprieties ... And again, with the new development of education our young Girton girls may study Juvenal and Catullus in the original, and laugh over the plain speaking of Aristophanes; while French novels, of which the translation lands a man in prison, may be sold by their hundreds in the original language wherein every decently educated girl is a proficient. (pp. 11–12)

Hardy's bitter attack is well known and needs no rehearsal, but one detail not often considered is his anxiety to make (twice) a moral distinction regarding the freedom to tell the truth that he is demanding:

Were the objections of the scrupulous limited to a prurient treatment of the relations of the sexes, or to any view of vice calculated to under-mine the essential principles of social order, all honest lovers of litera-ture would be in accord with them. (*THPV*: 100)

Nothing in [literature that tells the truth about life] should for a moment exhibit lax views of that purity of life upon which the well-being of society depends. (*THPV*: 102)

What investment does Hardy have in these ideas of 'the essential principles of social order' (whatever they are) or the 'purity of life upon which the well-being of society depends'? Is he more con-servative on such issues than we might have supposed, or is he covering his back in a public forum? Would he, in this light, have condemned, say, Swinburne's 'Anactoria' if it had been published as a short story?[6] Norman Feltes asserts that the candour in fiction debate had no significance in itself as 'a historical stage toward some greater candor or truthfulness in fiction overall', but is rather symptomatic of a crisis in novel production.[7] But this is simply inaccurate; both Joyce and Lawrence were clear that if Hardy had not pushed in practice and in theory against the boundaries of what the mainstream media of publication would allow, the way would not have opened for the (limited) acceptance of their yet more candid work.

It is the anger flaring out at the edges of his carefully control-led text that makes what Hardy wrote in 'Candour' so compelling, and what persuaded the editor that he would be a good choice to contribute to another *New Review* symposium, on 'The Science of Fiction' (1891). Again Besant kept him ill-assorted company, while the other view presented was that of the French novelist and critic Paul Bourget. In 'Candour' there had at least been agreement between the participants on what the title meant, but in 'Science' there was none. Besant wrote an abbreviated version of his 'Art of Fiction' of seven years earlier, advocating creative writing classes for embryonic novelists in which they would be taught the uni-versal principles of the construction of narratives. Bourget must have disappointed the editor, who no doubt thought that in invit-ing a French novelist to discuss the topic he would get an analysis of Zola's scientific naturalism; but instead Bourget offers a single definition of the art (not the science) of fiction as 'the art of imag-ining and depicting persons' (*New Review* 4, p. 306), and provides a brief critical summary of how good a range of French and Russian novelists are at doing it.

Both pieces are journalism written without any apparent sense that there is a significant literary issue at stake. On the other hand Hardy, in much the shortest essay of the three, is well aware that he is entering the ongoing public enquiry into the present nature and the future of the novel. He it is who takes on Zola, differentiating between his theoretical essays (untenable) and his fictional practice (powerful):

The most devoted apostle of realism, the sheerest naturalist, cannot escape, any more than the withered old gossip over her fire, the exercise of Art in his labour or pleasure of telling a tale. Not until he becomes an automatic reproducer of all impressions whatsoever can he be called purely scientific, or even a manufacturer on scientific principles. If in the exercise of his reason he select or omit, with an eye to being more truthful than truth (the just aim of Art), he transforms himself into a technicist at a move. (*THPV*: 107)[8]

The narrative voice implicitly asserts that the writer is separated by a wide gap from the realist or naturalist, proposing instead that acuteness of intuition and strength of imagination are required to create the illusion that alone communicates truth to experience. When Hardy writes, 'To see in half and quarter views the whole picture, to catch from a few bars the whole tune, is the intuitive power that supplies the would-be story-writer with the scientific bases for his pursuit' (*THPV*: 110), he places himself surprisingly close to James, who celebrates 'the power to guess the unseen from the seen, to trace the implication of things, to judge the whole piece by the pattern, the condition of feeling life, in general, so completely that you are well on your way to knowing any particular corner of it'.[9]

In the same year *Tess of the d'Urbervilles* was published, and Hardy's place in the literary field as a consequence dramatically shifted upwards; another writer would have capitalised on such widespread recognition to stake out further advances through polemical or theoretical articles in journals, but Hardy did not. He did, however, contribute briefly to a third *New Review* symposium, called 'The Tree of Knowledge', in 1894. Though it was not specifically literary, the topic might have been drawn directly from *Tess*, focussing as it did on how much and when daughters should be told about the sexual facts of life, and whether they should have the right to demand of any prospective husband details of his sexual experiences. The large majority of responses recommended full disclosure on all fronts. As might be expected, though, since at the time he was working on *Jude the Obscure*, Hardy argued that young men ought to receive the same instruction, for 'it has never struck me that the spider is invariably male and the fly invariably female', nor that he was the only contributor to question the assumption that marriage as it was currently constituted was the best way of establishing long-term relations between men and women (*THPV*: 132).[10]

Though his celebrity (or notoriety) after 1896 did not transform him into a public man, it should come as no surprise to anyone who has read *Jude* that when he felt anger, bitterness, disdain on public issues, he was still prepared to express it to the World. He was not as witty in his disgust at hunting as Oscar Wilde, but in 1901 he wrote with distaste that he held it 'immoral and unmanly to cultivate pleasure in compassing the death of our weaker and simpler fellow-creatures by cunning, instead of learning to regard their destruction, if a necessity, as an odious task, akin to that, say, of the common hangman' (*THPV*: 167). In a paper for the Society for the Protection of Ancient Buildings on 'Memories of Church Restoration' (1906), he was cynical about the current state of the Church of England: 'If the ruinous church could be enclosed in a crystal palace ... and a new church be built alongside for serv-ices (assuming the parish to retain sufficient earnest-mindedness to desire them), the method would be an ideal one' (*THPV*: 242). Later in the same piece he writes sarcastically of priests and churchwardens anxious to 'pull out old irregular pews to fix math-ematically spaced benches for a congregation that never comes' (*THPV*: 253). In 1909, five years before the First World War, he was invited by members of a German university to give a sense of his 'Weltanschauung'; which he did with anticipatory anger:

We call our age an age of Freedom. Yet Freedom, under her incubus of armaments, territorial ambitions smugly disguised as patriotism, superstitions, conventions of every sort, is of such stunted proportions in this her so-called time, that the human race is likely to be extinct before Freedom arrives at maturity. (*THPV*: 304)

In 1912, revising his work for the Wessex edition, he was asked by *Nash's Magazine* to express his opinion concerning 'How shall we solve the divorce problem?' He was direct and violent:

As the present marriage laws are, to the eyes of anybody who looks around, the gratuitous cause of at least half the misery of the commu-nity, that they are allowed to remain in force for a day is, to quote the famous last word of the ceremony itself, an 'amazement', and can only be accounted for by the assumption that we live in a barbaric age, and are the slaves of gross superstition. (*THPV*: 332)

The First World War and its aftermath drew from Hardy an indict-ment of British society that brought all these issues and more into a collective anticipation of catastrophe, in the 'Apology' he wrote in 1922 to *Late Lyrics and Earlier*:

The thoughts of any man of letters concerned to keep poetry alive can-not but run uncomfortably on the precarious prospects of English verse at the present day. [...] Whether owing to the barbarizing of taste in the younger minds by the dark madness of the late war, the unabashed cultivation of selfishness in all classes, the plethoric growth of knowledge simultaneously with the stunting of wisdom, 'a degrading thirst after outrageous stimulation' (to quote Wordsworth again), or from any other cause, we seem threatened with a new Dark Age. (*CP*: 560)

1922 was also the year in which Eliot's *The Waste Land* was published; in 1923 Yeats got his Nobel prize. Neither poet would fundamentally have disagreed with Hardy's assessment, and those who today anticipate a new dark age might find Hardy's analysis still conveniently apposite.

## NOTES

1 Cambridge: Cambridge University Press, 1997. See especially pp. 9–21.
2 In this context it is worth noting that Andrew Lang published in 1890 a wry lecture entitled 'How to Fail in Literature' in which he considers every aspect of the business of being an author from handwriting (preferably typewriting) to negotiations with publishers and the suborning of critics. Lang was much more aware of the complexity of the conditions of authorship than the one-dimensional Besant.
3 See John Goode, 'The Art of Fiction: Walter Besant and Henry James', in *Tradition and Tolerance in Nineteenth Century Fiction*, ed. D. Howard, J. Lucas, and J. Goode (London: Routledge and Kegan Paul, 1966), and N. N. Feltes, *Literary Capital and the Late Victorian Novel* (Madison: University of Wisconsin Press, 1993), pp. 65–103. George Moore is not usually included in this list, but his *Confessions of a Young Man* (1886) importantly though independently introduces the theories of French naturalism into the debate.
4 Hardy's first substantial forays into public discussion were also related to an aspect of this enterprise – defences of his treatment of Dorset dialect in his novels (*THPV*: 14 and 28–9) and an anonymous review of William Barnes's dialect poems (*THPV*: 17–27). This last is presented by Millgate not as it appeared in the *New Quarterly Magazine*, but as Hardy originally wrote it; it is suggestive that almost every passage of interest to a reader concerned with the nature and presentation of the dialect in Barnes's work was excised for the magazine, the editor of which, Kegan Paul, was also the publisher of the collection.

5 For a recent account of the affair, arguing that much of the energy driving the prosecution came as a consequence of increasing literacy since 1870, see Anthony Cummins, 'Emile Zola's Cheap English Dress: The Vizetelly Translations, Late-Victorian Print Culture, and the Crisis of Literary Value', *Review of English Studies* 60 (2009), pp. 108–132.

6 A similar debate was in progress concerning the representation of human relations on the stage, generated in both England and France by Ibsen's plays. In the case of the theatre, there was an official censor, and Hardy wrote in support of the establishment of a theatre club, a 'free stage' in London, following the model of the Parisian *Théâtre Libre*, that would evade the blue pen of the Lord Chancellor (*THPV*: 93–4). Here too he was following George Moore, who had made a similar proposal in *Confessions of a Young Man* (1888).

7 Feltes, *Literary Capital*, p. 104.

8 George Gissing makes the same point in *New Grub Street* through the characterisation of the impoverished novelist Biffen and his naturalist work 'Mr Bailey, Grocer', which attempts to put into practice Zola's theory.

9 'The Art of Fiction' (1884), transcribed from www.wsu.edu/~campbelld/amlit/artfiction.html, accessed 27 April 2010.

10 It is a detail as far as I know yet to be noted that the article following this symposium, written by Eveline M. Forbes and called 'Some Noteworthy Hands', has a reproduction and chiromantic analysis of Hardy's hands.

## 5

# From Serial to Volume

ANDREW NASH

The final third of the nineteenth century was a period of expansion and diversification in the fiction market. Novels were published in a variety of material forms targeted at different audiences. In the serial market there were shilling monthly magazines, sixpenny weeklies and penny newspapers. In the book market there were expensive multivolume library editions, cheap one-volume reprints, and, by the 1890s, sixpenny paperbacks. There were also continental, colonial, and American serial and volume editions. To maximise profits, novelists needed to master the serial form. All but the first two of Hardy's novels were serialised. He paid to see *Desperate Remedies* published and received only £30 for the copyright of *Under the Greenwood Tree*. For *A Pair of Blue Eyes*, however, he received £200 for serial and three-volume rights. This figure doubled for *Far From the Madding Crowd* and rose to £700 for *The Hand of Ethelberta*. For the latter Hardy also received £550 for American serial rights. His payments peaked in 1880 when he was paid £1300 from *Harper's New Monthly Magazine* for *A Laodicean*.

In addition to financial remuneration, serialisation generated publicity. Periodicals and newspapers gave running commentaries on the monthly contents of major magazines. The early speculation that the anonymous author of *Madding Crowd* might be George Eliot was initiated by the *Spectator* review of the first instalment. On 10 October 1874 the *Examiner* reported that 'comparatively little had been written' of the story since it was discovered not to be the work of Eliot but confirmed that it was 'one of the most remarkable that has appeared in any magazine for years'. Such publicity would have increased demand for the novel when it appeared in volume form at the circulating libraries.

Serialisation influenced the writing process in various ways. Hardy was often still composing his stories after early instalments had been printed. He had completed less than half of *The Hand of Ethelberta* when the first episode appeared in the *Cornhill*, and finished *The Woodlanders* just two months before the final instalment appeared in *Macmillan's Magazine*. Hardy was warned about the drawbacks of this working method in 1873 by the American publisher Henry Holt: 'you can't take your time about it, you can't afford to be sick or lazy ... You lose all benefit of the happy second thoughts that may arise as the work progresses.'[1] These words must have occurred to Hardy when he fell ill during the writing of *A Laodicean*. As he recalled, 'the story had to go on somehow' and a rough draft was completed from his sickbed midway through the serial run (*LW*: 149–50).

Hardy's first four serials appeared in shilling monthly magazines, which had long dominated the market. There was, however, considerable difference in reputation between *Tinsleys' Magazine*, which ran *Blue Eyes*, and the *Cornhill*, which commissioned *Far From the Madding Crowd* and *The Hand of Ethelberta*. Tinsley Brothers had already issued Hardy's first two novels in volume form. The firm had built its commercial success and dubious reputation upon Mary Braddon's *Lady Audley's Secret* and remained closely associated with sensation fiction. It was common for new authors to drift towards Tinsley having failed to attract more prestigious firms. *Desperate Remedies* was initially offered to Macmillan but William Tinsley later suggested that no other publisher than himself would have printed such a 'blood-curdling story' (*LW*: 91).

Hardy's graduation to the *Cornhill* represented a significant advance. It was here, however, that he first experienced on a significant scale the kind of editorial censorship that coloured his career as a novelist. The editor, Leslie Stephen, requested that he omit several passages in the manuscript of *Madding Crowd*, including softening the references to Fanny Robin's pregnancy. Rosemarie Morgan has shown the extent to which he altered Hardy's style and language, often without the author knowing until instalments were published.[2] Nevertheless, at this stage of his career Hardy was 'anxious ... to be considered a good hand at a serial'. In words that may owe something to retrospect, he recalled writing to Stephen: 'Perhaps I may have higher aims some day, and be a great stickler for the proper artistic balance of the completed work' (*LW*: 102). Stephen's interventions were not wholly motivated by prudishness: his objection to the length of the description of the sheep-shearing supper was that '[f]or periodical purposes … it rather delays the action unnecessarily'.[3] He himself suggested that Hardy might restore the cuts for volume publication.

Most magazines were conducted with an acute sense of audience. Stephen's censoring pencil had been sharpened by '[t]hree respectable ladies and subscribers' who had written in complaint of 'an improper passage'. He told Hardy that in responding to these objections he was speaking 'as an editor, not as a man' (*LW*: 101–2). Macmillan also received a letter from a reader during the serialisation of *The Woodlanders* regretting that such a story had been admitted into a magazine that might be 'put without hesitation into the hands of our daughters'.[4] Both examples are a reminder of how perceptions of the reading public were gendered. In his 1891 essay 'Candour in English Fiction', Hardy argued that by catering for 'household reading … the magazine in particular and the circulating library in general do not foster the growth of the novel which reflects and reveals life' (*THPW*: 128).

In his early career Hardy was willing to respond to the guidance of editors and publishers. His first two novels were directly shaped by advice given by two publishers' readers (George Meredith and John Morley) on the strengths and weaknesses of 'The Poor Man and the Lady', the unpublished novel he finished in 1868. His later concessions to Stephen and others have been judged by T. R. Wright as 'almost embarrassingly subservient (or perhaps cynically pragmatic)'.[5] As an apprentice author, however, he viewed editors as arbiters of literary taste from whom there was much to learn. When he submitted a portion of an early version of *The Return of the Native* to *Blackwood's Magazine* in 1877, he gave the editor liberty to 'strike … out' any 'word or reflection' that was 'not in harmony with the general tone of the magazine' (*CL* I: 49). William Blackwood admired the story and, though he had no opening for it, offered Hardy some constructive criticisms, principally on the opening chapters, which he thought might 'fail to catch popular interest'. Hardy promised to apply his 'valuable hints' to the remainder of the story and evidence suggests he did.[6] *The Return* was eventually published in *Belgravia*, a monthly magazine owned by Chatto & Windus, which accepted Hardy's offer without seeing any of the story. Though he subjected his manuscript to a thorough rewriting, there is no evidence that Hardy was required to make alterations specifically for *Belgravia*. Significantly, he made few substantive changes when revising this story for volume publication. Morgan wonders if he had 'lost interest' in the novel, but on this occasion without the intervention of an editor there was perhaps no need for revision.[7] It had been serialised, if not wholly in the form Hardy might have wanted, in one with which he could be content.

*Belgravia* was less puritanical than the *Cornhill* but also less prestigious. Edited until 1876 by Mary Braddon, it still carried her reputation for scandal. It is significant, however, that on the one occasion Hardy was not required by an editor to modify his serial it was for a somewhat disreputable magazine with a falling circulation. It is one of the ironies of the late-Victorian literary marketplace that the most culturally highbrow sites of publication and reading – the premier magazines and the circulating libraries – were also the most prudish. Ostensibly lower forms of publication, such as *Tinsleys'* and *Belgravia*, granted authors more freedom. For a novelist keen to build a reputation, however, these publications carried the wrong sorts of literary associations.

The contrasting tone and content of the different magazines in which Hardy's novels appeared meant that his audience was not homogenous. The *Cornhill* and *Macmillan's* were literary miscellanies; *Belgravia* was subtitled *An Illustrated London Magazine*. At a further extreme, *Good Words*, which serialised *The Trumpet-Major*, was a religiously oriented magazine that worked to construct as well as to serve its audience. The editor, Donald Macleod, requested that Hardy avoid 'everything likely to offend the susceptibilities of honest religious and domestic souls'.[8] Several amendments to Hardy's manuscript were made including, most famously, the transfer of a lovers' meeting from a Sunday to a Monday. As has been widely argued, part of the meaning of a serialised novel lies in the meanings generated by the other contents of the magazine, including the layout and use of illustration as well as the textual material. Linda M. Shires argues that the illustrations to *The Trumpet-Major*, like the choice of magazine itself, 'dulled the originality of the text'.[9] The first instalment of Hardy's story appeared alongside another serial by Jean Ingelow, a sermon, two other religious papers, and essays on such subjects as 'Food for the Economical' and 'Health at Home'. Just as the sensational associations of *Belgravia* contributed to the textual meaning of *The Return*, the domestic and religious emphasis of *Good Words* inflected *The Trumpet-Major*.

At sixpence, *Good Words* had a more popular appeal than the shilling magazines that ran Hardy's previous novels. Like the *Cornhill* and *Belgravia*, however, its readership was in decline by the 1870s. Hardy's serial history illustrates how monthly magazines were outmanoeuvred in the market by cheaper formats such as illustrated weeklies, newspapers, and American publications. His next two serials, *A Laodicean* and *Two on a Tower*, were published in American magazines,[10] and three of the subsequent four appeared in weekly publications. The duration of serials became shorter. *The Mayor of Casterbridge* appeared in the *Graphic* over a five-month period, less than half the duration of Hardy's monthly serials, and *The Pursuit of the Well-Beloved* occupied only twelve short weekly instalments of the *Illustrated London News*. Weekly serialisation presented different demands. Hardy felt he had 'damaged' *The Mayor* 'recklessly as an artistic whole' (*LW*: 185) by striving to get an incident into each weekly part, and in later revisions he worked to reduce the number of narrative events.

The *Illustrated London News* and the *Graphic* had circulations that touched 250,000: more than ten and twenty times, respectively, that of the *Cornhill* and *Belgravia* in the 1870s. The expansion of newspaper syndication opened Hardy up to an even larger audience. Publication in provincial newspapers became an increasingly significant mode of serialisation from the 1870s, offering greater remuneration to authors. The Bolton firm of Tillotson & Son pioneered the practice of buying up serial rights in novels and leasing them out to British and foreign newspapers. '[T]he plan of publication as a *feuilleton* in newspapers read mainly by adults' (*THPW*: 132) was a suggestion Hardy made in 'Candour in English Fiction' for overcoming market censorship. His own dealings with Tillotson, however, were brief and unrewarding. In the 1880s he sold some short stories, which were published in the *Bolton Weekly Journal* and the *Manchester Weekly Times*, and then, in June 1887, signed a contract for the exclusive world serial rights in a new novel. The payment, 1,000 guineas (£1,050), was the largest sum offered to Hardy by a British publisher. Portions of the manuscript were sent in September 1889 and set up in print but once the content of this early version of what became *Tess of the d'Urbervilles* was discovered Tillotson refused to publish and cancelled the contract. *Tess* nevertheless appeared in several provincial newspapers after Hardy had produced the bowdlerised version that ran in the *Graphic* from July to December 1891. It was common in this period for novels to be serialised in metropolitan magazines and provincial newspapers simultaneously. The sale of *Tess* (as 'A Daughter of the D'Urbervilles') to the *Nottinghamshire Guardian*, the *Birmingham Weekly Post*, and the *Sydney Mail* was conducted by the literary agent A. P. Watt acting on behalf of the *Graphic*, which had purchased British serial rights from Hardy for £550.[11]

Hardy's early novels had already been serialised in newspapers in America. Holt arranged for the issue of *Blue Eyes* and *Madding Crowd* in the *Semi-Weekly Tribune*. In the absence of copyright protection for British authors in America before 1891, however, other newspapers could print texts from the British serial versions, and *Madding Crowd* also appeared in at least three other papers. Increasingly, however, American publishers were willing to pay British authors for serial rights to get ahead on the market. The *New York Times* dealt directly with Hardy over *Ethelberta*, paying him £50 for each instalment. The widespread newspaper publication was matched by the availability of cheap volume editions. Holt published his first editions at $1.25 (approximately 5s) but was soon undercut by other publishers printing texts from the serial versions. The *Semi-Weekly Tribune* distributed a bound edition of *Blue Eyes* for just 10 cents (5d). In the predominantly book-borrowing culture of Britain, readers could not purchase a Hardy novel at a comparable price until sixpenny editions of the more popular works appeared in the new century. Unauthorised American printings (they were not, technically, pirated) proliferated in cheap, often paperback, series such as the Lakeside Library, the Fireside Library, and the Seaside Library. Six different editions of *The Mayor* appeared in one year.[12] All this meant that Hardy's readership in America was much larger than in his home country.

By the late 1880s Hardy had ceased to invest artistically in the serial form. Self-bowdlerisation had become a habit as he 'began consciously to address a dual audience' of serial and volume.[13] Having preempted editorial objections to *The Woodlanders*, he adopted a plan for *Tess* 'unprecedented in the annals of fiction' (*LW*: 232).

Having failed to place the story with *Murray's Magazine* and *Macmillan's* – which detected, respectively, too many 'immoral situations' and 'too much succulence' – he sent the story to the *Graphic* with chapters omitted and further changes indicated.[14] The story was bowdlerised to the point of absurdity, with no seduction taking place and the heroine instead being tricked into a phoney marriage. The violation and baptism scenes were cut out and published as two separate stories elsewhere. Hardy recalled that the 'sheer drudgery' of performing this act of dismemberment prompted him 'to get away from the supply of family fiction to magazines as soon as he could conveniently do so' (*LW*: 232). Even so, he began his next novel (what became *Jude the Obscure*) for *Harper's New Monthly Magazine* with the intention of writing a story that 'would not bring a blush to a school-girl's cheek'.[15] Finding that he could not fulfil this self-imposed directive, he agreed to make any necessary changes on the assumption that these would be restored for volume publication. Much of the composition of the novel was thus undertaken with two versions of the text and two audiences in mind.

The hostile critical reception of *Jude* in 1895–6 led to the end of Hardy's career as a novelist but not his career in fiction. At the time of publication, he was busy revising his works for a collected edition issued by Osgood, McIlvaine. *Jude* was first published as Volume 8 of that edition, completed in 1897 with *The Well-Beloved*, a much revised version of the *Illustrated London News* serial. Like James, Hardy was an inveterate reviser, and the publication of his novels in book form amounts to a complicated history of revision and re-revision.

With the exception of *Jude* and *The Well-Beloved*, all Hardy's novels were first published in book form in two- or three-volume sets. Artificially priced at 21s or 31s/6d, these sold almost entirely, at a substantial discount, to the circulating libraries. Less affected by library censorship than magazine censorship, Hardy still had to conform to the 'select' nature of the two main libraries: Mudie's and Smith's. Multivolume novels were published in small print runs, and excess sets were commonly remaindered after a year at prices below the cost of production. Tinsley issued 500 sets of *Desperate Remedies*, selling just over half at the normal discount rate.[16] Once established, however, Hardy did well at the libraries. To sell almost nine-tenths of the 1,000 sets of *The Return* was not commercially 'a disaster'.[17]

The diversification of the market was a significant factor in generating the widespread textual variation that characterises Hardy's fiction. Inconsistencies between American and British serial versions are explained in part by geographical distance. The absence of copyright protection allowing American firms to print editions from British serial instalments made it essential for material to reach the authorised American publisher quickly. Not all the changes Hardy made on the proof-sheets of the British serial edition of *Ethelberta* made their way into the *New York Times*, for example, and the American serial run was frequently interrupted when proof-sheets failed to reach the publisher in time. For *Two on a Tower*, serialised exclusively in the American *Atlantic Monthly*, Hardy arranged for a duplicate manuscript to be sent across the Atlantic but distance forced him to delegate proof-reading to the editor. American texts of the novels frequently contain unique variants. Hardy's revisions for Holt's 1874 edition of *Desperate Remedies* were not included in subsequent British editions. Similarly, the version of *The Trumpet-Major* serialised in *Demorest's Monthly Magazine* includes not only some manuscript passages cut from the British serial in *Good Words*, but also additional matter not then included in the British book editions.

Because volume editions in Britain and America were issued just before the completion of a serial run there was limited time for revision. Hardy made more than five hundred revisions to Holt's edition of *The Mayor* but none pertained to the final five chapters owing to the need to publish before unauthorised printings of the serial appeared.[18] Furthermore, book editions were usually printed from marked copies of the serial texts rather than manuscripts, which probably explains why the volume edition of *The Trumpet-Major* does not restore all of the manuscript passages omitted from *Good Words*. In the case of *Madding Crowd*, the manuscript was never returned to Hardy, making restoration of deleted passages almost impossible. Nevertheless, Hardy frequently made revisions at this stage of the textual process. For example, he deleted the self-reflexive opening of *Blue Eyes*, where the heroine is introduced reading a three-volume novel, and cancelled the section in *The*

*Mayor* when Henchard returns to Casterbridge for Elizabeth-Jane's marriage, whereas the American edition retained this passage.

In Britain, the publication of a library edition was followed by a cheap one-volume reprint. Hardy's early novels took several years to reach this form. *A Pair of Blue Eyes* only appeared in a 6s edition after four years and even the popular *Madding Crowd* took over two years to reach a 7s6d edition. By the 1880s, however, publishers were issuing cheap reprints more quickly: A one-volume edition of *The Woodlanders* appeared just five months after the three-decker. Because these editions were resettings of the novels, Hardy had the opportunity for further revision, and in the early novels in particular he sometimes made changes in response to criticisms by reviewers.

At the end of the century, publishers began issuing recently published works in paperback sixpenny editions (which would actually retail at 4½d). Printed on low-grade paper in double columns, these had an ephemeral quality with the look and feel of a newspaper. Harper published sixpenny editions of *Madding Crowd* and *Tess* in 1900 and 1901, the latter selling 100,000 copies in twelve months (*CL* III: 14). Textual variation was exacerbated since not all of the amendments Hardy made to these editions could be incorporated in the 1902–3 uniform edition of the works, published by Macmillan, as the plates of the Osgood, McIlvaine edition from which it was printed could bear minimum disruption.

The Osgood, McIlvaine edition represents Hardy's first sustained attempt to fashion his works as a whole. He used it chiefly to further his developing vision of Wessex.[19] The volumes were published under the title 'The Wessex Novels' and carried a map of the fictional area. The introduction of more precise fictional topography altered the style of the early novels in particular. *Under the Greenwood Tree* was transformed 'from an idyll set in some indeterminate pastoral realm into a novel of Wessex'.[20] Because Hardy had sold the copyright in this work, however, editions of the original 1876 cheap reprint continued to circulate alongside the substantially different versions of the text included in the uniform and collected editions. The novel was only included in the Osgood, McIlvaine edition after Hardy negotiated a royalty agreement with Chatto & Windus, which had purchased the copyright from Tinsley.

Hardy's revising hand refused to tire. The transfer of his novels in 1902 to Macmillan produced a revised uniform edition, which was followed in 1912–14 by the Wessex Edition and in 1919–20 by the Mellstock Edition, limited to 525 sets. The texts underwent substantial revision for the Wessex Edition, and in addition to writing a new set of prefaces Hardy divided his fictional works into categories: 'Novels of Character and Environment', 'Romances and Fantasies', and 'Novels of Ingenuity'. The texts of this edition formed the basis of most editions of Hardy's novels, popular and scholarly, published in the twentieth century. In the closing decades, however, two major series, the Oxford World's Classics and the new Penguin Classics, produced newly edited texts and triggered ongoing debates about editing Hardy.

The main feature of the Oxford volumes is the reproduction, where possible, of Hardy's manuscript punctuation. It was customary for Victorian compositors to follow a house style and novelists expected their punctuation to be altered in the transition from manuscript to print. This explains why many of Hardy's manuscripts are inconsistently punctuated, something that requires the Oxford editors, ironically, to replicate the role of the compositor. Nevertheless, the decision to restore Hardy's distinctively light use of the comma can be justified artistically as well as in terms of authorial intention, and Hardy's extensive removal of commas for the Wessex Edition suggests a desire to '[return] the text towards the manuscript'.[21] Most volumes in the series use the manuscript – where available – for the accidentals but incorporate all subsequent revisions that can be judged authorial. They are thus eclectic texts and do not correspond to any edition published or read in Hardy's lifetime. By seeking to present the works in a form that the author 'might have wished had he been able to collate all the texts himself',[22] the series follows the Greg-Bowers school of editing, with its theories of copy-text. By contrast, the Penguin series follows a 'social text' approach by using, with one exception (*Madding Crowd*), the first volume edition as the base-text, presenting each novel as 'the creation of its own period' rather than of later authorial revision.[23] The ready availability of two paperback series based on contrasting textual principles is actually a benefit to Hardy studies, since no student can ignore the complex history of the texts, a history that was fuelled by Hardy's insatiable appetite for revision but substantially created by the diverse nature of the literary market outlined in this chapter.

NOTES

1 Carl Weber, *Hardy in America* (Waterville: Colby College Press, 1946), p. 21.
2 Rosemarie Morgan, *Cancelled Words: Rediscovering Thomas Hardy* (London: Routledge, 1992).
3 Quoted by R. L. Purdy, *Thomas Hardy: A Bibliographical Study* (Oxford: Clarendon, 1968), pp. 337–8.
4 Simon Nowell-Smith, *Letters to Macmillan* (London: Macmillan, 1967), pp. 130–1.
5 T. R. Wright, *Hardy and His Readers* (Basingstoke: Palgrave Macmillan, 2003), p. 14.
6 Simon Gatrell, *Hardy the Creator: A Textual Biography* (Oxford: Clarendon, 1988), p. 33.
7 'Editing Hardy', in *Thomas Hardy Studies*, ed. Phillip Mallett (Basingstoke: Palgrave Macmillan, 2004), p. 99.
8 Quoted by Gatrell, *Hardy the Creator*, p. 53
9 *The Trumpet-Major*, ed. Linda M. Shires (London: Penguin, 1997), p. 341.
10 *Harper's New Monthly Magazine*, which published *A Laodicean*, appeared simultaneously in a European Edition; the *Atlantic Monthly*, which serialised *Two on a Tower*, was published simultaneously in London, the American sheets in an English wrapper: see Purdy, *Thomas Hardy*, pp. 37, 42.
11 Graham Law and John Stock Clarke, 'More Light on the Serial Publication of *Tess of the d'Urbervilles*', *Review of English Studies*, 54 (February 2003), pp. 94–101.
12 Weber, *Hardy in America*, p. 37.
13 Wright, *Hardy and His Readers*, p. 16.
14 *Tess of the d'Urbervilles*, ed. Tim Dolin (London: Penguin, 1998), pp. xlvii–xlix.
15 Joseph Henry Harper, *I Remember* (New York: Harper, 1934) pp. 164–5.
16 Purdy, *Thomas Hardy*, p. 5
17 Wright, *Hardy and His Readers*, p. 110.
18 *The Mayor of Casterbridge*, ed. Dale Kramer (Oxford: Oxford University Press, 1987), p. xxxvii.
19 Simon Gatrell, *Thomas Hardy's Vision of Wessex* (Basingstoke: Palgrave Macmillan, 2003).

20 *Under the Greenwood Tree*, ed. Tim Dolin (London: Penguin, 1998), p. xxiv.
21 Gatrell, *Hardy the Creator*, p. 218.
22 *A Pair of Blue Eyes*, ed. Alan Manford (Oxford: Oxford University Press, 1985), p. xxviii.
23 Patricia Ingham, 'General Editor's Preface' to the Penguin Classics series.

# 6

# Illustration

PAMELA DALZIEL

'what is the use of a book,' thought Alice, 'without pictures
or conversations?'

Alice's frequently cited question concludes the opening paragraph of
one of the most famous Victorian illustrated books, Lewis Carroll's
*Alice's Adventures in Wonderland*, published in 1865 with John
Tenniel illustrations engraved by the Dalziel brothers. That same
year the publication of 'How I Built Myself a House' in *Chambers's
Journal* brought Hardy his first literary earnings. Although his
story, like all *Chambers's* contributions, was unillustrated, Hardy
would have been well aware that success as an author in the 1860s,
in the midst of the 'golden age' of wood-engraving, often depended
upon publication in periodicals and books that exploited the power
of the visual to attract readers, and that the stature of the illustrator
could be equal or even superior to that of the author. Throughout
the 1860s Alexander Macmillan, to whom in 1868 Hardy sent the
manuscript of his first (and now lost) novel 'The Poor Man and
the Lady', published numerous books with illustrations by leading artists, including *Alice's Adventures in Wonderland*, Christina
Rossetti's *Goblin Market and Other Poems*, illustrated by Dante
Gabriel Rossetti (1862), and Charles Kingsley's *The Water-Babies*,
illustrated by Joseph Noel Paton (1863). While the Macmillan
venue for serial fiction, *Macmillan's Magazine*, was not illustrated –
and therefore neither was Hardy's first Macmillan publication,
*The Woodlanders* (1886–7) – all but one of the other magazines in
which Hardy's serialised novels appeared, beginning with *Tinsleys'
Magazine* (*A Pair of Blue Eyes*, 1872–3), were illustrated, as were
most of the periodicals that published his short stories and poems.
During his long publishing career, spanning seven decades from
the mid-1860s to the late 1920s, Hardy's work was illustrated by
some of the most celebrated visual artists of his time, including

George du Maurier, Hubert Herkomer, and Rockwell Kent – and also by a celebrated author, Thomas Hardy himself.

Hardy's visual sensibility found expression during his youth in his topographical drawings and watercolours and was further developed by his architectural training and experience. The sketches in his surviving architectural notebook demonstrate that he was a skilled draughtsman, while those torn from the pocket-sized notebooks that he carried with him from his early twenties onward bear witness to his continuing graphic skills. In later life he is said to have remarked that ideas 'frequently ... presented themselves to his mind in the first instance more in the guise of mental pictures than as subjects for writing down'.[1] The rich visuality of those ideas is evident in many of the extracts from the pocket notebooks incorporated in *Life and Work* or transcribed in the 'Memoranda I' ('Prose Matter') and 'Poetical Matter' notebooks, including:

Sept 11, 1872. In London.
Saw a lady who when she smiled smiled too much – over all her face, chin, round to her ears, & up among her hair, so that you were surfeited of smiling, & felt you would never smile any more. ('Memoranda I', *PN*: 11)

Moon like a gold bill hook, or the nail-paring of a goddess. (c. 1882, *PM*: 11)

Wind pulls at trees like a termagant seizing another termagant's hair; whizzes like a relaxing spring, combs the grass violently. Oct 13. 1891. (*PM*: 18)

During his later years, after decades of success and celebrity, Hardy wished to be remembered as 'a man who used to notice such things' ('Afterwards', *CPW* II: 308). At the beginning of his literary career, eager though he was to establish himself even if that required the occasional artistic compromise, he was concerned that the illustrators of his work also 'notice' – and of course realise effectively – things, specifically the details and significance of his novels' scenes and characters. He preempted the need for his first illustrator J. A. Pasquier to be particularly observant, however, by sending the publisher William Tinsley sketches for the illustrations to the first two *A Pair of Blue Eyes* instalments (September and October 1872) before sending the text. Although the sketches do not survive, that Pasquier made use of them is suggested by the resemblance between Elfride, at least as depicted in the first two illustrations, and her 'original', Hardy's future wife Emma Gifford. Since Hardy seems not to have sent sketches for the subsequent instalments, it is worth noting that the first two illustrations are the most successful: sympathetic in their representation of Elfride and dramatic in composition (see Figure 1).

Hardy was less actively involved in the illustration of his next novel, *Far from the Madding Crowd*, submitted to the prestigious *Cornhill* at the invitation of the editor Leslie Stephen and serialised January–December 1874. Hardy knew that the *Cornhill* was the premier magazine for fiction and that its authors and illustrators were among the most distinguished. Its first editor, W. M. Thackeray, whom in 1863 Hardy had recommended to his sister Mary Hardy as 'the greatest novellist [*sic*] of the day' (*CL* I: 5), had after all included in the first (1860) issues fiction by himself, Anthony Trollope, Elizabeth Gaskell, and George MacDonald, as well as signed poems by Alfred Tennyson, Washington Irving, Emily Brontë, Matthew Arnold, Elizabeth Barrett Browning, and Charlotte Brontë, and illustrations by John Everett Millais, Frederick Sandys, and Frederic Leighton. By the time Hardy began writing *Far from the Madding Crowd* in 1873 – indeed throughout the 1870s and much of the 1880s – the most consistently featured *Cornhill* illustrator was George du Maurier, best known then and now, in spite of his extensive illustration of fiction, for his *Punch* cartoons satirising the social pretensions of London society and all who transgressed conventional boundaries of aesthetic sensibility, gender, or class. Hardy could well have thought that, if du Maurier were to illustrate *Far from the Madding Crowd*, his renderings of the rural characters and scenes were unlikely to be overly sympathetic or even particularly accurate in detail. In December 1873, with the first instalment of the novel scheduled to appear at the end of that month for January 1874, Hardy wrote twice to the *Cornhill* publishers Smith, Elder:

With regard to the illustrations perhaps I may be allowed to express a hope that the rustics, although *quaint*, may be made to appear *intelligent, & not boorish* at all.

I have sketched in my note-book during the past summer a few correct outlines of smockfrocks, gaiters, sheep-crooks, rick-'staddles', a

Figure 1. J. A. Pasquier, *A Pair of Blue Eyes* illustration, *Tinsleys' Magazine*, September 1872.

sheep-washing pool, one of the old-fashioned malt-houses, and some other out-of-the-way things that might have to be shown. These I could send you if they would be of any use to the artist, but if he is a sensitive man and you think he would rather not be interfered with, I would not do so. (*CL* I: 25)

Implicit in Hardy's somewhat hesitantly expressed request and offer of assistance is an acknowledgement that the illustrator was likely to be a well-known artist, hence more valuable to the publishers than a fledgling author. Leading illustrators had always been featured in the *Cornhill*; most of them – along with the engravers – signed their work, whereas the serialised fiction was published anonymously, and indeed the advertisements for the magazine both named and gave primacy of place to the illustrators rather than the authors. The 30 May 1874 *Academy* advertisement is typical:

THE CORNHILL MAGAZINE for JUNE,
With Illustrations by GEORGE DU MAURIER and HELEN PATERSON.
CONTENTS: –
Far from the Madding Crowd. (With an Illustration.) ...

The short advertisements placed in newspapers did not refer to the fiction at all, only to the illustrations.

In spite of what most of the advertisements might suggest, *Far from the Madding Crowd* was not illustrated by du Maurier but by the then relatively obscure Helen Paterson, who during the course of the novel's serialisation married the poet William Allingham and only subsequently, beginning in the 1880s, began to paint the cottages and cottage gardens that would establish her as the most successful of the Idyllist school of watercolourists.[2] Thus when in May 1874 Hardy met Paterson he was not intimidated by her artistic reputation and, emboldened by the favourable reception of his novel's early instalments, did not hesitate to offer her 'a few points' (*LW*: 103) or to emphasise, even while being 'fairly complimentary', that 'it was difficult for two minds to imagine scenes in the same light'.[3] He subsequently sent her 'a few particulars of the story' and offered to provide 'any other information, or any sketch' (*CL* I: 30) – sketches of a milking bucket and shepherd's crook still accompany the draft letter – thereby demonstrating a concern for the accurate representation of details, which would continue unabated throughout his career.

During his later years Hardy consistently described Helen (Paterson) Allingham as the 'best illustrator I ever had', a judgement, as I have suggested elsewhere, which perhaps owed as much to his having developed 'romantical' feelings for her as it did to his appreciation of her work.[4] Paterson's illustrations, if well-executed, largely ignore the more dramatic – indeed sensational – aspects of *Far from the Madding Crowd*, limitingly defining it as a rural idyll, both in the *Cornhill* and in the two-volume Smith, Elder edition, which includes all of her full-page drawings, though not her initial capitals. Her illustration of Gabriel's asking Bathsheba if she wants a shepherd, for example, is distinctly Arcadian: a pastoral scene cleansed of all traces of the rick fire, complete with an unsooty shepherd in a pristine smock-frock neither burnt into holes nor dripping with water (Figure 2).

The genre of Hardy's next novel, *The Hand of Ethelberta*, serialised in the *Cornhill* July 1875–May 1876, was also defined rather narrowly by the illustrator, who on this occasion was du Maurier. As with *Far from the Madding Crowd*, that definition continued beyond the serialisation with the inclusion of the full-page illustrations in the two-volume edition. One of the earliest reviewers correctly observed that the illustrations 'are in Mr. Du Maurier's well-known style', while Ethelberta 'appears as the familiar lady of *Punch*' (*Athenæum*, 15 April 1876). To define this 'Comedy in Chapters' as *Punch*-like social satire is of course appropriate; however, the social conservative du Maurier did not represent – perhaps did not even recognise – the novel's subversion of class and gender norms. In his February 1876 illustration, for example, he depicted the republican artisan Sol and his brother Dan as Hodge-like caricatures with rounded shoulders and dazed, unintelligent expressions, thereby reinscribing class stereotype and ensuring that by the time Sol articulates his radical views the middle-class reader has already been encouraged to dismiss him as a person of no account.

Hardy seems not to have had any contact with du Maurier until after the serialisation of *Ethelberta* concluded, at which point, far from criticising the illustrator's limited interpretation, he sent him a 'kind & flattering letter'.[5] Hardy would have recognised

Figure 2. Helen Paterson, *Far from the Madding Crowd* illustration, *Cornhill Magazine*, February 1874.

the distinction that the association with du Maurier brought to the novel, and in any case he never objected to his illustrators' simplistic definition of genre, focusing instead on ensuring that details were depicted accurately and characters sympathetically. Attractive and engaging illustrations that would draw readers were particularly desirable for *The Return of the Native*, since its 1878 serialisation in *Belgravia* 'of all places' (*LW*: 120) represented a significant loss of status and income for Hardy at a time when he was still attempting to establish his career as a novelist. *Belgravia's* imitation of the *Cornhill* in name (a London location), price (one shilling), and format (illustrated monthly) did not extend to the quality of fiction or illustration, sensation and sentiment being the distinguishing characteristics of most *Belgravia* contributions. Although the *Return of the Native* illustrator Arthur Hopkins had previously contributed to a number of leading illustrated periodicals, including the *Cornhill* and the *Graphic*, he had neither the reputation of du Maurier nor the skill of Paterson, and Hardy did not hesitate to criticise his less than sympathetic initial drawing of Eustacia, sending him a sketch of his 'Queen of Night' as he imagined her and subsequently suggesting that she be 'represented as more youthful in face, supple in figure, &, in general, with a little more roundness & softness than have been given her' (*CL*: I:52) – in other words, as more conventionally feminine.[6] If Hardy's letters and sketches ensured that details such as the mummers' costumes were represented accurately, they did not entirely succeed in sparing his 'wayward & erring heroine' (*CL* I: 53) from being visually punished through unattractive representation by an illustrator who, in spite of his desire 'to supply some drawings of a strength and character in keeping with the strength and character of the story', was clearly more comfortable portraying the 'good' characters, especially Thomasin and Venn.[7]

Hardy's awareness of the importance of illustration and his continuing focus on accurate detail can be seen in his letter accepting William Isbister's offer for the 1880 serialisation of *The Trumpet-Major* in *Good Words*: 'I hope you will provide me with a skilful artist, & that he or she will not be above accepting from me rough sketches of any unusual objects that come into the tale' (*CL* VII: 92). Hardy subsequently recommended and then himself wrote to Charles Keene, celebrated for his *Punch* illustrations and 'considered by army men to draw soldiers remarkably well' (*CL* I: 66). Keene declined Hardy's invitation, which was in due course issued to and accepted by the realist painter John Collier. As a novice illustrator, Collier welcomed assistance, promising 'to insure correctness in the costume and accessories' and making extensive use of Hardy's sketches: 'They are just what I want the interior of the old kitchen being especially serviceable to me.'[8] However, as Linda M. Shires has observed, Collier's static illustrations are realistic only in detail and define the novel as an historically accurate romance rather than, as illustrations by Keene might have done, as 'experimental, anti-realist, anti-romantic, celebratory, [and] highly imaginative'.[9]

Having Hardy select and work closely with the illustrator was also less than successful for *A Laodicean*, serialised in the inaugural issues of the European Edition of *Harper's New Monthly Magazine* December 1880–December 1881, and illustrated by du Maurier after being offered to Helen Allingham, Frank Dicksee, and William Small. Harper & Brothers had asked Hardy to find a first-class artist, and du Maurier, 'by far the most popular illustrator' in England, was an obvious choice, since, as Hardy pointed out,

Figure 3. George du Maurier, *A Laodicean* illustration, *Harper's New Monthly Magazine*, December 1881.

'apart from the merit of his drawings, his name would carry a great deal of weight in placards or advertisements of the new edition of the *Magazine*, & would help greatly to attract attention here' (*CL* I: 74). Hardy also knew what he had not known during the serialisation of *Ethelberta*: that du Maurier preferred to work collaboratively and would welcome comments and suggestions. Until the onset of his serious illness in the midst of work on the third *Laodicean* illustration brought to an end the frequent luncheons and lengthy correspondence, Hardy actively assisted du Maurier, providing photographs and sketches and even approving drawings in draft and final form. Although Henry Harper was disappointed with the illustrations, some of the later, noncollaborative drawings of *Punch*-like social situations (see Figure 3) are in fact quite effective, if, as with *Ethelberta*, limiting in their definition of the novel as social satire.

In June 1883 Hardy's first illustrated story, 'The Romantic Adventures of a Milkmaid', appeared in the *Graphic*, which subsequently published *The Mayor of Casterbridge* (2 January–15 May 1886), *A Group of Noble Dames* (unillustrated, 1890 Christmas Number), and *Tess of the D'Urbervilles* (4 July–26 December 1891). Established in 1869 by the wood-engraver W. L. Thomas, the

*Graphic* was an illustrated weekly newspaper distinguished from its primary competitor the *Illustrated London News* by the exceptionally high quality of its large – often folio-sized and sometimes double-page – engravings of contemporary paintings and illustrations commissioned by leading artists. During its first decade the *Graphic* was also known for its pictorial social realism; however, by the 1880s most of its illustrations were characterised by the kind of sentimental idealisation embodied in Millais's now-famous painting *Cherry Ripe*, reproduced as a double-page colour supplement to the 1880 Christmas Number and printed in half a million copies, which did not come close to meeting demand. Although the extraordinary success of that issue was never repeated, subsequent issues exploited the marketability of similar types of images. The 1883 Summer Number, for example, featured engravings of sentimental pictures from the Graphic Exhibition of Animal Paintings; its advertisements listed Hardy's 'Romantic Adventures' last, giving primacy of place to 'TWO WHOLE SHEETS OF PICTURES, MOSTLY PRINTED IN COLOURS, ALSO A LARGE PRESENTATION PLATE, 31 inches by 22, entitled "A MUTE APPEAL"'.

The 'Romantic Adventures' illustrator, C. S. Reinhart, was not named in the *Graphic* advertisements; nor were his admittedly undistinguished drawings advantageously placed, the first three appearing in the midst of the story's final chapters and the fourth buried among advertisements. The situation was quite different for *The Mayor*, illustrated by Robert Barnes, and *Tess*, illustrated by Hubert Herkomer and his students, in part because fiction illustration was prominently featured in the regular weekly *Graphic* issues, but primarily because Barnes and Herkomer were so well known. In a 7 February 1891 list of one hundred *Graphic* artists headed by Leighton, Herkomer appears tenth and Barnes, immediately preceded by Helen Allingham, thirty-seventh; the parallel writers' list awards Hardy thirty-ninth place after George MacDonald. The more celebrated the contributor the more prominence he was awarded: 'DRAWN BY ROBERT BARNES' is included, albeit in relatively small type, below each of the *Mayor* illustrations, whereas 'DRAWN BY PROFESSOR HUBERT HERKOMER, R.A.' dwarfs all else in the captions for the opening double-page *Tess* illustration.

Figure 4. Robert Barnes, *The Mayor of Casterbridge* illustration, *Graphic*, 2 January 1886.

Barnes's and Herkomer's illustrations clearly achieved their intended purpose of attracting readers; they are also the most consistently successful in both literary and visual terms of all the illustrations to Hardy's fiction. Barnes's striking, if at times ideal-ised, drawings (see Figure 4) represent sympathetically the novel's drama of relationships and significantly influenced contemporary readers' responses, even prompting Hardy to revise his represen-tation of the principal female characters.[10] Although Herkomer produced only six of the twenty-five *Tess* illustrations, his first – 'the best one' (*CL* I: 255) – defined Hardy's most famous heroine in all her complexity for at least two generations: it was repro-duced in full or in part (Figure 5) in the 1891 *Harper's Bazar* serial, numerous Harper's volume editions, an 1895 London exhibition of 'Wessex Paintings', the 1919 *Book Monthly* Christmas Number, the 1925–6 *John o' London's Weekly* serial and the Hardys' 1925 Christmas cards.

Hardy knew Herkomer and could certainly have discussed the *Tess* illustrations with him; he probably also met Barnes when the

Figure 5. Hubert Herkomer, detail of *Tess of the D'Urbervilles* illustration, *Graphic*, 4 July 1891.

artist visited Dorchester in 1885 after receiving Hardy's list identifying the 'originals' of the *Mayor* locations. No assistance seems to have been offered, however, to either Walter Paget or William Hatherell, the respective illustrators of *The Pursuit of the Well-Beloved* (*Illustrated London News*, 1 October–17 December 1892) and *The Simpletons/Hearts Insurgent* (*Harper's New Monthly*, December 1894–November 1895), which did not prevent Paget from creating a distinctly Hardy-like Jocelyn or Hatherell from representing 'Jude at the Milestone' so effectively that Hardy wrote: 'The picture is a tragedy in itself: & I do not remember ever before having an artist who grasped a situation so thoroughly' (*CL* II: 94).

Although almost half of Hardy's short stories were illustrated when first published, he apparently assisted only one illustrator, the landscape painter Alfred Parsons. Hardy had suggested Parsons, along with Allingham, Charles Green, and Small, for 'The First Countess of Wessex' (*Harper's New Monthly*, December 1889); Harper & Brothers assigned the 'figures, in the costume of George the Second's reign', to Reinhart, and the 'old English manor-house architecture, & woodland scenery, with large gnarled oaks &c.' (*CL* I: 181), to Parsons, who was invited to stay at Max Gate and visited with Hardy at least one of the scenes of the story. Hardy's assisting Parsons, like his specifying Dorchester locations for the *Mayor* illustrations and purchasing local photographs for 'Ancient Earthworks at Casterbridge' (*English Illustrated Magazine*, December 1893), reflects a shift in focus as the increasing Wessexisation of his fiction led him to direct his concern for accurate detail toward ensuring that fictitious settings, even if only '*suggested* by … real places' (*CL* III: 172), were correctly identified.[11] He closely collaborated with both Henry Macbeth-Raeburn and Hermann Lea, indicating locations and even vantage points for their topographical frontispieces to his first two collected editions, appropriately entitled 'The Wessex Novels' (Osgood, McIlvaine, 1895–6) and 'Wessex Edition' (Macmillan, 1912–31). The inclusion of '*Drawn on the spot*' following the identification of each of Macbeth-Raeburn's evocative Osgood, McIlvaine etchings (see Figure 6) functions much as the use of Lea's photographs in the Wessex Edition, blurring the line between real and imaginary, as did the maps of Wessex that Hardy drafted for the two editions. Years earlier Hardy had drawn the sketch-map frontispiece to the three-volume *Return of the Native*

Figure 6. Henry Macbeth-Raeburn, *The Woodlanders* frontispiece, Osgood, McIlvaine, 1896 [1895].

(1878) and the vignettes of encampment and mill blocked on the cover of the three-volume *Trumpet-Major* (1880). His predilection for geographical and architectural illustration is also evident in his detailed sketches of Tintagel Castle for *The Famous Tragedy of the Queen of Cornwall* (1923) and indeed in his famously enigmatic drawings for *Wessex Poems* (1898), that extraordinary first volume of verse originally subtitled 'With Sketches of their Scenes by the Author' (*LW*: 302).

Hardy recognised that illustrations could 'really help ... poems' (*CL* I: 208). He requested that 'An Ancient to Ancients' (*Century Magazine*, May 1922) be illustrated by Rockwell Kent, whose powerful Blakeian two-page headpiece adds a mythical dimension to the poem. Kent's opening image (Figure 7), reworked as 'Twilight of Man' (1926), is the best known of all the Hardy illustrations. Two other celebrated twentieth-century artists also produced striking and evocative illustrations: Arthur Wragg's elegant Klimtian border enhances the haunting eroticism of 'The Last Leaf' (compare his lyrical interpretation of 'Vagrant's Song'), whereas Harry Clarke's Beardsleyesque drawings define 'The Portraits' as

Figure 7. Rockwell Kent, 'An Ancient to Ancients' illustration, *Century Magazine*, May 1922.

Symbolist nightmare (*Nash's and Pall Mall Magazine*, November 1924, January 1925, December 1924).

The complex interplay of word and image is of course most evident when the author is also the illustrator, as several *Wessex Poems* reviewers recognised. Arthur Quiller-Couch, for example, insisted that Hardy's illustrations are 'packed with meaning, and reveal something which the poems they decorate are also trying to reveal' (*Speaker*, 24 December 1898); the *Glasgow Herald* reviewer observed that the drawings, 'themselves poems', 'give force to the poetry' and 'compel thinking' (4 January 1899), and the *Athenæum* that they are 'a new light on Wessex', 'full of poetry' (14 January 1899). Hardy acknowledged that the 'novel occupation of making the drawings' had so absorbed his interest that he neglected to 'remove defects of form in the verses' (*CL* II: 214). Sketching was a natural mode of expression for Hardy: had his pocket notebooks survived his illustration of *Wessex Poems* would doubtless have seemed less extraordinary. If it is a satire of circumstance that the illustrations he so valued (see Figure 8) were excluded from later editions, it is no less a moment of vision that some of the

Figure 8. Thomas Hardy, 'She, to Him' illustration, *Wessex Poems*, 1898.

original drawings, their luminosity undimmed by nineteenth-century reproductive processes, are included in the Birmingham Museums and Art Gallery's online database, enabling the appreciation of Hardy's ability to create nuanced complexity in pen and wash as well as in prose and verse.

NOTES

1 Clive Holland, *Thomas Hardy, O.M.: The Man, His Works and the Land of Wessex* (London: Herbert Jenkins, 1933), p. 60.
2 Only the advertisements for the January and February 1874 *Cornhill* issues listed Paterson first, preceding du Maurier and Marcus Stone, respectively.
3 Marcus B. Huish, *Happy England as Painted by Helen Allingham, R.W.S.* (London: Adam and Charles Black, 1903), p. 39.
4 *CL* I: 181, III: 218; "'She matched his violence with her own wild passion'": Illustrating *Far from the Madding Crowd'*, in *Reading Thomas Hardy*, ed. Charles P. C. Pettit (Basingstoke: Macmillan, 1998), pp. 25–8.
5 Du Maurier to Hardy, no date (subsequently misdated "'80 ?'"), Dorset County Museum; an inaccurate partial transcription is included in Arlene M. Jackson, *Illustration and the Novels of Thomas Hardy* (Totowa, N.J.: Rowman and Littlefield, 1981), p. 38.

6  Hopkins claimed that the illustration had been poorly engraved, while acknowledging that Joseph Swain usually produced 'capital work' for him (to Hardy, 5 Feb. 1878, Dorset County Museum). High-quality engraving was essential to the success of wood-engraved illustrations – the majority of the Hardy illustrations published in periodicals – even when the engraver, like Swain, specialised in facsimile, attempting to reproduce precisely the artist's drawing, rather than in interpretive engraving. During the 1870s and early 1880s most artists' drawings were photographed on to the wood-blocks (see *CL* I: 74–5); the engravers then cut away the parts of the designs that were to be white, leaving the black parts in relief for printing. Although Swain was one of the best of the Victorian wood-engravers, he and his son kept up with technological advances, using process (photo-mechanical) engraving to produce line blocks and half-tone blocks. The Swain firm engraved the illustrations to *Far from the Madding Crowd*, *The Return of the Native*, *The Hand of Ethelberta*, *A Laodicean*, 'The Grave by the Hand-post', and 'A Changed Man'.

7  Hopkins to Hardy, 19 Feb. 1878 (Dorset County Museum); see *CL* I: 52–5, 59, and Dalziel, 'Anxieties of Representation: The Serial Illustrations to Hardy's *The Return of the Native*', *Nineteenth-Century Literature* 51 (1996), pp. 84–110.

8  Collier to Hardy, 29 Aug. and 20 Nov. 1879, Dorset County Museum.

9  'Good Words, the Illustrations, and Critical Interpretation', in *The Trumpet-Major*, ed. Linda M. Shires (London: Penguin, 1997), p. 342.

10  See Dalziel, 'Whatever Happened to Elizabeth Jane? Revisioning Gender in *The Mayor of Casterbridge*', in *Thomas Hardy: Texts and Contexts*, ed. Phillip Mallett (Basingstoke: Palgrave Macmillan, 2001), pp. 64–86.

11  See Simon Gatrell, *Thomas Hardy's Vision of Wessex* (Basingstoke: Palgrave Macmillan, 2003).

# PART II

# Critical Fortunes

# 7

# Critical Responses I: The Novels to 1970

SARAH E. MAIER

From the outset of his career as a novelist, Hardy's style, character-ization, philosophy, and intentions were variously discussed by crit-ics with a mixture of praise and distaste. An unsigned review in the *Athenaeum* greeted *Desperate Remedies* (1871) as an 'unpleasant' but 'very powerful' story, 'worked out with considerable artistic power'.[1] The *Spectator* found 'no fine characters' and 'no display of passion except of the brute kind, no pictures of Christian virtue', despite a 'very happy facility in catching and fixing phases of peasant life'; the reader was advised to 'step in silence over the corrupt body of the tale', ignoring its 'common-place' and 'clumsy' machinery, for the sake of its 'sensitiveness to scenic and atmospheric effects'.[2] The *Saturday Review* applauded the author's skill in the 'evolution of character', particularly in the working out of the women, but foreshadowed criticism to come in finding 'a little too much of laboured epigram'. Even so, it concluded, the anonymous author's 'deserts are of no ordinary kind'.[3]

*Under the Greenwood Tree* (1872) again found the reviewers wel-coming the 'graphic pictures of rustic life somewhere in the West Country', but warning of the author's tendency to 'make his char-acters now and then drop their personality, and speak too much like educated people'. The subtitle, 'A Rural Painting of the Dutch School', seemed pertinent: Hardy had the 'ability to paint', but not as yet 'the power of composition'.[4] This identification of Hardy as a painter in a realistic or even naturalistic manner ('a series of rural pictures full of life and genuine colouring, and drawn with a dis-tinct minuteness') becomes a recurring motif; his work was to be associated with a spectrum of painterly styles, from Dutch realism to Decadence.[5] The tenor of these reviews of the as yet unnamed author behind the novels anticipates the concerns of the next dec-ades of criticism of Hardy's prose fiction.

*A Pair of Blue Eyes* (1873), the first of Hardy's works to carry his
name, was seen by the *Saturday Review* as a 'thoroughly matured
work of its kind', free from 'traces of viciously stimulated workman-
ship', albeit still containing 'cumbrous' diction and inappropriate
language from certain persons in the text. The critic (anonymous,
as usual in the *Saturday*) lauds the way that from 'simple materials'
there has been 'evolved a result of really tragic power', but provides
two points of caution: first, that Hardy 'designs the mode of life led
by the heroine and her lovers with a kind of defiance of conventionality, though in each case the circumstances go far to justify what
is done'; and second, that he creates a 'tragedy of circumstance,
the power of mere events on certain kinds of character', exhibiting
'no moral obliquity, no deliberate viciousness of choice', but only
the 'social barriers of actual life'. Elfride's rescue of Knight is written with 'extraordinary force', akin to the 'intense minuteness and
vivid concentration of the most powerful among French writers of
fiction'.[6] In the coming years, in an effort to locate Hardy's subject
matter, his morality, his peasants, and his women, numerous critics
would refer to French realism and Naturalism, both in excoriation
and in praise.

The first of Hardy's great novels, *Far from the Madding Crowd*
(1874), appeared to a new level of critical interest. Now past
the neophyte stage, Hardy was taken to task by critics including Richard Holt Hutton at the *Spectator*, Henry James in the
*Nation*, and Andrew Lang in the *Academy*, each of whom was to
write on his work more than once in his career. Whereas Hutton
finds Gabriel Oak and Bathsheba Everdene wanting as heroes,
he values Hardy as a painter of the Dorsetshire labourers, despite
his suspicion about the 'more cultivated metaphors' in the speech
of characters such as Liddy, Jan Coggan or even Bathsheba:
he accuses Hardy of 'an intellectual graft on coarse and vulgar
thoughts' of ideas 'too clever' and 'too original' for such speak-
ers.[7] This 'cleverness which is only cleverness' is, for James, 'the
difference between original and imitative talent'. Hardy 'produces
a vast deal of sound and commotion', but it is merely 'a pound of
shadow': 'a decidedly delusive performance [with] a fatal lack of
magic', 'singularly inartistic' and full of 'ambitious artifice'. James's
one acknowledgement of Hardy's ability to capture the natural
is to admit that the 'genuine thing in his book, to our sense, is a

certain aroma of the meadows and lanes', less a compliment than a backhanded insult.[8]

The most significant account of Hardy's work before *Tess of the d'Urbervilles* came from the young medical student and future sexologist Havelock Ellis, in an essay on 'Thomas Hardy's Novels' for the *Westminster Review* in 1883. Ellis admits that Hardy 'moves within a limited range, but he is yet capable of producing many variations', replete with depth, irony and humour. Applauding Hardy's 'Nature-painting', he notes the 'microscopical minuteness' of his vision of a natural world, 'rich with all the complex possibilities of an organic life'. He also praises Hardy's 'peasants, for the like of whom, in strong and living individuality, in wealth of quaint humour, we must go back to Shakspere'. Challenging those earlier critics who found the rustics' speech unnatural or ridiculous, Ellis argues that a large part of their humour 'is bound up with their use of scriptural language', and no one 'will be prepared to assert that Mr. Hardy has herein departed from the truth of Nature'. But he finds Hardy's real greatness in his 'gallery of women – "Undines of the earth", they have been felicitously called – whose charm is unique; they have no like anywhere; he has added a fresh delight to certain aspects of Nature.' These 'instinct-led women' – Fancy Day, Elfride Swancourt, Bathsheba, Eustacia and Anne Garland – have, Ellis claims, 'an instinctive self-respect, an instinctive purity'. When they err, 'it is by caprice, by imagination'; there is 'something elemental, something *demonic* in them'; they have 'no souls', but instead have 'inimitable grace'. This 'absence of moral feeling' derives from their 'direct relation to the wild and solitary character of their environment'; they are, as yet, 'untamed' by social conventions. 'Woman, in Mr. Hardy's world, is far from being "the conscience of man"'; it is with the men that 'moral strength' ultimately lies. The men undergo no 'process of development one way or another'; Hardy's 'hero' is a 'sensitive being, gentle and pure as a woman, characterized by nothing so much as his receptivity'. But primarily, for Ellis, Hardy is great as a writer who has 'little or nothing to say about either morals or passion, and yet thinks love is the chief business of life'. His flaw is that he 'has not trained himself, as Mr. Henry James has, on the moderation, the precision, the perfect good sense of the French school':[9] a claim rejected by Richard le Gallienne, who parried that 'French authors [are] having a strong influence on Mr. Hardy's work', and that 'realism which is not theory but a necessary artistic instinct' is one of his strengths.[10]

Bathsheba Everdene is the first of Hardy's women whom readers found complex and fascinating but to whom the critics took exception.[11] The *Westminster Review* accused Hardy of creating her as a 'vain and selfish creature': 'Mr. Hardy may be proud of having drawn such a character. But she is a character not to be admired, as he would seem to intimate.'[12] Lang contests that 'we cannot easily pardon Bathsheba', because 'we have some difficulty in being much moved by [her] character and mischances'; nor is the dialogue authentic, which leads Lang 'to question the truthfulness' of the scenes in which she is involved.[13] From *Far from the Madding Crowd* onwards, Hardy's portraits of women are commented on by most reviewers. The *Athenaeum* continues the charge of questionable morality in the 'selfish and sensual' Eustacia Vye, who 'belongs essentially to the class of which Madame Bovary is the type', and 'compromises herself by vulgar indiscretions'.[14] W. E. Henley defends Hardy's delineation of character, particularly Eustacia: 'prescient, imaginative, insatiably observant, and at the same time so rigidly and so finely artistic that there is scarce a point in the whole that can be fairly questioned, he seems to me to paint the woman and the place as no other living writer could have done.'[15] The critical discomfort is that the men and women 'hang by each other in consequence of their weaknesses' but 'are not indissolubly united through their virtues'.[16] J. M. Barrie sees Hardy's 'fixed ideas about young women, whatever their rank or upbringing' as 'so original, adhered to with such tenacity from book to book, and so cunningly illustrated as to cry for comment'.[17]

What Edmund Gosse claims for Hardy's women is that they 'are moulded of the same flesh as his men', a 'feminine realism' that Hardy foregrounds in his 'proclivity towards placing a more unique and singular species of womanhood as the central figure' in his novels.[18] Nowhere is this more true than in *Tess of the d'Urbervilles* (1891). Le Gallienne defended Hardy's subtitle, 'A Pure Woman Faithfully Presented', arguing that Tess is 'a fine Pagan, full of humanity and imagination, and, like them, though in a less degree, flawed with that lack of will, that fatal indecision at great moments'.[19] Others denied that Hardy had made out his case for Tess. Richard Hutton believed she 'could only have been conceived as the outcome of a pantheistic philosophy'.[20] W. P. Trent agreed, seeing her as 'the greatest character in recent fiction', but warning that Hardy's 'method of reproduction is not that of the photographer, but of the painter'. Hardy is at once 'realistic' and 'idealistic'; he is an artist, to be given license in his portraiture of life, even if the 'tendency to paint life as repulsive' leads to a pessimism that 'imparts no *spring* to anything': 'pessimism is but another name for the deadly languor that accompanies the *malheur du siècle*, is, in fact, the symptom by which one is usually enabled to diagnose the disease.'[21]

Such assessments were not new. An early review of *Return of the Native* admired 'the touches which describe the life and spirit of the great heath' and its 'very considerable power of plot', but complained: 'Hardy's gloomy fatalism lowers the effect of his tragedy, by lowering almost all the passion and sentiment in his book to something rather near the same dead-level of dreary light, or not much more dreary shade.'[22] Clym Yeobright and Eustacia Vye act as 'if they were puppets of a sort of fate', expressing Hardy's Schopenhauerian pessimism.[23] The discomfort with 'fashionable pessimism' continues through reviews of *The Mayor of Casterbridge* (1886)[24] and *The Woodlanders* (1887), stories 'written with an indifference to the moral effect' they convey. As a corrective, the reviewers urge 'a little less "abstract humanism" and a little more of human piety'.[25] The critical reaction to *Jude the Obscure* (1895), was vehement; a 'titanically bad book', according to the *Athenaeum*, in which Hardy, 'in his anger against Destiny and in his desire to make Destiny and its offspring Society odious, has overreached himself'.[26] William Dean Howells admitted that Hardy 'heightens the pathos to almost intolerable effect', but insisted that Jude's character is 'in spite of all his weakness and debasement, one of inviolable dignity'; although 'the sport of fate', he is 'never otherwise than sublime'.[27] Mrs Oliphant notoriously linked Hardy with Grant Allen as members of 'The Anti-Marriage League', denouncing the novel as an 'exposition of the unclean', full of the 'grossness, indecency, and horror' of Hardy's fatalistic philosophy.[28] In the *Life* Hardy insisted that with his 'quick sense of humour' he could readily see the 'ludicrous side' to such 'booings', but he also remembered them as 'outrageously personal, unfair, and untrue', and they helped turn him from prose fiction to poetry (*LW*: 287–8).

Even more sympathetic critics were troubled by *Jude*. Edmund Gosse noticed a blending of science, philosophy, and psychology in the novel, with Jude 'a neurotic subject in whom hereditary degeneracy takes an idealist turn', and Sue 'a strange and unwelcome product of exhaustion' whose '*vita sexualis*' compounds this 'terrible study in pathology'. Gosse located a 'jarring note of rebellion': 'What has Providence done to Mr. Hardy that he should rise up in the arable land of Wessex and shake his fist at his Creator?' He urged Hardy to return to the 'calm and lovely pantheism … full of rural gods, all homely and benign' of the early romances.[29] Another reviewer balked at Hardy's 'Olympian ruthlessness towards his own creations'.[30] The strongest objections to the philosophical underpinning of the novel focused on Little Father Time, where the 'tragedy of the children strains … belief'. The 'horror of the infant pessimist' is not plausible: 'baby Schopenhauers are not coming into the world in shoals.'[31] Hardy's development from the historian of pastoral Wessex[32] to a writer of 'strenuous purpose'[33] was defended by Ellis, who argued that 'Mr. Hardy was not proposing to himself a study of gross pathological degenerescence', but 'a work of art as art'.[34]

The first full-length study of Hardy's work, Lionel Johnson's *The Art of Thomas Hardy*, appeared in 1894, just before the publication of *Jude*.[35] Johnson argues that Hardy's novels should be grouped according to narrative development: the 'tragic', the 'idyllic', and the uncategorized.[36] This perhaps prompted Hardy's own division of his work, in the 'Wessex Edition' of 1912, into three categories: Novels of Character and Environment, Romances and Fantasies, and Novels of Ingenuity, the first of which contains those novels that continue to feature most heavily in critical discussion, reading lists, and film or television adaptations: *Under the Greenwood Tree*, *Far from the Madding Crowd*, *The Return of the Native*, *The Mayor of Casterbridge*, *The Woodlanders*, *Tess of the d'Urbervilles*, and *Jude the Obscure*. In both cases, the effect was to sanction the relative lack of critical interest in particular novels. Lascelles Abercrombie, in *Thomas Hardy: A Critical Study* (1912), chooses to see the 'architectural image' in the novels as a means of evaluation. The great novels have a 'woven intricacy' that carries the 'threaded lives of several persons through a single complicated pattern of destiny', whereas the epic form applies to both *Tess* and *Jude* because they follow an individual, a 'thematic difference' from which 'formal difference naturally follows'.[37] Joseph Warren Beach's *The Technique of Thomas Hardy* (1922) voiced the widely held critical opinion that the 'most remarkable thing about Mr. Hardy's novels, for anyone who takes them in sequence, is their extreme unevenness of quality',[38] perhaps indicating why there was an attempt to grasp for a system, to exclude as much as include those narratives worthy of attention.

After a period in which the novels were set aside in favour of attempts to evaluate his poetry, this nexus of concerns – Hardy's implausible yet glorious rustics, his strategic yet compelling structures, his pagan or fatalistic philosophy and his flawed but captivating women – continues into the considerations of his work after his death in 1928. Virginia Woolf's 'The Novels of Thomas Hardy' (1928/1932) begins by lamenting his death and the loss of his genius. Hardy, she argued, regarded the novel as 'a means of giving truthful if harsh and violent impressions of the lives of men and women'. He understood 'Nature' as a force, feeling in it 'a spirit that can sympathize or mock or remain the indifferent spectator of human fortunes'. Like Dickens and Scott, but unlike Flaubert and James, he belonged to the class of 'unconscious writers': 'His own word, "moments of vision", exactly describes those passages of astonishing beauty and force' which fill his novels. His 'genius was uncertain in development, uneven in accomplishment, but, when the moment came, magnificent in achievement'. His 'peasants are the great sanctuary of sanity, the country the last stronghold of happiness': 'When they disappear, there is no hope for the race.' His major characters 'stand up like lightning conductors to attract the force of the elements'; they have 'something symbolical about them which is common to us all', in their relation to 'time, death, and fate'. Hardy, 'at his greatest ... gives us impressions; at his weakest, arguments'; *Jude*, the most argumentative of the novels, is also the most painful and the most pessimistic.[39]

In 1940, The *Southern Review* published a still valuable centennial volume on Hardy's work. Donald Davidson argues that 'almost three generations of critics' have not so much underrated or overrated his achievement as 'missed him' through failing to recognise his 'comparative isolation ... in modern literary history', as the creator of traditional, nonliterary narrative, or 'told' stories.[40] Jacques Barzun argues for the strength of Hardy's philosophy and narrative construction; rather than a realist per se he sought to expand 'the limits of reality by showing plausible characters enmeshed in unusual events'. Hardy writes 'tragedy in which we are not meant to acquiesce', but if the result of the 'characters' self-will and the world's indifference' is 'conflict and catastrophe, that too is natural, and no preference for a rational order should induce the artist to sketch in a preëstablished [*sic*] harmony or contrive a "logical" or "deserved" dénouement'.[41] Herbert J. Muller argues that nostalgia was the 'matrix' of Hardy'.[42] Arthur Mizener, in his consideration of *Jude*, urges the reader to see that Hardy's philosophic 'attitude was not complex and inclusive but simple and exclusive'; he merely 'contrast[s] the ideal life with the real life, not of man but of *a* man'. The novel tries but fails to break through the limits of naturalistic form, and because of that failure is rather the history of one obscure but worthy man than a fully worked out tragic fiction.[43]

The infamous snubbing of Hardy in F. R. Leavis's *The Great Tradition* (1948), as one of a pair with George Meredith, each 'supposed to be philosophically profound about life' but without the ability to 'support his reputation', marks the low point in the consideration of Hardy in the twentieth century. Leavis defers to James's dismissal of Hardy, particularly *Tess*, and leaves his own patronizing appraisal of *Jude* with the remark that 'in its clumsy way' it is 'impressive'.[44] Albert Guerard opposes this view in his important *Thomas Hardy: The Novels and Stories* (1949), seeing Hardy as a 'traditional teller of tales' who includes the 'distortions of popular storytelling – exaggeration, grotesque horror, macabre coincidence – to achieve his darker truth'. Rather than dismiss them as unrealistic, Guerard views Hardy's juxtapositions of the fantastic and the everyday 'as highly convincing foreshortenings of the actual and absurd world'.[45] Roy Morrell, in *Thomas Hardy: The Will and the Way* (1965), argued that readers had been 'conditioned by misunderstandings' to accuse Hardy of pessimistic determinism. Morrell instead sees continual contrasts that provoke either action or passivity in Hardy's characters: 'Hardy blames man, in short, for *choosing* to be a puppet; the Will does not make him so'.[46]

Perhaps the initiating moment for the more theorized reappraisals of Hardy's work in the 1970s was Philip Larkin's essay, 'Wanted: Good Hardy Critic' (1966). Contrary to 'the century's principal critics' who are hostile, patronizing, or neglectful of Hardy, or themselves 'mediocre perpetrators' without 'the penetration of intelligence and sensibility that would command confidence', Larkin finds Hardy 'simple; his work contains little in thought or reference that needs elucidation, his language in unambiguous, his themes easily comprehensible'. He interprets the 'sensual cruelty' and a relish for the macabre and the cruel in *Tess* as evidence of Hardy's participation in an 'ancient tradition' of 'suffering beauty'. It is for his 'consideration of the centrality of suffering' that Larkin regards Hardy as not merely truthful, but an indicator of 'superior spiritual character'. The interpretation of this character 'should be the first duty of the true critic for which the work is still waiting'.[47] The attempt to answer that call underlies the reassessments of Hardy in the later twentieth century.

### NOTES

1 [Anon] *Athenaeum* (1 April 1871), pp. 398–399 (*CH*: 1–2).
2 [Anon] *Spectator* (22 April 1871), pp. 481–483 (*CH*: 3–5).
3 [Anon] *Saturday Review* 32 (30 September 1871), pp. 441–2 (*CH*: 6–8).
4 [Anon] *Athenaeum* (15 June 1872), pp. 748–9 (*CH*: 9–11).
5 [Horace Moule] *Saturday Review* 34 (28 September 1872), p. 417 (*CH*: 11–14). Annie Macdonell, in one of the first monographs on Hardy, notes that he had 'the vision and [uses] the methods of a painter': *Thomas Hardy* (London: Hodder & Stoughton, 1894), p. 16.
6 [Anon] *Saturday Review* 36 (2 August 1873), pp. 158–9 (*CH*: 15–19).
7 R. H. Hutton, *Spectator* (19 December 1874), pp. 1597–99 (*CH*: 21–7).
8 Henry James, *Nation* (24 December 1874; *CH*: 27–31).
9 Havelock Ellis, *Westminster Review* 119, n.s. 63 (April 1883), pp. 334–64 (*CH*: 103–32).
10 Richard le Gallienne, *Star* (23 December 1891; *CH*: 178–81).
11 Edmund Gosse comments that 'the bulk of [Hardy's] readers [are] from the class of adult male persons', and notes the distinct 'unpopularity of [his] novels among women', which he finds 'a curious phenomenon': *The Speaker* 2 (13 September 1890), p. 295 (*CH*: 167–71). Certainly, the novelist Mrs Oliphant makes 'a great many objections' to *Tess* in *Blackwood's Magazine* 61 (March 1892), pp. 464–74 (*CH*: 203–14), notably that Tess is 'forced' to act out of character to suit Hardy's 'indignant anti-religion'.

12 [Anon] *Westminster Review* 103:47 (January 1875), p. 265 (*CH*: 315).

13 Andrew Lang, *Academy* 7 (2 January 1875), p. 9 (*CH*: 35–9).

14 [Anon] *Saturday Review* 47 (4 January 1879), pp. 23–24 (*CH*: 50–55).

15 W. E. Henley, *Academy* 14 (30 November 1878), p. 517 (*CH*: 48–50).

16 William Wallace, *Academy* 31 (9 April 1887), p. 251–2 (*CH*: 153–5).

17 J. M. Barrie, 'Thomas Hardy: The Historian of Wessex', *Contemporary Review* 61 (1889), p. 57 (*CH*: 156–66).

18 Gosse, 'Thomas Hardy', *CH*: 170.

19 Le Gallienne, *Star, CH*: 181.

20 R. H. Hutton, *Spectator* (23 January 1892), pp. 121–2 (*CH*: 191–4).

21 W. P. Trent, 'The Novels of Thomas Hardy', *Sewanee Review* 1 (November 1892; *CH*: 221–37). Trent's comment on the fin-de-siècle dis/ease in Hardy's novels is considered in A. J. Butler's 'Mr. Hardy as a Decadent', *National Review* 27 (May 1896), pp. 384–90 (*CH*: 284–91).

22 [Anon] *Spectator* (8 February 1879), pp. 181–2 (*CH*: 55–9).

23 The complexities of Hardy's philosophy provide early interest for scholars with varying degrees of success, including Helen Garwood's *Thomas Hardy: An Illustration of the Philosophy of Schopenhauer* (Philadelphia: John C. Winston, 1911), Ernest Brennecke's *Thomas Hardy's Universe: A Study of a Poet's Mind* (London: T. Fisher Unwin, 1924), and A. P. Elliott's *Fatalism in the Works of Thomas Hardy* (1935). There is a distinctive chapter on the place of philosophical readings in John Holloway's *The Victorian Sage: Studies in Argument* (London: Macmillan, 1953; New York: Russell and Russell, 1966).

24 R. H. Hutton, *Spectator* (5 June 1886), pp. 752–3 (*CH*: 136–40).

25 R. H. Hutton, *Spectator* (26 March 1887), pp. 419–20 (*CH*: 142–5). Hutton quotes from the penultimate paragraph of *The Woodlanders*.

26 [Anon] *Athenaeum* (23 November 1895), p. 709 (*CH*: 249–52).

27 W. D. Howells, *Harper's Weekly* (7 December 1895; *CH*: 253–6).

28 Mrs [Margaret] Oliphant, 'The Anti-Marriage League', *Blackwood's Magazine* 69 (January 1896), pp. 135–49 (*CH*: 256–62).

29 Edmund Gosse, *Cosmopolis* 1 (January 1896), pp. 60–9 (*CH*: 262–70).

30 [Anon] *Athenaeum* 711 (29 May 1886), (*CH*: 133–4).

31 [Anon] *Illustrated London News* 108 (11 January 1896), p. 50 (*CH*: 274–6).

32 Following Barrie's description of Hardy as the 'Historian of Wessex', early monographs on this aspect of his novels include Wilkinson Sherren's *The Wessex of Romance* (1902) and Hermann Lea's *Thomas Hardy's Wessex* (1913).

33 Richard le Gallienne, *Idler* 9 (February 1896), pp. 114–15 (*CH*: 277–8).

34 Havelock Ellis, 'Concerning *Jude the Obscure*', *Savoy* 6 (October 1896), pp. 35–49 (*CH*: 300–15).

35 Lionel Johnson, *The Art of Thomas Hardy* (New York: Russell & Russell, 1894).

36 Respectively, *DR*, *PBE*, *FFMC*, *RN*, *MC*, *W*, *Tess* and *Jude* (tragic); *UGT* and *T M* ('idyllic'); and *HE*, *AL*, and *TT* (uncategorized).

37 Lascelles Abercrombie, *Thomas Hardy: A Critical Study* (1912; New York: Russell & Russell, 1964), pp. 103–4.

38 Joseph Warren Beach, *The Technique of Thomas Hardy* (1922; New York: Russell & Russell, 1962), p. 3.

39 Virginia Woolf, 'The Novels of Thomas Hardy', in *The Common Reader: Second Series* (1932; London: Hogarth Press, 1962), pp. 245–7.

40 Donald Davidson, 'The Traditional Basis of Thomas Hardy's Fiction', *Southern Review* 6 (1940), pp. 162–78.

41 Jacques Barzun, 'Truth and Poetry in Thomas Hardy', *Southern Review* 6 (1940), pp. 179–92.

42 Herbert Muller, 'The Novels of Hardy Today', *Southern Review* 6 (1940), pp. 214–24.

43 Arther Mizener, '*Jude the Obscure* as a Tragedy', *Southern Review* 6 (1940), pp. 193–213.

44 F. R. Leavis, *The Great Tradition* (New York: George W. Stewart, 1950), pp. 22–3.

45 Albert Guerard, *Thomas Hardy: The Novels and Stories* (1949; New York: New Directions, 1964), pp. 1–4.

46 Roy Morrell, *Thomas Hardy: The Will and the Way* (Kuala Lumpur: University of Malaya Press, 1965), pp. ix, 75.

47 Philip Larkin, 'Wanted: Good Hardy Critic', *Critical Quarterly* 8:2 (June 1966), pp. 174–9.

# 8

# Critical Reponses II: The Novels from 1970

TIM DOLIN

Thomas Hardy's critical reputation as a novelist, although relatively stable since his death in 1928, dipped in the 1940s and 1950s. Measured against the Jamesian criteria of 'formal perfection' and 'moral intensity' dominant then,[1] Hardy's fiction provoked some disquiet. For all its tragic power, its 'singular beauty and charm', it was also held to be 'chock-full of faults and falsity',[2] as James had complained in the 1890s: the autodidact's 'abomination of the language';[3] the instability of character, especially those 'conjectural' creatures, female characters (*W*: 5); Hardy's offenses against probability and verisimilitude; the unconscionable combination of *fin-de-siècle* gloom and rustic geniality; and the inappropriate or incompatible discourses – poetic realism, amateur anthropology and social history, tragedy, folklore and myth, farce, and melodrama. In the 1970s, however, Hardy benefited from two radical approaches to criticism that swept away the old verities of textual unity and stability and attacked the complacent humanism of the liberal imagination. They were poststructuralism, with its analyses of the unsettling play of language and the repressive power of discourse, and Marxist (or materialist) criticism, with its suspicion of false unities affecting to resolve the historical contradictions that generated, and continue to generate, literary meaning. In 1970 two revisionary books appeared, in their different ways at the forefront of upheavals in the discipline. Both had a profound influence on Hardy criticism.

In the United States, J. Hillis Miller's *Thomas Hardy: Distance and Desire* was among the first studies of an English author to engage (albeit circumspectly) with the radical ideas introduced by Derrida in the 1960s. Still under the sway of Georges Poulet's Husserlian 'criticism of consciousness', Miller retained the characteristically phenomenological interest in immanence and the existential condition, literature as an intersubjective world, and the 'spontaneous withdrawal of the mind to a position of detached watchfulness' in Hardy's writing.[4] These interests were, however, supplemented by a structuralist's regard for the 'single design in the totality of the author's work' – the distance and desire of the title, through which Miller illuminates the underlying structures persisting through all its variations.[5] Structuralism was congenial to the New Critical tradition of close reading, and so too was deconstruction, whose watchwords are evident in *Distance and Desire*. Miller's theme – 'distance as the source of desire and desire as the energy behind attempts to turn distance into closeness' – identifies writing as 'part of that energy of desire', a desire 'to close the gap between words and what words name or create'.[6] This is Derridean *différance* by another name: 'The pre-text of a given text is always another text open in its turn to interpretation. There is never an extra-linguistic "origin" by means of which the critic can escape from his labyrinthine wanderings within the complexities of relationships among words.'[7]

In Britain, meanwhile, Raymond Williams's *The English Novel: From Dickens to Lawrence* also appeared in 1970. Its popularity attests to its socialist-humanist author's commitment to the role of literary studies in what he called 'the long revolution': 'If man is essentially a learning, creating, and communicating being, the only social organization adequate to his nature is a participating democracy, in which all of us, as unique individuals, learn, communicate, and control.'[8] *The English Novel* was conceived as a polemical corrective to Leavis's *The Great Tradition*, and particularly to the glaring omission of Hardy from that tradition. Reflecting on Leavis's patronising snub, Williams later remarked that Hardy must have been 'very disturbing for someone trying to rationalize refined, civilized, balancing judgment. [He] exposes so much which cannot be displaced from its social situation.'[9] This recognition – that literature cannot be displaced from its social situation – ensured that Hardy became an important figure in the New Left criticism, where Williams's concerns were rethought through the theories of Continental Marxism, emerging feminisms, and poststructuralism. At the same time, Williams's cultural studies gave readers of Hardy powerful new ways of thinking about contemporary cultural uses and meanings of Wessex and the material and symbolic reproduction of Hardy in film, television, tourism, and other cultural forms and practices. It also gave them cause to consider the consequences, trenchantly articulated in *Jude the Obscure*, of the gap between academic thinking and lived experience.

Miller and Williams came to Hardy from very different places, and their work would not be expected to share much ground. As a leading member of the 'Yale School' deconstructionists, Miller was outspoken in defence of poststructuralism's 'vigilant and sophisticated rhetorical analysis'[10] and disdainful of the sociologism of political and historical criticism. Far from being nihilistic, he argued, deconstruction's destabilisation of literary meaning (or rather demonstration of the ways texts destabilised themselves in the endless play of deferred meaning) was highly ethical in its linguistic attentiveness. With the advent of the 'historical turn' in the 1980s, however, Miller came to view literary language not as self-contained and remote from historical forces, but as a form of praxis: 'a human project, its meaning and significance bound up with the human community and its structure of values.'[11] Hardy has remained important to the developments of Miller's thought, exemplifying the deconstructive 'lateral dance of interpretation'[12] in his discussion of *Tess of the d'Urbervilles*, and the social effects of language in his later work on the 'linguistic moment' and on speech acts in literature.[13]

Perhaps unexpectedly, given its obvious receptiveness to the hermeneutics of suspicion, Hardy's fiction has received few deconstructive readings,[14] but poststructuralism (understood broadly as a series of distinct though closely related responses to structuralism) has undeniably transformed the way his work was interpreted. Deconstruction's reorientation of criticism from the 'philosophy of the subject to a philosophy of the sign'[15] had a profound impact on the rise of new historicism and its English Marxist partner, cultural materialism, in the 1980s. New historicism holds that expressive acts are embedded in networks of material practices and that 'literary and non-literary "texts" circulate inseparably'.[16] Its indebtedness to deconstructive thought is evident in some of the Hardy criticism it generated. In 1983, Ramón Saldívar applied what Greenblatt called the 'poetics of culture'[17] to *Jude the Obscure*, showing how its formal dynamics – 'whether one calls the trope governing the structure of the narrative metaphor, metonymy, chiasmus, or simply a "geometric construction"' – are determined by the contextual systems of Victorian marriage and civil law.[18] Also in 1983, Elaine Scarry identified Hardy's 'essential subject' as the 'reciprocal alterations' effected between humans and their world by their immersion in physical work.[19] And in 1995 Forest Pyle took up the ideas of Hayden White and Fredric Jameson to analyze the 'historicizing impulse and the textual resistances posed by the narrative medium through which history is to be conveyed'.[20] Shifting the hermeneutics of suspicion from text to history, Pyle averred that the 'desire to restore a living memory to the sites of history and to remake a narrative community' in *Jude the Obscure* 'becomes as much a "dream" as Jude's futile longings for Christminster'.[21]

Surprisingly, the work of Michel Foucault, a key theorist for new historicism, has had marginal impact on Hardy criticism. Foucault's critique of industrial modernity through revisionary 'genealogies' and 'archaeologies' of knowledge and power is especially relevant to Hardy, one might think, as is the Foucauldian notion of discourse: the exercise of power through the imposition of limits on what is sayable and can therefore be taken to be true, which also imposes certain 'correct' vocabularies, grammars, and styles. Yet, apart from some innovative essays invoking Foucault's ideas of spectacular power and the history of sexuality,[22] Foucault is largely ignored. The only squarely poststructuralist reading to explore language and power in any comparable way is Jean-Jacques Lecercle's Deleuzian reading of *Tess*, which examines the 'striking parallel between Tess's relation to language and Hardy's',[23] seeing in the tragic fate of Hardy's heroine the operation of the same power relations that marginalised Hardy for his 'linguistic plurality and contradiction', the lack of 'polish' that would erase 'all dialectical variations ... in the perfection of a unified text'.[24] Lecercle's take on the 'violence of repression' enacted and resisted in the polyphonic language of Hardy's novel reframes in Deleuzian terms what were, however, already established arguments about Tess's victimisation by language, and Hardy's stylistic ungainliness (see discussion later). Lecercle's approach is not Deleuzian enough for D. E. Musselwhite, who maps onto *Tess* the different 'regimes of signs' detailed in Deleuze and Guattari's *Anti-Oedipus* and *A Thousand Plateaux* and anticipated in Deleuze's earlier work on sadism and masochism.[25]

The reappraisal of Hardy's 'bad writing' by poststructuralism – the elevation of his unstable language and 'mannered, echoic style'[26] into an aesthetic of contingency that begins with Hillis Miller – is taken further by the generation of poststructuralist Marxists who built on Williams's foundational analysis of the dilemma of the returned native no longer at home in the countryside of his family or ever completely at home in metropolitan literary London. Terry Eagleton refocused this problem through the theoretical lens of Louis Althusser and Pierre Macherey in the introduction to the New Wessex edition of *Jude* in 1974, in *Criticism and Ideology* (1976), and in a section of his book on Walter Benjamin (1981). For Althusser and Macherey, literature is, in Margaret Higonnet's words, 'a social form that contributes to the reproduction of a ruling ideology but that also offers us telltale gaps and occlusions corresponding to social contradictions'.[27] Eagleton accordingly examines Hardy's 'unusually complex mode of insertion into the dominant ideological formation and its span of possible literary forms' as a result of his ambiguous social position as a petty bourgeois alienated equally from the 'declining rural enclave' of his upbringing and the metropolitan republic of letters.[28] This predicament prevents Hardy from continuing George Eliot's project of reconciling 'mutually conflictual modes' in a new kind of moral realism (which is, for Eliot, the aesthetic expression of liberal reformism). Where she can recast 'historical contradictions into ideologically resolvable form',[29] Hardy's class and professional contradictions prevent him from resolving the conflicts between 'pastoral, melodrama, social realism, naturalism, myth, fable, [and] classical tragedy',[30] which compete with and undermine each other. Ultimately Hardy ran up against the limits of realism itself. As Edward Said also argued, *Jude the Obscure* marks the end of Hardy's career as a novelist *and* the exhaustion of the 'dynastic principles' of nineteenth-century narrative itself.[31]

If Eagleton was the first critic to offer a cogent theoretical explanation (and vindication) of the unevenness and unrefinement of Hardy's language, he was also the first to comprehend the ideological character of the tendency among readers to impose coherence on Hardy's fiction from outside by isolating and securing its meanings, lauding the 'novels of character and environment' as monuments of tragic humanist realism and conveniently sweeping the

'lesser' novels – the 'novels of ingenuity' and 'romances and fantasies' – under the mat. The name '"Thomas Hardy"' Eagleton wrote,
'signifies a particular ideological and biographical formation …
[through which] certain texts, by virtue of their changing, contradictory modes of insertion into the dominant "cultural" and peda-
gogical apparatuses, are processed, "corrected" and reconstituted so
that a home may be found for them within a literary "tradition"
that is always the "imaginary" unity of the present.'[32]

Eagleton's ideas were developed by George Wotton and Peter
Widdowson, both exploring how 'Thomas Hardy' is reproduced
as both genius and aesthetic failure by educational and cultural
institutions. Wotton's unjustly neglected book contains the most
thoroughgoing analysis of Wessex as both a representation of particular historical socioeconomic contradictions and 'a system of
reality which is produced out of a combination of elements – the
time, place, relations and means of production – involved in the
productive process of writing itself'.[33] For Widdowson, too, the
'profound alienation that marks all Hardy's work – the clash of
modes, the mannered style, the derisive irony, the "satires of circumstance" – is determined by the *anomie* of his class and professional contradictions'.[34] His *Hardy in History* (1989) set out to
expose and critique 'the history which has carried [Hardy's nov-
els] down to us in the present as "profitably readable"':[35] that is,
as realist. Widdowson deplored the 'striking absence within for-
malist-humanist criticism of work dealing with Hardy's manifestly
non-realist discourses',[36] especially the lesser novels (notably *The
Hand of Ethelberta*). He traces the social and political forces underlying the critical construction of Hardy as a humanist-realist icon
of English national culture through detailed analyses of the various
texts and techniques that perpetuated the myth of Hardy's tragic
realism, including images and artworks used on book covers, questions in examination papers, and period details in films and TV
serials. Realism, he concludes, is what happens to Hardy's novels in
history, when they are coopted by liberal-humanist ideology.

John Goode's fine *Thomas Hardy: The Offensive Truth* (1988) is
interested, as his subtitle suggests, in the ideologically challenging Hardy, whose self-reflexive and alienating novels impede and
confront their readers. This Althusserian approach situates social
radicalism, or at least dissent, in textual self-consciousness, setting

aside the complicated question of Hardy's own participation in commercially motivated 'straight' misreadings of his fiction. Much has since been made of the double-voiced discourse in Hardy's writing. Constrained by market forces to produce two versions of his later novels, a serial version for conservative middle-brow periodicals and a book version for the more liberal (or at least more policeable) circulating libraries, Hardy was also constrained to conceal his social radicalism and artistic experimentalism. He adopted what Joe Fisher calls 'trading strategies' (a seeming compliance in his own suppression) and 'narrative strategies' ('antithetical counter-texts' of sociosexual subversion).[37] Hardy's paramount 'trading strategy', in Fisher's argument, is the artifice of the pastoral Wessex, an 'anthropological travelogue' which has been 'robbed of its "reality" (the work practices and class divisions which really make it) and rebuilt for the market'.[38] These questions are pursued in Roger Ebbatson's poststructuralist (and materialist) *Thomas Hardy: The Margin of the Unexpressed*, which uses readings of minor works to effect the 'dislocation of the liberal-idealist tradition which has successfully reproduced Hardy as a kind of cultural monument' and finds in the fiction (and elsewhere) a 'surplus of undecidability, [a] willingness of writer or reader to rest in uncertainty'.[39]

Hardy's fiction has always been associated with matters of gender, but it was not until 1982 that Penny Boumelha, applying Machereyan Marxism, wrote the first full-length feminist study of women in Hardy. Boumelha argued that the fiction was driven not solely by class alienation and instability but also by gender: The 'radicalism of Hardy's representation of women resides ... in their resistance to reduction to a single and uniform ideological position.'[40] Situating the major novels in the complex history of Victorian sexual ideology (as Jane Thomas was to do for the 'minor' novels),[41] Boumelha showed how Hardy's writing refuses to effect 'an imaginary resolution of actual (but displaced) social contradictions'.[42] The social contradictions immanent in shifting constructions of gender are produced and reproduced, Boumelha argued, as internally conflicted literary effects in Hardy.[43] This enables her to recuperate Hardy for feminism, a project inaugurated by Kate Millett's trailblazing (and incendiary) *Sexual Politics* of 1970. Millett demanded a paradigm shift: we must view the relation of the sexes in a political light and recognise that literature participates in those politics. She takes the character of Sue Bridehead in *Jude* to exemplify the sexual politics of the 'first phase' of the sexual revolution. Millett commends Hardy 'for creating in Sue an intelligent rebel against sexual politics and in understanding the forces which defeat such a rebel' but warns he is not really committed to that revolution. He makes Sue into a victim of 'a cultural literary convention (Lily and Rose) that in granting her a mind insists on withholding a body from her', and ends up, as she does, 'troubled and confused.'[44]

Mary Jacobus's response to Millett set the tone for much subsequent feminist commentary. Where does Hardy stand in relation to (Sue's) feminism? Does he dodge or bungle the issues he raises in her character?[45] Sue is not to be viewed as a failure of imaginative conception, Jacobus concludes, nor a failure of Hardy's political nerve. She is, rather, the novel's great achievement: we engage with her as with few other women in fiction because her 'timidity, irresolution, and inconsistency' offer a 'realistic sense of the gap between what [one] thinks and what [one] does, between belief and behaviour'.[46] Jacobus was the most important feminist Hardyan of the 1970s. Her observation that 'Tess's silence, like her purity, makes female desire dumb; places her on the side of unconsciousness and, finally, death',[47] was particularly influential for feminist critics interested in the dynamics of objectification and desire in Hardy's intensely visual writing. Most notably, Kaja Silverman, also a film critic, drew on the poststructuralist psychoanalytic theories of Lacan and Kristeva to explore the 'supremacy of the male gaze'[48] in *Tess*: how it 'never innocently alights on its object' but '*constructs* [it] through a process of colonisation, delimitation, configuration and inscription'.[49]

Feminist criticism subsequently broadened into gender studies, which drew in masculinity studies and queer theory. To date there have been a number of essays but no book-length study of Hardy's men as cultural signs[50] – meeting points of contradictory historical values, attitudes, and social practices – and the need remains for a study of the gender system in Hardy, 'embedded in and ruled by language and narrative structure':[51] along the lines, perhaps, of Patricia Ingham's work. Ingham applied expertise in sociolinguistics and Marxist-inflected textual scholarship to an influential study of woman as 'sign' and as an element in the 'narrative syntax' of

Hardy's novels. Essentially a form of semiotic analysis, this methodology extrapolates from sentence structure to narrative structure, on the grounds that 'a particular narrative language' existed when Hardy began writing: It was 'already there with signs and the necessary syntax of patterns for narrative sentences as sequences'. Its subjects (in this case female subjects) are 'created by the language, which in turn is a product of ideologies', a process that is, however 'disturbed by contradictions.'[52]

Surveying Hardy criticism in 1998, Peter Widdowson noted the paucity of postcolonialist readings of 'notions of national and racial consciousness' in Hardy.[53] Since then, the explosive growth and near collapse of transnational capitalism have led to a rethinking of ideas of national literatures, and a consolidation of critical approaches founded in postcolonialism, globalism, and ecocriticism. Among the most interesting for Hardy are Michael Valdez Moses' reading of Wessex as a temporal entity – 'the fictional presentation of a premodern historical epoch that has effectively come to an end in the relatively recent past' – and the significance of the creation of Wessex at a time when 'the process of modernization would have seemed irreversible to most Victorians', and when those processes were being imposed on 'remote imperial domains in the undeveloped world'.[54] As a poet Hardy participated directly, and critically, in debates over the Anglo-Boer conflict; his fiction, however, only silently reinforces the intimate interrelationship between imperial power and domestic crisis.[55]

The 'irreconcilable clash between the forces of tradition and of innovation' has also informed ecocritical readings of Hardy. For Jonathan Bate, Hardy anatomizes the 'condition of the modern man' who, 'with his mobility and his displaced knowledge ... will always be an outsider; his return to nature will always be partial, touristic, and semi-detached'.[56] Lawrence Buell takes much the same view, suggesting (in a way that would surely have troubled Raymond Williams) that the 'basic life-rhythms' of Hardy's Wessexers 'have scarcely changed for years and seem unlikely to do so in the future'.[57] Richard Kerridge offers a more subtle and knowledgeable reading, arguing that Hardy is ecological in that he depicts networks of mutual responsibility in which the reader is part of an 'implied moral community':[58] not a 'ghostly, free-moving figure who watches and leaves no imprint but a bodily presence engaged in an act of consumption that will have material consequences'.[59] Hardy's great value is that he 'will not allow anything, place or person, to stabilize in meaning; its meaning is always the product of a shifting set of relations and always seen in the act of generation by those relations.'[60] He therefore 'shows the possibility of a nature writing not always in search of stability, not simply hostile to change and incursion.'[61]

Inevitably, I have disregarded much important work in this overview: reader-centred interpretations,[62] and Bakhtinian readings;[63] studies of archaeology and anthropology;[64] of science – especially Darwin and evolutionary narrative, but also astronomy;[65] of philology, geography, and religion;[66] of music, photography, and film and television.[67] I have also set aside some important books and essays written since 1970 which, although they did not take up theoretical advances (some of them remaining resolutely antitheoretical), profoundly influenced Hardy studies: notably, books by John Bayley, Michael Millgate, and Ian Gregor.[68] Finally, over the past four decades Hardyans everywhere have profited from the great opening up of the field by bibliographers, textual critics, scholars, and biographers: the volumes of letters, the establishment of texts, the all-important notebooks, and right back at the beginning, in 1970, the appearance of that indispensable work of reference, the Hardy volume in Routledge's *Critical Heritage* series.

NOTES

1 F. R. Leavis, *The Great Tradition: George Eliot, Henry James, Joseph Conrad* (London: Chatto & Windus, 1948), pp. 8–9.
2 Henry James, *Letters*, ed. Leon Edel (London: Macmillan, 1978), II:194.
3 Ibid., p. 204.
4 J. Hillis Miller, *Thomas Hardy: Distance and Desire* (Cambridge, Mass.: Belknap Press, 1970), p. 5.
5 Ibid., pp. ix–x.
6 Ibid., pp. xii, xiv.
7 Ibid., pp. vii–viii.
8 Raymond Williams, *The Long Revolution* (Harmondsworth: Penguin, 1965), p. 118.
9 Raymond Williams, *Politics and Letters: Interviews with New Left Review* (London: New Left Books, 1979), p. 246.

10 J. Hillis Miller, *The Ethics of Reading* (New York: Columbia University Press, 1987), p. 7.

11 Alan Swingewood, 'Literature and Praxis: A Sociological Commentary', *New Literary History* 5:1 (Autumn 1973), p. 173.

12 J. Hillis Miller, 'Fiction and Repetition: *Tess of the d'Urbervilles*', *Forms of Modern British Fiction*, ed. A. W. Friedman (Austin: University of Texas Press, 1975), p. 59.

13 J. Hillis Miller, 'Introduction', *The Well-Beloved: A Sketch of Temperament* (London: Macmillan, 1975); 'Topography in *The Return of the Native*', *Essays in Literature* 8:2 (1981), pp. 119–34; 'Speech Acts, Decisions, and Community in *The Mayor of Casterbridge*', *Thomas Hardy and Contemporary Literary Studies*, ed. Tim Dolin and Peter Widdowson (Basingstoke: Palgrave, 2004), pp. 36–53.

14 In the spectral criticism of Julian Wolfreys, for example – see *Victorian Hauntings: Spectrality, Gothic, the Uncanny* (Basingstoke: Palgrave, 2002) – or in John Paul Riquelme, 'Echoic Language, Uncertainty and Freedom in *Tess of the d'Urbervilles*', *Tess of the d'Urbervilles*, ed. John Paul Riquelme (Boston: Broadview, *1998*), pp. 506–21. See also Christine Brooke-Rose, 'Ill Wit and Sick Tragedy: *Jude the Obscure*' (*1991*), *New Casebook: Jude the Obscure*, ed. Penny Boumelha (Basingstoke: Macmillan, 2000), pp. 122–44.

15 Terry Eagleton, 'Flesh and Spirit in Thomas Hardy', *Thomas Hardy and Contemporary Literary Studies*, ed. Dolin and Widdowson, p. 15.

16 H. Aram Veeser, 'Introduction', *The New Historicism*, ed. H. Aram Veeser (New York: Routledge, 1989), p. xi.

17 Greenblatt, 'Towards a Poetics of Culture', *The New Historicism*, ed. Veeser, pp. 1–14.

18 Ramón Saldívar, '*Jude the Obscure*: Reading and the Spirit of the Law', *English Literary History*, 50:3 (1983), p. 615.

19 Elaine Scarry, 'Work and the Body in Hardy and Other Nineteenth-Century Novelists', *Representations* 3 (1983), p. 94.

20 Forest Pyle, 'Demands of History: Narrative Crisis in *Jude the Obscure*', *New Literary History: A Journal of Theory and Interpretation* 26:2 (1995), p. 360.

21 Ibid., p. 375.

22 Jeff Nunokawa, 'Tess, Tourism, and the Spectacle of the Woman', *Rewriting the Victorians: Theory, History, and the Politics of Gender*, ed. Linda M. Shires (New York: Routledge, 1992), pp. 70–86; Robert Kiely, 'The Menace of Solitude: The Politics and Aesthetics of Exclusion', *The Sense of Sex: Feminist Perspectives on Hardy*, ed.

Margaret R. Higonnet (Urbana: University of Illinois Press, 1993), pp. 188–202; Richard Dellamora, 'Male Relations in Thomas Hardy's *Jude the Obscure*', *Papers on Language and Literature* 27:4 (1991), pp. 453–72.

23 Jean-Jacques Lecercle, 'The Violence of Style in *Tess of the d'Urbervilles*', *New Casebooks: Tess of the d'Urbervilles*, ed. Peter Widdowson (London: Macmillan, 1993), p. 153.

24 Ibid., p. 154.

25 D. E. Musselwhite, '*Tess of the d'Urbervilles*: "A Becoming Woman", or Deleuze and Guattari Go to Wessex', *Textual Practice* 14:3 (2000), pp. 499–518. See also Brett Neilson, 'Hardy, Barbarism, and the Transformations of Modernity', *Thomas Hardy and Contemporary Literary Studies*, ed. Dolin and Widdowson, pp. 65–79.

26 Riquelme, 'Echoic Language', p. 512.

27 Margaret R. Higonnet, 'Introduction', *Sense of Sex*, ed. Higonnet, p. 5.

28 Terry Eagleton, *Criticism and Ideology: A Study of Marxist Literary Theory* (London: Verso, 1976), p. 131. See also Eagleton's *Walter Benjamin, cor Towards a Revolutionary Criticism* (London: Verso, 1981).

29 Eagleton, *Criticism and Ideology*.

30 *Ibid.*, p. 131.

31 Edward W. Said, *Beginnings: Intention and Method* (New York: Basic Books, 1975), p. 84.

32 Eagleton, *Walter Benjamin*, p. 126.

33 George Wotton, *Thomas Hardy: Towards a Materialist Criticism* (Totowa, N.J.: Barnes & Noble, 1985), p. 40.

34 Peter Widdowson, *Hardy in History: A Study in Literary Sociology* (London: Routledge, 1989), p. 138.

35 Ibid., p. 5.

36 Ibid., p. 8.

37 Joe Fisher, *The Hidden Hardy* (Basingstoke: Macmillan, 1992), p. 4.

38 Ibid., p. 14. See also N. N. Feltes, *Modes of Production of Victorian Novels* (Chicago: University of Chicago Press, *1986*).

39 Roger Ebbatson, *Hardy: The Margin of the Unexpressed* (Sheffield: Sheffield Academic Press, 1993), p. 7.

40 Penny Boumelha, *Thomas Hardy and Women: Sexual Ideology and Narrative Form* (Brighton: Harvester, 1982), p. 7.

41 Jane Thomas, *Thomas Hardy, Femininity and Dissent: Reassessing the 'Minor' Novels* (Basingstoke: Macmillan, 1999).

42 Boumelha, *Women*, p. 6.

43 Ibid., p. 6.

44 Kate Millett, *Sexual Politics* (New York: Doubleday, 1970), pp. 133–4.

45 Mary Jacobus, 'Sue the Obscure', *Essays in Criticism* 25 (1975), p. 305.

46 Ibid., pp. 313, 325. See also Kathleen Rogers, 'Women in Thomas Hardy', *Centennial Review* 19 (1975), pp. 249–50, and Patricia Stubbs, *Women and Fiction: Feminism and the Novel 1880–1920* (Brighton: Harvester, 1979).

47 Jacobus, 'The Difference of View', *The Feminist Reader: Essays in Gender and the Politics of Literary Criticism*, ed. Catherine Belsey and Jane Moore (Oxford: Blackwell, 1989), p. 53. See also Jacobus, 'Tess: The Making of a Pure Woman', *Tearing the Veil: Essays on Femininity*, ed. Susan Lipshitz (London: Routledge & Kegan Paul, 1978), pp. 77–92.

48 Kaja Silverman, 'History, Figuration and Female Subjectivity in *Tess of the d'Urbervilles*', *Novel: A Forum on Fiction* 18:1 (1984), p. 27.

49 Silverman, 'History', p. 7. See also Judith Wittenberg, 'Early Hardy Novels and the Fictional Eye', *Novel: A Forum on Fiction* 16 (1982), pp. 157–64, and T. R. Wright, *Hardy and the Erotic* (Basingstoke: Macmillan, 1989). The significance of Lacan in feminist readings of Hardy is considerable, informing, for instance, Marjorie Garson's illuminating study of 'somatic anxiety' in Hardy: its 'anxieties about wholeness, about maleness, and particularly about women'. Marjorie Garson, *Hardy's Fables of Integrity: Woman, Body, Text* (Oxford: Clarendon Press, 1991), p. 3.

50 Higonnet, 'Introduction', p. 1. See Elaine Showalter, 'The Unmanning of the Mayor of Casterbridge', *Critical Approaches to the Fiction of Thomas Hardy*, ed. Dale Kramer (Basingstoke: Macmillan, 1979), pp. 99–115; Elizabeth Langland, 'Becoming a Man in *Jude the Obscure*', *Sense of Sex*, ed. Higonnet pp. 32–48; and Richard Dellamora, 'Male Relations', a queer-theoretical study of desire between men in Hardy informed by Foucault, and by Eve Sedgwick's *Between Men: English Literature and Male Homosocial Desire* (New York: Columbia University Press, 1985).

51 Higonnet, 'Introduction', p. 2.

52 Patricia Ingham, *Thomas Hardy* (London: Harvester Wheatsheaf, 1989), p. 7.

53 Peter Widdowson, 'Hardy and Critical Theory', in *The Cambridge Companion to Thomas Hardy*, ed. Dale Kramer (Cambridge: Cambridge Univresity Press, 1999), p. 89.

54 Michael Valdez Moses, *The Novel and the Globalization of Culture* (Oxford: Oxford University Press, 1995), p. 30.

55 Edward Said, *Culture and Imperialism* (New York: Knopf, 1993), pp. 189–90; Daniel Bivona, *Desire and Contradiction: Imperial Visions and Domestic Debates in Victorian Literature* (Manchester: Manchester University Press, 1990), pp. 92–93.

56 Jonathan Bate, 'Culture and Environment: From Austen to Hardy', *New Literary History* 30:3 (1999), pp. 551–4.

57 Lawrence Buell, *The Future of Environmental Criticism: Environmental Crisis and Literary Imagination* (Oxford: Blackwell, 2005), p. 88.

58 Richard Kerridge, 'Ecological Hardy', *Beyond Nature Writing: Expanding the Boundaries of Ecocriticsm*, ed. Karla Armbruster and Kathleen R. Wallace (Charlottesville: University Press of Virginia, 2001), p. 132.

59 Ibid., pp. 129–30.

60 Ibid., p. 140.

61 Ibid., p. 138.

62 Wayne C. Anderson, 'The Rhetoric of Silence in Hardy's Fiction', *Studies in the Novel* 17:1 (Spring 1985), pp. 53–68; Garrett Stewart, *Dear Reader: The Conscripted Audience in Nineteenth-Century British Fiction* (Baltimore: Johns Hopkins University Press, 1996).

63 John P. Farrell, 'Crossroads to Community: *Jude the Obscure* and the Chronotope of Wessex', *Dialogue and Critical Discourse: Language, Culture, Critical Theory*, ed. Michael Macovski (Oxford: Oxford University Press, 1997); Mark Hennelly, 'The 'Original Tess': Pre-Texts, Tess, Fess, Tesserae, Carnivalesque', *Thomas Hardy Yearbook* 25 (1998), pp. 26–68.

64 Patricia O'Hara, 'Narrating the Native: Victorian Anthropology and Hardy's *The Return of the Native*', *Nineteenth-Century Contexts* 20:2 (1997), pp. 147–63; Andrew Radford, *Thomas Hardy and the Survivals of Time* (Aldershot: Ashgate, 2003); Michael A. Zeitler, *Representations of Culture: Thomas Hardy's Wessex and Victorian Anthropology* (New York: Peter Lang, 2007).

65 Gillian Beer, *Darwin's Plots: Evolutionary Narrative in Darwin, George Eliot, and Nineteenth-Century Fiction* (London: Routledge, 1983); George Levine, *Darwin and the Novelists: Patterns of Science in Victorian Fiction* (Cambridge, Mass.: Harvard University Press, 1988).

66 Dennis Taylor, *Hardy's Literary Language and Victorian Philology* (Oxford: Clarendon Press, 1993); John Barrell, 'Geographies of Hardy's Wessex', *The Regional Novel in Britain and Ireland,*

*1800–1990*, ed. K. D. M. Snell (Cambridge: Cambridge University Press, 1998), pp. 99–118; Timothy Hands, *Thomas Hardy: Distracted Preacher?: Hardy's Religious Biography and Its Influence on His Novels* (Basingstoke: Macmillan, 1989).

67  John Hughes, *Ecstatic Sound: Music and Individuality in the Work of Thomas Hardy* (Aldershot: Ashgate, 2001); Mark Durden, 'Ritual and Deception: Photography and Thomas Hardy', *Journal of European Studies* 30:1 [117] (2000), pp. 57–69; Paul J. Niemeyer, *Seeing Hardy: Film and Television Adaptations of the Fiction of Thomas Hardy* (Jefferson, N.C.: McFarland & Co., 2003); T. R. Wright, ed., *Thomas Hardy on Screen* (Cambridge: Cambridge University Press, 2005).

68  John Bayley, *An Essay on Hardy* (Cambridge: Cambridge University Press, 1978); Michael Millgate, *Thomas Hardy: His Career as a Novelist* (London: Bodely Head, 1971); Ian Gregor, *The Great Web: The Form of Hardy's Major Fiction*, (Totowa, N.J.: Rowman and Littlefield, 1974).

# 9

# Hardy's Poets as His Critics

## PETER ROBINSON

On 20 November 2009, the *Times Literary Supplement* made a feature of Thomas Hardy's critical standing as a poet. It published Seamus Perry on Hardy's *'Poetical Matter' Notebook*, and, in the 'Then and Now' column, republished the opening of a sustained rejoinder in the 5 February 1904 issue from Hardy to negative reviews of *The Dynasts*.[1] Had he read Perry's review, the poet would surely not have felt a need to reply. Perry cites the opening quatrain of 'Afterwards' (*CPW* II: 308–9) with its self-epitaph 'He was a man who used to notice such things', and comments: 'The play between an assiduously cultivated language of poetry ("Delicately-filmed as new-spun silk") and a more ordinary register of village speculation (what "will the neighbours say"?) catches one unmistakable Hardy effect – an unresolved comedy of idioms, in which the literary and the commonplace find themselves entangled, each implicated within the life of the other.' Hardy's embedding of such multiple, unresolved perspectives within the textures of his verse characterizes it as the product of a plotting novelist. William Empson called such unresolved contradictions 'complacence',[2] though the recognition of intractable difference in life need not mean indifference to its consequences, as Hardy's novels amply demonstrate.

His achievement in 'Afterwards' had, over the decades before Perry's writing, been ratified by a number of prominent poets, including two Nobel laureates. Joseph Brodsky, in 'Wooing the Inanimate' (1995), explores the poem's 'peregrination of stresses and suddenly halting caesuras' which is why (as he argues by means of a characteristic association of rhythmic distinction and immortality) the 'bell of quittance' in the poem's final stanza 'never stops – not Mr. Hardy's, anyway'.[3] In the same year Seamus Heaney published *The Redress of Poetry*, which alights upon 'Afterwards' as exemplary of his theme, noting that Hardy's 'bewitching' poem, though 'an expression of solidarity with the ordinary world where people stand around after the news of a death', also gives readers 'access to a dimension beyond the frontier where an overbrimming, totally resourceful expressiveness becomes suddenly available; and this entry into a condition of illuminated rightness becomes an entry into poetry itself.'[4] Such a rise in the status of his verse is underlined by recalling that W. B. Yeats, also a Nobel poet, had selected just four of Hardy's poems, 'Weathers', 'Snow in the Suburbs', 'Song: The Night of Trafalgár' from *The Dynasts* (*CPW* III: 285–6) and 'Former Beauties', for *The Oxford Book of Modern Verse 1892–1935*, choosing half as many as from Dorothy Wellesley, and two-thirds less than Walter James Turner. [5] Yeats's eccentric choice contrasts sharply with a 1921 anthology dedicated to 'Thomas Hardy, O. M. Greatest of the Moderns', offering seven distinctive poems including 'Beeny Cliff', 'The Oxen', and 'Afterwards'. [6]

Perry notes that W. H. Auden cited this last as among his favourites in 'A Literary Transference' (1940),[7] while the poet's allusive phrase 'my Joy in noticing these things' appears among his juvenilia, in 'Ploughing' from 1925 to 1926.[8] Perry also associates the instability of Hardy's rhythmic and dictional registers with those conflicting perspectives on experience: 'The poem is sane enough to concede that its subject's observational genius might well go entirely unremembered, while nevertheless it deploys an ostentatious verbal inventiveness ("some nocturnal blackness, mothy and warm") which touchingly implies that noticings of such quality really ought to matter to *someone*.' The viewpoints of a literary man's eloquent attention to nature and that of his imagined neighbours are contiguous but neither combined nor reconciled. Yet 'Afterwards' is entirely an expression of Hardy's composite outlook. 'The mixture of self-assertion and self-abnegation,' Perry adds, 'is also wholly characteristic', for 'the poem shows such triumphs of the artistic life unceremoniously folded within the uncertain rhythms of continuing, unaesthetic lives: "a gazer may think, / 'To him this must have been a familiar sight'" – the studied metrical imprecision of that line (how would you scan it?) delightedly enacts the honest prosey artlessness of the neighbours.'[9] How would I scan it? It's a twelve-syllable pentameter made of three iambs and two anapaests, with a light caesura after the third foot, dividing the two-syllable feet from the three-syllable ones. Hardy's rhythmic subtlety carefully deploys the neighbours' felicities of directness to act as a necessary foil for his own high-wrought observational diction. Even Perry's referring to his 'studied metrical imprecision' shows how far we have come from the *Saturday Review* critic writing on 11 January 1902 that 'Mr Hardy has never written with flowing rhythms … and his verse often halts' (*CH*: 331). What were once technical weaknesses are now what make his poetry so skillfully distinctive, and, it might be added, canonically established, as Perry's pages make abundantly evident.

Looking back to the decade from the mid 1960s, though, we find Hardy's verse recruited into a debate about what British poetry should be, and to what extent his work could be taken as exemplary, or as not measuring up to the highest standards. Philip Larkin and Donald Davie, both self-proclaimed Hardyesque poets, were its principal antagonists. In the final paragraph of his 1966 review, 'Wanted: Good Hardy Critic', Larkin turns to the reputation of the writer's verse: 'Perhaps the oddest thing … is the way in which its mediocre perpetrators consider themselves justified in patronizing Hardy's poems.' He criticizes Carl J. Weber for making 'very merry with the early poems in general and "Hap" in particular', and notes that Roy Morrell 'parrots the usual stuff about "the number of poems meriting serious attention is not large in relation to the bulk of his collected verse"':

To these two gentlemen (and also to Samuel Hynes, author of *The Pattern in Hardy's Poetry*) may I trumpet the assurance that one reader at least would not wish Hardy's *Collected Poems* a single page shorter, and regards it as many times over the best body of poetic work this century so far has to show?[10]

Larkin contrasts various disparaged critics with poets such as Auden, Betjeman, and Dylan Thomas who admired Hardy's verse, observing that the distinguished critics have only been neglectful. Among these he lists Empson, who reviewed Hardy's poetry in 1940, expressing, as noted above, irritation at the 'flat contradictions' of the philosophy, his seeing 'no need to try and reconcile the contradictions': this showed 'the same complacence which could be satisfied with a clumsy piece of padding to make a lyric out of a twaddling reflection'. Empson speculates that Hardy 'needed this quality to win through as he did. Most people who are admired for "unpretentious integrity" have it.' We can enjoy the good ('you want their honesty and find their beauty') because he had to write them all.[11]

Yet there's no contradiction in acknowledging what Empson notices here, while feeling as Larkin does that he wouldn't wish the *Collected Poems* any shorter. As Empson allows, Hardy needed his working methods to 'win through as he did', and we can follow his winning ways in the *'Poetical Matter' Notebook* when he reminds himself 'after reading some of Sh—y's "Fragments["]' that he might write 'Short poems of the emotions arising from situations adumbrated but unexplained.' He had already done so many times, as in 'A January Night', adding in his notebook an aside that the idea of the 'unexplained' had come to him in 1905 and that it 'anticipates the modern fashion of poems'.[12] Hardy's more usual method was to give the situation, tell the story, and round everything off, as, for example, in the double explanatory stanzas at the end of 'On the Departure Platform'.[13] Thus, though some critics thought just a few poems were worth considering, while others, such as Empson, insisted on a limiting judgment but acknowledged we couldn't have the good without the rest, there were poets who, like Bernard Spencer[14] and Larkin, appeared to like them all. Auden's response was similarly to acknowledge that 'I cannot write objectively about Thomas Hardy because I was once in love with him,' adding that for more than a year from the summer of 1923 'I read no one else, and I do not think that I was ever without one volume or another of the beautifully produced Wessex edition in my hands.' The following summer 'there was a palace revolution after which he had to share his kingdom with Edward Thomas, until finally they were both defeated by Eliot at the battle of Oxford in 1926'.[15] But Larkin's praise for Hardy, though presented with an air of adulation not unlike Auden's, was staged in the mid 1960s with the further intention of reengaging in the 'battle of Oxford' to disparage T. S. Eliot, Ezra Pound, and their followers from the middle of that neo-modernist decade.

Larkin's praise was, thus, angled to target a set of dislikes, identifiable from the terms of his praise for Hardy's poetry in a radio talk from 1968. In 'The Poetry of Thomas Hardy', originally entitled 'A Man Who Noticed Things', Larkin states that 'what I like about him primarily is his temperament and the way he sees life.

He's not a transcendental writer, he's not a Yeats, he's not an Eliot; his subjects are men, the life of men, time and the passing of time, love and the fading of love.' Despite the implausibility of Yeats's or Eliot's work not including such subjects, Larkin associates nontranscendent poetry with the permission to 'simply relapse back into one's own life and write from it'. He echoes Auden in acknowledging that 'Hardy taught one to feel rather than to write – of course one has to use one's own language and one's own jargon and one's own situations – and he taught one as well to have confidence in what one felt.' Why such confidence building should not also encourage a 'transcendental' writer such as D. H. Lawrence is unexplained by Larkin's assertions, whose view is not merely that poets should write the poetry they can, but that the poetry they can should have the cultural values that he associates with his own and Hardy's. Yet we cannot read and appreciate a poet's work without taking note of that poet's aims, whether transcendental or not. Larkin wants his natural approach to be simply what poetry is, rather than what *his* kind of poetry might be. Poets need such a projected sense of what poetry *should* be so as to write the poetry they are able to write – even if this sense of a project risks their failing to do so because stymied by obligations. Yet this is a necessary risk, not one that you can banish by appearing not to have a projected kind of poetry that is yours, even if your aim *appears* only to be writing poems.

To illustrate Hardy's ability to be 'extremely direct', Larkin cites 'Not a line of her writing have I, not a thread of her hair' and adds that 'Donne couldn't be more' so.[16] Reading 'Thoughts of Phena' (*CPW* I: 81–2) had been Larkin's road-to-Damascus experience as reported in the 'Introduction' to the second edition of *The North Ship* (1965):

I knew Hardy as a novelist, but as regards his verse I shared Lytton Strachey's verdict that 'the gloom is not even relieved by a little elegance of diction'. This opinion didn't last long; if I were asked to date its disappearance, I should guess it was the morning I first read 'Thoughts of Phena At News of Her Death'.[17]

Larkin's 'Statement' (1955) of intent chimes with his conversion to Hardy: 'I write poems to preserve things I have seen/thought/felt (if I may so indicate a composite and complex experience) both for myself and for others, though I feel that my prime responsibility is to the experience itself, which I am trying to keep from oblivion for its own sake.' He adds that 'Generally my poems are related, therefore, to my own personal life' and 'every poem must be its own sole freshly created universe' – which is what appears to exclude Modernism, for he has 'no belief in "tradition" or a common myth-kitty or casual allusions in poems to other poems or poets'.[18] Yet to read 'A Singer Asleep', Hardy's 1910 elegy for Swinburne, is to find the poet breaking most of these Movement-style rules for the kind of poet he is supposed to be. Though Larkin was making a high claim for Hardy's poetry, he was doing so by selectively characterizing those near one thousand poems, all of which he claimed to value.

Donald Davie's first tacit response to Larkin's aesthetic-cultural attitudes appeared in a 1972 Thomas Hardy Special Issue of the poetry magazine *Agenda*. Guest edited by Davie, it featured such poets as Thom Gunn and C. H. Sisson from both sides of the Atlantic, and made a point of presenting a revisionary Hardy, in for example the first essay, John Peck's 'Pound and Hardy',[19] or one on American poet-critics' views of his work,[20] and especially in the allusiveness of Davie's own extremely fine 'Hardy's Virgilian Purples'.[21] The poet of 'Poems 1912–1913' is there presented as a modernist-like writer, one steeped in the epics of Virgil and Dante (as if a follower of T. S. Eliot's 'Tradition and the Individual Talent') and one who allows himself references to the common myth kitty of, for instance, visits to the underworld. Davie also makes a point, especially in *Thomas Hardy and British Poetry* (1973) of his rhythms being far more experimental and technically expert than had been acknowledged to date – as, for example, in his moving account of the form in 'After a Journey'.[22]

Yet Davie's ambivalence in responding to Larkin's position can be noted throughout, as in the similarity of his disappointment at the concluding poems of the 1912–1913 sequence, outlined in 'Hardy's Virgilian Purples', which chimes with Larkin's preferring to 'simply relapse back into his own life', and it is reiterated in his chapter on 'Landscapes of Larkin', prompting Davie's 'lowering of his sights'[23] criticism, and attributing it to the influence of Hardy: 'if he is Hardy's heir, he sells out or sells off a great deal of his inherited estate. Yet Hardy had provided the precedent for such a sell-out.'[24] Davie's view is that the final three 'Poems of 1912–1913', such as the concluding 'Where the Picnic Was', withdraw from his phantasmagoric encounter with the dead Emma into an inert memorializing of that past life.[25] Davie's strategy in *Thomas Hardy and British Poetry* of dividing his discussion into a chapter on 'Hardy as Technician' followed by 'Hardy Self-Excelling' similarly acknowledges Empson's distinction between the true and the laboured. Thus the falling off that is said to occur in the 'Poems of 1912–1913' (which might equally be a dramatizing of mourning stages), and the 'lowering of his sights' accusation both converge on whether Hardy's poetry can be attributed with a 'transcendental' dimension.

Davie's writings on Hardy underline how *unlike* Hardy's practice as a poet Larkin's account of him might be; and Tom Paulin's *Thomas Hardy: The Poetry of Perception* (1975) follows up this truth with a sustained account of his poetry's conflicted metaphysics of spiritual yearning and down-to-earth perceptual scepticism, as in the application of David Hume's 'effect of repeated perceptions' on the 'immortality which the agnostic poet anticipates' in 'Afterwards'.[26] Larkin's dislike of the neo-modernists and their sources had not only travestied what the high modernists were attempting to do (and his own debts to Eliot, Lawrence, and Auden), but also undervalues the complexities of Hardy's poetry so as, in effect, to express an increasing disillusion with the direction taken by British society and its poetry in the third quarter of the twentieth century. Davie's criticism of Larkin and his poetics, with its version of Hardy, of modernism's legacy, and Larkin's poetry itself in *Thomas Hardy and British Poetry* had erupted in public over Davie's 1973 review in *The Listener* of Larkin's selections for *The Oxford Book of Twentieth-Century Verse*.[27] Yet Davie's own ambivalence about those neo-modernist strategies equally characterizes his use of poetry by Roy Fisher and J. H. Prynne as an instance of Hardy's influence, for his discussions include limiting judgments about how far their strategies can be taken before 'the game is hardly worth the candle'.[28] The shame is that both Larkin and Davie attempt to recruit a partial Hardy for an idea about British poetry, and its conflicts in the 1970s, while the latter bends other poets' writings to a polemic about the presumed character of British society with Hardy as its laureate:

Fisher's opting for pathos and compassion as his objectives, [has] everything to do with the history of our times, which has shown that the political alternatives to social democracy on the British model – mean-spirited as that undoubtedly is – are too costly in terms of human suffering for any man of humane feeling, least of all a poet, to find them real alternatives any longer.[29]

Davie's words have much 'to do with the history of his times', with the Cold War, and decline of British prestige in the world. Both Larkin and Davie are turning to Hardy as an English poet whose work subliminally corresponds to this decline. Yet whereas Larkin appears to embrace such a change in poetry (though, increasingly, not in politics) Davie appears to be fighting a rear-guard action in which Hardy is claimed as just such a poet of the times, not only because he sponsors a reduction of ambition, but, more resistant, because his best work in all its complexity can stand comparison with any poetry.

The elegiac melancholy in Hardy's writings may thus have chimed with the times: 1973, the year of both *Thomas Hardy and British Poetry* and Larkin's *The Oxford Book of Twentieth-Century Verse*, is also when Britain joined the European Common Market. This further indication of the nation's changing position in the world was responded to in Larkin's case by his polemic for a specifically English kind of poetry. Davie, though, was invested in American literature too, had recently begun teaching in the United States, and his argument concerns making British poetry hold its ground on an international stage (within its own terms and traditions). Yet the history of poetry need not be wedded and inexorably parallel to that of general and political culture. How might Hardy's poetry tacitly comment on such a posthumous concern with British global decline? The poet of 'Under the Waterfall' memorializes loss within a stark acknowledgement of how complete it may be; nevertheless, his work puts the powers of memory and ghostly haunting at the disposal of grief, and in poem after poem homeopathically treats the fact of being 'past love, praise, indifference, blame' as in 'Your Last Drive' (*CPW* II: 48–9). When he writes that 'if way to the Better there be, it exacts a full look at the Worst' in

'In Tenebris II' (*CPW* I: 207–8), it hardly follows that 'the Worst' of global decline cannot be a 'way to the Better', or that military-technological progress such as the 'poison gas' of 'Christmas: 1924' (*CPW* III: 256) might not equally exact a full look. Similarly, 'In Time of "the Breaking of Nations"' (*CPW* II: 295–6) contradicts its Biblical source in Jeremiah 51:20–23, making the 'story' of 'the maid and her wight' what will principally survive when the nations are broken. If the extremely long, multiple, unresolved perspectives in Hardy's poetry foreshadow the political concerns of a little England isolationism in the wake of imperial decline, or of the British poetry that grew out of such circumstances, they also can and do make them look limited and parochial.

Yet since 1975 and Paulin's *The Poetry of Perception*, writing on Hardy's poetry has developed away from seeing him as the stand-ard bearer for an embattled tradition of verse, and concentrated on discussing the complex works that Hardy actually wrote. Dennis Taylor has, for one example, explored the poet's familiarity with 'dipodic rhythm' and 'the same line's susceptibility to different met-rical norms' with a detailed study of 'After a Journey' in *Hardy's Metres and Victorian Prosody*.[30] Looking back to the final third of the last century, though, it is fair to say Hardy's poets, by exemplify-ing in their own work and arguing for his contested poetic legacy, were crucial in confirming his oeuvre's place in the canon of British poetry. 'Hardy taught one to feel,'[31] wrote Philip Larkin, and, before him, W. H. Auden confessed that 'Hardy comforted me as an ado-lescent, and educated my vision as a human being.'[32] Writing from America as the Luftwaffe prepared its aerial bombardment, with Britain's position in the world about to change for ever, he con-cluded that Hardy 'is dead, the world he knew has died too, and we have other roads to build, but his humility before nature, his sym-pathy for the suffering and the blind, and his sense of proportion are as necessary now as they ever were'.[33] Seventy years after these words were first published, they are not a whit less true.

NOTES

1 *THPV*: 194–8; see also *CPW* V: 385–96.
2 William Empson, 'Selected Poems of Thomas Hardy', *Argufying: Essays on Literature and Culture*, ed. John Haffenden (London: Chatto & Windus, 1987), p. 421.

3  Joseph Brodsky, 'Wooing the Inanimate', *On Grief and Reason: Essays* (London: Hamish Hamilton, 1995), p. 373.

4  Seamus Heaney, *The Redress of Poetry: Oxford Lectures* (London: Faber & Faber, 1995), pp. xvi, xvii.

5  W. B. Yeats, ed., *The Oxford Book of Modern Verse 1892–1935* (Oxford: Oxford University Press, 1936), pp. 7–10.

6  A. Methuen, ed., *An Anthology of Modern Verse* (London: Methuen, 1921), pp. 97–107.

7  W. H. Auden, 'A Literary Transference', *The Complete Works of W. H. Auden: Prose: Volume 2, 1939–1948*, ed. Edward Mendelson (London: Faber & Faber, 2002), pp. 48.

8  W. H. Auden, *Juvenilia: Poems 1922–1928*, ed. Katherine Bucknell (London: Faber & Faber, 1994), p. 116.

9  Seamus Perry, 'Not Unnoting All Things', *TLS* no. 5564, 20 November 2009, p. 7.

10  Philip Larkin, *Required Writing: Miscellaneous Pieces 1955–1982* (London: Faber & Faber, 1983), pp. 173–4.

11  Ibid. pp. 421, 423.

12  Pamela Dalziel and Michael Millgate, eds., *Thomas Hardy's 'Poetical Matter' Notebook* (Oxford: Oxford University Press, 2009), p. 46.

13  See my 'Thomas Hardy', *The Cambridge Companion to English Poets*, ed. Claude Rawson (Cambridge: Cambridge University Press, 2011), pp. 439–56.

14  Asked in 1963 about his poetic influences, Bernard Spencer replied, 'I think Thomas Hardy, very, very especially', *The Poet Speaks: Interviews with Contemporary Poets*, ed. Peter Orr (New York: Barnes & Noble, 1966), p. 234.

15  Auden, 'A Literary Transference', pp. 43–4.

16  Larkin, *Required Writing*, pp. 175–6.

17  Ibid. pp. 29–30.

18  Ibid. p. 79.

19  Donald Davie, ed., *Agenda: Thomas Hardy Special Issue* 10: 2–3 (Spring–Summer 1972), pp. 3–10.

20  Robert Pinsky, 'Hardy, Ransom, Berryman: A "Curious Air"', ibid., pp. 89–99.

21  Ibid., pp. 138–56.

22  Donald Davie, *Thomas Hardy and British Poetry* (London: Routledge & Kegan Paul, 1973), pp. 57–60.

23  Ibid., p. 73.

24  Ibid., p. 82.

25  See 'Hardy's Virgilian Purples', *Agenda*, pp. 153–6.

26  Tom Paulin, *Thomas Hardy: The Poetry of Perception* (Basingstoke: Macmillan, 1975), pp. 95–6.

27 Donald Davie, 'Larkin's Choice', *The Listener* 89: 2296 (29 March 1973), p. 420, and see the subsequent six weeks of correspondence.

28 See Davie, *Thomas Hardy and British Poetry*, p. 167 and 'What sorts of poetry were you reading?', conversation with Ian Brinton, *The Use of English* 60:3 (Summer 2009), pp. 215–23.

29 Davie, *Thomas Hardy and British Poetry*, p. 172.

30 Dennis Taylor, *Hardy's Metres and Victorian Prosody* (Oxford: Oxford University Press, 1988), pp. 82–100.

31 Larkin, 'The Poetry of Hardy', *Required Writing*, p. 174.

32 Auden, 'A Literary Transference', p. 47.

33 Ibid., p. 48.

# PART III

# The Literary Scene

# 10

# Thomas Hardy and Realism

## FRANCIS O'GORMAN

One distinguished nineteenth-century novelist was bold enough to observe that 'realism', though much championed by the most celebrated fiction writers of the century, was 'an unfortunate, an ambiguous word'. It had been, he continued, 'taken up by literary society like a view-halloo'.[1] It was too capacious, too ready to mean different things: it had, in turn, been chased all over literary culture like a fox over the countryside. And it was liable, unlike most Victorian fox hunts, to be freighted with moral judgment.

Plotting Thomas Hardy's realism is to see with unusual clarity the availability of the term for alternative meanings at the end of the Victorian period. He makes its potential visible as he proposes across his life alternative versions for where the 'real', for the literary writer, might lie. The subject of Hardy and realism is not straightforward. And we have Hardy's own warning about this: he was the distinguished novelist.

In the period that saw the establishment of the novel as the dominant literary form in British culture, the Victorians gave powerful and complicated consideration to the idea of fiction as representing the 'real'. They were theorists about and practitioners of imaginative prose that described itself, in one way or another, as representing the textures and experiences of lived life. Realism is, at least at the headline level, the imaginative counter of romance. Unlike realism, romance does not have its feet on the ground. Realism claims itself as a language of the earth; romance of what might lie beyond it. Realism lives with history and politics and tragedy; romance with myth and fantasy and comedy. Realism, as a literary practice in the nineteenth century, is habitually a discourse of the agnostic because it concerns itself with things empirically knowable; romance readily makes way for the theological, because it admits into its textures the nonempirical, the extraordinary, the supernatural, the possibilities of what might be beyond the globe.

Realism offers itself as an imaginative discourse that makes its material from the observed world: romance offers itself as imaginative discourse.

The origins of realism as a literary practice lie early in the surviving histories of Western thought. They are with Aristotle and empiricism, whereas Plato, who envisaged forms beyond the earth, is the ancient figurehead of romance. But these broad brush statements are immediately in need of qualification. For the Victorians, to remain at the level of generalization, the writer who defined realism as the central mode for the English novel was George Eliot. Victorian realism and Marian Evans belong together. Sir Walter Scott had described a practice of realism that was committed to the representation of historical events – to things that had demonstrably happened. Eliot was interested in realism not primarily as testable by historical records (of the '45, the Old Tolbooth Prison, of Claverhouse and the Covenanters), but as narration that could be tested by something as instinctive as felt experience. Eliot's touchstone of what was real in fiction was the reader's sense of what was real beyond it (though that is not to say that she did not experiment with Scott's mode: *Romola* is her historical novel, as *The Trumpet-Major* is Hardy's). Eliot's narrator in *Adam Bede* (1859) observes that Adam, when he sees the preacher Dinah Morris, feels the contrast with the worldlier Hetty Sorrel. Dinah appears, Eliot's narrator says, with 'all the force that belongs to a reality contrasted with a preoccupying fancy'.[2] That summed up the ambitions of Eliot's fiction itself – the 'force' of realism as the novel's unique source of energy and moral grounding.

Eliot's practice admitted symbolism (*Silas Marner*), sensationalism (*Daniel Deronda*), and the structuring of moral fables (*Silas* again, and *Brother Jacob*). She was intrigued by (what appear to be) supernatural powers in *The Lifted Veil*. Even for its major architect in the nineteenth century, realism never refused the shaping hand of the artist. But its substance was primarily the observable and the empirical, nevertheless. And as part of that, Eliot's distinctively provincial realism sought, and in *Middlemarch* (1871–2) made central, the narrative allure of the unremarkable. 'Something real, cool, and solid lies before you; something unromantic as Monday morning,' said Charlotte Brontë, on the first page of her 'industrial' novel, *Shirley*. That was a tougher description of a realist practice, but it was not in essence different from Eliot's fondness for the meaning of the seemingly mundane, for the fact that the mundane had meaning in which others might be interested.

Thomas Hardy was intrigued by the ordinary, provincial, and day-to-day. Some of his fiction could easily have borne Eliot's unmetropolitan subtitle for *Middlemarch: A Study of Provincial Life*. The subtitle of *Under the Greenwood Tree, A Rural Painting of the Dutch School*, more obviously saluted Eliot's fondness for Dutch realism as a model for the new fiction. Realism for Anthony Trollope in the Palliser novels was concerned with the grand, the titled, and the parliamentary (though almost always with the desires and feelings of those men and women, rather than, in any detail, their heroic public deeds or their intellectual life). But Hardy, learning in part from Eliot and Elizabeth Gaskell, looked to the plots that could be made from unexalted forms of life, even as he sometimes made – in *Jude the Obscure* – the failure to leave lowly forms of existence the plot itself. What was real in this form of fiction, which is most clearly evidenced in *Under the Greenwood Tree*, seemed to inhere in the ordinary lives of the out-of-the-way. In *Tess of the d'Urbervilles*, Hardy's desire to write a domestic tragedy of the provinces resonated more specifically with Gustave Flaubert's realist experiment, *Madame Bovary* (1857), which proposed the tragic capacity of the apparently unremarkable. Tess is, reshaped and reimagined, an English version of Emma Bovary.

A reader of fiction, Hardy said relatively early in his career in 1881, must be persuaded 'to believe the personages true and real like himself', and to this end a 'work of fiction should be a precise transcript of ordinary life'. But he knew that would not do on its own. Such transcripts, for a start, are likely to be without the driving compulsion of fictional plots, the allure of narrative, the good story. In a mere transcript (assuming for a moment such a thing to be possible), 'the uncommon would be absent and the interest lost'. The lives of the day-to-day, the provincial, jeopardised the success of fiction if they were not made engaging by incident. Of course, Hardy knew and always exploited the fact that 'ordinary' life was perfectly capable of containing the uncommon, the surprising, the unexpected, as matters to be – expected. The oddities of the seemingly regular were part of the natural order of things. But, he went on in his autobiography:

The writer's problem is, how to strike the balance between the uncommon and the ordinary so as on the one hand to give interest, on the other to give reality.

In working out this problem, human nature must never be made abnormal, which is introducing incredibility. The uncommonness must be in the events, not in the characters; and the writer's art lies in shaping that uncommonness while disguising its unlikelihood, if it be unlikely. (*LW*: 154)

Hardy's aesthetic as a writer of fiction circles around this self-declared problem. The uncommon events in the life of the common person might be the swiftest summary of the major fiction, and the challenge many of Hardy's readers have felt is the 'likelihood' of the result. Many a critic and teacher of Hardy has been frustrated by readers' comments about the 'impossibility' or 'absurdity' of Hardy's plots, for such a crude sense of whether a novel is 'true to life' is no very useful tool in thinking sophisticatedly about the fiction. Yet likelihood, the judgment of verisimilitude, bothered Hardy himself. Henchard's drunken decision to sell his wife in *The Mayor of Casterbridge* begins a novel that places an ordinary man in exceptional positions: as that drunken act helps make his life, so it ends it. The plot exemplifies a form of realism that examines and exposes the responses of 'ordinary' individuals to extraordinary circumstances. Likelihood mattered to Hardy, but it was the likelihood of human reaction – as for Shakespeare in, for instance, *Othello* or *The Winter's Tale* – more than the likelihood of the events. As he said himself of *The Mayor*: 'it is not improbabilities of incident but improbabilities of character that matter' (*LW*: 183).

The notion of a mere 'transcript' remained both challenging and productive. That which was slavish in its following of the empirical was not art: it was neither pleasurable nor educative. The 'most devoted apostle of realism', Hardy said in the *New Review* in April 1891, 'the sheerest naturalist, cannot escape, any more than the withered old gossip over her fire, the exercise of Art in his labour or pleasure of telling a tale' (*THPV*: 107). French naturalism and the novels of Emile Zola in particular were implicitly too much a 'transcript of ordinary life'. To 'advance realism as complete copyism', Hardy said, 'is the hyperbolic flight of an admirable enthusiasm' (*THPV*: 109). But it went too far. Select and omit, Hardy advised: realism is an art of tact. And then, like John Ruskin on the paintings of J. M. W. Turner, he claimed the higher ground: the 'just aim of Art', Hardy declared, is representation that has 'an eye to being more truthful than truth' (*THPV*: 107). The substance of the real must be manipulated by the artist to articulate meanings that lie deeper than appearances, surfaces, materialities.

At the most extreme point, the real did not seem, sometimes, to inhere for Hardy in the observed, tangible world at all. He could on occasions sound like a visionary, looking at the externalities of terrestrial life, and at times could hardly be further away from suggesting the novel as a mere transcript. 'I was thinking,' he said in 1887, 'that people are somnambulists – that the material is not the real – only the visible, the real being invisible optically' (*LW*: 192). Of course, part of the force of that observation was in relation to his realist practice as a describer of the empirical world. But Hardy the realist could transmute into something like Hardy the visionary with such felicity because his exploration of the meanings, verities, and 'realities' with which prose fiction properly dealt remained restless and serious. The location of the real, like the location of the ideal in *The Well-Beloved*, was not stable, and Hardy is distinctive among the Victorians as a theorist of fiction, and a practitioner of it, in part because he permits the reader to know so wide a range of conceptions of the real in a single body of writing. Hardy's interest in modes of perception, frames of observation – exemplified by *The Hand of Ethelberta* or *Tess* – included, at the amplest level, a readiness to expose realism as a representational act based on choice. He helped make realism self-conscious.

Matters could become more complicated still. In one of his most important critical statements, 'The Profitable Reading of Fiction' (1888), Hardy did not think about the artist alone as he moved away from considering modes of writing to modes of reading. A writer engaged with the materiality of the real world, and he or she adapted it to express more deeply located values, meanings, pleasures. But the *reader* added a new level of meaning. Reading a novel, Hardy said, in now celebrated words:

should be the exercise of a generous imaginativeness, which shall find in a tale not only all that was put there by the author, put he it never so awkwardly, but which shall find there what was never inserted by him, never foreseen, never contemplated. Sometimes these additions which are woven around a work of fiction by the intensitive power of the reader's own imagination are the finest parts of the scenery. (*THPV*: 76)

In this expressive theory, Hardy was not envisaging the irrelevance of the author: this is not Roland Barthes *avant la lettre*. But he was, modestly, looking to good readers to find 'parts of the scenery' the author had not. The words quietly acknowledge that there are such things as good and (by implication) bad readers, and that acknowledgement arose in part from Hardy's ongoing frustration with the reception of some of his writing. But, in this depiction of the role of the reader's reality, realism as a writer's product is always ready to be woven around with the imagination of someone else, so that the reading experience becomes a compound of creative powers. Another set of distancing or self-conscious speech marks are put around 'realism' in this reflection, for here the best part of a novel arises from its capacity to bring, potentially, the realism of any fictional representation into contact with others' associations, fantasies, and imaginings.

If Hardy was interested in personal associations, was, perhaps, his realism grounded in what was distinctively real *to him*? Eliot's form of realism did not make a claim about autobiography. Indeed, a defining feature of Victorian realism as a practice of writing is that it usually assumes a collective or universalised point of view. Realist prose offers itself typically, like much of *Middlemarch*, as constituted from abstracted generality, from a perspective that does not claim to be that of a named individual. Certainly, Hardy was wary of permitting a reader to think the author's private life, his own experience, was prominent in the fiction. He did not like the idea of the self as the 'key' to the novels, or of the 'real' of his own life as any obvious foundation for his fiction's claims to represent reality, even as he once welcomed the addition of the reader's personal imagination to the fabric of his novels' meaning. Inevitably, there was knowledge in Hardy's fiction drawn from personal experience – of landscapes, towns and cities, buildings, architectural practice. But that was not the private life of the author in any intimate way. As he said himself, he had 'ever been shy of putting his personal characteristics into his novels' (*LW*: 76). Even Hardy's autobiography was narrated in the third person, and issued – as he had required – under his wife's name. Yet for all the 'impersonality' of the fictions, individual they remain. His tragic plots, characterisation, fondness for the unexpected and melodramatic, and his celebrated 'unlikelihood', are his alone. If Hardy's realism avoided personal testimony, it was personal in other, but still real, ways. 'Art consists of so depicting the common events of life,' he remarked plainly, 'as to bring out the features which illustrate the author's idiosyncratic mode of regard' (*LW*: 235).

'Am I awake? / Or is this all a dream?', says Napoleon in Part Third of *The Dynasts*, before realising: ' – Ah, no. Too real!'[3] And Hardy, to some readers, could seem 'too real', as well. The contradiction in that criticism is always obvious, but the inquiry about the scope of art that lies beneath it is demanding. As Hardy laid out for his audience a set of alternatives about where the real might be found, so he invited his readers, as Zola did, to reflect at times on what the legitimate scope of art is, the legitimate reach of realism as a practice of writing, the legitimate nature of what word art could say, what feelings it could evoke, what scenes it could or should make public. 'All great art is praise,' said John Ruskin boldly, in the opening chapter of *The Laws of Fésole* (1877–8);[4] Robert Browning envisaged the imagination of the poet as the bringer of life in almost literal terms; Henry James, in *The Art of Fiction* (1888), thought the central commitment of fiction was to nothing other than life itself. But what were the borders of that life? Darkness, sorrow, and suffering were one thing; but what of the sordid, the violent, the shocking? Hardy disapproved of literary censorship that was undertaken on moral grounds, and said so in his gloomy article on 'Candour in English Fiction' for the *New Review* in January 1890. But *were* there things that realism should not say? Questions of the moral responsibilities of art were serious for the late nineteenth century, as indeed they remain. Here, certainly, was a challenge to the discretion of realism as a practice of writing, and a large question about what readers were doing reading fiction in the first place. Hardy's account of hard and degrading labour (*Tess*), child death (*Tess*), child suicide (*Jude*), human hopelessness (*The Mayor of Casterbridge*), the slaughter of a pig (*Jude*), the suffering of a rabbit in a gin (*Jude*), to name but a few instances, provoke the reader to think more about what George Eliot's realism of the provinces has become in Hardy's hands – and to think about the kinds of pleasure and responsibility realism can or *should* offer.

Hardy was, he believed, first and foremost a poet, and to poetry he eventually returned. Looking back, he would narrate his venture into fiction as driven by a perception of what he thought a late Victorian audience would prefer to read, a response to a market that had more room for novels than for poems. That more than usually acute sense of the novel's relation to audience was, perhaps, one of the factors that encouraged his readiness to exploit different modes, to adopt a manner that was inquiringly experimental and speculative. But as a poet, he reflected diversely on the world that Eliotian realism had described too – the world of material knowledge, human experience, terrestrial destinies, terrestrial understandings – and mourned it as lacking, as necessarily and tragically detached from the chances of vision. Nowhere was that sense of the diminished, the limited, more evident than in poems on death. 'A Sign-Seeker' from *Wessex Poems* considers the absence of prophetic knowledge in a world without the romance of hope or vision. Prophetic powers are beyond this poet's reach, Hardy concluded:

> I have lain in dead men's beds, have walked
> The tombs of those with whom I had talked,
> Called many a gone and goodly one to shape a sign,
>
> And panted for response. But none replies;
> No warnings loom, nor whisperings
> To open out my limitings,
> And Nescience mutely muses: When a man falls he lies. (*CP*: 50)

What was 'real' was dependent on the absence of knowledge of things beyond the earthly, an absence of faith or Christian surety about the immortal life. Hardy's sense of 'limitings' was, in this poem, a small but still suggestive episode in his ongoing, lifelong consideration of what realism involved for an artist as a practice of representation that was rooted in things of the earth. Here, empirical, experienced, terrestrial existence was the primary, and perhaps the only, reality. In 'A Sign-Seeker' knowledge was uncomforted by vision. Realism was not merely an ambiguous word: its implications for Thomas Hardy stretched starkly between two opposites. At one end, realist practice expressed a rich faith in the meaningfulness of lived, ordinary, observable existence. At the other, it admitted the awfulness of a life seemingly without meaning beyond such an existence.

### NOTES

1 Thomas Hardy, 'The Science of Fiction', *New Review* 4 (April 1891), pp. 315–19; *THPV*: 106–110.
2 George Eliot, *Adam Bede* (Harmondsworth: Penguin, 1980), pp. 161–2 (Chapter 11).
3 *The Dynasts*, *CPW* V: 86.
4 *The Library Edition of the Works of John Ruskin*, ed. E. T. Cook and Alexander Wedderburn, 39 vols. (London: Allen, 1903–12), 15:351.

# Tragedy and the Novel

K. M. NEWTON

Although it is common for the terms 'tragedy' or 'tragic' to be used in critical discussions of novels, do these terms have any critical substance or even legitimacy when applied to the novel as a form? It has been argued that they are problematic enough in themselves, and that it is critically counterproductive to try to construct concepts of tragedy even in relation to Greek drama when the plays are so different from each other.[1] Clearly if one takes this view, it would seem fruitless to discuss the novel in relation to tragedy, as any extension of tragedy or the tragic beyond classical drama will necessarily create more difficulties. Even if one argues that there are formal elements which give substance to tragedy as a critical term, that does not help in applying it to the novel as a form, since the most obvious of the formal aspects associated with tragedy are verse and a highly structured plot. Aristotle in his *Poetics* thought plot was the most significant formal element in tragic drama and created such terms as 'peripeteia', 'anagnorisis', 'catastrophe', 'catharsis' in describing its nature. Their relevance to plot as it functions in the novel may seem limited at best. George Steiner implicitly dismisses the novel's claim to be tragic as he sees verse as an essential feature of tragedy, since prose inevitably brings into play the contingencies of the real world, distracting the mind from the fundamental existential issues that tragedy is concerned with.[2]

However, there are some novels that set out to incorporate some of the formal elements of classical tragedy into their narratives, such as George Eliot's *Felix Holt* and Hardy's *The Mayor of Casterbridge*.[3] This does not necessarily mean that Eliot or Hardy believed that only by adopting the formal devices of classical tragedy could the novel aspire to the tragic, but may rather suggest that both these novelists believe the novel has sufficient artistic power to achieve tragic status. Arguably in *The Mill on the Floss* or *Tess of the d'Urbervilles*, which do not draw so explicitly on the conventions of classical tragedy, a more powerful tragic effect is achieved.

This raises the question in what way novels can be tragic if they generally disregard the formal elements of tragedy and use prose rather than verse. Philosophers have of course been interested in tragedy almost from its emergence as a dramatic genre. Though Aristotle saw Sophocles' *Oedipus the King* as the ideal tragedy, his main reason was philosophical rather than formal since it exemplifies most powerfully his concept of the tragic. Many other philosophers have also focused on tragedy and the tragic, most notably Hegel, but also Schopenhauer and Nietzsche in his *Birth of Tragedy*, as well as numerous less well known figures. Though the novel may have only marginal connections with the form of tragic drama, I shall suggest that tragedy as philosophy has had a major impact on it. Yet philosophy has thrown up many theories of the tragic, so there may seem little chance of agreement as to what criteria should apply in determining what novels can be legitimately described as tragic. But though there seems little likelihood of one particular theory of the tragic gaining complete critical ascendancy, it may be possible to establish some minimal criteria that would elicit a degree of critical agreement sufficient to discuss the relation between tragedy and the novel. The most influential philosophers to have discussed tragedy are Aristotle and Hegel. I shall suggest that a basic idea from each may supply the minimal criteria that would allow a discussion of tragedy and the tragic to be extended beyond drama to the novel.

The basic idea from Aristotle necessary to his concept of the tragic is his claim that neither a good nor a wicked person falling into misfortune is a suitable vehicle for tragedy. Neither one nor the other would inspire the 'pity and fear' that for Aristotle are fundamental to the tragic effect. This can be connected with Hegel's basic idea that though tragedy is founded on conflict, a conflict in which good and evil are clearly demarcated would not have tragic potential, since the conflict must have an ethical basis with both parties to the conflict believing that their opposed beliefs or actions are justified. The disastrous working out of the conflict between irreconcilable positions, both of which the audience can sympathise with, even if not equally, creates the tragic effect. Clearly Aristotle and Hegel are not far apart because an unequivocally good or wicked person being party to a conflict would not create any sense of ethical undecidability for an audience, and the destructive consequences would not produce pity and fear.

Yet all concepts of the tragic are contestable, even the most minimal, and there is no alternative but to confront objections. It has been argued, for example, that the presence of evil or 'morally dubious'[4] forces in many tragedies is problematic for Hegel's theory since 'evil' is not reconcilable with moral undecidability. The 'good' may be even more difficult to reconcile with my minimal criteria: in *King Lear*, widely regarded as Shakespeare's greatest tragedy, Cordelia is generally seen as an unequivocally 'good' character destroyed by the 'evil' forces of her monstrous sisters and the amoral Edmund. One can, however, question whether the latter characters are 'evil' in any absolute sense since their actions can be seen as responses to being disadvantaged by gender and bastardy, respectively. The sisters' lack of love for their father is understandable in the light of the kind of sexist language Lear uses towards Goneril when she resists his will, and Edmund's bastardy makes him a victim of the injustice and prejudice that lead him to believe that the only way he can rise in the world is by craft and ruthlessness.

But how can Cordelia be reconciled with the minimal criteria for the tragic I have drawn from Aristotelian and Hegelian tragic theory? I would contend that identifying Cordelia with a goodness that should gain the audience's entire sympathy leads to a simplistic view of the play. Though one may sympathise with her refusal to match her sisters' extravagant declarations of love for their father, it is this action that precipitates the tragedy. In a ceremonial speech situation she both proclaims sincerity as a value independent of circumstances and applies logical argument in a context that can be seen as inappropriate. Indeed, in such a public forum a particular form of rhetoric – one in which sincerity and logic have little or no place – is expected in addressing a king. Cordelia's response that when she marries, since her husband 'shall carry / Half my love with him', she cannot 'love my father all', is an application of logic that is irrefutable in the abstract but in the concrete situation in which it is uttered, it is inevitably seen as an insult and sets in train events which lead to tragedy. Though Cordelia may seem to be the polar opposite of her sisters and Edmund, she is linked to them by the fact that they also apply logic to disastrous effect. When Lear and Goneril have their altercation over her objection to the behaviour of the king and his knights in her household, Goneril, supported by Regan, asks, with logical force, why Lear should demand so many knights when he no longer needs them as he no longer has regal power. Regan's comment that he does not even 'need one' provokes the play's most powerful rebuttal of the abstract application of logic to human life: 'O, reason not the need.' The most ruthless applier of logic is, of course, Edmund, whose contempt for portents and astrology is persuasive from a rational point of view, but who goes on to use such abstract rationality to justify a philosophy of total self-seeking. But without Cordelia's initial refusal to respond to the king in the way he and his court expect tragedy need not have resulted from their 'morally dubious' tendencies.

However, my purpose in such a brief discussion is merely to show that even *King Lear* is not resistant to my minimal criteria for the tragic, despite initially appearing to be. If one applies these minimal criteria to the novel, one can argue that tragedy is at the centre of the novel's modern origins in the eighteenth century. On the face of it, Richardson's *Clarissa* may, like *King Lear*, appear to be a work in which good and evil are clearly demarcated, with an innocent woman being driven to death by the unforgivable actions of a rapist, Lovelace. Richardson is also generally associated with a moralism based on Christian precepts, and a novel based on those might appear to be outside the orbit of the tragic. Yet Richardson's stated intention in his preface to *Clarissa* – 'to warn the inconsiderate and thoughtless of the one sex, against the base arts and designs of specious contrivers of the other' – provides the potentially tragic foundation not only of this novel but of much subsequent fiction, since the relationship between the sexes was seen as one of intrinsic conflict that could never be fully resolved and that at the extreme could be destructive to both parties. What is particularly interesting in *Clarissa*, however, is that Christianity, far from helping, makes matters worse.

Much of Christian morality is, of course, concerned with sexual behaviour, not only condemning fornication and adultery but also lustful thoughts. According to Jesus, 'whoever looks at a woman to lust for her has already committed adultery with her in his heart' (Matthew 5:28). The value attached to chastity and celibacy in the Christian tradition implicitly downgrades sexuality even within marriage – one recalls St Paul's comment, 'better to marry than to burn' (1 Corinthians 7:1). Clarissa believes her fundamental relationship is to God, and one feels that given the choice she would choose a chaste life. She resists marriage to the man her parents have chosen for her, but the extremity of her resistance suggests little if any attraction to marriage as such. After the rape she rejects any pragmatic solution to her situation, either by marrying Lovelace or by becoming his mistress. On one level Lovelace is a conventional villain, but his desire for Clarissa goes beyond pure lust. He embodies and represents a sexuality that no moral or religious system can fully control. Ironically, the Christian moral view of sex makes virtuous and beautiful women such as Clarissa even more desirable for men such as Lovelace, driving them even to rape. There is of course no approval or justification for Lovelace's behaviour in the novel, but in representing so powerfully the drives that underlie it, any easy categorisation of him as merely evil is undermined, and his life as well as hers is destroyed by the action.

Jane Austen, however, is a Christian writer who has little attraction to tragedy, even though one can discern tragic potentiality in her fiction. In *Pride and Prejudice*, Elizabeth Bennet is confronted with a situation in which she can save her family from probable future ruin if she accepts the proposal of the man who will inherit her father's estate, an eventuality that could leave his widow and daughters homeless and virtually destitute. If any of the Bennet sisters married a rich man that fate could be averted, but their lack of dowry makes that possibility remote. When Mr Collins proposes to Lizzie she has the opportunity to safeguard the prosperity and status of her family at the expense of sacrificing her own happiness by marrying a man she not only has no respect for but regards as ridiculous. The potential for disaster is clear whatever she chooses: her family's likely ruin if she does not, and her own misery if she does. But in the world of Austen's fiction God is to be trusted; indeed, it would be unchristian to believe in a God who could present human beings with a choice of evils. Lizzie's implicit trust in God eventually leads to the match with Darcy in which not only is the well-being of her family secured but she finds both wealth and personal happiness.

Such trust in God's providence comes under stress in the midnineteenth century, which gives scope for tragedy to become a major force in fiction. In Matthew Arnold's most famous poem, 'Dover Beach', begun in 1851 though not published until 1867, the 'Sea of Faith' is famously on the wane and the poet creates a parallel between himself and the tragedian Sophocles who also heard the sound of the waves 'on the Aegean, and it brought / Into his mind the turbid ebb and flow / Of human misery'. Tennyson's *In Memoriam*, published in 1850, raised doubts about God's providence when confronted by a 'Nature, red in tooth and claw' (lyric 56) and archaeological evidence of mass extinctions of species. Tragedy in the fiction of Eliot and Hardy emerges from such a context, though in their case Christianity and the idea of providence or order in the universe had been further undermined by Darwin, whose theory of evolution by natural selection clearly called into question the argument from design.

There are significant differences between Eliot and Hardy, however, in their treatment and attitude to the tragic. Eliot's major attempt at tragedy in the full sense was her dramatic poem, *The Spanish Gypsy*, which also has a preface in which she discusses tragedy in general. The Hegelian influence on Eliot's thinking about tragedy is clear but in her fiction, though tragedy is a recurrent element, its impact is always qualified. What is distinctive about classical tragedy and later tragedy influenced by it is that endings tend to be absolute; there is no going beyond the culminating catastrophe, though Aristotle of course tried to overcome pure negativity through his concept of catharsis. But though Tennyson, Arnold and many of those who responded negatively to Darwinian theory may have promoted a pessimism about the world and life that provided the basis for tragedy, Eliot in contrast refuses to equate tragedy with such pessimism. Her writing implies that the concept of finality, or absolute notions of catastrophe that are part of tragedy in the traditional sense, are undermined by modern thought's undermining of finality. Though there may have been mass extinctions of species in evolutionary history, new species have replaced them. Would humanity as a species have emerged if the dinosaurs had not been wiped out? However, Eliot also rejects teleological concepts that attempt to overcome the notion of the tragic, a position that Tennyson appears to support at the end of *In Memoriam*.

The extinction of the dinosaurs can still be seen as tragic, even though it may have led to the emergence of the human species, but unremitting pessimism is at least qualified.

Eliot is sometimes blamed for not following through the tragic implications of her thought, for example in such novels as *The Mill on the Floss* or *Middlemarch*. Maggie Tulliver's life seems doubly tragic, forced to make a choice that will create unhappiness and pain for both herself and others no matter what she chooses, and then killed by an indifferent nature when trying to rescue her brother in the flood scene. Yet the novel does not end there. The last page suggests that just as nature recovers from apparently destructive events, so do human beings, or at least some of them. Two of the victims of the tragic events involving Maggie appear to be on the verge of rebuilding their lives. And in *Middlemarch*, Dorothea Brooke's life has a tragic dimension, in that someone who had similar qualities to heroic women of the past such as Saint Theresa is forced to settle for a limited life because she lives in a cultural context that provides little scope for such qualities. Yet though Ladislaw, the man she finally marries, may be more of a parody of a Romantic than the real thing, and thus a disappointment to many readers, Dorothea makes him become a more socially responsible individual. And as the narrator points out in the Finale, even those whose lives seem to be unfulfilled, who have lived 'a hidden life', may have contributed to the good of human beings in the future.

In Hardy's fiction, however, there is a much stronger sense of finality than in Eliot's, and this gives his work a more powerful tragic effect. Though in *Tess of the d'Urbervilles* Tess dreams of her sister being a substitute for her and marrying Angel Clare after her death, this prospect has little impact compared with her execution on the gallows. And though life goes on for Sue Bridehead after the death of Jude in *Jude the Obscure*, this future offers only a horror story, with Sue remaining united to a man for whom she has a physical loathing.

Like Richardson, Hardy finds the tragic in the relationship between the sexes. Tess resisting the sexual advances of Alec d'Urberville is structurally similar to Clarissa resisting Lovelace, and of course a rape is involved in both cases, even though with Hardy there is some ambiguity. However, in Hardy as a post-Darwinian writer, the nature of the conflict is fundamentally different from that represented by Richardson writing in a Christian context. Whereas Lovelace's sexuality is associated with original sin or man's fallen nature, Alec's sexuality derives from an evolutionary process; he is programmed by nature to be attracted by the physical charms of Tess, charms that have evolved to arouse such male attraction. Nature can still be resisted by the human will, but there is an intrinsic opposition between the individual will and forces within nature, which include the human body and may overwhelm the will of any individual. The novel's Darwinian aspect creates a new context for what Hardy, in the preface to the first edition of *Jude the Obscure*, famously called 'a deadly war waged between flesh and spirit' and to 'the tragedy of unfulfilled aims' that resulted from it (*Jude*: viii).

Unlike Clarissa, Tess does not wish to transcend or reject sexuality or the body but rather to relate them to a human ideal of reciprocated love in which body and spirit are unified. Her love for Angel Clare embodies this ideal. But nature and the evolutionary process have made her attractive not only to Angel but to men like Alec in whom she has little or no sexual interest, and this discordance sets in train a set of events that has a tragic outcome. In *Jude the Obscure*, Jude is also an idealist, though unlike Tess's ideal of sexual fulfilment in love, his ideal is religious and focused on Christminster, where he hopes that religion and knowledge will be reconciled and the contradictions he perceives in the world overcome. But nature enters his life with a vengeance when Arabella, 'a complete and substantial female animal – no more, no less', enters his life, and forces him to confront the body and sexuality which, when he first encounters her, form no part of the 'dreams of the humaner letters' with which he is preoccupied (*Jude*: I.6). Though he succumbs to Arabella's sexuality, he remains unreconciled to this force within himself, and attempts to overcome the conflict between flesh and spirit through his relationship with Sue Bridehead, a woman lacking the attributes of female sexuality that characterise Arabella, and whose interest in sex is intermittent at best. Since Sue does not seem a bodily creature like Arabella, and because her sexual desires are so limited, his love for her seems to transcend the body and animality.

Oppositions, contradictions, discordances are rooted in Hardy's fiction and underlie its tragic perspective. His major characters are tragic figures because they refuse to accept or come to terms with such forms of apparent disorder, but resist them and aspire beyond them. Characters like Tess and Jude show that human beings cannot reconcile themselves to the fact – and Hardy does not seek to deny it – that they are merely higher types of animal. They resist the idea that they are the product of an impersonal and humanly indifferent evolutionary process, and that religious or spiritual values are irreconcilable with the world. For Hardy spiritual aspirations define the human, but these aspirations inevitably encounter that which is resistant to them, both within and beyond the dimension of the human, and out of this confrontation emerges the tragic.[5]

D. H. Lawrence admired Hardy's novels but criticised what he saw as his negative representation of Arabella, Hardy's Darwinian character who accepts without guilt her animal sexuality and who has no moral qualms about doing what is necessary to survive in the world by adapting to changing circumstance. The 'war between flesh and spirit' is manifested in Jude's and Arabella different responses to the killing of the pig, with her declaration that 'Pigs must be killed!' contrasting with Jude's belief that it is almost equivalent to murder (*Jude*: I.10). For Lawrence, Hardy's negative treatment of Arabella is ideological as it reveals Hardy's rejection of the body and of life: 'he must have his personal revenge on her for her coarseness, which offends him, because he is something of an Angel Clare.'[6] Lawrence, however, by seeing Arabella positively as on the side of life, is rejecting, under the influence of Nietzsche's writing on tragedy, conceptions of the tragic that identify it with human defeat or pessimism about life. Like Hardy, Nietzsche did not deny Darwinian theory or the fundamentals of Schopenhauerian philosophy, but he interpreted them against the grain to create new experimental forms of humanism which seek to go beyond Christian and Christian humanist ideas. This Nietzschean influence is particularly strong in *Women in Love* which can be seen as experimenting with ideas of the tragic. Gerald Crich ultimately becomes a traditional type of tragic figure, while the other characters experiment through Dionysian yea-saying to life in a Nietzschean manner, or by holding pessimism at bay through irony.

Tragedy has continued to be a significant preoccupation for modern novelists but just as for the most influential of these novelists the writing of narrative in terms of story, character, and the various other elements associated with the novel as a form, becomes fused with self-conscious reflection about the writing of fiction, so the representation of the tragic in modern fiction is not objective in the sense that it involves a particular content, treatment and the use of formal devices traditionally associated with tragedy. The tragic in modern fiction as content interacts with a self-conscious reflection on what tragedy is, for example whether as both a form and a philosophy it is still viable and of value, or whether it has no authenticity any longer and has been superseded. If this makes modern fiction 'post-tragic' rather than tragic, with polarities such as those evident in Hardy being subject to deconstruction, then perhaps Hardy is the last novelist whom one can call a tragic writer without serious qualification.

NOTES

1 David Gervais takes this view in his article 'Tragic Endings', *PN Review* 35:4 (2009), pp. 19–26.
2 See George Steiner, *The Death of Tragedy* (London: Faber and Faber, 1963).
3 See Fred C. Thomson, '*Felix Holt* and Classical Tragedy', *Nineteenth-Century Fiction* 16 (1961), pp. 47–58, and Jeanette King, *Tragedy in the Victorian Novel: Theory and Practice in the Novels of George Eliot, Thomas Hardy and Henry James* (Cambridge: Cambridge University Press, 1978).
4 See Adrian Poole, *Tragedy: A Very Short Introduction* (Oxford: Oxford University Press, 2005), p. 61.
5 For further discussion of Eliot and, especially, Hardy in relation to the tragic see K. M. Newton, *Modern Literature and the Tragic* (Edinburgh: Edinburgh University Press, 2008).
6 D. H. Lawrence, *Selected Critical Writings*, ed. Michael Herbert (Oxford: Oxford World's Classics, 1998), p. 51.

# 12

# Hardy and the Short Story

SOPHIE GILMARTIN

Such was the debate in the 1880s and the 1890s over the shape and definition of the short story that one could be forgiven for imagining women and men of letters wholly engrossing talk at the club or the 'at home' with the finer distinctions between the short story, the tale, and the anecdote. Oscar Wilde may have been telling anecdotes, brilliantly and incessantly, but others were talking about them, about what they were, which is quite a different thing. Henry James wrote in 1898 that the short story had become 'an object of such almost extravagant dissertation'.[1] Looking back on this period, H. G. Wells wrote in 1911 of distinctions that he found stifling and arbitrary:

It was either Mr Edward Garnett or Mr George Moore in a violently anti-Kipling mood who invented the distinction between the short story and the anecdote. The short story was Maupassant, the anecdote was damnable … Anyone could say of any short story, 'A mere anecdote', just as anyone can say 'Incoherent!' of any novel or of any sonata that isn't studiously monotonous.[2]

In 1885 Brander Matthews distinguished between the 'Short-story' with a capital S, and the 'story which is merely short':

Like the brief tales to be seen in the British monthly magazines and in the Sunday editions of American newspapers into which they are copied, they are, for the most part, either merely amplified anecdotes or else incidents which might have been used in a Novel just as well as not.[3]

The American novelist and critic William Dean Howells argued that the anecdote is 'too palpably simple and single', and cannot 'expand … to dramatic dimensions' as the short story can.[4] In the same spirit, Henry Harland, editor of the controversial, prestigious and short-lived *Yellow Book* (1894–97), aggressively sought to redefine the short story within the pages of his magazine. The *Yellow Book* was to carry no serials, only short stories, but he made it abundantly clear that this was not to be 'the usual short story for the usual magazine': that 'meaningless little coincidence' which could be told 'in two minutes'. Harland holds up Henry James as 'the supreme prince of short story writers', but, he cautions, his writing 'is not to be approached by people whose interest in literature is superficial or unenlightened'. It must not 'be recommended either to the man in the street or to the man in the train'.[5]

Meanwhile men and women on the train were happily absorbed in those 'usual magazines', purchased before boarding at W. H. Smith's station bookstand; in them they were reading stories by authors such as R. L. Stevenson, Vernon Lee, Kipling, Thomas Hardy, and even Henry James.

Hardy wrote more than forty stories for a wide variety of Victorian periodical magazines, most of them published in the 1880s and 1890s in popular fortnightly, monthly and quarterly magazines such as *Blackwood's Edinburgh Magazine*, the *New Quarterly Magazine*, *Tinsleys'*, and the *Illustrated London News*. He collected them into four volumes: *Wessex Tales* (1888); *A Group of Noble Dames* (1891); *Life's Little Ironies* (1894), and *A Changed Man* (1913). A journal entry in the autumn of 1891 discovers him considering the current ferment over the short story:

October 30. Howells and those of his school forget that a story *must* be striking enough to be worth the telling. Therein lies the problem – to reconcile the average with that uncommonness which alone makes it natural that a tale or experience would dwell in the memory and induce repetition. (*LW*: 251)

This entry is full of allusion to aspects of fiction which exercised Hardy: his thinking about realism, about the role of memory, and also about the oral tradition, in which the ability to remember and to repeat, and to want to repeat, is crucial. It is also a response to some of the directives and strictures at this time concerning the short story. The watchwords of these 'rules' were 'singleness' and 'impression', and the methods were compression, and according to Henry Harland, an almost alchemical extraction: the 'artist's difficulty will be, by distilling and purifying his impression, to present it to us in a phial.'[6]

Much of this language of singleness, unity, compression and impression, originated with Edgar Allan Poe in the 1840s, but was only properly taken up by literary studies in the 1880s and 1890s, notably by Henry James and Robert Louis Stevenson. In a review of Hawthorne's *Twice-Told Tales* in 1842 Poe declared that 'without unity of impression, the deepest effects cannot be brought about'. However, it is also the case that James and Stevenson frequently broke with these 'rules' of composition: James's stories are often not brief, and not always succinctly phrased; many would require more than the 'one sitting' that Poe recommends for 'unity of impression'.[7] The same could be said of Stevenson's stories, and both authors and their contemporaries had to put up with the fact that even if they succeeded in producing a story which could be read in one evening, editors usually divided the stories over two or more issues, often ignoring the author's wishes as to where the divides should occur. While many short story writers of the period were attracted to a theory of a new and 'modern' short story, they interpreted theories of compression, singleness and impression fairly freely. Indeed, not to do so would risk the production of absurdly programmatic tales: Winnie Chan has noted that 'the *Yellow Book*'s debut coincided with the first in a new genre of instructional handbooks for writing the short story', the first of many.[8] In 1911 Wells poured scorn on such manuals:

I will confess I am all for laxness and variety in this as in every field of art. Insistence upon rigid forms and austere unities seems to me the instinctive reaction of the sterile against the fecund … I refuse altogether to recognize any hard and fast type for the short story.[9]

The tight grip that British magazine editors kept on the 'three-decker' mode of novel publication meant that writers contributing to magazines needed to write novels – and novels of a clearly prescribed length – to make a living writing. As Brander Matthews wrote in 1885:

The Short-story is of very great importance to the American magazine. But in the British magazine the serial novel is the one thing of consequence, and all else is termed 'padding' … It is the three-volume Novel which has killed the Short-story in England.

He dismisses the short story in England as 'only a little British novel': it is, in other words, highly plotted, full of incident and description, lacking what its American counterpart has: 'originality, ingenuity and compression.' Matthews admitted in 1901 that since this 1885 assessment, the work of Stevenson and Kipling had shown him 'how dangerous it is to argue from special conditions'.[10]

Hardy's battles with magazine editors, with the 'Grundyism' of the periodical machine and its conventions are clear from the tone of the endnote he added in 1912 to 'The Distracted Preacher' (1879):

Note: – The ending of this story with the marriage of Lizzy and the minister was almost *de rigueur* in an English magazine at the time of writing. But at this late date, thirty years after, it may not be amiss to give the ending that would have been preferred by the writer to the convention used above ... Lizzy ... stuck to Jim the smuggler, and emigrated with him after their marriage ... They both died in Wisconsin between 1850 and 1860.

Hardy here gives his preferred ending, which he also states, 'corresponds more closely with the true incidents of which the tale is a vague and flickering shadow'.[11] It is a long short story, fragmented by the editors, divided into chapters, ignoring 'unity of impression'. In its length, its ellipses of time and its ending, it takes its place alongside the more conventional fare of the British magazines, the tradition of the highly plotted 'short British novel'. In its basis on 'true incidents' passed down, it looks back to a far older oral tradition familiar to Hardy from his Dorsetshire upbringing. But while some of his short stories would seem to belong to conventional, or even ancient traditions, the effect of many of them is more closely aligned with what is most current in the short story at the fin de siècle, both in form and theme. As one contemporary noted in the *Athenaeum* of his story 'On the Western Circuit',[12] Hardy succeeds in a sort of 'impressionism', so central to these early ideas of the modernist short story: he 'excels pre-eminently in those little half-sketched glimpses that suggest the whole horror of a situation.'[13] Thematically, his stories discover many alignments with the contemporary enthusiasm for the supernatural tale, and with the subject matter of New Woman fiction.

One short story genre which was especially popular in the magazines of the 1880s and 90s was the colonial or imperial tale, with its emphasis on adventure in far-off lands and the trials and testing of British masculinity. Hardy's fiction rarely leaves English soil and his short stories are, without exception, set in England. All that comes from the colonies or America in his fiction arrives from 'off-stage' and carries with it an impossible vagueness and vulnerability. At the close of 'The Fiddler of the Reels', Ned Hipcroft searches for years for Carry, 'his' little girl who has been abducted by her biological father:

That Carry and her father had emigrated to America was the general opinion; Mop, no doubt, finding the girl a highly desirable companion when he had trained her to keep him by her earnings as a dancer. There, for that matter, they may be performing in some capacity now, though he must be an old scamp verging on three-score-and-ten, and she a woman of four-and-forty.[14]

Here, the inability to imagine that American place, its unknowability, intensifies the tragedy of Ned's helplessness and loss, but also the story's indeterminacy and lack of closure. The otherness of those places that can only exist off-stage in Hardy's stories contributes to those 'half-sketched glimpses' of a more modernist sensibility.

Rudyard Kipling's 'On Greenhow Hill', first published in *Harper's Weekly* in 1890, makes an interesting point of comparison with Hardy's stories and their failure to imagine those remote places, so central to the colonial or imperial tale. Published three years before 'The Fiddler of the Reels', the title of Kipling's story evokes an English landscape – possibly a Wessex place – but the tale develops as three soldiers lie in wait on a Himalayan hillside to shoot a native deserter. The privates, who appear in several of Kipling's stories, have distinctive regional (or national) accents – Yorkshire, Cockney and Irish – but despite this, their dialects and their slang seem only vaguely and uncertainly linked to an actual place in England or Ireland. This is the inverse of the case in Hardy, in which the Dorsetshire dialect is so earthed in a sense of place. Nevertheless, 'On Greenhow Hill' differs from the other stories that feature these soldiers; in this tale, the Yorkshireman Learoyd tells a story which is rooted in place, of the woman he loved and lost. This 'tale within the tale' sparks a glimmer of anticipation in the reader that this love story may deter the soldiers' bloodthirst for the native deserter, who has, it is rumoured, deserted for a woman.

But Learoyd's story of longing is brutally interrupted by Ortheris's 'clean shot': "'See that beggar? ... Got 'im.'" The tale from 'home' is seen to have no weight or influence in a place which British readers imagine as 'other', yet is the only reality that the soldiers know. Learoyd does not have a home to which he may return from India: if he does go back, his Greenhow Hill will not be the same Greenhow Hill. Kipling's Anglo-Indian background means that he understands, as Hardy did, the problems and even the impossibility of 'the return of the native'.

But the returned native, however difficult to place, also carries with him or her a powerful relationship to story-telling. Such was the judgement of Walter Benjamin, who wrote that it was in the 'artisan class' that was 'combined the lore of faraway places, such as a much-travelled man brings home, with the lore of the past, as it best reveals itself to the natives of a place'.[15] Benjamin regarded the most 'intimate interpenetration' of these two types as necessary to the expansion of the short story into 'its full historical breadth'. Hardy recognized – and regretted – that in his own time the artisan class, his own father's class, was in its demise, and his stories reflect this in the gaps they open up when that 'intimate interpenetration' is prized apart. These are gaps in empathy and understanding between classes, and between an urban readership and rural otherness. A sense of the other, and also of displacement, exists as strongly in Hardy's stories as it does in the Scottish and the South Seas tales of Robert Louis Stevenson, in Kipling's Indian stories, or Joseph Conrad's Malaysian and African stories of the 1890s.

Many stories by these writers have a strong narratorial presence. As Benjamin wrote, to distinguish the 'isolation' of the novel reader from the reader of the short story: 'A man listening to a story is in the company of the storyteller; even a man reading one shares this companionship.'[16] Benjamin privileges and is nostalgic about the oral tale: for these short story writers of the 1880s and 1890s, Hardy included, the written short story is 'fixed' on paper and can no longer change with retellings across the generations. Hardy wrote that a story must be 'striking' enough 'to dwell in the memory and induce repetition', but he evokes a near-lost oral tradition in saying so. The story may be remembered, but it is unlikely to be repeated until the reader rereads it. A distinctive narratorial voice gives the illusion of the oral – that the reader is not alone – but for

Hardy, Conrad, Kipling, Stevenson, and James, the narrator also becomes a sophisticated narrative tool, creating polyphony, uncertainty, and sometimes indecipherability. His deployment of the narrator is just one of the ways in which Hardy's short stories are in the company of those writers of the 1880s and 90s whose work anticipates or lies on the cusp of what is commonly understood as the modernist short story.

The supernatural tale was popular throughout the Victorian period, and standard fare in the magazines and especially in the Christmas numbers. Many ghost stories engaged, often comically, with the late nineteenth-century fascination with spiritualism and the 'exact and unimpassioned inquiry' into the supernatural that was one of the objects of the Society for Psychical Research, founded in 1882.[17] In 'A Castle Dangerous', published in the *Cornhill* in 1886, a self-obsessed ghost informs the country house guest he is haunting that his appearances are really a type of 'aphasia': 'By the way, I've had an idea about my apparitions in disguise. Perhaps it is my "Unconscious Self" that does them. You have read about the "Unconscious Self" in the *Spectator*?'[18] The tone here is reminiscent of Oscar Wilde's 'The Canterville Ghost: A Hylo-Idealistic Romance', its subtitle referring to a current 'scientific' theory about the relationship between mind and matter. Leslie Stephen advised Hardy to provide a 'scientific' explanation for the urban readership of his supernatural story, 'The Withered Arm' (*Blackwood's Edinburgh Magazine*, 1888). Hardy rejected this advice, and left the supernatural 'overlooking', and the resultant withering of a love rival's arm, unexplained, and therefore the more disturbing, carrying traces of the oral tradition from which it came. In Hardy's story, this oral tradition is framed by a seemingly educated narrator, possibly a returned native, who gives only the reported speech in dialect. Stevenson's tale 'Thrawn Janet' (*Cornhill*, 1881) is introduced by an outsider in standard English, but continued in Scots dialect by an old native. Neither writer mitigates the sense of evil with a rational explanation, or other conciliation to an urban readership. Both stories also centre upon women whose bodies have been marred or misshapen by diabolical forces ('thrawn' means distorted or deformed in Scots). Hardy and Stevenson intensify regional or national otherness in their tales through a depiction of the other on many levels: dialect, gender, class, and a terrifying supernatural force.

The writing of the 'New Woman' in the 1890s is especially associated with the short story: the form itself was less married to marriage as closure, and allowed for more freedom both in structure and the choice of its often controversial subject matter. Although the *Yellow Book* claimed to be the first journal dedicated to short fiction, in fact by this time many journals eschewed the serial novel to promote the short story: 'new journals dedicated to short fiction, such as *The Strand*, *The Idler*, *Black and White* and *The Graphic* all published their first editions in the 1890s' and a 'proliferation' of new British and American magazines for women, often edited by women, provided another outlet for New Woman short stories.[19] New Woman writing was often set in the city, mapping that territory for women as they travelled more freely on foot, omnibuses, train and underground. Hardy's 'A Son's Veto' (*Illustrated London News*, 1891), set in a London suburb, bears comparison with Ella D'Arcy's 'At Twickenham' (*Yellow Book*, 1897) in its exploration of the suburban as a place where women got left behind, separated from urban freedom and opportunity. In D'Arcy's story, two sisters are so bored in Twickenham that they take a first-class ticket to Waterloo one dull Sunday evening, only to return as soon as they have arrived – just to be going somewhere; however, their physical mobility belies the fact that they are really going nowhere, hemmed in by their own lack of imagination and ambition. In Hardy's story, Sophy Twycott, relict of a cross-class marriage, lives in a polite and impersonal suburban wasteland: she literally cannot go anywhere, as she is crippled. But it is really the strictures of gender and class inequality, represented by her cruel and snobbish son, that keep her immobile, unable to return to the Wessex home and to the man for whom she yearns.

Sophy is offered a journey out from this dessicated suburban life, when her old love Sam courts her again as he passes under her window by night, headed with his vegetable cart for Covent Garden market. In the early hours of the morning he gives her a ride on his cart before London and its suburbs have awoken. This predawn flotilla of carts is a scene vividly depicted in this Hardy story and also in two of Oscar Wilde's best-known tales: *The Picture of Dorian Gray* (1890) and 'Lord Arthur Savile's Crime' (1897). In Hardy's version, the dawn procession holds a 'charm' for Sophy: 'these semi-rural people and vehicles moving in an urban atmosphere, leading a life quite distinct from that of the daytime toilers on the same road.'[20] In Wilde's story, Lord Arthur is 'curiously affected' by it:

Rude as they were, with their heavy, hobnailed shoes, and their awkward gait, they brought a little of Arcady with them. He felt that they had lived with Nature, and that she had taught them peace. He envied them all that they did not know.[21]

Hardy's story reveals that these country people know life and its problems, and struggle to find peace as much as the urban sophisticate. Wilde's Arthur Savile is movingly obtuse in thinking these men disindividualized – both 'Hodge' and classical constructs at the same time. Something of the unknowability of the rural for the urban reader is implied by this comparison. Interestingly, both Hardy and Wilde call up the Eastern 'other' in their descriptions of the market carts: to the aesthete Savile, the 'great piles of vegetables looked like masses of jade against the morning sky',[22] and in Hardy's story they are 'pyramids of snow-white turnips, swaying howdahs of mixed produce'.[23] Both writers seem to register an essential strangeness in this injection of the countryside into a sleeping London, and map this otherness onto the East.

Marital breakdown; women's independence, sexual desires and fantasies; the working woman: these are some of the preoccupations of New Woman writers both in the pages of *Yellow Book* and also in its 'offshoot' the experimental *The Savoy* (1896). Hardy's stories, although never published in these magazines, were often concerned with the same themes. In his short story 'An Imaginative Woman', Ella is bored by her husband and children. Her poetic aspirations and sexual fantasies come together one night as she imagines a spiritual and sexual union with her favourite poet: 'she was sleeping on a poet's lips, immersed in the very essence of him, permeated by his spirit as by an ether.'[24] Although there is sympathy for the aspiring and frustrated Ella, she is not quite the 'New Woman': Hardy rather mocks her poetic affectations, as when she dresses herself to meet 'her' poet in an aesthetic *chiton*, fashioned by an expensive Bond Street dressmaker, and paid for by her prosaic husband. These women who are not quite ready for independence or to flout convention are seen also in stories such as Netta Syrett's 'A Correspondence' (*Yellow Book*, October 1895), which bears much resemblance to Hardy's 1891 'On the Western Circuit'. There is both sympathy for and impatience with women who are not 'New', and occupy a limbo in which they aspire to independence but lack the courage and encouragement to break the old moulds.

'What past can be yours, O journeying boy / Towards a world unknown ...?': this question, in Hardy's poem, 'Midnight on the Great Western' (*CP*: 514) imagines a story that lies on the cusp of a hidden past and an uncertain future. Hardy's stories lie on this borderland between the ancient past of oral tradition, the so-called certainties of realism, and an ambivalently imagined future which endows his writing with the indeterminacies of a new age.

### NOTES

1  Henry James, 'The Story-teller at Large: Mr Henry Harland', *The Fortnightly Review* LXIII (April 1898), p. 652.
2  H. G. Wells, 'Introduction' to *The Country of the Blind and Other Stories* (1911), reprinted in H. G. Wells, *The Country of the Blind and Other Selected Stories*, ed. Patrick Parrinder (London: Penguin Classics, 2007), p. 397.
3  Brander Matthews, 'The Philosophy of the Short-story', *Lippincott's Magazine* (October 1885). Reprinted in Hans Bungert, ed., *Die Amerikanische Short Story: Theorie und Entwicklung* (Darmstadt: Wissenschaftliche Buchgesellschaft, 1972), p. 14.
4  William Dean Howells, 'Some Anomalies of the Short Story', *North American Review* CLXXIII (September 1901). Reprinted in Bungert, *Die Amerikanische Short Story*, p. 43.
5  Henry Harland, 'Concerning the Short Story', *The Academy* 51, Fiction Supplement (June 1897), p. 6.
6  Ibid, p. 6.
7  Edgar Allan Poe, 'Nathaniel Hawthorne: Twice-Told Tales', *Graham's Magazine* (April–May 1842); reprinted in Bungert, *Die Amerikanische Short Story*, p. 3.
8  Winnie Chan, *The Economy of the Short Story in British Periodicals in the 1890s* (New York and London: Routledge, 2007), p. 56.
9  Wells, 'Introduction', p. 398.
10  Matthews, *The Philosophy of the Short-story*, pp. 2–6.
11  Thomas Hardy, 'The Distracted Preacher', *New Quarterly Magazine* (April 1879), pp. 324–76; this quotation, *WT*: 286–7.
12  Thomas Hardy, 'On the Western Circuit', *English Illustrated Magazine* (December 1891), pp. 275–88; *LLI*: 109–37.
13  'Literature', *Athenaeum* No. 3465 (24 March 1894), p. 367.

14 Thomas Hardy, 'The Fiddler of the Reels', *Scribner's Magazine* 13 (May 1893), pp. 597–609; this quotation, *LLI*: 185.

15 Walter Benjamin, 'The Storyteller' (1936), in *Illuminations*, ed. Hannah Arendt, trans. Harry Zorn (London: Pimlico, 1999), p. 84.

16 Ibid., p. 99.

17 *Proceedings of the Society of Psychical Research*, 1 (London 1883), p. 4.

18 'In Castle Dangerous', *Cornhill Magazine*, New Series VI (May 1886), pp. 514 and 523.

19 Emma Liggins, Andrew Maunder, and Ruth Robbins, *The British Short Story* (London: Palgrave Macmillan, 2010), p. 69.

20 Thomas Hardy, 'The Son's Veto', *Illustrated London News* (December 1891); this quotation, *LLI*: 44.

21 Oscar Wilde, 'Lord Arthur Savile's Crime', *Court and Society Review* Vol. 4 Nos. 149–151 (May 1887); this quotation, *Oscar Wilde: The Complete Short Stories*, ed. John Sloan (Oxford: Oxford University Press, 2010), pp. 13 and 14.

22 Ibid., p. 13.

23 Thomas Hardy, 'The Son's Veto', *LLI*: 44.

24 Thomas Hardy, 'An Imaginative Woman', *Pall Mall Magazine* (April 1894), pp. 951–69; this quotation, *LLI*: 17.

# 13
# Poet, Poetry, Poem
FRANCESCO MARRONI

It would be hardly an exaggeration to claim that between Hardy's birth in 1840 and his death in 1928 poetry moved ideologically from the centre to the periphery of British culture. The change is not self-evident if we consider it from an exclusively literary viewpoint: twentieth-century poets had the same vocational drives and inspirations as the Romantic poets. Essentially, the transformation concerns the poet's role as a credible interpreter of new axiological horizons. Despite their doubts and anguished reflections on the destiny of humanity, Victorian poets no less than the Romantics felt that they were voicing concepts and visions whose shaping force was an apt response to a changing society. If Tennyson complained that 'there is a mighty wave of evil passing over the world',[1] he was nevertheless convinced that the best weapon to use to fight against impending anarchy and moral degeneration was poetry, which he felt had an ennobling function and a responsibility for the nation and its future. This was not the stance taken by the intelligentsia of the early twentieth century. Even though moral issues continue to be debated, the main aim seems to have been to combine individual aspirations for a rejection of the past with a modernist search for new modalities of artistic representation. The embodiment of these ideas implies an uncompromising breach with literary tradition as well as aesthetic choices often equated to a shocking experience.

The futurist movement set the most extreme agenda for the artist of the new century. In his first manifesto (1909), F. T. Marinetti maintained the absolute supremacy of 'the beauty of speed' over the set of values on which Europe had so far founded its moral edifice: 'A racing car ... a roaring car, which seems to run over a machine-gun fire, is more beautiful than the *Victory of Samothrace*.'[2] Futurism configured a radical and subversive transformation in art and society. It fostered a change of sensibility that emphasized the centrality of machinery and the celebration of speed as a quintessential

paradigm of modernity. In opposition to bourgeois conservatism and self-satisfaction, the futurists' programme included the
destruction of 'museums, libraries, academies of every kind': poetry
meant *parole in libertà* – 'words set free'. Futurism sought to inau-
gurate a new approach to the aesthetic process that rejected the
past as a repository of platitudinous ideas, musty literary models
and creative paralysis, and proclaimed the worship of a technological future and the triumph of excess and dynamism. Considering
the political implications of Futurism together with its direct
involvement in Mussolini's Fascism, it is not a banal generalisation
to say that futurist exaltation of speed was, above all, a flight both
from moral responsibility and from society and its historical and
political complexities.

1909 was also the year in which Swinburne and Meredith both
died. While Futurism exalted war and technological beauty, the
69-year-old Hardy was endeavouring to reply as neatly as he could
to reviews, comments, and letters stimulated by the publication of
his idiosyncratic and ambitious poem, *The Dynasts* (1904–8). It has
been amply recognised that he regarded this undertaking as one of
the highest moments of his poetical inventiveness. Hardy's definition of epic-drama reveals not only the fascination exerted on him
by Napoleon's military triumph and downfall, but also his determined programme to inscribe *The Dynasts* in the Western epic
tradition. Leaving aside critical investigation as to its success or
failure in technique and invention, it is worth pausing on the role
Hardy envisaged for himself as he planned his epic-drama. The
most obvious remark is that he firmly believed in poetry, since he
regarded it as a literary form superior to the novel. His effort was
directed at relocating the poet's voice at the centre of British society. Despite his own autobiographical minimalism in so doing, he
was more or less consciously portraying himself as a new Milton, if
not a new Shelley, whose *A Defence of Poetry* (1820) had crowned
poets as 'the unacknowledged legislators of the World'.[3] It is in this
context that the famous note of October 1896 should be read:

Poetry. Perhaps I can express more fully in verse ideas and emotions
which run counter to the inert crystallized opinion – hard as a rock –
which the vast body of men have vested interests in supporting. To cry
out in a passionate poem that (for instance) the Supreme Mover or

Movers, the Prime Force or Forces, must be either limited in power, unknowing, or cruel – which is obvious enough, and has been for centuries – will cause them merely a shake of the head; but to put it in argumentative prose will make them sneer, or foam, and set all the literary contortionists jumping upon me, a harmless agnostic, as if I were a clamorous atheist, which in their crass illiteracy they seem to think is the same thing. (*LW*: 302)

On the face of it, Hardy's note seems to be inspired by personal confession and intellectual honesty. The reflection is a way of controlling his own image as a poet, while keeping in sight the twentieth-century reader. In this light, his attitude is symptomatic of a personality who feels himself besieged by misunderstandings and prejudiced reservations. But to say that poetry was a means of freeing himself from the binding chains of convention would be simplistic. Victorian in culture and outlook though he was, Hardy was also a man who loved to go against the grain: orthodoxy, complacency and conformity were his archenemies, which means that he either questioned or rejected Victorian institutions, while endeavouring to imagine alternative views and solutions. This is why poetry was the artistic form he adopted to express his stance of 'a harmless agnostic', prepared to discover and record the 'unadjusted impressions' stimulated by the everyday world – impressions which were 'the road to a true philosophy of life' (*CP*: 84).[4]

In this respect, a poem like 'The Darkling Thrush' can be interpreted as a multilayered metaphor both on England in the nineteenth century and on the situation of poetry at its close. Dated 31 December 1900, the lyric focuses on the gaze of a spectator who cannot help feeling the spectral atmosphere of a winter landscape whose pessimistic overtones are voiced almost exclusively through the visible:

> The land's sharp features seemed to be
> > The Century's corpse outleant,
> His crypt the cloudy canopy,
> > The wind his death lament. (*CP*: 150)

The underlying meaning is not difficult to decode.[5] The desolation of the scene subsumes the spiritual wasteland of the dying century: Hardy conveys the sensation that he is living in a time devoid of meaning, marked by the end of a culture. Paradoxically, the only voice that, however humbly and unpretentiously, does its best to break the surrounding deadly silence belongs to an isolated thrush, whose song is an attempt to infuse a new hope into humankind. Hence, Hardy's message to the century about to be born: peripheral and unheeded as they may be, poets remain true to their mission as a bulwark against spiritual barrenness and ethical starvation. Briefly, starting from the tradition of ornithological verse (Keats, Milton, Cowper, Wordsworth, Shelley, and Swinburne), Hardy writes a destabilising text, which is also a problematised revisitation of the nightingale trope, with a well-defined intention: the urgency of reaffirming the fundamental importance of poetry for modernity, no matter whether the poet will be forced to assume a marginalised stance or a strategy of self-defence. Indeed, what matters is the persistence of his voice.

Of course, the poet's isolation is partly a consequence of the appearance of the masses which, in Hardy's view, configured a society heading towards 'the utter ruin of art and literature' (*LW*: 247). But, what is important to underline here is that his terrified aloofness from the urban crowds implied a nostalgic look at a rural England that, in his poetry, meant much more than a mental place in which to find solace and tranquillity. Ruralism was really a way of life in which, in his maturity, Hardy seemed to discover a gratifying link between the individual and the community. His perception of the masses as 'a monster' (*LW*: 141) is already an anticipation and an index of another monster: war. It is no surprise that Elias Canetti charts a natural relationship between war and crowds: 'The outbreak of a war is primarily an *eruption of two crowds*.'[6] And in its combination of a multiplicity of masses, the First World War had a disheartening effect on Hardy's humanism and pacifist sensibility, as he concedes in the *Life*: 'It may be added here that so mad and brutal a war destroyed all Hardy's belief in the gradual ennoblement of man, a belief he had held for many years' (*LW*: 398). It is the much anthologized 'In Time of "The Breaking of Nations"' that best epitomises his philosophical attitude towards the war and its absurdities. The poem contrasts warfare with the positive continuity in human daily experience and feelings, emphasized by the anaphoric structure of the first two stanzas: 'Only a man harrowing clods', 'Only thin smoke without flame.' The third and last verse configures Hardy's relativism, with a lexical simplicity, in a succinct antirhetorical manner:

> Yonder a maid and her wight
>   Come whispering by:
> War's annals will cloud into night
>   Ere their story die. (*CP*: 543)

Written in 1915, this poem implicitly suggests that every war is an act of discontinuity, entailing a negation of humanity, whose true values are not based on bloodshed, raging artillery, bayonets and dying bodies on the frontline. Real life expresses its meaning by more eternal and intimate axiologies. Ironically, 'Dynasties pass' together with their pomp and popular applause, whereas the converging scenes deftly portrayed (a man 'with an old horse' in the field performing his daily tasks and two happy young lovers) are still there to testify to the continuity of human feelings and toil.

What is clear is that Hardy is far from embracing the patriotism and enthusiasm which permeated the nation. Hence, he never appealed to martial splendour. The unexpected opportunities offered by Great War set the soil for the newborn ambitions of the war poets who, against boredom and spiritual stasis, felt themselves in the aura of a romanticised heroism. Still, in a poem like 'Men Who March Away', first published in *The Times* on 9 September 1914, Hardy is compliant with the belligerent national mood, and his quadruple evocation of 'the faith and fire within us' (*CP*: 538–539) is an index of his appropriation of the language of the propaganda characterising the early phase of the War. But he soon abandoned the tone of a recruiting anthem. Thus, in a letter to Arthur Symons dated 13 September 1914, he was only too anxious to distance himself from 'Men Who March Away':

I am glad to hear that you liked the verses, though I fear they were not free from some banalities which it is difficult to keep out of lines which are meant to appeal to the man in the street, & not to "a few friends" only. The army badly wants some new marching songs, being at present compelled to fall back on those that have no bearing on circumstances. (*CL* V: 48)

From one viewpoint, nationalistic attitudes and a degree of patriotic spirit are legitimate in a general crusading atmosphere that envisaged military glory and acclaim rather than the expenditure of life. But the First World War did not conform to traditional views of war and its effects. It was a new kind of conflict in which every code of honour was broken, as instanced in the use of poison gas at Ypres on 22 April 1915, for the first time in military history: the English army was gassed, and ten thousand soldiers died without understanding why they were stifling to death in their shelters. A decade later, Hardy would pen a poem, 'Christmas: 1924', in which his scepticism and scorn against Church hierarchies are explicitly voiced:

> 'Peace upon earth!' was said. We sing it,
> And pay a million priests to bring it.
> After two thousand years of mass
> We've got as far as poison-gas. (*CP*: 914)

Hardy had an irony that the Georgian poets mostly did not possess. Irony implies not only a modality of distancing oneself from phenomena, but also a philosophical frame of mind and a self-knowledge that such young poets as Rupert Brooke and Charles Sorley lacked. Hardy was ready to perceive that the 'Georgian Poets' were nothing new in the literary panorama. An entry from the *Life* dated 27 May 1915 evinces his suspicion about the new acclaimed voices of British poetry: '"Georgian Poets". – It is a pity that these promising young writers adopted such a title. The use of it lacks the modesty of true genius' (*LW*: 401). If we consider the aspects of language and poetic diction, it is easy to conclude that the Georgian poets interpreted warfare and its victims, trench life, barbed wire and soldiers in action, by means of linguistic devices and rhetorical instruments which showed to a high degree the limits of their imagination. Their traditional forms, their search for smooth sonorities and iconic clichés, were too poor instruments to stage such a traumatic event as the First World War. In brief, as young poets, they were unable to look beyond their scholarly formation and their classical models, mainly because the conviction that the theme itself offered sufficient material for originality prevailed in their artistic programme. No matter whether it is the shadow of Donne or that of Keats: what is clear is that the Georgian poets' gaze is towards the literary past, connecting their voices to old forms (for example, the frequent adoption of the sonnet) and traditional poetic genealogies.

Even the work of poets like Siegfried Sassoon, Wilfred Owen, and Isaac Rosenberg is arguably diminished by an unwillingness to face the necessity of finding the right words, and to steer clear of clichés in order to express the absurdities of war. Although they saw the urgency of breaking with the received poetic modality, they did not achieve the fervid awareness which, for example, can be found in the war poems of Giuseppe Ungaretti in the same years, while fighting on the northern front of Italy. Ungaretti worked hard to condense to the bare verbal minimum the sensations and thoughts derived from his experience during trench warfare on the eastern Alps. His poetics was based on the pursuit of a few dried and densely encoded words; he often resorted to the technique of the one-word line, uninterested in mellifluous sonority, but ready to capture the spiritual disorientation of a soldier's trench life through lexical fragmentation, drastic dissonances and a high degree of word-essentialisation. By contrast, British war poets seem to have been, as it were, gratified and satisfied with the representation of their 'heroic' experience, producing only a very few original instances in terms of poetic achievement. Naturally, no direct parallel may be drawn between Hardy and Ungaretti, but Hardy had the same attitude in his use of vocabulary as well as in the quest for lexical density. It was this peculiar focus on the renovation of British poetry, together with a permanent confrontation with the Romantic and Victorian traditions, that made his verse so innovative in its textual striving for a valence of universality.

Such lyrics as 'Channel Firing', 'A Plaint to Man', 'At Day-Close in November', 'The Year's Awakening', 'Under the Waterfall', 'A Poet', along with the 'Poems of 1912–13', exemplify Hardy's control over his linguistic medium, not to mention his deftness in combining semantic universality with a compact semiotic construction. In this connection, Hardy the poet occupied a territory which no literary school or avant-garde movement could destabilise: too solid to change, too vast to be charted in all its underlying ramifications towards the past and towards the future. Characteristically, F. R. Leavis did not consider the thematic complexity and technical experimentation of Hardy's poetry. His critical approach is drastically reductive: hence Leavis's wish to establish an ideological opposition between 'Hardy's Victorian solidity' and Edward Thomas's work, marked by 'the modern disintegration, the sense of directionlessness'. Even so, and while emphasising that 'Thomas's negativeness has nothing in common with the vacuity of the Georgians',[7] Leavis has to concede that 'Edward Thomas, Owen, and Rosenberg together … could hardly have constituted a challenge to the ruling poetic fashions'.[8]

That Hardy's poetry can be reduced to an ideological formula ('Victorian solidity') is an oversimplification which reveals a prejudiced interpretation and, even more seriously, a fundamental inability to read Hardyan poems – and especially those written in his maturity – as an expression of a modernity which, as well as dramatising a pervading sense of precariousness, entails a profound awareness of the human predicament. Faced with the paradox of human phenomenology, Hardy prefers to confess his helplessness and to adopt an unsystematic method based on '"questionings" in the exploration of reality' ('Apology', *CP*: 557). In other words, he seems to subscribe to modernist fragmentation, while rejecting any form of easy solace or consolatory responses to the crises and dilemmas of humanity. In this sense, a parallel investigation of Hardy's and Thomas's poetry, more than a consideration of their diverging points, may shed light on the extent to which a dialogic line can be drawn between the two poets. A first important element is their focus on reality: the glimpse of an insignificant scene, gesture or person can trigger visions and suggestive visual combinations in their respective imaginations. Not for nothing did Hardy tell Elliott Felkin in 1919 that 'the characteristic of all great poetry [was] the general perfectly reduced in the particular' (*IR*: 115). It is true that Thomas was born in 1878 when Hardy was thirty-eight, and a different generation meant a different sensibility and responsiveness to certain phenomena. And yet some of his lyrics stimulate in the reader the same upsetting reaction as we can find in Hardy's. For example, 'Gone, Gone Again':

> And now again,
> In the harvest rain,
> The Blenheim oranges
> Fall grubby from trees
> As when I was young –

> And when the lost one was here –
> And when the war begun
> To turn young men to dung.[9]

Under the visionary gaze of the poet, anxiously searching for 'the footsteps of life', the dichotomy of past and present epitomises the human impossibility of experiencing the essence of reality – its appropriation is pure delusion. While 'reality' vanishes into nothingness, we are still anchored to images of our immediate personal past which are themselves part of the vast mechanism of illusion. Hence, the exaltation of moments of vision, which, brief and transitory as they may be, delineate a scene of continuity as opposed to the discontinuities of the real. Even though Hardy's relationship with his personal past is painful and often spectralised, it is a dialogue more tragically problematic than Thomas's. Thomas's retrospective look seems too weak and too fragmentary to reach a full appropriation of past experiences. However, a prevailing sense of loss and displacement, often interwoven with threads of pessimism culminating in despair, characterises both poets' voices – as in the final line of Thomas's oft-quoted lyric, 'Old Man': 'Only an avenue, dark, nameless, without end.'[10]

It would be too simple here to conclude that Hardy is a greater poet because of his overarching tragic vision. Hardy's greatness lies in his deep-rooted artistic awareness, which makes his verse a crucial moment, even an unavoidable crossroads, in the history of British poetry. On the other hand, in decades of radical artistic transformations, he resisted emerging poetic fashions and remained extremely coherent in his literary endeavour of exploring reality. He held to his faith that a poet could play a role in the betterment of humanity, and in this connection, what he writes in the 'Apology' is very clear:

It may indeed be a forlorn hope, a mere dream, that of an alliance between religion, which must be retained unless the world is to perish, and complete rationality, which must come, unless also the world is to perish, by means of the interfusing effect of poetry – 'the breath and finer spirit of all knowledge; the impassioned expression of science', as it was defined by an English poet who was quite orthodox in his ideas.

(*CP*: 561–2)

As well as revealing the influence of Wordsworth on his poetics, the comment is symptomatic of Hardy's pursuit of an authority from the past whose words give poetic credibility and genealogical continuity to his ideas on the poet's role. And here it is noteworthy that, through 'the interfusing effect of poetry', Hardy envisages a future in which religion and science will adopt a dialogic language able to create a higher level of harmony. Ultimately, this is the mission of poetry, whose spiritual centrality Hardy is not prepared to renounce. At the same time, it is significant that the segment 'the world is to perish' is repeated emphatically, as if Hardy's imagination cannot separate the positive function of poetry from an underlying conviction that mankind and all living creatures on earth are doomed to extinction. It is in this persistence of a pessimistic world-view that Hardy is a poet portraying a densely dichotomic territory in which hope and despair, harmony and disharmony, life and death, are in eternal strife. It is not a modernist wasteland but, metaphorically speaking, its fragmented scene is in itself part of the same continent.

NOTES

1  Hallam Tennyson, *Alfred Lord Tennyson: A Memoir* (New York: Macmillan, 1906), p. 701. Tennyson's talk was given in 1887. In the same talk, significantly, Tennyson also observed: 'All ages are ages of transition, but this is an awful moment of transition.'
2  Filippo Tommaso Marinetti, 'Fondazione e Manifesto del Futurismo', *Marinetti e il Futurismo*, ed. L. De Maria (Milano: Mondadori, 1973), p. 6: my translation.
3  P. B. Shelley, *A Defence of Poetry*, ed., Donald H. Reiman and Sharon B. Powers, *Shelley's Poetry and Prose* (New York and London: W. W. Norton, 1977), p. 508.
4  'Preface' to *Poems of the Past and the Present* (1901).
5  For a semiotic analysis of the poem, see Francesco Marroni, 'Thomas Hardy e l'"esplorazione della realtà": una lettura di "The Darkling Thrush"', *Strumenti critici*, 8.1 (Gennaio 1993), pp. 87–111.
6  Elias Canetti, *Crowds and Power*, trans. Carol Stewart (Harmondsworth: Penguin, 1973), p. 83.
7  F. R. Leavis, *New Bearings in English Poetry* (Harmondsworth: Penguin, 1972), p. 57.
8  Ibid., p. 58.
9  Edward Thomas, *Selected Poems and Prose*, ed. David Wright (Harmondsworth: Penguin, 1981), p. 265.
10  Ibid., p. 172.

# 14

## *The Dynasts* in Epic Context

### HERBERT F. TUCKER

Examining Hardy and context, one could do worse than approach *The Dynasts* (1904–8) as a vast and circumstantially illustrated meditation on context itself. That is another way of putting this chapter's major and minor claims: that the genre to which Hardy's masterpiece belongs is epic; and that attention to epic's ambition to compass contextuality can highlight *The Dynasts'* innovative relation to the traditions of the genre. On the premiss that the encyclopedic charter of epic disposes it to assimilate lesser genres – enlist them as its constituents, contextualize them with each another, become their horizon – I begin by reviewing some ingredient sources for *The Dynasts*, returning thence to its larger epic bearings.

To write a poem including history (Pound's catchphrase for epic) was to plunge into historiographical seas whose tide ran high at the turn of the twentieth century, thanks chiefly to the nineteenth's predilection for narrative as the way to understand everything from the origin of species to the intimacies of the psyche. To focus such a poem, moreover, on the 1805–1815 history of Napoleonic warfare was to choose the definitive contest of the century, whose cause in the French Revolution and outcome in the Pax Britannica had set the terms in which Europe struggled to grasp its modern situation. This is the matrix in which to locate, not only Hardy's gestation from 1875 of a Napoleon epic that should be 'an Iliad of Europe' (*LW*: 110), but what nourished the project: the fascination exerted on him, as on other Victorians who were witnesses to its surviving witnesses, by a swiftly mythologised recent past whose upheavals seemed in retrospect the birth pangs of their own culture.

As writers since Byron had done, Hardy went on pilgrimage to Waterloo and other sites. More important, he perused the histories written by Hazlitt, Gifford, Napier, Alison, Capefigue, and Thiers among others. A still stronger influence was Carlyle's *French Revolution*, which while never reaching Hardy's terminus of 1805 nevertheless emplots the blinkered agency of Revolution-era individuals within fields of transpersonal force (*dynamis* in Greek, whence the Biblical *dynastos* that provided Hardy's title). Carlyle's grim preference for charismatic or armed Might over liberal or procedural Right as a way of explaining the past anticipates the evocation of the Immanent Will in Hardy: only the currency of power suffices, for either author, to confer on history a meaningful shape.

The fact that these histories were undertaken before 1850 may make Hardy's century-long retrospect look retrograde: an attempt to breathe belated life into matters historians had left behind. It is nearer the truth, though, to say that by 1850 the nineteenth-century mind had internalized the Revolution and Napoleonic wars as both long-range causes and default repositories of images for whatever new crisis the years from 1848 (European insurgencies) to 1899 (Second Anglo-Boer War) might bring. A cardinal context for *The Dynasts* is the underappreciated fact that British regiments were actively engaged, somewhere in the world, more often than not throughout the half-century before its publication. The poet who revived the Hundred Days at a hundred years' distance was reactivating material that was perennial because still traumatic for wide reaches of the British public. Some recognition that his century's inaugurating events had gradually mutated from conscious attention into the collective unconscious – from history into mythology – may have underlain Hardy's 1908 decision not to furnish the bibliographic 'list of the chief authorities' he had promised in 1904. *The Dynasts* was scrupulously rooted in documented realities; yet its compelling authority came from something more abstract, and at the same time more visceral, than documents.

One history Hardy seems not to have read was Scott's massive *Life of Napoleon*. But then he took Scott's influence by other generic means: the verse romance and especially the historical novel. What prose fiction modelled on Scott might do with the matter of Napoleon shows clearly in *The Trumpet-Major*, a near-textbook instance of the genre according to Lukács, wherein the world-historical potency of France's threat to the Wessex coast exerts inciting and conditioning pressure on the novel's domestic-rustic plot. Impingement rather than incursion on ordinary lives by extraordinary events is a rule Hardy here obeys if anything more gingerly than Scott in the Waverley novels – or, to take just two intervening novels with kindred historical settings, than Thackeray in *Vanity Fair* and Gaskell in *Sylvia's Lovers*. All these novels, Hardy's included, adumbrate a large history, but do so after the fashion of British fiction: in the diminished key of familial and personal relations conditioned by historically and socially specific structures of relationship.

To this rule the conspicuous exception was Tolstoy's *War and Peace*, which requisitions enough Napoleonic scope to urge comparison with *The Dynasts*, which Hardy manifestly knew and drew on, yet which matters most for his work as a negative context, a model for *The Dynasts* to differ from. 'Novels grow inadequate,' Hardy judged in 1906 (*CL* III: 221) – much as he had mused in 1886 (when *War and Peace* appeared in English) how 'Novel-writing as an art' might now 'transcend' the 'analytic stage' it had attained 'by going still further in the same direction. Why not by rendering as visible essences, spectres, &c. the abstract thoughts of the analytic school?' (*LW*: 183). Not the Phantom Intelligences of *The Dynasts*, exactly, but close. In view of Tolstoy's embodied analysis of the thick web of history, Hardy's speculation throws a bridge between his work in the novel and what can seem its stubborn repudiation in the epic work to which he turned in earnest during the later 1890s. 'The President of the Immortals, in Aeschylean phrase, had ended his sport with Tess': aligning this last paragraph from *Tess of the d'Urbervilles* with the vantage embraced in *The Dynasts*, we again trace, not the wholesale rejection of fictional narrative, but rather its refinement, along a line of continuity 'in the same direction' that Hardy and his best contemporaries in the art of fiction had marked out – albeit a continuation by newly adapted means.

For those alternative means, we might even say alternative media, there lay rich resources in the adjacent generic tradition of nineteenth-century epic. Today this tradition is obscured within received literary history, although most readers know a few of its congeners (*The Prelude*, *Idylls of the King*). Indeed it was obscure even to the Victorians, although most authors, especially poets, paid homage to its undiminished prestige. One obscuring factor is the protean character of Romantic and Victorian epic: isolated as it largely was from market considerations, the genre exhibited far more internal diversity and modal experimentation than the novel could risk. Thus each of the formal options Hardy considered during his Napoleonic project's long incubation was already represented within recent British epic writing. Straight-up narratives, from Hannah Cowley's six books of 1801 (*The Siege of Acre*) to William Richard Harris's twelve of 1845 (*Napoleon Portrayed*), would have sufficed to show Hardy, who may or may not have seen either work, how futile any commitment to unrelievedly heroic couplets or blank verse must prove.

The 'Iliad of Europe' first shaped itself to his mind in 1875 as 'A Ballad of the Hundred Days. Then another of Moscow. Others of earlier campaigns' (*LW*: 110). The unprepossessing idea that serial balladry might amount to an epic resonated with a nineteenth-century controversy that swirled around the imputed folk origins of Homer's and even Virgil's classics, a controversy that, as it affected epic translation, pitted Arnold in theory against Morris in practice. Apparently siding with the populist Morris, Hardy toyed in the 1880s with 'a Napoleonic chronicle in Ballad form – a sequence of such making a lyrical whole', a 'Homeric Ballad, in which Napoleon is a sort of Achilles' (*LW*: 150, 152) – although here his phrasing squares more neatly with the practice of Victorian conservatives: William Maginn's *Homeric Ballads* (1838, 1850), W. E. Aytoun's *Lays of the Scottish Cavaliers* (1849). In any case the idea went nowhere. For a poet of even Hardy's technical resourcefulness to conduct in ballad stanzas a narrative even half as long as *The Dynasts* would have been a fool's errand, and the handiwork of errant fools survives to prove it. *The Imperial Captive* (1817) by John Gwilliam dragged over 700 pages that very 'Ballad of the Hundred Days' whose idea later kindled in Hardy; and in the early 1890s Charles Rathbone Low's insatiable patriotism produced one chronicle epic on the army and two on the navy. All these works assumed balladic form; none is readable.

The choral effect of collective epic spokesmanship, to which Hardy's fumbling after a 'lyrical whole' in balladry formed a false start, eventually came to him through a reimagination of dramaturgical conventions. The theatre after all was where in classical times choral odes had arisen to high civic purpose, brought before the Athenian polis 'in Aeschylean phrase' that managed to be noble and ironic at once. Drama in and of the mind had also more recently formed a long, sometimes mischievous intimacy with the experimental restlessness of nineteenth-century epic. Since Hardy's remarks on *The Dynasts* remain coy to the point of disingenuousness about his place in this tradition, it is well to recall how distinguished – and checkered – a context it was. Shelley in *Prometheus Unbound* and *Hellas* had rehearsed the overthrow of dynasties; Byron's turbid *Cain* and *Heaven and Earth* had sluiced the Miltonic fountainheads of Genesis into the currents of soliloquy and rapids of dialogue, whither one imitator, John Edmund Reade, had followed him with a double bill of plays anticipating Hardy's subtitle: *The Revolt of the Angels; and The Fall from Paradise: An Epic Drama* (1830). Goethe's *Faust* had claimed for Romantic genius a generalizing Everyman power; his dark English heir Thomas Beddoes, striking a common denominator in gallows humour, had in a climactic scene for *Death's Jest-Book* (posthumously published in 1850*)* surrounded living revellers with the sardonic mockery of skeletal ghosts. The literally riotous advent of Hugo's *Cromwell* in Paris established a precedent for London writers of the 1830s (Taylor, Talfourd, Browning) to stage the premisses of parliamentary Reform in a mental auditorium that played historical incidents back to private readers keen to imagine the forensic public sphere. If the big-top elephantiasis of Bailey's *Festus* (1837) did not outdo Goethe, it was not for want of confidence on the part of the poet or his many readers. Bailey's most loyal followers were the 1850s spasmodists Alexander Smith (*A Life-Drama*, 1853) and Sydney Dobell (*Balder*, 1854), who sought through a dramatic format to prolong, across an entire book, something not unlike Hardy's desired 'lyric whole': the immediacy of staged presence, where action is not recounted at leisure but enacted on the page in real time.

Such effacement of historical distance had always been one feature of epic narrative, where sudden reversion from past to present tense resumed by fits the improvisatory scene of oral epic. Carlyle employed this feature in his histories, and it was newly grafted onto epic stock when Barrett Browning adopted a diaristic mode for *Aurora Leigh* (1857) and Clough an epistolary one for *Amours de Voyage* (1858). Hardy surely noted the epic performativity in these works, as in the more nearly dramatic innovation of Browning's *The Ring and the Book* (1868–69), which was not a script but rather a carousel of monologues performing feats of historiographic perspectivism. Another example holding particular interest lies in the one firmly epic venture of a novelist with every claim on Hardy's attention, George Eliot. To say that *The Spanish Gypsy* (1868) was a hybrid work is only to insist that it stood in the mutant tradition of nineteenth-century epic; what matters here is how, like *The Dynasts*, it mingles verse with prose and dramatically scripted scenes with sweeping diegetic overviews. Eliot's medley bespeaks a bold if not altogether successful concern, like Hardy's, to coordinate her principal characters' passions and choices with larger ethnic and national considerations – to which, in fact, the characters' eventual accommodation forms the plot. This tragic result inverts the ratio between individual figure and social ground that typifies historical fiction, and in so doing gainsays the whiggish disposition that routinely goes with it. The very mixture of media in *The Spanish Gypsy* serves to expose a social-scientific algebra that also lies at the bone of Eliot's more fleshed-out novels: the 'abstract thoughts', in Hardy's query cited earlier, of the 'analytic school' to which both novelists belonged, and from which their advances into epic made a faithful departure.

Epic's ambition to epitomise history in its plot and summarise culture in its theme sponsored, during the decades when Hardy was pondering what to make of the matter of Napoleon, a frankly imperialist turn to transcend nationalism and tell the story of the world. In practice that meant the story of western civilisation, with no more oriental seasoning than a genuflection to Christianity required; and even this retrenched scheme was practicable only through a judicious sampling of episodes linked within a framing argument. Such was the loosely shared plan of *Chronicles and Characters* (1868) by Owen Meredith, *The Epic of Hades* (1876) by Lewis Morris, and *The Ascent of Man* (1889) by Mathilde Blind, each in its way boasting a (de)moralized outline-of-history scope that H. G. Wells might respect. When epoists from this imperial phase drew on resources of the drama, they dusted off the elder forms of pageant and masque, in order to parade history past the reviewing stand of a climactic Victorian modernity towards which each symbolic entrant was understood to have been marching all along. One practitioner of this self-congratulatory genealogy, Robert Buchanan, in *The Drama of Kings* (1871) and *The City of Dream* (1888) displayed a visionary cultural history that stations

him midway between Shelley and Yeats. Hardy, who was reading Buchanan's long poems alongside those of Shelley, Scott, and
Byron during the 1860s,[1] fingered Buchanan's impact in a note
from 1889: 'I feel continually that I require a larger canvas ... A
spectral tone must be adopted ... Royal ghosts ... Title: "A Drama
of Kings"' (*LW*: 231).

Detection of this fingerprint does not belie Hardy's claim that
*The Dynasts* was 'not a copy of something else' (*LW*: 343), or a *Times*
drama critic's praise that it was 'unique in literature, an epic-drama
without predecessor in its own kind' (*LW*: 524). As late as 1909,
the poet remained unsure just what to call it, proposing in rapid
sequence 'A mental drama', 'A vision-drama', 'A closet-drama', 'An
epical drama', and 'A chronicle poem of the Napc wars, under the
similitude of a drama' (*CL* IV: 5). As Hardy's perplexity suggests,
the poem was indeed 'unique in literature', so far as anything can
be, which is to say that it was in the company of a remarkable
set of congeners but not in thrall to them: while hardly without
forerunners, *The Dynasts* was forerun by the tradition of a modern
genre in which the most conspicuously eligible species all looked
*sui generis* and knew it. The advantage of placing Hardy's work in
this reconstructed generic context is to reveal with what powerful originality it redirected the predominant tendency of epic in
the waning nineteenth century. There was a 'spectral tone' about
Buchanan's dynastic masques, all right, and it clung as well to most
nondramatic epics at the approach of the fin de siècle. It was a
tone that befitted human exhibits within civilisation's parade, who
were blown up and down time by the zeitgeist, and dwarfed by the
tectonic heaves of cultural change – or paralyzed by the millennial
inertia of cultural stasis – and who in the final analysis each represented their epoch by virtue of their passivity as its mere exponent.
The implied reader of such works was likewise a 'royal ghost': one
whelmed by spectacular pageantry into a passivity like that which
he beheld, flattered by assurances that all was for the best, and that
life at the Victorian pinnacle was, even if it did make a ghost of
you, still the royal treatment while it lasted.

To this spectatorial indulgence *The Dynasts* put paid, and in literature's noblest cause: epic was not a commodity that gratified
audiences but an honour they were challenged to deserve. Hardy
issued this riposte by activating representational potentials that had

gone dormant within the epic-dramatic tradition. For what the fin-de-siècle epic mode had surrendered was the dramatic quality of conflict: the wars it glanced at were pas-de-deux stepping in compulsory harmony to the foregone conclusion whose renewable name was progress. This forfeit quality of dramatic conflict Hardy revived at the level of historical content and also at the level of mediating form. Most of the 130 scenes of *The Dynasts* render battle, intrigue, or debate; and in this primary sense the poem reinstates energies of motivated dialogue that its recent predecessors had relinquished. But Hardy also imposes, over and above the represented action, a sustained level of articulate dialectical response to it, in the spectral-toned and semichorally partial voices of his Phantom Intelligences. These bickering witnesses can no more agree about how to *react* – what constitutes right responsiveness to history's ongoing spectacle – than the human agents can agree about how to *act* – what constitutes right behaviour within the ever-shifting field of history's limited options.

Moreover, and despite the formal and epistemological difference between the stage of human history and the loft whence spirits behold it, Hardy's postulate of the Immanent Will thins to scrim-like translucence the moral and ontological difference between action and reaction. Given the ubiquitous if witless omnipotence of the Will, these two conditions are functionally equipollent: much as Nelson, Napoleon, and the meanest footsoldier at Borodino believe themselves free agents but are impelled in fact by the Will, so conversely the Spirits of the Pities and the Years believe themselves detached from the fabric of history but are in fact a part of it. Whether impassive, ironic, or sympathetic, their reaction to the spectacle forms part of the Will's work – and to that extent it affects that work, by superadding, if only incrementally, new dimensions of consciousness and conscience. The Phantom Intelligences' tissue of antiphonal, often contradictory reaction itself participates in the meta-representational history, the context of contexts, that *The Dynasts* ultimately comprises.

And so, crucially, does the reaction experienced by the reader, for whom by analogy the surveillant spirits are implanted proxies, not in spite but because of the internal dissidence they voice. By this surrogation Hardy put the reader also into question – into *context*. Turning the spectatorial passivity of imperial epic outside-in, he drafted the reader back into a living continuum, the observation of which is itself a species of participation. This conscription, while peculiarly dramatic, is also deeply and radically epic. For it has always been epic's charter to tell its audience the tale that is most their own, to rehearse a narrative that declares their condition as denizens of a common culture. By 1900 in Britain that culture was multiform, diversified, and famously racked with doubt. Where Hardy's epic congeners had addressed this condition with swollen anthems commending the panacea of civilising progress, *The Dynasts* met it instead head-on. Hardy's epic machinery was designed to dramatize doubt as the modern feature of greatest moment, its Will 'a tentative theory of things which seemed to accord with the mind of the age', its quarrelsome onlooking spirits 'embodying the real, if only temporary, thought of the age' (*LW*: 343–4). The respect Hardy pays here to the transience of ideology is matched only by his conviction that it remains existentially inevitable even when, in the case of modern liberalism, it is always at odds with itself, caught in the internal dialogue of the mind. In 1875, the year in which the work was conceived, Hardy jotted down with approval A. W. Schlegel's remark that the 'deficiency of all modern Art lies in the fact that the Artists have no mythology' (*LN* I: 14). Three decades later he turned this deficiency to brilliant account by performing it within *The Dynasts*' split-level, multi-media theatre of the mind. He projected in visionary cinema the dubious grandeur of history-baffled men who would be myths, and must fail; and an anatomy of the process whereby, out of that failure, their successors make a myth anyway, and call it history.

The reception of a masterpiece is its last and unruliest context, as is evident from the century of response that separates us from *The Dynasts* – more years than separated the work from its represented events. Early reviewers were puzzled about the plan of the author when not flatly affronted by the amorality of the Will; but with each published part the historical plot gained traction, and the balance of opinion shifted from consternation to congratulation at the immensity and stamina of Hardy's invention. These are the features that have continued to draw admirers, for the most part among ambitious general readers in the first half of the twentieth century and among literary critics and scholars thereafter. A taste for immensity and stamina having, however, fared little better in the academy since 1950 than in the culture at large, *The Dynasts* is not well known even among lovers of Hardy's verse, who in turn constitute a fraction of the many who read his novels.

Reviewers whose insight Hardy himself acknowledged include Lascelles Abercrombie, Arthur Quiller-Couch, and Henry Newbolt; not long after the poet's death a kindred appreciation entered formal literary history with B. Ifor Evans's *English Poetry in the Later Nineteenth Century* (1933). Serious scholarship on *The Dynasts* dates from William R. Rutland's *Thomas Hardy* (1938). Midcentury studies of note include a sequence of research articles by Emma Clifford (1956–61), J. O. Bailey's *Thomas Hardy and the Cosmic Mind* (1956), and Samuel Hynes's *The Pattern of Hardy's Poetry* (1961) – two books whose titles mark a persistent scholarly tendency to emphasise either the philosophical conception of *The Dynasts* or its formal execution. Harold Orel brought these two together in *Thomas Hardy's Epic-Drama* (1963), and Walter F. Wright followed suit with *The Shaping of 'The Dynasts'* (1967), which offers a running commentary on the historical substance of the work. One-third of *Thomas Hardy and History* by R. J. White (1974) discusses *The Dynasts* from a working historian's standpoint. In 1977 Susan Dean brought into freshly argued and illustrated synthesis the strands pursued in critical scholarship to that point, and her *Hardy's Poetic Vision in 'The Dynasts'* remains the best single book on the poem. New light has been struck since in occasional essays and chapters, notably by Charles Lock and Keith Wilson.[2] There are sharp and original remarks in Paul Turner's 1998 *Life of Thomas Hardy*, and I have had my say in the final section of *Epic* (2008). G. Glen Wickens's *Thomas Hardy, Monism, and the Carnival Tradition* 2002), brings out the poem's larger structural dialectics by way of Bakhtinian dialogism, and thus underscores the address with which a modern epic can wield arts ordinarily associated with the novel.

It is one hundred years since Hardy's work finally took the name of epic; and it is high time we did more with *The Dynasts* in the library and the classroom, in practical criticism and in theory, in trying the power of genre to renew the literary history of modernity. The tools are there. In 1995 Samuel Hynes's edition of *The Dynasts* formed volumes 4 and 5 of the *Complete Poetical Works*, with textual variants, appendices, and explanatory notes that make this the scholar's edition of choice. John Wain (1965) and Harold Orel (1978) wrote, respectively, provocative and informative prefaces to teaching editions that still reward consultation, at a time when our apprehension of dynasty-strength entities like the Matrix, the System, and the Military-Industrial Complex could stand some imaginative reinforcement.

One word more, on the poem's suggestive afterlife in creative hands and in other media. The Great War turned the remarkable trick of converting a posttheological, postnationalist, antiwar strife epic into a quarry for patriotic encouragement and survivors' consolation. The presence within the work of elements suitable for such appropriation cannot be denied – the death of Nelson, the Wessex scenes, the cherishing of the English language throughout the text – yet they emerge with salience in the wake of Granville-Barker's 1914 London production, in which Hardy collaborated, albeit reluctantly and insisting to correspondents that he had never meant it for the stage. A modest Dorset fundraiser that same year for the Red Cross had his blessing, as did the postwar staging in his honor of selected scenes by the Dramatic Society at Oxford (1920). This whole episode in reception history, retraced more faintly during World War II, illustrates with ironic pungency *The Dynasts'* motivating insight into the unforeseeable plasticity of historical conditions – to which we may in conclusion add one more illustration. Hardy rebuffed overtures from early cinema companies to put *The Dynasts* on the silver screen: had the contemplated films been made, they might possess considerable period interest but could hardly, especially in days before the film soundtrack, have done justice to the visualisations and voiceovers that animate the text. Only recently has digital imaging reached a point where the zooms, closeups, and special effects of Hardy's uncannily prescient shooting-script might find adequate realization at last. Is it, ironically, too late?

### NOTES

1 Pamela Dalziel and Michael Millgate, eds., *'Studies, Specimens &c.' Notebook* (Oxford: Clarendon Press, 1994), p. 46.

2 Charles Lock, 'Hardy Promises: *The Dynasts* and the Epic of Imperialism', *Reading Thomas Hardy*, ed. Charles Pettit (London: Macmillan, 1998), pp. 83–116; Keith Wilson, '"We thank you … most of all, perhaps for *The Dynasts*": Hardy's Epic-Drama Re-Evaluated', *Thomas Hardy Journal* 22 (Autumn 2006), pp. 235–54.

# PART IV

# The Historical and Cultural Context

# 15

# Hardy and Social Class

CHRISTINE DEVINE

'Modern developments have shaken up the classes like peas in a hopper.'

Lord Mountclere, *The Hand of Ethelberta.*

Chained in a convict ship and transported to Australia in 1834 – just six years before Hardy's birth – six agricultural labourers from Tolpuddle, a village just a few miles northeast of the author's birthplace, quickly became known as the 'Tolpuddle Martyrs'. Ostensibly they were convicted of swearing illegal oaths, but in reality for harboring thoughts of forming a union.[1] They were sentenced in a Dorchester court presided over by wealthy land-owners who felt they could deter others who might be nurtur-ing similarly subversive ideas. As the word 'martyrs' suggests, the transportation of these men symbolized to thousands of low-paid workers the repressive stance the government was taking to those demanding better wages through the nascent union movement. It was a transformative moment, inciting other workers to action, and crowds gathered in London and elsewhere to protest that they had no voice in the government of their country. The transporta-tion of the Tolpuddle men along with other actions to quash the unions, the New Poor Law's punitive measures intended to crack down on the 'lazy' poor who were seen as wanting to live off the parish, the failure of the Chartist movement to remedy the prob-lems of the working class through parliamentary reform, and the reduction of wages of agricultural labourers, combined together to create a sense of powerlessness and resentment in wage earners in both the rural areas and urban centres in the first half of the nine-teenth century in England. The workers responded with the Swing riots[2] and rick burnings in the countryside and an ongoing series of strikes and marches in the cities, adding to the growing conscious-ness of class identity on both sides of the divide.

That Hardy should be born in the vicinity of such an episode in union history and class conflict seems appropriate and perhaps telling, since class constitutes part of the fabric of both Hardy's fiction and much commentary on the author himself. Like Gissing, Bennett, and Wells after him, Hardy was not born into the privileged, well-educated, financially independent class that dominated Victorian culture. Instead, he was from a rural artisan family, one whose specific class status has been analyzed minutely by critics over the years. Peter Widdowson writes that 'the pressure and suppression of acute class consciousness are intimately related in Hardy's work', but goes on to add: 'Hardy's social origins in a specific class fraction in mid nineteenth-century Dorset are, of course, important, but only within the frame of the upwardly mobile professional writer operating in a metropolitan, upper-class-dominated social and literary culture.'[3] Nevertheless, Hardy's own class status and its effect on his work continue to be the focus of critical attention. Widdowson describes him as a 'writer obsessed by class'.[4] But one might equally describe him as a writer whose critics were, and to some extent still are, obsessed by *his* class. In fact, it is difficult to read about class in discussions of Hardy's novels without biographical considerations being brought into play. Roger Ebbatson, for example, argues that the 'disturbances in Hardy's texts' are 'related to [an] act of class repression' by the author, while '[t]he splitting of the self that begins with Smith/Knight and culminates with Angel/Alec or Jude/Sue is the signature of an author who is self-divided in respect to social class'. He adds: 'The figure of the double in Hardy emerges ... from the writerly attempt to contain elements of social shame and impoverishment in his own family history.'[5]

But as Mary Eagleton and David Pierce point out, 'the class origin of the writer is only one of many ways in which class and fiction interpenetrate'.[6] So bound up together are class and fiction that 'However much novelists themselves might wish to avoid class in their work ... the interpenetration of fiction and social class is deep, wide ranging, and inevitable.'[7] Little wonder, then, that Hardy should have focused on class issues to a great degree in his novels, as did many other nineteenth-century novelists. Indeed, one could argue that class issues were so pervasive in Victorian England that a realist novelist would be hard put to invent a convincing character that was not dealing with class issues in some form. And to see *only* lower-middle-class writers who are concerned with class issues as doing so because of their own personal class anxieties is to see the middle-class viewpoint as 'normal' or invisible in the same way. Hardy's work is not simply an expression of his own class anxiety; rather it is a critique of the class system itself, a system that continued to be supported in part by the literary establishment – even by those middle-class novelists who were ostensibly sympathetic to the so-called 'lower' classes, and whose fiction sought to tell their story and the story of class conflict.

No doubt, the century in which Hardy was born, grew up and became a successful novelist was one marked by class conflict and worker unrest – not only in England, but across Europe, too. Early in the century enclosure laws in England, added to the rules of primogeniture, had helped consolidate and strengthen the position of the already wealthy. By the 1870s just over four hundred individuals owned 16 percent of the land of England and Wales. Nearly three-quarters of the land in the British Isles was in the hands of fewer than five thousand people.[8] Some aristocrats lived on an impressive scale: it is estimated that in the 1880s at least seventeen landowners had an annual income from their rentals of over £100,000, while the Duke of Westminster received about £350,000 per annum from the property he owned in London as well as his holdings in the north of England.[9] Others were nearly as rich. Lord Egremont kept three hundred horses at Petworth House in Sussex; the cost of stabling so many and the number of people needed to maintain them would have been enormous.[10] By contrast, Hardy received £30 for the copyright of *Under the Greenwood Tree* in 1872, and many agricultural workers eked out a living on less than 10 shillings a week, an intolerably low wage and the very problem that had provoked the Tolpuddle Martyrs to form a union.

With great wealth came great power, and to those who had it talk of democracy and the widening of the franchise threatened to challenge the seemingly immutable class hierarchy. Inevitably, then, it was hard to get democratic ideas off the ground. Whereas it was viewed positively in nineteenth-century America, in England democracy was seen by many as unpalatable Jacobinism. British travellers like Charles Dickens and Fanny Trollope visited the United States to see what the 'the great experiment' looked like in action. Dickens had high hopes for it, but once there was disappointed. Even though the idea of democracy appealed to him, he disliked the reality because every man in the street saw himself as the famous author's equal. Trollope's book about her travels, *Domestic Manners of the Americans* (1832), is written from an antidemocratic viewpoint. In her view, democracy in England would bring 'the jarring tumult and universal degradation which invariably follow the wild scheme of placing all the power of the state in the hands of the populace'.[11] The 1832 Reform Act increased the franchise, but still only allowed one in six adult males to vote. Subsequently, there were fears that the Second Reform Act of 1867 would usher in an era in which working-class leaders would confiscate private property, and anarchy would reign. In his speech on the bill, Disraeli expressed his hope that it would 'never be the fate of this country to live under a democracy'.[12] But despite these reforms, large numbers of working-class men and all working-class women had no voice in their country's government for most of the century. It was not until 1872 that the secret ballot was used for national elections, making it less likely that elections would be won because those with money and power exerted pressure on their underlings. Despite the claim of Henry James's protagonist, Hyacinth Robinson, in *The Princess Casamassima* (1886) that 'the flood of democracy was rising over the world … [and] would sweep all the traditions of the past before it',[13] even in the 1880s the flood of democracy was more like a trickle. It was not until 1874 that the first two working-class Members of Parliament – both miners – took their seats in the House of Commons. In many working-class constituencies, one in two adult males still lacked the vote. Even after yet another Reform Act in 1884, adding millions more to the voting rolls, middle-class males carried perhaps twice the electoral weight they would have had under a 'one man, one vote' system.[14] It was only in 1918 that some women finally won the right to vote in national elections.

Despite the protests and reforms, and the efforts of writers of both fiction and nonfiction to alleviate the problem of poverty, Charles Booth's investigation of the London poor revealed that 35 percent were still living in poverty at the end of the century.[15] In its last decades, when Hardy's reputation was at its height, so divided had the classes become that those in the wealthy West

End of London feared 'invasion' from those in the poverty-stricken East End. The rumblings of disgruntlement among the working class, especially in the big cities, were getting louder. Henry James wrote on 26 September 1884 to his friend T. S. Perry, 'Nothing *lives* in England today but politics. They are all-devouring, their mental uproar crowds everything out [...] the air is full of events, of changes of movement (some people wld. say of revolution).'[16] Dynamite explosions on the London Underground, a bomb explosion in the House of Commons in January 1885, and international incidents such as the assassinations of President Garfield and the Tsar Alexander II in 1881 combined to put the British middle and upper classes on edge, in fear of revolution. The workers' discontent came to a head in February 1886 when, after a particularly hard winter that had exacerbated unemployment and worsened the conditions for those out of work, a group of the hungry and angry met in Trafalgar Square to protest. The gathering ended with protesters heading for Hyde Park, but along Pall Mall some members of the gentlemen's clubs shouted abuse at the marchers. At this point the peaceful march turned into a riot; windows were broken and shops looted. For several days rumours spread of a crowd spilling out of the East End and heading towards the West End destroying property along the way, rumours that exploited the already strong division – both physical and metaphorical – between the two ends of London. No such riot materialized, but that the rumours were believed suggests how far an uprising was feared.

Hardy was not in London at the time of the Pall Mall debacle, but he often spent time there, writing to friends from the Savile Club on Piccadilly. In May, June, and July 1886, he took a flat in Bloomsbury and frequented the British Museum Reading Room. That summer George Gissing sent him copies of two of his novels; in his note of thanks Hardy referred to Gissing's *Demos*, published that same year, which works with the idea of socialist revolution (*CL* I: 149). Hardy was clearly aware of the edgy atmosphere, and recent events must have been in his mind as he worked on *The Woodlanders*, a story that seems far removed from this mostly urban conflict. But his novels increasingly address the trials and tribulations of those on the lower rungs of society; in *The Woodlanders* the focus is not on the town dwellers but on the class consciousness and equally threatening financial uncertainties experienced by rural workers.

As the nineteenth century drew to a close and Hardy turned from fiction to poetry, the economic and political climates were bringing ill winds for the very wealthy. They, too, were experiencing financial uncertainty. By the time Edward VII took the throne in 1901, estate rentals were beginning to drop in response to the world-wide collapse in agriculture prices, resulting in falling land values. Simultaneously, business and industry were producing plutocrats with vast fortunes that far exceeded those of some of the largest land owners. Then, in 1909, Lloyd George as Chancellor of the Exchequer deployed his People's Budget, aimed at undermining the already weakened position of the landed rich.[17] The great British country house system was about to collapse. The third Reform Act in 1884–85 had changed the balance of power in government, and during Edward's reign the landed elite were under siege in Parliament as well as at home in the country. Democracy was becoming a reality; the working classes were finally having their say. The class system was under pressure, though class divisions were by no means being eradicated.

Hardy's sympathy for the rural working class has been considered self-evident from his novels because he apparently paints them so realistically, while often depicting the middle and upper classes unsympathetically. But as Ebbatson points out, more recent critics have questioned the accuracy of Hardy's account of country life in both his fiction and his essay on 'The Dorsetshire Labourer'.[18] As Michael Millgate remarks, Hardy handles the economic hardships of agricultural labourers 'somewhat gingerly' in this essay, explaining that while Hardy 'personally supported the Liberals in their undertaking to give agricultural workers the vote', he avoided 'any appearance of espousing a particular political viewpoint'.[19] In the essay, Hardy berates the middle-class city dweller for stereotyping country people, rather than recognising them as individuals, whose language was a valid dialect, not simply 'a vile corruption of cultivated speech'. He goes on: 'A pure atmosphere and a pastoral environment are a very appreciable portion of the sustenance which tends to produce the sound mind and body, and thus much sustenance is, at least, the labourer's birthright' (*THPW*: 170–1). But even though he acknowledges the insecurity threatening rural workers, he presents an idealized portrait of life in the country. And, of course, he knows this: his portrait fits the scene at Talbothays Dairy, for example, where Tess and the other dairy maids are bonnie and happy, but not Tess's experience at Flintcomb-Ash. Ebbatson argues that 'Hardy's portrayal of the rustic class is mediated by his internalization of bourgeois values – he is sympathetic to their class subordination whilst at the same time distancing himself from them.'[20] In other words, he depicts rural life, in his novels and in his essay, from a particular political viewpoint, even though he is not writing the realist fiction espoused by authors such as Gissing, intended to reveal the shocking living conditions of the lower classes. Merryn Williams notes that some of the rural workers in *Tess* clearly contradict urban idealizations of pastoral life. Of the scene immediately before the rape of Tess she writes: 'The picture of the women staggering drunkenly home from their weekly orgy, making a jealous scene with Tess over Alec … and then roaring with laughter when she escapes with him "out of the frying pan into the fire" shows just how far the Arcadian stereotype was removed from the facts.'[21] True, Car Darch and her sister do not fit the idyllic image of the country maid, but are they any more 'real' than that other stereotype?

In the end Hardy's rustics are designed not to comment on the condition of the poor, but to be part and parcel of the depiction of a class system that determined the fates of people's lives, whether rich or poor. They are the people who supposedly keep the farms productive, who, as evidenced in *Far from the Madding Crowd*, appear to fill the pubs and villages, and who perform a myriad small tasks in order to keep rural life ticking along. Hardy constructs his 'nature' to suit his fictional purposes and his rustics are integral to that constructed milieu. Whether they are 'true to life' portrayals is neither here nor there: what matters is Hardy's ability to create a living and lively rural world around his main characters, a portrayal that while appealing to his middle-class, urban readers, often questions the class system and its power over people of all classes.

Class division in the novels is not simply a rift between the rich and the poor, or master and worker, nor is it a straightforward tripartite division between the upper, middle and lower classes. As Ebbatson has noted, 'Classes are not to be conceived as static "entities": they are the product of struggle or conflict, and it may be argued that Hardy's fiction demonstrates increasing awareness of this factor as a determinant in his characters' lives.'[22] In *Far from the Madding Crowd* and in *The Return of the Native* especially, the isolated communities in Weatherbury and on Egdon Heath contain a fluid, less stable class system than one might expect to find in a Victorian novel. The class status of some of the main characters is constantly in a state of flux: Bathsheba goes from poor woman to wealthy farmer, Gabriel Oak's fortunes rise and fall and rise again, as do Clym Yeobright's. Clym is an educated man who has worked in Paris, and yet he spends some time as a poor man gathering furze on the Heath. Diggory Venn, too, is in a changeable class position and ends up literally as well as financially no longer in the red. This class fluidity is evident in other novels such as *The Mayor of Casterbridge*, in which all the main characters undergo a dramatic change in social status at some point in the novel, with Henchard's rise and fall the extreme example. This fluidity – the possibility of a move downward in class status being just as likely as a move upward – suggests instability rather than the absence of class boundaries.

A desire for upward mobility, the driving force behind much of the narrative movement in Hardy's novels as for many a Victorian triple-decker, is more than a plot device; it also suggests a cultural concern. One of the most obvious ways in which Victorians outside the novel, as well as Hardy's fictional characters, were able to move up in social class was through cross-class marriage. Hardy explores the issue of women marrying either above or below their class status in a series of novels – *Under the Greenwood Tree*, *A Pair of Blue Eyes*, *Far from the Madding Crowd*, *The Hand of Ethelberta*, *Two on a Tower*, and *The Woodlanders* – in which the plots revolve around a woman having to choose between men of different classes. In *Tess of the d'Urbervilles*, whereas Tess is hardly faced with a choice, the men in her life both bring the possibility of a rise in class. In most cases – Fancy Day and Bathsheba Everdene are the exceptions – the women end up married to the higher-class men, but not with a happy outcome, indicating that, at least in Hardy's view, marrying a prince doesn't guarantee a fairy-tale ending. As Penny Boumelha points out, 'This could be seen as the mark of a deep conservatism, a glorified version of knowing your place and sticking to it.' But this is not how Boumelha reads it, and I agree. She writes: 'It suggests, rather, a complex understanding of class differences that sees further than simple variations in manners or grammar.'[23] Terry Eagleton notes that 'Hardy is the first of the major male English novelists to explore sexual politics with such a keen eye to the relations between gender and class',[24] and Hardy's working of this theme becomes increasingly complicated through his career.

*The Hand of Ethelberta* necessarily has a key place in any account of class and Hardy's fiction. The relationship between gender and class, the destructiveness of the class system, and the fiction of class embodied in the performance of class, form the complicated subject both of Hardy's novel and of Ethelberta's storytelling, for she earns money by telling stories on the stage professionally. One of the stories she tells publicly, apparently invented, is that of living a fiction with regard to class. Her manipulation of the tricky relationship between class and fiction stands as an appropriate figure for the complicated relationship Hardy had with such issues both as a person and as a writer: from the artisan class, he lived most of his life in the middle class, though unable to shrug off labels derived from his class origins. While he is accused by some of patronizing his rustic characters, to others his work speaks for the plight of the agricultural worker.

The conviction and transportation of the Tolpuddle Martyrs provoked cries of injustice, causing them to be pardoned and returned to England, but they did not return to their Dorset homes to enjoy a better standard of living won by their efforts. Five of them eventually emigrated to Canada; the sixth died in a Dorchester workhouse. But their story reveals the power that class wields over people's lives. Hardy writes in his preface to *Tess* that 'a novel is an impression, not an argument' (*THPW*: 27). Nevertheless, his novels do interrogate class issues. And the growing bleakness of outlook in his work was to some extent a response to the lack of progress made in improving the lives of labourers so many years after the sacrifice made by the Tolpuddle men.

NOTES

1 Unions were in fact legal at this time.
2 Riots and uprisings in the arable south and east in 1830 were known from the name 'Captain Swing' sometimes appended to threatening letters sent to farmers and landlords.

3 Peter Widdowson, *Hardy in History: A Study in Literary Sociology* (London: Routledge, 1989), p. 130.

4 Ibid., p. 154.

5 Roger Ebbatson, "'A Thickness of Wall'': Hardy and Class', *A Companion to Thomas Hardy*, ed. Keith Wilson (Oxford: Wiley-Blackwell, 2000), p. 170.

6 Mary Eagleton and David Pierce, *Attitudes to Class in the English Novel from Walter Scott to David Story* (London: Thames and Hudson, 1979), p. 14.

7 Ibid., p. 9.

8 David Cannadine, *The Decline and Fall of the British Aristocracy* (New York: Vintage, 1999), p. 55.

9 W. D. Rubinstein, *Britain's Century: A Political and Social History 1815–1905* (Oxford: Oxford University Press, 1998), p. 281.

10 Richard D. Altick, *Victorian People and Ideas* (New York: Norton, 1973), p. 22.

11 Fanny Trollope, *Domestic Manners of the American* (London: Penguin, 1997), pp. 7–8.

12 Quoted in Donald Read, *The Age of Urban Democracy: England 1868–1914* (London: Longman, 1994), p. 145.

13 Henry James, *The Princess Casamassima* (London: Penguin, 1987), p. 478.

14 Read, *Urban Democracy*, pp. 302–3.

15 Published initially as *Life and Labour of the People* (1889), Booth's work eventually filled seventeen volumes.

16 Virginia Harlow, *Thomas Sergeant Perry: A Biography and Letters to Perry from William, Henry and Garth Wilkinson James* (Durham, N.C.: Duke University Press, 1950).

17 Cannadine, *Decline*, p. 48.

18 Roger Ebbatson, 'Hardy and Class', *Palgrave Advances in Thomas Hardy Studies*, ed. Phillip Mallett (Basingstoke: Palgrave, 2004), p. 124. 'The Dorsetshire Labourer' was first published in *Longman's Magazine* in July 1883.

19 Michael Millgate, *Thomas Hardy: A Biography Revisited* (Oxford: Oxford University Press, 2004), p. 219.

20 Ebbatson, 'Hardy and Class', p. 125.

21 Merryn Williams, *Thomas Hardy and Rural England* (London: Macmillan, 1972), p. 93.

22 Ebbatson, 'Hardy and Class', p. 113.

23 Penny Boumelha, *Thomas Hardy and Women: Sexual Ideology and Narrative Form*, (Brighton: Harvester Press, 1985), pp. 43–4.

24 Terry Eagleton, *The English Novel: An Introduction* (Oxford: Blackwell, 2005), p. 212.

# 16

# 'The Dorsetshire Labourer'

## FRED REID

Hardy's essay on 'The Dorsetshire Labourer' appeared in *Longman's Magazine* in 1883. It has often been discussed in terms of 'realism', representing, more or less, the impact of agricultural depression on Dorset labour. Most commentators have concluded that the article was descriptive rather than politically prescriptive.[1] Such readings seem naïve. Close reading and historical contextualisation suggest it can be better situated in an emergent discourse of 'progressive' politics, and read as a political meditation on early globalization.

Discussion of Hardy's realism has a long pedigree, from at least as far back as the sociological criticism of Douglas Brown and Arnold Kettle in the mid-twentieth century. Sympathetic to agricultural protection, Brown read Hardy as a 'faithful witness' to 'the ruin of English agriculture' in the depression of 1873–96.[2] For the Marxist Kettle, *Tess of the d'Urbervilles* represented the tragedy of the English 'peasantry', in its final struggle with capitalist farming.[3] These claims were undermined by 'economic and social' history, then fairly new. It produced knowledge of social formations from statistical sources like census records. It did not veto reference to literary sources, but warned that these could be misleading unless checked against quantitative data. In the 1950s and 1960s historians argued that nothing like universal ruin befell English agriculture in the late nineteenth century, and that the 'peasantry', in the strict sense of family farmers with manorial title to their holdings, had disappeared in England by 1850.[4]

Barbara Kerr applied this to the history of Dorset. She did not dismiss Hardy, and her statistical evidence on wage rates and demographic fluctuations was enlivened by the remarks of characters like Joseph Poorgrass, but she criticised him for dwelling nostalgically on a vanishing past. By 1860, the 'peasantry' had all but disappeared, many having joined the ranks of the labourers, who were 'bound to the soil' by poverty.[5] After 1860 agricultural mechanisation and railways permitted escape by migration.[6]

Until 1860, labourers and farmers looked back nostalgically to the 'good old times' before the defeat of Napoleon in 1815. Hardy, Kerr argued, adopted this nostalgia and despised those enterprising spirits who understood that escape from poverty lay in estate improvement, commercial farming, steam power, migration to the towns and the colonies. Hardy's tragic vision was misleading. The middlemen, contractors, and engineers who came to Dorset in the late nineteenth century were not 'invaders', like Alec d'Urberville, corrupting village innocence, but made farming more businesslike and stimulated migration.

By the 1960s, both historians and formalist critics were warning readers against trusting the novelist. Interest in 'realism' was, however, rekindled by the 'New Left' after 1968. Raymond Williams and his daughter Merryn turned to economic history to argue that the 'peasantry' had disappeared before Hardy wrote, and that agriculture was dominated by the three class system of landlords, tenant farmers and labourers. They pointed, however, to 'intermediate classes', some of them 'lifeholders', which survived in the interstices between large farmers and labourers. These were the groups which interested Hardy – farmers cum tradesmen in a small way of business, working their holdings mainly with family labour. Such intermediaries did indeed survive into the late nineteenth century, as in the Weald of Sussex.[7] The Williamses treated Hardy's writings as a source, not for Dorset agriculture generally, but for small tradesmen who clung on through depression in the 1880s and 1890s. Conscious of Hardy's strictures on photographic 'realism', they praised his fiction as 'the highest kind of realism'[8] – not literal correspondence, but signification of what would be essential for the future, the 'border' (Raymond),[9] or cooperation (Merryn).

But the 'highest realism' satisfied economic and social historians no more than the older version of Brown and Kettle. The most radical critique came from K. D. M. Snell.[10] Snell dismissed critics who insisted on Hardy's intimate knowledge of the Dorsetshire labourer: His upbringing as the son of a master builder and subsequent literary success distanced him from the class, and the novels offer only incidental observations of the labourer's conditions. They rarely enter seriously and sympathetically into the area of labourers' values, priorities, and subjective experience, and are revealingly reticent on the actual conditions of life in Dorset: on the low wages and unemployment; on the prevalence of and reasons for religious nonconformity; on the reality and character of political belief; on the agricultural unionism and bitterness of class antagonism; on labourers' attitudes to work and the use of the land; on working-class sexuality; on familial relationships and the treatment of the elderly; on the notorious hostility to the New Poor Law and its administrators. For Dorset, these and other matters bearing on social relations and the standard of living were being brought constantly to the attention of contemporaries by parliamentary blue books and newspaper reportage. But one finds them ignored in Hardy, and replaced by a romanticising and pastoral gloss which, from the viewpoint of the social historian, is simplistically misrepresentative in suggesting an amiable docility of labourers seen largely as bucolic clowns; a misrepresentation which held reassurance for the agricultural employing class and Hardy's readership, and which reveals its political partiality in all that it deliberately omits and discounts.[11]

'The Dorsetshire Labourer' is included in this sweeping criticism.

Snell is rightly esteemed by historians of rural England for his analysis of change over three centuries. His scholarship is massive, giving full weight to the psychological impact of enclosure and poor law reform. The final chapter, 'Thomas Hardy, Rural Dorset, and the Family' argues convincingly that Hardy was interested in the lifeholders because their marriage customs reflected the participation of women alongside men in work, compared to the extreme sexual division of labour in his own time. That theme, however, is not present in 'The Dorsetshire Labourer'. When Snell deals with the article it is to deny Hardy's rural 'realism', and here two serious criticisms must be offered.

First, the polemical style, though justified by the sweeping claims of some critics, leads Snell to belittle the accuracy of Hardy's observations. Space allows only one example. Noting correctly that female labour on threshing machines would have been 'very unusual'[12] in the Dorset of the 1870s and 1880s, he fails to mention Alec d'Urberville's recognition of this fact: 'I have told the farmer that he has no right to employ women at steam-threshing.... on all the better class of farms it has been given up, as he knows very well' (*Tess*: 46).

Second, Snell argues that the inadequate realism of 'The Dorsetshire Labourer' stemmed from Hardy's explicit assumptions (also implied in the novels). They were 'reassuring' to the 'agricultural employing class' and are explicable in terms of his own class situation, as 'a detached and educated member of the Dorset market-town middle or professional class, with close literary connections in London'.[13] This is regrettably reductionist, suggesting that no variation of political outlook can be found among the members of a social class. The political historian commonly finds within the same social formation a range of assumptions: reactionary, progressive, revolutionary. Hardy was no revolutionary. 'The Dorsetshire Labourer', closely read and contextualized, leans towards progressive politics and this is easily overlooked by a reductionist literary sociology.[14]

Hardy begins his essay by criticizing those who view the Dorsetshire labourer stereotypically as 'Hodge'. Any visitor from London who passed some weeks in a labourer's cottage would find that his host, family and neighbours had the same diversity of character traits as the rest of humanity: 'some happy, many serene, a few depressed; some clever, even to genius, some stupid, some wanton, some austere; some mutely Miltonic, some Cromwellian.' And Hardy does not rest with this language of universal types. Having asserted the brotherhood of man, he proceeds to particular social observation, not presented as scientific realism, but as a political meditation on the ignorance of social superiors concerning the life choices of the labourers and the motives underlying them. Ignorance is not confined to town dwellers. It is equally prevalent among superior figures in rural society, many of them self-styled benefactors. Hardy instances the 'philanthropic lady' who notes the 'squalor' of a cottage she visits in the role of social improver, firmly believing that whiteness is the mark of general cleanliness. A white apron or whitewashed cottage might conceal the dirtiest bedrooms, whereas the cottage dwelling painted in any variety of 'mud colour' is taken to be an 'abode of filth'. She fails to understand that use of drab colours might be a matter of taste or economy and might be accompanied by bed linen and underclothes 'like the driven snow'.[15]

How reassuring could this have been to upper-class readers, so often implicated in rural philanthropy? If anyone was romanticizing it was they, not Hardy, who proceeds immediately to read them another lesson concerning their inability to 'see below the surface of things'. They cannot understand that the dependent wage labourer is often forced to affect respectability, fearing the disaster of eviction as arbitrary as that of 'Burns's field-mouse'. 'Copyholders, cottage freeholders, and the like,' Hardy adds, 'are as a rule less trim and neat, more muddling in their ways, than the dependent labourer; and yet there is no more comfortable or serene being than the cottager who is sure of his roof.'

Far from ignoring the labourer's desire for security of tenure, Hardy cunningly emphasizes it by pointing up the contrast between some English labourers and some French 'peasant proprietors'. We must guard, he writes,

against the inference that because these peasant proprietors are in a slovenly condition, and certain English peasants who are not proprietors live in model cottages copied out of a book by the squire, the latter are so much happier than the former as the dignity of their architecture is greater [...] When we know that the Damocles' sword of the poor is the fear of being turned out of their houses by the farmer or squire, we may wonder how many scrupulously clean English labourers would not be glad with half-an-acre of the complaint that afflicts these unhappy freeholders of Auvergne.

He then turns to wages and growing labour market flexibility. Recent historical research corroborates the precision and subtlety of his observations. Rejecting the propaganda of writers who held that 'Hodge' existed everywhere in misery and despair, he drew distinctions by age, gender and marital status, an early identification of the poverty cycle described by Joseph Rowntree after the end of the century. Thus a shepherd, whose skill in 'ovine surgery' would have ensured continuous employment in early manhood is passed over, in old age, for a younger man. Hardy elucidates the importance of family earnings, to which maturing offspring and wives contribute, somewhat mitigating the impact of low wages.[16]

Mobile younger men are no longer dependent on the hiring fair. Increasingly they find work in 'the penny local papers' and they are prepared to move as far as fifteen miles each year to better themselves on another farm. They and their families are anything but destitute, as anyone who observes their treasured household goods on the removal wagon can see. There is the dresser, 'importantly in front ... in its erect and natural position, like some Ark of the Covenant, which must not be handled slightingly or overturned'. Carefully stowed is their vital garden produce: 'The hive of bees', 'the roots of garden flowers' and 'budding gooseberry bushes'. Among the furniture and the barrels of crockery, there are pieces of conspicuous consumption, the clock and the looking glass, proudly protected by the mother and her eldest daughter. Even the husband may sport a shaving mirror, replacing older contrivances such as 'placing the crown of an old hat outside the window-pane, then confronting it inside the room and falling to'.

Mobility brings more than economic gain. The 'habitually-removing man' is 'shrewder and sharper', capable of holding his own 'with firmness and judgment'. Alongside the 'old-fashioned stationary sort, who are still to be found' he is 'much more wide awake'. If there is nostalgia here for the immobile farm labourer, for the 'humorous simplicity' of the men and 'the unsophisticated modesty of the women', it is not Hardy's: 'It is the common remark of villagers above the labouring class', in which there is 'some exaggeration', and of 'romantic spectators' who deplore the disappearance of smock frocks and 'nice homely labourers'.

Some historians have thought the charge of romantic nostalgia buttressed by Hardy's next topic, landlord paternalism:

> Not so very many years ago, the landowner, if he were good for anything, stood as a court of final appeal in cases of the harsh dismissal of a man by the farmer. 'I'll go to my lord' was a threat which overbearing farmers respected, for 'my lord' had often personally known the labourer long before he knew the labourer's master.

Again, the historical evidence corroborates Hardy. From the 1850s to the 1870s, Dorset landowners sought to create a 'new paternalism' in response to class conflict in the 'hungry forties'.[17] Conservative organs like the *Dorset County Chronicle* represented this as the revival of an ancient organic community[18] and Hardy has been seen as endorsing the myth. A closer reading reveals that he undermines the myth at many points. He followed the radical economist Thorold Rogers in recognizing that economic conflict between landlord and peasant is also part of rural history:[19] many of the landless wage labourers of Dorset are, 'no doubt, descendants of the old copyholders who were ousted from their little plots when the system of leasing large farms grew general'. Hardy rightly sees that the 'new paternalism' is breaking down in the depression. 'The landlord does not know by sight, if even by name, half the men who preserve his acres from the curse of Eden. They come and go yearly, like birds of passage, nobody thinks whence or whither.' The farmer himself may well be a 'new comer', having taken over the tenancy from one who had failed. As such, he 'takes strictly commercial views of his man and cannot afford to waste a penny on sentimental considerations'. The agricultural labourer, in consequence has become 'nomadic' and the result is 'a less intimate and kindly relation with the land he tills'. This was not sentimental. 'Dirty farming' was a phenomenon often noticed, as depression forced farmers to cut down labour and nonessential maintenance.[20]

Hardy did not endorse the myth of the ancient community. His focus was on the depression and its disturbance of villagers. The 'pecuniary condition' of labourers 'in the prime of life' has improved, but Hardy senses the loss of 'happiness' that comes from insecurity of housing and deplores the end of 'long local participancy ... one of the pleasures of age.' Isolating passages like this reinforces the idea of Hardy as a romantic, hostile to modernity, but that reading is immediately undermined by the comment standing just after:

On the other hand, new varieties of happiness evolve themselves like new varieties of plants, and new charms may have arisen among the classes who have been driven to adopt the remedy of locomotion for the evils of oppression and poverty – charms which compensate in some measure for the lost sense of home.

Hardy was no simple pessimist about modernity. But did he have in mind any political action to further the evolution of a happier, more secure, more environment friendly society? Commentators have often answered in the negative, yet to read 'The Dorsetshire Labourer' in the historical context of debate over the land question suggests that Hardy leans to the side of reformist socialism and progressive politics emerging in the 1880s.[21] The 'great depression', as contemporaries called it, was an effect of early globalisation on primary industries as well as agriculture.[22] In the old world and the new, rural workers were forced off the land, swelling unemployment in industrial centres.[24] One response was terrorism. Tsar Alexander II was assassinated in 1881, and in 1882 two ministers of the British Crown were murdered in Phoenix park, Dublin. Closer to home was the 'dynamite war' on British cities, waged by 'Fenians' for Irish independence.[25] Such violence was associated with 'anarchism', contributing to a sense of impending revolution.

Hardy preferred reform to revolution. He responded sympathetically to reform of land ownership. Key to this was the thought of John Stuart Mill, whose ideas were taken up by the Irish leader, Michael Davitt, as the solution for the 'land war' raging in his country from 1879 to 1882. Ireland was the springboard for political action aimed at reform of land ownership, which took various forms, from peasant proprietorship to abolition of private ownership by land nationalization. It deeply influenced British politics, for example in Gladstone's Land Act of 1881 and the Liberal party's Newcastle programme of 1891.

It is in this context that we should read the remainder of 'The Dorsetshire Labourer'. Hardy spoke approvingly of French peasant proprietorship. Towards the end of his article he associates himself with two prominent land reformers, Joseph Arch, English leader of agricultural trade unionism, and Emile de Laveleye, a Belgian economist whose works were frequently cited in connection with the land question in Ireland.[25] Arch's views, wrote Hardy, 'showed him to be rather the social evolutionist – what M. Emile de Laveleye would call a "Possibilist" – than the anarchic irreconcilable'.[26]

These political references have received little attention from critics and historians.[27] They show Hardy aligning with an emergent reformist socialism, characterized by the 'Possibilist' Party in Paris and the Fabian socialists in London.[28] These proposed to use municipal powers for urban and rural improvement, such as housing, land tenure and municipal farms, which would bring comfort and security – in a word, happiness – to the working classes and restore balance between town and country.

To sum up, it was always simplistic to discuss 'The Dorsetshire Labour' in terms of 'realism'. It should be recognized as a political meditation on the dangers of class alienation. It is neither argumentative nor partisan. In modern critical parlance it resists closure and is multi-vocal throughout, viewing the question from many historical and social perspectives; a woven texture, in the manner of his fiction, rather than a structure of logic. Yet it is not simply relativistic. It opens the way to an alignment of new thinking, reformist, socialistic, later to be dubbed 'progressive'. That Hardy hoped to influence this tendency can be seen from the fact that he sent Gladstone a copy of his article and publicly 'identified himself as a Liberal' in the General Election of 1885.[29]

He was well aware that his meditations had virtually global significance. Rural depopulation was not wholly voluntary. The life-holders who were being forced from Dorset villages to the towns had their counterparts throughout Europe, not least in Ireland. As Emile Zola had shown in *Germinal*, their experience was a major reason for the spread of anarchism and the terrorist bomb throwing which accompanied it.[30] The system of eviction, wrote Hardy,

is much to be deplored, for every one of these banished people imbibes a sworn enmity to the existing order of things, and not a few of them, far from becoming merely honest Radicals, degenerate into Anarchists, waiters on chance, to whom danger to the State, the town – nay, the street they live in, is a welcomed opportunity.

And so the meditation ends with a characteristic feint which resists closure. The reader may read 'The Dorsetshire Labourer' as merely descriptive but is reminded of what has already been hinted, that 'the question of the Dorset cottager here merges in that of all the houseless and landless poor, and the vast topic of the Rights of Man'.

### NOTES

1 See, e.g., Merryn Williams, *Thomas Hardy and Rural England* (London: Macmillan, 1972), pp. 103ff.

2 Douglas Brown, *Thomas Hardy* (London: Longmans, 1954, rev. edn 1961), pp. 36, 101ff.

3 Arnold Kettle, *Introduction to the English Novel II: Henry James to the Present Day,* (London: Hutchinson, 1953), p. 49.

4 See, e.g., T. W. Fletcher, 'The Great Depression in English Agriculture', *Economic History Review* 13, Issue 3 (April 1961), p. 417.

5 Barbara Kerr, *Bound to the Soil: a Social History of Dorset, 1750–1918* (London: Baker, 1968; reprinted Tiverton, Dorset, 1993), p. 93.

6 Ibid., pp. 24ff.

7  Alun Howkins, *Reshaping Rural England: a Social History, 1850–1925* (London: Routledge, 1991), p. 15; M. Reed, 'The Peasantry of Nineteenth Century England: a Neglected Class?', *History Workshop Journal* 18 (Autumn 1984), pp. 5–6.

8  Williams, *Thomas Hardy and Rural England*, p. 200.

9  Raymond Williams, *The English Novel from Dickens to Lawrence* (London: Chatto and Windus 1970, reprinted 1974), pp. 78–96.

10  K. D. M. Snell, *Annals of the Labouring Poor: Social Change and Agrarian England, 1660–1900* (Cambridge: Cambridge University Press, 1987).

11  Ibid., p. 392.

12  Ibid., p. 378.

13  Ibid., p. 399.

14  See Roger Ebbatson, *Hardy: The Margin of the Unexpressed* (Sheffield: Sheffield Academic press, 1993), pp. 129–53.

15  In *The Mayor of Casterbridge*, a white apron signals prostitution among the denizens of Mixen Lane: 'A white apron is a suspicious vesture in situations where spotlessness is difficult' (*MC*: 36).

16  Howkins, *Reshaping Rural England*, p. 105.

17  Ibid., pp. 74ff, 86ff.

18  Fred Reid, 'Art and Ideology in *Far from the Madding Crowd*', *Thomas Hardy Annual* IV, ed. Norman Page (London: Macmillan, 1986), pp. 95ff.

19  William Greenslade, ed., *Thomas Hardy's 'Facts' Notebook: a Critical Edition* (Aldershot: Ashgate, 2004), p. 3.

20  Howkins, *Reshaping Rural England*, pp. 148ff.

21  See, e.g., P. C. Gould, *Early Green Politics: Back to Nature, Back to the Land and Socialism in Britain, 1880–1900* (Brighton: Harvester, 1998), pp. 67–74, 105–22; Tristram Hunt, *Building Jerusalem: The Rise and Fall of the Victorian City* (London: Weidenfeld & Nicolson, 2004), pp. 266–80.

22  E. J. Hobsbawm, *Age of Empire* (London: Weidenfeld & Nicolson, 1987; reprinted 2005), pp. 35–7.

24  Ibid., pp. 112–17.

25  Perhaps the only commentator to link 'The Dorsetshire Labourer' to Irish terrorism is Simon Trezise, '"Here's Zixpence Towards That, Please God!": Thomas Hardy, Joseph Arch and Hodge', *Thomas Hardy Journal* VI (1990), pp. 48–61.

25  T. W. Moody, *Michael Davitt and the Irish Revolution, 1846–82* (Oxford: Oxford University Press, 1982), p. 504.

26  E. de Laveleye, 'The European Terror', *Fortnightly Review* XXXIII (1883), pp. 548–561.

27 For the French 'Possibilists', see G. D. H. Cole, *History of Socialist Thought:*
28 *The Second International, 1889–1914* (London: Macmillan, 1956), pp. 326–34; Roger Magraw, *France 1814–1915: The Bourgeois Century* (London: Fontana, 1983), pp. 296–300.
29 Michael Millgate, *Thomas Hardy: A Biography Revisited* (Oxford: Oxford University Press, 2004), pp. 225, 219.
30 Mark Leier, *Bakunin: the Creative Passion* (New York: Thomas Dunne Books, 2006), pp. 201ff.

## 17

# Education and Social Class

JANE MATTISSON

The view of education offered in Hardy's novels is consistently dark: both access to and the quality of the education received are determined by one's social class and not by merit, placing the working or artisan classes at a disadvantage. Any attempt to improve one's social standing through education results in failure or a painful dislocation from one's environment, values and traditions. This is, in varying forms, the experience shared by Fancy Day, Stephen Smith, and Clym Yeobright in the earlier novels, and by Grace Melbury, Tess, and Jude in the later ones.

Hardy himself was educated in rural Dorset, one of the most backward counties in England. He was forced to rely on self-help, and received no university education. Pushed on by his mother, he entered the National (i.e., Church of England) School in Bockhampton aged 8, where according to his own recollection, he excelled at arithmetic and geography (*LW*: 21–30), moved to the British School (Nonconformist) in Dorchester when he was 10, and then at 13 progressed to three years of further study at Isaac Last's independent commercial academy for more advanced pupils: itself a major achievement, since only five percent of all pupils attending school up to 1861 continued after the age of eleven.[1] In the *Life* he recalls becoming 'deeply interested' in a periodical called *The Popular Educator*, published by 'that genius in home-education, John Cassell' (*LW*: 29–30).[2] It was not until late in his writing career that he was given the academic recognition – including honorary doctorates from Aberdeen (1905), Cambridge (1913), and Oxford (1920) – for which he had striven all his life. As I argue elsewhere,[3] Hardy's novels valorise traditional wisdom and skills while simultaneously recognising the importance of 'modern' formal – often scientific – knowledge for industrial development and social progress. Access to 'modern' knowledge is limited for Hardy's characters, as a consequence both of social class and geographical location.

Educational developments in nineteenth-century England can be seen from two perspectives: that adopted by, among others, sociologist Pierre Bourdieu and many prominent historians,[4] namely that education is designed by those in power to reinforce class distinctions by training leaders and followers; and that propounded by Victorian educational reformers, who focused on the potential of education for intellectual and social development. Both perspectives can be found in Hardy's novels, though the former is the more prominent. It thus comes as no surprise that Clym Yeobright (*The Return of the Native*), for all his idealistic theories about education for the poor, is ultimately forced to abandon them: his liberal ideas come too early and fail to win the support of the rustics.

Hardy was not averse to challenging and antagonising his middle-class readers. Recent studies have recognised that he was a great deal more subversive in his views than earlier biographers had supposed.[5] His characters are more often than not victims of the educational system rather than beneficiaries. The benefits of economic progress are passing them by, and there is a distinct danger that educational reform will do the same, thanks to their isolated geographical situation and colonisation of education by the middle classes, 'either because it reflected their culture or because the educated middle class was better equipped to take advantage of it'.[6] As Merryn and Raymond Williams demonstrate, Hardy was concerned that learning and privilege had become interchangeable in the educated world.[7] He was particularly conscious of this as one born into a artisan family.

Hardy's early childhood coincided with major developments in the educational system, exemplified by the introduction of the pupil-teacher system in 1846. By the time of his death in 1928, compulsory education for children up to 12 years of age had been introduced; it was established that all children had the right to secondary-school education from the age of 11; and the universities had undergone major reforms both in terms of curriculum and teaching methods. Hardy's novels reflect many of these developments. School reforms of relevance to such characters as Fancy Day, Grace Melbury, and Tess Durbeyfield, as well as those relating to adult education, are reviewed later. Hardy is at his most eloquent in revealing the injustices of the educational system for the working class.

In order to understand the philosophy behind the educational developments of the nineteenth century and their effect on social mobility, it is necessary to consider the impact of the doctrine of self-help as expounded by Samuel Smiles and the Utilitarians. The pronounced class differences that characterised Victorian society required 'a rationale which showed such conditions to be necessary and to be compatible with a Christian society's view of itself'.[8] Self-reliance was part of this picture. Samuel Smiles's best-selling *Self-Help* (1859) promoted diligence and condemned idleness. Self-help was seen as a prerequisite both for the growth of the individual and the development of the nation. Only will power and a degree of talent were needed to achieve economic and social success. Perseverance was a key quality. In Hardy's novels, two characters stand out as examples of self-help: Clym Yeobright and Jude Fawley (*Jude the Obscure*), both of whom share Hardy's thirst for knowledge.[9]

The Utilitarians were keen promoters of self-help. Formulated by Jeremy Bentham among others, Utilitarianism was at the height of its influence between the 1830s and 1850s, the chronological setting of many of Hardy's novels. Its philosophy of producing the greatest happiness for the greatest number had profound implications for national educational developments. The Utilitarians were preoccupied with useful knowledge, and instrumental in establishing monitorial schools for the poor (later replaced by the pupil-teacher system). They subsequently influenced secondary school reform, proposing that children should be educated for specific social roles: the poor to work and the middle classes to govern. John Stuart Mill, more liberally inclined than some of his fellow Utilitarians, was admired by Hardy because he recognised the potential of education for social mobility, arguing that 'a firm foundation may be laid for a life of mental action, a life of wisdom, and reflection, and ingenuity, even in those by whom the most ordinary labour will fall to be performed'.[10] This was a new way of looking at education for the working class, designed to foster a liberal democracy.

The Utilitarians also promoted higher education. Above all, they were concerned with fostering science at colleges and universities. It was much thanks to them, for example, that new universities were established in the north of England. They saw to it that most

middle-class occupations and professions had their own prepara-
tory institutions: teacher training colleges, agricultural colleges,
scientific colleges, and so on. Indeed, Utilitarianism permeated science and political and economic philosophy for much of the time
Hardy lived and wrote.

By the mid-nineteenth century, education had become an important and long-term investment in the future, thanks to increased
life expectancy (for men this increased by eleven years between
1838 and 1902, and for women by fourteen years).[11] Inspectors'
reports from the 1830s onwards show a significant increase in
the number of children from labourers' homes attending school.
Between 1833 and 1851, for example, there was a national increase
of over 23 percent for children of the labouring classes as against 9
percent for children from other homes.[12] There was some opposition to the spread of education to the working classes, both from
themselves and from the upper strata of society. Working-class
parents resented their children attending school when they could
be assisting them in supporting the family. The older generation of
both the lower and upper classes was afraid that children would
learn inappropriate behaviour while at school. Captain Vye in *The
Return of the Native* expresses this fear clearly:

Ah, there's too much of that sending to school in these days! It only
does harm. Every gatepost and every barn's door you come to is sure
to have some bad word or other chalked upon it by the young rascals:
a woman can hardly pass for shame sometimes. If they'd never been
taught how to write they wouldn't have been able to scribble such vil-
lainy. Their fathers couldn't do it, and the country was all the better for
it. (*RN*: II.1)

The two rustics with whom Captain Vye is talking do not disagree.
Not only the rustics but also the upper classes were unprepared for
the scope and speed of the transformation, as exemplified by Miss
Aldclyffe: 'like a good many others in her position' she is unable
to understand how Edward Springrove, 'a son of her tenant and
inferior could have become an educated man' (*DR*: XI.4).[13]

However, neither the lower nor the upper classes could stand in
the way of the inevitable. With the Industrial Revolution came a
demand from employers for a more skilled workforce. There was
also a growing desire to understand the fundamental changes

taking place in society, particularly with regard to scientific and technological innovations. As Roger Fieldhouse observes, the increasing number of literary, philosophical, and scientific societies found in every town and in many villages represented a desire to understand and control the environment. Public funds were pumped into education from 1833 onwards, marking what Fieldhouse describes as an 'ideological drift from self-help individualism to social collectivism'.[14] Fear of foreign competition bolstered the view that education should no longer be left to individualist self-help. The following brief discussion of state-regulated school reforms is limited to those areas which are of direct relevance to Hardy's novels.

The Committee of the Privy Council on Education, created in 1839, began a series of improvements in school buildings, furniture and apparatus. It also introduced a new era in teacher training with the inauguration of the pupil-teacher scheme, marking a new state concern for teaching standards. Candidates were to be not younger than 13 years of age; able to read with fluency, write neatly, spell and punctuate correctly; know the tables of weights and measures; possess an elementary knowledge of geography; and be able to teach a junior class to the satisfaction of the Inspector. They served a five-year apprenticeship, at the end of which they sat an examination that entailed writing an essay on didactics, studying the rudiments of algebra or the practice of land surveying, as well as using globes and the geography of the British Empire and Europe. In the fifth year the girls also sat an examination in the Scriptures, Liturgy and Catechism of the Church of England. Theoretical and scientific subjects were prioritised for boys and more practical and arts-orientated ones for girls. The pupil-teacher scheme was the system under which the majority of Hardy's fictional characters would have been taught. Fancy Day in *Under the Greenwood Tree* is educated under this system: she is the best scholar of her year, completes teacher training with a first-class pass, and gains employment as an elementary school teacher. In real life, though, it has to be said that standards were extremely low.[15]

Sixteen years after the establishment of the pupil-teacher system, the Revised Code was introduced. With this came the notorious payment-by-results scheme, under which children were drilled and examined in the three 'Rs': reading, writing, and arithmetic.

The Newcastle Commission (1858–61) had reported that few children attended school past the age of 12, and only 25 percent of older children received an acceptable education.[16] The Revised Code gave rise to an over emphasis on rote learning and a neglect of other subjects, since school grants were wholly dependent on successful performance in the three 'Rs'. Tess Durbeyfield is a product of the Revised Code. Its effects were dramatic, causing a rift between mother and daughter:

Between the mother, with her fast-perishing lumber of superstitions, folk-lore, dialect, and orally transmitted ballads, and the daughter, with her trained National teachings and Standard knowledge under an infinitely Revised Code, there was a gap of two hundred years as ordinarily understood. When they were together the Jacobean and Victorian ages were juxtaposed. (*Tess*: I.3).

The Code was revised in 1882. Additional subjects for examination were added and schools were graded 'fair', 'good' or 'excellent'. These changes signalled a new attitude towards education.

By the 1870s, when Hardy was writing his first novels, education had become a significant part of social policy. William Forster's Education Act of 1870 attempted to establish compulsory education in all districts. School boards supervised the building of new schools, a scheme in which Hardy was directly involved in his capacity as an architect. The new board schools were opposed by local farmers of the type represented by Groby in *Tess of the d'Urbervilles*; child labour was, as already indicated, an indispensable complement to the workforce. The 1870 Act created a considerable demand for teachers. Teacher training colleges such as Salisbury College (the original of the Training College at Melchester, which Sue Bridehead attends as a 'Queen's Scholar' in *Jude*) attempted to cater for this demand, offering opportunities for among others Hardy's own sisters, Mary and Kate.[17] As Hardy shows, the quality of trainees varied: Sue comments bitterly on 'the rough living, and the mixed character of her fellow-students, gathered together from all parts of the diocese' (*Jude*: III.1). Adult education too was only in the very early stages of development, and clearly reflected the social inequalities of Victorian society. One of its major functions was teaching the three 'R's to the large illiterate section of the population, particularly during the first half of the century. This was part of an attempt made by the middle classes to help the working classes assimilate themselves more completely into the new and more complex industrialised society. By the 1860s the system of informal, non-institutionalised, working-class autonomous adult education and popular culture prevalent in the first half of the century had been extensively undermined by more formal adult education in the adult schools, the Sunday schools and night schools, Mechanics' Institutes and Working Men's Colleges.

A number of radical working-class movements promoted school and adult education, such as Robert Owen's 'The Universal Community Society of Rational Religionists' (1835) and the early Co-operative Societies of the 1820s through to the 1840s. Educational activities were also organised by the Chartists, whose spirit of free enquiry and social purpose attracted and influenced large numbers of working people.[18] By the mid-century, with the defeat of Chartism, independent working-class education – like the political movements that harboured it – found itself increasingly isolated. The notion of an alternative working-class education was replaced by demands for more equal access to facilities provided by the middle classes and the State.

Sunday schools spread rapidly, especially in the 1830s and 1840s; Hardy himself taught Sunday school in Stinsford. In addition to their religious purpose, the schools provided many with a basic training in literacy (Hardy wrote – from dictation – letters for local girls). Meanwhile, an adult school movement emerged, closely allied to Sunday Schools but devoted exclusively to the education of grown-ups. From the 1830s onwards an increasing number of elementary day schools opened in the evenings, for adult students as well as children and adolescents. These were small, private institutions run on the same lines as the day schools and used the same teachers and premises. 'More than any other form of adult education, they met the needs of large numbers of adults for basic literacy and therefore played an important part in nineteenth century adult education.'[19]

University education was open to the middle and upper classes only. From the 1830s onwards, there was increasing pressure to reform the ancient universities of Oxford and Cambridge to make them comply better with the demands of contemporary society. In due course, from the 1850s onwards, both Oxford and

Cambridge began to offer extension lectures in towns and cities, vying with each other and with the newly-established London University. Interestingly, neither Jude nor Sue appears to notice the system, though in 1865 Hardy himself enrolled in French evening classes at King's College London (*LW*: 52). University extension was predominantly middle class, and particularly popular with women.

One positive effect of university extension was the university settlement movement, which began in 1883. This aimed to extend social harmony and build bridges between the social classes. Middle- and working-class students mingled, and the idea of a people's university was planted. The movement was also characterised by a strong Christian socialist basis. As a member of the working classes and self-educated, Jude's dream of entering Oxford is doomed to failure.[20] It was not to Oxford ('Christminster') that Jude should have turned, but to one of the universities emerging from the university-settlement movement. Jude is isolated.[21] He asks the question, 'who knoweth what is good for man in this life?' (*Jude*: VI.1). In a sense, Hardy had already answered that question in *The Hand of Ethelberta*: Ethelberta's superior education (briefly described on the first page of the novel) combined with an iron will ensures that she will cross the class divide, even if she must leave her siblings on the other side (her brothers, for their part, are content to stay there). Jude is not so wise. This is no coincidence: *Jude the Obscure* is Hardy's final and most bitter statement on the role of education in socially divided nineteenth-century England.

The nineteenth century saw a shift from self-help to state provision of education. Hardy's rustic characters benefit little from either the Industrial Revolution or educational reforms. When they do receive a more thorough education, as in the case of Grace Melbury in *The Woodlanders*, they become alienated from traditional values and from their environment. Jude Fawley learns that it is impossible to cross the class divide: a stonemason he is, and a stonemason he will remain. Oxford is not for the likes of him. This is the harsh reality, which Hardy portrayed in his novels and one which he had encountered at first hand, not least in his own writing career, where the absence of a university degree was a constant source of regret.

NOTES

1　See T. W. Heyck, *The Transformation of Intellectual Life in Victorian England* (London: Croom Helm, 1982).

2　*The Popular Educator* began publishing in *1852*. John Cassell (1817–65), himself an autodidact, was committed to the moral and social improvement of the working classes.

3　See Jane Mattisson, *Knowledge and Survival in the Novels of Thomas Hardy* (Lund: Lund University, 2002), pp. 102–52.

4　See Helen Merrell Lynd, *England in the Eighteen-Eighties. Toward a Social Basis for Freedom* (London: Oxford University Press, 1945), p. 360.

5　Edward Neill, for example, argues that Hardy was 'mischievous and subversive, not cowed and compliant': *The Secret Life of Thomas Hardy: 'Retaliatory Fiction'* (Aldershot: Ashgate, 2004), p. viii.

6　Roger Fieldhouse et al., *A History of Modern British Adult Education* (Leicester: National Institute of Adult Continuing Education, *1998*), p. 44.

7　Merryn and Raymond Williams, 'Hardy and Social Class', *Thomas Hardy: The Writer and his Background*, ed. Norman Page (London: Bell & Hyman, 1980), p. 37.

8　Patricia Ingham, *Thomas Hardy* (Oxford: Oxford University Press, 2003), p. 44.

9　Stephen Smith in *A Pair of Blue Eyes* is a different case. He too seeks knowledge, but his goals are primarily social. See John Goode, *Thomas Hardy. The Offensive Truth* (Oxford: Basil Blackwell, 1988), p. 2, and Phillip Mallett, 'Hardy and Masculinity', *Ashgate Research Companion to Thomas Hardy*, ed. Rosemarie Morgan (Aldershot: Ashgate, 2010), pp. 387–403.

10　'Education', *Supplement to the Encyclopedia Britannica*, pp. 18–19. Quoted in John Lawson and Harold Silver, *A Social History of Education in England* (London: Methuen, 1973), p. 231.

11　J. M. Goldstrom, *The Social Content of Education 1808–1870: A Study of the Working Class School Reader in England and Ireland* (Shannon: Irish University Press, 1972), p. 1.

12　*Reports from Commissioners, Inspectors and Others. Education. Special Reports. Session 8 February 1889–12 August 1898*, XXIV, p. 446.

13　*Desperate Remedies* was written while the 1870 Education Act was being implemented, in the early days of far-reaching educational reforms: see Philip Collins, 'Hardy and Education', *Thomas Hardy*, ed. Page, pp. 47–8.

14　Fieldhouse et al., *A History of Modern British Adult Education*, p. 3.

15  See Jane Mattisson, *Knowledge and Survival*, pp. 66–70, 85–7, 185–6.

16  For further details see J. M. Goldstrom, *Social Content of Education*, pp. 153–9.

17  See Michael Millgate and Stephen Mottram, 'Sisters: Mary and Kate Hardy as Teachers', *Thomas Hardy Journal*, 25 (Autumn 2009), pp. 4–24.

18  Brian Simon, *The Two Nations and the Educational Structure, 1780–1870* (London: Lawrence & Wishart, 1974), pp. 254–5.

19  Fieldhouse et al., *A History of Modern British Adult Education*, pp. 32–3.

20  See Mattisson, *Knowledge and Survival*, pp. 365–85.

21  On Jude's isolation, see Roger Ebbatson, '"A Thickness of Wall": Hardy and Class', *A Companion to Thomas Hardy*, ed. Keith Wilson (Oxford: Wiley-Blackwell, 2009), pp. 162–77.

# 18

# Hardy and the Sociological Imagination

### ROGER EBBATSON

As social integration [formation into societies] advances, the increasing aggregates [bodies of people] exercise increasing restraints over their units – a truth which is the obverse of the one ... that the maintenance of its integrity by a larger aggregate implies greater cohesion.[1]

'But my father and friends?' said [Ethelberta].
'Are nothing to be concerned about. Modern developments have shaken up the classes like peas in a hopper. An annuity, and a comfortable cottage – '
'My brothers are workmen.'
'Manufacture is the single vocation in which a man's prospects may be said to be illimitable. Hee hee! – they may buy me up before they die! And now what stands in the way? It would take fifty alliances with fifty families so little disreputable as yours, darling, to drag mine down.'[2]

Thomas Hardy, whose career coincided with the rise of academic sociology, here embeds Herbert Spencer's theory of social development in an exchange between Ethelberta Petherwin and Lord Mountclere. Writing primarily about the rural economy, Hardy's work portrays the trajectory of communal individualism towards the more faceless aggregation of the 'administered society' through the impact of 'metamorphic classes' (*HE*: 39). An early novel like *Under the Greenwood Tree* offers the reader a portrait of a community of individuals, 'five men of different ages and gaits', representing 'the chief portion of Mellstock parish choir' (*UGT*: I.1). This 'chief portion' is then rendered in all its specificity: 'a bowed and bent man, who carried a fiddle' (Michael Mail); 'a little man, who ... walked as if that fact had not come to his own knowledge'

(Robert Penny); one 'who walked perpendicularly and dramatically' (Elias Spinks); and 'a weak lath-like form, trotting and stumbling along' (Thomas Leaf). The Quire are presented as embodying, in their observation of ancient custom, folkways undermined by the tremors of modernity:

'Times have changed from the times they used to be,' said Mail [...] 'we must be almost the last left in the county of the old string players. Barrel-organs, and the things next door to 'em that you blow wi' your foot, have come in terribly of late years.' (*UGT*: I.4)

These ambiguous portents of change, dramatised by the ascension of Fancy Day and the new church organ, resonate throughout the middle novels, as in George Somerset's tour of Stancy Castle in company with the displaced aristocrat, Charlotte De Stancy:

They walked on, and came opposite to where the telegraph emerged from the trees, leaped over the parapet, and up through the loophole into the interior.

'That looks strange in such a building,' said her companion.

'Miss Power had it put up to know the latest news from town. It costs six pounds a year for each mile. She can work it herself, beautifully: ... And did you hear the new clock? ... Paula says that time, being so much more valuable now, must of course be cut up into smaller pieces.' (*AL*: 4)

The homology between Hardy's creative project and the rise of sociology is traceable in his interest in the writings of Herbert Spencer, with its amalgam of Lamarckian and Darwinian thought. Spencer's early interest in geology persuaded him that organic forms had arisen by progressive modification. He supplemented this with a Malthusian understanding of population growth and competition to propound his influential formula of the 'survival of the fittest', first defined in *Social Statics* (1850). The articulation of the development hypothesis would characterise a career devoted to the compilation of a 'Synthetic Philosophy'. His reconfiguration of Lamarck enabled him to read the principles of inheritance and variation as the laws of genesis and individuation. For Spencer, a higher degree of individual evolution entailed a lower degree of 'race multiplication', as Jude and Sue discover to their cost. With limited amounts of energy, development of brain and personality is bought at the expense of fertility:

> A time there was – as one may guess
> And as, indeed, earth's testimonies tell –
> Before the birth of consciousness,
> When all went well. [3]

Hardy's fiction critically scrutinises and dramatises the Spencerean scenario of the impact of 'the disease of feeling' upon 'primal rightness' – hence, for instance, Clym Yeobright's baffled educational programme on Egdon, Angel's fatal idealism, or the consequences of the union of Sue and Jude.

Spencer's theory also possessed wide-ranging political and social ramifications, entailing, in his view, laissez-faire liberal capitalism and a society in which the battle of life would eliminate the unfit, 'weeding out those of lowest development' and 'subjecting those who remain to the never-ceasing discipline of experience':

nature secures the growth of a race who shall both understand the conditions of existence, and be able to act up to them. It is impossible in any degree to suspend this discipline by stepping in between ignorance and its consequences, without, to a corresponding degree, suspending progress.[4]

Hardy ironises this 'beneficent' Spencerean 'law' and explores its human implications: comedically in the demise of the Mellstock Quire and the survival of the Egdon rustics, tragically in the sacrifice of Tess, or in Arabella's ability to flourish at the expense of Sue and Jude. Both Spencer and Hardy were 'evolutionary meliorists', whose work bears traces of the principle of individuation, which, functioning as the primary motif of evolution, is central to the development hypothesis. The Lamarckian strand in Spencer's thought prompted the view that living animals and humans could be positioned on an evolutionary scale of increasing complexity. Complication arose out of simple elements: Lamarckian evolution through the inheritance of acquired characteristics combined with the principle of the conservation of energy. Change was inevitably in the direction of either Evolution (coherence) or Dissolution (incoherence). Spencer applied this thesis to society, which would become ever more complex, after originating in a 'primal horde'.

The social division of labour was more efficient, and increased the ratio of survival. Peace, free trade, and unfettered competition would be the inevitable goals of social evolution. Greater heterogeneity paradoxically implied a higher level of cohesion.

Spencer's *First Principles* (1862) exerted a seminal influence upon the young Hardy. According to Spencer, 'matter passes from an indefinite incoherent homogeneity to a definite coherent heterogeneity',[5] and this pattern is widely in evidence in Hardy's Wessex. At the same time the contrary laws of entropic reversal undermine progression:

there is always a differential progression towards either integration or disintegration. During the earlier part of the cycle of changes, the integration predominates – there goes on what we call growth. The middle part of the cycle is usually characterised, not by equilibrium between the integrating and disintegrating processes, but by alternating excesses of them. And the cycle closes with a period in which the disintegration ... eventually puts a stop to integration.[6]

The equilibrium of the social structure, and its trajectory towards coherence, is always unstable in Hardy. In the early novels balance is achieved through adaptation and adjustment – the voluntary withdrawal of the Mellstock Quire, or the inventive capability of Gabriel Oak or Ethelberta Petherwin – but in the later work the tone darkens with portents of Spencerean dissolution, as in the Hintock woods, at Flintcomb-Ash or Christminster. In terms of the delineation of social consciousness and the formulation of a 'world view' Spencer proved fertile for Hardy in suggesting evolutionary movement from incoherence to coherence, homogeneity to heterogeneity, change within continuity, and, in the poetry and *The Dynasts*, the persistence of a universal driving force designated 'the Unknowable'. Spencer's system is replete with contradictions, but his *oeuvre* resonated creatively in Hardy's imagination, as I have argued elsewhere:

The imprecision of Spencer's thought ... mattered less for his original readers than the insights into agencies of human and social change. Incorporation of speculative philosophy into the life of the imagination was essential artistic strategy for Hardy, whose whole habit of understanding formed itself out of his reading and experience in the eighteen-sixties. Behind the exaggeration and coincidence of the novels there is a sense of the pressures of the new thought being translated into the experience of men and women in isolated rural communities.[7]

Hardy's most overtly 'sociological' text, however, his 1883 essay on 'The Dorsetshire Labourer', shows little trace of Spencer's influence. He suggests that there is now a general post in the countryside on Old Lady Day (6 April), when the labourers' belongings are piled onto a wagon sent by the new employer. At such times the roads bear witness to Hardy's sense of an increasing migratory tendency in the countryside, though he balances this with the apothegm that 'Change is also a certain sort of education.' Nonetheless, the field labourer is losing individuality and adopting an 'increasing nomadic habit', which leads inevitably to 'a less intimate and kindly relation with the land he tills' (*THPV*: 48–50). Tim Dolin has explored the political background to this essay, stressing its origins in Hardy's ambivalent response to the Radical land programme of the early 1880s, and concluding that the author was 'unwilling to put himself forward as a spokesman for rural labour'. Whilst Hardy's stress fell differently, his concerns 'overlapped with the Radicals' emphasis on rural depopulation, the deceptive appearance of cottages, and real wages and conditions'. Nonetheless, Dolin observes, the essay as a whole 'presents a compelling case against the enfranchisement of agricultural labourers as a class'.[8]

Hardy's essay might be read off against the wide-ranging contemporary sociological account given in Ferdinand Tönnies's 1887 *Community and Society*, a study of the evolution from *Gemeinschaft* (community) to *Gesellschaft* (association). Tönnies suggests that 'Men change their temperaments with the place and conditions of their daily life, which becomes hasty and changeable through restless striving.'[9] Like Hardy, Tönnies in his native Schleswig-Holstein had witnessed the gradual dissolution of the old rural order, and he postulated a central distinction between *Gemeinschaft*, defined by blood, place and kinship, and *Gesellschaft*, dominated by money, competition and the cash-nexus. The engine of social change for Tönnies is the clash between the 'primordial will' and the 'mechanical' – a diagnosis Hardy would at times endorse. There exists 'a *Gemeinschaft* of language, or folkways or mores, or of beliefs', whereas *Gesellschaft* 'exists in the realm of borders, travel, or sciences'. Life in the community is marked by an 'intimate, private and exclusive living together', so that the individual moves towards *Gesellschaft* 'as one goes into a strange country' (*CS*: 33–4).

Tönnies attempts to present his two types impartially, but the weight of his valuation falls upon *Gemeinschaft*. In *Gesellschaft* the defining elements of egoism, competition and ruthless acquisitiveness combine to generate the development of the modern metropolis as 'a society of strangers'. Under *Gemeinschaft* Tönnies blends features of the ancient village commune and the medieval town with its craft associations. In Tönnies's thesis we may detect three types of community: kinship (the household), locality (the village), and fellowship (the craft guild), and these combine in his thought to form a unified social experience.

Hardy's fiction independently explores the implications of this sociological diagnosis, not only in his delineations of rootedness, but also in the traversal of borders, the impact of the *Gesellschaft*, upon such figures as Clym Yeobright, Edred Fitzpiers or Angel Clare. Tönnies depicts a sense of 'concord' in the experience of 'living together in the rural village' and the concomitant 'co-operation in labour' (*CS*: 43), such as that which characterises work in the Marlott harvest fields or at Talbothays Dairy:

the domicile becomes immovable like earth and soil. The human being becomes bound in a twofold way, through cultivated fields and through the house in which he lives; that is to say, tied down by his own work. (*CS*: 51)

Beginning with his earliest poem, 'Domicilium', Hardy frequently recreates this sense of dwelling, centred in his memories of the cottage at Higher Bockhampton:

The window-shutters were not yet closed, and the fire- and candle-light within radiated forth upon the bushes of variegated box and thick laurestinus ... The walls of the dwelling were for the most part covered with creepers, though these were rather beaten back from the doorway – a feature which was worn and scratched by much passing in and out, giving it by day the appearance of an old keyhole. (*UGT*: I.2)

By contrast, in the world of *Gesellschaft*, founded in the principle of exchange, Tönnies discerns a situation in which 'everybody is by himself and isolated, and there exists a condition of tension against all others' (*CS*: 65). This experience of an urbanised sense of aliena-tion reverberates in Hardy, as in the pattern discerned by Manston as he gazes at the 'lively thoroughfare of the Strand':

Each and all were alike in this one respect, that they followed a soli-tary trail like the inwoven threads which form a banner, and all were equally unconscious of the significant whole they collectively showed forth. (*DR*: XVI.4)

London, Hardy would reflect elsewhere, 'appears not to *see itself*: 'Each individual is conscious of *himself*, but nobody conscious of themselves collectively, except perhaps some poor gaper who stares round with a half-idiotic aspect' (*LW*: 215). But the condition of uprooting and homelessness discerned by Tönnies would also transform the rural economy, as refracted in the exchange between 'Sir' John Durbeyfield and Parson Tringham:

'And where do we raise our smoke now, parson, if I may make so bold; I mean, where do we d'Urbervilles live?'

'You don't live anywhere. You are extinct – as a county family.'

'That's bad.' (*Tess*: 1)

The entire trajectory of Hardy's work as a novelist, from the com-munal portrait of *Under the Greenwood Tree* to the existential *anomie* of *Jude the Obscure*, is a richly imagined elaboration of the ambiguous implications of Tönnies' sociological thesis:

For a settled people, the real substance of the will of *Gemeinschaft* which is the basis for numerous individual customs is its folkways and mores ... to the blood *Gemeinschaft* is added the *Gemeinschaft* of the land, of the home country (*Heimat*) ... The people see themselves sur-rounded by the inhabited earth. It seems as if, in the beginning of time, the earth itself had brought forth from its womb the human beings who look upon her as their mother. (*CS*: 206)

It would be left to another sociological contemporary of Hardy's to develop the full implications of this historic movement. For Max Weber, in the drive towards modernity, the 'idyllic state' charac-terised by the 'old leisured comfortable attitude toward life gave way to a hard frugality'.[10] Weber's *The Protestant Ethic and the*

*Spirit of Capitalism* proposed that capitalist activity was motivated by the transmutation of religious ideas, especially the doctrines of Calvinism, into a secular ensemble stressing duty, economic diligence, thrift and productivity. Weber's tripartite model of social evolution ostensibly demonstrated how first a traditional and subsequently a charismatic order would give way to a rational sociality governed by calculation. The Calvinist notion of a religious 'calling' is transposed, in Weber's thought, into a machinic principle: 'The Puritan wanted to work in a calling; we are forced to do so' (*PE*: 181). The onset of administrative structures has led to the 'disenchantment' of modernity and the gradual disappearance of the communal life-world. Without bureaucracy, capitalism itself would have been impossible of realisation. Whilst Weber's reading of history as a process of ineluctable rationalisation has been the subject of debate and critique,[11] it retains a potency which may fruitfully be related to issues and themes in Hardy's fiction.

Weber's concept of the charismatic personality and its supersession by economic rationality is relevant to a reading of *The Mayor of Casterbridge*, a novel 'centrally concerned with the operation of market forces upon social relationships'.[12] The action of the novel, in which the individualistic Henchard is supplanted by Farfrae with his 'secular worldly asceticism', refracts some of the tenets of Weber's thesis. In the wife-sale which inaugurates the novel, Henchard acts out Weber's contention that the charismatic individual 'must stand outside the ties of this world', 'outside the routine obligations of family life',[13] with the consequent alienation and loneliness which blights his affective relations with Lucetta and Elizabeth-Jane, and leads to his suicidal thoughts at Ten-Hatches-Hole. What Weber characterises as the 'unprecedented loneliness of the single individual' (*PE*: 104) leads towards the 'rationalisation' of the world staged in Henchard's abortive visit to Conjuror Fall. Weber's diagnosis aptly mirrors Henchard's predicament here in relation to Donald Farfrae: 'The radical elimination of magic from the world allowed no other psychological course than the practice of worldly asceticism' (*PE*: 149).

As Hardy remarks, the early 'traditionalist' form of capital enterprise undertaken by Henchard with his 'old crude *viva voce* system ... in which everything depended upon his memory, and bargains were made by the tongue alone, was swept away' (*MC*: 14).

'The pen and all its relations', we are told, 'were awkward tools in Henchard's hands' (*MC*: 36). The 'traditional manner of life', Weber observes, would be 'suddenly destroyed' when 'some young man' transforms his workforce 'from peasants into labourers', and institutes a system of 'rational book-keeping' (*PE*: 67, 22). Instead of the 'dare-devil speculations' Henchard enters into with Jopp, the new economic order is characterised by agents who are 'calculating and daring at the same time, above all temperate and reliable ... with strictly bourgeois opinions and principles' (*PE*: 69). Farfrae's brief outbursts of Scottish song are calculatingly controlled, bearing out Weber's contention that 'Impulsive enjoyment of life' was 'the enemy of rational asceticism' (*PE*: 167): efficiency consists in 'eliminating from official business love, hatred, and all purely personal, irrational, and emotional elements which escape calculation'.[14]

Within the traditional economy, Weber notes, a 'flood of mistrust' would have 'regularly opposed itself to the first innovator' (*PE*: 69), and the cancellation of spontaneity and charisma by a secular worldly asceticism is marked by 'specialisation of work and labour discipline' which, he argues, 'formed a predisposing condition, even an impetus toward the increasing application and import of machines'.[15] Farfrae's advocacy of the new seed-drill creates 'as much sensation in the corn-market as a flying-machine would create at Charing Cross' (*MC*: 24). The machine is decried by Henchard, whilst Farfrae is seen 'pushing his head into the internal works to master their simple secrets', and goes on to declare, 'It will revolutionise sowing heerabout' (*MC*: 24). As Andrew Radford observes, Farfrae discovers in Casterbridge 'the perfect ethnographic "laboratory" for his experiments in impersonal business methods'.[16] If Henchard's death on the heath signals the waning of charisma, his wedding gift of a goldfinch in a 'wire prison' (*MC*: 44) gestures towards Weber's famous image of the demands of bureaucracy functioning as an 'iron cage' for humanity. Indeed this diagnosis resonates widely in Hardy's writing: in 'A Tragedy of Two Ambitions', the Halborough brothers' worldly aim of rising in the church is set in contradistinction to their father's fecklessly charismatic career and leads them to allow the old man to drown. 'Do you think human hearts are iron-cased safes?' Cornelius demands, to which Joshua ominously replies, 'Yes, I think they are, sometimes' (*LLI*: 104).

But it is the steam-threshing machine which most potently embodies the implications of Weber's thesis for Hardy's Wessex. At the outset of 'An Indiscretion in the Life of an Heiress', the heroine, in her curiosity about the new machine, risks being 'whirled round the wheel as a mangled carcase'.[17] This scenario takes on greater intensity at Flintcomb-Ash:

Close under the eaves of the stack ... was the red tyrant that the women had come to serve – a timber-framed construction, with straps and wheels appertaining – the threshing-machine which, whilst it was going, kept up a despotic demand upon the endurance of their muscles and nerves. (*Tess*: 47)

Despite the field labourers' hatred of machines, the work proceeds apace, 'the inexorable wheels continuing to spin, and the penetrating hum of the thresher to thrill to the very marrow all who were near the *revolving wire cage*' (*Tess*: 47).[18] However, what differentiates Hardy from his sociological contemporaries is his scrupulous reorientation of the predominant male gaze. If, as Janet Wolff argues, women 'only appear' in classical sociological texts 'through their relationships with men in the public sphere, and in their illegitimate or eccentric roles in this male arena',[19] Hardy, by contrast is alert and empathic in his registration of women's predicament in rural Wessex:

> How it rained
> When we worked at Flintcomb-Ash,
> And could not stand upon the hill
> Trimming swedes for the slicing-mill.
> The wet washed through us – plash, plash, plash:
> How it rained! [20]

To sum up: in his analysis of the transfer of the ascetic principle from the monastery to the economic conditions of machine production Weber offers a sociological gloss upon Hardy's life-world, with its intensely rendered range of responses to change in nineteenth-century Wessex. As Raymond Williams argued, in Hardy's lifetime 'identity and community became more problematic' as 'the scale and complexity of the characteristic social organisation increased'. Thus it was that 'any assumption of a knowable community – a whole community, wholly knowable – became harder and harder to sustain'.[21] In the ousting of Mayor Henchard, in Tess's pilgrimage from Talbothays dairy to Flintcomb-Ash, or Jude and Sue's endless peregrinations, we may discern an imaginative refraction of, but also heroic resistance to, Weber's bleak sociological prophecy for the coming century, a time in which, as he phrases it, 'all the weather signs point in the direction of diminishing freedom':[22]

Together with the inanimate machine, the living machine constructs the cage of future bondage. Perhaps men will be forced to fit themselves helplessly into this cage if a technically good, that is, a rational bureaucratic administration and provision of services, is to be the ultimate and only value.[23]

Hardy's writing bears eloquent witness to communal praxis, inventiveness and adaptability to nature, which counters, even in defeat, the monolithic process of reification posited by his more fatalistic sociological contemporaries:

'Whenever I plant the young larches I'll think that none can plant as you planted; and whenever I split a gad, and whenever I turn the cider wring, I'll say none could do it like you. If ever I forget your name let me forget home and heaven! ... But no, no, my love, I never can forget 'ee; for you was a good man, and did good things!' (*W*: 45)

#### NOTES

1 *LN* I: 139, quoting Herbert Spencer, 'Political Integration', *Fortnightly Review* XXIX (1881). Square brackets and ellipses are Hardy's.
2 *HE*: 38.
3 'Before Life and After', *CP*: 277.
4 Herbert Spencer, *Social Statics* (New York: Appleton, 1882), p. 119.
5 Herbert Spencer, *First Principles* (New York: Burt, 1880), p. 343.
6 Ibid., p. 246.
7 Roger Ebbatson, *The Evolutionary Self* (Brighton: Harvester, 1982), pp. 43–4.
8 Tim Dolin, 'Liberal Politics and the Origins of Wessex', in *Thomas Hardy and Contemporary Literary Studies*, ed. Tim Dolin and Peter Widdowson (Basingstoke: Palgrave, 2004), pp. 123–7.
9 Ferdinand Tönnies, *Community and Society*, trans. P. A. Sorokin (New Brunswick, N.J.: Transaction Publications, 1988), p. 225. Subsequently cited as *CS*.

10  Max Weber, *The Protestant Ethic and the Spirit of Capitalism* (1904), trans. Talcott Parsons (London: Allen & Unwin, 1976), p. 68. Subsequently cited as *PE*.

11  For a useful overview see Jack Barbalet, *Weber, Passion and Profit* (Cambridge: Cambridge University Press, 2008).

12  Michael J. Franklin, '"Market-Faces" and Market Forces: [Corn] Factors in the Moral Economy of Casterbridge', *Review of English Studies* 59 (2008), p. 427.

13  *Max Weber on Charisma and Institution Building*, ed. S. N. Eisenstadt (Chicago: Chicago University Press, 1968), p. 21.

14  Max Weber, *Economy and Society*, ed. Guenther Roth and Claus Wittich (Berkeley: University of California Press, 1978), II:975.

15  *Weber on Charisma*, p. 137.

16  Andrew Radford, 'Excavating an Empire of Dust in *The Mayor of Casterbridge*', *Thomas Hardy Journal* 25 (2009), p. 66.

17  Thomas Hardy, *An Indiscretion in the Life of an Heiress and Other Stories*, ed. Pamela Dalziel (Oxford: Oxford University Press, 1994), p. 45.

18  Italics added. See Roger Ebbatson, 'Landscape and Machine: Hardy, Jefferies and the Question of Technology', *Writing Technologies* (online) 2:2 (2009), pp. 35–54; Zena Meadowsong, 'Thomas Hardy and the Machine: Mechanical Deformation of Narrative Realism in *Tess of the d'Urbervilles*', *Nineteenth-Century Literature* 64:2 (2009), pp. 225–47.

19  Janet Wolff, 'The Invisible Flâneuse', *Theory, Culture and Society* 3 (1985), p. 44.

20  'We Field-Women', *CP*: 881

21  Raymond Williams, *The Country and the City* (London: Chatto & Windus, 1973), p. 165.

22  Cited in Alan Swingewood, *Marx and Modern Social Theory* (London: Macmillan, 1975), p. 150.

23  Cited in Karl Löwith, *Max Weber and Karl Marx* (London: Routledge, 1993), p. 74.

19

# Folklore and Anthropology

ANDREW RADFORD

'I may say, once for all,' Thomas Hardy wrote in April 1894, 'that every superstition, custom, &c., described in my novels may be depended on as true records of the same (whatever merit in folklorists eyes they may have as such) – & not inventions of mine' (*CL* II: 54). Hardy's lifelong fascination with folklore reflects his precarious position on a cultural fault-line: keenly alert to the dislocating complexities of a hectic modernity yet impelled by a historical responsibility to exhume, record, and reanimate forgotten traditions. He registered early the destabilizing outcome of his rural sociology in the imaginative patterns of his work; nevertheless, his fiction and poetry both shadowed and foreshadowed the nascent science of anthropology.

Edward W. Brabrook, President of the Folk-Lore Society, declared in 1901 in a memorial on the death of Queen Victoria that 'the very existence' of 'the study of folklore' was 'bounded by Her Majesty's reign'.[1] William John Thoms, writing in the *Athenaeum* (22 August 1846) under the pseudonym Ambrose Merton, proposed the term 'folk-lore' as a 'good Saxon compound to refer to what we in England designate as Popular Antiquities'. That Hardy incorporated the still modish term into his Preface to *Far from the Madding Crowd* (1874) reveals the extent to which contemporary peasant customs, hitherto belittled as the worthless wreckage shunned by a supposedly enlightened society, had become an object of acute antiquarian curiosity – indeed a residuum key to the recovery and classification of archaic British political institutions.

The 'instincts of merry England' (*RN*: VI.1), enshrined in the pastimes of children, riddles, gambling games, nurses' fables and the arts of divination, were known to Hardy first of all as experienced folk-traditions, not simply as objects of detached scrutiny for collectors of ancient and medieval antiquities. He grew up in a region that still preserved the agricultural and ecclesiastical calendars, making it ideal, according to John Symonds Udal, for the preservation of practices of immemorial provenance. Udal, who corresponded frequently with Hardy concerning local customs, remarked in his 1892 essay 'Witchcraft in Dorset' that 'there is no part of England … more prone to belief in the supernatural … than the West; and, of the western counties, none more so than Dorset'.[2] Hardy's paternal grandmother Mary Hardy, who lived with the family until her death in 1857, regaled the young Thomas and his siblings with vivid stories of yearly maypole festivities, village dances and forgotten ballads. The poem 'One We Knew' evokes Mary as a woman for whom 'Past things retold were to her as things existent', dwelling 'on such dead themes, not as one who remembers, / But rather as one who sees' (*CP*: 275).

Thomas Hardy drew on personal memory to render those conceptions and fancies of primitive superstition that had been varnished over by Christianity but scarcely hidden by it: for instance, bonfire-lighting in *The Return of the Native*, consulting the weather-prophet in *The Mayor of Casterbridge*, the Midsummer sowing of hemp-seed in *The Woodlanders*, and club-walking in *Tess of the d'Urbervilles*. From the outset of his career Hardy grasped the signal role feasting played in both the secular and religious life of human assemblies: bringing people together and helping produce the changes which take place within them. William Hone's *Every-Day Book and Table Book*[3] treated the sheep-shearing feast as a ritual which offered rare insight into a hoard of intellectual and cultural oddities – that 'fast-perishing lumber of superstitions, folk-lore, dialect and orally transmitted ballads'– gathered together in such arcane volumes as Joan Durbeyfield's *Compleat Fortune-Teller* (*Tess*: 3).

Hardy extended his first-hand knowledge of folklore, as well as its role in the recovery of the origin of social institutions, from conversation with his early mentor, the philologist and poet William Barnes (1801–86). Barnes was, in Hardy's view, 'probably the most interesting link between present and past forms of rural life that England possessed […] a complete repertory of forgotten manners, words, and sentiments, a store which he afterwards turned to such good use in his writings on ancient British and Anglo-Saxon speech, customs, and folklore'.[4] In 1863, the Philological Society published Barnes's first edition of *A Grammar and Glossary of the Dorset Dialect*, with, as the subtitle declared, *The History and Outspreadings and Bearings of the South-Western English*.

Whereas Barnes habitually saw the newest views of life intruding with predatory pervasiveness on the ordered serenity of his poetic terrain, Hardy reacted as an enlightened cosmopolite: paradoxically perhaps, the latest ideas were to him often the soundest. Through the *Glossary*, Barnes indulged both his scholarly exactitude and his less scientific relish in casually amassing words and phrases contributed by readers of the *Dorset County Chronicle*. It was this combination of serious-minded enquiry and dilettante dabbling that resonated with Hardy, as evinced by his letter to the Dorset antiquarian Rev. Charles Bingham in September 1877, requesting archives of local newspapers from the early part of the nineteenth century as part of initial research for his Napoleonic romance, *The Trumpet-Major* (*CL* I: 51).

Hardy's experiences as a member of the Dorset Natural History and Antiquarian Field Club, which he joined in 1881, as well as his frequent visits to Rushmore, the estate of General Augustus Lane Pitt-Rivers, founder of the Museum of Archaeology at Oxford University, encouraged him to regard folklore fragments such as ballads, folk medicines, love potions and fairy lore as precious though misconstrued 'documents': faded and worn by time, yet a means by which primitive humankind's philosophical system might be salvaged. Hardy's recollections of the more eccentric habits of local societies influenced his droll depiction of 'the South-Wessex Field and Antiquarian Club' in *A Group of Noble Dames* (1891). In *The Hand of Ethelberta*, when his heroine joins members of the 'Imperial Association' for a visit to Corvesgate Castle (Corfe), he remarks on the pursuits which characterized antiquarian fieldwork as a popular pastime for the country parson or gentleman of leisure (*HE*: 31).

Hardy's deep familiarity with the ancient beliefs enshrined in the annual round of calendar customs, along with the imaginative tactic of amassing residual relics from various periods which is such a unique and deep-rooted facet of his art, also drew its authority from the spirit of haphazard data gathering epitomized by John Brand (1744–1806). Brand's *Observations on the Popular Antiquities of Great Britain* was a vital resource for the founding fathers of British anthropology Edward Burnett Tylor (1832–1917) in

*Primitive Culture* (1871) and James George Frazer (1854–1941) in the multivolume *Golden Bough* (1890). Frazer was, in Margaret Hodgen's opinion, 'a collector of popular and primitive antiquities in the tradition of Brand'.[5] *Popular Antiquities* became for Hardy and other erudite, nonacademic Victorians 'an automatic reference' on 'antique custom and odd superstition'.[6] Brand's attempt to translate the complex codes underlying communal events would enable Frazer to attain detailed knowledge about submerged social attitudes. Sigmund Freud, whose *Totem and Taboo* (1914) owes an immense debt to Frazer's discussion of sacrifice as a totemic communion sacrament, stressed how a feast was rooted in archaic ideas of the importance of eating and drinking as a group.

One of Hardy's favourite books was John Hutchins's *The History and Antiquities of the County of Dorset*, referred to impishly as 'the excellent county history' in *The Trumpet-Major* (*TM*: 6). A copy of the third edition (4 vols., London, 1861–73) was in Hardy's Max Gate library. Like Brand, Hutchins construed the 'County of Dorset' as a key focus for folkloric investigation: 'the advantages of its situation, fertility of its soil, rare productions, the many remains of antiquity with which it abounds ... well deserves an Historian.'[7] Hardy offers versions of this local 'Historian' in his fiction, poetry and journalistic writings. Indeed, a measure of Hutchins's dizzying eclecticism – deliberately derailing any scholarly endeavour to pinpoint a straightforward 'scientific theory' in it – imbues Hardy's correspondence with the folklorist and mythologist Andrew Lang, as well as his speech to the Dorset Antiquarian Society concerning the 'Romano-British Relics' unearthed while digging the foundations of his home Max Gate (*THPV*: 61–4).

Hutchins and Brand, though they lacked Tylor and Frazer's magisterial breadth of vision, argued with limpid clarity that many customs of the calendar year derived from 'the times of Paganism' whose 'annual festivals were celebrated in honour and memory of their gods, goddesses and heroes, when the people resorted together at their temples and tombs'.[8] It was partly owing to Brand's indefatigable industry that the nineteenth century registered with increasing formality that folklore and the anthropological myths to which it related exposed as much of the remote past as the dolmens, hillforts and tumuli dotting the distant uplands around Hardy's birthplace. To that extent Hutchins and Brand functioned as signal links between amateur antiquarianism, archaeology and the autonomous, comprehensive 'science' of anthropology embodied by Tylor, Frazer and the 'Cambridge Ritualists' in the early twentieth century.

Hardy's preoccupation with folklore, myth and communal narrative history undoubtedly received a vital stimulus from Tylor's two-volume *Primitive Culture*, published the same year as *Under the Greenwood Tree* in 1871, and now judged by Robert Ackerman and George W. Stocking as a 'founding document in modern British anthropology'.[9] Tylor contended that all societies passed through a unilinear, three-stage cultural development of savagery, barbarism and civilization. From this he concluded that vestiges of primitive belief and custom, which he termed 'survivals', illuminated a clear and definite evolutionary connection between the untutored rural masses of modern Europe and ancient tribes: 'Look at the modern European peasant using his hatchet and his hoe, see his food boiling or roasting over the log-fire ... hear his tale of the ghost in the nearest haunted house ... If we choose out in this way things which have altered little in a long course of centuries, we may draw a picture where there shall be scarce a hand's breadth difference between an English ploughman and a negro of Central Africa.'[10]

Tylor contested that probing the provincial lore of the village community, a 'now unfamiliar social institution', was no 'profitless task', and he gave superstitions a documentary significance already attributed to the shattered urns and petrified organic remains uncovered by excavators in the fossil-rich soil of Dorset, Wiltshire and Cornwall.[11] Tylor's work crucially informed Hardy's lifelong concern with regional attachment and especially the patriarchal family as the means of calibrating the locus of authority, the tracing of descent and the provenance of civil society. Tylor's querying of the patriarchal clan as the enduring and fixed foundation of advanced culture – extended by John F. McLennan's *Primitive Marriage* (1876) and Lewis Henry Morgan's *Ancient Society* (1877) – dominates the fiction and sociology of the nineteenth century and after.

Middlebrow magazines and periodicals such as *The Gentleman's Magazine*, *Saturday Review*, *Cornhill* and *Blackwood's Magazine* reflected this intensified interest by offering more discussion of 'survivals'. Tylor posited that the findings of anthropology would enable the 'great modern nations to understand themselves, to weigh in a just balance their own merits and defects, and even in some measure to forecast ... the possibilities of the future'.[12] There is compelling evidence in the *Literary Notes* and the *Life* that Hardy monitored with avid curiosity these learned and lively debates over the emergent science of anthropology in the 1870s and 1880s. He may have extracted a great deal of information from an 1885–86 discussion in the pages of *The Nineteenth Century* journal between Max Müller and other anthropological luminaries on mythography.[13] Moreover, Hardy's reading, for example, of John Addington Symonds's *Studies of the Greek Poets, Second Series* (1876) alone would have acquainted him with most of the recent approaches to the investigation of ancestral lore.

The publication of *Primitive Culture* prompted Hardy, along with a new generation of amateur antiquarians, to compile the folklore 'survivals' of European peasant life and to gauge their similarities with arcane tribal rites. Hardy adroitly weaves Tylor's coinage into the imaginative fabric of *The Return of the Native* when describing the mummers' play: 'A traditional pastime is to be distinguished from a mere revival in no more striking feature than in this, that while in the revival all is excitement and fervour, the survival is carried on with a stolidity and absence of stir which sets one wondering why a thing that is done so perfunctorily should be kept up at all' (*RN*: II.4). In this novel, the material expanse of the heath itself is imagined as a Tylorian survival, given its non-conformity with the existing pattern of advanced culture: 'To many persons this Egdon was a place which had slipped out of its century, generations ago, to intrude as an uncouth object into this. It was an obsolete thing, and few cared to study it' (*RN*: III.2). But Hardy's antiquarian narrator *does* study it, finding in its austere contours myriad instances of ethnographic significance. Indeed, his fiction can be read as the crowning imaginative assimilation and recreation of the 'proceedings' of the new sciences of humankind that evolved during the Victorian age.

Hardy's close friend, the rationalist propagandist and President of the Folk-Lore Society Edward Clodd, seized upon the theoretical potential of Tylor's coinage and enthused: 'The early history of man shows us how wonderful his progress has been when we compare the Age of Stone with our present happy lot.'[14] Many Victorian sages and anthropologists, Hegel, Auguste Comte and

Herbert Spencer included – all thinkers whose work Hardy carefully read – were driven by a staunch belief in progressive enlightenment and postulated historical advance as logically natural, universal and inevitable.

For the Hardy whose antiquarian imagination was inquisitive about time, Clodd's confident optimism, evident from their first meeting in 1890, was peculiarly problematic. Hardy's presentation of the rambunctious skimmity-ride from *The Mayor of Casterbridge* (1886), for instance, far from demonstrating Clodd's sense of 'our present happy lot' indicates rather the opposite: a culture locked into a history of provincial prejudice which evidences not steady progress but rather the dreary repetition of error. The skimmity-ride is an insular atavism, a lamentable fragment of a community's former brio as a highly integrated social structure. Instead of the quaint caretaker of a disappearing Dorset, we have here a diagnostician of the frailties and insecurities which beset what Charlotte Burne called in 1911 the 'non-official' culture of the 'unlettered classes'.[15] Indeed, as Arthur Mitchell reflected nearly a decade after the publication of Tylor's *Primitive Culture*, 'there is no intrinsic tendency in human societies … to pass ever on and ever up to something better and higher and nobler'.[16] In 1880, the west country antiquarian William Bottrell believed that 'the folk-lore student, in collecting the myths, the proverbs, the traditions, the customs of the peasants of many lands, is doing an important work in accumulating facts bearing on the history of mankind; not the mere records of the wars and doings of kings and generals, but of the beliefs, aspirations, thoughts and feelings of the working classes of various nations'.[17] But what if the Wessex 'working classes' uphold beliefs and rites 'more naturally belonging to barbaric culture' – to use Tylor's phrase?[18]

Hardy responded to Tylor's anthropological enterprise because it was not, in any simplistic sense, attempting to preserve 'traditional values' or 'the poetry of existence' (*RN*: I.9). Tylor's clear-sighted perception of cultural inertia reveals 'how large a share stupidity and unpractical conservatism and dogged superstition have had in preserving for us traces of the history of our race'.[19] So many vestigial relics of ancient practice are exposed as 'diseased' and morbid in Hardy's fiction, such as the sinister occult practices in 'The Withered Arm' and Susan Nunsuch's 'ghastly invention of superstition, calculated to bring powerlessness, atrophy, and annihilation on any human being against whom it was directed' (*RN*: V.7). The ailing John South's arboreal paranoia concerning his 'totem-elm' in *The Woodlanders* (1887) not only leads to his 'debilitation and death', but also becomes a perverse source of suffering for Marty South and Giles Winterborne.[20] These habits and ideas, falling beyond Tylor's category of 'fond and foolish customs,'[21] comprise the introverted articulation of a desiccated mode of life. Hardy utilizes these moments of anthropological import to probe, with a searching and sophisticated scepticism, the utility of those folklore fragments which literally and materially connect the strata of the unrecorded and forgotten past to the modern moment.

Nevertheless, the roving historical consciousness at work in Hardy's art located intellectual sustenance in Tylor's definition of modern anthropology's purpose: 'Civilization, being a process of long and complex growth, can only be thoroughly understood when studied through its entire range; that the past is continually needed to explain the present, and the whole to explain the part.'[22] Yet Tylor's sense of the need for structure was strong too: he argued vehemently that the new science of man depended upon the painstakingly rational processes of minute observation, inference, and generalization. His books and articles exhorted students of the past to eschew the patchy, piecemeal speculations of the old-fashioned folklorists by setting themselves 'to walk on the solid ground of inductive reasoning'.[23]

Yet Hardy's temperamental inclination and artistic tactic are promiscuous, rather than systematic or methodical. In the novels and poetry, he incorporates into his artistic vision both the tenacious resolve of a Tylor, and the jovial dilettantism of an amateur antiquarian such as John Hutchins. For instance, Hardy's quarrying of disparate bygone moments during the Stonehenge scene in *Tess* with a mixture of solemn intensity and playful wit epitomizes the eclectic spirit and strategy of a novel absorbed by multiple time-schemes. Indeed, the whole countryside in the Wessex Novels is symbolic of an infinitely stratified sense of place. Hardy broods over 'survivals' not as the laureate of a lost rural tradition, but as a writer obsessed by relics which are crusted with ancestral imprints and so open up vitalising possibilities for his art. The Tylorian 'survival' is essentially moribund matter, 'battered like [a] pebble' and carried along 'the stream of time'[24] into a future epoch, incongruously residing beside more modern concepts, customs and habits. The mummers' play and skimmity-ride could be construed so. But this underestimates Hardy's radical redefinition of Tylor's term, especially in poems such as 'Old Furniture' (*CP*: 485–6). He invokes the relics of time – the tangible artefacts and occasions which are the 'survivals' of history – and makes them play tantalizingly round the immediate object of his concern, so prompting his audience to extract the implications of the elaborate standpoints that result. At a personal level, Hardy's rendering of 'survivals' gratifies his own idiosyncratic sense of imaginative excitement. He locates a counterforce to his stricken sense of social and historical severance in an art that involves irony, incongruous juxtaposition and 'black' humour to promote unusual angles of vision.

When Hardy read Frazer's *The Golden Bough* in the 1890s, the most extended attempt at the time to interpret and relate folk customs to the great myths and legends of the past, he saw that 'survivals' afforded irreplaceable insight into the earliest habits of thought. Andrew Lang, whose prolific years closely paralleled those of Tylor, spoke for the majority of late Victorian anthropologists when he announced that 'we explain many peculiarities of myths as survivals from an earlier social and mental condition of humanity'.[25] Freud, an archaeologist of the mind, developed this research to show how the prehistoric impulses of the race were replicated in the unconscious layers of the individual psyche, tracing basic neurotic traits back to a common prehistory.

The questions raised by Hardy's reinflection of E. B. Tylor's anthropological doctrine are many and various. Lionel Johnson's 1894 monograph on Hardy's fiction, *The Art of Thomas Hardy*, first noted how his subject's ethnographic, philological and antiquarian interests closely paralleled contemporary 'students of anthropology'.[26] Very little was done to canvass the implications of this parallel prior to Robert Squillace's 1986 article 'Hardy's Mummers',[27] which subjected the Tylorian 'survival' in *The Return of the Native* to searching and subtle critique. Subsequent commentators have paid increasing attention to the continuing existence in Hardy's corpus of the distant past as a mythically relevant force in the present. George W. Stocking's *Victorian Anthropology* (1991) and *After Tylor* (1998) examine how the divisions proposed in cultural commentary between self and other, and between 'here' and 'there', imbue the new social sciences, as they do Hardy's own writing enterprise. Throughout his fiction, the division adumbrated between bustling metropolitan hub and rustic hinterland, and the notion of recuperating a lost collective identity are, according to Allison Adler Kroll, highly significant;[28] a persistent anthropological motif is the infiltration of a sheltered bucolic enclave from the outside. Recent studies such as Michael A. Zeitler's *Representations of Culture: Thomas Hardy's Wessex and Victorian Anthropology* (2007) demonstrate that the Tylorian 'survival' still provides a richly suggestive lens through which to calibrate Hardy's unresolved and fascinated musing on those customs, landmarks and beliefs which transmit the climate of a lost locality, communicating experiences beyond the confines of the social language.

NOTES

1 Edward W. Brabrook, 'Memorial Address', *Folk-Lore* 12 (1901), p. 98.

2 J. S. Udal, 'Witchcraft in Dorset', *Proceedings of the Dorset Natural History and Antiquarian Field Club*, 13 (1892), pp. 35, 38.

3 William Hone, *The Every-Day Book and Table Book or, Everlasting Calendar of Popular Amusements, Sports, Pastimes, Ceremonies, Manners, Customs, and Events*, 3 vols. (London: T. Tegg & Son, 1835), pp. 559–61.

4 'The Rev. William Barnes, B.D.' (*THPV*: 66–7).

5 Margaret T. Hodgen, *The Doctrine of Survivals: A Chapter in the History of Scientific Method in the Study of Man* (London: Allenson, 1936), p. 116.

6 Richard M. Dorson, *The British Folklorists: A History* (London: Routledge & Kegan Paul, 1968), p. 17.

7 John Hutchins, *The History and Antiquities of Dorset (interspersed with some remarkable particulars of natural history; and adorned with a correct map of the country, and view of antiquities, seats of the nobility and gentry)*, 3rd edition, corrected by William Shipp and James Whitworth Hodson, 4 vols. (Westminster: John Bowyer Nichols & Sons, 1861), I:vii.

8 John Brand, *Observations on the Popular Antiquities of Great Britain: chiefly illustrating the Origin of our Vulgar and Provincial Customs, Ceremonies, and Superstitions*, revised with introduction by Sir Henry Ellis, 3 vols. (1848–49; republished New York: AMS Press, 1970), II:1–2.

9 Robert Ackerman, *J. G. Frazer: His Life and Work* (Cambridge: Cambridge University Press, 1987), p. 77.

10 E. B. Tylor, *Primitive Culture: Researches into the Development of Mythology, Philosophy, Religion, Art and Custom*, 4th edition, 2 vols. (London: John Murray, 1903), I:6.

11 E. B. Tylor, 'Maine's Village Communities', *Quarterly Review* 131 (1871), p. 176.

12 Quoted in Henrika Kuklick, *The Savage Within: The Social History of British Anthropology, 1885–1945* (Cambridge: Cambridge University Press, 1991), p. 7.

13 Hardy's *Literary Notebooks* show that he encountered Müller's work in the 1870s (*LN* I: 19, 59); see Michael Millgate, 'Hardy's Fiction: Some Comments on the Present State of Criticism', *English Literature in Transition* 14 (1971), pp. 230–38.

14 Edward Clodd, *The Childhood of the World. A Simple Account of Man in Early Times* (London: Macmillan, 1873), p. 50.

15 Charlotte Sophie Burne, 'The Essential Unity of Folk-lore', *Folk-Lore* 22 (1911), pp. 16, 20–21.

16 Arthur Mitchell, *The Past in the Present. What is Civilization?* (New York: Harper & Brothers, 1881), pp. 228.

17 William Bottrell, *Traditions and Hearthside Stories: Third Series* (Penzance, 1880; privately published), p. iii.

18 Tylor, *Primitive Culture*, II:449.

19 Tylor, *Primitive Culture*, I:150.

20 Kevin Z. Moore, *The Descent of the Imagination: Post-Romantic Culture in the Later Novels of Thomas Hardy* (New York: New York University Press, 1990), pp. 118ff.

21 Tylor, *Primitive Culture*, I:94.

22 E. B. Tylor, *Researches into the Early History of Mankind and the Development of Civilization* (London: John Murray, 1865), p. 2.

23 E. B. Tylor, 'William von Humboldt', *Quarterly Review* 124 (1868), p. 524.

24 Tylor, *Primitive Culture*, I:271.

25 Andrew Lang, 'Myths and Mythologists', *Nineteenth Century* 19 (1886), p. 59.

26 Lionel Johnson, 'Wessex' (Chapter III of *The Art of Thomas Hardy*), reprinted in *Thomas Hardy: Critical Assessments, Volume III*, ed. Graham Clarke (London: Helm, 1993), pp. 387–88.

27 Robert Squillace, 'Hardy's Mummers', *Nineteenth Century Literature* 41 (1986), pp. 172–89.

28 Allison Adler Kroll, 'Hardy's Wessex, Heritage Culture, and the Archaeology of Rural England', *Nineteenth-Century Contexts* 31:4 (2009), pp. 335–52.

# Archaeology

REBECCA WELSHMAN

... swift hands, on strings nigh overhead,
Began to melodize a waltz by Strauss:
It stirred me as I stood, in Caesar's house,
Raised the old routs Imperial lyres had led,

And blended pulsing life with lives long done,
Till Time seemed fiction, Past and Present one.[1]

The reconstructive potential of archaeology and its capacity to bridge the present and the past appealed to Hardy, who had grown up close by what was once the Roman capital of the southwest, Durnovaria. In Dorset, as in towns and cities around the world, archaeological discoveries began to assume new importance in the late Victorian era as archaeology developed as a discipline of its own. Lecturing on 'The Development of Archaeology in the Nineteenth Century' in February 1900, Reverend Professor Mahaffy, Knight Grand Cross of the Order of the British Empire and Provost of Trinity College Dublin, remarked that 'in no science had success been more marked than in archaeology'.[2] Transcending the domain of the amateur antiquary, archaeology had become what the archaeologist and ethnologist Sir Daniel Wilson termed in 1851 'an indispensable link in the circle of the sciences'.[3] In light of its broad appeal to enthusiasts, thinkers, and artists alike, archaeology became one of the most popular topics in the periodical press during the 1870s, leading to the launch in 1880 of the *Antiquary: A Magazine devoted to the Study of the Past.*

In the last decades of the nineteenth century, archaeology was a generic term for the study of the past, including a wide range of activities such as bell-rubbings, the study of classical and Latin texts, and genealogy. The nineteenth century brought about developments in all areas of archaeological practice and thought – Classical, Biblical, mediaeval, and prehistoric – inviting exploration of its intersection with geology, history and anthropology. Whereas many sites in Britain remained unexcavated and inaccurately dated during the early part of Hardy's career, more were uncovered by the beginning of the twentieth century. The public interest roused by the mid nineteenth century excavations of lost cities abroad, such as Nineveh and Troy, contributed to the British desire to explore the origins of what was then considered the race of the ancient Britons, through the burial sites which remained. Destruction of the archaeological record, and the unregulated excavation and plundering of sites in Wessex, resulted in many objects becoming lost. Hardy's concern for this lack of regulation is clearly expressed in his short story 'A Tryst at an Ancient Earthwork',[4] which describes the exploits of a local archaeologist, believed to be the Dorset antiquary Edward Cunnington, who pocketed archaeological finds rather than donating them to the Dorset County Museum. It was only during the last two decades of the nineteenth century, through the work of Hardy's friend General Augustus Fox Pitt-Rivers (1827–1900), that the practice of planned excavation with the aim of answering specific questions began to be more widely adopted.[5]

It was to be the science of prehistory, emerging in the 1860s, that increased the scientific credibility of archaeology. Sir Daniel Wilson, archaeologist, ethnologist, and author, formally introduced the term 'prehistoric' into the English language in *The Prehistoric Annals of Scotland*, published in 1851.[6] In 1859, the year of Darwin's *Origin of Species*, a series of articles in the periodical press represented increasing public fascination with the debates on the prehistoric origin of mankind. The French antiquary, Boucher de Perthes (1788–1868), was initially discredited for claiming that human remains found in Abbeville among those of mammoths and other extinct animals strongly suggested that mankind had existed contemporaneously with these species. It was not until William Pengelly's excavation in 1858–9 of a further site at Brixham in Devon, now recognised as part of the Jurassic Coast,[7] that de Perthes's hypothesis was taken seriously.[8]

The mystery and ambiguity of prehistory motivated the late Victorian urge to identify and as far as possible reconstruct a picture of how previous cultures lived and died. For Hardy, whose work was deeply grounded in a landscape shaped by prehistoric earthworks and tumuli as well as Roman remains, archaeology provided a rich imaginative and physical context for his novels, short stories and poetry. Less alienating than considering human life in the context of geological or astronomical time, the new dimension to human history afforded by archaeology encouraged an imaginative reassessment of the relationship between humans and the landscape.

In 1878 an article in the *Academy* observed the untiring interest in 'the so popular ... science of prehistoric archaeology' at the Paris Exhibition, which included flint weapons 'from almost every part of the world'.[9] In *The Return of the Native*, published the same year, Hardy uses the phrase 'prehistoric times',[10] the title of Sir John Lubbock's landmark *Pre-Historic Times as Illustrated by Ancient Remains,* first published in 1865 and one of the most influential archaeological text books of the century.[11] Hardy writes:

To recline on a stump of thorn in the central valley of Egdon, between afternoon and night, as now, where the eye could reach nothing of the world outside the summits and shoulders of heathland which filled the whole circumference of its glance, and to know that everything around and underneath had been from prehistoric times as unaltered as the stars overhead, gave ballast to the mind adrift on change, and harassed by the irrepressible New. (*RN*: I.1)

In this passage the unchanging nature of the heath gives weight to the mind 'adrift on change'. Late-nineteenth-century archaeology was disturbing ground – on a practical and imaginative level – at an unprecedented rate, altering landscapes which had been unchanged for thousands of years. Hardy's concern about the impact of late Victorian industrial and agricultural change on his locality extended to an interview printed in *The Daily Chronicle* in 1899, defending the need to protect Stonehenge from being sold (*THPV*: 153–5).

Michael Millgate notes how Hardy's interest in local archaeology developed alongside other local interests during the 1880s when Max Gate was built.[12] In laying the foundations for the house, significant discoveries were made of Romano-British human remains and grave goods, which formed the subject of a paper Hardy gave to a meeting of the Dorset Natural History and Antiquarian Field Club on 13 May 1884.[13] Hardy's name and address appear in the membership lists for the club from 1882 to 1892. His interest in the archaeology of his local area fostered friendships and acquaintances with H. J. Moule, curator of Dorset County Museum, and Edward Benjamin Cunnington,[14] whose excavations of prehistoric Wiltshire, together with his wife Maud, rediscovered the Neolithic site on Overton Hill called The Sanctuary, not seen since the work of William Stukeley in the eighteenth century.

A still more significant friendship, and one that also contributed to Hardy's developing interest in archaeology, was with his neighbour, the poet and antiquarian William Barnes. When the Hardys were staying in Shire-Hall Place in Dorchester in 1883, waiting for the construction of Max Gate to be completed, Hardy records visiting Barnes with his friend Edmund Gosse. It is likely that they would have discussed the remains found at Max Gate with Barnes, who had led the Archaeological Institute excursion to Maiden Castle during the first week of August 1865,[15] and was a member of the Somerset Archaeological Society and the London Archaeological Institute.

Hardy's interest in the archaeology of the local area encouraged a more personalised vision of the past in his work. In *The Mayor of Casterbridge,* published in 1886, Maumbury Rings – a Neolithic henge[16] used as an amphitheatre during Roman times – functions as a significant feature of the landscape, much as it had done for centuries. A place of reunion for the estranged Henchard and his wife Susan, the enclosed tract of land is heavily reminiscent of a violent human past – specifically the execution of the young Mary Channing in the seventeenth century – and in keeping with the themes of trial and retribution throughout the novel.[17]

The discovery of archaeological phenomena in the nineteenth century often occurred through expansion of towns and cities, the laying of roads and railways, and during agricultural work, such as ploughing or digging for chalk. It was particularly significant for Hardy, writing in rural Wessex, that chance archaeological discovery could lead to new understanding and appreciation of the landscape. This element of chance and surprise he worked into his novels through his use of archaeological sites as settings. In *Far from the Madding Crowd*, for example, chance plays a significant part in shaping the fortunes of Troy and his estranged wife,

Bathsheba Everdene, when Troy appears as the masked actor at the fair held at the Iron Age fortification, Woodbury Hill.

The unprecedented rate of archaeological discovery during the late nineteenth century, and the sudden insights it afforded into how past cultures lived, worshipped and died, caused a reassessment of the relationship between nineteenth century and earlier societies, imbuing the process of excavation itself with new imaginative potential. Hardy's affinity with archaeology was part of a wider late-nineteenth-century ambition to understand more deeply the significance of the past. The discovery of buried objects in a particular context and the accompanying process of imaginative reconstruction seemed to shorten time, connecting the present to the past with sudden and illuminating consequences. Hardy records his own experience of the wafting 'fan of time'[18] at Maiden Castle in 'A Tryst at an Ancient Earthwork' (1885), in which he imagines Roman activity at the site lingering in the form of inarticulate 'airborne vibrations'. He refers to Maiden Castle as an animate feature of the landscape withholding a past that is still very much alive and that 'looms out of the shade by degrees, like a thing waking up and asking what I want there'.[19] Late-nineteenth-century admiration and reverence for Roman society was particularly encouraged in Wessex, where the Roman occupation of Dorchester was known through the presence of Christian burials, Romano-Celtic temples, forts, and the use of Maumbury Ring as a Roman amphitheatre. In the poem 'The Roman Gravemounds' Hardy refers to Rome as 'vast … in the world's regard, / Vast it looms there still' (*CP*: 397). In both the short story and the poem the idea of a past that 'looms' denotes a human history that waits to be fully understood; one that is at once immanent and threatening, more so because the archaeology of the time had not yet developed reliable dating techniques for objects and remains, thus hampering clear interpretation. As expressed in an article for the magazine *Once a Week,* relics of the past were deemed to speak a 'language' to which antiquaries had no 'sure key'.[20] As a result the true significance of past events for the contemporary psyche remained unrealised, as is implied in Hardy's description of a Roman burial in *The Mayor of Casterbridge* as 'a chicken in its shell' (*MC*: 11).[21]

For Hardy, archaeology afforded a point of reconciliation between the individual human life and the natural world – all the more significant in light of the increasing estrangement from landscape encouraged by the industrial revolution. Frank Giordano notes that the first appearance of Eustacia Vye in *The Return of the Native* on one of the Rainbarrows of Egdon Heath immediately associates her with 'pre-Christian paganism'. Away from her contemporary community, in the death-world of prehistoric ancestors, Eustacia embodies an otherworldliness that is achieved through her engagement with her native landscape. The Rainbarrow, more than just a feature of the landscape, is a phenomenological point of contact between mankind and the natural world; an embodiment of past human cares and desires carried through time to impact upon the modern mind in new and unpredictable ways. Giordano argues that the land itself, 'so nearly resembling the torpor of death', causes Eustacia to seem 'alien in a world inimical to her temperament'.[22] Hardy suggests that Eustacia is one of the last upholders of what he terms in *The Well-Beloved* the 'last local stronghold of the Pagan divinities' of south Dorset (*WB*: I.2), referring to her as 'a sort of last man among them, musing for a moment before dropping into eternal night with the rest of his race' (*RN*: I.2) The transformative potential of archaeology to illumine previous ways of life – to shed light on ordinary objects that emerged through excavation from 'eternal night' to assume new significance in modern times – is an idea that Hardy explores in *A Pair of Blue Eyes* (1873). In the novel the dishonesty of Henry Knight's fiancée, Elfride Swancourt, is brought to light by his chance excavation of her earring, which 'shine[s] weakly' in the sun from its place in a rocky crevice (*PBE*: 31). The irreversible implications of this discovery cause her gradual demise, suggesting that the location and recovery of a relatively mundane object has potential to transform fundamental human perceptions about the relationship between the material and the emotional world.

The phenomenon of the small object of study holding greater significance occurred widely in scientific developments of the late nineteenth century; not just in biology with the development of more sophisticated microscopes, but in palaeontology and archaeology too. Whereas larger grave goods such as urns, bronze metalwork, and weapons were often collected by more unscrupulous archaeologists as trophies, excavations by archaeologists such as Wake Smart in the 1870s were part of a newly emerging consciousness of the significance of small remains, the interpretation of which had potentially greater implications for the understanding of human progress. Fragments of bone, pollen grains, tools, and beads informed archaeologists about the sophistication of past societies, including trade links with Europe, methods of subsistence, and religious practices. For example, the collection of shale beads found by William Greenwell during his excavations at the Aldbourne Four Barrows in the late 1880s was recognised as having been procured and manufactured on the Dorset coast at a much earlier date. Aldbourne formed part of a chain of archaeological sites along the Ridgeway to Stonehenge, the scene of the finale in *Tess in the d'Urbervilles*, and is known best for its Bronze Age finds, including incense cups, a dagger, and a gold plaque. As late-nineteenth-century archaeologists worked with the developing understanding that the small could hold greater consequences for understanding human activity within a landscape, so Hardy wrote with recognition of the importance of the most minute details of the material world – and the significance of that scale in understanding the human condition.

Hardy's firsthand experience of the significance of small remains was developed through witnessing excavations where objects, once removed from the place of discovery, assumed new value when considered in the wider context of knowledge of the human past. Such insights added valuable dimensions not only to human thought and history but to phenomenological understandings of place itself. In an article written for *The Times* on excavations taking place at Maumbury Ring in 1908, Hardy records that 'the blood of us onlookers ran cold' when prehistoric finds, including chipped flints and horns were recovered, casting sudden doubt over the idea of Roman occupation. 'The obvious explanation,' Hardy reassures the nonspecialist, 'seems to be that here, as elsewhere, the colonists, to save labour, shaped and adapted to their own use some earthworks already on the spot.'[23] The article goes on to list the phases of human history that the site has withstood, noting the 'congregational masses' that have gathered there over centuries for different reasons. The strong interpretative capacity of this article, which a report in the *Antiquary* magazine termed 'non-archaeological',[24] would today have a rightful place in landscape archaeology, a subject in its own right that was not recognised as such until the

1950s.[25] Hardy's concern that these excavations confirmed the Roman use of the site as a gladiatorial arena suggests that his own understanding of that spot – as explored and expressed through the writing of *The Mayor of Casterbridge* – was informed by archaeology. The article suggests a sense of security in the knowledge of the origin of Maumbury Ring – a security reinforced by the years during which Hardy had regularly walked past the spot, and which in a moment during excavation suddenly became threatened by the throwing up of prehistoric implements. It was through experiencing archaeology in a landscape, rather than simply reading about it, that the ambiguity of archaeological discovery and the fascinating potential to suddenly turn perceived facts on their head were to be fully appreciated.

Yet consonant with the potential of archaeology were negative implications for the disturbance and removal of material remains. Although barrows held a sepulchral charm that contributed to the popularisation of archaeology, superstition still very much surrounded the removal of burial treasures from the tomb or body. The opening line of Hardy's poem 'The Clasped Skeletons' – 'Oh why did we uncover to view / So closely clasped a pair?' (*CP*: 873) – suggests his concern for the intrusive nature of excavation. The 'bedded' couple amongst the 'chalky bedclothes' of the Wessex downs suggest close affinity between the remnants of human life and the earth itself, akin to the description of the weathered Rainbarrows in *The Return of the Native*. These burial mounds, which bear 'the very finger-touches of the last geological change', suggest only a faint degree of separation between the ancient mound created by human hands and the surrounding landscape, crafted by the slow methodical hand of time – a gradually formed relationship between the natural and human worlds, which can be suddenly and irretrievably displaced by the action of a 'pickaxe, plough, or spade' (*RN*: I.1).

Hardy experienced archaeology as a practical and imaginative exploration into the complexities of the relationship between the individual, living in the present, and the long history of human life upon an ancient earth. It afforded insight into the nature of past activity within a setting and imbued that place with a magic and meaning that transcended ordinary time. As he observed the 'finger touches of the last ice age' to have gently shaped the contours of Egdon Heath, he recognised archaeology to have awakened the slumbering human past, endowing the present with new imaginative consequences. The 'strange spell' of the past that touches the mind with a 'yet living hand' (*AL*: III.4) suggests that archaeology for Hardy, perhaps even more than other sciences, had the potential to strengthen the position of the self in the world, rather than alienate, connecting the individual psyche to the grand human past and the more nebulous cosmic future.

### NOTES

1 'Rome: On the Palatine (April 1887)' (*CP*: 102–3).
2 Quoted from a summary of the lecture in *Freeman's Journal and Daily Commercial Advertiser,* 17 February 1900.
3 Sir Daniel Wilson, *The Archaeology and Prehistoric Annals of Scotland* (Edinburgh: Sutherland and Knox, 1851), p. xii.
4 First published in the *Detroit Post* in 1885, but not printed in England until 1893.
5 R. H. Cunnington, *From Antiquary to Archaeologist,* ed. James Dyer (Buckinghamshire: Shire Publications, 1975), p. xvi.
6 The earliest use cited in the *OED* (hyphenated, as 'pre-history') is from the *Foreign Quarterly Review* in 1832.
7 For Hardy and the Jurassic Coast, see Rebecca Welshman and Patrick Tolfree, *Thomas Hardy and the Jurassic Coast* (Creeds: Bridport, 2010).
8 See 'Alpha', 'Man among the Mammoths', *Once a Week* 1:1 (July 1859), p. 3. For the debates on the antiquity of man, see A. Bowdoin Van Riper, *Men Among the Mammoths: Victorian Science and the Discovery of Human Prehistory* (Chicago: Chicago University Press, 1993).
9 'Anthropology', *Academy,* 329 (August 1878), p. 200.
10 The term 'prehistoric' is used in both *Two on a Tower* (1882), e.g., chapter 8, and *Tess of the d'Urbervilles* (1891), chapter 55.
11 Lubbock became 1st Baron Avebury in 1900, commemorating the largest Stone Age site in Europe. He also invented the terms 'Paleolithic' and 'Neolithic'. He was one of the first archaeologists to provide an anthropological context for discoveries by comparing tribal nineteenth-century cultures and prehistoric ancestors. Later editions of *Pre-Historic Times* dispensed with the hyphen.
12 Michael Millgate, *Thomas Hardy: A Biography Revisited* (Oxford: Oxford University Press, 2004), p. 238.
13 It was later reprinted in the club's proceedings in 1890, with a note referring to its omission in those of 1884 (*THPV*: 61–4).

14 Usually known as Benjamin, for sixty years the honorary curator of Devizes Museum, and not to be confused with the Dorset antiquary Edward Cunnington (a relative) whose integrity Hardy called into question in 'A Tryst'. He and his wife Maud (for whom, see *DNB*) excavated The Sanctuary in 1930.

15 *The Gentlemen's Magazine*, 1865, p. 331.

16 Originally a term for monuments akin to the stone circle at Stonehenge; later, more generally, a monument enclosing an area by means of a bank and internal ditch.

17 For the function of Maumbury Rings in the novel see Andrew Radford, 'Excavating an Empire of Dust in *The Mayor of Casterbridge*', *Thomas Hardy Journal* 25 (2008), pp. 57–8.

18 In *A Pair of Blue Eyes* Hardy refers to Knight's experience of imagining back through the ages as opening 'the fan of time' (*PBE*: 22).

19 *A Changed Man and Other Tales*, p. 173.

20 Richard King, 'Folk-lore of Barrows', *Once a Week*, 1:25 (June 1866), p. 693.

21 Hardy first used this phrase in his paper to the Dorset Natural History and Antiquarian Field Club in 1884, in which he remarked that the bodies were 'fitted with ... perfect accuracy into the oval hole ... strongly suggestive of the chicken in the egg shell' ('Some Romano-British Relics Found at Max Gate, Dorchester': *THPV*: 62).

22 Frank R. Giordano, *I'd Have My Life Unbe: Thomas Hardy's Self-Destructive Characters* (Alabama: University of Alabama Press, 1984), p. 58.

23 'Maumbury Ring', *THPV*: 284–90; this quotation, p. 285.

24 An article in the *Antiquary* acknowledges Hardy's article ('Notes of the Month', *Antiquary* 44 [January–December 1908], p. 402), wryly commenting that Hardy's reference to the director of the project, Mr St George Gray, underplays the technicality and responsibility that such supervision entails.

25 In *Interpreting the Landscape: Landscape Archaeology and Local History* (London: Routledge, 1997), Michael Ashton recognises that much of what is visible in the landscape today is the result of a chain of social and natural processes.

# The Victorian Philological Contexts of Hardy's Poetry

DENNIS TAYLOR

The first readers of Hardy's poetry quickly observed that there was something anomalous about much of his language. William Archer, in an influential comment on Hardy's first volume of poetry, *Wessex Poems*, said:

There are times when Mr. Hardy seems to lose all sense of local and historical perspective in language, seeing all the words in the dictionary on one plane, so to speak, and regarding them all as equally available and appropriate for any and every literary response.[1]

A reviewer in 1927 began to discern contextual reasons for Hardy's vocabulary but remained troubled: 'It is a difficult pleasure which the ear can take, if it can take any, in such locutions as *noonshine, mindsight, scareless, bloomage, wormwood-worded, foredame, phasmal,* however skillfully they may be fitted in their context; the somewhat problematical charm of freshness which they achieve seems hardly to compensate for their summary buffeting of one's established expectations.'[2] This theme continued after Hardy's death, typified in F. R. Leavis's comment in the Hardy centennial issue of the *Southern Review*: 'There is something extremely personal about the gauche unshrinking mismarriages – group-mismarriages – of his diction, in which, with naïf aplomb, he takes as they come the romantic-poetical, the prosaic banal, the stilted literary, the colloquial, the archaistic, the erudite, the technical, the dialect word, the brand-new Hardy coinage.'[3] But in order to appreciate Hardy's 'local and historical perspective in language', we need to understand his historical contexts, including developments in the field of philology, and in the idea of a standard language.

Victorian philology was rooted in an age deeply immersed in history, in the writing of history, and in the belief in history as the key to understanding the present. This distinctive Victorian historicism was clearly represented in its philology, which connected with other historical and comparative disciplines, from geology to anthropology, where we see a 'number of formations superimposed upon one another, each of which is, for the most part, an assemblage of fragments and results of the preceding condition'.[4] Words, like men and women, had their ancestors, wrote Richard Trench: 'If we would know what they now are, we must know what they have been ... the date and place of their birth, the successive stages of their subsequent history, the company which they have kept, all the road which they have travelled, and what has brought them to the point at which now we find them; we must know, in short, their antecedents.'[5] It was in the 1860s, the decade when Hardy began his literary career, that a new philology became widely publicized, mainly through the influence of Max Müller's *Lectures on the Science of Language* at the Royal Institution in 1861 and 1863. The new sense of history helped turn the old philology into the 'new philology', attentive to the actualities of history and to careful comparison of known languages and sound changes. Where the old philology had assumed that it could recover the ultimate sources of language, namely the Adamic language, the primal significant sounds, the new philologists increasingly put aside the question of ultimate origins as hopeless of resolution. They focused instead on known records and reconstructed the history of language as it could be realistically recovered. An 1862 review of Müller's *Lectures* proclaimed in its first sentence: 'The Ptolemaean theory of the universe was not more completely set aside by the system of Copernicus, than all previous conceptions of grammar and speech by the new-born science of language.'[6]

The development of dictionaries in the late nineteenth century reflected this new science, as the naïve etymologizing of Horne Tooke (1736–1812) was discarded, and a new dictionary on historical grounds was envisioned. In 1859 the Philological Society issued its *Proposal for the Publication of a New English Dictionary*. Readers from all over the world began contributing slips that would later help fill the 'blocks of pigeon-holes' in the famous Scriptorium constructed by James Murray after he became editor of what was now to be known as the *Oxford English Dictionary* in 1879, with the first fascicle (*A – Ant*) appearing in 1884. The magnitude of the work was an inspiration to contemporary writers, who were inspired and intimidated by it. Hardy and Hopkins are perhaps the two Victorian authors most conspicuously influenced, though studies of the relation of other writers to the *OED* have also proven illuminating. Hopkins was led by the *OED* and related philological works to seek out an Anglo-Saxon substrate for poetic language. He thus retained a longing to find the original sources of language, at least of English.

Hardy's reaction was very different. One of his favourite analogies for his language was that of an ancient building often rebuilt. It was but a step from the architectural analogy to a geological and thence to a mental analogy. 'It is no wonder, then,' Hardy read in Leslie Stephen, 'if the belief, even of cultivated minds, is often a heterogeneous mixture of elements representing various stages of thought; whilst in different social strata we may find specimens of opinions derived from every age of mankind.'[7] One more analogy was philological: in *On the Study of Words* (1851), Trench said that language 'is the amber in which a thousand precious thoughts have been safely embedded and preserved. […] Here too are strata and deposits, not of gravel and chalk, sandstone and limestone, but of Celtic, Latin, Saxon, Danish, Norman, and then again Latin and French words.'[8] The ancients had been aware of the changing language: Horace had recommended poets to 'Command old words that long have slept, to wake.'[9] But the new philology gave a whole new reach and dimension to this insight. One explanation of the anomalies of Hardy's language is that he attempted to reflect the historicity of the *OED*, through the interaction of his words drawn from multiple historical moments, and from multiple classes. The effect, to present English as a complex historical collage, was 'seeing all words on one plane': not a synchronic plane, but an historical plane.

But the same science that opened new doors closed others. Contemporary geologists and naturalists had opened up huge expanses of history and prehistory. These were not only religiously troubling discoveries but intellectually puzzling, since knowledge itself now seemed subject to sources that it could not know. Complementing this perplexity was the Victorian interest in the proto-Whorfian notion that language conditions thought, given a weak form by William Whitney, a stronger one by Max Müller.

Intermediate between them was John Addington Symonds, writing at the turn of the century: 'Language does not create thought,' he argued. 'On the contrary, thought demands language for its utterance':

But language once created, the words which have been launched on their career, pregnant with antecedent thoughts, react upon the minds of those who use them [...] the stuff to be expressed, cannot be disentangled from its verbal vehicle.[10]

The new philology, along with such notions, reinforced the Victorian theme that old language may trap us in ideas that have become obsolete. In *An Essay on The Origin of Language* (1860), Frederic Farrar wrote: 'our words become the tyrants of our convictions, and our phrases "often repeated, ossify the very organs of intelligence" ... a mistaken theory embalmed in a widely-received word has retarded for centuries the progress of knowledge.'[11]

Hardy's use of diction thus reflects both the history of words and their obscure origins. His language conjures up an ancient and variegated history whose sources are lost. The universe seems to say to him, in 'The Masked Face':

> 'O vassal-wight,
> There once complained a goosequill pen
> To the scribe of the Infinite
> Of the words it had to write
> Because they were past its ken.' (*CP*: 522)

In another poem, 'In a Former Resort after Many Years', the speaker describes his mind as

> scored with necrologic scrawls,
> Where feeble voices rise, once full-defined,
> From underground in curious calls[.] (*CP*: 702)

In 'The Masked Face,' the meanings of the old curious words are 'past its ken' in two senses: outside of comprehension, and temporally past. As language proliferates, the knowledge of our origins is endlessly deferred. Deferring, 'différance', has been one of the most influential insights of deconstructive criticism. The important distinction is that Hardy focuses on differentiation as an historical process moving away from sources that are real but largely irrecoverable. He roots his larger sense of loss and irrecoverability in this linguistic process.

Hardy's linguistic oddities, both in diction and phrasing, often assault the idiomatic structures of the standard language, and do so in a way that seems consciously antistandard. Of course, many literary writers denormalize the language, but we need the Victorian contexts to understand the distinctive nature of Hardy's technique. He showed in his novels and in many poems that he could master the standard language if he wanted to: indeed, his earliest known poem, 'Domicilium,' is in an accomplished Wordsworthian idiom (by Hardy's time naturalized as part of the standard language). Hardy defended 'provincialism' against Arnold, and also defended dialect which he saw, as in the case of William Barnes, as a legitimate form of language. But while he wrote a few poems in dialect, and was an important source of the first written transcriptions of many words recorded in the *English Dialect Dictionary*, he himself mostly avoided dialect, because he was in search of a deeper dimension underlying the standard language and its presumptions. The poem which he put at the head of his first volume, *Wessex Poems*, and of his *Collected Poems*, was not his earliest, 'Domicilium', but 'The Temporary the All', undated but probably a poem of the 1860s, that represented his new style:

> Change and chancefulness in my flowering youthtime,
> Set me sun by sun near to one unchosen;
> Wrought us fellowlike, and despite divergence,
>     Fused us in friendship. (*CP*: 7)

The theme and language of this poem are remarkably cooperative: The idea of a chance meeting become a firm fellowship is compared to a random coinage become an entrenched idiom. In such a poem, Hardy creates a poetic idiom that seems a permanent challenge to the hegemonic standard. 'I have no sympathy,' he told William Archer, 'with the criticism which would treat English as dead language – a thing crystallized at an arbitrarily selected stage of its existence, and bidden to forget that it has a past and deny that it has a future.'[12] Thus Hardy challenges not just the decorums of a given genre but the decorums of the language itself.

Literary writers exist at a frontier where language is in flux; some of their innovations become standard, some remain non-standard.

To assess the nature of their linguistic creativity, and its influence, we need a knowledge of the existent language as the poet changes it. Here the dictionary becomes an important tool for literary estimation. With the help of the *OED*, we can characterize Hardy's and other writers' contribution to the state of the language: the ways they influence its development, the dead ends into which they are led, the experiments that eventually prove or do not prove normative. We can profile the characteristics of their vocabulary. Of course, some literary works like *Finnegans Wake* remain more or less permanently counterstandard; but the existence of the standard language, so exhaustively recorded in the *OED*, remains a valuable gauge of what is counter to the standard. Other sources help define the reigning standard: grammars, usage guides, rhetorics, specialized dictionaries, histories, theories of language, encyclopedias, and the like, but much of this is filtered into a good dictionary.

But a question remains: is the dictionary a good record of the standard language? A persistent modern critique is that the dictionary reflects less the state of the language than the biases of its lexicographers and the quirks of its readers, who may neglect whole areas of literature (in the case of the first *OED* – *OED*1 – these included much of the eighteenth century and women's literature). Nevertheless, the increased coverage and accuracy of the new *OED* (*OED*3) has corrected many of these biases, leaving it a good measure of the nature of a poet's vocabulary. Thus Charlotte Brewer: 'To date, the revision of *OED* significantly illuminates the vocabulary of Auden, Joyce and no doubt hundreds of other poets and writers whose works it quotes: not least, this is a result of the lexicographers casting their nets far wider, over nonliterary as well as literary texts, than was ever possible for (or thought proper by) their predecessors.'[13]

The Hardy profiles analysed in *Hardy's Literary Language*, drawn from *OED*1, show that he used a highly labelled diction (obsolete, archaic, rare, etc.) and that he was 'a leader in using unique words, one of the last in using first words, and low to moderate on the scale for using revivals'. There have been very few changes so far in label status in *OED*3, so in the absence of further revisions the conclusion stands that 'Hardy's first words were not picked up and used by later writers but remained unique words', contrary to the influence that other writers may have on the language.[14] What this confirms is that Hardy's language was deliberately anomalous, consciously challenging the standard language, and has remained a challenge over the years.

Critical justification of Hardy's style began with the notion that his roughened language represented a revolution against what Edmund Gosse called 'the glittering femininity of the "jewelled line"': 'It is writing that should help to give backbone to a literature which certainly errs on the side of flabbiness.'[15] But Hardy's literary language cannot be fully and satisfactorily explained by local *explications de texte*. As the 1927 reviewer cited earlier put it, however skillfully Hardy's words are deployed, 'the somewhat problematical charm of freshness' is not enough in itself to 'compensate for their summary buffeting of one's established expectations'. More than the intrinsic context is needed.

Hardy's language persistently exhibits a pervasive historic dimension as well as an intrinsic aesthetic function. For example, in 'The Pedigree', the speaker studies his genealogical family tree, and then turns to look in the mirror:

> And then did I divine
> That every heave and coil and move I made
> Within my brain, and in my mood and speech,
>     Was in the glass portrayed
> As long forestalled by their so making it;
> The first of them, the primest fuglemen of my line,
> Being fogged in far antiqueness past surmise and reason's reach.
>
> (*CP*: 460)

The language is characteristic of Hardy's verse. There is the jarring of mentalist 'divine' and physicalist 'brain'; the string 'heave and coil and move', lacking idiomatic collocation; the self-distorting awkwardness of 'made / Within my brain'; the artificiality and near solecism of 'their so making it'; the archaism of 'fugleman' and 'antiqueness'; the slightly anomalous combination of 'surmise and reason'. Aesthetically the choice of language beautifully embodies the sense of the poet's enclosure in a web of language that acts both as vehicle, and limiter, of perception. Hardy is trapped in a synchronic system whose artifice is evident in the violation of collocation. But on a more historical plane, he is also controlled by ancient words whose origins he cannot know. His self-understanding is thus forestalled and deferred by the shifting of signifiers on both synchronic and diachronic planes. The personal experience recapitulates the historical reality. Hardy challenges not only the norms of a given genre or register but also the norms of the standard language in a more fundamental sense.

The modern transition from Victorian diachronism to modernist synchronism has made it difficult to read Hardy adequately. A practical consequence of the new synchronism was a dismissal of the importance of etymology and emphasis on the 'etymological fallacy'. The synchronically inclined philologist William Whitney proclaimed: 'our knowledge or our ignorance of their etymology do not determine our use and understanding of the terms.'[16] To this kind of critique, Trench in turn would reply: 'But while it is quite true that words may often ride very slackly at anchor on their etymologies, may be borne hither and thither by the shifting tides and currents of usage, yet are they for the most part still holden by them [...] The etymology of a word exercises an unconscious influence upon its usages.'[17] This comment opens up a *mise en abyme* where an etymon is unconscious of its later derivations, and later words unconscious of their etymons, as language goes its own way irrespective of conscious control. As George Marsh put it in 1860: 'the origin of language is shrouded in the same impenetrable mystery that conceals the secrets of our primary mental and physical being.'[18] But these are the secrets that the Victorians were inexorably driven to seek, and which still impel the modern dictionary reader who wants to know where words come from.

The dispute between the synchronist and the historicist was well represented in the late Victorian age by the arguments between William Whitney and Max Müller. The fact is that both points of view are needed. We use language as a system of meaning without fully knowing the sources of our words; yet we also retain a diachronic sense that continues to influence usage. Saussure knew this, and distinguished the two axes of language, both needed for its study. His defense of the synchronic dimension was needed against the heavy hand of some historicists, a defense earlier made by Whitney (credited by Saussure for recognising the arbitrary nature of linguistic signs) and embodied in the work of Alexander Ellis and Henry Sweet.[19] But misuse of Saussure caused a kind of simplistic synchronism that annulled history, a synchronism motivated perhaps by the fact that that the ultimate sources of history could not be found. The Victorians, however, did not abandon the endless search, but held to their qualified epistemology. Purist synchronism gave up the search, and transformed its open-endedness into a synchronic textuality that is never stable. In this new context, Hardy's language has remained a puzzle. Hardy is a fascinating figure because he shares fully in the scepticism of our own period, and yet remains very much the high Victorian quester, in transition from the loss of one absolute but still in search of another that eludes him. He is Arnold's transition figure, 'Wandering between two worlds, one dead, / The other powerless to be born.'[20] We are discovering that there are things to be said for that transitional place.

Hardy's literary career, from the mid 1860s to 1928, embraced the period in which historical philology was eventually overshadowed by the new synchronic linguistics. So the historical context for understanding Hardy's language was lost. Whitney's point of view became dominant in the synchronic era, but in fact the two points of view overlap – and this is what Hardy embodies. Whether language began as pure conventionalism with no organic relation to reality, or as organic symbols soon conventionalized, conventions become fixed and institutionalized, and their relation to the signified becomes cemented and potentially obsolete under changing conditions. Thus Wittgenstein spoke of the 'bewitchment of our intelligence by means of language'.[21]

We cannot argue with the need for two different languages, of synchrony and diachrony; when talking of language as a current system, we cannot at the same time be talking of it as an historical product.[22] But the two kinds of discussion represent two dimensions which in fact intersect; and this is the intersection Hardy seeks to expose. Like the wave and particle theory of quantum mechanics, both synchronic and historical understandings are necessary if the reality is to be perceived. History awakes the present system from its spell, while the present system keeps revising history. There is a constant temptation for standard language and understanding to lapse either into systematic or into historical sleep. In the collision between the present and the past of language, a new consciousness occurs. It is this spark of consciousness that Hardy seeks in the artifices of his phrasing and the heterogeneities of his diction.

NOTES

1 Archer, *Daily Chronicle* (21 December 1898). The present chapter is partly a retrospect and assessment of Dennis Taylor, *Hardy's Literary Language and Victorian Philology* (Oxford: Clarendon Press, 1993; corrected edition, 1998).

2 *The Dial*, June 1927, p. 525.

3 F. R. Leavis, 'Hardy the Poet', in *The Critic as Anti-Philosopher: Essays and Papers*, ed. G. Singh (Athens: University of Georgia Press, 1983), p. 99; reprinted from the *Southern Review* 6 (1940–1), pp. 85–98.

4 William Whewell, *History of the Inductive Sciences* (1840), cited in Hans Aarsleff, *The Study of Language in England 1780–1860* (Minneapolis: University of Minneapolis Press, 1983), p. 207.

5 Richard Trench, *English, Past and Present*, 7th edition (London: Macmillan & Co., 1870), p. 276.

6 *Edinburgh Review* 115 (June 1862), p. 67.

7 Leslie Stephen, *History of English Thought in the Eighteenth Century*, 2 vols. (London: Smith, Elder & Co, 1876), I:5.

8 Richard Trench, *On the Study of Words*, 4th edition (London: John W. Parker and Son, 1853), pp. 23, 62.

9 Alexander Pope, 'Second Epistle of the Second Book of Horace', I:167; *Poems of Alexander Pope*, ed. John Butt (London: Methuen, 1963), p. 654.

10 John Addington Symonds, *Essays Speculative and Suggestive* 3rd edition. (London: John Murray, 1907), p. 190.

11 Frederic Farrar, *An Essay on The Origin of Language* (London: John Murray, 1860), pp. 114–15.

12 William Archer, *Real Conversations* (London: Heinemann, 1904), pp. 29–50 (*IR*: 71).

13 Charlotte Brewer, 'The Use of Literary Quotations in the *Oxford English Dictionary*', *Review of English Studies* 61 (2010), p. 125.

14 Taylor, *Hardy's Literary Language*, pp. 126–7.

15 Edmund Gosse, 'Mr Hardy's Lyrical Poems', *Edinburgh Review* 229 (April 1918), p. 274; [Anon] 'Mr Hardy's Book of Verse', *Athenaeum* 3716 (14 January 1899), p. 42.

16 William Whitney, *Language and the Study of Language* (New York, 1867), pp. 128–9.

17 Trench, *On the Study of Words*, pp. 164–5.

18 George Perkins Marsh, *Lectures on the English Language* (New York: Charles Scribner, 1860), p. 38.

19 For discussion, see Taylor, *Hardy's Literary Language*, pp. 370–1.

20 'Stanzas from the Grande Chartreuse' (1855), II:85–6; *The Poems of Matthew Arnold*, ed. Miriam Allott (London: Longman, 1979), p. 305.

21 Ludwig Wittgenstein, *Philosophical Investigations*, trans. G. E. M. Anscombe (Oxford: Blackwell, 1972), §109.

22 Roman Jakobson argued against the radical divorce of synchronic and diachronic linguistic analysis, since each synchronic state of the language retains elements of earlier ones. (*Selected Writings*, 8 vols. (The Hague: Mouton, 1971–87), I:502.

# Physics, Geology, Astronomy

## ADELENE BUCKLAND

On 23 March 1875 Thomas Hardy arrived by invitation at the Kensington home of Leslie Stephen, editor of the prestigious *Cornhill Magazine* which had recently published *Far from the Madding Crowd*. Cambridge-educated, a respected man of letters, Stephen represented everything the novelist aspired to become, and as his editor he held the key to his future success. Hardy 'found him alone, wandering up and down his library in slippers; his tall thin figure wrapt in a heath-coloured dressing-gown.' Hardy's task was to bear witness to Stephen's renunciation of holy orders, an increasing inevitability since he had stopped attending chapel in 1862. 'The deed ... executed with due formality,' Hardy remembered, 'our conversation then turned upon theologies decayed and defunct, the origin of things, the constitution of matter, the unreality of time, and kindred subjects. He told me that he had "wasted" much time on systems of religion and metaphysics, and that the new theory of vortex rings had "a staggering fascination" for him' (*LW*: 108–9).

These topics were not unrelated. The theory of vortex rings, widely discussed on the pages of periodicals and at dinner parties and clubs, was 'staggering' to Stephen precisely for its new insights into 'the constitution of matter' and 'the origin of things'. Following earlier work by Hermann von Helmholtz, the properties of vortex rings had been demonstrated by Peter Guthrie Tait at the University of Edinburgh in 1867 in a visual experiment comprising two boxes each expelling rings of smoke at different angles. These fluid rings, when moving through a perfect or frictionless fluid, were immune to destruction, retaining their integrity even if forced into contact, glancing off and going into violent vibration if propelled toward each other at oblique angles. In such a fluid they could not under any circumstances be cut, altered or destroyed. For one audience member, William Thomson, later Lord Kelvin, the phenomenon possessed tantalising affinities with the properties considered essential to the structure of atoms: permanence, elasticity, and the power to act on one another in a shared medium. In his paper 'On Vortex Atoms' in 1867 Thomson argued against the prevailing Lucretian view of the atom as solid particles in empty, featureless space to claim instead that atoms were rotating vortex rings.[1] These rings were only permanent in a perfect fluid, the 'ether', which Thomson, like many of his contemporaries, proposed permeated all space. There was no material difference between the ether and the vortex ring. The only difference was the motion of the rings themselves. And since they could be neither created nor destroyed in the ether, a supernatural act of creative power must have set them into motion. The 'staggering fascination' of the vortex rings lay both in their capacity to explain the constitution of the universe and in the mysteriousness of the creative act that had brought them into existence.

It is precisely this kind of cosmological speculation that is often thought to define Hardy's engagement with the astronomical, geological and physical sciences. Citing a passage Hardy copied into his notebook, that 'To look on our own time from the point of view of history, on history from the view of geological periods, on geology from the point of view of astronomy – this is to enfranchise thought' (*LN* I: 162), critics have emphasised his use of geological and astronomical proportions to shift temporal and spatial perspective in his writing, dramatising the triviality of humanity in a boundless, uncaring universe.[2] While this cosmological perspective could be intellectually exciting, it was also horrifying: the astronomer Swithin St. Cleeve in *Two on a Tower* (1882) reveals to his lover the terrible formlessness of the universe through his telescope; in *A Pair of Blue Eyes* (1872) Henry Knight is confronted by the insignificance of humanity in geological time as he clings for life to a denuding cliff face. The image is one of Romantic individualism: Hardy and his heroes stand alone on emotional precipices gazing at the stars or into the depths of time, terrified and energised by its immensity.

Cosmology was indeed an important dimension of scientific thought in the nineteenth century. In two papers delivered before the Royal Society in 1811 and 1814, William Herschel, famous for his discovery of Uranus, argued that the universe had begun as swirling dust, gradually contracting into nebulae, which finally resolved into stars and planets.[3] By 1844 this 'nebular hypothesis' was vehemently debated across the culture, in pamphlets, novels and at dinner parties, following the anonymous publication of a literary sensation, *Vestiges of the Natural History of Creation*, which gave dramatic form to the nebular hypothesis by extending its story of the evolution of the universe to explain life on earth: new forms, from stars to species, constantly evolved from old in ever-more complex configuration.[4] Astronomy could explain the workings of the entire universe from the furthest star to the tiniest creature. At the same time, astronomers like the Herschels produced catalogues of comets and double stars and the Royal Observatory at Greenwich mapped the heavens for timekeeping and navigation. Astronomy was 'queen of the sciences'.[5]

In 1844 no geologist in Britain publicly contemplated the notion that the fossil record revealed an evolving pattern of life on earth, and few agreed with it even in private. Many reacted against *Vestiges* both for its evolutionary speculations and for its cosmological narrative form. Geologists had spent three decades attempting to build a science of 'geology' from the wreckage of cosmological 'theories of the earth' popular in the eighteenth century. Such theories were thought by many both to have contributed to the materialism of the French revolution, and to have brought science into disrepute, as the proponents of rival theories publicly ridiculed one another and destroyed one another's reputations. The Geological Society of London, founded in 1807, was one sign of the emergence of 'geology' as a distinctive science forged from a rejection of these competing theories the earth, and by the more sober pursuits of mineralogy and physical geography.[6] The new science would be defined by its rhetoric of strict induction, with gentleman practitioners claiming to forego cosmology and commit themselves to direct observation of nature, classifying the strata and mapping them across the globe, just as the stars had been mapped across the skies.

Though cosmology was officially pushed into the future of the science, which could only hope to tell the story of the earth once all this inductive work had been done, astronomical and physical cosmologies nonetheless continued to inform geological speculation. Much work on mapping and unravelling the strata was tacitly underpinned by theories of heat proposed by Joseph Fourier in the 1820s, who speculated that planets were formed as fiery molten fluids which cooled over the course of ages to a life-sustaining equilibrium. Fossil evidence and the character of the rocks seemed to suggest, likewise, that the oldest strata represented the beginning of earth history (being apparently devoid of life and once molten) and that there had been a progressive sequence of more complex life forms occupying an increasingly habitable earth. This was not evolution, for most geologists agreed that species were fixed, and often identified particular species as characteristic of the geological epochs in which they lived.

For one of the most important geologists of the period, Charles Lyell, this progressive sequence was still too cosmological. In his *Principles of Geology* (1830–3) he argued that the beginning of the rock record was not the beginning of earth history, because the oldest rocks must have been destroyed. Evidence for the earliest periods of the earth simply did not exist. And the fossil record was so badly mutilated that it was impossible to reconstruct the overall pattern or direction of geological change.[7] Instead, geologists should only speculate on the ancient past by reasoning from those geological processes that were acting in the present. Acting over a long enough span of time, even a stream had the power to carve out a valley; the combined action of volcanoes, floods, and a host of other commonplace geological agents could explain everything that had ever happened, or would happen, on the earth. Though he could not account for how new species might be introduced in such a system, Lyell rejected evolutionary theory until 1867. For him, beginnings and endings, or teleology, lay outside the domain of scientific reasoning. In turn, he was accused of purveying a new cosmology in disguise: why should earth processes not have once have been more intense than they now are? For many of his contemporaries, Lyell had not escaped the cosmological determination to explain everything by a single, simple law.[8]

Thomson, of vortex ring fame, offered a different view of earth history from Lyell. In the 1850s and 1860s, just as Hardy moved to London, Thomson, Tait, and others attempted to turn studies of the physical basis of the universe from an existing focus on forces and particles to a new property called 'energy', stored in the ether and travelling through it in waves at the speed of light.[9] Many proponents of 'energy' taught at Scottish universities and worked in northern industrial cities, and they sought an *applied* science that could help make more efficient steam engines. The science of thermodynamics emerged from this work as an explanation of the conservation and dissipation of the new 'energy' during mechanical work. Just as vortex rings suggested a beginning for the universe, the second law of thermodynamics, articulated by Thomson in 1851, proposed that in anything but a perfect machine (which could not exist) energy would be lost when converted into useful work. 'Entropy', energy unavailable for useful work, was perpetually increasing in a universe that was slowly winding down to its death.[10]

It is easy to demonstrate Hardy's interest in all these ideas, though it is harder to judge the precise nature of his engagement with them. His notebooks reveal a lifetime of reading frequently encompassing astronomical, geological and physical questions, but which, as notes are apt to do, reveal as many contradictions as answers. There is a lengthy entry copied from a periodical essay on the 'luxuriant' vegetation of the Carboniferous period, for instance, in which there was a 'high temperature of the globe' and, correspondingly, 'none of the higher animals: no birds rested on the branches of the trees: no mammal in the forests. The air was sultry & full of vapour, the soil hot & steaming: & the stillness was profound' (*LN* I: 89–90). This verbal recreation of an ancient world radically different from the cooler, more complex present endorses Fourier's cooling globe and geological progression. But we find elsewhere quotations such as that from the *Daily Chronicle* on Ernst Haeckel's argument that such 'anthropism' and 'teleology' should be discarded from scientific thought, for man, the apex of any progressive scheme of creation, 'sinks to the level of a placental mammal, which has no more value for the universe at large than the ant, the fly of a summer's day, the microscopic infusorium, or the smallest bacillus' (*LN* II: 99). (Both the *Daily Chronicle* and Hardy add that the human capacity for morality is an exception to this rule.) And while astronomy threatens to overwhelm Hardy, as he wonders that our knowledge of it 'has not dwarfed & crushed ambition' (*LN* I: 104), elsewhere we find astronomical irreverence: 'Uranus's circuit = 84 years', he notes, paraphrasing the popular astronomical writings of Richard Proctor, '[so that a man of three-score & ten w$^{d.}$ be only 10 months there – or a man at the ripe old age of 84 w$^{d.}$ be just 1 year old in Uranus]' (*LN* I: 16). The notes reveal emotional and stylistic responses to the shifts in scale suggested by cosmological patterns, responses reflected in 'At a Lunar Eclipse' (*CP*: 116), or 'The Comet at Yell'ham' (*CP*: 151). Competing cosmologies sit side by side, and Hardy's contribution to them is often as wry as appalled.

But all this merely encourages us to keep rooting Hardy to the earth, gazing at the heavens. Notebooks, with their emphasis on grand ideas, obscure the fact that Hardy was an active member of a society for whom 'science' was never a monolithic entity. Both the notions that the earth was ancient, stretching back beyond human life and into infinity, and that the universe was boundless, were as old (at least in written form) as Aristotle. What was new in the nineteenth century was the sense that science could be a potential mode of cultural self-advancement. Vortex rings are not the most important aspect of Hardy's conversation with Stephen on that evening in 1875. Stephen's library, his Kensington address, and his heath-coloured dressing gown have as much to do with Hardy's contemplation of 'the origin of things' as atomic theory. They were not only engaging in debate about the nature of the universe, but signifying their shared membership in an educated body of men, the kinds of men who attended lecture series in the metropolis, who read periodical essays in which those lectures were summarised or excerpted and who picked up and read the scientific tomes on the bookshelves of their literary clubs.

'Science' was thus a constituent element in the most prestigious quarters of the literary culture of the day, and it was also embedded in a wide range of social spaces and practices. The sciences considered here took place at different times throughout Hardy's life in large-scale observatories, government surveys, laboratories, museums, gardens, universities, periodicals, theatres, lecture halls, galleries, at dinner parties, learned and local societies and Mechanics' Institutes, and they encompassed a wide variety of methods, values, aims, and practices.[11] As Hardy and Stephen discussed vortex rings, for example, they may have tested the theory, as Thomson asked his lecture audiences to do, by dragging a teaspoon over the surface of a cup of tea and watching two vortex rings swirl around its edges, dying out as they came into contact with air and the end of the fluid that sustained them. Such a test was an image by which Thomson could make physics democratic: the 'energy' pulsing in waves through the 'ether' was the same energy driving the new, powerful steam engines, and could be tested in that most ubiquitous of English drinks, the cup of tea. The experiment claimed the universe of 'energy' physics as the property and product of industrialism, not of the Anglican clergymen and anti-Anglican metropolitan gentlemen who also appropriate 'science' for their own, and attempted to determine its values, methods, and results according to their own agendas.

This interest in science as a means of cultural gain – and of social competition for ownership of it – is central to Hardy's writing. While researching *Two on a Tower*, in which he sends his hero on one of the real-life expeditions to record the Transits of Venus in 1874 and 1882, Hardy visited the Royal Observatory at Greenwich. In his letter of application, he claimed to have 'written astronomical passages which are quoted both in England and America', presumably referring to his descriptions of Gabriel Oak's knowledge of the stars in *Far from the Madding Crowd*. When asked to 'State the name of any gentleman of either the Scientific Societies of London, or who has repute in Science to whom you are known', Hardy entered the anatomist 'Professor Huxley', politician and poet 'Lord Houghton' and 'Mr Tennyson' (*CL* I: 96). As the sciences sought to define themselves, and to gain the popularity and authority that was essential to their survival, it was not disingenuous for Hardy to consider himself a scientific man on the basis of 'astronomical passages' written in fiction, or to cite his acquaintance with Tennyson, frequently lauded as a champion of the sciences, as a scientific qualification. He may have been selling himself a little eagerly, but he expected to be taken seriously as a man of science *because* he was a man of letters. Science was part of the intellectual property he had worked so hard to acquire.

Later in life Hardy read and took notes on some of the many books and popular articles discussing the work of Albert Einstein.[12] Einstein's theories contradicted common-sense notions of the universe even more profoundly than the wave theories of light and energy of the nineteenth century. The first postulate of Einstein's 'special' theory of relativity was that motion is relative: two people sitting on a train appear stationary to one another because both move with the same relative motion. The second was that the speed of light is constant in a vacuum, meaning that the speed of light is the absolute physical boundary for motion: it is the only speed at which a moving body would *appear* to move at the same speed relative to *any* observer, whatever his or her own speed or position. From this Einstein deduced that objects travelling near the speed of light would slow and shorten in length from the point of view of an observer on earth, that clocks moving near the speed of light operate more slowly than stationary clocks, and that things appearing to happen at the same time to one observer may appear to happen at different times to another. Time was relative, and it operated on a continuum with space as a fourth dimension. As Hardy wrote in his notebooks, 'The dynamic universe with time outside is replaced by a static world with time inside. Events do not happen, they are just there & we come across them in the voyage of life'; there is 'no absolute physical reality which can be contemplated in entire detachment from the position of the contemplator', and 'a three-dimensional solid' is 'a mere slice of something four-dimensional' in space-time. 'An indiv$^l$ as he grows from childh$^d$ to old age makes up such a four-dim$^l$ figure; what we see of him at any time is just the 3-dim$^l$ figure sect$^n$ correspon$^g$ to that time' (*LN* II: 228–9). Here again is Hardy's preoccupation with scale, style, and idiosyncratic narrative patterns, preoccupations he shared with men of science and which gave his work so much of its intellectual vitality.

But Einstein also irritated Hardy. 'I have lately been getting out of patience, if not with philosophers, with men of science', he wrote to a friend in 1919. 'Really after what he [Einstein] says the universe seems to be getting too comic for words.' Einstein was a riddle to understand, thinking 'queerly of time & space', despite the fact that his ideas also chimed agreeably with Hardy's long-held notion that '*motion* is merely relative' (*CL* V: 353). Three years later Hardy refused to write a preface to a work called *Living Nature* for, while he 'might have had the temerity to try [his] hand on it 20 or 30 years ago … it is rather beyond my energies nowadays, & anyhow somewhat outside my compass, for I know really nothing about Nature scientifically'. Perhaps 'some English Einstein' would do better (*CL* VI: 173). This grumpy retort tells us less that science had gone beyond public understanding, than that Hardy was an elderly and busy man trying to get out of a project that did not interest him (*Living Nature* never made it to press). Einstein's ideas were widely reported on through the 1920s, and men like Hardy could still, as his invitation to write for this scientific book suggests, contribute to the debate. At other times he was keen to do so: In his 'Apology' to *Late Lyrics*, he presented himself as a man 'concerned to keep poetry alive' as an instrument of cultural improvement, bringing rational science into creative and fertile dialogue with human feeling and faith, to the benefit of both. Einstein was for Hardy a black comedian of the universe, but the new physics continued to energise his belief in a poetic vocation.

Physics, geology, and astronomy were the glories of nineteenth-century science. But they were part of a culture continually grappling with the best methods by which the universe could be seen, known, and understood. Hardy and the other scientific men and women of his day interrogated the complexities of the scale and style of the universe, the narrative patterns that would best describe its workings, and the best language through which to describe and classify it – questions that preoccupied writers and thinkers of all kinds, and which always carried political and social assumptions about who could be entrusted to see the world accurately, and by what means. As he attempted to become a respected man of letters, the sciences were a key component of the language Hardy would have to learn, and they made him happy, grumpy, nostalgic, gloomy, and excited by turns. And this active, interrogative engagement with the sciences is a more vital feature of Hardy's work than any certainties they may have promised about the farthest reaches of the universe or the deepest depths of time.

NOTES

1 William Thomson, 'On Vortex Atoms', *Philosophical Magazine* 34 (1867), pp. 14–16.
2 See Pamela Gossin, *Thomas Hardy's Novel Universe: Astronomy, Cosmology and Gender in the Post-Darwinian World* (Burlington: Ashgate, 2007); Anna Henchman, 'Hardy's Stargazers and the Astronomy of Other Minds', *Victorian Studies* 51:1 (Autumn 2008), pp. 37–64; Gillian Beer, 'The Death of the Sun: Victorian Solar Physics and Solar Myth', *The Sun is God: Painting, Literature,*

*and Mythology in the Nineteenth Century*, ed. J. B. Bullen (Oxford: Clarendon Press, 1989); Andrew Radford, *Thomas Hardy and the Survivals of Time* (Aldershot and Burlington: Ashgate, 2003).

3  See Simon Schaffer, 'Uranus and the Establishment of Herschel's Astronomy', *Journal for the History of Astronomy* 12 (1981), pp. 11–26; Simon Schaffer, 'Herschel in Bedlam: Natural History and Stellar Astronomy', *British Journal for the History of Science* 13 (1980), pp. 211–39; Simon Schaffer, 'The Nebular Hypothesis and the Science of Progress', *History, Humanity and Evolution: Essays for John C. Greene*, ed. James R. Moore (Cambridge: Cambridge University Press, 1989), pp. 131–64.

4  [Robert Chambers], *Vestiges of the Natural History of Creation* (London: Churchill, 1844). This paragraph paraphrases James A. Secord's *Victorian Sensation: The Extraordinary Publication, Reception and Authorship of Vestiges of the Natural History of Creation* (Chicago: University of Chicago Press, 2000).

5  See Michael J. Crowe, *The Extraterrestrial Life Debate 1750–1900: the Idea of a Plurality of Worlds* (Cambridge: Cambridge University Press, 1986).

6  See Martin Rudwick, *Bursting the Limits of Time: The Reconstruction of Geohistory in the Age of Revolution* (Chicago: University of Chicago Press), for the emergence of 'geology' as a distinctive science. For counterpoint, see Rachel Laudan, *From Mineralogy to Geology: the Foundations of a Science, 1650–1830* (Chicago: University of Chicago Press, 1987).

7  Charles Lyell, *Principles of Geology*, 3 vols. (London: Murray, 1830–3).

8  See, for instance, Martin Rudwick, *Worlds Before Adam: The Reconstruction of Geohistory in the Age of Reform* (Chicago: University of Chicago Press, 2008).

9  See Crosbie Smith and M. Norton Wise, *Energy and Empire: A Biographical Study of Lord Kelvin* (Cambridge: Cambridge University Press, 1989). On energy physics, see Crosbie Smith, *The Science of Energy: A Cultural History of Energy Physics in Victorian Britain* (London: Athlone Press, 1998).

10  See Stephen Brush, *The Temperature of History: Phases of Science and Culture in the Nineteenth Century* (New York: Franklin, 1978).

11  See Bernard Lightman, *Victorian Popularizers of Science: Designing Nature for New Audiences* (Chicago: University of Chicago Press, 2007) and Peter J. Bowler, *Science for All: The Popularization of*

*Science in Twentieth-Century Britain* (Chicago: University of Chicago Press, 2009).

12  See David C. Cassidy, *Einstein and Our World* (Chicago: University of Chicago Press, 2004), and Richard Staley, *Einstein's Generation: the Origins of the Relativity Revolution* (Chicago: University of Chicago Press, 2008).

23

# Culture

MARY RIMMER

The primary current meaning of 'culture' – 'Refinement of mind, taste, and manners; artistic and intellectual development. Hence: the arts and other manifestations of human intellectual achievement regarded collectively'[1] – is a relatively recent one. The older senses of the word – 'the action or practice of cultivating the soil' and 'the cultivating or rearing of a plant or crop' – dominated until the late eighteenth century.[2] The agricultural meaning remains embedded in the current one, which stems in part from the long-standing habit of using 'culture' metaphorically for 'the cultivation or development of the mind'.[3] That metaphor remained a living one well into the nineteenth century, doubtless because so many people still had some connection with agriculture, but as the current sense emerged 'culture' gradually severed itself from agriculture.

The new meaning gained ground in the early nineteenth century, in part influenced by German. *Kultur*, itself a new term, was being used by German ethnographers and others to refer to national and ethnic cultures in ways that approximated to 'intellectual achievement regarded collectively', and translators reached for 'culture' as an English equivalent.[4] Using Google Books to follow the word's evolution, one finds 'culture' in something like its current sense appearing most often in German translations, periodical articles, and American works in the earlier nineteenth century.[5] The shift seems to have happened more rapidly in the United States than in Britain: the *OED* cites Ralph Waldo Emerson's journal (1837) as an early use.[6]

In his seminal works *Culture and Society* (1958) and *Keywords* (1976), Raymond Williams tracks 'culture' over several centuries, arguing that its nineteenth-century shift in meaning reflected the transformation that industrial capitalism produced in everything from workplaces to literature. By the 1860s, a crucial decade for the redefinition of 'culture', the concept had become for many writers a way of resisting perceived 'mechanical' tendencies in mid-Victorian society.[7] Matthew Arnold, for instance, in *Culture and Anarchy* (1869), defined culture as a 'harmonious expansion of those gifts of thought and feeling which make the peculiar dignity, wealth and happiness of human nature'.[8] *Culture and Anarchy* was widely influential, and yet also resisted: Williams suggests that 'the common English hostility to the word' began as a response to Arnold's 'priggish intonation' of it.[9] Arnold sees culture as aiming to shape minds, 'to draw ever nearer to a sense of what is indeed beautiful, graceful, and becoming, and to get the raw person to like that'.[10] Despite references to 'fresh and free thought',[11] he leaves little room for debate over what makes something beautiful, graceful or becoming. As W. A. Knight pointed out in a review of *Culture and Anarchy*, 'respect for your pupils ... [is] a condition of successful teaching', and Arnold did not show much of it.[12]

When Arnold took up 'culture' in the 1860s, it had not only been changing its meaning for decades, but was also a controversial term, embedded in, among other things, the debates leading up to the Reform Bill of 1867, one of the largest single extensions of the franchise in British history. Arnold begins *Culture and Anarchy* by quoting an 1866 Parliamentary speech by Radical MP John Bright, who was opposing educational qualifications for voting: 'People who talk about what they call *culture!* ... by which they mean a smattering of the two dead languages of Greek and Latin.'[13] Hansard's version of Bright's words reveals the electoral connection that Arnold elides: 'Those literary gentlemen ... who are all for what they call culture because they happen to have a smattering of two dead languages, talk of culture and say the great body of working men of this country should be permanently excluded from the franchise.'[14] The proposed educational qualification was defeated, but the issue of the franchise continued to spark arguments about culture, class and education, even after the 1867 Reform Bill passed. Robert Lowe's speech deploring its imminent passage was frequently quoted in the aftermath of 1867: 'I believe it will be absolutely necessary that you should prevail on our future masters to learn their letters' (usually rendered as 'we must educate our masters').[15] 'Culture' appears frequently in comments about the limitations of the newly enfranchised; as one writer put it in 1868, if some new voters might 'compete with any class of the community for virtue, intelligence, and even a rough kind of culture', these were 'vastly in the minority'.[16]

Discussions of curricular reform in middle- and upper-class boys' schools also involved debates about culture.[17] T. H. Huxley repeatedly challenged the notion that culture meant knowledge of 'one particular form of literature, namely, that of Greek and Roman antiquity', and argued for science as an indispensable element of modern culture, and hence of curricula.[18] Knight's review links 'culture' specifically to these debates, praising a 'many-sided education' as opposed to a 'partial and utilitarian' one, and noting that both 'the advocates of scientific culture' and 'the partisans of classical study' proposed 'partial' curricula.[19] The place of religion in curricula and culture was also in dispute; Knight objected to Arnold's 'unwise' separation of culture from religion.[20]

Around the same time anthropologists such as E. B. Tylor were making another sense of 'culture' current, namely 'the distinctive ideas, customs, social behaviour, products, or way of life of a particular society, people, or period'.[21] The first occurrence of this sense in the *OED* is from 1860, but it does occur earlier, no doubt influenced by the German uses of *Kultur* mentioned above.[22] Anthropologists' sense of cultures as multiple and diverse reacted with and gradually modified the Arnoldian notion of culture as 'refinement of mind, taste, and manners'. Early anthropology was by no means pluralistic: even in its title, Tylor's *Primitive Culture* (1870) assumes a hierarchical contrast between the 'civilised' and the 'primitive'. Yet once 'culture' is seen as something every tribe and nation has, it becomes harder to see it only as the 'high' culture of 'the beautiful, the graceful and the becoming'.

'Culture', then, was disputed ground in the mid nineteenth century, especially during the 1860s and early 1870s, when a young Thomas Hardy was learning and practising architecture in Dorchester, London and Weymouth, and later poised 'Between Architecture and Literature' (*LW*: 57). The word's current meaning was emerging out of a struggle for control of everything from the franchise to education. Indeed, 'culture', even in its agricultural sense, has inherent overtones of conflict, not to say violence. The culture of any crop involves more than natural growth. Agriculturalists must first prepare the soil by clearing ground, breaking up the earth with plough or hoe, and rooting up weeds;

after planting they cultivate again to destroy any new weeds, and struggle against insects, birds, blights, and the elements. When 'culture' refers metaphorically to education or character formation the violence of the process is muted, but the metaphor still implies eradicating unwanted growths in order to foster desired ones. In the nineteenth century and earlier education routinely involved corporal punishment, and even at its most benign, the culture of a mind entails shaping and disciplining a learner.

Hardy's middling social and educational position made him especially aware of the implicit conflicts of cultivation; he was, in Angelique Richardson's words, 'ambivalent, conflicted, contradictory on the place of culture'.[23] He did not need to 'learn his letters': he had more schooling than most people below the middle class in his generation, along with professional training and some classical learning. Yet he did not have a gentleman's education: His Latin and Greek were largely self-taught, and he never realized his dream of going to Oxford or Cambridge. Most of those debating culture, the franchise, or education would have seen him neither as one of themselves nor as a problem to be solved. To some extent he was a culture seeker, habitually reading into the night, and upon his arrival in London seizing opportunities to attend the theatre and concerts and to see paintings. So far he resembles many nineteenth-century working-class people who sought knowledge and self-improvement through reading and study of various kinds.[24] At first he had vocational ends in mind, studying classical languages with a view to a clerical career, and systematically studying art, either to acquire credentials for writing about it or to advance as an architect.[25] Poetry reading was a pleasure – he read Swinburne's *Poems and Ballads* in the street, risking being knocked down (*CL* II: 158) – but also preparation for a literary career. His reading notes were taken with future novels in mind: many notes on Macaulay, for instance, collect examples of human traits, such as 'Kind cruelty' (*LN* I: 128) or 'Dexterity' (*LN* I: 140).

Aspiring as he did to careers that few young men of his class contemplated, Hardy knew that acquiring more than a 'rough' form of culture required guidance, and he looked for that guidance. Horace Moule, the clergyman's son who had known him from adolescence, helped him with Greek, gave him reading lists, lent him books, and suggested ways for him to move into literary work.[26] Hardy also sought advice from others, even asking Alexander Macmillan, 'Would you mind suggesting the sort of story you think I could do best, or any literary work I should do well to go on upon?' (*CL* I: 8). Yet such facts do not make the young Hardy one of Arnold's 'raw people', waiting to be drawn by others towards the graceful and becoming. He did not always accept authority, even when he sought it out. Although his notes record few reactions to his reading, when he used the material in his notebooks he adapted it audaciously.[27] He read Newman's *Apologia* because Moule urged him to but one of his notes shows that he read critically:

A great desire to be convinced by him, because H.M.M. likes him so much ... Only – and here comes the fatal catastrophe – there is no first link to his excellent chain of reasoning, and down you come headlong. Poor Newman! His gentle childish faith in revelation and tradition must have made him a very charming character. (*LW*: 50–1)

Both the logical analysis and the comment on Newman's childishness and charm register Hardy's confidence in his ability to come to his own conclusions and to withhold consent from a mentor's cultural judgements.

In Hardy's own writing, he often seems most interested in the feeling of homelessness acquired culture creates. For characters such as Stephen Smith in *A Pair of Blue Eyes* (1873) and Ethelberta Petherwin in *The Hand of Ethelberta* (1876), 'refinement of mind, taste and manners' assists social mobility. Yet both have to hide their rustic and servant-class relatives, and their eventual successes are Pyrrhic. Both ultimately improve their social and material standing, and Ethelberta even marries into the aristocracy, but neither her projected epic nor Stephen's success as a colonial architect can make up for their losses – of loved ones and of a sense of belonging. Stephen moves restlessly between India and various parts of England. His rising status spurs his parents to leave his native village: that move, coupled with Elfride's death, effectively severs his ties to the place where he was born. Ethelberta, at 'home' with Lord Mountclere, is separated from most of those she loves and distanced from narrator and reader: Third parties relate her life as Lady Mountclere.

After finishing *The Hand of Ethelberta*, Hardy paused from novel writing 'to broaden his general education', as Lennart Björk puts it (*LN* I: xxi), by reading a wide range of contemporary and near-contemporary authors, including Arnold, Carlyle, Comte, De Quincy, Macaulay, Newman, and George Sand, and numerous periodicals such as the *Fortnightly Review*, the *Cornhill*, and the *Saturday Review*. Likely the reading sharpened Hardy's sense of the debates over 'culture' and 'cultivation', for it is in the novels of the next two decades that he most often uses those words. They are especially resonant in *The Return of the Native* (1878) and *The Woodlanders* (1887), books in which the figure of the returning native highlights the conflicts between 'high' culture and 'old association', the 'almost exhaustive biographical or historical acquaintance' with a particular place that only those born in it can have (*W*:17). In between these two books Hardy performed the return himself after several peripatetic years, settling in Dorchester in 1883 and building a house at Max Gate in 1885, within walking distance of his birthplace. To an extent, then, he is examining in these novels his own desire both to leave and to return: to possess, like *The Woodlanders'* Grace Melbury, 'intellectual light and culture far beyond those of any other native', and yet return to 'the local life which was once to [him] the movement of the world' (*W*: 8).

Culture, class and locality are intricately connected in Grace's and Clym Yeobright's stories. Having acquired culture elsewhere, they will be seen as failures by their old neighbours if they return for good rather than 'keep straight on' (*RN*: III.2) into remote middle-class lives. Both novels begin by emphasizing the distance between their fictional worlds and cultivated society. In the first chapter of *The Return of the Native* we learn that Egdon Heath is a 'furzy, briary wilderness' (*RN*: I.1), almost impossible to farm. 'Civilisation' is 'its enemy' (*RN*: I.1) – 'civilisation' was often synonymous with 'culture' in the nineteenth century – and it resists intellectual movement as much as it resists agriculture. Little Hintock in *The Woodlanders*, though more cultivated in the sense that its trees are planted and harvested for timber and apples, is remote from other kinds of culture. To find it, travellers must turn up 'a half-invisible little lane' to 'a yet smaller lane' at the bottom of which is the village, a 'sequestered [spot] outside the gates of the world' (*W*: 1).[28]

Despite these openings, Hardy sets up the nature/culture opposition only to query it. 'Sequestered' Hintock sells products far beyond its woods: profits from such sales enable George Melbury to give Grace a middle-class education. Egdon, despite being 'away from comparisons, shut in by the stable hills' (*RN*: II.1), is in touch with the outside world: Eustacia Vye's grandfather is a retired sea-captain, and her father a Budmouth bandmaster. (In the serial and book editions from 1895 her father is also a foreigner.) Clym has worked in Paris; Wildeve's shadowy background includes 'travels' (*RN*: I.6); Diggory Venn frequently leaves and reenters Egdon. Moreover, like Hardy's own, the characters' loyalties are divided: Clym plans to raise the cultural level of the heath's inhabitants, but his 'culture scheme' (*RN*: IV.2) is undercut from the start by the 'barbarous satisfaction' he takes in seeing places on Egdon where agriculture has 'receded ... in despair, the ferns and furze-tufts stubbornly reasserting themselves' (*RN*: III.2). Egdon is Eustacia's 'Hades', but her hair, which closes 'over her forehead like nightfall extinguishing the western glow', reflects the heath's own darkness, and her sensuous appreciation of its vegetation extends to using 'the large Ulex Europaeus' as a hairbrush (*RN*: I.7). Grace enjoys coming home to half-forgotten Hintock scenes, which are to her 'as an old painting restored' (*W*: 7), but she watches the dancing at Giles's Christmas party thinking 'of a very different measure' that she remembers dancing at school, 'with a bevy of sylph-like creatures in muslin' (*W*: 10). Marty South, apparently the complete woodland native, has fingers that could have 'skilfully guided the pencil or swept the string, had they only been set to do it in good time' (*W*: 2). By describing them in terms drawn from science and the arts (the Ulex Europaeus, an old painting, the pencil, and string), Hardy ironically undercuts the claims that these worlds are 'sequestered'.

In *The Return of the Native* and *The Woodlanders* as elsewhere in Hardy, the relationship between imported culture and local life is further complicated by erotic desire, which feeds on cultural glamour. Clym first attracts Eustacia as a man from Paris who knows 'glorious things' and has 'mixed in brilliant scenes' (*RN*: IV.3). Different from everyone around her, he appeals in part because their cultured difference seems mutual. As the heath dwellers put it, their 'thinking about high doctrine' would make them 'a very pretty pigeon-pair' (*RN*: II.1). Approaching Bloom's End with the mummers, Eustacia jealously imagines Clym dancing with a woman 'far beneath herself in culture' (*RN*: II.5): like the heath dwellers, she thinks her culture will tell if she can reach him soon enough. In the event he is indeed drawn to her difference from the other mummers and party guests, defining it not only as her disguised gender, but also as a cultivation that makes her seem his natural mate (*RN*: II.6); he even thinks that Eustacia might want to assist his culture scheme by teaching children (*RN*: III.3).

Culture is still more clearly an erotic lure in *The Woodlanders*. Melbury educates Grace to make her a more desirable guilt offering to Giles, in recompense for having tricked Grace's mother away from Giles's father. Grace's cultivation enhances her gift-value but also complicates her relations with the men around her, who are intensely aware that culture raises her value. Melbury thinks that it would be '*wasting her* to give her to a man of no higher standing' than Giles (*W*: 3; original emphasis). Giles himself worries that Grace is now priced beyond his reach, swiveling between admonishing her for talking over his head and thinking that she will necessarily look higher than him, 'a yeoman, immersed in tree planting' (*W*: 9). Edred Fitzpiers responds to Grace's reminder that her blood is no better than Giles's by claiming that she has been 'refined and educated into something quite different' (*W*: 25). Neither a comic spectacle like the others Fitzpiers watches approach a freshly painted gate, nor a source of casual sexual satisfaction like Suke Damson, Grace is a precious 'creature' who must be stopped from soiling even 'the tip of her glove' (*W*: 16) with paint. She stands out from the 'crude rusticity' of Hintock (*W* 16): For Fitzpiers as for Clym, the cultivated woman's 'difference' from others and apparent similarity to himself strengthens the fascination. Grace herself is drawn to people unlike the Hintock norm, such as Felice Charmond. She notices Fitzpiers because he is 'a specimen of creation altogether unusual' in Hintock (*W*: 18), associated both with the culture of science and with that of idealist philosophy and poetry. Although the 'influence' (*W*: 22, 23) he exercises over her seems to owe as much to physical arousal as to 'the possibilities of a refined and cultivated inner life' (*W*: 23), his ability to meet her on the ground of culture boosts his attractiveness in her eyes. Accordingly, when he turns out to be serially unfaithful, she turns not only against him but against cultivation itself, telling her father that it has 'only brought [her] inconveniences and troubles' (*W*: 30).

In Hardy's novels, then, culture most often proves to be a specious good. Its glamour and the bonds it is supposed to create between the cultivated are more apparent than real: relationships based on them leave many dead and others, like Grace and Clym, with blighted lives. Yet the counter attraction of places like Egdon and Hintock may be equally misleading; rustic lives are not only less sequestered than they seem, but also less idyllic than returning natives tend to imagine. Giles and Marty, hymned near the end of *The Woodlanders* as the only two who have seen the 'wondrous world of sap and leaves' with 'a clear gaze', remain solitary, he in death and she in a life of perpetual mourning for him, and the narrator ironises the hymn by calling Grace's echoes of it 'mournful fancies' (*W*: 44). For if his characters tend to set up binary oppositions between cultivated and natural worlds, Hardy recognised that culture in its older and newer senses remains in conflict but also in dialogue with nature, and that the porous boundaries between the two are nowhere more evident than in the experience of hybrid characters like Grace, Clym, Eustacia – and Thomas Hardy.

NOTES

1 'Culture', def. 6, *The Oxford English Dictionary* (*OED*), Draft revision June 2010, online (Oxford: Oxford University Press, 2010). See def. 5 in *OED* 2nd edition (Oxford: Oxford University Press, 1989).

2 'Culture', def. 1a and 2a, *OED* 2010 (def. 2a and 3a in *OED* 2nd edition).

3 'Culture', def. 5a, *OED* 2010 (def. 4 in *OED* 2nd edition). The *OED* sees 'culture' as an exact synonym for 'cultivation', and until at least the end of the nineteenth century the two words were often used interchangeably, in extended senses as well as agricultural ones: accordingly, 'cultivation' will be discussed along with 'culture'.

4 See Raymond Williams, *Keywords: A Vocabulary of Culture and Society* (London: Fontana/Croom Helm, 1976), pp. 78–80, for a more detailed account.

5 Frequent dating errors make conclusions drawn from Google Books searches necessarily tentative. In order not to rely much on the metadata, I have looked at the scanned text of all instances that seemed likely to show changes in the usage of 'culture', and checked each date.

6 'Culture', *OED* 2010, def. 6 (def. 5a in *OED* 2nd edition).

7 Williams, *Keywords*, p. 79.
8 Matthew Arnold, *Culture and Anarchy: An Essay in Political and Social Criticism*, ed. Jane Garnett (Oxford: Oxford University Press, 2006), p. 36.
9 Raymond Williams, *Culture and Society 1780–1950* (Harmondsworth: Penguin, 1966), pp. 134–5.
10 Arnold, *Culture and Anarchy*, p. 38. For further discussion of Arnold in relation to Hardy, see Mary Rimmer, 'Hardy, Victorian Culture, and Provinciality' *Thomas Hardy Studies*, ed. Phillip Mallett (Basingstoke: Palgrave, 2004), pp. 135–55.
11 Arnold, *Culture and Anarchy*, p. 5.
12 [W. A. Knight], 'What is Man's Chief End?', review of *Culture and Anarchy*, *North British Review*, o.s. 50, n.s. 11 (1869), pp. 190–225.
13 Arnold, *Culture and Anarchy*, p. 31.
14 Hansard, 3rd ser., vol. 183, 30 May 1866, col. 1518. Hansard 1803–2005 (http://hansard.millbanksystems.com).
15 Hansard, 3rd ser., vol. 188, 15 July 1867, col. 1549. Hansard 1803–2005.
16 [Sheldon Amos or J. S. Blackie], 'Dangers of democracy', *Westminster Review*, o.s. 89, n.s. 33 (1868), pp. 1–37.
17 A simultaneous and sometimes overlapping debate was being conducted on curricula for girls.
18 Thomas Henry Huxley, 'Science and Culture', *Science and Culture and Other Essays* (London: Macmillan, 1888), p. 8. Huxley's essay was originally delivered as a speech in 1880; he made similar arguments in many writings and public appearances.
19 Knight, 'What is Man's Chief End?', pp. 199–200. Though Arnold does not focus on the curricular implications of 'culture', they are certainly present in *Culture and Anarchy*, and his thinking was influenced by his work as Inspector of Schools.
20 Knight, 'What is Man's Chief End?', p. 220.
21 'Culture', *OED* 2010, def. 7a. See def. 5b in *OED* 2nd edition.
22 To cite one example of many, there is a reference to 'German culture' in 'Conversations with Goethe', a review of Johann Eckermann, *Gespräche mit Goethe in den letzten Jahren seines Lebens*, in *Westminster Review* 50:2 (1849), pp. 555–568.
23 Angelique Richardson, 'Hardy and the Place of Culture', *A Companion to Thomas Hardy*, ed. Keith Wilson (Oxford: Wiley-Blackwell, 2009), p. 55.
24 See Jonathan Rose, *The Intellectual Life of the British Working Classes* (New Haven, Conn.: Yale University Press, 2001). Most of the people Rose quotes speak of desiring 'knowledge' or

'improvement' rather than 'culture', though they sometimes mention 'self-culture'.

25 Michael Millgate, *Thomas Hardy: A Biography Revisited* (Oxford: Oxford University Press, 2004), p. 78.

26 Millgate, *Biography Revisited*, pp. 66–70, 83, 92.

27 On Hardy's unorthodox uses of his reading, see Mary Rimmer, 'A Feast of Language: Hardy's Allusions' *The Achievement of Thomas Hardy*, ed. Phillip Mallett (Basingstoke: Macmillan, 2000), pp. 58–71.

28 The references to the 'half-invisible little lane' and the 'yet smaller lane' appear in all versions of the text up to the one-volume edition of 1887.

24

# Hardy and Hellenism

SHANYN FISKE

In November 1895, shortly after the publication of *Jude the Obscure*, A. C. Swinburne, the controversial author of *Poems and Ballads*, wrote encouragingly to Hardy, who was reeling from the scorching criticism for his latest novel: 'The tragedy – if I may venture an opinion – is equally beautiful and terrible in its pathos [...] I will risk saying how thankful we should be (I know that I may speak for other admirers as cordial as myself) for another admission into an English paradise "under the greenwood tree". But if you prefer to be – or to remain – ποιητων τραγικώτατος no doubt you may; for Balzac is dead, and there has been no such tragedy in fiction – on anything like the same lines – since he died' (*LW*: 288–9). Whether Hardy merits the title 'the most tragic of authors' will be considered later, but it is significant and ironic that Swinburne, a graduate of Eton and Oxford, should bestow upon him a Greek accolade. The gesture indicates acceptance into the exclusive discourse of classical learning to which Jude Fawley fails to gain admission and from which Hardy himself felt irreconcilably alienated (a feeling reinforced by at least one critic of *Jude* who lambasted the author for his 'affectation of scholarship' and erroneous Greek transliterations).[1] Largely self-educated in the classics, Hardy was fascinated by the literary and cultural traditions of the Greeks, but his lack of a university education prevented him from participating with writers like Matthew Arnold, Walter Pater, and Swinburne in discussions of the significance of Greek antiquity to Victorian England.

It is precisely his disengagement from any formal theory or school of Hellenism, however, that makes Hardy a useful lens on the multi-faceted and evolving interpretations of Greek antiquity in Victorian Britain. In a lifetime spanning the second half of the nineteenth and the first three decades of the twentieth century, Hardy witnessed the midcentury peak of humanistic Hellenism, the appropriation of the Greeks by the artistic philosophies of the fin de siècle, and the introduction of archaeological and anthropological approaches to the ancient world. The conflicting views between and within each of these movements reveal the incohesion of a tradition so many Victorians felt to be essential to an understanding of their own age. If, as Pater wrote in *The Renaissance*, 'Hellenism is not merely an absorbed element in our intellectual life; it is a conscious tradition in it,'[2] the many allusions to Greek mythology, epic, tragedy, philosophy, and art in Hardy's works evidence the author's struggle to reconcile the conscious and unconscious elements of an at once inescapable and inaccessible heritage.

Hardy was born into an England already thoroughly Hellenized. James Stuart's and Nicholas Revett's *The Antiquities of Athens* (1762) kicked off the Hellenic revival by igniting enthusiasm for Athenian architecture; F. A. Wolf's *Prolegomena to Homer* (1795) gave birth to the Homeric Question, which was to exercise scholars and critics throughout and beyond the nineteenth century; the 1807 display and 1816 purchase of the Elgin Marbles decisively shifted artistic favour from Roman idealism to Greek realism and originality.[3] Keats, Shelley, and Byron, who died fighting in the movement for Greek independence, all valorized the Greeks and featured Hellenic themes in their poetry. As Richard Jenkyns observes, 'for agnostics and atheists [in the early nineteenth century] Hellas was the supreme example of a non-Christian society that had reached the highest degree of humane civilization; for radicals Athens was the state that had come closest to political perfection.'[4]

For the Victorians, the appeal of ancient Greece was not limited to the ranks of the culturally unorthodox. By the time Hardy was growing up in the 1840s and 1850s, Greek language, literature, art, and philosophy had become central to the educational trajectory and the sociopolitical discourse of the upper classes. The new focus on ancient Greece replaced the Romanism of the seventeenth and eighteenth centuries with a classical model that was considered more original, purified of the utilitarianism and mundanity that had begun to taint Latin, and – because of its relative abstruseness – ripe with the possibility of symbolic reinvention.[5] 'Greece could represent almost any value or outlook that a writer wished to ascribe to it', notes Frank Turner, describing ancient Greece as 'an imaginative landscape on which [writers, artists, and critics] might discover artistic patterns, ethical values, and concepts of human nature that could displace those of Christianity and ossified French classicism.' The variety of interpretations and applications of Greek antiquity to Victorian politics and society certainly testifies to the malleability of Greece as a symbolic structure, but perhaps its over-riding significance for the Victorians was social privilege: 'Writers appealed to Greece as an allegedly universal human experience, but the moral and social values of genteel upper-class English society set the parameters of that prescriptive experience.'[6] Members of these upper classes were drilled in their conjugations, declensions, and recitations of Homer and Thucydides from childhood, prepar-ing them with heroic values they would later apply to the running of the nation and its expanding empire.

While Hardy received honorary degrees from Cambridge and Oxford later in his life, his formal education was limited, and his classical knowledge almost entirely self-taught. Instilled by his mother with an early love of reading, he started to learn Latin when he was 12 years old, under the direction of Isaac Last in Dorchester, where Hardy was a student until 1856. His depar-ture from school (to be apprenticed to an architect) left a lasting intellectual scar: as Michael Millgate has observed, 'an imperfect knowledge of Latin combined with an almost total ignorance of Greek' left him badly prepared for university admission. If he was to acquire a classical education, it would come only through a 'slow and painful' process of self-training: in the event, his plan to study for the ministry was not fulfilled, and he 'never quite lost the sense of inferiority and resentment stemming from the incompleteness of his schooling – especially as symbolized by the lack of a univer-sity degree – and from his bitter memories of the long hours of sterile private labour he had wearily invested and the social barriers he had had to confront'.[7] Harboring 'every instinct of a scholar' (*LW*: 38), Hardy took pains to learn Greek after leaving school, reading the *Iliad* and the Greek Testament in the early morning before heading to the office. The excitement of these autodidac-tic efforts was later captured in his descriptions of Jude Fawley's struggles: 'To acquire languages, departed or living, in spite of such obstinacies as he now knew them inherently to possess, was a herculean performance which gradually led him on to a greater interest in it than in the presupposed patent process. The mountain-weight of material under which the ideas lay in those dusty volumes called the classics piqued him into a dogged, mouselike subtlety of attempt to move it piecemeal' (*Jude*: I.5). His quest ends, however, in his failure to gain admission to Christminster: 'It was next to impossible that a man reading on his own system, however widely and thoroughly, even over the prolonged period of ten years, should be able to compete with those who had passed their lives under trained teachers and had worked to ordained lines' (*Jude*: II.6). Hardy himself reached the same discouraging conclusion in the early 1860s when, at the advice of Horace Moule – a friend and classical scholar trained at both Oxford and Cambridge – he abandoned the systematic study of Greek.[8] While Moule had served as a mentor and model, his opinion that translating Aeschylus and Sophocles would hardly help advance a wage-earning career put a stop to Hardy's pursuit of the literary-linguistic knowledge that would qualify him for university entrance.[9]

Fortunately for Hardy, Jude, and other Victorians inclined toward the classics but unable to access formal education, the venues for acquiring classical knowledge were expanding. In an 1858 lecture on 'Oxford and the Middle Class Examinations', Moule himself explained 'how recent changes at Oxford would make its advantages available to a wider middle-class public'.[10] Extension lectures – begun in the 1870s and delivered by university scholars in provincial cities – were one example of the increased accessibility of higher education.[11] Aside from the universities, numerous publications were made available to the lay public seeking to further their classical knowledge. One reviewer of *Jude* noted: 'it may interest [the reader] to learn that today in the second-hand book-shops old out-of-date text-books are sold by the thousand.'[12] For those interested in reading the Greeks in translation, Dryden's, Pope's and Chapman's versions of Homer were widely available, and Lemprière's *Classical Dictionary* (1788) offered guidance on unfamiliar names and terminology. Collections like A. J. Valpy's Family Classical Library (1830–4) and Bohn's Classical Library (1848–1912) included thorough introductions to translated classical works. Histories of ancient Greece – Thirlwall (1835), Grote (1846), and Mahaffy (1874) – proliferated, evidencing the turn

toward Greece from Rome. In addition, magazines and periodicals contained commentary, translations, and criticism of classical
texts and debates in almost every issue. Even for the casual reader,
some knowledge of the ancient world – and of ancient Greece in
particular – was nearly unavoidable. As Sue Bridehead tells Jude:
'I know most of the Greek and Latin classics through translations'
(*Jude*: III.4).

That Hardy too drew extensively from widely available forms of
classical knowledge is evident from his *Literary Notebooks*, which
indicate that he was as interested in his contemporaries' reflections
on the Greeks as he was in the Greeks themselves. A flurry of quotations from Mahaffy's *Social Life of Greece* suggests his interest in
the widely accepted equivalence of the Greeks and the Victorians:
'If one of us were transported to Periclean Athens, provided he were
a man of high culture, he would find life and manners strangely
like our own, strangely modern, as he might term it.'[13] Further
evidence of his readings indicates a certain urgency to establish
dialogue with the Greeks. In addition to Mahaffy, he made notes
on Max Müller's sun theory, J. A. Symond's view of the Greek
poets and the genius of the Greeks versus the Romans, Gilbert
Murray's interpretations of Euripides, Pater's *Appreciations* (1889),
Robert Bridges's *Demeter* (1905), and other Greek texts and scholars. What is clear from the *Literary Notebooks* is that while Hardy
may have given up study of the Greek language early in his life,
Victorian popular culture made the Greeks both unavoidable and
essential to an understanding of his own time. Hellenism formed a
strong, if fragmented, foundation for his work.

The appearance of Greek influence in Hardy's novels reflects the
piecemeal nature in which his classical knowledge was acquired as
well as his struggles to formulate contemporary views of Hellenism
into a cohesive image. These efforts are apparent in *Return of the
Native* (1878), which Lennart Björk identifies as the first of Hardy's
novels 'to employ "Hellenism" as a criterion against which modern
life is assessed' (*LN* I: xxviii). In doing so, Hardy was reflecting on
and responding to several prominent critics for whom the Greeks
served as a measure of Victorian culture. The second edition of
Matthew Arnold's *Culture and Anarchy* had been published in
1875, containing a new Preface that exhorted the need to Hellenize
and 'praise knowing'. For Arnold, the ancient Greeks exemplified

the unity of beauty and intelligence ('sweetness and light') that English society must reclaim in order to escape from the spiritually paralyzing effects of Christian moral stringency. Two years earlier, Walter Pater had published *Studies in the History of the Renaissance*, which, while similarly valorizing Hellenism as 'the principle pre-eminently of intellectual light', argued that the Greeks' production of superior art and literature stemmed from their vision of a 'sombre world' in which exist 'irresistible natural powers, for the most part ranged against man.'[14]

Despite their divergent interpretations, both Arnold and Pater believed that the greatness of the Greeks could only be captured and comprehended in the 'refined light which a great education creates for us'.[15] While Hardy may have shared a deep appreciation for Greek culture and art – and in particular sympathized with Pater's impression of Hellenism's darker side – he was far less convinced of the utility or recoverability of the Greek legacy in the modern world. 'The truth seems to be that a long line of disillusive centuries has permanently displaced the Hellenic idea of life,' Hardy wrote in *Return*. 'What the Greeks only suspected, we know well; what their Aeschylus imagined our nursery children feel. That old-fashioned revelling in the general situation grows less and less possible as we uncover the defects of natural laws, and see the quandary that man is in by their operation' (*RN*: III.1). Whereas, as John Paterson and others have noted, *Return* strives more than any of Hardy's other novels to capture the artistic unities of time, place, and action delineated by Aristotle, the novel ultimately implies the impossibility of recreating the Hellenic ideal. For the modern man, the shadowy underworld that haunted the Greek consciousness has risen to obscure any possibility of a light that might bring the 'blitheness and repose' Pater claimed for Greek art. Even when the possibility of Grecian glory emerges in a modern character, it gives off a tarnished and incomplete glow at best, as exemplified in this description of Eustacia:

The new moon behind her head, an old helmet upon it, a diadem of accidental dewdrops round her brow, would have been adjuncts sufficient to strike the note of Artemis, Athena, or Hera respectively, with as close an approximation to the antique as that which passes muster on many respected canvases.

But celestial imperiousness, love, wrath, and fervour had proved to be somewhat thrown away on netherward Egdon. Her power was limited, and the consciousness of this limitation had biased her development. Egdon was her Hades, and since coming there she had imbibed much of what was dark in its tone, though inwardly and eternally unreconciled thereto. (*RN*: I.7)

Here, the light of art not only fails to match the radiance of antiquity and meliorate pagan gloom but is engulfed by the very underworld it is supposed to vanquish. According to Paterson, *Return* does not fulfill the tragic promise created by its various evocations of antiquity because, 'unpersuaded of the existence of a just cosmic order, it fails to command, in the presence of human defeat, the detachment and equanimity of the classical imagination'.[16]

Hardy's pursuit of a successful tragedy for his times was firmly rooted in a larger cultural revaluation of the Greeks. Stimulated by the enthusiasm of the German Romantics – Lessing, Winckelmann, the Schlegel brothers – for Greek drama, the Victorians began revisiting the works of Aeschylus, Sophocles and to a lesser extent Euripides, as examples of the naturalism, originality, and intensity toward which literature should strive. This artistic reappraisal occurred not only in the elite halls of government and academia but in popular fora easily accessible to the reading public. A year after the purchase of the Elgin Marbles, *Blackwood's Edinburgh Magazine* published in its inaugural volume a four-part series of 'Remarks on Greek Tragedy'. Greek tragedy, the article states, 'was drawn directly from nature, and the likeness was pleasing because it was the faithful copy of a fair original; not, as too frequently happens among the ancient Romans and the modern nation of Europe, a servile imitation – a tame copy of a copy. [...] Its whole interest arises out of the simple expression of natural feeling in situations of suffering and sorrow.'[17] That Hardy took a keen interest in adapting Greek tragedy into an aesthetic model for his own time is evident from his *Literary Notebooks*, which drew ideas about Greek tragedy from popular journals as well as more scholarly publications. In his 1890 essay on 'Candour in English Fiction', he expounded more directly on the relationship between Greek tragedy and modern literature: 'All really true literature directly or indirectly sounds as its refrain the words in the *Agamemnon*: "Ælinon, Ælinon! But may the good prevail'" (*THPV*: 100). In his later novels – as in the *Agamemnon* – the significance of the prayer hinges on the ambiguity of 'the good' and on acknowledgement of the frequent absence of reliable moral measures. Demonstrating the tragic potential of moral uncertainty, Hardy's more mature characters, such as Henchard, Tess and Jude, suffer primarily from (as Hardy states in his own reflection on tragedy) 'the gradual closing in of a situation that comes of ordinary human passions, prejudices, and ambitions' (*LW*: 123).

A number of critics hailed Hardy's success as a tragedian. William Dean Howells, for instance, commended 'the return of an English writer to the Greek motive of tragedy in a book [*Jude*] which seems to me one of the most tragical I have read'.[18] But Hardy was far more profoundly affected by the flood of negativity that met his later works. Indeed, however much he may have believed in the necessity of a modern appreciation for Greek tragedy, however successful may have been his attempts to adapt the tragic mode of antiquity for his own age, it became increasingly obvious that his readership and the publishing environment could not accept in contemporary authors what they seemed to celebrate in ancient ones: 'the magazine in particular and the circulating library in general do not foster the growth of the novel which reflects and reveals life. They directly tend to exterminate it by monopolizing all literary space' (*THPV*: 98). This bitterness towards the unreceptive nature of his audience to what he believed to be true tragedy became more vehement after the publication of *Jude*: 'Tragedy may be created by an opposing environment either of things inherent in the universe, or of human institutions. If the former be the means exhibited and deplored, the writer is regarded as impious; if the latter, as subversive and dangerous; when all the while he may never have questioned the necessity or urged the non-necessity of either' (*LW*: 290). While Hardy saw the potential for Greek tragedy's service to humanity, the wounding criticism of his greatest works impressed on him the impossibility of its realization as well as the irony that his own career might stand as the ultimate testimony to his tragic vision.

Hardy's exasperation with the rigidity of his public and his disillusion with the widely-accepted idealization of the Greek world is starkly apparent in *The Well-Beloved*, which functions as a critique not only of the ideas of specific individuals – like Pater and Benjamin Jowett (Master of Balliol College, and an avid Platonist) – but of a socially exclusive Hellenism that fails to account for the realities of human emotional experience and physical need. Chronicling the struggles of a sculptor who wastes his life searching for a woman to embody his concept of aesthetic perfection, the novel vigorously rejects Pater's admiration for the 'sexless beauty' of Greek statuary[19] and, along with it, his utopian vision of 'an ivory tower [...] where a few fortunate and superior persons are blissfully sequestered from the grossness of modern life'.[20] Like Pierston's futile pursuit of Platonic love, such a vision can only yield an impotent existence. As Annette Federico remarks, 'The danger of pursuing an Ideal is that we can be led to despise what is human and ordinary, to edit the everyday out of our stories.'[21]

Deeply attuned to the struggles and failures that comprise ordinary existence, Hardy objected to an ideal of the ancient world that failed to provide either consolation or a sense of continuity for the majority of the population. His own novels attempt to understand Greek antiquity as contributing to an aspect of human experience at once separate from and more integral than an intellectual apprehension of linguistics and philosophy. For Hardy, a sterile, academic approach to Hellenism only widened the gulf between the ancients and moderns, disenabling the intercourse so many of his contemporaries were seeking. His 1905 poem 'Christmas in the Elgin Room' expresses the enforced impotence of the ancient Greeks in the modern world, with its carefully guarded vaults of knowledge:

> O it is sad now we are sold –
> We gods! for Borean people's gold,
>   And brought to the gloom
>   Of this gaunt room
> Which sunlight shuns, and sweet Aurore but enters cold. (*CP*: 928)

### NOTES

1 R. Y. Tyrrell, *Fortnightly Review* LXV (June 1896), pp. 857–64 (*CH*: 298).

2 Walter Pater, *The Renaissance: Studies in Art and Poetry* (London: Macmillan and Co., 1922), p. 199.

3 The Homeric Question involved debates over the authorship, genesis, and unity of the *Iliad* and *Odyssey*. On the Elgin Marbles and Victorian ideas of realism, see my *Heretical Hellenism: Women Writers, Ancient Greece, and the Victorian Popular Imagination* (Athens: Ohio University Press, 2008), pp. 86–92.

4 Richard Jenkyns, *The Victorians and Ancient Greece* (Cambridge, Mass.: Harvard University Press, 1980), p. 14.

5 On the ascension of Greek studies over Roman in the nineteenth century, see G. W. Clarke, ed., *Rediscovering Hellenism: The Hellenic Inheritance and the English Imagination* (Cambridge: Cambridge University Press, 1989); Christopher Stray, *Classics Transformed: Schools, Universities, and Society in England, 1830–1960* (Oxford: Oxford University Press, 1998); Frank Turner, *The Greek Heritage in Victorian Britain* (New Haven, Conn.: Yale University Press, 1981).

6 Turner, *Greek Heritage*, pp. 1–3, 51.

7 Michael Millgate, *Thomas Hardy: A Biography* (New York: Random House, 1982), p. 55.

8 Moule never attained a degree from either university.

9 Commenting on the autobiographical elements of *Jude*, Hardy notes: 'I was not altogether hindered going, at least to Cambridge, and could have gone up easily at five-and-twenty' (*LW*: 216).

10 Millgate, *Thomas Hardy*, p. 68.

11 See Isobel Hurst, *Victorian Women Writers and the Classics: The Feminine of Homer* (Oxford: Oxford University Press, 2006), p. 27.

12 *Saturday Review* lxxxi (8 February 1896), pp. 153–4 (*CH*: 281).

13 J. P. Mahaffy, *Social Life in Greece from Homer to Menander* (London: Macmillan, 1913), p. 2. See *LN* I: 51–60.

14 Walter Pater, *The Renaissance: Studies in Art and Poetry* (London: Macmillan and Co., 1922), pp. 188, 202, 201.

15 Ibid., p. 226.

16 John Paterson, 'The "Poetics" of *The Return of the Native*, *Critical Essays on Thomas Hardy: The Novels*, ed. Dale Kramer (Boston: G. K. Hall & Co., 1990), pp. 134–5.

17 'Remarks on Greek Tragedy', *Blackwood's Edinburgh Magazine* 1 (April–September 1817), p. 39.

18 *Harper's Weekly* (7 December 1895) (*CH*: 253).

19 Pater, *Renaissance*, p. 220.

20 Jenkyns, *The Victorians and Ancient Greece*, p. 257.

21 Annette Federico, 'Thomas Hardy's *The Well-Beloved*: Love's Descent', *English Literature in Tranition* 50 (2007), p. 287.

# 25

# Faith and Doubt

NORMAN VANCE

Hardy's generation encountered affirmations of faith and doubt in different forms, in church and at public meetings, in art and music, in hymns and poems, in novels and pamphlets and in essays and books of reminiscence and argument.

Despite the growing problem of the unchurched masses, caused as much by urbanization as by religious doubt, religion remained a power in the land throughout the nineteenth century.[1] Fellows of Oxford and Cambridge colleges were required to take orders in the Church of England, leading conscientious doubters to resign their fellowships rather than live a lie, among them J. A. Froude, author of *The Nemesis of Faith* (1849), and Hardy's editor and mentor Leslie Stephen, author of *An Agnostic's Apology* (1893). In addition to the Church of England, the national church as by law established, there were nonconformist groups such as the Baptists, Congregationalists and Methodists, and a growing number of Catholic churches mainly serving Irish immigrant communities. The village church was, or was supposed to be, at the heart of rural society, and the parish unit was the basis for welfare provision. Even in the towns, parish churches had once served relatively stable and knowable communities. But the system crumbled under the pressure of rapid urbanization in the wake of the industrial revolution. Old preindustrial parishes in Manchester or Leeds were powerless to cope with the multitude of workers drawn to the new industrial centres.

Eventually ambitious church-building programmes were launched to serve the new urban communities and to provide visible evidence of the continuing existence of the institutional church. Massive new churches were erected, such as Leeds Parish Church (1841), the largest new church in England since Wren's St Paul's Cathedral, and St Barnabas, Oxford (1869), built to serve a slum district. The architect was Sir Arthur Blomfield, who specialised in churches, and Hardy had worked with the Blomfield practice in London from 1862 to 1867. The church of St Barnabas features in *Jude the Obscure*, lightly disguised as St Silas.

There were other visible and audible signs of faith. The long tradition of Christian art was continued or revived by the Pre-Raphaelites in popular works such as Holman Hunt's *The Light of the World* (1851–3) and Dante Gabriel Rossetti's *Ecce Ancilla Domini* (1849–50). Christina Rossetti, the model for the Virgin Mary in her brother's painting, published religious poetry and *The Face of the Deep: a Devotional Commentary on the Apocalypse* (1892). Congregational hymn-singing, emotionally satisfying and important in nonconformist worship but somewhat looked down on in the Church of England, became respectably Anglican with the publication of *Hymns Ancient and Modern* in 1861, one of the many hymn books Hardy possessed. It contained translations of ancient and medieval Latin hymns and German chorales as well as such modern hymns as those by John Henry Newman and John Keble. Keble's *The Christian Year* (1827), modestly subtitled 'Thoughts in Verse', was enormously popular: an 1873 reprint is described as the 'hundred and fifty-fourth edition'.

Newman and Keble, both Oxford scholars, haunt Christminster, Hardy's version of Oxford, in *Jude the Obscure*. Together with E. B. Pusey, Professor of Hebrew, they led the Oxford Movement of the 1830s and 1840s, a controversial attempt to return the Church of England to a more Catholic understanding of doctrine and devotion and church tradition.[2] The movement undoubtedly enriched the spiritual life of the church, and Anglo-Catholic priests did invaluable work in the inner cities, but it provoked strenuous opposition. It fuelled anticlerical prejudice, in Hardy and in others, by encouraging a doctrinaire attitude to church principles, particularly apparent in clerical opposition to the modest divorce reforms of 1857.[3] Among its severest critics were the Evangelicals, who stressed England's protestant heritage, the authority of scripture, and what they called 'Bible preaching', rather than Catholic tradition. The Reverend Henry Moule and his family, who befriended the young Hardy, were Evangelicals of this stamp.[4]

The hymn writer and translator John Mason Neale was more sympathetic to the Catholic vision of the national church. He helped to found the Cambridge Camden Society in 1839. This had considerable influence on the revival of interest in church architecture, particularly Gothic, and in Catholic traditions of worship and ceremonial. It stimulated church restoration, carried out with varying degrees of historical sensitivity, which was good news for practising architects such as Hardy and stonemasons such as Hardy's Jude Fawley. But it added to tensions within the national church, already divided on doctrinal issues, by introducing or reintroducing what were sometimes felt to be alien practices, such as elaborate vestments for officiating clergy. Keble and Pusey stayed within the Church of England, but Newman became a Roman Catholic in 1845, and there were other defections to Rome.

Newman's conversion and the vigorous debate about the nature and identity of the Church of England that ensued were seen as matters of national importance. There was a ready market for Newman's novels of religious conversion *Loss and Gain* (1848), set in contemporary Oxford, and *Callista, a Tale of the Third Century* (1856), followed by his autobiographical *Apologia pro Vita Sua* (1864). The sense of crisis in the church produced other novels of religious controversy, such as Elizabeth Harris's painfully topical *From Oxford to Rome, and how it Fared with Some who lately Made the Journey* (1847), and Anthony Trollope's more readable novel of church politics *Barchester Towers* (1857), in which the Oxford scholar Mr Arabin considers following Newman to Rome but ends up as Dean of Barchester instead.[5]

Newman's long poem about a religious death, *The Dream of Gerontius*, became more widely known in Edward Elgar's musical setting (1900).[6] Religious sentiment reached audiences beyond the churches when the great Victorian and Edwardian choral societies mounted regular performances of Bach's *St Matthew Passion*, Handel's *Messiah* and Haydn's *The Creation*, as well as more modern works such as Mendelssohn's *St Paul* (1836) and *Elijah* (1846), composed for the Birmingham Festival, and John Stainer's once-popular cantata *The Crucifixion* (1887). Many of these works included chorales and hymn settings, which found their way into hymn books such as *The English Hymnal* (1906), for which Ralph Vaughan Williams was the music editor. Williams was an agnostic, like Hardy, whose work he admired, but religion still influenced his creative imagination, giving rise to some splendid hymn tunes and a life-long fascination with Bunyan's *Pilgrim's Progress*. He incorporated a setting of Hardy's half-doubting Christmas poem 'The Oxen' in his Christmas cantata *Hodie* (1954), a reminder that in music (as in poetry) the believer and the doubter shared and exploited a common heritage.[7]

It is tempting to think that the doubt experienced by Vaughan Williams and Hardy was a specifically Victorian phenomenon. It certainly had its own new-minted vocabulary, including terms such as 'secularist' and 'secularism' (dating from 1851) and 'agnosticism', apparently coined by T. H. Huxley in 1869. But Victorian doubt built on an earlier substratum of religious questioning inherited from the previous century.

Perhaps the most important inherited question for doubting souls and tragic novelists was the problem of innocent suffering and how a just God could permit it, sometimes referred to as 'theodicy'. The issue was age-old, addressed if not exactly resolved in the book of Job, but it entered on its modern phase in Leibniz's *Essais de Théodicée sur la bonté de Dieu, la liberté de l'homme et l'origine du mal* (1710). If Leibniz, and Voltaire's savage parody of him, Dr Pangloss in *Candide* (1759), could claim that all was for the best in the best of all possible worlds, the appalling disaster of the Lisbon earthquake of 1755 provided a powerful counterargument, which Voltaire found persuasive. So did the young Goethe. Hardy's notebooks, which include many extracts from his friend John Morley's *Voltaire* (1872, reprinted 1886), also record, from the 1855 edition of G. H. Lewes's *Life of Goethe*, that 'Goethe's religion was all taken out of him by the Lisbon earthquake' (*LN* I: 14).

Enlightenment sages raised other matters of concern, particularly miracles. The mysterious or nonrational aspects of Christianity were dismissed as relics of paganism perpetuated by a priestly caste for their own purposes in John Toland's controversial *Christianity not Mysterious* (1696). David Hume's *Philosophical Essays Concerning Human Understanding* (1748) included an influentially sceptical 'Essay on Miracles', which prompted clerical responses such as Richard Whately's ingenious *reductio ad absurdum*, *Historic Doubts Relative to Napoleon Bonaparte* (1819). Edward Gibbon's *The Decline and Fall of the Roman Empire* (1776–88), approached the evidences of early Christianity from the rational and scientific perspective of the critical historian. Alert to pious fraud, he noted the various miracles claimed in the New Testament and in the early church, not confirmed from other sources, and dryly observed how 'the laws of Nature were frequently suspended for the benefit of the church'.[8] Hardy relished and sometimes quoted Gibbon's subtly lethal sentences, and admired him as a much-maligned champion of the truth. He visited his home in Lausanne in 1897, commemorated in his poem 'Lausanne. In Gibbon's Old Garden: 11–12 p.m.' (*CP*: 105–6). An even more sweeping approach to church tradition and self-interested priests was represented by the Deist Matthew Tindal's *Christianity as Old as the Creation, or the Gospel a Republication of the Religion of Nature* (1730), which seemed to bypass the biblical record and church history altogether. Later in the century the revolutionary writer Tom Paine published *The Age of Reason* (1794–5), which ridiculed the institutions and beliefs of revealed religion.

None of this fundamental questioning had very immediate impact on religious life in England. There was, however, a tradition of reading Hume, Gibbon, and Paine in radical and freethinking circles. The printer Richard Carlile was prosecuted for republishing Paine's *The Age of Reason* in 1819. But later generations were undeterred. The secularist G. J. Holyoake published an *Essay on the Character and Services of T. Paine* in 1861. Gibbon's popularity among freethinkers continued into the twentieth century: Hardy's militantly secularist friend Edward Clodd, a renegade from Congregationalism, delivered the Moncure Conway Memorial Lecture of 1916 on the subject of 'Gibbon and Christianity', and J. M. Robertson's edition of the most anti-Christian chapters of *Decline and Fall* was still in print in 1930 as *Gibbon on Christianity*. Hume's scepticism about miracles influenced Huxley, who published a short book about Hume in 1878.

English Deists were soon largely forgotten in England, at least until Leslie Stephen wrote about them in his *History of English Thought in the Eighteenth Century* (1876). They were, however, more influential in Germany: Tindal and others were soon available in German translation and their work contributed to disturbing departures in biblical and historical studies, particularly the study of Christian origins.[9] It became clear that there were considerable difficulties involved in taking scriptural narratives at face value as reliable history. The usual solution was to treat them as poetic or mythic rather than historical, designed to convey religious teaching rather than factual information. Awkward questions came back from Germany to disturb Victorian believers. In 1846 George Eliot published her translation of David Strauss's demythologising *Leben Jesu* (1835), a massive work, which Hardy seems to have read as far as page 192.[10] Ernest Renan's Strauss-influenced *Vie de Jésus* (1863) was available in English translation from 1864. For Strauss and Renan and for other advanced thinkers the main obstacle to taking the Bible at face value was miracle and the supernatural. This was the view adopted by Matthew Arnold in *Literature and Dogma* (1873). For him miracles did not happen and the super-natural had to be discounted: the natural truth of Christianity was its best defence. The Bible was still important, but it needed to be approached with critical discrimination rather than taken literally or treated as some kind of magical book.

There were other causes for religious concern. One of the stand-ard arguments for the existence of God, the argument from design, had been lucidly presented by the mathematician and clergyman William Paley in *A View of the Evidences of Creation* (1794). The intricate design of a watch implied a watchmaker and the evidence of design and order in nature and the universe implied a Creator God, a kind of divine watchmaker. But what if the design was actu-ally rather less than perfect? Darwin's *The Origin of Species* (1859) offered a disturbing theory of development in nature. This chal-lenged traditional notions of a benign providence at work in the natural world by outlining a struggle for existence which ruthlessly eliminated creatures and species ill-adapted for survival. Huxley, 'Darwin's bulldog', was much more aggressive than Darwin himself, baiting conservative churchmen with the new scientific knowledge, most famously at the Oxford meeting of the British Association for the Advancement of Science in 1860 when he dealt effectively with the condescending mockery of Samuel Wilberforce, Bishop of Oxford. In later years Huxley amused himself by poking holes in miraculous Bible stories such as the account of the Gadarene swine. But it is easy to exaggerate the role of Darwin and Huxley. The great poems of Victorian doubt, Alfred Tennyson's *In Memoriam* (1850) and Matthew Arnold's 'Dover Beach' (1851, published 1867) were written before Darwin.

Tennyson and Darwin were both influenced by Charles Lyell's *Principles of Geology* (1830–3), which argued that the earth's crust had acquired its current form through the operation of still-continuing natural processes such as volcanic action, sedimentation and erosion. This approach, known as 'uniformitarianism', called for immense abysses of geological time, millions rather than thousands of years, which made the earth much older than the computations of Bible-reading late renaissance chronologists such as James Ussher. Darwin realised that this provided him with a time-frame to accommodate the slow but inexorable processes of evolution. The fossil evidence of extinct life-forms preserved in geological strata suggested a mindless process of development and destruction, which haunted the melancholy speaker of Tennyson's *In Memoriam*. Bewildered, he asks 'Are God and nature then at strife?' The ruthless violence of 'Nature, red in tooth and claw' challenged the traditional belief that 'God was love indeed / And love Creation's final law'.[11] Tennyson and Darwin, and their readers, including the young Thomas Hardy, were fascinated and appalled by the grim realisation that the seeming abundance of nature might be largely unsustainable, involving an economy of waste. 'Social Darwinist' theories, which owed more to the sociologist Herbert Spencer than to Darwin, sought to apply the ruthless competition of the natural world to human affairs. Some of Hardy's unfortunate characters seem to be victims of social-Darwinist struggle, raising the issue of theodicy once again, but Huxley refused to accept evolution as a basis for social ethics.[12]

Disconcerting scientific discoveries, and new thinking about Christian origins and the nature of the Bible record, were usually accommodated rather than resisted by the more liberal churchmen, though their reward could be public outcry. *Essays and Reviews* (1860), provides a case in point. The seven contributors, six of them Anglican clergymen, were pilloried as the 'Seven against Christ'. Men of faith, they were accused of instilling doubt because they seemed to challenge the supreme authority of scripture and the unchanging nature of religious truth in the name of science and modern knowledge. The Old Testament scholar Rowland Williams's contribution, on 'Bunsen's Biblical Researches', began by using the geological principle of uniformitarianism as a way of stressing 'the Divine energy as continuous and omnipresent', linking it with 'the law of growth, traceable through the Bible, as in the world'. He praised the voluminous Biblical researches and other writings of the Prussian scholar and diplomat Baron Bunsen, a Lutheran, commending his awareness of process and the sometimes erratic development of religious ideas, necessarily different at different times and in different contexts. Bunsen traced the continuity of faith from earlier ages, when it was reflected or expressed only in the imperfectly credible narratives and propositions of scripture that would hardly stand the test of time.[13]

The Bible as popular religion understood it was given a hard time in *Essays and Reviews*. H. B. Wilson, discussing 'The National Church', pointed out that no scriptural author actually identified the books of the Old and New Testaments as the 'Word of God'. While this ultra-Protestant claim was made in other credal statements such as the Helvetic Confession (he might have added the seventeenth-century Westminster Confession still used by many nonconformists), it was not to be found in the Thirty-Nine Articles of the Church of England. As far as he was concerned this represented a 'comparative freedom' of interpretation which was entirely beneficial, though he regretted the 'many evils' entailed by 'an extreme and too exclusive Scripturalism'.[14]

Benjamin Jowett, Oxford Professor of Greek, was even more severe in his essay 'On the Interpretation of Scripture'. He anticipated Arnold by insisting that it was seldom interpreted properly. Protestants habitually claimed biblical support for their teaching from particular verses at the cost of ignoring others: 'The favourite verses shine like stars, while the rest of the page is thrown into the shade.' Jowett felt the Bible should be read like any other book, 'by the same rules of evidence and the same canons of criticism'.[15] He noted that despite popular superstitions to the contrary the Bible, or rather the generally accepted original text and English translation of the Bible, was not immune from human errors and misinterpretations, sometimes perpetuated because they seemed to support preconceived opinions and traditional religious teaching. One instance of convenient error preserved for doctrinal reasons, which he could have taken from Gibbon's examples of pious fraud, was the persistence in the King James version of 1611 (though not in Luther's Bible) of a spurious verse, the so-called 'Johannine comma' (1 John 5:7), referring to the three witnesses in heaven, the Father, the Word and the Holy Ghost. This was habitually used as a proof-text for the orthodox doctrine of the Trinity. It appeared in the Latin Vulgate translation but there was no authority for it in the best Greek manuscripts. But conservative Oxford did not thank Jowett or the other essayists for raising difficulties.

It was a mixed blessing for J. W. Colenso, Bishop of Natal, that his biblical researches began to appear in 1862, with the publication of *The Pentateuch Examined as an Historical Narrative*, in the middle of the furore attending *Essays and Reviews*, while Rowland Williams was still being prosecuted in the church courts. Boldly taking as his motto 'We can do nothing against the Truth' (2 Corinthians 13:8), Colenso deliberately linked his work with *Essays and Reviews* and responses to it. He had found his moment and his sales were enormous, but so was the trouble he brought upon himself. In the course of working on a Zulu translation of the Bible for use in his missionary diocese he had become acutely aware of anomalies in the text which he found it impossible to explain away to his African assistant William Ngidi. Detailed engagement with particular passages brought home to him inconsistency and incoherence which demonstrated the unhistorical nature of much Old Testament narrative. He drew attention to problems such as the story of the departure from Egypt and the miraculous crossing of the Red Sea (Exodus12–15). A mathematician, he noted the impossible numbers involved, nine times Wellington's army at Waterloo, not counting women and children. How could so many people have been mobilised so quickly?[16] Here, and elsewhere in the Pentateuch, scripture quite literally did not add up.

The very public controversy about biblical authority associated with *Essays and Reviews* and Colenso was renewed when modern textual and philological scholarship was deployed to produce a revised version of the English Bible. After 270 years of the King James Bible there was considerable suspicion of the distinctly overdue Revised Version of the New Testament (1881), based not on the old inadequate Greek text but on a scientifically reconstructed critical text prepared by two distinguished Professors of Divinity at Cambridge, B. F. Westcott and F. J. A. Hort. Their textual labours followed the work of German scholars such as J. J. Griesbach and Constantin Tischendorf, who had compared all the available manuscripts. As a young man Hardy had purchased Griesbach's Greek text, probably the third edition, with additional variant readings, published in Bohn's Collegiate Series in 1859, and he bestowed the same volume on his self-taught protagonist Jude Fawley (*Jude*: I.7) For biblical literalists it was symptomatic that the revisers of 1881 had changed the familiar wording of 2 Timothy 3:16 ('All scripture is given by inspiration of God, and is profitable for doctrine, for reproof, for correction, for instruction in righteousness') to 'Every scripture inspired of God is also profitable for teaching, for reproof, for correction, for instruction which is in righteousness.' The new phrasing seemed dangerously weaker, as if the translators were doubtful about the inspiration of scripture, even though it more accurately translated the Greek. The revisions were usually very minor, but the critics had little sense of proportion. The revisers, devout and scholarly men, were attacked, outrageously, for having 'sown broadcast over four continents doubts as to the truth of Scripture, which it will never be in their power either to remove or to recall'. As if that were not enough, the new 'ill-advised practice' of recording alternative readings in the margins 'can only result in hopelessly unsettling the faith of millions'.[17]

This was of course totally unfair. Neither science nor biblical scholarship should take all the blame for religious doubt. The problem of innocent suffering was more important, particularly during and after the First World War. Temperament and personal feeling played their part. Doubting poets and artists were often driven by passion or melancholia rather than Darwin or German criticism. Romantic rebellion rather than textual problems lies behind Algernon Swinburne's colourful neo-paganism and his disparagement of Jesus as the 'pale Galilean' ('Hymn to Proserpine'). Private perplexity may explain the strange late paintings of G. F. Watts with titles such as 'The Sower of the Systems' (1902) or 'Hope' (1885). 'Hope' is a surprisingly gloomy painting of a downcast figure, contradicting the traditional religious iconography of 'Hope', usually grouped with Faith and Charity. And yet for Watts as for Hardy some kind of religious hope can still be entertained. The painting may have influenced Hardy's sombre poem 'The Darkling Thrush' with its unexpected hint : 'Some blessed Hope, whereof he knew / And I was unaware.'[18]

NOTES

1  See A. D. Gilbert, *Religion and Society in Industrial England: Church, Chapel and Social Change 1740–1914* (Longman: London, 1976).

2  R. W. Church, *The Oxford Movement: Twelve Years, 1833–1845* (London: Macmillan, 1891).

3  See Allen Horstman, *Victorian Divorce* (London: Croom Helm, 1985).

4  Michael Millgate, *Thomas Hardy: a Biography Revisited* (Oxford: Oxford University Press, 2004), p. 65.

5  For religious fiction see Robert Lee Wolff, *Gains and Losses: Novels of Faith and Doubt in Victorian England* (London: Murray, 1977).

6  On Newman and Elgar's *Gerontius*, see Michael Wheeler, *Death and the Future Life in Victorian Literature and Theology* (Cambridge: Cambridge University Press, 1990), pp. 305–39.

7  On Vaughan Williams and Hardy, see Wilfred Mellers, *Vaughan Williams and the Vision of Albion* (London: Barrie and Jenkins, 1989), p. 26.

8  Edward Gibbon, *Decline and Fall of the Roman Empire*, ed. David Womersley, 3 vols. (London: Allen Lane, 1994), I:512.

9  Thomas Albert Howard, *Protestant Theology and the Making of the Modern German University* (Oxford: Oxford University Press, 2006), pp. 46, 99.

10  *LN* I: 381. Apparently the pages were uncut after page 192.

11  Alfred Tennyson, *In Memoriam* LV, line 5; LVI, lines 13–15.

12  See T. H. Huxley, *Evolution and Ethics and Other Essays* (London: Macmillan, 1895).

13  Rowland Williams, 'Bunsen's Biblical Researches', *Essays and Reviews*, 7th ed. (London: Longman, 1861), pp. 50, 52, 82–5.

14  H. B. Wilson, 'Séances Historiques de Genève. The National Church', *Essays and Reviews*, pp. 175–7.

15  Benjamin Jowett, 'On the Interpretation of Scripture', *Essays and Reviews*, pp. 366, 375.

16  *The Pentateuch and Book of Joshua Critically Examined*, 7 vols. (London: Longmans, 1862–79), I:xiv, xx, 48–50, 63.

17  [J. W. Burgon] 'New Testament Revision: The New English Version', *Quarterly Review* 153 (January 1882), p. 2.

18  *CP*: 150. See Norman Vance, 'Hardy's "The Darkling Thrush" and G. F. Watts's *Hope*', *Victorian Poetry* 33 (Summer 1995), pp. 295–8.

# Hardy's Philosophy

MARK ASQUITH

'I have no philosophy', Hardy noted towards the end of his career, merely 'a confused heap of impressions, like those of a bewildered child at a conjuring show' (*LW*: 441). For Michael Millgate this form of 'Laodiceanism' – a quality that enabled him 'to see virtue in all sides of a question' – is indicative of a mind 'not naturally equipped to move easily in realms of philosophical discourse'.[1] Hardy certainly provides easy pickings for those seeking philosophical inconsistency: look no further than Robert Schweik's collation of philosophical blunders in *Tess*.[2] Although not seeking to deny Hardy's philosophical limitations, a more generous critical tradition, exemplified by the work of Brian Green and Deborah Collins, has sought to distil from Hardy's novels a 'master theme' around which the various strands of his thought are woven.[3] This position can be summarised as follows. Hardy conceives of a world governed by deterministic laws, such as those of the Immanent Will, Darwinian sexual selection, materialist laws of determinism, and the principle of heredity. Humanity is part of this deterministic universe, but possesses an evolving consciousness which allows the individual to glimpse the harshness of his situation, and also use his free will to attempt of overcome those forces, both internal and external, that dictate their behaviour. This creates the tragic tension that lies at the centre of Hardy's tragedies.

Green's reluctance to proceed beyond the 'themes' is surely right, just as it is surely wrong to appraise Hardy's novels through the lens of systematic philosophy. Read in the light of Walter Pater's ultra-Romantic manifesto, *The Renaissance*, which transforms the spirit of 'tentativeness' into something approaching a philosophical methodology, Hardy's narratives can be seen as offering a virtuous acknowledgement of the complexity of the world without falsifying it through simplification and systematisation. In his conclusion to the second edition, Pater argues that although deterministic laws may govern man's activities, the artist should resist Enlightenment attempts to discover their nature and focus on the momentary manifestation of these forces.[4] In this context a letter written by Hardy to Alfred Noyes is of interest: he chastises Noyes for picking contradictory passages from his poems, noting that although he 'called this Power [the Cause of Things] all sorts of names' they are mere 'expression[s] of fancy' and are not to be confused with the 'expression of belief' (*LW*: 439). The reasoning seems entirely Paterian: his attempts to capture the isolated moment do not preclude his 'belief' in a coherent metaphysical universe, while his 'belief' in the latter does not annihilate his impression of the moment. Essentially, he offers his readers the main threads of a coherent view, whilst never losing the bemusement of the child before the conjuror.

Hardy's philosophical 'tentativeness', then, is less a reflection of theoretical uncertainty than the product of an aesthetic perspective that made a virtue of perplexity. And Hardy certainly lived in perplexing times, the long shadow of evolutionary theory replacing the static certainty of a benevolent god with a world of 'process'. For Pater, in *Plato and Platonism*, Darwin had vindicated the fear of the Ancients of a world in 'flux'.[5] And if, as Herbert Spencer argues in his essay 'Progress: its Law and Cause', species continued to evolve in a Lamarckian fashion from the 'homogeneous to the heterogeneous', then the sense of confusion could only get worse.[6] Furthermore, as Spencer makes clear in *First Principles*, this pattern of increasing diversity was not confined to biology but was to be found in political, economic and cultural spheres, and even in the increasing specialism exhibited by the new sciences such as psychology, physiology and anthropology.[7] Diversity also reflected the profile of those participating in intellectual endeavour (fossil hunting, for instance, was popular with gentlemen and ladies alike) and the means by which cultural knowledge was disseminated, signalled by the growth in popularity of the midcentury periodical press. Such journals catered for the new market of the educated and would-be-educated middle classes by publishing academically rigorous essays on a range of scientific, political and artistic controversies. It was through such articles that the reading public was introduced to some of the most groundbreaking ideas of the day; articles which were then annotated, and found themselves classified and dissected in the pages of personal notebooks.

The Notebook proved another peculiarly Victorian response to the midcentury malaise, and note taking, through its process of careful selection and rejection, offered a suitably evolutionary mechanism for bringing the world into focus. Hardy was an inveterate note taker; adapting his working practices in a desire not to be labelled a purely rural writer following the success of *Far from the Madding Crowd*, he began a campaign of journal reading in 1876 that was to provide the intellectual foundation for a more serious literature. A comment from Emma's brother during a visit to their Sturminster Newton home in 1876, to the effect that Hardy was not getting on with his next novel, seems to have resulted in his abandonment of larger texts in favour of short articles from the mainstream journals of the day.[8] Here Hardy was exposed to many of the theories that moulded his own cosmic vision; competing theories selected because they provided variations on a common theme.

One theme that appears to have preoccupied Hardy from the outset is the autonomy of the individual in a world of flux. In 1876 the influential physicist John Tyndall gave his popular 'Belfast Address', in which he presented the world as a molecular vortex in which even man's thoughts and feelings are reducible to the 'separation and remarshalling of the atoms of the brain'.[9] The following summer Hardy was introduced to a similar theory while reading John Morley's analysis of 'Holbach's System of Nature' in the *Fortnightly Review*. Here the world of flux is imaged as a raging sandstorm in which, despite the apparent chaos, every grain of sand obeys the laws of molecular necessity. Hardy was evidently drawn to this conception, marking this passage in his copy of Morley's works and copying into his *Notebook* the assertion that '*All phenomena are necessary*. No creature in the universe, in its circumstances & according to its given property, can act otherwise than as it does act' (*LN* I: 114). These sentiments echo a long entry copied from John Tulloch's 'Morality without Metaphysic' (*Edinburgh Review*, October 1876), in which it is argued that man's supposedly independent will or conscience is simply the 'last transformation of the great natural forces of light & heat & electricity, passing through the mysterious involvements of the human nervous system' (*LN* I: 88).

What this meant for thinkers like Spencer is that there was no transcendent 'self', simply a series of 'psychical states' that conform to laws just as easily as simple reflex action. In the *Principles of Psychology* he argues that it is an 'illusion' to suggest that 'at each moment the *ego* is something more than the composite state of consciousness which then exists'.[10] Hardy remained a fervent supporter of Spencer throughout his life, and was reading and noting very similar conclusions in Frederic Myers's 'Human Personality' in the *Fortnightly Review* of 1885 (*LN* I: 167). Myers argues that human beings have a multiplex nature, human as other; what we suppose to be choice is reflex action only. Describing the self as a 'colony of cells, Myers asked: 'Does my consciousness testify that I am a single entity?' This question Hardy seems to answer in the *Life*: 'I am more than ever convinced that persons are successively various persons, according as each special strand in their characters is brought uppermost by circumstances' (*LW*: 241).

It is this combination of mutability and physiology that seems so apparent in the way that Hardy crafts his characters. They seldom, as Phillip Mallett has observed, exhibit the kind of introspective reflection employed by a more psychological novelist to demonstrate continuity of subjective experience.[11] They are, according to Gilles Deleuze, not so much 'people or subjects' as 'collections of intensive sensations' that exist in a state of perpetual 'becoming'.[12] However, it is not simply an aesthetic ploy that the emotional turmoil of Hardy's characters is continually presented in terms of palpitations, vibrations, trembling and flushes; rather, his characters are little more than a product of these transient physiological states. Tess observes that 'There are very few women's lives that are not – tremulous', and under the power of Angel she becomes 'such a sheaf of susceptibilities that her pulse was accelerated by the touch, her blood driven to her finger-ends, and the cool arms flushed hot' (*Tess*: 29; 28). Similarly, the sensitivity of Sue Bridehead is characterised in physical rather than psychological terms: 'the fibres of her nature seemed strained like harp-strings' which 'the least wind of emotion from another's heart could make to vibrate' (*Jude*: IV.3; V.3). In both cases, the notion of love is removed from the ethereal and relocated in the nervous system; a system which seems to demonstrate the dangers of overspecialisation and refinement inherent in Spencerian ideas concerning progress from the 'homogeneous to the heterogeneous'. It is a bleak view made even darker in Hardy's writing through his knowledge of Darwinian sexual selection (in which man is driven by the procreative instinct), and his contact with the idea of the 'will to life' in the work of the German philosopher, Arthur Schopenhauer.

Hardy's debt to Darwin is well known; his debt to Schopenhauer is more speculative. R. H. Hutton noted as early as 1879 that Hardy seems to speak 'with the calm confidence of one who has found Schopenhauer far superior to all the prophets and all the seers'.[13] Yet modern criticism has tended to diminish his influence, largely because Hardy did not read German and Richard Haldane's translation of *The World as Will and Idea* (first published in 1819 but largely ignored) did not appear until 1883. However, Schopenhauer was enjoying something of a vogue in Britain in 1876, largely because of his connection with Wagner, whose first Bayreuth Festival was being widely reported. The contemporary philosopher Robert Adamson could write that 'one can scarcely open any philosophical work without finding reference to [Schopenhauer's] name and thoughts'.[14] Articles appeared in the *Fortnightly Review* and the *Cornhill*,[15] whilst the philosopher and psychologist James Sully and the writer and translator Helen Zimmern produced book-length reviews,[16] in response to a growing public curiosity about his philosophy. It is almost inconceivable that a writer of Hardy's interests would have been ignorant of these articles; furthermore, he owned a copy of Sully's *Pessimism* and took notes from Edmund Gurney's outline of Schopenhauer's ideas published in the *Fortnightly Review* in 1876 (*LN* I: 51).[17] This is not to say that he had a full appreciation of the subtleties of Schopenhauer's thought, but rather that he found points of contact which both confirmed and stimulated his own thinking. For, as with Darwinism, one does not need a detailed understanding of Schopenhauer's philosophy to grasp Schopenhauerism.

What Schopenhauer offered a Victorian intellectual community generally suspicious of German metaphysics was a solution, emerging from empirical observation of the human body, to the problem of the self dissolving into a Paterian jumble of fragments. From his observation of the body's extension into the world (an object in the phenomenal world over which we have a special knowledge), he argued that the Kantian 'thing in itself' (that element independent of the perceiving mind which prevents the phenomenal world from becoming merely the product of individual perception) is the 'will to life' – a cluster of primal sensations and desires experienced by the individual through his own body; often primarily sexual. Since, Schopenhauer reasons, there is no difference between our body and any other object of perception in the phenomenal world, the will must constitute the inner state of all things, both animate and inanimate. The phenomenal world, therefore, from the smallest crystal to the most complex animal, is an objectification of the constantly striving will.

The similarity between Schopenhauer's 'will' and Darwinian instinct is clear, and for a Victorian public acculturated to the empirical tradition Schopenhauer simply offered a vindication of what they already thought; as the contemporary philosopher David Asher noted: 'Schopenhauer taught deductively what Darwin has proved inductively.'[18] This is proved most clearly in the elasticity with which terms specific to the work of both men – 'will', 'impulse' and 'adaptation' – are used: and nowhere is this tendency clearer than when considering their writing on sexual relations, a subject particularly significant for any late Victorian novelist. Love becomes, in Asher's essay, 'what Schopenhauer has defined it to be; viz., the law of natural selection implanted within us for the purpose of preserving the type of the human race.'[19] For Sully, love is reduced to the will of the unborn child manifesting itself through its parents; sentiments which we find echoed in Hardy's late verse 'The Mother Mourns', in which a personified Nature laments that desire is nothing more than the 'lure that my species / May gather and gain' (*CP*: 112).[20]

In Hardy's work, falling in love is described continually by means of metaphors drawn from biology and metaphysics that emphasise the element of compulsion, transforming the experience into something to be endured rather than enjoyed. Jude experiences 'a momentary flash of intelligence, a dumb announcement of affinity' between himself and the 'complete and substantial female animal' Arabella Donn (*Jude*: I.6); Grace Melbury suffers 'the compelling power of Fitzpiers's atmosphere', which derives from the 'strange effect upon her nerves'. His own diagnosis of 'Grace's 'curious susceptibility to his presence', formulated while carrying out his medical investigation of John South's brain, is that 'the currents of her life were disturbed rather than attracted by him' (*W*: 18, 19). In *The Well-Beloved*, a casual conversation about laundry between Jocelyn Pierston and the second incarnation of Avice Caro is transformed into an illustration of the laws of attraction: Hardy's reference to a capitalised 'Nature ... working her plans for the next generation under the cloak of a dialogue on linen', invokes directly the sacrifice of the individual to the species discussed by both Asher and Zimmern (*WB*: II.6). The milkmaids in *Tess* are particularly acute victims of the 'oppressiveness of an emotion thrust on them by cruel Nature's law'. They become merely a 'portion' of a vast semi-anthropomorphised 'organism called sex', which causes them to 'writhe feverishly' in their cots at night (*Tess*: 23). This last image is significant because it invokes both the Darwinian struggle for sexual selection and the 'brain-like network of currents and ejections, twitching, interpenetrating, entangling, and thrusting hither and thither the human forms' that makes up 'the controlling Immanent Will' in Part First of *The Dynasts* (*CPW* IV: 163).

All the milkmaids suffer, but the suffering of Tess is greater because it is the product of a more highly refined nervous system. Such is its complexity, that, according to Hardy, we have the emergence of consciousness; a potentially positive development, which, in Hardy's hands, becomes a means of amplifying rather than ameliorating her pain. Hardy's views on consciousness are difficult to tease out, but again he seems entirely in harmony with an intellectual community struggling to make sense of how sentience may have emerged in a materialist world. In the *Fortnightly* of August 1876, for example, James Sully published an analysis of Edward von Hartmann's *Philosophy of the Unconscious* in which he argues that the will is not blind but consists of an unconscious energy existing in all phenomena becoming conscious.[21] It is a view that Hardy was later to praise in an interview with William Archer, speculating whether there may be some 'consciousness, infinitely far off, at the other end of the chain of phenomena, always striving to express itself'.[22] Similar ideas are to be found in the work of the contemporary theorist W. L. Clifford, who proposed the existence of 'mind-stuff' in all inorganic and organic phenomena, which combines in such a way in complex organisms that sentience emerges.[23] Hardy claimed in a letter to Roden Noel that he found this idea 'very attractive' (*CL* I: 262), and in 1882 noted from a discussion of materialism in the *Spectator* that 'unless you assume the ultimate atom or molecule to have some inner qualities analogous to those which we call mental – qualities such as the late Prof. Clifford used to speak of as those of mind-stuff – there is no explaining how the mental universe is developed out of the physical' (*LN* I: 148).

Tragically, for Hardy's sensitive characters, this process is in its embryonic stage, meaning that they possess just enough sentience to perceive their powerlessness to control the determining forces working upon and through them. Hence, they are continually presented as perplexed observers of their own actions: in the poem 'He Wonders About Himself' the speaker describes himself as 'Tugged' by an invisible force of 'the general Will', wondering 'What I shall find me doing next!' *(CP:* 510). It is a bemused statement echoed by many of Hardy's characters: Napoleon in *The Dynasts* excuses the bloodshed he has caused by claiming 'Some force within me, baffling my intent, / Harries me onward, whether I will or no' (*CPW* IV: 233); Henchard lies to Newson out of impulse and then, 'amazed at what he had done', resolves to commit suicide (*MC:* 41); and Jude never develops from the perplexed young figure lying on his back contemplating the fact that 'Nature's logic' was 'too horrid' (*Jude:* I.2).

Yet there is worse. In the *Life* Hardy extrapolated from Darwin that man is continually evolving 'a degree of intelligence which Nature never contemplated when framing her laws' (*LW:* 169), a sentiment echoed in Sully's summary of Schopenhauer's ideas in *Pessimism:* 'all progress as intellectual development necessarily increases the amount of suffering, so that the world is tending to become worse instead of better.'[24] Schopenhauer's a priori conclusions were also reached through Hartmann's inductive methodology, according to which human existence is 'growing more and more miserable as intelligence increases and the true value of human ends becomes calmly recognised'.[25] This unique conspiracy of determinism and evolution brings to Hardy's novels a concept of tragedy that not only highlighted the perpetuation of human misery, but asserted with scientific justification that things could only decline further.

The only escape, according to Hartmann and Schopenhauer, is a 'common act of will annihilation', which is not suicide, but the submersion of the individual will within the wider will, or the abandonment of consciousness to instinct. Hardy takes a similar view, arguing in the 'Apology' to *Late Lyrics and Earlier* that suffering can only be reduced if the individual uses his 'modicum of free will' in harmony with the wider will (*CP*: 558). Hardy explains this view through the image of a pianist whose 'fingers are free to go on playing the pianoforte of themselves when he talks or thinks of something else' (*LW*: 361). Man is transformed into the digit of a universal melodist – an image reflected in the Spirit of the Years' observation that 'the Will heaves through Space, and moulds the times, / With mortals for Its fingers!' (*CPW* IV: 248). The image is entirely appropriate, because throughout his work Hardy represents the abandonment of the individual to the wider will through the analogy with dancing, a communal activity in which the individual loses himself to the music according to predestined steps. Hardy's characters are continually presented as bemused, envious or censorious onlookers of the many dances that punctuate his narratives: having read the 'terribly sensible advice' contained in the letter from Dr Tetuphenay, a bleary-eyed Jude (alcohol numbs the conscious self) finds himself standing at Fourways, an envious observer of the dancing 'book of humanity' (*Jude*: II.6). During the East Egdon dance we are told that Eustacia began 'to envy those pirouetters, to hunger for the hope and happiness which the fascination of the dance seemed to engender within them'. When she eventually joins in, her proximity to Wildeve does not lead to the palpitations that characterise their passionate relationship; rather, her face is 'rapt and statuesque, empty and quiescent' – the face of a tormented individual giving into her instinct to be loved to madness (*RN*: IV.3).

Paradoxically, then, consciousness entails the freedom to act within the constraints of the will. Such a conclusion invites the question why Hardy should allow it to exist at all. The answer given in the 'Apology' asserts that when the forces of the universe are in equilibrium man is able to exercise his 'modicum of free will' to decide for himself what a morally correct course of action is, and therefore keep pain and suffering 'down to a minimum' (*CP*: 558). This ability to adapt becomes one of the key themes running through Hardy's fiction. Tess, for example, remains pure in Hardy's eyes because her free will constantly struggles against her sexual instinct and the hereditary disposition of her barbarous ancestors. Conversely, the tragedy of Michael Henchard stems from his attempts to impose his own small portion of the will upon the universe through a series of acts both impulsive and massive in scale. In essence, in a world which rewards flexibility and adaptability Henchard, and characters like Eustacia, Clym and Jude are too forceful. Those characters who manage to survive, such as the more passive Thomasin and Elizabeth-Jane, do so because they use their will to minimise the excesses caused by the vicissitudes of the determined world.

NOTES

1 Michael Millgate, *Thomas Hardy: His Career as a Novelist* (London: Macmillan, 1994), p. 176.

2 Robert Schweik, 'Moral Perspectives in *Tess of the d'Urbervilles*', *College English* 24 (1962), pp. 14–18.

3 Brian Green, *Hardy's Lyrics: Pearls of Pity* (London: Macmillan, 1996), p. 3; Deborah Collins, *Thomas Hardy and his God: A Liturgy of Unbelief* (London: Macmillan, 1990).

4 Donald L. Hill (ed.), *The Renaissance, Studies In Art and Literature*, 2nd edition, (Berkeley: University of California Press, 1980), pp. 150–1.

5 Walter Pater, *Plato and Platonism: A Series of Lectures*, 3rd edition (London: Macmillan, 1910), pp. 14, 18–19.

6 Herbert Spencer, *Westminster Review*, 67 o.s., 11 n.s. (1857), pp. 445–85.

7 See Herbert Spencer, *First Principles* (1862), II, Chapter 24.

8 See Robert Gittings, *The Older Hardy* (London: Heinemann, 1978), pp. 6–7.

9 *Fragments of Science: A Series of Detached Essays, Addresses and Reviews*, 5th edition (London: Longman, Green & Co., 1876), p. 560.

10 Herbert Spencer, *The Principles of Psychology*, 3rd edition, 2 vols. (London: Williams and Northgate, 1881), I: 617–18.

11 Phillip Mallett, 'Hardy and Philosophy', *A Companion to Thomas Hardy*, ed. Keith Wilson (Oxford: Wiley Blackwell, 2009), p. 25.

12 Gilles Deleuze and Claire Parnet, *Dialogues*, trans. Hugh Tomlinson and Barbara Habberjam (New York: Columbia University Press, 1987), pp. 39–40.

13 *Spectator* (5 February 1879), pp. 181–2 (*CH*: 58).

14  Robert Adamson, 'Schopenhauer's Philosophy', *Mind* 1 (1876), pp. 491–509.

15  Francis Hueffer, 'Arthur Schopenhauer', *Fortnightly Review* 20 (1876), pp. 773–792; James Sully, 'The Pessimist's View of Life', *Cornhill Magazine* 33 (1876), pp. 431–43.

16  James Sully, *Pessimism: A History and a Criticism* (London: Henry S. King and Co., 1877); Helen Zimmern, *Arthur Schopenhauer: His Life and His Philosophy* (London: Longmans, Green and Co., 1876).

17  *Fortnightly Review*, 26 o.s., 20 n. s. (July 1876), pp. 106–30, pp. 121–2 (see *LN* 1: 170).

18  David Asher, 'Schopenhauer and Darwinism', *The Journal of Anthropology* I (1871), pp. 312–32.

19  Ibid., p. 331.

20  Sully, *Pessimism*, p. 92.

21  James Sully, 'Hartmann's Philosophy of the Unconscious', *Fortnightly Review* 26 o. s., 20 n. s. (August 1876), pp. 242–62.

22  See William Archer, 'Real Conversations. Conversation I – With Mr Thomas Hardy', *The Critic* 38 (April, 1901), p. 316.

23  W. L. Clifford, 'On The Nature of Things-in-Themselves', *Lectures and Essays*, ed. Leslie Stephen and Frederick Pollock, 2 vols. (London: Macmillan, 1879), II: 85.

24  Sully, *Pessimism*, p. 97.

25  Sully, 'Hartman's Philosophy', pp. 252, 254.

# 27

# Positivism: Comte and Mill

### T. R. WRIGHT

Hardy's attitude towards Positivism, which has been relatively neglected by critics, was complicated. His *Literary Notebooks* show that he studied Comte very carefully, while in his autobiography he describes himself as one of the students of the mid-1860s who revered Mill and knew *On Liberty* 'almost by heart' (*LW*: 355). It is impossible, however, to find unequivocal endorsement of Positivism or any other system of philosophy in his work. He was not that kind of a writer, preferring 'representations of life' to 'views *about* life',[1] 'a confused heap of impressions' to 'philosophy' (*LW*: 441).[2] 'I am not a Positivist,' he assured Lady Grove in 1903, but added, 'no person of serious thought in these times could be said to stand aloof from Positivist teaching & ideals' (*CL* III: 53). He occasionally attended Positivist services at Newton Hall, praising both the lectures there and the singing (*LW*: 230; *CL* I: 133–4). His work, as we shall see, contains some of the technical terms of Positivism and several characters who can be identified as Positivists. Here, after outlining the main tenets of Positivism as they appear in the works of Comte and Mill, I will summarise Hardy's explicit comments on them before considering how they enter some of the novels.

Comte's major works comprise the *Cours de philosophie positive* and the *Système de politique positive*, which Hardy read in their English translations of 1853 and 1875–7. The *Système* contains within the first of its four volumes a summary of the whole philosophy, published separately in 1865 in English as *A General View of Positivism*. Horace Moule gave Hardy his copy of this, which is heavily marked by both.[3] The *Life* suggests as a 'possible reason' for a reviewer attributing *Far from the Madding Crowd* to George Eliot the fact 'that he had latterly been reading Comte's *Positive Philosophy*, and writings of that school' (*LW*: 100). That Hardy also studied the third volume of the *Système*, entitled *Social Dynamics*, later in the 1870s is evinced by twelve pages of notes in the *Literary*

*Notebooks*, more than for any other writer (*LN* I: 67–78). It is worth focussing on these three volumes, therefore, to clarify what Hardy would have understood by Positivism.[4]

The point of the *Cours* is to show that all of the sciences have gradually become positive, that is, based upon demonstrable scientific laws. Most relevant to Hardy is probably the last of the six books, which explains Comte's theory of morality and history. The former was based upon the supposed 'science' of phrenology, with its belief that the innate altruistic 'social instincts', like the egoistic 'personal instincts', can be strengthened by exercise and weakened by disuse, forming a supposedly scientific basis for a belief in moral progress. The advance of the whole human race, according to Comte, involved three stages : first, the 'theological', beginning with fetishism, that is, the attribution of will to inanimate objects, before passing through polytheism to monotheism, and reaching its zenith in medieval Catholicism; second, the 'metaphysical' or negative stage, in which Catholicism was questioned and finally abandoned; and finally the 'positive', in which became known the invariable laws of society, on which the reconstruction of society could be based.[5]

*A General View of Positivism* contains six chapters, the first of which outlines the observable laws of the external world. The second chapter, on society, makes explicit Comte's aim 'to make our sympathetic instincts preponderate as far as possible over the selfish instincts'.[6] The two middle chapters explain the importance of the working classes and women, the former having been preserved from the selfish ambitions of the bourgeoisie, the latter representing 'the affective elements in our nature' (I:164). Chapter 5 explains the importance of art in the cultivation of human nature, while the conclusion outlines the main features of the Religion of Humanity, which it presents as 'the successor of Christianity', carrying into effect what that religion left unfinished (I:280–1). Worship in Comte's religion is directed at Humanity itself, the whole of the race, in particular its great men, for which Comte designed a Positivist Calendar. The book ends with a strong attack on monotheism and 'its servile terrors' (I:320–1).

It was the third volume of the *System* which Hardy annotated in detail, with frequent underlinings. Entries 724 to 769 in his *Literary Notebooks* are all taken from the first three chapters of this volume, which outline 'The Positive Theory of Human Evolution' (*LN* I: 74–8). After observing the point of Comte's cerebral theory, Hardy moves on to the law of the three stages, noting in particular the current 'Theological stage of social phenomena'. He observes that the 'Metaphysical spirit' is 'a mere solvent of the Theological: a transition to Pos[itivism]' and is particularly taken with the notion that 'Social Progress' is like "a looped orbit," sometimes apparently backwards, but really always forwards', even drawing a diagram of how this works.

Hardy's notes dwell at some length on the second chapter, 'The Positive Theory of the Age of Fetichism', observing Comte's view that it remains partly valid since 'we shall never know the Real order well enough to be able to dispense entirely' with it. 'There is no harm in Fetichist hypotheses now,' Comte observes, because their 'error [is] too easily perceived to be dangerous', unlike those of 'Theologism', whose 'error [is] not so apparent'. Hardy's notes become more sketchy at this point, as he follows Comte's own somewhat selective analysis of ancient history through polytheism to monotheism and Greek philosophy. He ends this block of notes with a diagram representing Comte's 'Encyclopedic Hierarchy', or chart of the rise of the sciences.

The second main batch of notes from Comte's *Social Dynamics* (entries 645 to 698; *LN* I: 67–71) resumes with Greek philosophy (chapter 4) and continues through the foundation of Christianity in chapter 5. Hardy passes over Comte's attribution of this to St Paul, 'the real founder of Catholicism', with Christ being merely a figurehead. But he notes 'St Paul's theory of the Antagonism of Nature and Grace', anticipating what Positivism explains as the struggle between egoism and altruism. He also summarises the 'self-contradiction in the conception of a single God. "For omnipotence, omniscience, & moral perfection are irreconcilable" with a radically imperfect world.' In a rare extended comment of his own, Hardy recognises there is 'Much in a name – "Western Monotheism" may be proved … a worn-out superstition in the most respectable households, < minds > where an attack on Christianity wᵈ be received with qualms of conscience.' He notes a number of Comte's attacks on 'The Deity' and 'his caprices' and on the doctrines of salvation and damnation. He also notices ways in which Comte sees Catholicism as preparing the way for the Religion of Humanity, in particular through the 'Worship of Saints', and also 'the conception of Humanity' symbolised as it is by the figure of the Virgin Mary. A final batch of notes relates to the French Revolution, the climax of the negative stage (entries 706–17), and the Religion of Humanity to which it led, 'the replacement of supernatural creeds by a demonstrable faith'.

The fourth volume of the *Positive Polity* goes on to expound *The Theory of the Future of Man* in painstaking detail, complete with instructions on private worship, focussed upon the 'angels' in the house (mother, wife and daughter) and the festivals Comte prescribed for the public worship of Humanity. Hardy seems to have taken little interest in this, copying just one paragraph from its preface into his notebook (*LN* I: 133). That he found 'Comte's theory of <u>Modern History</u>' worth dwelling on, however, is evident from the elaborate diagram he constructed illustrating the transition from the 'Catholic-Feudal Power' in 1100 to the 'Scientific or Positive' Power in 1900 (*LN* I: 133).

These notebooks, surprisingly, contain only one extract from Mill, the only external evidence we have of Hardy's study of Mill other than his marked copy of *On Liberty*. It is highly likely, however, that Hardy studied other works by a writer he made so many of his characters read. Mill, as well as being a revered philosopher in his own right, provided Hardy with a model for a broad Positivism less open to ridicule than Comte. Mill was the most respectable British thinker to espouse Positivist principles within the field of science, morality and religion. Reticent as Mill was about his own hostility to Christianity, there can be little doubt about 'the seriousness of his intent to found a new secular or nontheological religion', a revised and less ridiculous version of Comte's Religion of Humanity.[7] Mill had written to Comte in 1841 to express his desire to co-operate in the spread of Positivism. Their correspondence, which continued for another six years, would reveal differences over psychology (which Mill regarded as a separate science) and politics (in which he was far more liberal than Comte, especially on the role of women), but never any doubt about the fundamental principles of Positivism.[8]

Many of Mill's works of the 1840s and 1850s warmly advocate Positivism. The final book of his *System of Logic* (1843), 'On the Logic of the Moral Sciences', retains a Comtean belief in the modifiability of human character through the development of altruistic habits. It also accepts the principles of social statics and dynamics, giving an enthusiastic account of the law of the three stages.[9] *Utilitarianism,* written in 1854 though not published until 1863, reiterates Mill's belief in the possibility of developing 'the nobler feelings' by exercise and 'giving to the service of humanity, even without the belief in a Providence, both the psychological power and the social efficacy of a religion'.[10] *On Liberty* (1859) expresses serious doubts about the 'despotism of society over the individual' to be found in the later Comte.[11] The chapter 'Of Individuality', listed by Hardy in 1868 as one of his three 'Cures for despair' (*LW*: 59), continues to adhere to a Comtean belief in 'the better development of the social part of his nature rendered possible by the restraint put upon the selfish part' but places limits upon the extent to which an individual should be controlled by others. The final chapter turns Comte's morals against his politics, arguing that too much state interference prevents men 'strengthening their active faculties'.[12] But Mill's critique of Comte is mild in comparison with his attack on the servile and conformist morality of Christianity.[13]

Mill's most sustained commentary upon Comte can be found in *Comte and Positivism* (1865), which praises his systematisation of the philosophy of science and finds 'no fundamental errors' in his 'general conception of history'. Mill also expresses complete sympathy with the general aims of the Religion of Humanity, finding 'nothing really ridiculous in the devotional practices Comte recommends towards a cherished memory or an ennobling ideal, when they come unprompted from the depths of the individual feeling'.[14] Shorn of its prescriptive details, in other words, Mill found much of value in Comte's religion. His continuing disagreement with Comte over the role of women is apparent in *The Subjection of Women* (1869), which deplores the view that it is both 'the duty of women' and 'their nature' to 'live for others ... and to have no life but in their affections'.[15] His posthumously published *Autobiography* (1873) again deplores the 'spiritual and temporal despotism' evident in the *Système*.[16] But his *Three Essays on Religion* (1874) restate his sympathy with the basic idea of a Religion of Humanity, the notion that 'the idealization of our earthly life' is 'capable of supplying a poetry and ... a religion', as well fitted 'to exalt the feelings' and 'ennoble the conduct' as 'any belief respecting the unseen powers'.[17] These later works, unlike Comte's, continue to present Christ as a model of human goodness.

Mill was by no means the only midcentury British thinker familiar to Hardy who engaged seriously with Comte's work. A whole range of scientific and literary figures who feature in his intellectual development, such as John Morley, Leslie Stephen and George Eliot, felt it necessary to read and comment on Comte. Hardy also knew a number of card-carrying members of the Positivist Society, including Frederic Harrison, a friend for forty years (*CL* VI: 180), E. S. Beesly the historian, J. H. Bridges, another 'Dorset man' (*LW*: 178), and James Cotter Morison, long passages from whose book on *The Service of Man* (1887) appear in the *Literary Notebooks*.[18]

Hardy's interest in Positivism, in other words, initiated by Moule in the 1860s and reinforced by his study of Comte in the 1870s, was maintained through the 1880s. The death of George Eliot at the end of 1880, for example, 'set him thinking about Positivism', about which he wrote:

If Comte had introduced Christ among the worthies in his calendar it would have made Positivism tolerable to thousands who, from position, family connection, or early education, now decry what in their heart of hearts they hold to contain the germs of a true system. (*LW*: 150–1)

Hardy explained to Morley in 1885 that what he '& other thoughtful people who have ceased to believe in supernatural theology' wanted was not the disestablishment of the Church of England but its being 'made to modulate by degrees (say as the present incumbents die out) into an undogmatic, non-theological establishment for the promotion of that virtuous living on which all honest men are agreed' (*CL* I: 136–7). At other times, however, he agreed with Comte that there could be no compromise with Christianity. He urged Frederic Harrison in 1888 to attack 'the New Christians (or whatever they are)' as he had done earlier in an article of 1860 on 'Neo-Christianity', criticising the liberal theologians responsible for *Essays and Reviews* (*CL* I: 176).[19] Both publicly, in his essay on 'Candour in English Fiction' of 1890, which refers very positively to Comte's view of human progress,[20] and privately, in a note from the same year which discusses 'Altruism' and the concept of

Humanity, the idea that 'Mankind ... may be, and possibly will be, viewed as members of one corporeal frame' (*LW*: 235), Hardy indicated clear agreement with key Comtean ideas.

When Frederic Harrison wrote in 1891 to claim that *Tess* was so 'saturated with human and anti-theological morality' that it read 'like a Positivist allegory or sermon', Hardy assured him that the first draft of the novel had contained 'much more on religion as apart from theology' (*CL* I: 251). He also attributed to 'the Positive view of the Universe' expressed in *The Dynasts* the '*odium theologicum*' it had raised in the critics (*CL* III: 98), and accepted that he and Harrison were in philosophical (if not temperamental) agreement (*CL* III: 231). This difference rose to the surface when Harrison attacked Hardy's poems for their consistent pessimism,[21] causing Hardy to defend himself in an 'Apology' to *Late Lyrics and Earlier*, in which he repeated his allegiance to 'evolutionary meliorism', with another reference to Comte's notion that 'advance is never is a straight line, but in a looped orbit' (*CP*: 557, 562).

Those looking for Positivism in Hardy's work are likely to be disappointed if they expect unequivocal endorsement of the kind Harrison wanted. They will find, however, a general sympathy with its central belief in the possible development of altruism without recourse to the supernatural. They will also find a number of characters who are identifiably Positivist in attitude, of whom the most important are Clym Yeobright, Angel Clare, and, to some extent, Sue Bridehead.

*The Return of the Native*, the first novel Hardy wrote after his detailed study of Comte's *Système*, describes Clym Yeobright's as 'the typical countenance of the future', expressing the essential Positivist virtue of resignation, 'the view of life as a thing to be put up with' rather than enjoyed (*RN*: III.1). His beliefs are presented as a product of 'his studious life in Paris, where he had become acquainted with ethical systems popular at the time' (*RN*: III.2). Paterson, noting that this last phrase, like the 'growth of fellow-feeling' which Clym evinces (*RN*: II.6), was in the first edition but not in the serial, argues that these beliefs were a late addition to the manuscript, covering the powerful anti-Christian core of the novel with 'a basically irrelevant and superficial humanitarianism'.[22] But the two come together in Comte, whose ideas appear to feed into the discourses Clym delivers at the end of the novel. He even practises a form of Positive worship, dwelling on the memory of his mother as a 'sublime saint' (*RN*: VI.4). By presenting Clym as 'a Comtean paradigm', however, Hardy does not necessarily endorse all of his views,[23] leaving his readers to judge how effective Clym's work is likely to be.

The same can be said of Angel Clare, whose first words on his reappearance in the novel at Talbothays are in praise of 'medieval times, when faith was a living thing' (*Tess*: 17). Again, Hardy gives a clear hint as to the source of Angel's views when he recounts the story (adapted from the experience of Horace Moule) of a book shocking his father on its arrival at the vicarage, only for Angel to explain that 'it is a system of philosophy. There is no more moral, or even religious, work published.' Angel insists with Comte, 'I love the Church as one loves a parent', but rejects her 'untenable redemptive theolatry'. 'My whole instinct in matters of religion,' he proceeds, 'is toward reconstruction', replacing work for 'the glory of God' with work 'for the glory of man' (*Tess*: 18). Both the sentiments and the vocabulary clearly derive from Positivism, as does his critique of 'creeds which futilely attempt to check what wisdom would be content to regulate' (*Tess*: 25).

This debt to Positivism is even more apparent when Tess echoes Clare's beliefs to Alec, insisting that she too has a religion, 'Though I don't believe in anything supernatural' (*Tess*: 46). Tess echoes not only Clare but Morison's *Service of Man,* reproducing his argument that 'Primitive religion had little or no connection with morals'(*LN* I: 190): 'She tried to ... tell him that he had mixed in his dull brain two matters, theology and morals, which in the primitive days of mankind had been quite distinct.' Not all Tess's views can be attributed directly to Positivism, of course; the narrator notes that a saying of Clare's which she repeats 'might possibly have been paralleled in many a work of pedigree ranging from the *Dictionnaire Philosophique* to Huxley's essays' (*Tess*: 46). There is also a suggestion that Clare, like Comte, does not go far enough in his rejection of Christian morality, and that his rejection of Tess reflects the 'ethereal' and 'imaginative' nature of his Positivistic worship of her, 'creating an ideal presence that erroneously drops the defects of the real' (*Tess*: 36). Only in Brazil does he recognise this, abandoning 'the old appraisements of morality' along with 'the old systems of mysticism' (*Tess*: 49). Positivism, in other words, can be seen to feed into Clare's character, but not always in ways that are to be admired.

Sue Bridehead has been identified as another of Hardy's somewhat questionable Positivists by the terms she uses, as for instance when she dismisses Oxford as 'a place full of fetichists'.[24] She is also given to quoting Mill against the 'apelike ... imitation' of convention (*Jude*: IV.3). It is possible too to detect in *The Dynasts* in particular and in Hardy's poetry in general a Positivist view of history (culminating in the French Revolution) and a belief in the possible amelioration of Humanity. The Pities, Hardy explains in his Preface, represent 'the Universal Sympathy of human nature' while the Years represent the 'Insight of the Ages'.[25] But the relation between Positivism as a system of thought and the imaginative work of a writer as unsystematic, impressionistic and conflicted as Hardy remains irreducible to any straightforward conclusion. The most one can say is that Positivism made a significant impression on Hardy, informing his thinking about religion, morality, history and society. Its traces recur not only in his vocabulary but in his construction of character and in the questions about the future of religion which pervade his work.

NOTES

1  Thomas Hardy, 'The Profitable Reading of Fiction' (*THPV*: 21).
2  See Phillip Mallett, 'Hardy and Philosophy', *A Companion to Thomas Hardy*, ed. Keith Wilson (Oxford: Blackwell, 2009), pp. 21–35.
3  Michael Millgate, *Thomas Hardy: A Biography Revisited* (Oxford: Oxford University Press, 2004), p. 88.
4  For a full discussion of Comte see Mary Pickering, *Auguste Comte: An Intellectual Biography* (Cambridge: Cambridge University Press, 1993), and T. R. Wright, *The Religion of Humanity: The Impact of Comtean Positivism on Victorian Britain* (Cambridge: Cambridge University Press, 1986).
5  *The Positive Philosophy of Auguste Comte,* trans. Harriet Martineau, 2 vols. (London: John Chapman, 1853). This and the *General View* were reissued by Cambridge University Press in 2009.
6  Auguste Comte, *System of Positive Polity,* trans. J. H. Bridges and others, 4 vols. (London: Longmans, Green and Co., 1875–7), I.72–3.
7  Linda C. Raeder, *John Stuart Mill and the Religion of Humanity* (Columbia: University of Missouri Press, 2002), p. 1. See also Alan P. F. Snell, *Mill on God* (Aldershot: Ashgate, 2004) and Alan Millar,

'Mill on Religion', *The Cambridge Companion to Mill*, ed. John Skorupski (Cambridge: Cambridge University Press, 1998), pp. 176–202.

8 Oscar A. Haac, ed., *The Correspondence of John Stuart Mill and Auguste Comte*, (New Brunswick: Transaction Publishers, 1995).

9 John Stuart Mill, *A System of Logic*, 2 vols. (London: J. W. Parker, 1843). Later editions of the *Logic* remove or tone down the many enthusiastic references to Comte in the first edition.

10 John Stuart Mill, *Utilitarianism* (London: Longmans, Green and Co., 1863), pp. 15, 48.

11 John Stuart Mill, *On Liberty* (London: J. W. Parker, 1859), p. 29.

12 Ibid., pp. 114, 196–7.

13 Joseph Hamburger, 'Religion and *On Liberty*', *A Cultivated Mind: Essays on John Stuart Mill Presented to John M. Robson*, ed. Michael Laine (Toronto: University of Toronto Press, 1991), pp. 139–81.

14 John Stuart Mill, *Auguste Comte and Positivism* (London: Longmans, Green and Co., 1865), pp. 113–18, 153.

15 John Stuart Mill, *The Subjection of Women* (London: Longmans, Green and Co., 1869), p. 27.

16 John Stuart Mill, *Autobiography* (London: Longmans, Green and Co., 1873), p. 213.

17 John Stuart Mill, *Nature, The Utility of Religion and Theism* (London: Longmans, Green and Co., 1874), pp. 104–5 and 257.

18 James Cotter Morison, *The Service of Man. An Essay Toward the Religion of the Future* (London: Kegan and Paul, 1887). Passages from this book also appear in *Thomas Hardy's 'Facts' Notebook*, ed. William Greenslade (Aldershot: Ashgate, 2004), pp. 273–5.

19 Reprinted in Frederic Harrison, *The Creed of a Layman* (London: Macmillan, 1907).

20 *THPV*: 96–7.

21 Reprinted in Frederic Harrison, *Novissima Verba* (London: T. F. Unwin, 1921), pp. 27–34.

22 John Paterson, *The Making of 'The Return of the Native'* (Berkeley: University of California Press, 1960), pp. 63–6. Later editions read 'emotional development' in place of 'growth of fellow-feeling'.

23 Hillary Tiefer, 'Clym Yeobright: Hardy's Comtean Hero', *Thomas Hardy Journal* 16:2 (2000), p. 43.

24 Robert Gittings, *Young Thomas Hardy* (London: Penguin, 1978), p. 140; *Jude*: III.4.

25 Thomas Hardy, Preface to *The Dynasts*, *CPW* IV: 7.

## 28

# Hardy and the Law

### MELANIE WILLIAMS

Hardy's interest in the law is well known. He dined with the judiciary, took a keen interest in the human stories manifesting in the courtroom and served as a magistrate himself. Legal characters appear throughout his work and legal themes are extensive.[1] Though Hardy often demonstrates what William Davis describes as a 'justice plot' in the greater narrative fabric, the role of the law in the delivery of formal justice is frequently arbitrary.[2] As a Magistrate, Hardy must have had occasion to deliver a 'fair' judgement and sentence; as a human being and novelist however, he was alive to the injustices of class, education and chance frequently creating terrible inequalities endorsed by the law. 'Cruelty is the law pervading all nature and society; and we can't get out of it if we would!' says Phillotson in *Jude the Obscure* (*Jude*: V.8), and this harsh reality is reflected again and again in the novels, echoing Hardy's frequent intimation of the apparently malevolent 'play' between the laws of man and the laws of nature.

Where Hardy might have been tempted to use the law, like Dickens, as an illustration or source of social injustice, he instead works it into the fabric of lives lived subject to the play of more powerful human forces. Though the legal motifs in his work are often far from minor, Hardy tends to situate them in terms of their primary genesis, as instances of social and human catastrophe in the relentless interplay between character, agency and fate befalling his human creatures. Thus *The Mayor of Casterbridge*, though dealing with transposed identities and wife-sales – topics clearly capable of interesting jurisprudential treatment – is recognised essentially as a tragedy of power, flawed character and custom. The terrible concatenation of events leading to the murder in *Far from the Madding Crowd* is focussed more upon the notion of spiritual growth: of Bathsheba learning that her power over men can have untold consequences, and that quiet loyalty is deeper than status, wealth or dashing shows of gallantry. *Jude the Obscure* is a grid of marital arrangements – marriage, co-habitation, separation, and divorce – yet the legal issues are intimately directed by the personal sensitivities of the characters concerned.[3] From the very beginning we learn that Jude himself comes from a family not suited to marriage; Sue Bridehead is tormented by qualms about the spiritual meaning of the contract of marriage whilst Arabella calculates the utility of the deed in planning her worldly strategies. These human responses are treated much more extensively than the technical legal questions. Most significantly, perhaps, *Tess of the d'Urbervilles* is a story of at very least a seduction, perhaps a rape, of the eventual murder of one character and hanging of another, yet virtually no textual space is spent upon examination of the legal issues, nor is any narrative provided of the murder trial itself.[4] Indeed, many would argue that *Tess* is not a tale of legal significance; it is not, after all, 'about' the law.

What is most significant, therefore, in Hardy's treatment of legal issues is his refusal to situate the law as a central plank of his narratives *from the point of view of the law*. This is clearly deliberate. Hardy recognizes that the role played by the law in the lives of ordinary people is frequently peripheral to the driving forces of their lives and, where it does impinge upon them, is more likely than not to be just one more source of those ironies, obstacles and fateful twists so critical to the world view implicit in the texts. 'Once victim, always victim: that's the law!' is Tess Durbeyfield's bitter cry, and we learn its relentless truth (*Tess*: 47).

Hardy's jurisprudential subtlety is evident when one considers the interpretations possible in relation to the legally significant events in *Tess of the d'Urbervilles*. In his essay 'Was Alec a Rapist', John Sutherland suggests that Tess is more a seductress than victim, engaging in sexual risk taking and eventually murdering Alec d'Urberville in a vengeful and unjustified pique.[5] Sutherland's essential thesis is that, at the time the book was published, Hardy's audience would have understood that Tess was, at worst, a party to 'seduction', but that a cultural shift towards a kind of gender-political correctness had altered that reading: 'She who was seduced in 1892 is she who is raped in the permissive 1960s.'[6] However, it may be argued that Hardy was wholly calculating in his depiction of events and that the scenario was, and remains, pertinent to the construction of 'rape', and an eventual killing in response to the persistently malign shadow thrown by Alec over the life of Tess. With his rural background, Hardy understood, practically and intellectually, the hardship and privations of peasant life and the pretences of the bourgeoisie. He was alive to the likely repercussions of his writings: textual ambiguities, as exemplified in this sexual encounter, at least in part reflect the social constraints imposed upon him as author *and* upon the experiences to which his characters could lay claim.

Sutherland's analysis is focused upon the textual evidence of the sexual encounter and appears similar to the analysis that would take place in a legal context; certain facts, circumstantial evidence, points of view and verbal statements made by the parties to the encounter are selected as material to the case. The selectivity of Sutherland's account is crucial to his conclusions: reading this in conjunction with the text of the novel provides an opportunity to test his reading of the evidence. After the sexual encounter Tess, we may recall, rebukes her mother:

'How could I be expected to know? I was a child when I left this house four months ago. Why didn't you tell me there was danger in men-folk? Why didn't you warn me? Ladies know what to fend hands against, because they read novels that tell them of these tricks.' (*Tess*: 12)

Sutherland dismisses this extensive plea (which indicates real anatomical ignorance – 'Ladies know what to fend hands against') with the gloss: 'Nor, when upbraiding her mother for not warning her against men, does Tess claim that she has been raped': for Sutherland, failure to use the *word* 'rape' is conclusive.[7] Yet had the plot so centred upon the crime of rape, clear rape in Tess's mind and published abroad by her as such, insuperable demands would have been made upon the plot; the complex tale of emotional and social dislocation that is *Tess of the d'Urbervilles* would have been denied. Nevertheless, the whole novel centres upon her unwitting victimhood and her status, as the subtitle has it, as 'a pure woman', despite society branding her otherwise. It is an indictment of Victorian double standards, which by the 1890s a few enlightened members of society could begin to critique. It is also a reflection of the more usual circumstances obtaining in such cases. The text explores the subtleties of victim experience, strongly mirrored by modern accounts: the exploitation of unequal gender and power relations; the fatalism of the rural working class; the scepticism and readiness of wider society to judge and condemn in error; the isolation and sense of guilt experienced by the victim. Even after the sexual assault scene, Tess remains subject to d'Urberville's power and influence, as he continues to be her employer and the benefactor of her destitute family; a destitution which Tess blames in part upon herself.[8] She allows Alec to kiss her on the cheek, but remains 'indifferent', and repeats her assertion that she cannot love him, despite her apprehension that future events might justify her being less than truthful on the point.

Even today, a vast proportion of rape cases either go unreported or collapse at trial because victims are all too readily undermined. Like Tess, victims excoriate themselves with unwarranted feelings of guilt for having 'allowed' events to occur, and courts – and society – play into this. The case of Tess is miserably typical of the type of case that might well then, as now, have failed. For although 'successful' case law is similar in *some* facts (as we shall see), Tess's account would be undermined firstly by having allowed herself to be led without witness into a wood, and secondly by her lowly status as against that of her attacker.[9] Tess's tale is thus largely *untold* by precedent, like many hundreds of cases unreported or unpursued. Moreover, the word 'rape' was virtually unsayable in the Victorian mouth, whilst 'seduction', 'ruination' and the like were words used broadly, with little reference to the presence or absence of consent. As a creature of the patriarchal *logos*, the word served a multitude of material and ideological purposes.

Of contextual relevance is the subtle interplay of values and assumptions revealed by the laws of the period. Sutherland's view is coloured by the verbal and conceptual anomaly that was played out in Victorian law, in the ambiguous relationship between the words 'seduction' and 'rape'. For some Victorian commentators, as for Sutherland, 'seduction' more readily implies mutuality, complicity. In present assumptions of sexual liberation and equality, 'seduction' is no longer a crime,[10] yet we may still find ourselves speaking of a 'victim' of seduction. At the time of *Tess*, seduction could be subject to legal notice. In English law, the terms of this legal response were rooted in the history of women as property.[11] The language and forms of these cases reveal that women were very far from being the autonomous beings that Sutherland's use of the word 'seduction' assumes;[12] in some cases the masculine 'duel' over ruined property occludes evidence bearing a close resemblance to the facts of rape.

The case is of additional interest for lawyers and scholars because it involves the suggestion, as in some 'real life' sexual offence cases, that the act took place while the victim was asleep: that 'penetration' began whilst Tess was sleeping soundly and that, given her anatomical ignorance she was, on waking, confused enough for completion of the act to occur, 'succumb[ing] to adroit advantages he took of her helplessness' (*Tess*: 12).[13] Like many rape victims, Tess feels foolish and guilty for having allowed herself to fall into such a trap and is unsure as to whether she has any claim to moral integrity. When she later meets a religious slogan-writer inscribing 'THY, DAMNATION, SLUMBERETH, NOT', and asks: 'suppose your sin was not of your own seeking?' (*Tess*: 12), the question independently classifies the act as *unsought*. Once the deed is done, she lapses into a state of fatalistic apathy. This is a credible response: Aware of the contribution made by her own ignorance, a girl in her lowly position would also have had difficulty sustaining a complaint against a gentleman, albeit a gentleman who has proved himself calculating and amoral.[14]

In criminal trials for rape, there is a clear motive for construing the evidence either to strengthen or undermine the case against the accused. It is the *raison d'être* of prosecution and defence counsel, the very purpose of the theatre of law, to test the credibility of conflicting accounts. In the text *Tess of the d'Urbervilles* there exists an additional source of evidence to which the real-life courtroom cannot advert, in the philosophically enlightened and reliably clairvoyant eye of the omniscient narrator. Those events obscured or unsayable in the Victorian text are made more transparent by judgments offered by the omniscient narrator. The voice vindicates Tess as an innocent who is consumed first for her beauty and then again for daring to hope that the absence of agency in her own sexual fate will preserve her from further harm. The plot confirms this view: Alec is a cad who admits full blame, her husband Angel Clare rejects her because of the mechanical fact of her lost maidenhood, notwithstanding the blameless context of that loss.

The transcendent importance of preserving virginity as the emblem of unsullied property meant, as Hardy clearly knew, that women were divided into two basic groups, determined not by the modern emphasis upon whether intercourse was consensual or not but by whether anatomical invasion had occurred.[15] Whereas Tess's rural companions clearly understand that the protections vouchsafed to bourgeois females do not extend to them, writers of critical essays languished in the deluded certainties of middle-class prejudice. It was believed that girls who found themselves in compromising situations at the very least contributed to, if not actively sought, their fate.[16]

Tess herself was little more than a child at the time of the encounter; the text describes her bastard offspring as 'a child's child' (*Tess*: 14).[17] But this was at a time when childhood was fleeting, in fact and law, and sexual maturation all too easily implied a guilty mind. Tess's sensual appeal and her downfall lie partly in that very combination of childish womanliness:

'Here was I thinking you a new-sprung child of nature: there were you, the belated seedling of an effete aristocracy!' (*Tess*: 35)

rails her husband. Yet the evidence throughout the book suggests that Tess is the victim of her own sexual ignorance and innocence, that the encounter is unwanted, but that in Victorian terms 'The Woman Pays'.

Hardy's insights into the complex psychological landscapes especially prevalent in the unequal power relations between men and women extend beyond his vision of the sexual encounter. A similarly compelling perspective is offered in the circumstances surrounding the eventual killing of Alec. Hardy's depiction of the long-suffering Tess demonstrates a prescient understanding of the state of mind which might have led to such an act – a state of mind still very much debated by the law.[18] Hardy divined the degree of emotional alienation caused by such psychological damage, describing how Angel sees that

his original Tess had spiritually ceased to recognize the body before him as hers –allowing it to drift, like a corpse upon the current, in a direction dissociated from its living will. (*Tess*: 55)

In modern murder trials, especially those resulting from a culmin-
ation of psychological or physical suffering by the accused at the
hands of the victim, a 'dissociated' state of mind has only recently
come to be recognized as pertinent to assessment of the state of
mind of the accused and to their subsequent responsibility for
their acts. In the very detail of this state of mind, Hardy produces
a remarkable correlation between the piteous notes sent by Tess
to Angel – whose love she hopes to regain – and those sent by
the accused in a modern British murder trial,[19] demonstrating an
instinct for portraying this particular but relevant state of mind
that continues to pose a challenge to modern jurisprudence and
psychiatry.[20]

Hardy was of course a master in the art of dramatizing the profound connections between the worlds of the ideal and the real, of
Nature as cruel mistress, of human nature as flawed entity, of the
ironies and paradoxes obtaining between notions of the laws of
man, of nature and of 'Natural Law'.[21] More specifically, in touch-
ing upon scenarios relevant to the law, his contribution was much
greater than the straightforwardly 'technical' knowledge – of wills,
insurances, divorce rules, inquests – overtly displayed throughout
the novels. Subtly and more profoundly, Hardy recognized a fact
still deeply material to debates in criminal justice today and even
more so in days gone by: that social constraints and prejudices
inscribe the individual agent with a pre-determined identity which
undoubtedly affects the 'classical' model of the 'free-willing' agent,
contributing to the 'production' of the crime to a degree more
fundamental than the law – and our vision of the autonomous
subject – will admit. The entire doctrinal framework in criminal
law, with its attempt to identify those 'characteristics' or 'lapses',
which will separate the 'deviant' from the 'reasonable' is miscon-
ceived; little or no account is taken, for example, of the entirely
uncharacteristic turn of behaviour exemplified when abused persons finally 'break'.[22] As Hardy divines, the issue is not entirely
clinical or doctrinal, but also philosophical and linguistic.[23] In
particular, as he so masterfully reveals, the collision of such factors
with the uncertain impact of contingent events, social power and
an antic moral landscape, renders the individual vulnerable indeed
to the less than rational impact of the world of man and, thereby,
the world of law.

NOTES

1 Harold Orel, *The Unknown Thomas Hardy* (London: Palgrave Macmillan, 1987), pp. 141–2, reproduces in alphabetical form the list of such characters first compiled by Frank Pinion in *A Hardy Companion* (London: Macmillan, 1968).

2 William A. Davis, *Thomas Hardy and the Law: Legal Presences in Hardy's Life and Fiction* (Newark: University of Delaware Press, 2003). Davis melds research into Hardy's personal links to the law with the fictional accounts, unearthing cases pertinent to the twists of various plots from the English common law record. He traces legal issues on a kind of evolutionary basis: of *Desperate Remedies*, for example, he notes (p. 54) the 'principal metaphor which holds the novel together – the woman's life viewed as an evolving, confusing legal spectacle'.

3 For the debate upon marriage in *Jude the Obscure*, see Melanie Williams, *Secrets and Laws* (London: UCL Press, 2005), ch. 7.

4 For legal issues in *Tess*, see Melanie Williams, *Empty Justice: One Hundred Years of Law, Literature and Philosophy* (London: Cavendish Publishing, 2002), ch. 2.

5 John Sutherland, 'Was Alec a Rapist?', *Is Heathcliff a Murderer – Puzzles in Nineteenth Century Fiction* (Oxford: Oxford University Press, 1996). A considered legal response to Sutherland appears in Melanie Williams, *Secrets and Laws*, ch. 9.

6 Sutherland, 'Was Alec a Rapist?', p. 203.

7 Ibid., p. 208. However, the word 'rape' is frequently avoided in Victorian century culture: From writers of fiction to witness statements, euphemisms are preferred to the precise noun.

8 Tess attempts to retain some shred of dignity in this aftermath, wearing only the clothes she can pay for herself and working in the fields. Despite Alec's protestation that she need not work and can 'clothe herself with the best', Tess replies 'I *should* be your creature to go on doing that; and I won't!' (*Tess*: 12)

9 For defence based on the 'character' of the accused, see Carolyn Conley, 'Rape and Justice in Victorian England', *Victorian Studies* 29:4 (Summer 1986), pp. 519–36.

10 Note however the recent resurrection of the notion of criminalising 'seduction' in England and Wales in the context of schoolteachers and their 16 to 17-year-old charges: 'Teachers criticise "seduction law" plan', *The Times*, 4 September 1998.

11 Note for example the language used in *R v. Mycock* [1871] Cox C.C. 28, an action for abduction: 'the prisoner had no more right to deprive the father of the girl of his property, as it were,

in her, and his possession of her, than he would have a right to go into his shop and carry away one of his telescopes or optical instruments.'

12 The focus of the action was upon the preservation of *physical* integrity; whether the girl consented or understood was irrelevant to the men of law. Not only might seduction be classified as a trespass against property, a tort; in 1921, thirty-seven American jurisdictions maintained statutes defining seduction as a crime.

13 As has been noted, Victorian case law gives clear indications that women could be tricked into allowing intercourse as a result of their sexual ignorance. The case law that most closely mirrors the case of Tess established that rape can occur whilst the victim is asleep. In *R v. Young* (1878) 14 Cox C.C. 114, the prisoner 'proceeded to have connexion' with the victim, she 'then being asleep'. Held, the prisoner was guilty of the crime of rape. In *R v. Mayers* (1872) Cox C.C. Vol. XII (1871–4) 311 Sarah Mayers testified (note the euphemistic terms used) that she 'fell asleep; the first thing after that which I remember was finding the prisoner in bed with me, he was agate of me when I awoke.' See also the sad case of *R v. Page* (1846) Cox C.L.C. 133, on the trial of an indictment for rape: 'it appeared that the prisoner had commenced having connexion with the prosecutrix, his own daughter, a girl about thirteen years of age, while she was asleep, but that she awoke before it was at an end and made no resistance, until she saw that a third person was present watching her.'

14 Consent remained 'in issue' in crimes against young children. Little wonder perhaps that rape claims by ordinary women of the period seem singularly rare; for this paradoxical reference to consent may be resolved by viewing it as involving an unspoken *presumption* of consent, as opposed to the modern ideal of establishing whether consent was real or, from diverse pressures, apparent. The case of Woodhurst (1870) Cox C.L.C. 443 adverted to the negation of consent through terror because it involved a ten year old child; such 'psychological' pressure has only lately come to be recognised as a viable negating factor for adult women.

15 The fact of such damage raised a presumption in the minds of 'respectable' souls, still exploited today. As Helena Kennedy explains, 'The persistent cross-examination ploy of defence counsel is to deny that fear might paralyze the victim and to insist that a woman guarding her virtue would fight like a lioness': Helena Kennedy, *Eve was Framed: Women and British Justice* (London: Vintage, 1993), p. 123.

16  Sutherland relies on the views of the Victorian critic Mrs Oliphant, who, as Sutherland must know, represented extreme sanctimony.

17  On the significance of Tess's age and virginity at the time of the encounter, see Phillip Mallett, 'The Immortal Puzzle: Hardy and Sexuality', *Thomas Hardy Studies*, ed. Phillip Mallett (London: Palgrave Macmillan, 2004), pp. 181–202.

18  See debates surrounding the production of the Coroners and Justice Act 2009 and Law Commission Consultation Summary Paper no. 173 (2003) on Partial Defences to Murder at http:// www.lawcom.gov.uk/docs/cp173sum.pdf.

19  See letters reproduced in Melanie Williams, *Empty Justice*, at p. 54, comparing the description and pleas of Tess with those of Mrs Ahluwalia in *R v Ahluwalia* [1992] All ER 889, p. 893.

20  See Melanie Williams, 'A Normal Man ... Hardly Exists', *Current Legal Problems 2009*, ed. Colm O'Cinneide (Oxford: Oxford University Press, 2009).

21  References, often ironic or tragic, to the laws of nature and natural law abound in the works of Hardy. Tess is told that Alec d'Urberville is her 'husband in nature', that is, that he was first to 'mate' with her. (Formally, 'Natural Law' refers to the conception of a body of universal moral principles from which are derived the ethical and *legal* norms by which human conduct is sometimes understood and ruled.)

22  The commitment of the criminal law of England and Wales to the abstracted notion of the free-willing agent has compromised consideration of the relationship between ill-treatment, reactive violence, and lack of fit with prior good character; the Coroners and Justice Act 2009 makes some attempt to allow recognition of such issues (see note 18, this chapter).

23  Rhetorical force and devices may still steer the doctrinal equation, with 'interpretation' of facts remaining an art closer to the domain of fiction than to the claimed territory of forensic science.

# 29

# Hardy, Darwin, and *The Origin of Species*

## PHILLIP MALLETT

Recalling in his autobiography that in April 1882 he had attended the funeral in Westminster Abbey of Charles Darwin, Hardy added that 'As a young man he had been among the earliest acclaimers of *The Origin of Species*' (*LW*: 158). In what sense an architectural pupil in out-of-the-way Dorchester, of avowedly 'churchy' tendencies, might have acclaimed the *Origin* is unclear; nor is it wholly evident what he might have been acclaiming. In the 1860s Hardy studied Newman's *Apologia*, the French utopian socialist Charles Fourier, and Comte's *A General View of Positivism*, but there is no record of his reading Darwin. In 1875, when he witnessed Leslie Stephen's renunciation of holy orders, the two men discussed together 'the origin of things, the constitution of matter, the unreality of time, and kindred subjects', the latter perhaps including Stephen's 1873 essay on 'Darwinism and Divinity' (*LW*: 109). Evolutionary biology was in the air, and its presence can be felt in Hardy's work from the 1860s on – the chanciness noted in his early poem 'Hap' (1866), for example, is at the least consonant with Darwin's emphasis on the power of random variations – but not, it seems likely, because of an early encounter with the *Origin*.[1]

The received account of the writing and impact of the *Origin* holds that during his voyage on HMS *Beagle* Darwin's study of the variously shaped beaks of related species of finch in the Galápagos archipelago compelled him towards a new and dangerous idea: the evolution of species by descent along diverging lines from a common progenitor, and in particular the descent of the human race from a simian ancestor. This idea, the story goes, disproved the Bible and 'destroyed God'. In the resulting battle between religion and science, Thomas Huxley, Darwin's bulldog, routed the Church establishment so decisively that two decades later evolution by natural selection had triumphed, and Darwin was accorded the honour of burial in the Abbey. The story is, unfortunately, as misleading as it is engaging. To unpick it is to get closer to what Darwin called the 'one long argument' of the *Origin*, and to an estimate of its influence on his contemporaries.

HMS *Beagle* set sail in December 1831, and returned in October 1836. Darwin's chief concern at the outset was geology rather than zoology, and he immersed himself in Charles Lyell's *Principles of Geology* (1830–3). He took from it two essential insights. First, Lyell's methodological insistence on the study of proximate causes still observably at work was to become Darwin's own: it was never his ambition to construct an ultimate theory of origins. Second, Lyell's theory of gradual geological change extended the dark backward and abysm of time to the hundreds of millions of years that would be required by the theory of natural selection. But while uniformitarian geology and the concept of deep time helped explain the elevation of the Andes, and prompted Darwin's own theory about the formation of coral islands, he could not share Lyell's belief that the distribution of species proved separate acts of creation. In particular, he puzzled over the presence of distinct but related species in overlapping territories, like the several kinds of Argentinean rhea, or inhabiting separate islands, like the different types of finches, mockingbirds, and tortoises of the Galápagos archipelago. Elsewhere he found living animals in the same area as fossilized mammals whom they closely resembled. It was only on his return, however, when the ornithologist John Gould helped him link the separation of species to the geographical barriers between them, that he concluded that each had diverged from a common ancestor. The key to the classification of species, Darwin came to understand, was genealogical. Structural and functional resemblances derived from consanguinity, not from the Divine preference for a few recurring patterns. The 'law of evolution,' as Hardy was to summarise it in 1909, 'revealed that all organic creatures are of one family' (*LW*: 373) – a family in which 'man' was 'not "higher" than the other animals' (*LN* II: 225).[2]

There was then no eureka moment on board the *Beagle*. Nor was there a sudden loss of faith. Natural selection did and does make nonsense of the argument from design, but the *Origin* still admits the possibility of a Creator who impressed life into all living things, albeit through natural laws rather than a series of discrete acts. It was not 'Darwinism' but the age-old problem of pain and still more the doctrine of damnation that turned Darwin himself into an agnostic (the word coined by Huxley), if not quite an atheist. True, according to the faith of his much-loved wife Emma, their daughter Annie, who died aged ten in 1851, was a soul in bliss, but in the severer versions of that belief his father and his brother were in torment, and that was a 'damnable doctrine'. Disbelief 'crept over me at a very slow rate', he wrote later, but it was 'at last complete'.[3]

Meanwhile, other Victorian thinkers were finding ways to accommodate evolution and religious belief. To do so, however, they typically sidestepped natural selection as the mechanism of evolution; it is at least arguable that those who hated Darwin's theory because it worked with random variations, like the astronomer John Herschel ('the law of higgledy-piggledy'), or the novelist Samuel Butler, for whom the undirected evolution of the *Origin* exhibited the world as 'a nightmare of waste and death',[4] understood it better than apologists such as Frederick Temple, the future Archbishop of Canterbury, whose Bampton Lectures on Science and Religion (1884) insisted that there was no antagonism between evolution and Christian teaching. Darwin's burial in Westminster Abbey paid tribute to a hero of science, but it did not mean that evolution by natural selection had swept all before it.

Nor was the idea of evolution as novel as the familiar story suggests. Darwin's own grandfather, Erasmus Darwin, had speculated in *Zoonomia* (1794–6) that rather than immutable products of a benevolent Deity, species were constantly developing, with all warm-blooded animals descended from one 'living filament'. The French naturalist Jean-Baptiste Lamarck proposed a similar but more coherent theory in his *Philosophie zoologique* (1809). Lyell challenged Lamarck's arguments in detail in the second volume of *Principles*, but essentially his critics offered three main objections. Lamarck's belief that the first living things had been produced by 'spontaneous generation' was rejected by conservative thinkers as blasphemous and materialist – and, therefore, likely to encourage political radicals eager to strike at Church and State. His view that evolution was linear, following a necessary path, admitted the suggestion that human beings were no more than highly developed animals. He also argued for the 'inheritance of acquired characteristics': that is, that bodily changes achieved by effort in one generation – the giraffe's long neck provides the notorious example – could be passed on to the next. In the absence of a proper account of the mechanism of inheritance, this was not necessarily implausible, but it too smacked of materialism: precisely what was later to make it attractive to those like Herbert Spencer for whom evolutionary change in the past provided the justification for political reform in the future.

Equally disturbing to conservative thinkers was Robert Chambers's anonymous but widely read *Vestiges of Creation* (1844). Beginning with William Herschel's theories of the formation of stars, Chambers argued for a divinely instituted process forcing life to rise to ever higher levels of intelligence and organisation. Humanity was not the result of a single act of divine creation, but it was the outcome intended by a wise Providence: the 'principle of development', not an ideal stasis, was built into the structure of the cosmos. It is in this spirit that lyric 118 of Tennyson's *In Memoriam* (1850) moves in a single nineteen-line sentence from the 'tracts of fluent heat' in which ('They say') the earth began, through 'seeming-random forms', on to 'man' and the prospect that the humanity of the nineteenth century might be the 'herald of a higher race' yet to come.[5] Despite furious attacks on its 'degrading materialism', *Vestiges* could be read to show that evolution and teleology were compatible. The problem for Darwin, who thought the work scientifically illiterate, was that natural selection discarded teleology altogether.

It was in this context that Darwin began first to frame his theory, and then to consider how he might present it. He was confident that species were not immutable, but what drove evolution? He found the answer in Thomas Malthus's *Essay on the Principles of Population* (1798), which argued that population tends to grow geometrically, outstripping the resources needed to support it. In the human economy, the balance was maintained only through such 'checks' as war, disease, famine and sexual abstinence. Without these checks, there would be unceasing competition for the means of life. So too, Darwin saw, in the natural world. In this ruthless economy, any creature born with even a slight advantage would have a greater chance of surviving and reproducing. Its offspring would tend to inherit that advantage; over time, the resulting differential survival rate would lead to the extinction of some forms, and their replacement by others. Extended over the vast lapse of time that Lyell's geology opened up, the principle of divergence would create new species.

In 1838 Darwin began a series of notebooks on the transmutation of species, then in 1842 wrote a thirty-five-page sketch of his theory, extended in 1844 to 230 pages. But as the reception given to *Vestiges* had shown, to publish a work of radical scientific materialism, especially in the politically turbulent 1840s, was to risk alienating family and friends. Instead, he undertook two decades of intense detailed study, including eight years on the taxonomy of barnacles, refining his theory and occasionally testing it, cautiously, with trusted scientific colleagues. Then, in 1858, came news that the naturalist Alfred Wallace had found his own route to a theory of natural selection, threatening to pre-empt the work on which Darwin had been engaged for so long. Friends rallied round, and papers illustrating his theory were read to the Linnaean Society, together with Wallace's essay: Both men, in later years, were generous about the achievement of the other. But Darwin's hand had been forced, and in November 1859 the publisher John Murray brought out *On The Origin of Species by Means of Natural Selection, or The Preservation of Favoured Races in the Struggle for Life*.[6]

The first sentence of the Introduction to *Origin* disarmingly recalls Darwin's time as naturalist on board HMS *Beagle*; the second remarks that the facts encountered then 'seemed to me to throw some light on the origin of species – that mystery of mysteries, as it has been called'. Without referring to 'evolution' or 'transmutation', Darwin suggests that the only difficulty in accepting that species were not independently created was the absence of a convincing account of 'the means of modification and coadaptation'. This is, in effect, the rationale for the organisation of the *Origin*. It begins by demonstrating that natural selection is such a means, and that it can and indeed must occur. It then rehearses and rebuts the possible counterarguments, and in the concluding chapters shows how otherwise baffling phenomena can be explained on the assumption of common descent by adaptive modification over long periods of time.

The first chapter, 'Variation under Domestication', draws attention to the remarkable changes produced by artificial selection – for example, tumbler, fantail, and pouter pigeons, all descended from one species of wild dove, but now so far differentiated as to blur the distinction between variety and species. The 'key', as animal and plant breeders knew, is 'man's power of accumulative selection': Nature 'gives successive variations; man adds them up in certain directions useful to himself' (p. 27). Darwin concedes that the cause of such variations is unknown, but demonstrably they exist, and they are heritable. Crucially, they are also cumulative: there is no inherent tendency for varieties to return to an original, 'natural' type or form. chapter 2, 'Variation under Nature', extends the argument to the variability of species in the wild, evident in the problems faced by taxonomists. One author's species is another's variety: 'a well-marked variety may be called an incipient species' (p. 44).

The next two chapters set out Darwin's central argument. Chapters 3 deals with the 'Struggle for Existence'. Since species reproduce in excess of the resources available for their support, they necessarily compete for the means of subsistence. This is 'the doctrine of Malthus applied with manifold force to the whole animal and vegetable kingdom': 'manifold', because Nature has no equivalent to the 'prudential restraint from marriage' Malthus had urged on the nineteenth-century poor (p. 54). The struggle is most intense between members of the same or related species: two seedling mistletoes on the same tree (such a one as might have stood in Hardy's woodlands, 'wrestling for existence' against its neighbours)[7] may 'truly be said to struggle with each other', as they tempt birds to eat and thus disseminate their seeds rather than those of other plants (p. 53). In later editions, Darwin recalled here a sentence from his 1838 notebooks:

The face of Nature may be compared to a yielding surface, with ten thousand sharp wedges packed close together and driven inwards by incessant blows, sometimes one wedge being struck, and then another with greater force.

The image of a face struck with tens of thousands of blows remains shocking, and must have been still more so to readers who had grown up with the poetry of Wordsworth, or the Bridgewater Treatises (1833–40), intended to show the power and wisdom of God manifested in creation. Even the reassurance with which the chapter ends, that 'the war of nature is not incessant, that no fear is felt, that death is generally prompt, and that the vigorous, the healthy, and the happy survive and multiply' (p. 66), invites the thought that Darwin's happily multiplying readers are those whose ancestors had struck hardest.

Chapter 4 turns to 'Natural Selection'. Given that more individuals are born than can possibly survive, any useful variation to an individual of any species, however slight, will assist it in 'the great and complex battle of life'; just as surely, any hurtful variation will be 'rigidly destroyed' (pp. 66–7): 'This preservation of favourable variations and the rejection of injurious variations, I call Natural Selection' (p. 68). Such 'infinitesimally small inherited modifications' gradually accumulate to produce new species; there is no more need to assume 'the continued creation of new organic beings', or the dramatic modification of existing ones, than there is to assume that a great valley must have been excavated by a catastrophic flood rather by than the steady processes of erosion described by Lyell (p. 79).

The rest of the chapter explores the conditions most favourable to natural selection, such as geographical isolation. Two points are worth underlining. First, adaptive modification works for the benefit of each species separately, never for the advantage of another: there is no prevision, and no overarching force working for the collective good.[8] Second, the differentiation of species ensures that the maximum amount of life is supported: 'the more diversified in habits and structure' species become, the more places can be occupied in 'the polity of nature' (p. 93). The plenitude which obliges Nature to be so ruthless in disposing of the unfit is also a source of endless opportunity. So too, Hardy was to suggest, in the human economy: Gabriel Oak, Diggory Venn, Elizabeth-Jane, perhaps even Liza-Lu, all move into the niche prepared for them by the death of their predecessor.

The following chapters are increasingly rich in illustrative detail. Chapter 5 deals with the 'Laws of Variation', while acknowledging that little was yet known of the subject. Some part is played by climate, some probably by habit, including the use and disuse of organs (as in the blindness of the mole); some visible external modifications may be correlated to internal ones. In chapter 6, 'Difficulties on Theory', Darwin turns to possible objections to his arguments. The absence of transitional forms between known species is explained by the extermination of the less specialised forms.

On the appearance of complex structures such as the eye, often adduced as evidence of design, Darwin shows that light-sensitive organs such as the ocelli of jellyfish, if understood as intermediate stages in the development towards full vision, are consistent with natural selection.

Chapter 7 deals with 'Instinct'. Twelve years later, in *The Descent of Man* (1871), Darwin was to argue that our moral life is derived from conjugal, parental and social instincts that we share with other creatures, and that there is accordingly no hard boundary between human morality and animal instinct.[9] Chapter 40 of *Far from the Madding Crowd*, 'On Casterbridge Highway', which brings together an unnamed woman (the heavily pregnant Fanny Robin) and a dog of unspecified breed which struggles to assist her, can be read as Hardy's exploration of this thesis. In the *Origin*, however, it is enough for Darwin's purpose to show that natural selection acts to modify instincts or behaviours as it does physical structures. The cuckoo's instinct to lay its eggs in the nests of other birds reflects the survival benefits of what among its ancestors was probably aberrant or occasional behaviour. In the complex case of the elaborate structures built by the hive-bee, natural selection again provides the 'motive power', operating through the differential survival rate of the swarms which use least wax, and thus transmitting to future generations 'its newly acquired economical instinct' (p. 191). The problem presented by sterile or neuter insects (which cannot transmit helpful variations) is explained by selection working on families as well as individuals (p. 193). Where the tendency to produce some neuter offspring has been beneficial, the colony that does so is more likely to survive.

The significance of 'Hybridism' (chapter 8) is that hybrid sterility preserves barriers between populations: varieties within species can be cross-bred, but not distinct species. Darwin shows that the division between species and varieties is not absolute, and that the attempt to cross-breed species produces varying (and disputed) degrees of infertility. The gradual divergence through natural selection of two related forms is accompanied by their diminishing ability to interbreed, eventually reaching complete sterility.

The two following chapters deal with geological evidence. Contrary to the gradualism of Darwin's argument, the fossil record appears to show that both individual species and groups of species appear suddenly. In reply, Darwin notes the 'Imperfection of the Geological Record': only a small portion of the globe has been explored; not all rocks bear fossils, and those that do may be deposited at long intervals; evolutionary changes may take place in areas or during periods where fossils are not being laid down. Discussing the 'Geological Succession of Organic Beings', Darwin observes that extinct species often prove intermediate in character between those now living, suggesting a common progenitor from which the modern forms have evolved. Turning next to two chapters on 'Geographical Distribution', he draws on his experiences on the *Beagle*, and his subsequent studies to find how far seeds can be transported across the oceans, to argue that the main factor determining dispersal is the existence of physical barriers to migration, which will accordingly define groups of species. Hence too the affinity between productions of the same continent or sea, evidence of 'some deep organic bond, prevailing throughout space and time': 'This bond, on my theory, is simply inheritance' (p. 283).

Chapter 13, on the 'Mutual Affinities of Organic Beings', argues that 'propinquity of descent', partially hidden by modification, explains why species are grouped together into genera, genera into families, and so on (p. 335). So too with morphology: such homologous forms as the human hand, the mole's paw and a bat's wing are better accounted for by community of descent than the nonexplanation of Divine preference for a five-digit pattern (pp. 351–2). Embryology too suggests common descent. The embryos of different creatures resemble each other more than the adults because 'the embryo is the animal in its less modified state', and that state harks back to 'the structure of its progenitor' (p. 363). Darwin recognised that there were no experimental tests or verifiable predictions to 'prove' the theory of natural selection, any more than Lyell could prove that the forces which shaped the surface of the globe had operated with constant force; but each could show that their theories made sense of phenomena that were otherwise without explanation.

The closing sentence of the Conclusion is well known, but can hardly too often be quoted:

There is grandeur in this view of life, with its several powers, having been originally breathed by the Creator into a few forms or into one;

and that, whilst this planet has gone cycling on according to the fixed law of gravity, from so simple a beginning endless forms most beautiful and most wonderful have been, and are being, evolved.

There is considerable rhetorical subtlety here. Reference to 'the fixed law of gravity' recruits for Darwin's cause earlier discussions of how the Creator might act by intermediary laws rather than through repeated separate interventions. Evolution, not mentioned under that name elsewhere in the first edition, has literally the last word, in a sentence which hints that the process has no end, and no goal. If there is little comfort, there is indeed grandeur in such a view.

Comprehensive as it was, *Origin* left many questions unanswered. Darwin grants a single magnificently understated sentence to the place of humanity: 'Light will be thrown on the origin of man and his history' (p. 394). He had no need to say more: as the clash between Huxley and Bishop Wilberforce at Oxford was soon to illustrate, his readers knew how much was at stake. But other issues too, less dramatic but vital to the argument, had been left unresolved: how and at what point varieties are irreversibly separated as species, what causes the variations on which selection depends, how variations are passed on through inheritance. This last was seized on in a hostile review by Fleming Jenkin, who argued that even beneficial variations would be swamped by interbreeding.[10] The answer to Jenkin lay in the theory of particulate inheritance: heritable characteristics are passed through the generations in discrete particles (or genes), and do not blend. Like natural selection itself, particulate inheritance was to be discovered by two independent researchers, by Gregor Mendel cross-breeding peas in a Brno monastery, and later by August Weismann, but it was not available to Darwin.[11]

The objections of William Thomson, the future Lord Kelvin, were equally troubling. Thomson's studies of the dissipation of heat from the sun convinced him that if the earth were as old as Lyell's theories claimed, and Darwin's argument needed, it would long since have been too cold to sustain life, unless 'the great storehouse of creation' contained sources of energy 'unknown to us'.[12] In Victorian England more prestige attached to physics than to biology, and it seemed Thomson had, as he intended, struck a powerful blow against natural selection. Fifty years later the discovery of radioactivity in the 'storehouse of creation' was to make his calculations irrelevant, but in the 1860s Darwin and his supporters had no answer to them.

Others critics, such as the palaeontologist Richard Owen and the Catholic scientist St George Mivart, could accept evolution, but not in its Darwinian, undirected form, and either sought evidence of patterns in the fossil record too artful to be other than designed, or saw evolution not as adaptive but as the predetermined or 'orthogenetic' unfolding of tendencies inherent in the constitution of individual forms of life. Herbert Spencer, who as early as 1852 had argued deductively (and in Darwin's view unhelpfully) for what he termed 'The Development Hypothesis',[13] continued to argue that development must embody the efforts of each generation; as several critics have noted, the 'social Darwinism' with which Spencer is associated might better be termed 'social Lamarckism'. Even Alfred Wallace, once he embraced spiritualism in 1866, concluded that the moral and intellectual life of humanity could not have arisen by natural selection. Thomas Huxley was a tireless defender of Darwin's work, but unlike Darwin he was willing to accept leaps or mutations ('saltations') alongside the slow process of adaptive modification.

Both Huxley and Wallace might fairly have termed themselves, like Hardy, 'among the earliest acclaimers of *The Origin of Species*', but in 1882, when all three attended Darwin's funeral in the Abbey, the theory of natural selection, or the preservation of favoured species in the struggle for life, was still only one of several competing accounts of evolution. Not until the 1940s, with the 'Modern Synthesis' of the *Origin* and genetics, would it take its proper place as one of the most powerful ideas ever known to science.

NOTES

1 The foundational studies are Gillian Beer, *Darwin's Plots: Evolutionary Narrative in Darwin, George Eliot and Nineteenth-Century Fiction* (Cambridge: Cambridge University Press, 1983; 3rd edition 2009), which examines the 'two-way' traffic between literature and science of 'not only *ideas* but metaphors, myths, and narrative patterns'; and George Levine, *Darwin and the Novelists: Patterns of Science in Victorian Fiction* (Chicago: University of

Chicago Press, 1988), which describes 'a gestalt of the Darwinian imagination', detectable in fiction as in science (p. 13).

2 Both Darwin and Hardy grasped the ethical implications of this. For Darwin it constituted an argument against slavery; for Hardy, more radically, it 'shifted the centre of altruism from humanity to the whole conscious world collectively' (*LW*: 373).

3 *The Autobiography of Charles Darwin, 1809–1882*, ed. Nora Barlow (London: Collins, 1958), pp. 85–96. Emma herself rejected 'the doctrine of everlasting punishment for disbelief' (p. 87).

4 Samuel Butler, 'The Deadlock in Darwinism – III' (June 1890), *Essays on Life, Art and Science* (New York: Kennakar Press, 1970), p. 308.

5 Tennyson denied being influenced by *Vestiges*: see Hallam Tennyson, *Alfred Lord Tennyson: A Memoir* (London: Macmillan, 1897), I:223.

6 The second edition (January 1860), including Darwin's immediate response to his critics, is cited here, as edited by Gillian Beer (Oxford: Oxford University Press, 1996). Succeeding editions replied to objectors in more detail, in the view of most scholars conceding too much to them. The sixth (1872) was the first to adopt Herbert Spencer's phrase, 'the survival of the fittest'.

7 'Next were more trees close together, wrestling for existence, their branches disfigured with wounds resulting from their mutual rubbings and blows' (*W*: 42).

8 'I do not believe that any animal in the world performs an action for the exclusive good of another of a distinct species' (p. 171).

9 See chapters 3 and 4, 'Comparison of the Mental Powers of Man and the Lower Animals'.

10 Fleming Jenkin, 'The Origin of Species', *The North British Review*, 46 (June 1867), pp. 277–318.

11 See Angelique Richardson, 'Heredity', in this volume.

12 William Thomson, 'On the Age of the Sun's Heat', *Macmillan's Magazine*, 5 (March 1862), pp. 388–93.

13 *The Leader*, 20 March 1852; reprinted in Herbert Spencer, *Essays Scientific, Political & Speculative*, 3 vols. (London: Williams and Norgate, 1891), I. 1–7.

# 30

# Heredity

ANGELIQUE RICHARDSON

Lucy Snowe remarks on the first page of *Villette* (1853) that Graham Bretton has inherited some aspects of his mother's features, including the promise of her stature, her health and equable temperament. But, she notes, it is regrettable that he has not inherited her complexion. Inheritance seems relatively straightforward, if inconclusive, and of value to a novelist whose task is to develop characters from an infinite set of possibilities. In a literary form concerned with the development of the individual over time heredity was an obvious plot device. *Villette*, though, is a novel about 'nobody's daughter' – a woman with no family, who must make her own way, and about whose ancestry we know nothing.[1] Being nobody's daughter sets Lucy Snowe free. Characters who bring nothing of their past abound in the nineteenth century novel; it either remains unknown, as with Heathcliff; appears only in the form of material inheritance, as with Jane Eyre; or, in the case of Oliver Twist, ensures that a set of middle-class values and virtue remains inviolate as he moves through the London underclass: 'But nature or inheritance had implanted a good sturdy spirit in Oliver's breast.'[2]

This chapter will outline developments in hereditarian thought, but note the extent to which heredity remained a question through the nineteenth century, and suggest this as a new context for reading Hardy's work. The novel thrives on unpredictability and complexity and these were – and remain – the characteristics of heredity. In *The Origin of Species* (1859) Charles Darwin expressed uncertainty on the subject: 'The laws governing inheritance are quite unknown; no one can say why the same peculiarity in different individuals of the same species, and in individuals of different species, is sometimes inherited and sometimes not.'[3] A year later,

I am grateful to the Arts and Humanities Research Council for supporting this research.

Mr Tulliver in *The Mill on the Floss* finds heredity 'an uncommon puzzlin' thing'.[4]

For the first half of the century, ideas of inheritance were governed largely by the work of the French naturalist and transformist Jean-Baptiste Lamarck (1744–1829). His evolutionary treatise, *Philosophie zoologique* (1809), sought to account for the transmutation of species, advancing a purposive view of nature, privileging environmental effects. In the words of the biologist and popular writer Grant Allen, who corresponded regularly with Hardy, Lamarck 'openly proclaimed under the Napoleonic reaction his profound conviction that all species, including man, were descended by modification from one or more primordial forms'.[5] Lamarck had argued for the tendency of living organisms to develop without struggle into more complex forms through what he termed 'the inheritance of acquired characteristics', or 'use-inheritance'. For Lamarck the environment would create an organism's needs, and those would determine how it used its body. Organs that were used would develop, disused organs would degenerate.[6] Darwin would continue to emphasise the role of the environment. The *Origin* opened with the assertion:

When we reflect on the vast diversity of the plants and animals which have been cultivated, and which have varied during all ages under the most different climates and treatment, I think we are driven to conclude that this great variability is simply due to our domestic productions having been raised under conditions of life not so uniform as, and somewhat different from, those to which the parent-species have been exposed under nature.[7]

Equally, Darwin made use of Lamarck's idea of acquired characteristics. In his chapter on the 'Laws of Variation', discussing the 'effects of use and disuse', he stated 'there can be little doubt that use in our domestic animals strengthens and enlarges certain parts, and disuse diminishes them; and that such modifications are inherited'.[8]

By the time he wrote *The Variation of Animals and Plants under Domestication* (1868), Darwin was drawing more directly on Lamarckian ideas: here he outlined his own theory of heredity, the concept of 'pangenesis', which held that hereditary material was gathered from all parts of the body and collected into the

'germ cells' from which it was passed on to subsequent generations. It was in this work that Darwin set out what Müller-Wille
and Rheinberger have referred to as the two hallmarks of modern
hereditarian thought. First, the carriers of properties to be inherited were not the parents but 'submicroscopic entities that circulate, from generation to generation, among individuals within
one and the same species'. Second, Darwin broke away from early
modern conceptions of descent which emphasised vertical relations, invoking instead the horizontal;[9] he referred to a range of
traits from 'a long line of male and female ancestors separated by
hundreds or even thousands of generations from the present time'.
He remarked: 'these characters, like those written on paper with
invisible ink, lie ready to be evolved whenever the generation is
disturbed by certain known or unknown conditions'.[10] The analogy with writing suggests the appeal of such ideas to the novelist,
who must script character from an almost infinite variety of possibilities, choosing which conditions to bring to bear. This increased
the element of unpredictability and considerably broadened the
time scale – both merits as far as the novelist was concerned. In
*The Mayor of Casterbridge* the single direct reference to inheritance
occurs when Elizabeth-Jane is sleeping: 'buried genealogical facts,
ancestral curves' become visible, confirming for Henchard that he
is not her father (*MC*: 19). But even this novel counters aspects of
inheritance and biology as much as it courts it; Henchard shows
his greatest affection for a child that is not his biologically.

The term heredity acquired its biological sense relatively late, in
the decade following the *Origin of Species*, which saw a more general shift towards biological inquiry and explanation. The *Oxford
English Dictionary* gives the first use as 1540, where the sense is
of hereditary succession, and marks this meaning as obsolete. The
legal sense of the term continues, but is less frequent. The first
appearance of the now prevalent biological sense occurs in Herbert
Spencer's *Principles of Biology* (1863). Darwin's cousin Francis
Galton outlined his ideas on racial improvement in an essay on
'Hereditary Talent and Character' two years later,[11] while preparing
material for his book *Hereditary Genius: An Inquiry into its Laws
and Consequences* (1869).

The mid-Victorian novel reflects the shift from inheritance as
the transmission of material possessions to the transmission of

character. In *Under the Greenwood Tree* there is little talk of inheritance; though Fancy Day is assumed unlikely to 'inherit [her father's] closeness', his silence, 'she may have a few dribblets from his sense'. Local discussion refers at once to heredity and material possession: one character adds: 'And his pocket, perhaps' (*UGT*: I.5). Heredity intrudes more in his next published novel, *A Pair of Blue Eyes*, in part at a comedic level. The reader is informed, 'That trick of running away seems to be handed down in families, like craziness or gout. And they two women [Elfride and her grandmother] be alike as peas,' and must wait to see what consequence this must have for Elfride (*PBE*: 26). Two years later, in *The Hand of Ethelberta*, heredity is one of the opening themes of the novel.

There was wide resistance to the idea of the influence of heredity. In the same year as the *Origin*, Samuel Smiles published *Self-Help; with Illustrations of Character and Conduct*. Smiles emphasised the capacity for autonomy and self-development, opposing hereditarian ideas of social hierarchy: 'it may be observed how greatly the character may be strengthened and supported by the cultivation of good habits.'[12] Long-term habits might be difficult to break, but Smiles quoted Joseph Butler: '"As habits belonging to the body," he says, "are produced by external acts, so habits of the mind are produced by the execution of inward practical purpose".'[13] Similarly, John Stuart Mill argued in his *Autobiography* that 'the prevailing tendency to regard all the marked distinctions of human character as innate, and in the main indelible … is one of the chief hindrances to the rational treatment of great social questions, and one of the greatest stumbling blocks to human improvement'.[14] For George Eliot too character can be delible. In *Middlemarch*, Lydgate walks 'by hereditary habit'.[15] The phrase is significant, undercutting the sense of a determining heredity. Habits are not hereditary in the sense of inevitable but learned, somehow; they are ultimately chosen rather than given, and may be thrown off.[16] As Farebrother assures Dorothea, 'character is not cut in marble – it is not something solid and unalterable. It is something living and changing' (chapter 72). Fred Vincy sets out to undo the way he has been taught to write, and follows Caleb Garth's instructions: 'Why, you must learn to form your letters and keep the line […] Every man can learn to write. I taught myself. Go at it with a will, and sit up at night if the day-time isn't enough' (chapter 56).

Heredity was gaining scientific attention and social valency. But quite what heredity meant was an open question. George Lewes observed in a discussion of 'Mr Darwin's Hypothesis' in 1868 that Lamarck had increased focus on the environment, but had given too little attention to the organism: 'naturalists before his time had been wont to consider the Organism apart from the Medium in which it existed; he clearly saw that vital phenomena depended on the relation of the two; but in his hypothesis he sacrificed the one factor somewhat to the other; he paid too little regard to the Organism and its laws of development.'[17] Lewes pointed to the complexity and depth of environmental influence: 'by "conditions" we are not to understand geographical or climatal influences simply, or even mainly; but the whole group of conditions, external and internal, physical, organic, and social, which determine the result.'[18] George Romanes, the zoologist and close follower of Darwin, remarked in the *Contemporary Review* that when we speak of 'heredity' as a cause, 'what we mean is that in the complex and obscure physiology of generation there are a number of unknown causes at work'.[19]

But in the 1880s, rising concern over poverty, degeneration and imperial rivalries drove changing perceptions of human nature. Heredity was accorded a more decisive role as increasingly troubling social questions were displaced onto the biological. The British zoologist Ray Lankester, with whom Hardy spent an evening at the Royal Society in 1893, had published the profoundly deterministic *Degeneration: A Chapter in Darwinism* in 1880, and the *Lancet* conducted a debate on whether the British race was degenerating.[20] The degrading effects of slum-life and factory work, and the conditions of the poor, were receiving sensational coverage in such articles as 'How the Poor Live' by George Sims, which became a regular feature of *The Pictorial World*, and these fuelled fears of degeneration. 'London. Four Million forlorn hopes!' wrote Hardy in his diary in 1889 (*LW*: 227). The journalist and eugenist Arnold White wrote in *Empire and Efficiency* (1901) of 'street-bred brains' and 'country-born labourers in the prime of life' becoming 'white-faced workmen living in courts and alleys'.[21] The upper classes were also held to be degenerating.[22] Tess shares with the other milkmaids at Talbothays her position as a descendant of a spent aristocracy, and in the *Life* Hardy considers his place at the end of the family line of 'Hardy' or 'Le Hardy', with the suggestion that (like the d'Urberville or Fawley line), it is a family of 'spent social energies' (*LW*: 9).

In his lecture 'On Heredity' (1883) the German zoologist August Weismann delivered a dramatic challenge to environmental influence by dismissing the effects of use or disuse or the inheritance of any acquired characteristics. Weismann argued resolutely in favour of nature over nurture, making a decisive break with past conceptions: 'the substance of the germ-cells … transfers its hereditary tendencies from generation to generation, at first unchanged, and always uninfluenced in any corresponding manner, by that which happens during the life of the individual which bears it.' Germ-plasm – which bore the factors determining the transmission of characters from parent – was isolated from the body of the organism that carried it and was transmitted unchanged from generation to generation; it simply passed through the organism, without contributions from the somatic cells, and apparently impervious to environmental influence. Organism and environment were cut off from each other. It followed that 'if these ideas … be correct, all our ideas upon the transformation of species require thorough modification, for the whole principle of evolution by means of exercise (use and disuse), as proposed by Lamarck, and accepted in some cases by Darwin, entirely collapses'.[23] The role of culture in this account of evolutionary development was redundant. Weismann's essays were among the books Hardy 'dipped into' in 1890 (*LW*: 240).

Shortly afterwards, George Romanes coined Neo-Darwinism as a negative term, to signal Weismann's departure from Darwin's views.[24] But while Weismann's ideas lent themselves to a shift towards hard-line hereditarian thought, Weismann himself was aware that organisms were vastly complex and that their environment profoundly affected them and their capacity to survive. Writing of horses introduced to the Falkland Islands, and the climatic varieties of butterflies, he observed 'there still remains a certain scope for the influence of external conditions upon the organism'.[25] In a later piece, 'Remarks on Certain Problems of the Day', he conceded that 'further investigation may show that we are on the wrong track and must abandon it; what the future of the question may be no one can foretell'; current ideas on heredity were not final, but rather 'a starting-point for further thought;

they constitute no complete theory ... they are rather "researches" which, if fortune favours, will, sooner or later, directly or indirectly, lead to the formation of a real theory.'[26]

In 1880 Darwin wrote a preface to a collection of essays on descent by Weismann, flagging up uncertainty around questions of variation and environment:

Several distinguished naturalists maintain with much confidence that organic beings tend to vary and to rise in the scale, independently of the conditions to which they and their progenitors have been exposed; whilst others maintain that all variation is due to such exposure, though the manner in which the environment acts is as yet quite unknown. At the present time there is hardly any question in biology of more importance than this of the nature and causes of variability. [27]

By the 1890s heredity was even more at the fore in literature. It appears as an idea, and means of explanation, in *Tess of the d'Urbervilles* and *Jude the Obscure*. There is to Tess 'a luxuriance of aspect, a fullness of growth, which made her appear more of a woman than she really was. She had inherited the feature from her mother without the quality it denoted' (*Tess*: 5). She shows also 'the slight incautiousness of character inherited from her race' (*Tess*: 14) and, less troublingly, 'that innate love of melody, which she had inherited from her ballad-singing mother' (*Tess*: 13). In 1895 Jude fears that he has 'the germs of every human infirmity' in him (*Jude*: V.2), and in the same year Grant Allen's notorious *Woman Who Did*, Herminia Barton, states frankly 'I regard myself as a living proof of the doctrine of heredity.'[28] But even Allen, committed to hereditarian ideas, notes that Herminia's daughter Dolores affords no such proof:

Heredity of mental and moral qualities is a precarious matter. These things lie, as it were, on the topmost plane of character; they smack of the individual, and are therefore far less likely to persist in offspring than the deeper-seated and better-established peculiarities of the family, the clan, the race, or the species. They are idiosyncratic. Indeed, when we remember how greatly the mental and moral faculties differ from brother to brother, the product of the same two parental factors, can we wonder that they differ much more from father to son, the product of one like factor alone, diluted by the addition of a relatively unknown quality, the maternal influence? However this may be, at any rate, Dolores early began to strike out for herself all the most ordinary and stereotyped opinions of British respectability.[29]

Allen's novel depends on this unpredictability. Purporting fixity, predictability, heredity was one of the most unfixed questions of the century.

Having acknowledged its uncertainty, Allen goes on to evoke weaker forms of heredity, drawing on Darwin's ideas in *Variation*. Dolores 'had never heard in the society of her mother's lodgings any but the freest and most rational ideas; yet she herself seemed to hark back, of internal congruity, to the lower and vulgarer moral plane of her remoter ancestry.' His explanation is expressed in the language of evolution; he suggests that her individuality is paradoxically, an expression of not being individual: 'She showed her individuality only by evolving for herself all the threadbare platitudes of ordinary convention.'[30] The moment points to a tension in the novel, and arguably to some degree in all fiction that engages with heredity. Circumstances necessarily impinge, thwart, nurture and shape. Even Emile Zola's characters, seemingly in thrall to heredity, find themselves in relentless environments. Lankester related his pessimistic model of development to environment: 'Degeneration may be defined as a gradual change of the structure in which the organism becomes adapted to less varied and less complex conditions of life [...] Any new set of conditions occurring to an animal which render its food and safety very easily attained, seem to lead as a rule to Degeneration.'[31]

There was resistance to hereditarian thought both within and outside the scientific community in the closing decades of the century. The zoologist Oscar Hertwig in *The Biological Problem of Today: Preformation or Epigenesis? The Basis of a Theory of Organic Development* (1896) saw Weismann's doctrine of determinants as 'a closed system, finding within itself a formal explanation of all development'. It was, he argued 'an abandonment of explanation rather than an explanation; for it explains by sign and tokens that elude verification and experiment, and that cannot encounter concrete investigation.' Hertwig defined epigenesis as the doctrine that the formation of a new individual was not simply the outgrowing of particles in the egg-cell, but the result of 'moulding external forces'.[32] In his introduction to Hertwig's study the zoologist Peter Chalmers Mitchell wrote: 'we are only at the beginning of inquiry into the problems of heredity' (p. xix). In Hardy's last published novel, *The Well-Beloved*, heredity is a central idea, but one expressed both as a compulsion and an absurdity, as Pierston successively falls in love with three generations of women from the 'island race' of Portland.

I have written elsewhere of Hardy's interest in the eugenics movement in the twentieth century, but his notebook entries and comments make clear he did not support it; it formed part of his wider engagement with contemporary ideas in science. Galton defined eugenics as 'the science of improving stock, which is by no means confined to questions of judicious mating, but which, especially in the case of man, takes cognisance of all influences that tend in however remote a degree to give to the more suitable races or strains of blood a better chance of prevailing speedily over the less suitable than they otherwise would have had'.[33] Even eugenists had to acknowledge that environment had a part to play, though nature separated from nurture remained their chief preoccupation. In 1908, Galton reflected that 'the study of agencies under social control that may improve or impair the racial qualities of future generations, either physically or mentally'.[34] The eugenists had difficulty over individuality; there were a number of strands of eugenics, from the social reformist libertarian to the right-wing authoritarian, with varying and often contradictory emphasis placed on heredity.

When Hardy came to assess the impact of Darwin, it is significant that he saw the implications as ethical, emphasising kinship between species rather than competition. Questions of heredity and competition opened up by Darwin remained open for Hardy and perhaps of greatest value for broadening the franchise of creative possibility. Heredity forms the focus of a number of his poems, providing the title to one.[35] Through his engagement with ideas of heredity and his sustained questioning of inherited privilege, from 'The Poor Man and the Lady', which remained too radical to be published, and *Jude the Obscure*, which appeared too radical to his readers, his work plays out the struggle for individual autonomy, and the complex set of circumstances which threaten its realisation, and which are most insistently social, centred on poverty and class inequalities.

NOTES

1 Charlotte Brontë, *Villette*, ed. H. Rosengarten and M. Smith (Oxford: Oxford University Press, 2008), ch. 14.
2 Charles Dickens, *Oliver Twist*, ed. Stephen Gill (Oxford: Oxford University Press), ch. 2.
3 Charles Darwin, *On the Origin of Species by means of natural selection, or the preservation of favoured races in the struggle for life* (London: John Murray, 1859), p. 13.
4 George Eliot, *The Mill on the Floss* (Oxford: Oxford University Press, 2008), Book First, ch. 3.
5 Grant Allen, *Charles Darwin* (London: Longmans, Green, and Co., 1885), p. 11.
6 See Peter Bowler, *Evolution: The History of an Idea* (1983; Berkeley and Los Angeles: University of California Press, 1989), p. 86.
7 Darwin, *Origin*, p. 7.
8 Ibid., p. 134.
9 Staffan Müller-Wille and Hans-Jörg Rheinberger, 'Heredity – The Formation of an Epistemic Space', *Heredity Produced. At the Crossroads of Biology, Politics, and Culture, 1500–1870*, ed. Müller-Wille and Rheinberger (Cambridge, Mass.: MIT Press, 2007), p. 24.
10 Charles Darwin, *The Variation of Animals and Plants under Domestication*, 2 vols. (London: John Murray, 1868), II.61.
11 Francis Galton, 'Hereditary Talent and Character', *Macmillan's Magazine* 12 (1865), pp.157–66, 318–27.
12 Samuel Smiles, *Self-Help; with Illustrations of Conduct, and Perseverance*, ed. Peter Sinnema (Oxford: Oxford University Press, 2008), p. 319.
13 *Analogy of Religion, Natural and Revealed* (1736), in Smiles, *Self-Help*, p. 319.
14 J. S. Mill, *Autobiography of John Stuart Mill* (New York: Columbia University Press, 1960), p. 184.
15 George Eliot, *Middlemarch*, ed. David Carroll (Oxford University Press, 2008), chapter 36.
16 See Paul White, 'Acquired Character: The Hereditary Material of the Self-Made Man', in Müller-Wille and Rheinberger, *Heredity Produced*, pp. 375–397.
17 'Mr Darwin's Hypothesis', Part I, *Fortnightly Review* 9 (1868), pp. 353–73, reprinted in *Versatile Victorian: Selected Critical Writings of George Henry Lewes*, ed. Rosemary Ashton (London: Bristol Classical Press, 1992), pp. 299–316.
18 'Mr Darwin's Hypothesis', p. 310.

19 George Romanes, 'Recent Critics of Darwinism', *Contemporary Review* 53 (1888), pp. 836–54 (p. 852).

20 'Are We Degenerating Physically?', *Lancet* (1 December 1888), pp. 1076–7.

21 Arnold White, *Efficiency and Empire* (Brighton: Harvester Press, 1973), pp. 95–7, 110–1.

22 Francis Galton, *Hereditary Genius: An Inquiry into Its Laws and Consequences* (1869; London: Watts & Co., 1892), p. 335; Henry Maudsley, *Body and Will* (London: Kegan Paul, Trench, 1883), p. 320.

23 August Weismann, *Essays upon Heredity and Kindred Biological Problems*, ed. E. B. Poulton, S. Schönland and A. E. Shipley, 2 vols. (Oxford, 1889–92), I.69.

24 *Darwin and After Darwin: An Exposition of the Darwinian Theory and a Discussion of Post-Darwinian Questions*, 3 vols. (London: Longmans, Green, 1892–1897).

25 Weismann, *Essays upon Heredity*, I.99.

26 Ibid., II.82.

27 Darwin, preface to August Weismann, *Studies in the Theory of Descent*, 2 vols. (London: Low, Marston, Searle, & Rivington, 1880), p. vi.

28 Allen, *The Woman Who Did* (Oxford University Press, 1995), ch. 2.

29 Ibid., ch. 18.

30 Ibid., ch. 18.

31 E. Ray Lankester, *Degeneration: A Chapter in Darwinism* (London: Macmillan, 1880), pp. 32–3.

32 Oscar Hertwig, *The Biological Problem of Today: Preformation or Epigenesis? The Basis of a Theory of Organic Development* (London: Heinemann, 1896), pp. 140, 143.

33 Francis Galton, *Inquiries into Human Faculty, and its Development* (London, Macmillan, 1883), p. 25.

34 Francis Galton, *Memories of My Life* (London: Methuen, 1908), p. 321.

35 Notably, 'Heredity' ('I am the family face') and 'The Pedigree' (*CP*: 434, 460–1).

# 31

# Psychology

JENNY BOURNE TAYLOR

In the fourth chapter of *The Woodlanders*, the inhabitants of Little Hintock speculate about the newly arrived doctor. 'Nonsense,' Mr Melbury retorts to the suggestion that 'he has sold his soul to the wicked one'; 'He's only a gentleman fond of science, and philosophy, and poetry, and, in fact, every kind of knowledge; and being lonely here he passes his time in making such matters his hobby' (*W*: 4). One of Edred Fitzpiers's 'hobbies' is craniology: he even flatters Grammer Oliver into selling him her brain to dissect after her death. 'A woman's is usually four ounces less than a man's; but your's [sic] is man's size,' she reports him telling her (*W*: 6). Yet despite his interest in the interior of their skulls, Fitzpiers shows little understanding of his patients' inner mental lives. Though he succeeds in dissecting John South's brain, he is unable to understand the living man's monomaniacal fear of the tree outside his window – which 'rather than any organic disease' is 'eating away [his] health' (*W*: 13) – and precipitates South's death by suddenly removing the object around which the man has morbidly woven his entire identity. Despite Grace's speculation after their marriage that his mind was 'in some region … of psychological literature' (*W*: 28), Fitzpiers fails to appreciate either the intricate interconnections between body and mind, or the complexities of impulse and motivation, whether in others, or himself. Yet throughout his fiction Hardy himself actively engages with much of the 'psychological literature' that Fitzpiers has failed to use wisely, as well as suggesting some of its limits in the doctor himself.

Hardy's familiarity with contemporary astronomy, philosophy, biology and evolutionary theory is well recognised; but his *Literary Notebooks* also display an enduring interest in discussion of the workings of the individual mind. He noted not only key midcentury psychological theorists such as Herbert Spencer, G. H. Lewes and John Stuart Mill, but also medical writers, such as A. L.

Wigan whose *A New View of Insanity: The Duality of the Mind* of 1844 played an influential part in debates on 'double consciousness' (*LN* I: 200), and John Kitto, whose *The Lost Senses* (1845) contributed to understanding how the deprivation of one sense can be compensated for by another (*LN* 1: 90). He read the work of contemporary writers on heredity, such as Francis Galton and Henry Maudsley; but also mentions more multifaceted figures, including the psychologist James Sully (*LN* I: 170) and F. W. H. Myers (*LN* I: 167), whose theories of the 'the subliminal consciousness' drew on the work of the French psychologist Paul Janet, and Janet himself, whose writing on mental dissociation and dual personality Hardy also quotes in the original (*LN* I: 209–10).

We may trace evidence of this reading, as well as of wider debates on selfhood circulating within intellectual and popular cultures, but it rarely takes the form of straightforward influence in his fiction. Hardy makes use of specific and at times conflicting psychological models and languages which emerged at different moments, as a multilayered and multifaceted set of reference points to suggest how characters are seen by others; to explore various forms of consciousness and subconscious motivation; to probe the scope and limits of the individual will; and to trace the role of individual and collective memory in shaping the individual and in forging family and community bonds and conflicts in the face of disruption and change.

The decade in which Hardy established his career as a novelist was crucial to the institutional establishment of psychology as a recognised discipline which focused on how the complex interconnections between mind, body and brain shaped consciousness and unconscious mental life. Maudsley's *Body and Mind: An Inquiry into Their Mutual Influence, Specially in Relation to Mental Disorder* appeared in 1870, Alexander Bain's *Mind and Body: the Theories of Their Relation* in 1872, and David Ferrier's enormously influential study of cerebral localization based on animal experiments, *The Functions of the Brain,* in 1876. Such work grew out of early nineteenth century physiological studies of the brain and nervous system, including Franz Joseph Gall's work on the brain in Austria, and research on reflex actions by Charles Bell in England and François Magendie in France, who both investigated the ways in which specific sensory and motor functions operated within the nervous system.[1] Although these materialist approaches became increasingly prominent through the century, mid nineteenth-century psychology, as Rick Rylance has shown, was 'an unshapely, accommodating, contested, emergent, energetic discipline', which addressed a diverse readership through the rich intellectual culture fostered by periodicals.[2] The study of the mind spanned the fields of physiology, philosophy and medicine, while reforms in the institutional treatment of insanity lead to the increasing respectability of mental pathology and mental science.

Midcentury psychology grew out of, and transformed, two principle tendencies in philosophy of mind: faculty psychology and associationist philosophy. Faculty psychology derived from Immanuel Kant's idealist philosophy and the 'Common Sense' school of the Scottish Enlightenment expounded by Thomas Reid. It posited a self composed of innate human attributes arranged in a hierarchy, and conceived the mind as autonomous, self-motivating and independent. In contrast, associationism elaborated John Locke's premise that there are no innate faculties, but that consciousness and therefore knowledge are derived from experience. Locke's analysis of the mind as linking chains of thought built up from childhood, binding together the self through memory, was given a physiological basis in the mid eighteenth century by David Hartley, who argued that the mind responds to vibrations transmitted to the nervous system, in a model of consciousness that was scathingly criticised as mechanistic and passive – most famously by Coleridge in the *Biographia Literaria*. Yet both schools of thought emphasised the fundamental role of memory, and deployed generic terms such as will and reason, while associationism itself could encompass very different approaches to the mind. While James Mill had highlighted the importance of rigid mental training, his early-nineteenth-century contemporary Thomas Brown emphasised the formative role of the emotions, replacing the notion of association with the more flexible one of suggestion.[3] And although associationist philosophy was criticised for its reliance on introspection, the figures who dominated physiological psychology at midcentury – William Carpenter, Bain, Lewes and Spencer – were all rooted in or drew on its fundamental premise: that the self is shaped through strands or streams of experience, built up through sensations, and through both conscious and unconscious memory.

These writers drew on developments in sensory-motor physiology and, from midcentury, evolutionary theory, but it was the popular science of phrenology that provided the most visible and accessible materialist model of the mind, and with its idealist counterpart physiognomy offered a crucial resource for the novel. Though it had lost much of its scientific credibility by the late 1840s, phrenology paved the way for studies later in the century of cerebral localisation, as well as for craniology (the study of brain size and capacity deployed in racial science), criminology and, more widely, studies of sexual difference. Phrenology evolved from Gall's influential treatise *On the Functions of the Brain* (1822–6), which argued that the mind had no existence beyond the physical brain, and that the brain itself consisted of many organs, each comprising specific faculties and functions, located in specific regions of the skull, and detectable in its outward shape.[4] Gall's theories were popularised by the Edinburgh lawyer George Combe, whose *The Constitution of Man Considered in Relation to External Objects* (1828) offered readers the means of scrutinising and classifying others and themselves. While Gall had conceived localised faculties as innate and static, Combe argued that they could be developed and exercised through active agency – that organs such as 'Amativeness', 'Adhesiveness' or 'Combativeness' could be identified and trained in a particular direction. It was this emphasis on potential, as much as the stress on classification and control, that contributed to phrenology's cultural resonance and popular appeal. Charlotte Brontë visited a phrenologist in 1851, and as Sally Shuttleworth and Nicholas Dames have explored, she draws heavily on phrenological concepts and terms in *The Professor* (written in 1846 but published posthumously in 1857), *Jane Eyre* (1847) and *Villette* (1853), as a means both to interpret others, and as a form of internal surveillance.[5]

However, Fitzpiers's interest in craniology is more symptomatic of his own personality than Grammer Oliver's, and it was physiognomy, phrenology's idealist counterpart, that provided Hardy with a more effective – albeit limited – visual language to describe character. Physiognomy remained popular through the century; shifting from a science of identity rooted in natural theology to one which in Charles Bell's work encompassed new physiological rationales for the expression of the emotions, culminating in Darwin's *The Expression of the Emotions in Man and Animals* of 1872.[6] Its classical roots were reworked in the 1790s by John Caspar Lavater, whose *Essays in Physiognomy* of 1789 (published in numerous editions through the nineteenth century) argued that all individuals possessed essential qualities that linked them to God and to natural creation, and could be discerned in facial features. Lavater's illustrated accounts of the meaning of the shape of the eye or forehead partly explained the method's enduring popularity: many manuals such as Samuel Wells's *New Physiognomy* (1867) laid emphasis on static features, as would Cesare Lombroso's studies of atavistic criminal 'stigmata' later in the century. But Lavater had also stressed the importance of fleeting facial expression, and this formed the core of Charles Bell's aim in *The Anatomy and Philosophy of Expression as Connected to the Fine Arts* (1844) to demonstrate the somatic and neurological basis of emotion.[7]

Hardy frequently adapts the language of physiognomy – *The Woodlanders* opens with 'the physiognomy of a deserted highway' – and Fitzpiers is described in Lavater's terms as 'finely formed': his face is 'rather soft than stern', and his nose 'artistically beautiful enough to have been worth modelling by any sculptor not over-busy' (*W*: 14). Like many midcentury novelists (including Collins and Braddon), though, Hardy is interested in the ambiguity of feature and expression, and the light the act of interpretation throws on the observer: a striking example is Jude Fawley's naïve selection of five Christminster wardens 'whose physiognomies seemed to say to him that they were appreciative and far-seeing men' (*Jude*: II.6). Hardy often echoes Bell's emphasis on the interconnections between nervous response, bodily movement and facial expression. 'The infinitesimal movement of muscle, curve, hair and wrinkle' of the reserved Giles Winterborne have the power of leaving the surrounding company 'charged' with his 'moods and meanings' (*W*: 15), while Jude's bitter sense of failure after his drunken visit to his cousin Sue Bridehead could have been taken from one of Bell's illustrations: 'If he had been a woman he must have screamed under the nervous tension which he was now undergoing. But that relief being denied to his virility, he clenched his teeth in misery, bringing lines about his mouth like those in the Laocoön, and corrugations between his brows' (*Jude*: II.7).

Hardy's use of nervous response to convey character is inseparable from his exploration of the multifaceted forms of unconscious activity that pick up on debates on automatic mental life through the second half of the century. These constitute unconscious bodily intelligence as an aspect of the intertwined mental, emotional and physical responses that make an individual at home in their surroundings. Fitzpiers lacks not only 'old association – an almost exhaustive biographical or historical acquaintance with every object, animate and inanimate, within the observer's horizon' (*W*: 17), but also unconscious bodily memory, in which 'the secondary intelligence of the hands and arms [can] carry on without the sovereign attention of the head' (*W*: 4). Both forms of memory are crucial to a sense of belonging. Lewes's observation in *The Physiology of Common Life* (1859–60) that 'Habits, Fixed Ideas, and what we call automatic actions' are built up by repetition creating patterns of habitual behaviour was widely shared, and midcentury physiological psychologists all in different ways stressed the dynamic interconnections between physiological and mental actions, and the role the emotions played within this process.[8] Bain, for example, acknowledged a distinction between intellectual and emotional response, noting that 'while we can check or diminish an outburst of feeling through voluntary restraint ... the whole brain, with all its connexions in the general framework of the body, is concurrent and participant in a state of mental emotion'.[9] Spencer argued that the mind, like all organic life, moves from simple to complex forms as consciousness evolves through a continual process of differentiation and integration, entailing emotional awareness as much as rational thought: 'Feelings are not, scientifically considered, divisible from other phenomena of consciousness ... [they] become nascent at the same time Memory and Reason do.'[10] All three, in particular Lewes, recognised that physiological explanations alone could not account for the complexities of the 'Thinking' and 'Feeling' self.

While automatic actions convey a sense of belonging in Winterborne or Marty South, Hardy also makes use of trance-like states to convey states of alienation and reveal hidden motivations. The half-waking, half-sleeping state in which Fitzpiers first meets Grace Melbury, or his semiconscious condition after falling from his horse when he unwittingly reveals his frustration to Grace's father – or Angel Clare's somnambulism on his disastrous wedding night in *Tess of the d'Urbervilles* – echo debates across the century on the significance of altered forms of consciousness, which dovetail with those on automatic actions, but extend their range. Both faculty psychology and associationism had recognised that large tracts of past experience are inaccessible to consciousness and are only revealed through dreams, dissociated states and some forms of insanity. In the *Biographia Literaria* Coleridge had cited a celebrated case of a young German woman, who, seized with a 'nervous fever', had inexplicably started speaking Greek and Hebrew (it was later revealed that as a child she had unknowingly absorbed the learned recitations of a lodger while asleep). William Hamilton coined the term 'latent mental modification' in *Lectures on Metaphysics and Logic* (1859) to describe how the mind unconsciously modifies and transforms experience, and his former student E. S. Dallas argued in his study of psychology and aesthetics *The Gay Science* (1866) that all creativity arose from the constant traffic between the conscious mind and the 'hidden soul'. From the midcentury, however, cases of mental dissociation were increasingly analysed in the growing field of psychiatric medicine in debates around mesmerism and in discussions of 'double consciousness'.

Anton Mesmer had claimed in the late eighteenth century that there existed a universal force or fluid (loosely allied to Luigi Galvani's concept of 'animal electricity') that when harnessed could cure diseases, and reveal extraordinary powers. In Britain mesmerism, like phrenology, peaked in popularity in the 1840s and 1850s – Charles Dickens and Harriet Martineau were among its supporters – though the practice been dismissed by the medical establishment by the late 1830s. Nonetheless, cases of 'artificial somnambulism' were widely discussed by mental scientists, precisely because they revealed both the power of suggestion and unconscious capacities and motivations. In the 1840s the physiologist Thomas Laycock had cited cases of mesmeric trance as examples of automatic mental reflex, and his ideas were developed by William Carpenter, who in 1855 coined the term 'unconscious cerebration' to describe the 'spontaneous' and 'automatic' motion of mental as well as physical activity. In a further analysis in *Principles of Mental Physiology* (1874), he stressed the need for early mental training to exercise and exert the power of the will.

The induced mesmeric trance was closely allied to the phenomenon of 'double consciousness', a condition of disordered perception, and in extreme cases the doubling or splitting of the personality. In the midcentury such cases had highlighted the tensions between physiological and associationist models of the mind, being seen either as a pathological response to the physical doubleness of the brain (as A. L. Wigan had claimed) or as the product of disordered association. The medical study of double consciousness was developed in the 1870s by Eugène Azam, who had been instrumental in establishing hypnotism (a term coined by James Braid in 1843) as a diagnostic and therapeutic method in France. Azam's reports of 'Felida X' – one of the most dramatic cases of alternating personalities – in the *Revue Scientifique* during the 1870s highlighted the interconnections between somatic state and psychological symptom, laying the foundation of the systematic study of memory and the effects of its repression which culminated in Pierre Janet's analysis of traumatic neurosis and Freud's studies of hysteria.[11] Their work was made available to an English readership by F. W. H. Myers, co-founder of the Society for Psychical Research (1882), who wished to 'track personality to its recesses' (as he put it in a letter to Robert Louis Stevenson) through the investigation of mental dissociation and other forms of amnesia.[12] In many ways Myers embodies Fitzpiers's unsuccessful ambition to 'carry on simultaneously the study of physiology and transcendental philosophy, the material world and the ideal' (*W*: 18). A brilliant classical scholar, his fascination with the limits of the self led him both to question the boundaries of scientific naturalism, and to embrace developments in French psychiatry and neurology. His explorations included cases such as 'Louis V' who oscillated between 'well-behaved' and 'violent' personalities, and more complex states in which the 'subliminal consciousness' forms part of a 'strata of personality' that include both subliminal elements and the 'supraliminal' workings of a 'higher self'.[13]

Myers concludes his 1886 article 'Multiplex Personality' by placing the individual in an evolutionary process that reaches back to 'my ancestor, the ascidian', and cerebral duality had been mapped onto evolutionary divisions between the 'savage' and 'civilised' self since the 1860s, when Pierre Broca located the capacity for language in a region in the brain's left hemisphere. In his revised 1870 edition of *The Principles of Psychology*, Spencer argued (following Lamarck rather than Darwin) that 'instinct is a kind of organised memory', as automatic actions are organically transmitted across generations. The concept of 'organic memory' was elaborated by T. A. Ribot in *Heredity* (1873), who combined it with Hermann Helmholtz's theories of the accumulation and dissipation of energy: 'Every family, every people, every race brings into the world at their birth a certain amount of vitality,' noted Ribot; 'when this sum of vitality and of attributes begins to fail, decay commences.'[14]

Ribot's claim that a finite amount of energy is distributed through a family or race contributed to the wide-ranging discussions of heredity and degeneration that pervaded biological, psychological and social theory during the late nineteenth century. In 1880 E. Ray Lankester's *Degeneration: A Chapter in Darwinism* proposed that the process of natural selection might be halted or even reversed in primitive life-forms. It formed part of a complex discussion on the mechanism of biological transmission carried on by Ernst Haeckel, August Weismann, George Romanes, Francis Galton, and T. H. Huxley, and Hardy's keen interest in these debates can be traced in his later novels of the 1890s – above all *Tess*, *Jude the Obscure*, and *The Well-Beloved*.[15]

Hardy was also familiar with key developments in evolutionary psychology. Though it is hard to establish his reading beyond that recorded in the *Literary Notebooks*, he certainly knew some work of the most polemical psychological writer of the late nineteenth century, Henry Maudsley.[16] An arch-materialist, Maudsley had established his reputation with *The Physiology and Pathology of Mind* in 1867. His gloomy account of mental disease combined B. A. Morel's argument that morbid traits accumulate in families with reflex physiology and post-Darwinian claims that idiocy represents a form of atavism, in which 'animal traits and instincts' are 'a faint echo from a far distant past, testifying to a kinship that man has almost outgrown'.[17] For Maudsley, insanity and imbecility represented retribution for ancestral misconduct; despite his agnosticism, he recalls the Old Testament pronouncement that the sins of the father are visited on the children: 'multitudes of human beings come into the world weighted with a destiny against which they have neither the will nor power to contend.'[18]

Hardy also became acquainted with the prominent psychiatrist James Crichton Browne in the early 1890s, even recording a conversation on the cerebral capacities of men and woman in

1893, some years after *The Woodlanders* appeared (*LW*: 275). A key figure in the development of both neurology and child psychiatry, Crichton Browne had set up a research laboratory with David Ferrier while Medical Director of Wakefield Asylum in the 1870s, which combined experimental work on brain structure and function with clinical observations of nervous disease. Appointed Lord Chancellor's Visitor in Lunacy in 1876, he combined a lucrative private practice with a public role as promoter of the nation's physical and mental health.[19] His concern with hereditary degeneration developed in this context, and forms part of the growing study of childhood, which had become an important branch of psychology by the 1890s. An early article, 'Psychical Diseases of Early Life' (1860), argued that children's undeveloped nervous system made them particularly susceptible to hereditary nervous disease which could even be acquired 'in utero'; in the 1880s he argued that the system of 'cramming' in schools was likely to lead to child neurosis.

In *The Mind of the Child*, Sally Shuttleworth explores the figure of Father Time in *Jude the Obscure* in the context of widespread concerns about the transmission and accumulation of morbid qualities, which amplified Crichton Browne's fears that children are particularly susceptible to both hereditary and acquired nervous disease. These concerns culminated in a series of reports on the apparent dramatic rise in child suicide: Shuttleworth cites an 1880 article in *Blackwood's*, noting the pressures of modernity, and one by Maudsley on 'Heredity in Health and Disease' in 1886.[20] Both pieces warned of the 'deep-lying' dangers of interbreeding, and both the morbid nature of Father Time and the disastrous results of Jude and Sue's liaison clearly chime with these concerns.[21] We need to place Hardy's late work within these contexts; but it is equally important to recognise his engagement with a wider range of psychological theories and perspectives that span the century. And while the discourses of degeneration and heredity may have been most prominent by 1880, they coexisted with other perspectives, such as those of James Ward, William James or that other prominent figure in the growing field of child psychology, James Sully.

James Sully placed his analysis of dreams and childhood in an explicitly evolutionary framework, but his close links with older writers such as Lewes enabled him to develop a more dynamic theory of consciousness than many of his contemporaries. Hardy took notes from Sully's 1877 study, *Pessimism: A History and a Criticism* (*LN* I: 170), and Sully's robust critique of Schopenhauer and Von Hartmann echoes and contrasts with Hardy's own engagement with these writers. Sully's rather sentimental view of childhood, too, is very different from Hardy's (or Crichton Browne's); but he also wrote on music and aesthetics, on dreams, on illusions and on laughter, and his work is an indication of the continuing range of writing on the mind. Despite the contrasts, Hardy's representation of mental states shares this range and flexibility, and he would surely have agreed with Sully's assessment that 'Modern psychology has taught us to regard the difference between a sensation and an idea, a perception and an imagination, as one of degree, and not of kind.'[22]

NOTES

1 See Edwin Clarke and J. S. Jakyna *The Nineteenth-Century Origins of Neuroscientific Concepts* (Berkeley: University of California Press, 1997), pp. 29–37.

2 Rick Rylance, *Victorian Psychology and British Culture 1850–1880* (Oxford: Oxford University Press, 2000), p. 7. Many of the writers discussed here are included in Jenny Bourne Taylor and Sally Shuttleworth, eds., *Embodied Selves: An Anthology of Psychological Texts 1830–1890* (Oxford: Oxford University Press, 1998).

3 See Thomas Dixon, *From Passions to Emotions: The Creation of a Secular Psychological Category* (Cambridge: Cambridge University Press, 2003), pp. 109–20.

4 On Gall's theories and their influence in the early nineteenth century, see Alan Richardson, *British Romanticism and the Science of the Mind* (Cambridge: Cambridge University Press, 2001), pp. 1–39.

5 See Sally Shuttleworth, *Charlotte Brontë and Victorian Psychology* (Cambridge: Cambridge University Press, 1996); Nicholas Dames, *Amnesiac Selves: Nostalgia, Forgetting and British Fiction 1810–1870* (Oxford: Oxford University Press 2001), ch. 2.

6 See Lucy Hartley, *Physiognomy and the Meaning of Expression in Nineteenth-Century Culture* (Cambridge: Cambridge University Press, 2001).

7 Hartley, *Physiognomy*, ch. 2 and 3. Bell's work was the third and enlarged edition of his *Essays on the Anatomy of Expression in Painting* (1806).

8  G. H. Lewes, *The Physiology of Common Life*, 2 vols. (London: Blackwood and Son, 1859–60), II.58.

9  Alexander Bain, *The Emotions and the Will* (London: Parker & Son, 1859), p. 8.

10 Herbert Spencer, *The Principles of Psychology* (London: Longman, 1855), p. 584.

11 See Ann Harrington, *Medicine, Mind and the Double Brain* (Princeton: Princeton University Press, 1987).

12 Letter of 28 February 1886, in Paul Maxner, ed., *Robert Louis Stevenson: The Critical Heritage* (London: Routledge, 1981), p. 212.

13 F. W. H. Myers, 'Multiplex Personality', *Nineteenth Century* 20 (November 1886), p. 649, and 'French Experiments on Strata of Personality', *Proceedings of the Society for Psychical Research* 5 (1888–9), pp. 374–97.

14 T. A. Ribot, *Heredity: A Psychological Study of its Phenomena, Laws, Causes and Consequences*, 2nd edition (London: Henry S. King, 1875), p. 303.

15 See, for example, Peter Morton, *The Vital Science: Biology and the Literary Imagination* (London: George Allen and Unwin, 1984), ch. 7; William Greenslade, *Degeneration, Culture and the Novel, 1880–1940* (Cambridge: Cambridge University Press, 1994), ch. 8; Laura Otis, *Organic Memory* (Lincoln: University of Nebraska Press, 1994), ch. 4.

16 Hardy notes Maudsley's *Natural Causes and Supernatural Seemings* in *LN* I: 195–7.

17 Henry Maudsley *Body and Mind*, 2nd edition (London: Macmillan, 1873), pp. 51–2.

18 Ibid., p. 43.

19 See Janet Oppenheim, *"Shattered Nerves": Doctors, Patients and Depression in Victorian England* (Oxford: Oxford University Press, 1991), ch. 2.

20 [Frederic Marshall], 'Suicide', *Blackwood's Edinburgh Magazine* 127 (1880), pp. 719–35; Henry Maudsley, 'Heredity in Health and Disease', *Fortnightly Review* 39 (1886), pp. 648–59.

21 Sally Shuttleworth, *The Mind of the Child: Child Development in Literature, Science and Medicine, 1840–1900* (Oxford: Oxford University Press, 2010), pp. 335–45.

22 James Sully, 'The Laws of Dream-Fancy', *Cornhill* 34 (November 1876), p. 538.

# Marriage

## ANN HEILMANN

Hardy's fiction offers a trenchant critique of Victorian marriage. Dubbed a leader of the 'anti-marriage league',[1] he systematically exposed marriage as a 'sordid' apparatus of social and legal control (*Jude*: IV.2), 'the gratuitous cause of at least half the misery of the community'.[2] As this chapter seeks to illustrate, the late-nineteenth-century axiom that the 'Woman Question is the Marriage Question'[3] found consistent expression in his work. While acknowledging that the 'woman mostly gets the worst of it in the long run' (*Jude*: IV.3), Hardy drew attention to the marital entrapment of both sexes, portraying men as agents of female oppression and as co-victims of the 'artificial system ... under which the normal sex-impulses are turned into devilish domestic gins and springes to noose and hold back those who want to progress' (*Jude*: IV.3). The metaphor of the trap tearing into living flesh is powerfully invoked in *The Woodlanders* (1887) and compounded by the image of slaughter in *Jude*.

Feminists and social purity writers saw male sexual corruption as the root cause of marital and societal breakdown. New Woman writer Sarah Grand's bestselling *The Heavenly Twins* (1893) features a syphilitic officer who infects mistress, wife, and children; similar scenarios shape Ibsen's *Ghosts* (1881) and Emma Frances Brooke's *A Superfluous Woman* (1894). The high incidence of venereal disease among the military, its spread into the domestic realm, and legislation like the Contagious Diseases Acts (1864, 1866, 1869), which incriminated women as the source of contagion[4] prompted some feminists to advocate male health screening as a legal precondition for marriage. In *Jude the Obscure*, Hardy responded to social purist demands by expressing through his hero his concern that 'instead of protesting against the conditions they protest against the man, the other victim' (*Jude*: V.4); the disastrous consequences of male victimisation are exemplified in Jude's exploitation by Arabella.

How closely Hardy's social critique was bound up with his authorial identity is suggested in his rare parodic treatment of marriage as a trade (a theme of popular and feminist debate)[5] in *The Hand of Ethelberta* (1876): a class satire which explores marriage as a catalyst of social advancement. Ethelberta marries a profligate peer, and far from contracting syphilis is eminently successful in her endeavours. A butler's daughter who starts out as a poet and earns her living by story-telling until her rise enables her to devote herself to epic drama, Ethelberta acts as a comic avatar of Hardy. Her ethic of social-as-moral improvement – 'I ought to do some good by marriage' (*HE*: 36) – may signal Hardy's unease about his own class ascent.

That marriage was fertile ground for late-Victorian writers is exemplified by the resonance of the subject in the periodical press. When Mona Caird, about to become a major New Woman figure, published her first article on 'Marriage' in 1888, her outspoken views on the 'united degeneration' effected by the matrimonial state and its moral, social, and legal 'degradation of womanhood' sparked off a reader exchange of extraordinary dimensions.[6] Within seven weeks, 27,000 letters had reached the *Daily Telegraph*; a selection was subsequently published as *Is Marriage a Failure?*[7] American readers conducted a similar debate in the *Cosmopolitan*.[8] *Punch* contributed a cartoon dubbed 'Marriage evidently not a failure', featuring a middle-aged wife lovingly tying her husband's shoelaces.[9] The *Police News*, however, supported Caird's contention, spotlighting upper-class commercialism and working-class domestic violence.[10]

Hardy's preoccupation with marriage reflects the wider concerns of the age. Many of Caird's respondents promoted a more liberal divorce law. The 'hideous' wording of the Anglican marriage service was condemned even by a practising minister.[11] This places Sue Bridehead's protest against a ritual which reduces the bride to a mere chattel (*Jude*: III.7) and her outcry against the absurdity of the marriage vows into context: 'And so ... the two swore that at every other time of their lives till death took them, they would assuredly believe, feel, and desire precisely as they had believed, felt, and desired during the few preceding weeks' (*Jude*: I.9). Nor was Hardy alone in highlighting the plight of illegitimate children. In the wake of the foundation, in 1893, of the Legitimation League, which lobbied for the legal recognition of children born out of wedlock,[12] a case was made for the equal rights of all children.[13] Another concern was the prohibition to marry a deceased wife's sister; until 1907 marriage between in-laws was treated as incest by the law.[14] Here, too, parallels arise in Hardy's work. When in *Tess of the d'Urbervilles* (1892) Angel Clare walks off with Tess's sister Liza-Lu, presumably to embark on a new marriage, Hardy does not capitulate to conventional morals (Angel getting his 'pure' wife) but, rather, launches a renewed assault on the moral, social, and legal fabric of Victorian marriage.

Marriage reform constituted one of the central campaigns of the Victorian women's movement, with both Barbara Bodichon's *A Brief Summary, in Plain Language, of the Most Important Laws Concerning Women* and Caroline Norton's *English Laws for Women in the Nineteenth Century* outlining the legal disabilities of women in 1854. Norton's high-profile case of marital abuse triggered a series of Infant Custody Acts (1839, 1873, 1886) which introduced limited rights for access and custody for wives considered blameless by the courts; coequal parental rights did not come into effect until the Guardianship of Infants Act of 1925.[15] That *Jude*'s Arabella returns her unloved son is an ironic reflection of the law: Jude is indeed Father Time's legal guardian (and has no formal rights to his children with Sue). Arabella displays considerable insight into married women's rights when she advises Sue to formalise her union: 'if you have rows, and he turns you out of doors, you can get the law to protect you [...] And if he bolts away from you ... you'll have the sticks o' furniture' (*Jude*: V.2). The Matrimonial Causes Act of 1878 included recommendations for the protection of battered wives as outlined by Frances Power Cobbe in 'Wife-Torture in England' (1878).[16] Married, separated, and divorced women's property rights came under consideration in the Matrimonial Causes Act of 1857 and the Married Women's Property Act of 1870, but not until 1882 were wives accorded full control over their own property and income.[17] In the 1890s Arabella could have recourse to the law; in *The Woodlanders*, set in the period following the Divorce Act of 1857, Grace is dispossessed on contracting marriage.

Prior to the act of 1857 divorce was available only through the ecclesiastical courts (precluding remarriage), followed by a private Act of Parliament, and thus the resort of wealthy and influential men.[18] As *Woodlanders* and *Jude* illustrate, the law sharply distinguished between the sexes. Until the Matrimonial Causes Act of 1923, husbands (Phillotson and Jude) could sue for divorce on the grounds of adultery, whereas wives (Grace) had to prove adultery combined with further aggravating causes, such as bigamy, cruelty, incest, sodomy, bestiality, or desertion without cause for over two years.[19] Fitzpiers returns in time and is not 'sufficiently' culpable of cruelty (*W*: 39) – he did not batter Grace – for divorce proceedings to go ahead. In seeking refuge with Giles, thus laying herself open to charges of adultery, Grace, by contrast, becomes 'guilty of desertion and forfeit[s] all claim to a share of his property (even that she might have brought to the marriage)'.[20]

While Hardy advocated that 'a marriage should be dissolvable at the wish of either party, if that party prove it to be a cruelty to him or her',[21] feminists were divided on the issue. Where radicals like Caird, socialists like Eleanor Marx, social purists like Grand, and conservatives like Dinah Mulock (later Craik)[22] saw eye to eye was in their opposition to legalised gender inequity. Many female activists believed that divorce was not in the interest of women and children. 'Greater facility for divorce,' Grand warned, would inevitably lead to 'more self-indulgence for those who are that way inclined, and more misery for the rest.'[23] To Rachel Mary Chapman, 'divorce, historically speaking, has been but another name for the subjugation of women'; it was 'marriage-reform, not marriage-rejection' that would advance civilisation.[24] Millicent Fawcett, leader of the National Union of Women's Suffrage Societies, went as far as equating divorce with political anarchy.[25] In Hardy's work, on the other hand, divorce is the beacon of hope in a world wrecked by marriage, whose 'Letter [law] killeth' (as the epigraph to *Jude* insists); no reform, however farreaching, was able to offer relief from its brutalising regime.

It is his late tragedies – *The Mayor of Casterbridge*, *Tess*, and especially *The Woodlanders* and *Jude* – that contain his most hard-hitting denunciations. The sexual double standard is exposed in the provocative subtitle of *Tess*, 'A Pure Woman'. Marriage's affinity with prostitution and sexual slavery is hinted at in Michael Henchard's sale of his wife (and daughter): an act with implied sexual undertones in a novel published in the year which saw the repeal of the Contagious Diseases Acts, and which still reverberated with the shock waves caused by the journalist W. T. Stead's revelations, in 1885, about the coerced prostitution and trafficking of under-age girls.[26] The sale of women shapes Henchard's affective life: years later, after he has symbolically 'bought [Susan] back again' (*MC*: 10), Lucetta is discarded with a cheque, Elizabeth-Jane dismissed with an annuity and a suggestive note to Farfrae. In *Woodlanders* the sexual barter of a girl by her father is made explicit when Melbury offers his daughter up for sexual-qua-marital consumption to two different men. Grace's terror at the thought of Fitzpiers's return and flight from the marital-cum-paternal home conceptually link father and husband as joint drivers of sexual oppression.

Grace becomes despoiled the moment she enters wifehood. As she realises almost instantly, 'she had made a frightful mistake … Acquiescence in her father's wishes had been degradation to herself' (*W*: 29). A matrimonial union founded on male physical and/or female emotional infidelity is, Sue exclaims, tantamount to 'adultery … however legal' (*Jude*: IV:3). Worse, Sue's retreat into an airless closet and leap out of the window are a potent example of how seamlessly marital sex could turn into an experience of rape. In invoking the sense of defilement – physical, psychological, moral – that arose from the wife's legal obligation to maintain conjugal relations, Hardy raised similar concerns as fin-de-siècle women writers. In the words of Iota (Kathleen Mannington Caffyn), George Egerton (Mary Chavelita Dunne), and Sarah Grand, the wife's duty to oblige her husband's sexual appetites was a 'horror made manifest',[27] the equivalent of 'legal prostitution, a nightly degradation',[28] 'as absolute, as repugnant, as cruel, and as contrary to nature as that of the streets'.[29] What these writers challenged was the unholy alliance of scripture and science in framing matrimonial law. Contemporary medical opinion held fast to the dictat, *pace* William Acton, that while a 'modest woman' was afflicted with little sexual desire (women who did were to be considered prostitutes or nymphomaniacs), a wife naturally 'submit[ted] to her husband's embraces … to gratify him' and to enjoy the pleasures of maternity; wives who 'maintain[ed] women's rights' to the extent of refusing sex were condemned for endangering their husbands' health.[30] The mathematician and eugenist Karl Pearson, founder of the Men and Women's Club (1885–9) established to debate matters of sexuality, propounded that 'Race-evolution has implanted in women a desire for children, as it has implanted in man a desire for woman', and that 'the penalty to be paid for race-predominance' was 'the subjection of women'.[31] The Catholic biologist St George Mivart deplored the 'false conscience' of wives led astray by the 'newest school' in literature, protesting that what degraded women was not undesired marital intercourse but an obsessive attention to their feelings: 'By submission ... the wife yields to the injunctions of reason and justice, and conforms to the moral law. If such submission is distasteful, her compliance acquires the increased merit of self-sacrifice to duty.'[32] Sue's shrunken, sackcloth-bound body and broken mind, together with Jude's crucifixion on the altar of marriage, act as a powerful indictment of the scientific, religious, and legal doctrines which conspired to enslave both sexes by turning 'Weddings [into] funerals' (*Jude*: VI.9).

*Jude* offers an alternative to institutionalised marriage. Hardy's 1912 Postscript contrasts legal marriage and the 'law of nature' (*Jude* x). Sue and Jude constitute a 'natural' union. Phillotson comments on their 'extraordinary affinity'; like him, Arabella is struck by the 'complete mutual understanding' which makes them 'almost the two parts of a single whole', and cynically infers that they cannot be married 'or they wouldn't be so much to one another as that' (*Jude*: IV.4, V.5). Ironically, it is only in their legally unsanctified state that they embody John Stuart Mill's blueprint for marriage outlined in *The Subjection of Women* (1869): 'two persons of cultivated faculties, identical in opinions and purposes, between whom there exists that best kind of equality, similarity of powers and capacities with reciprocal superiority.' The novel's legalised unions, in contrast, illustrate Mill's notion of 'primitive barbarism':[33] Sue's 'utter horror' at the sight of the ill-assorted couples at the registry office is exacerbated by witnessing a church wedding, whose flower-bedecked bride resembles a human sacrifice (*Jude*: V.4). This image is also invoked in Caird's *The Daughters of Danaus* (1894): why 'could not men and women have interests in common, without wishing instantly to plunge into a condition of things which hampered and crippled them so miserably?'[34]

The most crippling condition, for women, was the lack of the 'obvious right of the woman to *possess herself* body and soul, to give or withhold herself ... exactly as she wills'.[35] Although a landmark case in 1891 (of which Hardy must certainly have been aware)

dismissed the husband's right to imprison his wife,[36] rape continued to be defined as a man's non-consensual sex with a woman who
was '*not his wife*'.[37] In the words of Justice Hawkins, on marriage
a woman gave her husband 'an irrevocable right to her person ...
Consent is immaterial.'[38] This condition of sexual slavery prompted
Mill to add a clause to his marriage contract with Harriet Taylor in
which he formally abrogated his rights over his wife.[39] The efforts
of the feminist activist Elizabeth Wolstenholme Elmy to end
marital sexual coercion by lobbying MPs to introduce a bill which
would remove the matrimonial exemption proved unsuccessful.[40]
This provides a context for Sue's abhorrence of marriage. One of
the reasons why she shrinks from formalising her union with Jude,
Hardy wrote to Edmund Gosse, is her fear of placing herself under
a sexual obligation, 'though while uncontracted she feels at liberty
to yield herself as seldom as she chooses' (*CL* II: 99). Her inner
compulsion to do her 'duty' by the letter of the law propels her into
self-destruction.

Sue's aversion to sex even in her relationship with Jude indicates
the strength of the repulsion caused by her bodily dispossession.
Given Arabella's strong sex drive, Hardy was not suggesting, as
Victorian doctors did, that women knew no physical desire, but
that a 'fastidious' woman like Sue felt revolted by the legal denial
of her right to self-ownership. Sue later laments that 'We ought
to have lived in mental communion, and no more' (*Jude*: VI.3). To
many women of the time celibacy indeed held distinct advantages,
including professional advancement through freedom from maternity. This, New Woman author Ella Hepworth Dixon affirmed,
was the reason for women's reluctance to marry.[41] Even when in
the new century female sexual abstinence or 'self-control' came
under attack,[42] Kathlyn Oliver, a suffragist and unionist, protested
to the *Freewoman* that celibacy was far from injurious.[43] Oliver
sparked off a heated debate, but her views were supported by other
contributors who argued for continence in marriage as a means of
wider social and moral regeneration.

In that *Jude*'s only authentic and emotionally fulfilled union
remains noninstitutionalised, Hardy intimated that neither conventional marriage nor celibacy offered a viable foundation for heterosexual partnership. As a public figure, however, he was at pains
to distance himself from free love.[44] In the aftermath of the Hinton

trial for bigamy the free love movement was associated with promiscuity and sexual depravity.[45] Olive Schreiner, too, whose heroine Lyndall in *The Story of an African Farm* (1883) refuses to marry the father of her unborn child but consents to live with him ('then when we do not love any more, we can say good-bye'), hotly denied that she was condoning 'temporary unions'.[46] Eleanor Marx, herself engaged in a (fatal) free love relationship with Edward Aveling,[47] took care to establish in *The Woman Question* (1886) that the egalitarian sexual relationship of the future would be based on monogamy.[48] Women had more at stake than men: Elizabeth Wolstenholme was pressurised into legalising her union with Ben Elmy, and the socialist Edith Lanchester was committed to a lunatic asylum by her father for refusing to marry her lover.[49]

Hardy's disclaimer followed in the wake of Grant Allen's sensational 1895 novels *The Woman Who Did* and *The British Barbarians*, which promoted free love as 'the higher and purer ideals of life and art',[50] exculpating adultery on the grounds that 'every man and woman should be free to do as they will with their own persons'.[51] Like Hardy, Allen attacked the marriage laws, arguing that the mother had a 'natural' right to the custody of her children irrespective of her actions.[52] Like the hero of *The British Barbarians* Jude dismisses the 'beggarly question of parentage': 'What does it matter ... whether a child is yours by blood or not?' (*Jude*: V.3).

When Sue reflects that 'Everybody is getting to feel as we do' (*Jude*: V.4), Hardy referred to advanced thought which sought to challenge conventional morality. Thus Edith (Lees) Ellis (the lesbian wife of sexologist Havelock Ellis) proposed a marital 'apprenticeship' system 'as a preventive of unhappy unions', designed to hasten the end of 'prostitution ... and sexual repression'.[53] If Ellis stopped short of promoting cohabitation trials, Caird showcased a 'free' marriage conducted across two separate if adjoining flats.[54] 'That entire and unswerving refusal to "cage" another person,' the early gay theorist Edward Carpenter asserted in 1896, 'must inevitably bring its own price of mortal suffering with it; yet the Love so gained ... will be found in the end to be worth the pang.'[55] Given the virulence of the response to *Jude*, Hardy may have felt otherwise, withdrawing as he did from his novelistic career. Yet with their uncompromising dissection of marriage his novels had carried into practice his determination, as professed in a letter to

Millicent Fawcett of 30 November 1906 (*CL* III: 238), to 'break up the present pernicious conventions in respect of manners, customs, religion, illegitimacy, the stereotyped household': his novels throw the gauntlet at the moral, social, and legal status quo.

NOTES

1 Margaret Oliphant, 'The Anti-Marriage League', *Blackwood's Edinburgh Magazine* (1896), p. 138, in, *The Late-Victorian Marriage Question*, ed. Ann Heilmann, 5 vols. (London: Routledge Thoemmes, 1998), V; hereafter *LVMQ*.

2 'How Shall We Solve the Divorce Problem?', *Nash's Magazine* 5 (March 1912); *THPV*: 331–2.

3 Sarah Grand, 'The New Aspect of the Woman Question', *North American Review* 58 (1894), p. 276 (*LVMQ*: II).

4 These acts authorised nonuniformed police in specified naval and garrison towns to coerce any woman believed to be acting as a 'common prostitute' to undergo gynaecological examinations and formal registration: see Judith R. Walkowitz, *Prostitution and Victorian Society* (Cambridge: Cambridge University Press, 1980), pp. 1–2.

5 Marie Corelli, Lady Jeune, Flora Annie Steele, and Susan, Countess of Malmesbury, *The Modern Marriage Market* (London: Hutchinson and Co., 1898); Cicely Hamilton, *Marriage as a Trade* (New York: Moffat, Yard and Company, 1909).

6 Mona Caird, 'Marriage', *Westminster Review* 130 (July–December 1888), p. 197.

7 Harry Quilter, ed., *Is Marriage a Failure?* (London: Swan Sonnenschein, 1888); *LVMQ*: I.

8 Patricia Marks, *Bicycles, Bangs, and Bloomers* (Lexington: University Press of Kentucky, 1990), p. 51.

9 *Punch*, 15 September 1888, p. 130.

10 'Is Marriage a Failure? As a Rule – Yes!', *Police News*, 4 April 1891, p. 1.

11 Quilter, *Marriage*, pp. 153, 165, 232.

12 Lucy Bland, *Banishing the Beast: Sexuality and the Early Feminists* (London: Penguin, 1995), p. 156.

13 Quilter, *Marriage*, pp. 235–8.

14 Nancy F. Anderson, 'The "Marriage with a Deceased Wife's Sister Bill" Controversy', *Journal of British Studies* 21:2 (Spring 1982), pp. 67–86.

15 Mary Lyndon Shanley, *Feminism, Marriage, and the Law in Victorian England* (Princeton: Princeton University Press, 1989), pp. 131–55.

16 Maeve E. Doggett, *Marriage, Wife-Beating and the Law in Victorian England* (Columbia: University of South Carolina Press, 1993), pp. 130–1; Frances Power Cobbe, 'Wife-Torture in England' (1878), in Susan Hamilton, ed., *Criminals, Idiots, Women, and Minors* (Peterborough: Broadview Press, 1995), pp. 132–70.

17 Shanley, *Marriage*, pp. 103–30.

18 Shanley, *Marriage*, pp. 9, 36.

19 Lee Holcombe, *Wives and Property* (Toronto: University of Toronto Press, 1983), p. 99; Doggett, *Wife-Beating*, p. 100.

20 Shanley, *Marriage*, p. 9, p. 176.

21 Hardy, 'How Shall We Solve the Divorce Problem?' (*THPV*: 331–2). See also his 1912 Postscript to *Jude*.

22 Dinah M. Mulock, 'For Better for Worse', *Contemporary Review* 51 (1887), pp. 570–6 (*LMVQ*: II).

23 Sarah Grand, 'Marriage Questions in Fiction', *Fortnightly Review* 69 (1898), p. 389 (*LMVQ*: V).

24 Rachel Mary Chapman, 'The Decline of Divorce' and 'Marriage Rejection and Marriage Reform', *Marriage Questions in Modern Fiction* (London: Lane, the Bodley Head, 1897), pp. 163, 125 (*LMVQ*: II, V).

25 Millicent Fawcett, 'The Emancipation of Women', *Fortnightly Review* 50 (1891), p. 675.

26 W. T. Stead, 'The Maiden Tribute of Modern Babylon', *Pall Mall Gazette* for 6, 7, 8, and 10 July 1885. Stead's investigation hastened the Criminal Law Amendment Act of 1885, which raised girls' age of consent from thirteen to sixteen; Sheila Jeffreys, *The Spinster and her Enemies* (London: Pandora, 1985), p. 55.

27 Iota, *A Yellow Aster* (London: Hutchinson, 1894), p. 245.

28 George Egerton, 'Virgin Soil', *Discords* (London: Virago, 1983), p. 155.

29 Sarah Grand, *The Beth Book* (1897; Bristol: Thoemmes, 1994), pp. 424–5.

30 William Acton, *The Functions and Disorders of the Reproductive Organs* (1875), in Sheila Jeffreys, ed., *The Sexuality Debates* (New York: Routledge & Kegan Paul, 1987), pp. 61–4.

31 'The Woman's Question' (1885), quoted in Judith R. Walkowitz, *City of Dreadful Delight* (London: Virago, 1992), p. 148.

32 St George Mivart, 'The Degradation of Women', *Humanitarian* 9 (1896), pp. 251–2, 257 (*LMVQ*: II).

33 J. S. Mill, *The Subjection of Women* (1869; London: Virago, 1983), p. 177.

34 Mona Caird, *The Daughters of Danaus* (New York: Feminist Press, 1989), pp. 121, 169.

35 Caird, 'Marriage', p. 198.

36 *Regina v. Jackson*, Shanley, *Marriage*, pp. 177–83; Phillip Mallett, '"Smacked, and Brought to Her Senses": Hardy and the Clitheroe Abduction Case', *Thomas Hardy Journal* 8.2 (1992), pp. 70–3.

37 Shanley, *Marriage*, p. 184. UK law did not recognise marital rape until 1991.

38 Quoted ibid., p. 185.

39 Ray Strachey, *The Cause* (1928; London: Virago, 1988), p. 67.

40 Shanley, *Marriage*, p. 185.

41 Ella Hepworth Dixon, 'Why Women are Ceasing to Marry', *Humanitarian* 14 (1899), pp. 391–6 (*LMVQ*: II).

42 Lucy Bland, 'Heterosexuality, Feminism and the *Freewoman* Journal in Early Twentieth-Century England', *Women's History Review* 4:1 (1995), p. 15.

43 Kathlyn Oliver, 'Asceticism and Passion', *Freewoman*, 15 February 1912, p. 252.

44 See letter to Florence Henniker, 1 June 1896 (*CL* II: 122).

45 Inspired by James Hinton's *Life in Nature* (1862), Hintonians promoted polygamy as a mystic form of nature worship. Sharply gendered practices, however, demanded women's sexual availability. Hinton's son was tried for bigamy in 1886. See Ann Heilmann, *New Woman Fiction* (Basingstoke: Palgrave Macmillan, 2000), pp. 109–10.

46 Olive Schreiner, *The Story of an African Farm* (London: Virago, 1989), p. 220. Olive Schreiner to J. T. Lloyd, undated, in Richard Rive, ed., *Olive Schreiner: Letters* (Oxford: Oxford University Press, 1988), p. 260.

47 Aveling ensured he was the main beneficiary of Eleanor's will, married another woman while living with her, and helped procure the poison with which she killed herself. Ruth Brandon, *The New Women and the Old Men* (London: Secker & Warburg, 1990), pp. 133–59.

48 Edward and Eleanor Marx Aveling, *The Woman Question* (London: Swan Sonnenschein, 1886), pp. 15–16 (*LMVQ*: II).

49 Bland, *Banishing the Beast*, pp. 157–63; Shanley, *Marriage*, p. 115.

50 Grant Allen, Introduction to *The British Barbarians* (London: Putnam's, 1895), p. 17.

51 Ibid., p. 249.

52 Ibid., pp. 251–2.

53 Edith Ellis, *A Noviciate for Marriage* (Haslemere, 1894), p. 16 (*LMVQ*: II).

54 Mona Caird, *The Stones of Sacrifice* (London: Simpkin, Marshall, 1915).

55 Edward Carpenter, *Love's Coming-of-Age* (London: Methuen, 1914), p. 113 (*LMVQ*: II).

33

# The New Woman

CAROLYN BURDETT

The New Woman has flexed her muscles and grown over the last two decades. While a small number of important critical studies appeared in the 1970s and 1980s, the New Woman has since become the focus of extensive scholarship.[1] Her dominance in recent feminist literary criticism has echoes of her surge to prominence in the 1890s: the New Woman tag, then and now, risks the same co-option of diverse opinions, politics and texts under a single banner. But as the prolific forms of writing of the 1890s abundantly attest, part of the power of a newly coined label is precisely its ability to gather to itself and unify disparate positions. This essay will indicate the diversity of views which came to be identified with the New Woman, as well as clarifying the common aims and strategies which characterised debate about the position of women at the end of the nineteenth century. What emerges as the most important unifying characteristic of the New Woman is her modernity: she is a sign of the changing aspirations of women which gathered momentum through the second half of the nineteenth century. These aspirations were formed out of powerfully transformative ideas of liberal autonomy and self-realisation, scientific discovery and cultural experimentation. But the New Woman was also preeminently a representation, formed in energetic debate in the periodical press and in a variety of forms of fictional narrative where her qualities were applauded or vilified, and her image drawn, contested and redrawn.

So when did the distinctive figure of the New Woman first appear, and what was her relation to the diverse debates about the position of women? By the final decades of the nineteenth century, real social and political change was underway: a series of parliamentary acts had improved the legal status of married women, including their right to retain property; higher education institutions gradually opened to women; forms of female employment expanded; and female trades union membership significantly increased between the 1870s and the end of the century. By the mid 1880s, 'the Woman Question', which began to gather momentum from the midcentury, was widely debated: groups such as the Men and Women's Club, formed in 1885, gathered women and men together for supposedly 'free' discussion about issues of sex, informed by scientific principles. In this group and elsewhere, marriage and maternity, adultery and divorce, venereal disease, prostitution, birth control and sex education were discussed openly by unmarried, as well as married, women.

Women also proved themselves effective campaigners and lobbyists. The repeal in 1886 of the Contagious Diseases Acts, which from the 1860s had given police powers to arrest suspected prostitutes in port or garrison areas, provided a model for action which extended into many other areas of public life conceived as needing 'purification'. It also offered a model for subsequent suffrage campaigning. In addition, women formed a significant presence in labour agitation, and socialist women occasionally intersected with feminist debate dominated by middle-class concerns. The centrality of prostitution, and the public furore caused by W. T. Stead's sensational *Pall Mall Gazette* exposé of sexual traffic in English working-class virgins is one example of an event which united feminists, socialists and clergymen in common protest.[2] Cultural innovation, too, could bring together figures involved in feminist and class politics: Karl Marx's daughter, Eleanor Marx, for example, hosted a reading of Ibsen's *A Doll's House* in December 1885 and, with other prominent socialists, feminists and intellectuals attended the first performance in 1891 of *Hedda Gabler*, when Thomas Hardy was also in the audience.[3] Edith Lees, who later married the sexologist Havelock Ellis, wrote of the women and men gathering together after the first full production at London's Novelty theatre of *A Doll's House* in 1889: 'We were restive and almost savage in our arguments. What did it mean?... Was it life or death for women?'[4]

But it was in the pages of bestselling fiction that the New Woman really flourished and took on her distinctive characteristics. In an essay of 1979 John Goode accuses Hardy of being disingenuous when, in the 'Postscript' to *Jude the Obscure* written in 1912, he cites an 'experienced reviewer' from Germany who deemed Sue

Bridehead the 'first delineation in fiction of a woman who was coming in to notice in her thousands every year – the woman of the feminist movement' (*Jude*: xi–xii). Goode himself dates the emergence of this fictional feminist heroine as 1891, after the performance of *Hedda Gabler*, insisting that Hardy could not have been unaware of the burgeoning field of feminist fiction that followed.[5] More recently, critics have chosen to focus on the coining of the term 'New Woman' in Sarah Grand's essay 'The New Aspect of the Woman Question', and Ouida's response in the same issue of the *North American Review* of 1894.[6] However, W. T. Stead's 1894 review essay on 'The Novel of the Modern Woman' pushes the date of her inauguration rather earlier, to the publication in 1883 of South African-born Olive Schreiner's *The Story of an African Farm*. According to Stead, it established Schreiner as the 'the founder and high priestess of the school'.[7]

Schreiner's female protagonist, Lyndall, unfolds an eloquent if dismaying analysis of the position of women: the distorting socialisation of young girls, trained to value only the corrupted fragility of a power dependent on fleeting physical beauty; the ludicrously inadequate education of women for motherhood, the work most urgently and profoundly in need of a wide and expansive culture; and the disease of woman's economic dependency in marriage, which allies her with the prostitute. These issues, Stead insists, constitute the 'brief' of the Modern Woman, 'the leaven which is working directly and indirectly in all the women novelists of to-day'.[8] Certainly, Stead is correct in identifying these topics – of female 'nature', the effects of socialisation, economic inequality, and the vastly different stakes for men and women that love, marriage and parenthood imply – as central to the New Woman literature and debate. But it is also the case that Lyndall is a model for the New Woman as much for her restless, agitated subjectivity, her intelligence and her unconventional reading, and her conflicted relation to her own desire. When her lover questions her about why she is attracted to him, Lyndall answers: 'because I like to experience, I like to try. You don't understand that.'[9] Gwen Waring, in Iota's (Kathleen Mannington Caffyn) *The Yellow Aster* (1894) similarly tells the man she will marry, 'I like new sensations; I am curious.' Believing herself 'sexless', she embarks on marriage as an 'experiment'.[10]

For many critics of the New Woman, this 'unfeminine' tone allied her with wider culturally disruptive trends of the fin de siècle. The 'quickened, multiplied consciousness' advocated in Walter Pater's infamous Conclusion to *The Renaissance* (1873), and taken as a touchstone for the decadent imagination, was synonymous for some with a failure of moral discipline and healthy natural instinct.[11] The prolific antifeminist polemicist, Eliza Lynn Linton, deemed women who 'light up' cigarettes with the men, engage in 'male' pursuits like hunting, indulge in 'shopkeeping and slumming' in pretence of a need to work, 'insurgent to their finger-tips'. They are prey to 'the terrible restlessness with which this age is afflicted, part of the contempt for law in all its forms which certain women have adopted from certain men, themselves too effeminate, too little manly to be able to submit to discipline'.[12] Hugh Stutfield lampooned '"yellow" lady novelists' in his attack on the forms of 'debased emotionalism' diagnosed in Max Nordau's sensational critique of modern culture, *Degeneration* (1895). Women writers create characters who are pathologically introspective or erotomaniacs, obsessed with sex: 'some are "amorous sensitives," others are apparently sexless, and are at pains to explain this to the reader.'[13] New Woman writing was placed by its critics alongside the writing of both the Decadent movement and the Naturalist fiction and drama associated with Emile Zola and Ibsen. All were considered signs of cultural decay, social degeneration and a falling-away of moral value.

Argument about the representation of sex and sexuality was also closely linked to the commercial forms of Victorian publishing. The important debate conducted in the *New Review* on 'Candour in English Fiction', to which Hardy contributed in 1890, showed the power of moral sanction and censorship which belonged to publishers and the circulating libraries. The noisy condemnation to which authors such as Hardy felt subjected, however, was in fact a symptom of the waning power of traditional forms of Victorian publishing and book circulation. New, cheaper forms of fiction, and especially the one-volume novel, precipitated a swift collapse of the triple-decker novel in the 1890s and with it the ability to control and police a moral agenda through library control of the market. Although the long narrative fiction remained an important form for New Woman writers, some also experimented with new

literary forms, which in turn were in part a response to the burgeoning and competitive new magazine markets. From the 1880s,
commentators began to refer to the 'short story', a form successfully developed by George Egerton (Mary Chavelita Dunne) in
her 1893 *Keynotes*, and by Olive Schreiner and Ella D'Arcy.

Part of the restlessness which critics of the New Woman detected
and deplored was related to the urgency with which women –
both in fiction and in their lives – represented their hunger for
knowledge. Sarah Grand's enormously popular and influential *The
Heavenly Twins* (1893) opens with Evadne, aged 19, looking out
onto the world with inquiring eyes, impelled – perhaps by 'hereditary preparation' – to seek the truth which prejudice and convention
conceal: 'It was a need of her nature to know.'[14] This New Woman,
given to 'advanced reading', was a particular target of ridicule for
critics. An unsigned review of *Jude the Obscure* in the *Athenaeum* in
November 1895 is typical. It quotes Sue, quoting John Stuart Mill
on self-determination to Phillotson, and hoping that he might act
on those words as she 'wish[es] to always', whereupon the reviewer
adds acidly: 'No wonder the husband moaned, "What do I care
about J. S. Mill".'[15] Writing to her friend, the sexual radical and utopian socialist Edward Carpenter in 1889, Olive Schreiner defends
her reading of Mill and Herbert Spencer, insisting that her passion
for such work cannot be understood by those, like Carpenter, who
have taken for granted a privileged education: '*You have been over
fed*. We are starving to death.'[16]

But the New Woman's reading signalled more than a determination to be better educated and more knowledgeable. Many
New Women writers were profoundly influenced by recent scientific theory, and used to powerful effect the new languages of science. As Angelique Richardson has shown, sexual selection, seen
through the lens of Darwin's biology, gave a new shape to marriage narratives.[17] Issues of heredity and the social responsibility of
'healthy' marriage choices were foregrounded in the pro-eugenicist
feminism of writers such as Sarah Grand. In *The Heavenly Twins*,
Evadne Frayling, receiving information on her wedding day about
her new husband's 'character and past life', forbids sexual consummation. Studying the works of Herbert Spencer and Francis
Galton helps her to recognise her husband as 'unfit' and saves her
from Edith Beale's fate: Edith, also married to a dissolute man, is

infected with syphilis, gives birth to a 'monstrous' child, becomes insane and dies.[18] The home is rewritten in New Woman narratives as a place of corruption and infection, of frustration, discontent, lies and deception, where women and children suffer from prevalent sexual double standards. The biological determinism and hereditarianism in many of these narratives was incorporated into a feminist vision of women's duty as policers and purifiers of the public realm, above all in their role as mothers and educators of the next generation. Separate spheres rhetoric was reworked and radicalised in the light of current biological theory. It was able to combine traditional ideals of women as wives and mothers, with a very current emphasis on the dangers of social and cultural degeneration – ills which women could remedy as part of a newly conceived civic and domestic duty which demanded social and legal change and the transformation of male sexual behaviour.

But just as in wider social debate evolutionary theory was cited in support of divergent political positions, so too feminist writers contested meanings and crafted different arguments out of their engagements with contemporary science. Mona Caird, who became a prominent New Woman novelist after the publication in 1894 of *The Daughters of Danaus*, was incisively critical of what she deemed 'the fetish "nature"', arguing in response to Eliza Lynn Linton's articles on modern women's 'insurgency' that if they 'are really insurgents against human nature, and not the indications of a new social development, then their fatal error will assuredly prove itself'.[19] Maternal feeling, for Caird, was simply not innate in every woman: insisting it to be so narrowed women's life choices and fettered their individual freedoms.[20] Caird had caused shock waves when, in 1888, she declared marriage in its present form to be 'a vexatious failure' and sparked the famous controversy in which 27,000 letters from readers of the *Daily Telegraph* responded to the question 'Is Marriage a Failure?' In that essay, as in her subsequent writing, Caird robustly contextualised and historicised women's position, asserting the 'sacred' institution of marriage to be a late-invented bourgeois form.[21] 'Adaptation' becomes a key term in Caird's argument, evoking Darwin's key concept in his theory of natural selection to argue against the fixity of gender positions and relations, and the need instead to acknowledge context and environment. Olive Schreiner was later to make a similar evolutionary argument central to her 1911 *Woman and Labour*, where she characterised the movement for female emancipation as an evolutionarily inevitable response to the changing social and economic environment of modernity.[22]

New Woman writers were also affected by developments in psychology, which transformed traditional ways in which feelings were conceived. Minds were seen as part of evolved physiological and reflex systems, and emotions were uncoupled from conventional (often Christian) associations and understood as products of evolution. Some novelists – Hardy foremost amongst them – began to question whether an emotional state such as love, usually sparked initially by sexual instincts, could or should be brought to the sphere of the law. When Jude and Arabella make their swiftly contracted marriage vows, the narrator comments:

The two swore that every other time of their lives till death took them, they would assuredly believe, feel, and desire precisely as they had believed, felt, and desired during the few preceding weeks. What was as remarkable as the undertaking itself was the fact that nobody seemed at all surprised at what they swore. (*Jude*: I.9)

In Grant Allen's 1896 *A Splendid Sin* a wife tells her husband: 'Promise to *do* or not to do, if you will; but promise to *feel* or not to feel – what a transparent absurdity!', a sentiment which almost exactly repeats New Woman Herminia Barton's outburst to Alan Merrick in Allen's bestselling *The Woman Who Did* (1895): 'contract to feel or not to feel – what a transparent absurdity!'[23]

However, while critics of the 'anti-marriage league' – the title of Margaret Oliphant's 1896 article in *Blackwood's Edinburgh Magazine*, which criticised *Jude the Obscure* and *The Woman Who Did* – frequently indicted New Women as 'anti-marriage', narratives focused on 'free unions' remained largely the province of male writers. Representations ranged from the 'thin-skinned' fragile resistance of Sue and Jude on the day allotted for that 'most preposterous of all joint-ventures' (*Jude*: V.4) to Herminia Barton, the daughter of an Anglican Dean, declaring that the marriage ceremony is 'part and parcel of a system of slavery... I will not palter and parley with the unholy thing.'[24] In George Gissing's *The Odd Women* (1893), the refined Everard Barfoot tests New Woman Rhoda Nunn by challenging her to embark on a love relationship with him that dispensed with the legal bond. Gissing's own impatience with the gap between feminist critique and the willingness to dispense with marriage amongst educated middle-class women is perhaps eloquent of the fact that – as Olive Schreiner puts it in her story 'The Buddhist Priest's Wife' (1923) – 'For a woman, marriage is much more serious than for a man.'[25] Many women feared that free love would leave them vulnerable and unprotected. Instead, the energy of much of the fiction of the 1890s was spent in challenging existing conventions and exposing hypocrisies. As well as the 'syphilitic' narratives explored by Grand and by Emma Frances Brooke in *A Superfluous Woman* (1894), Ménie Muriel Dowie's *Gallia* (1895) satirized double standards in relation to men's premarital sexual experience, while George Egerton's 'Virgin Soil', from *Discords* (1894), is a coruscating attack on female sexual ignorance. It opens with a bridegroom awaiting his young bride, as she sobs farewell to her mother; five years later, the wife returns, a 'hollow-eyed, sullen' woman, to castigate her mother for marrying her for the sake of middle-class respectability to a worldly man: 'You sold me for a home, for clothes, for food.' More shocking still is the bitterness with which she condemns her mother for delivering her unprepared to the 'nightly degradation' of marital sex, ignorant of 'my physical needs, my coming passion, the very meaning of my sex'.[26]

However, even those women writers who opposed the pro-eugenic views of a figure like Sarah Grand often strenuously denied antagonism to marriage as such, affirming only their condemnation of its present form. This focus is perhaps in part responsible for the fact that New Woman narratives offered endings in which the difficulties of marriage were rarely resolved otherwise than in female conformity, suffering or death. The intense investment in female suffering so common to these narratives was in part an affective response to the felt and experienced difficulties of women's position – which now explicitly included issues of sexual desire. But it was also sometimes a strategic counter to charges of selfishness which shadowed claims for female self-realisation. Complaints came not only from conservatives and traditionalists. The socialist Karl Pearson, who founded the Men and Women's Club, and later became a leading eugenicist, attacked women for demanding 'equality of opportunity', accusing them of '[s]elf-interest and class-prejudice', of preferring John Stuart Mill's *Subjection of Women* to 'general social efficiency', thus avoiding the social duty imposed by maternity.[27] Emphasising women's willed (and temporary) renunciation of the pleasures of marriage, sexual relations, and maternity was one form of narrative and argumentative response to such accusations.

Despite their often punitive narrative endings, however, the fiction of the 1890s undoubtedly contributed to important new images of and for women. One of the significant effects of the debates was to suggest the *complexity* of women's desires, aspirations and identities. This was despite the fact that much commentary – exemplified in *Punch*'s cartoons – tried to limit the 'type' of the modern woman to stereotypes: sometimes of mannish, unattractive spinsters, or overbearing, vulgar and selfish harridans who threatened to bring about the end of civilization; or else of bicycle-riding Amazons, unstoppable in their pursuit of the latest theory or cause. The sheer energy of fiction writing, journalism, and discussion, however, opened spaces for imagining change and interrogating subjectivity and desire. Even the relentless focus on unconventional lifestyle which presented the New Woman as cigarette smoking, bicycle riding, and garbed either in sinuous decadent finery or else 'rational dress', could become material for new ways of imagining women's lives. In her short story 'A Woman in Grey' (1896), the poet Alice Meynell turns the stereotype of a bicycling modern woman into an image of female responsiveness, and of the human capacity to tolerate uncertainties and in-between states such as those which characterise profound social and psychic transformation. Cycling along Oxford Street, amidst omnibuses, carriages, cabs and carts, some going her way, others following different paths, absolutely part of the modern world, the (new) woman in grey maintains her 'unstable equilibrium' as she heads towards the twentieth century.[28]

NOTES

1 See, for example of earlier scholarship, Gail Cunningham, *The New Woman and the Victorian Novel* (Basingstoke: Macmillan, 1978).

2 W. T. Stead, 'The Maiden Tribute of Modern Babylon', *Pall Mall Gazette* of 6, 7, 8, and 10 July 1885; Lucy Bland, *Banishing the Beast: English Feminism and Sexual Morality 1885–1914* (London: Penguin, 1995), p. xvi.

3  See Yvonne Kapp, *Eleanor Marx: The Crowded Years 1884–1898* (London: Virago, 1979), pp. 100–3, 476.

4  Quoted in Sally Ledger, *Henrik Ibsen* (Plymouth: Northcote House, 1999), p. 2.

5  John Goode, 'Sue Bridehead and the New Woman', *Women Writing and Writing about Women*, ed. Mary Jacobus (London: Croom Helm, 1979), p. 108. Goode correctly insists that Hardy was aware of feminist writing. He wrote in 1890 to Percy Bunting, editor of the *Contemporary Review*, on behalf of Mona Caird, who was seeking a publisher for one of the articles which eventually formed her collection *The Morality of Marriage* (*CL* I: 207–8). Sarah Grand sent a copy of *The Heavenly Twins* and unexpectedly visited the Hardys in 1893 (*CL* II:12), and Hardy knew Grant Allen, writing in February 1895 to congratulate him on *The Woman Who Did* (*CL* II: 74–5).

6  Sarah Grand, 'The New Aspect of the Woman Question', *North American Review* 158 (1894), pp. 270–6; Ouida, 'The New Woman', also *North American Review* 158, pp. 610–19. Influential critical works foregrounding these essays include Sally Ledger, *The New Woman: Fiction and Feminism at the Fin de Siècle* (Manchester: Manchester University Press, 1997), p. 9, and Carolyn Christensen Nelson, ed., *A New Woman Reader: Fiction, Articles, Drama of the 1890s* (Hertfordshire: Broadview Press, 2001), p. ix.

7  W. T. Stead, 'The Book of the Month: the Novel of the Modern Woman', *Review of Reviews* 10 (July 1894), pp. 64–74.

8  Ibid., p. 66.

9  Olive Schreiner, *The Story of an African Farm* (Oxford: Oxford University Press, 1992), p. 206.

10  Iota [Kathleen Mannington Caffyn], *The Yellow Aster* (London: Hutchinson, 1894), pp. 129, 130–1.

11  Walter Pater, *The Renaissance: Studies in Art and Poetry* (Oxford: Oxford University Press, 1986), p. 153.

12  Eliza Lynn Linton, 'The Wild Women as Social Insurgents', *Nineteenth Century* 30 (October 1891), pp. 596–605.

13  Hugh E. M. Stutfield, 'Tommyrotics', *Blackwood's Edinburgh Magazine* 157 (1895), in Sally Ledger and Roger Luckhurst, eds., *The Fin de Siècle: A Reader in Cultural History c. 1880–1900* (Oxford: Oxford University Press, 2000) pp. 121, 123.

14  Sarah Grand, *The Heavenly Twins* [1893] (University of Michigan Press, 1992), p. 3.

15  Unsigned review, *Athenaeum* (November 1895) (*CH*: 251).

16  Olive Schreiner to Edward Carpenter, in Richard Rive, ed., *Olive Schreiner Letters: 1871–1899* (Oxford University Press, 1988), I:147.

17  Angelique Richardson, *Love and Eugenics in the Late Nineteenth Century: Rational Reproduction and the New Woman* (Oxford: Oxford University Press, 2003).

18  Grand, *Heavenly Twins*, pp. 68, 304–5.

19  Mona Caird, 'A Defence of the So-Called "Wild Women"', *Nineteenth Century* 31 (May 1892), pp. 819, 817.

20  Richardson, *Love and Eugenics*, has been central in reassessing Caird's place in the debate, pp. 179–214.

21  Mona Caird, 'Marriage', *Westminster Review* 130 (July 1888), p. 186.

22  Olive Schreiner, *Woman and Labour* (London: Virago, 1978), pp. 33–72.

23  Grant Allen, *A Splendid Sin* (London: White & Co., 1896), p. 101; Grant Allen, *The Woman Who Did* (Plymouth: Broadview Press, 2004), p. 4.

24  Ibid.

25  Olive Schreiner, 'The Buddhist Priest's Wife', *Stories, Dreams and Allegories* (London: T. Fisher Unwin, 1923), pp. 59–80, 69–70.

26  George Egerton, 'Virgin Soil', *Discords* (London: Virago, 1983), pp. 151, 157, 155, 157.

27  Karl Pearson, 'Woman and Labour', *Fortnightly Review* 55 (May 1894), pp. 563–4.

28  Alice Meynell, 'A Woman in Grey' [1896], in Angelique Richardson, ed., *Women Who Did: Stories by Men and Women, 1890–1914* (Harmondsworth: Penguin, 2002), p. 179.

# 34

# Hardy and Masculinity

ELIZABETH LANGLAND

Gender in the works of Thomas Hardy has proved a rich topic for exploration over the last few decades. Early feminist criticism and theory led to a focus during the 1970s on Hardy's representations of women and femininity, but within a few years such influential essays as Elaine Showalter's 'The Unmanning of the Mayor of Casterbridge' set the stage for interest in masculinity, in the fact that men too have a gender.[1] The rise of gender as a category of analysis and the emergence of queer theory in the 1980s ensured that critics intensified their analytical gaze on masculinity as a contingent, contested and constructed category, elucidating the process by which one becomes a man.

Masculinity is here, of course, distinguished from maleness, the fact of being born biologically male; it comprises values and expectations, shifting cultural negotiations and conflicts over how those born male are expected to behave. It is equally distinguished from manliness, a particular expression of a culture's expectations for those born male. Against those expectations, many of Hardy's most sympathetic characters struggle, like the eponymous hero of *Jude the Obscure*, Hardy's penultimate novel, who decides early 'He did not want to be a man' (*Jude*: I.2).

But, who or what, we might ask, is the man that Jude does not want to be? That concept itself is provisional, subject to shifting norms and values, shaped by changing historical circumstances that structured relationships between men and women.

Hardy is not alone in exploring this vexed and changing terrain. Conceptions of masculinity and manliness were being renegotiated throughout Victorian literature, as the rise of the middle and professional classes brought new expectations for men and work, men and the patriarchal family. Hardy's exploration of masculinity reflects not only those general changes but also his particular position, straddling working and middle classes, and his sensitivity about being self-taught rather than university educated. John Tosh proposes addressing the subject of masculinity in Victorian England from the perspective of three contexts: the man at home, at work, and in association with other men.[2] His categories suggest three contexts that characterize Hardy's explorations of masculinity, always as a relational concept: men and education, men and sexuality, men and work. Each of these complex relationships is inflected by class.

Richard Dellamora has underscored Hardy's educational and experiential status as an outsider to the educational-aesthetic-sexual culture on which Dellamora focuses. As he observes, Hardy 'was not a university man', and *Jude* 'is notable for the weakness within it of same sex bonding – at least for its protagonists, Jude and Sue. Jude has no male friends; he has no entry into the male homosocial enclaves to which he is so strongly drawn, especially Oxford.'[3] The pattern of uneasy, fraught, and even disastrous relationships between men that Dellamora observes in *Jude* is present from Hardy's earliest fiction and continues throughout his corpus. Even when those men love or desire the same woman, as is often the case in Hardy's novels, that common bond does not serve, in the terminology of Eve Kosofsky Sedgwick, as a mediator of male 'homosocial' desire, functioning as a medium through which men can authorize their feelings for each other.[4]

Conceptions of manliness in Victorian England had one important origin in schoolboy culture, articulated by Thomas Hughes's novel *Tom Brown's Schooldays* (1857). Hughes's novel is born of the same conception of manhood that produced the apocryphal 'Wellington *mot*': to wit, that the battle of Waterloo was won on the playing fields of Eton. The year that *Tom Brown's School Days* came out, the *Saturday Review* noted that 'it is in these sports that the character of a boy is formed. It is from them that the readiness, pluck, and self-dependence of the British gentleman is principally caught.' As Bruce Haley explains, in 1857 'that line of thought was quite new but was catching on everywhere: the function of a public school was to turn out gentlemen; a gentleman was a man of character; character consisted of readiness, pluck, and self-dependence; and these virtues were best learned on the playing field.'[5]

Some of Hardy's male protagonists born into the working classes initially define education as the route to a more congenial male identity. Stephen Smith and Jude Fawley, in *A Pair of Blue Eyes* and *Jude the Obscure* respectively, aspire to higher education to overcome a perceived social inferiority and achieve a manhood founded on the basis on intellectual rather than physical prowess. But their working-class backgrounds exclude them from the schoolboy culture that defines masculinity for those in that fraternity. Their educational aspirations, in contrast, are represented as allying them with feminine inclinations and tastes. Both initially resemble the women they love, and both are initially described as more feminine than masculine in their respective traits.

As Stephen advances in his profession and receives accolades, he increasingly sheds the 'girlishness' that early characterizes him, very like Elfride, the woman with whom he falls in love. Initially, however, he is 'but a youth in appearance, and not yet a man in years [...] His complexion was as fine as Elfride's own; the pink of his cheeks almost as delicate. His mouth as perfect as Cupid's bow in form, and as cherry-red in colour as hers' (*PBE*: 2). Although Elfride confides that she loves him because he is 'so docile and gentle' (*PBE*: 7), it appears likely that those qualities also denote to her his lack of manliness. The narrator remarks that he has a 'plastic adaptability more common in woman than in man' (*PBE*: 10). His deference to Elfride during their proposed elopement early dooms their relationship; his growth and increasing confidence borne of his work as an architect come too late.

Like Stephen, Jude is early linked with a woman, his cousin, Sue Bridehead, but unlike Stephen, he fails to emerge as successfully into the professional identity and success that Stephen achieves as an architect. Jude's Aunt Drusilla describes him as a 'poor useless boy,' with the sensibility and frame of a girl. Jude weeps easily and feels pain keenly: 'he was a boy who could not himself bear to hurt anything.' He quickly fastens on Christminster and becoming a 'university graduate' as 'the necessary hallmark of a man who wants to do anything in teaching' (*Jude*: I.1), and as the completion of his quest to be a man. His longing for that authority culminates in a fanciful idea of Christminster as a 'new Jerusalem' and as a 'mistress' (*Jude*: I.3) beckoning him to his fulfillment.

It is ultimately through kinship and twinship with Sue that Jude seeks a more satisfying alternative to the frustrating constructions of his masculinity that his culture holds out. Sue represents what is in him but also what he is not to seek in himself, which is here coded as the feminine. His desire to discover that alternative, of course, results from his frustrations with both lower-class social definitions of manhood and the conflicts introduced by middle-class codes. When he first locates Sue, he 'recognized in the accents certain qualities of his own voice' (*Jude*: II.2). Later Jude sees Sue, dressed in his clothes, as 'a slim and fragile being masquerading as himself on a Sunday' (*Jude*: III.3). Phillotson corroborates the 'extraordinary sympathy, or similarity, between the pair ... They seem to be one person split in two!' (*Jude*: IV.4) And as Jude flounders among social markers for masculine identity, he turns to Sue as the source of his 'authentic' meaning.

Increasingly, the novel focuses on the tension between Jude's need to be the man his culture demands and his desire to locate a more fulfilling existence outside custom and convention. When Jude argues his similarity to his cousin – 'for you are just like me at heart' – she demurs, 'But not at head.' And when he insists, 'We are both alike,' she corrects him: 'Not in our thoughts' (*Jude*: IV.1). Their disagreement arises because Sue's attractiveness as an alternative disrupts but cannot displace the categories of masculinity Jude has already internalized. Jude is drawn in two directions because he can never fully abandon the categories of thought he has imbibed from his culture. His sudden passion to return to Christminster for Remembrance Day, his fatal attraction for the very hierarchical, scholastic, masculinist conventions that have proven a source of self-alienation, and his seeming rejection of the egalitarian partnership with Sue, lead to the death of their children and the full destruction of their relationship. Jude aptly remarks that he is 'in a chaos of principles – groping in the dark – acting by instinct and not after example' (*Jude*: VI.1).

Just as educational attainment does not automatically ground one's masculinity, sexuality is also perilously fraught.[6] The robust sexual energy that a Tom Jones embodies in the eighteenth century novel has been reconfigured in the Victorian Age, and masculine sexuality has become a relational concept, defined by a man's relationship to a woman, often marked by ambivalence and reticence, especially with new rights for women that gave them more autonomy, such as the Married Women's Property Acts, and the emergence of a new icon, the spirited and independent New Woman, of which *Jude the Obscure*'s Sue Bridehead is often cited as an example.[7]

Jude's sexual impulses are initially held in abeyance by his infatuation with the scholastic life, until Arabella Donn temporarily displaces the authority of intellectual discourse by throwing a pig's
pizzle at him. Yet it is not the sexual response this elicits that traps
Jude; it is the middle-class ethic of chivalric or honourable love that
demands that he behave as a gentleman toward a woman constructed
as 'vulnerable', despite the reality of Arabella's predatory designs on
a hapless youth. Arabella uses her claim of pregnancy to trap him
into marriage and, when her plot is revealed, Jude ponders not his
own folly, but 'something wrong in a social ritual' (*Jude*: I.9). When
Sue asks, 'Why should you take such trouble for a woman who has
served you so badly,' he responds, 'But, Sue, she's a woman, and I
once cared for her; and [a man] can't be a brute in such circumstances' (*Jude*: V.2). Jude's determination to fulfill a 'man's' obligations
to Arabella exerts a sexual coercion on Sue, who precipitously agrees
to sleep with him to erase Arabella's claims. When Sue capitulates,
Jude transfers to her his sexual allegiance and chivalric defense. In
fact, Jude is betrayed by his own shifting constructions of manliness.
He summons up notions of manliness that caricature his relationships, describing himself as afflicted by 'two Arch Enemies … my
weakness for womankind and my impulse to strong liquor' (*Jude*:
VI.3). And he calls up established discourses of manliness to justify
remarrying Arabella: 'I'd marry the W – of Babylon rather than do
anything dishonourable … I am not a man who wants to save himself
at the expense of the weaker among us!' (*Jude*: VI.7)

There is a brief idyllic moment, when Jude and Sue consummate
their sexual relationship, that Jude marvels: 'All that's best and
noblest in me loves you, and your freedom from everything that's
gross has elevated me, and enabled me to do what I should never
have dreamt myself capable of, *or any man*, a year or two ago' (*Jude*:
V.2, my italics). Early in her relationship with Jude, Sue claims
that 'We are a little beforehand, that's all' (*Jude*: V.4). In fact, she is
only partly right; Jude and Sue are constructed by the very terms
they seek to transcend. The lingering sadness of this novel lies in
its apprehension of the way destructive cultural self-constructions
of masculinity and femininity ultimately reach out to claim them,
the ways, indeed, they are always already within, crucial to the formation and development of individual subjecthood and therefore
perilous to reject.

Like Jude, Angel Clare in *Tess* falls prey to conventional sexual attitudes regarding male and female roles. But unlike Jude, Angel's failure lies in his sexual reticence and fastidiousness. In this, he also resembles Henry Knight in *A Pair of Blue Eyes*. Although Henry initially displaces Stephen in Elfride's affection because he is both more mature and definitive than the younger man, he suffers from deficits of another kind. For Knight, like Clare, the fantasized version of his love's purity cannot survive the revelation that Elfride, like Tess, has had a previous lover. Indeed, the representation of Knight anticipates Hardy's depiction of Clare, and what the narrator says of Knight might well be said of Clare: 'It is a melancholy thought that men who at first will not allow the verdict of perfection they pronounce upon their sweethearts or wives to be disturbed by God's own testimony to the contrary, will, once suspecting their purity, morally hang them upon evidence they would be ashamed to admit in judging a dog' (*PBE*: 34). And what the narrator later says of Clare might well be said of Henry Knight: 'Some might risk the odd paradox that with more animalism he would have been the nobler man' (*Tess*: 36).

Knight's and Clare's limitation, their harshness and inability to be the nobler men, stems from deep veins of social and sexual conventionality. The narrator says of Clare: 'With all his attempted independence of judgment this advanced and well-meaning young man, a sample product of the last five-and-twenty years, was yet the slave to custom and conventionality when surprised back into his early teachings' (*Tess*: 39). Part of that conventionality shapes his sense of the proper relationship between men and women, as it does Knight's; both are discomfited in the face of superior female sexual experience. Hardy articulates the relational nature of gender roles, arguing of Knight that had Elfride 'been assertive to any degree he would not have been so peremptory' (*PBE*: 31). The drama between Clare and Tess echoes this earlier scene: 'There was, it is true, underneath, a back-current of sympathy through which a woman of the world might have conquered him. But Tess did not think of this' (*Tess*: 36). The way in which a man and a woman in a Hardy novel often stand like Clare and Tess, 'fixed, their baffled hearts looking out of their eyes with a joylessness pitiful to see' (*Tess*: 55), speaks to their frustration in the face of this gendered dialectic, their tendency to play out the sexual script written by their culture.

Occupations in which a man is comfortable with who and what he is are rare among Hardy's male protagonists. There are a few successful professional men who prosper through their own energies – like Stephen Smith and Donald Farfrae, Henchard's disciple and ultimately his successor as the Mayor of Casterbridge. And there are educated professional men – like Angel Clare and Clym Yeobright – who struggle to integrate their education with their diminished circumstances. Angel remains uneasily situated; Clym finally turns to itinerant outdoor preaching, in which he finds his 'vocation', although some of his neighbours remark 'that it was well enough for a man to take to preaching who could not see to do anything else' (*RN*: VI.4).

Certainly a man's ability to find work that fulfills him is, like his relationships with women, complicated by changing gender expectations and his shifting role within the family in response to new rights and opportunities for women. To find meaningful work challenges Hardy's male protagonists and only a small number are fulfilled though that work, so fulfilled that it provides a point of stability beyond their relationships with women. But there are a few who create a satisfying identity through their work on the land, perhaps reflecting a continuing value on physical strength as a measure of masculinity.[8] Three male protagonists in particular illuminate important patterns in Hardy's representations of masculinity: Gabriel Oak in *Far from the Madding Crowd*, Diggory Venn in *The Return of the Native*, and Giles Winterborne in *The Woodlanders*.

Farmer Gabriel Oak is Bathsheba Everdene's earliest suitor and his marriage proposal to her launches the novel. Once rejected, Oak resolves to ask no more; the narrator elucidates: 'No man like to see his emotions the sport of a merry-go-round of skittishness' (*FFMC*: 4). But Oak is, in fact, the exception rather than the rule in preserving his integrity in the face of rejection and in his ability to witness with some equanimity Bathsheba's emergence as a prosperous farm owner and boss. And he is explicitly contrasted to Bathsheba's other suitors: the philandering Sergeant Troy, whom to her sorrow she marries, and the middle-aged prosperous farmer Boldwood, whose unconsummated passion eats away at him like a canker and destroys his reason. Boldwood's subsequent murder of Troy extinguishes his own future with her even as it destroys the sergeant.

What is surprising is that this high melodrama succeeds to one of the most successful male/female relationships depicted in Hardy's entire corpus: the equitable marriage between Gabriel Oak and Bathsheba Everdene, the bailiff and the successful farmer, respectively, who have become close friends through working the land together over a long period:

This good-fellowship – *camaraderie* – usually occurring through similarity of pursuits, is unfortunately seldom superadded to love between the sexes, because men and woman associate, not in their labours, but in their pleasures merely. Where, however, happy circumstance permits its development, the compounded feeling proves itself to be the only love which is strong as death – that love which many waters cannot quench, nor the floods drown, beside which the passion usually called by the name is evanescent as steam. (*FFMC*: 56)

It is a rare moment in Hardy when a man and a woman are both fully comfortable in their work, sexuality, and achieved masculinity and femininity.

In contrast to Oak, Giles Winterborne, seemingly destined from childhood to win Grace Melbury as his wife, finds instead that their early compatibility has fallen prey to her education and created a social chasm between them. Feeling diminished as a man, he retreats in the face of that chasm, his hesitancy and backwardness with Grace contrasting sharply with the confidence and ease of the seductive and confident doctor, Fitzpiers, who becomes his rival and ultimately Grace's husband.

But Grace's unhappy marriage to Fitzpiers matures her, and late in the novel, when Winterborne encounters her in the woods, the narrator remarks, 'it was a new woman in many ways whom he had come out to see: a creature of more ideas, more dignity, and, above all, more assurance, than the original Grace had been capable of' (*W*: 38). Winterborne has always had the dignity of his work as a grounding point, and his integrity ensures that Grace continues to find him attractive despite his status as a labourer. Confronted with this more mature yet chastened Grace, he 'betray[s] a man's weakness ... he gave way to the temptation, notwithstanding that he perfectly well knew her to be wedded irrevocably to Fitzpiers ... deciding once in his life to clasp in his arms her he had watched over and loved so long.' His masculine assertion, in turn, evokes her lament: 'Giles, if you had only shown half the boldness before I married that you show now, you would have carried me off for your own' (*W*: 39).

Diggory Venn, first reddleman and then dairyman, like Gabriel Oak remains to claim the woman he loves, Thomasin Yeobright, whom he had also initially wooed and lost. Like Bathsheba, Thomasin marries a philandering husband who dies and finally marries the man, Venn, who has loved and served her steadfastly. Venn's assertion that 'what a man has once been he may be again' (*RN*: VI.2) is one that could be uttered with confidence by very few of Hardy's male protagonists, most of whom lack that centering integrity that is a stable point in their masculine identity. Both Bathsheba and Thomasin are initially pulled away from the worthy labouring man because he is not 'gentleman enough' (*RN*: VI.2), only to find the gentleman thoroughly unworthy and to return to the steadfast labourers, whose manliness bespeaks their rare, in Hardy's corpus, comfort with themselves as men.

Hardy's novels offer a trenchant examination and understanding of the way masculinity is always articulated within sociocultural contexts, and therefore perilous to negotiate. Indeed, a man with sensibility and sensitivity to possible alternatives – whether intuited or articulated – to his culture's norms finds his path the most fraught. Rather than discovering joy and affirmation in new ways of bonding with both men and women, Hardy's male protagonists typically struggle and fail to achieve equipoise and become pale shadows of the men they might have been.

NOTES

1 In *Critical Approaches to the Fiction of Thomas Hardy*, ed. Dale Kramer (London: Macmillan, 1979), pp. 99–115.

2 John Tosh, *Manliness and Masculinities in Nineteenth-Century Britain* (Harlow: Pearson Education, 2005), pp. 35–9.

3 Richard Dellamora, *Masculine Desire: The Sexual Politics of Victorian Aestheticism* (Chapel Hill: University of North Carolina Press, 1990), pp. 212–13.

4 *Between Men: English Literature and Male Homosocial Desire* (New York: Columbia University Press, 1985). See, however, Phillip Mallett, 'Hardy and Masculinity: *A Pair of Blue Eyes* and *Jude the Obscure*', *Ashgate Research Companion to Thomas Hardy*, ed. Rosemarie Morgan (Aldershot: Ashgate, 2010), pp. 387–402.

5 Bruce Haley, *The Healthy Body and Victorian Culture* (Cambridge, Mass.: Harvard University Press, 1978), p. 161.

6 James Eli Adams's *Dandies and Desert Saints: Styles of Victorian Masculinity* (Cornell University Press, 1995) explores masculine identities as 'multiple, complex, and unstable constructions' and proleptically describes a process in Hardy's novel through which 'reconfigurations of masculinity frequently compensated for the loss of traditional, more assured forms of masculine identity and authority' (pp. 3–5). Herbert Sussman's *Victorian Masculinities: Manhood and Masculine Poetics in Early Victorian Literature and Art* (Cambridge: Cambridge University Press, 1995) limits its study to the period of the 1830s through the 1860s, but comments insightfully on Angel Clare and Jude Fawley as 'evolutionary figures in the early Victorian anxiety about the destabilization of a heterosexual masculinity defined as sexual potency' (p. 186).

7 Martin Danahay's *Gender at Work in Victorian Culture: Literature, Art and Masculinity* (Aldershot: Ashgate, 2005) approaches masculinity as context-specific, mutable, and constructed through representations (p. 3), and further identifies a pattern enacted repeatedly in Hardy's novels, that is, the positing of 'men' as a relational category that must be analyzed in combination with the term 'women'. Mary Childers early observed that 'in the assertiveness of Hardy's pronouncements about the nature of women, the possession of masculinity is secured' ('Thomas Hardy, The Man Who "Liked" Women', *Criticism* 23 (1981), p. 334). Although it is true that when a man pronounces on woman's nature, he is often engaged in asserting his own masculinity, it is also true that such pronouncements point to efforts to construct that masculinity or repair it.

8 Tosh, *Manliness and Masculinities*, p. 37, notes that 'Among the manual working class, it seems highly likely that the aggressive celebration of physical strength as an exclusive badge of masculinity … prevailed in Victorian times too.'

35

# Hardy's London

KEITH WILSON

Chapter III of *The Life and Work of Thomas Hardy* opens with a memory whose prominent positioning indicates the magnitude of the transition it records: 'On Thursday, April 17, 1862, Thomas Hardy started alone for London, to pursue the art and science of architecture on more advanced lines' (*LW*: 40). The specificity with which Hardy recalls this departure from Dorchester, for what would be a five-year residence in the capital, suggests his sense of London's importance to his whole subsequent life. During this initial period he would experience it as 'only a young man in the metropolis can ... knowing every street and alley west of St. Paul's like a born Londoner, which he was often supposed to be' (*LW*: 64). By the summer of 1867, disabling enervation forced a return to Bockhampton, interpreted as a retreat by his less sympathetic neighbours. But as Hardy's professional ambitions turned from architecture to literature, London, as the centre of the English-speaking world's publishing industry, would inevitably be fundamental to their fulfilment, his ultimate social ease and acceptance there reflecting both literary success and the class ascent it enabled.

For the term 'Hardy's London' to carry genuine authority, both man and city need viewing against the passage of time. Hardy himself recognized that 'the metropolis into which he had plunged ... differed greatly from the London of even a short time after' (*LW*: 43). Equally, the 21-year-old trainee architect experiencing London for the first time,[1] after relocation from an area so remote as barely even to count as the provinces, was very different from the married man and established author who returned to live there from 1878 to 1881, and had even less in common with the national institution – member of the Athenaeum, recipient of the Order of Merit, decliner of a knighthood – who by 1910 was finding what had been for many years regular seasonal stays in London beyond both his energy and inclination. Thus this chapter will consider Hardy's changing identity as Londoner at three distinct stages of his life: the mid-1860s, the late-1870s, and the first decade of the new century.

London had been redefined in the public mind in the decade before Hardy's arrival there, and would undergo continual trans-formation in its infrastructure – architecture, street layout, systems of transportation, governance – for the rest of the century. In 1855 the Metropolitan Board of Works, London's first tentative attempt to establish a more centralized system of municipal administration, had been established.[2] When the limits of the Board's good inten-tions and powers had been reached, it was replaced by the London County Council (1889).[3] The creation of both bodies recognized that London had outgrown local vestry-based, and hence piece-meal and often self-interested, attempts to house, feed, transport, and keep moderately healthy the rapidly expanding population (over three million by the early 1860s) of a city frequently described as the capital of the world. This claim had been trumpeted more loudly since 1851, the year of the Great Exhibition, which gave many British their first experience of London in a context that assertively announced its centrality to world trade, manufacture, and design. For all its evident social problems, amply displayed in the publication, shortly before Hardy's arrival, of the final volume of Henry Mayhew's *London Labour and the London Poor*, London had become a very public embodiment of high-Victorian confi-dence, generating in the authors of proliferating guidebooks and collections of 'views' a celebratory pride often difficult to distin-guish from hubris.

The tone struck in the opening paragraph of Thomas Holmes's *Great Metropolis*, one of the many guides issued to coincide with the huge influx of visitors for the Exhibition, is typical of the genre: 'It has been attempted in the present work ... to exhibit in a concise form, and to demonstrate by statistical accounts, the population, opulence, resources and magnitude of the commerce of London, the emporium of the world; making manifest the means by which the British capital has attained a zenith of grandeur and importance unparalleled in the annals of civilized nations.'[4] While the emphasis here is brashly mercantile, other commentators provided the moral and political inflections often accompanying Victorian invocations of trade and commerce: 'London ... is at once the centre of liberty, the seat of a great imperial government, and the metropolis of that great race whose industry and practical application of the arts of peace are felt in every clime, while they exert an almost boundless influence over the moral and political destinies of the world.'[5] The complex reality of the London that Hardy encountered a decade later is not, of course, adequately encapsulated in such facile rhetoric. But it would be no less misrepresentative to underestimate the influence on his imaginative development of extended familiarity with a metropolitan centre that routinely elicited such panegyrics from those convinced of its uniqueness. The corresponding note of pride in Hardy's 'like a born Londoner' is difficult to miss.

Already equipped with the elegiac cast of mind that would distinguish much of his writing, Hardy placed the emphasis somewhat differently from such celebratory works, more responsive as he was to names redolent of London's past than to the imperial reach of its present. To read his account of being young, independent, and free to roam at will about the city is to sense what must have been for an impressionable mind, imbued with a strong sense of the power of association, an unrepeatable excitement. It was 'the London of Dickens and Thackeray' (*LW*: 43), of Evans's supper rooms in Covent Garden, of the Cider Cellars in Maiden Lane, of the Coal Hole in the Strand, of Willis's Rooms (late Almack's), Cremorne Gardens, and the Argyle, of the last appearances of Charles and Ellen Kean at the Princess's Theatre, John Baldwin Buckstone's management at the Haymarket, and Samuel Phelps's later Shakespeare series at Drury Lane. It is striking that so many of Hardy's early London memories relate to people and institutions already possessed of pasts substantially longer than their futures would be, and with the more risqué of which he may have had only glancing familiarity, whatever the wishful thinking implicit in his poem 'Reminiscences of a Dancing Man' (*CP*: 216–17).

Thackeray would be dead within two years, and Dickens would barely outlive the decade. Charles and Ellen Kean, Buckstone, and Phelps were all approaching the end of glittering stage careers. It had been nearly twenty years since Evans's had been run by W. C. Evans himself, who had sold out to the Irish entertainer Paddy Green in 1844.[6] By the late 1860s its end was in sight, although it outlasted both the Coal Hole and the Cider Cellars, which closed in the 1850s. Hardy may have preferred to call Willis's, in which he danced (perhaps on only the one occasion), by its earlier and more august name of Almack's, 'realizing its historical character' (*LW*: 45), but even under that original designation it had been in decline since before Victoria ascended the throne.[7] The Cremorne Gardens still flourished, though many of its Chelsea neighbours rather wished it didn't, and recurrent complaints about the disorderliness of patrons would eventually result in denial of a licence renewal in 1877. As for the Argyle (more conventionally the 'Argyll') Rooms, the fashionable Regency original had burned down back in 1830 and the relocated incarnation Hardy knew had inherited only the name and reputation for loucheness, possessing 'no history worthy of relation'.[8] And in any case, as with the Cremorne, 'he did not dance there much himself, if at all' (*LW*: 45).

This is not to suggest that as a young man in London Hardy always took a rearguard and romanticized view of things; this impression may well be a distortion created by his assembling memories for *Life and Work* more than fifty years after the experiences, or in some instances nonexperiences, they recall. In fact there is a somewhat Janus-like quality to his evocation of those years, manifest in his memories of his employer's Adelphi Terrace offices, where he both mused on such former Adelphi habitués as Garrick and Johnson and watched the adjacent Victoria Embankment and Charing Cross railway bridge being built (*LW*: 42). He responded to the volatility of London's change by figuring himself as witnessing equally a disappearing past and an emergent future:

There was no Thames Embankment. Temple Bar still stood in its place, and the huge block of buildings known as the Law Courts was not erected. Holborn Hill was still a steep and noisy thoroughfare which almost broke the legs of the slipping horses, and Skinner Street ran close by, with presumably Godwin's house yet standing in it, at which Shelley first set eyes on Mary. No bridge across Ludgate Hill disfigured St. Paul's and the whole neighbourhood. [...] There was no underground railway, and omnibus conductors leaving 'Kilburn Gate', near which Hardy lived awhile, cried 'Any more passengers for London!' (*LW*: 44).

This list outlines the future as much as the past. By the time Hardy left London in 1867, the Victoria Embankment and Holborn

Viaduct were both advancing fast, and the Metropolitan Railway – first leg of the London underground system – had opened (1863). Kilburn Toll-Gate had been removed (1864), only to be re-located, much to the indignation of many regular commuters, a mile to the south, finally disappearing entirely in 1872.[9] The London, Chatham and Dover Railway bridge (1865) already defaced the bottom of Ludgate Hill, not merely ruining the view of St. Paul's but, in Walter Thornbury's memorable image, lying as 'an enormous flat iron ... across the chest of Ludgate Hill like a bar of metal on the breast of a wretch in a torture-chamber'.[10] By the time Hardy moved to London again in 1878, Temple Bar had been sacrificed to road widening and carted off to country storage, and the Law Courts in the Strand were under construction.

As the bidirectional perspective of his early memories of London suggests, with the city's still-living past giving way to its emergent future virtually as he watched, Hardy developed an enduring awareness of the associational power of a city that spoke national history in its streets and buildings while undergoing changes that seemed overwhelming to many inhabitants. One of the most dramatic embodiments for Hardy of this aggressive thrust to change would have been provided by watching the construction of the Embankment, which literally pushed back the Thames, modifying not just an artificial urban streetscape but a natural force. Another more macabre experience of change was provided by his being required to supervise exhumation of human remains from Old St. Pancras churchyard to accommodate a railway cutting, a memory eventually incorporated into the poem 'In the Cemetery'. His viewing of these relentless modifications to the cityscape in the 1860s may well have contributed to his later representation of the operations of an Immanent Will that subsumes all matter, animate and inanimate, within its ceaseless movements.

If London introduced Hardy to such existential truths about massed humanity, equally important were the social truths it inculcated, among them the recognition that for classes more exalted than Hardy's own, private lives inevitably had public faces. The fortuitous introduction, within two weeks of his arrival in London, to Arthur Blomfield, his employer throughout these years, provided more than an enduring friendship. Blomfield, only eleven years Hardy's senior, came from a very different world.

Born into privilege, the son of a Bishop of London, educated at Rugby and Cambridge, and already a well-respected architect whose professional eminence would lead ultimately to a knighthood, Blomfield gave Hardy access to the fringes of a metropolitan society that he would not enter with full confidence until literary reputation granted him passage there in his own right. Blomfield's sponsorship gained him early membership of the Architectural Association (Blomfield was its president), which occasioned Hardy's presence at a '*conversazione*', described to his sister Mary in reverential tones ('Many ladies were there, and of course in full dress, Shaw lent me a dress coat as I did not possess one') that included instruction in how to pronounce *conversazione* (*CL* I: 2). He accompanied Blomfield to Windsor for the laying by the Crown Princess of Germany of the memorial stone of All Saints Church (*LW*: 50), one of Blomfield's earliest ecclesiastical commissions. It was through a Blomfield connection that Hardy received a ticket to the Westminster Abbey funeral of Lord Palmerston, again described in awed detail to his sister Mary: 'Only fancy, Ld P. has been connected with the govt off and on for the last 60 years, & that he was contemporaneous with Pitt, Fox, Sheridan, Burke &c' (*CL* I: 6). This occasion was given further piquancy by his having once heard Palmerston speak in Parliament. Such moments gave recurrent opportunities for private participation in the capital's public events.

Between 1867 and 1878, Hardy frequently visited and made occasional extended stays in London, including most of the nine months following his September 1874 marriage. But it wasn't until the late 1870s that he 'by degrees fell into line as a London man again' (*LW*: 125), albeit a very different one from fifteen years earlier. When between March 1878 and June 1881 Hardy lived again in London, he was sufficiently well-known for the continuum between private and public life to influence his own social position and sense of self. By the time he 'had decided that the practical side of his vocation of novelist demanded that he should have his headquarters in or near London' (*LW*: 121), his life had changed almost out of recognition. An established author, with five published novels to his credit, he was also a married man with a wife whose family background placed her, at least in her own eyes, rather closer to Blomfield's class origins than to his own.

Although conducted from the security of suburban Tooting –
'We might have ventured on Kensington, but for such utter rustics as ourselves Tooting seemed town enough to begin with' (*CL*
I: 57–8) – his life as a Londoner was now that of a public figure. His contacts in the literary world were already extensive and
continually expanding, with the result that by June 1878 he had
been elected to the Savile Club, whose membership was drawn
primarily from literature and the arts. He would soon be invited
by Walter Besant to be a founder member of the Rabelais, a club
established 'as a declaration for virility in literature' (*LW*: 136):
members included such variously virile writers and artists as
Edward Bellamy, George Du Maurier, Brett Harte, Oliver
Wendell Holmes, Henry Irving, Henry James, Andrew Lang,
George Meredith, John Everett Millais, George Augusts Sala,
Lawrence Alma Tadema, and Thomas Woolner.[11] One of Hardy's
neighbours at Tooting was Alexander Macmillan, earlier known to
him in the less sociable role of decliner of his first three novels, at
whose house he met T. H. Huxley, John Morley, and the American
publisher Henry Holt. Developing friendships with other publishers, most particularly Charles Kegan Paul and George Smith, must
have confirmed his sense that London was the place to cultivate
'the practical side of his vocation of novelist'. Matthew Arnold,
Browning and Tennyson all became part of his widening circle: if
not exactly friends, co-members of a London cultural milieu he
was himself now sufficiently secure to take for granted as a natural
extension of his own identity.

Michael Millgate's sense of these years is that this invigorating
social and professional context carried with it attendant dangers:
'London tempted him with journalistic opportunities, invited him
to be trivial, exacerbated his vulnerability to contemporary opinion, undermined him with sheer occupation – an excess of gossip,
shop-talk, dining out, and "keeping up."'[12] This view of the city's
adverse influence on his physical and mental well-being has an
echo in a suggestive note on 'Society' that Hardy wrote during the
harrowing period of illness that kept him confined to bed while
dictating *A Laodicean*:

Discover for how many years, and on how many occasions, the organism, Society, has been standing, lying, etc, in varied positions, as if it
were a tree or a man hit by vicissitudes.

There would be found these periods: –
1. Upright, normal, or healthy periods.
2. Oblique or cramped periods.
3. Prostrate periods (intellect counterpoised by ignorance or narrowness, producing stagnation.)
4. Drooping periods.
5. Inverted periods. (*LW*: 150)

Within a few months of writing this note, Hardy would effect his second retreat from London, returning to settle permanently in Dorset, having found that 'both for reasons of health and for mental inspiration … residence in or near a city tended to force mechanical and ordinary productions from his pen, concerning ordinary society-life and habits' (*LW*: 154). Paradoxically, the extension of such somatic musings from 'Society' to London itself had evoked mental images unsettlingly dissimilar from the customary attributes of 'ordinary society-life', including 'an eerie feeling which sometimes haunted him, a horror at lying down in close proximity to "a monster whose body had four million heads and eight million eyes"' (*LW*: 141).

Whatever the adverse effects of urban living on Hardy's work, return to Dorset constituted little impediment to his maintenance of ties to a fashionable London milieu distinguished as much by social as by specifically literary eminence. Notwithstanding the challenges to orthodoxy issued increasingly aggressively by his later novels, his advance towards what would eventually constitute quasi-institutional status was unswerving, its course demarcated by the names of London's social elite that decorate both his correspondence and *Life and Work*. In the mid 1880s he first met Lady Portsmouth, and through her the Carnarvons (Lord Carnarvon was to be prime mover in Hardy's election to the Athenaeum in 1891). At around the same time, he moved into the circle of Mary Jeune (later Lady St Helier). By the 1890s, such London milieus were sufficiently natural to him that he could afford to be somewhat cavalier in his prioritizing of engagements, writing to Florence Henniker in June 1893: 'I have accepted also an invitation to Lady Shrewsbury's dinner on the 29th but I can throw her over if necessary' (*CL* II :16). It was fortunate that he didn't, since that was seemingly the dinner at which he met Lady Shrewsbury's daughter, Lady Gwendolen Little, whose sister, Lady Londonderry, he first met this summer and who became not only a friend but also within a few years the most powerful society hostess in London.[13]

Thus by the turn of the century, Hardy's London bore little resemblance to the one he explored in the 1860s, for reasons distinct from the dramatic redevelopment the city itself had undergone. It is fitting that his creative life during the opening years of the new century should have been dominated by *The Dynasts*, a work that casual readers interpreted as a national epic celebratory of those virtues of liberty and 'influence over the moral and political destinies of the world' that for many of its more privileged inhabitants London itself had come to embody during the previous half-century. It was not just the exigencies of war and Harley Granville Barker's artful selectivity in adapting *The Dynasts* for the stage in 1914 that made Hardy appear 'as orthodox as a church warden' (*CL* V: 66). As early as 1909, Henry Newbolt had greeted the completion of *The Dynasts* with the observation that Hardy had written 'a poem of gigantic scale, and with the British nation for hero'.[14] Only careless misreading could have found in *The Dynasts* such uncomplicatedly patriotic sentiment. But imperial pride was in the process of indulging emotions not dissimilar from those Newbolt had identified in Hardy's epic in the reconstruction of the centre of London, creating a vista 'of gigantic scale' running all the way from Trafalgar Square, via Admiralty Arch, to the Victoria Memorial, tacitly declaring every inch of the way the heroism of the British nation. There was only one way to read this palpable topographical design, with no room at all for misinterpretation.[15]

Against such a context, appropriate convergences marked what was to be Hardy's last extended London season. He and Emma moved into a flat in the evocatively named Blomfield Court on 6 May 1910, and recalled looking out of the window on the morning after their arrival to see placards announcing Edward VII's death (*LW*: 377). A few weeks later George V's first Birthday Honours List admitted Hardy to the Order of Merit, selection for this most prestigious of British honours being in the personal keeping of the monarch. Since the lease of the flat had already ended, Emma had returned to Dorchester in mid July. Hardy stayed on at the Athenaeum in order to attend the investiture on 19 July. Thus his regular pattern of London stays was brought to a close by a few days of bachelor rooming in London's most intellectually and socially eminent men's club and a ceremony at which the new King admitted him to a fellowship whose first members in 1902, the year of its foundation, had been those imperial icons, the Lords Roberts, Wolseley, and Kitchener.

For the next ten years Hardy would continue to make occasional trips to London but for much shorter periods, and with little of the anticipatory relish he had once experienced. His last recorded visit was for an appropriately symbolic occasion uniting the worlds of metropolitan fashion, political power, and literature: the marriage at St. Margaret's Church, Westminster (the church of Parliament in the grounds of Westminster Abbey) of the young publisher and future Prime Minister, Harold Macmillan, great-nephew of Alexander Macmillan, to Lady Dorothy Cavendish, daughter of the 9th Duke of Devonshire.

NOTES

1 His only other, very brief, visit was on a childhood journey through London with his mother in 1849 (*LW*: 22).
2 For its establishment and evolution, see David Owen, *The Government of Victorian London 1855–89: The Metropolitan Board of Works, the Vestries, and the City Corporation* (Cambridge Mass.: The Belknap Press of Harvard University Press, 1982).
3 For its early history, see Gwilym Gibbon and Reginald W. Bell, *History of the London County Council 1889–1939* (London: Macmillan, 1939).
4 Thomas Holmes, *Great Metropolis: or, Views and History of London in the Nineteenth Century* (London: Thomas Homes, n.d. [1851]), p. 1.
5 [John Weale], *The Pictorial Handbook of London Comprising its Antiquities, Architecture, Arts, Manufacture, Trade, Social, Literary, and Scientific Institutions, Exhibitions, and Galleries of Art; Together with Some Account of the Principal Suburbs and Most Attractive Localities* (London: Henry G. Bohn, n.d. [1851]), p. 1.
6 For accounts of Evans's supper rooms, see George Augustus Sala, *Twice Round the Clock or the Hours of the Day and Night in London* (London: Houlston and Wright, n.d. [1859]), pp. 333–45, and Charles Douglas Stuart and A. J. Park, *The Variety Stage: A History of the Music Halls from the Earliest Period to the Present Time* (London: Fisher Unwin, n. d. [1895]), pp. 14–21.
7 See E. Beresford Chancellor, *Memorials of St. James's Street Together with The Annals of Almack's* (London: Grant Richards, 1922), pp. 195–279.

8  Henry B. Wheatley, *London Past and Present: Its History, Associations, and Traditions* (London: John Murray, 1891), vol. 1, p. 60.

9  Mark Searle, *Turnpikes and Toll-Bars* (London: Hutchinson, n.d. [1930]), vol. 2, pp. 692–3.

10  Walter Thornbury, *Old and New London* (London: Cassell, Petter, and Galpin, n.d. [1879]), vol. 1, p. 220.

11  See *Recreations of the Rabelais Club: 1882–1885* (London: privately printed, n.d.), pp. vii–x.

12  Michael Millgate, *Thomas Hardy: A Biography Revisited* (Oxford: Oxford University Press, 2004), p. 183.

13  For the remarkable influence of Lady Londonderry, see Jonathan Schneer, *London 1900: The Imperial Metropolis* (New Haven and London: Yale University Press, 1999), pp. 126–33.

14  Henry Newbolt, 'A New Departure in English Poetry', *Quarterly Review* 210 (1909), pp. 193–209; reprinted in R. G. Cox, ed., *Thomas Hardy: The Critical Heritage* (London: Routledge & Kegan Paul, 1870), p. 387.

15  For London as imperial capital see M. H. Port, *Imperial London: Civil Government Building in London, 1851–1915* (New Haven and London: Yale University Press, 1995).

# 36

# Hardy and Englishness

PATRICK PARRINDER

Introducing the Loveday family in *The Trumpet-Major*, the narrator tells us that they are descended from 'a vast body of Gothic ladies and gentlemen of the rank known as ceorls or villeins, full of importance to the country at large, and ramifying throughout the unwritten history of England' (*TM*: 2). Hardy's veiled irony at the expense of middle-class prejudice is firmly in the tradition of earlier English novelists such as Fielding and Dickens, and, like them, he claims to be recording the 'unwritten history of England'. Yet the sentence, and the sentiment it expresses, are rather untypical. Outside his 'epic-drama' *The Dynasts*, the words *England* and *English* are relatively uncommon in his writing. It may well be, as Jonathan Bate has written, that there are readers who associate Hardy's works with 'nostalgia for a simple, honest rustic way of life among hedgerows, haystacks and sturdy English oak trees'.[1] But his characters pass their mostly very ordinary lives within specific, not generic, landscapes, and hedgerows and haystacks do not often feature in them. Where we might expect generalisations about rural England as a whole, Hardy repeatedly confines his remarks to the southwestern region which, reviving the name of an ancient Anglo-Saxon kingdom, he calls Wessex.

'Wessex' for Hardy is an imagined community on the borders between fact and fiction. His attempts to give it an economic and social reality – for example, he supported a campaign to establish a University of Wessex – have (so far) been largely unsuccessful. The Wessex of his novels often seems part of a disunited kingdom, modelled perhaps on the Anglo-Saxon 'heptarchy' of Kent, Sussex, Wessex, Essex, East Anglia, Mercia, and Northumbria, without a strong central government or dominant national institutions. The land is scarred by prehistoric remains whose antiquity dwarfs the recorded history of the English and British monarchies. London, the distant metropolis, has little or no significance for most of his characters, and there are vast tracts such as Egdon Heath and (Cranborne) Chase in whose 'outlandish hamlets' (*RN*: VI.1) the church and the law have little purchase. When Clym Yeobright in *The Return of the Native* leaves Wessex, he makes not for London but for the 'centre and vortex of the fashionable world', Paris (*RN*: II.1). Jude Fawley's ambitions draw him to Christminster (Oxford), the intellectual capital of Wessex, even though he compares himself to the country boy Dick Whittington who became Lord Mayor of London. Hardy almost never opposes London to the provinces in the ways that his fellow 'provincial' novelists such as George Eliot, Arnold Bennett and D. H. Lawrence do.

It is true that he occasionally presents the remoter areas of Wessex as part of an almost legendary 'Old England'. Speaking of the maypole on Egdon Heath, for example, he writes that the 'instincts of merry England lingered on here with exceptional vitality' (*RN*: VI.1). This largely 'pagan' land is stalked by puritanical apostles such as Clym Yeobright in his final incarnation as an 'itinerant open-air preacher and lecturer' (*RN*: VI.4), Jude Fawley after he is denied entry to Christminster, and the false evangelist Alec d'Urberville. The ancient opposition between Puritan and Cavalier still survives in the more backward parts of Wessex, where it acts as a dynamic force and a modernising influence, part of the mechanism of social change that Hardy detects throughout his fiction. There is no 'English peasantry' in his novels; feudal divisions have given way to modern class distinctions, and the struggle between the pagan and the godly is overlaid with that between the half-educated and the hyper-intellectual.[2] Both Jude and Tess Durbeyfield – a National School pupil who might have trained as a teacher – are denied the educational opportunities that we nowadays take for granted. It is Tess's misfortune as a dairymaid to attract two very different versions of the nineteenth-century English gentleman, since both Alec d'Urberville and Angel Clare prove quintessential products of the Victorian age. In his later novels Hardy juxtaposes 'unwritten history' with up-to-date reporting on a raw and anguished modernity.

In discussing Hardy and Englishness we need to bear in mind not only the complexity of his literary career, but the distinction between the two broad categories of national character and national identity.[3] A person or a fictional character may be seen as 'typically English' by reference to a common stock of observations and prejudices about national characteristics. If you are 'typically English' you cannot help being so, nor, in all probability, are you fully aware of the fact; otherwise you will be acting a part and thus crossing the boundary between typical and stage Englishness. National identity, by contrast, always has a willed and subjective dimension. Even its purely bureaucratic aspect – the nationality stated on one's passport – requires individual acceptance or rejection, the latter leading to acts of subversion and rebellion or to the attempt to change one's identity through naturalisation. National identity implies a process of emotional and ideological identification, which in many cases takes the form of patriotism. Both national character and national identity are examined in Hardy's works, though more subtly and more unobtrusively than in many of his contemporaries.

Since national identification is usually at its strongest in wartime, it is important to give due weight to Hardy's often neglected body of writings about war. He looked back to the Napoleonic Wars, as we now look back to the Second World War, as an epoch-making global conflict whose decisive effects were still felt in the contemporary world. Britain had become the world's greatest economic and military power in the aftermath of the victory over Napoleon, but things could easily have gone otherwise. Above all, Hardy liked to recall the year 1805, when the French had assembled an invasion fleet at Boulogne. Wessex was in the front line both as a possible target for the Napoleonic assault and as a place of embarkation for the Royal Navy with its bases at Portsmouth and Plymouth. The English court was temporarily situated at Weymouth (Hardy's Budmouth), where King George III took his summer holidays. The invasion scare passed when Napoleon diverted his troops to the Eastern front, and in late October Nelson defeated the French fleet at Trafalgar. Trafalgar lived on in the popular memory thanks to the heroic death of the Navy's greatest commander, and – as every English schoolboy would know for the next century and more – Nelson was tended in his last moments by a Dorsetman, Captain Hardy, who was Thomas Hardy's namesake.

Trafalgar features in both *The Dynasts* and *The Trumpet-Major*, where Bob Loveday earns promotion for his bravery on board Nelson's flagship *Victory*. Bob finds his berth on the *Victory* by making a direct appeal to Captain Hardy when the latter is off-duty at his Dorset household. Such a personal encounter between an ordinary protagonist and a glamorous historical figure had been a staple of historical romance since Walter Scott's *Waverley* (1814), where Edward Waverley is overwhelmed by his meeting with Bonnie Prince Charlie. Hardy adds a second, still more romantic (though somewhat superfluous) encounter in the chance meeting between his lovelorn heroine, Anne Garland, and King George III. *The Trumpet-Major* thus incorporates the pomp and ceremony of state institutions and the British monarchy that Hardy so carefully excludes from all but one of his better-known Wessex novels. It presents local patriotism, as in Bob's reverence for his near-neighbour Captain Hardy, as part and parcel of national loyalty. This union of local and national was central to British military tradition in Hardy's lifetime, as any visitor to the First World War cemeteries in France and Belgium, with their headstones each bearing the name of the dead man's county regiment, can testify. Hardy's 1899 elegy, 'Drummer Hodge', makes this point forcefully. Hodge with his 'homely Northern breast and brain' and generic rustic surname is 'Fresh from his Wessex home'; his allegiance to the King and the British Army is, we suspect, no less real for being left unstated (*CP*: 91).

'Drummer Hodge' was one of a sequence of poems that Hardy wrote at the outbreak of the Boer War in 1899. As an artist, this moved him more than any other public event during his lifetime. In 'Departure', written in October 1899, he watches the troops embarking for South Africa at Southampton Docks. Like most of his more liberal contemporaries, he looks forward to a day when 'patriotism' will have come to mean a global, cosmopolitan loyalty surpassing attachment to the nation-state:

> When shall the saner softer polities
> Whereof we dream, have sway in each proud land
> And patriotism, grown Godlike, scorn to stand
> Bondslave to realms, but circle earth and seas? (*CP*: 87)

He repeated these sentiments a quarter of a century later in a message to the PEN Club in 1923 (*THPV*: 424).

As the Boer War continued, Hardy was taken aback by the outpouring of bellicose sentiments in poetry and prose. The Decadent movement of the early 1890s gave place to an undignified rush to the colours, as ageing poets produced volume after volume of patriotic verse. 1898 saw the publication of *The Island Race* by the Poet Laureate Alfred Austin, together with *Songs for England* by Henry Newbolt: two volumes which threatened to overshadow Hardy's more modestly titled *Wessex Poems*. W. E. Henley's *For England's Sake* appeared in 1900, and Sir William Watson named his 1904 collection *For England*. A younger poet, Lawrence Binyon, published *England and Other Poems* in 1909. No wonder that, when asked by the French *Revue Bleue* in 1902 to comment on the impact of the South African War on English literature, Hardy spoke of 'the vast multiplication of books on the war itself, books on former wars, books of action as opposed to reflection, and large quantities of warlike and patriotic poetry'. Works (like his own) that 'breathe a more quiet and philosophic spirit' had little chance of a hearing (*THPV*: 181).

The 'philosophic spirit' is exemplified by Hardy's much-quoted later public poems, 'Channel Firing' written in April 1914 and 'In Time of "The Breaking of Nations"' in 1915. The latter sets the young lovers and the immemorial field labourer in opposition to 'Dynasties' and 'War's annals' (*CP*: 543), while in 'Channel Firing' a naval gunnery exercise disturbs the dead

> As far inland as Stourton Tower,
> And Camelot, and starlit Stonehenge. (*CP*: 306)

Camelot, the seat of Arthur's Round Table, was customarily identified with Winchester (the Wintoncester of Hardy's Wessex), where the Saxon kings are buried. Stourton Tower commemorates Alfred the Great's victory over the Danes. Like 'Departure' this poem looks forward to a saner world, a world without contending nations in which there will be no more gunfire off the coast of Wessex. Yet Hardy is also looking back to the Anglo-Saxon heptarchy and, before that, to the ancient Britons. The modern state is bracketed by its past and future just as the target is bracketed by a ship's cannon finding its range.

Hardy may envisage a future of cosmopolitanism, but he did not write novels that hinge on a choice of national identity as many of his more well-travelled contemporaries did. Charlotte Brontë's *Villette* (1853), Trollope's *The Way We Live Now* (1875), and George

Eliot's *Daniel Deronda* (1876) are novels of this type. Henry James
built a whole career around his 'international theme' with its contrast of American, British, and European identities. Hardy comes
nearest to this in *The Return of the Native*, where Clym Yeobright
returns to Wessex only for his local bride, Eustacia Vye, to dream
of eloping to Paris with the 'Rousseau of Egdon', Damon Wildeve.
Early in the novel Wildeve appeals to Eustacia to 'turn our backs
upon this dog-hole of England for ever'; Clym's arrival on his
native heath, meanwhile, is being spoken of 'as if it were of national
importance' (*RN*: I.11). His life with its passages through Vanity
Fair (Captain Vye calls Paris 'that rookery of pomp and vanity')
and the Valley of Humiliation (his period as a furze-cutter) forms a
kind of Pilgrim's Progress in which, finally, he becomes an educator
working to raise the condition of the people of Wessex. The inhabitants of Egdon, who are Anglican parishioners only in name, now
have the opportunity to listen to regular Sunday afternoon 'moral
lectures or Sermons on the Mount' (*RN*: VI.4) from someone who
is, in 'provincial' terms, an advanced thinker. *The Return of the Native*
portrays a society riddled with stratification and division: class
divisions, cultural levels, and moral heights and depths, all framed
by the physical contrast between the featureless, low-lying Heath
and the 'commanding elevation' (*RN*: VI.4) of its surrounding hills.
Clym's influence should help to even out these inequalities and,
ideally, to reunite province and metropolis, however remote such a
prospect may seem.

To become an apostle to the English, like Clym, is very different from embodying or representing the English character. Can
any of Hardy's fictional personae be said to personify 'Englishness'
in this sense? Some influential recent critical approaches suggest
that Hardy moved away from a settled view of national character
if, indeed, he ever possessed one. For Raymond Williams in *The
Country and the City* (1973), 'the real Hardy country ... is that border country so many of us have been living in: between custom and
education, between work and ideas, between love of place and an
experience of change'.[4] In Roger Ebbatson's *An Imaginary England*
(2005) Hardy is one of a group of writers exemplifying the idea of
modern Englishness as 'a type of "border study"', in which what
was formerly seen as marginal is now considered 'central', and vice
versa.[5] David Gervais in *Literary Englands* (1993) links this to the

radical change from an early to a late style in Hardy's fiction: from *Far from the Madding Crowd* to *Jude the Obscure*. In the former novel 'social change is contained by locating the action inside a Wessex that seems cut off from the rest of England and self-sufficient', whereas 'The world of *Jude the Obscure* is in the grip of accelerated change and fragmentation; it allows no nostalgic backward glances to rural Wessex.'[6] It seems no accident, then, that the protagonist of *Far from the Madding Crowd* bears the symbolically 'Old English' name of Oak. Nevertheless, Hardy comes much closer to an explicit study of national character in a much later novel, *The Mayor of Casterbridge*.

When Raymond Williams speaks of the Hardy country as a metaphorical borderland, he is referring to both spatial and temporal transitions. Temporally Hardy stands at the junction of tradition and modernity, but the metaphor also points to the geographical position of Wessex on southern England's coastal edge – both a 'rural heartland' and a maritime district facing outwards to the Atlantic and to Europe. There is a tension in several of Hardy's novels between the seagoing and the landlocked: between the Loveday brothers, the soldier and the sailor, and the home-bound Anne Garland in *The Trumpet-Major*; between the Channel ferry to Paris and the benightedness of Egdon in *The Return of the Native*; and between the Wessex-bound Michael Henchard in *The Mayor of Casterbridge* and the sailor to whom he sells his wife and daughter – not to mention those disturbing immigrants to the Casterbridge world, the Jerseywoman Lucetta Templeman and the Scotsman Donald Farfrae.

Henchard is seen at first as an out-of-work labourer trudging with his family through rural Wessex. After losing his wife and child at a fair he pledges himself to twenty years' abstinence from strong drink. We next see him some nineteen years later in Casterbridge, where he has become both a prosperous corn-factor and Mayor of the town. His ex-wife returns secretly to find him lording it over a municipal banquet, with the band playing 'The Roast Beef of Old England' in the street outside. On the same evening Farfrae arrives in Casterbridge on his way to Bristol, where he intends to take ship for the New World. Late at night he enchants a small audience with haunting songs of Scotland; the following day Henchard offers him the position of manager and persuades him to stay. The two men are, briefly, bosom friends and then bitter commercial and personal rivals. Their mutual competition is, in part, a national contest, seen at first in their respective 'signature tunes' and then in the contrasting business methods which express their jarring personalities. The struggle between them is, Hardy observes at one point, 'in some degree, Northern insight against Southron doggedness – the dirk against the cudgel' (*MC*: 17). 'Southron' is a traditional Scots epithet for the English as a whole, but it came to be used in the nineteenth century to distinguish the south from the north of England. It identifies Henchard as a Wessex man and a native southerner. 'Doggedness', too, is a central feature of his nature, as underlined in the novel's subtitle: *A Story of a Man of Character*.

It is necessary here to remember that 'southernness' has been used to represent Englishness as a whole in countless national stereotypes, particularly during Hardy's lifetime. Historians such as Alun Howkins and Krishan Kumar have stressed the extent to which the image of 'unspoilt' rural England in the twentieth century drew on the southern landscapes of Hardy and a number of his younger contemporaries, notably W. H. Hudson, Richard Jefferies, Edward Thomas, and George Sturt. In Howkins's words, these writers 'created the world of the South Country and fixed it as a part of national ideology'.[7] In this perspective Hardy's Wessex belongs to the same world as Hudson's and Jefferies's attachments to Wiltshire, Sturt's to rural Surrey, and Thomas's to Hampshire. All five were students of social change and of a world that seemed to be disappearing before their eyes; but there are also sharp differences between them. Hudson, Jefferies, and Thomas, for example, lived in London for long periods. Thomas, one of the few modern rural poets comparable to Hardy, was Welsh by culture and family background, whereas Hudson was born to American parents in Argentina. At the outset of the First World War, Thomas seriously considered emigrating to the United States. Some, at least, of the elegists of the 'South Country' were outsiders whose identification with Englishness was more willed, more self-conscious, and in more pressing need of explanation and justification than Hardy's. The same could be said of many other patriotic writers among Hardy's contemporaries: for example, the French-born Hilaire Belloc who coined the expression 'the south country', the Anglo-

Indian Rudyard Kipling, and the half-German novelist Ford Madox Hueffer who changed his name to Ford Madox Ford.

To return to Michael Henchard: his rivalry with Farfrae comes to a head on the day of the 'Skimmity-ride', with Henchard engaging the Scot in man-to-man combat. Earlier the same day Farfrae, who has replaced Henchard as Mayor, officially welcomes an unnamed 'Royal Personage' (presumably Prince Albert) who is passing through the town. Henchard has asked the town council for permission to take part in the municipal welcome, but has been refused. Armed with a home-made Union Jack, and already drunk (his twenty years' abstinence is at last over), he barges in front of Farfrae and succeeds in buttonholing the royal visitor. Farfrae's subsequent criticism of Henchard's actions leads to their fight: "'Royalty be damned," said Henchard. "I am as loyal as you, come to that!'" (*MC*: 38). Hardy, as often, stops short of explaining Henchard's feelings, but it seems likely he thinks that a native Wessex man rather than an interloper from Scotland has the right to welcome royalty to the town.

Hardy, we remember, has characterised Farfrae versus Henchard as 'Northern insight against Southron doggedness – the dirk against the cudgel'. The dirk is a traditional Highland weapon while the cudgel was associated with the eighteenth and nineteenth centuries' favourite personification of Englishness, John Bull. This legendary figure, a staple of *Punch* and other illustrated papers, had been invented by John Arbuthnot a century earlier. His original characterisation appears in *The History of John Bull* (1712):

*Bull*, in the main, was an honest plain-dealing Fellow, Cholerick, Bold, and of a very unconstant Temper ... he was very apt to quarrel with his best friends, especially if they pretended to govern him: If you flatter'd him, you might lead him like a Child. ... *John* was quick, and understood his business very well, but no Man alive was more careless, in looking into his Accounts, or more cheated by Partners, Apprentices, and Servants: This was occasioned by his being a Boon-Companion, loving his Bottle and his Diversion.[8]

Henchard resembles John Bull in his impulsive generosity, his inconstancy, his carelessness and recklessness in business matters. After he has taken the pledge he is John Bull sober, but by the time of the royal visit he displays Bull's qualities in full measure.

Moreover, he is set against the modernising, Puritanical Scot who runs his business by cool calculation and observes conscious moral rectitude in his personal life. Insofar as Henchard is John Bull, he personifies Old England, the rural England that all Hardy's novels show to be slowly dying, to be replaced by new agricultural machinery, harder-faced business methods, and stricter and more impersonal standards of conduct. Farfrae, the harbinger of a more formal, managerial culture, is a good husband and a reliable employer, but it is the tempestuous, unpredictable Henchard who is the 'man of character' since, as a figure in a novel, he completely overshadows his strait-laced rival. Finally the tragedy of Henchard's self-destruction is complete, and he writes his will consigning himself – and, we might feel, Old England too – to utter oblivion.

Hardy, proud Dorsetman though he was, was not a Michael Henchard and still less a John Bull. Yet there was one remarkable moment in his later public life when he sounded like John Bull personified. In 1920 he wrote a letter to the Royal Society of St George (published in its journal *The English Race*) congratulating its members 'upon their wise insistence on the word "English" as the name of this country's people, and in not giving way to a few shortsighted clamourers for the vague, unhistoric, and pinchbeck title of "British", by which they would fain see it supplanted' (*THPV*: 407).

NOTES

1 Jonathan Bate, *The Song of the Earth* (London: Picador, 2000), p. 1.
2 Arnold Kettle in *An Introduction to the English Novel, Volume II* (London: Arrow, 1962), p. 50, describes the subject of *Tess of the d'Urbervilles* as 'the destruction of the English peasantry'.
3 For a more detailed account, see my *Nation and Novel: The English Novel from its Origins to the Present Day* (Oxford: Oxford University Press, 2006), pp. 20–8.
4 Raymond Williams, *The Country and the City* (London: Chatto and Windus, 1973), p. 197.
5 Roger Ebbatson, *An Imaginary England: Nation, Landscape and Literature, 1840–1920* (Aldershot: Ashgate, 2005), p. 2.
6 David Gervais, *Literary Englands: Versions of 'Englishness' in Modern Writing* (Cambridge: Cambridge University Press, 1993), p. 16.

7 Alun Howkins, 'The Discovery of Rural England', in Robert Colls and Philip Dodd, eds., *Englishness: Politics and Culture 1880–1920* (London: Croom Helm, 1987), pp. 62–88, especially p. 74. See also Krishan Kumar, *The Making of English National Identity* (Cambridge: Cambridge University Press, 2003), esp. pp. 209–12.

8 John Arbuthnot, *The History of John Bull*, ed. Alan W. Bower and Robert A. Erickson (Oxford: Clarendon Press, 1976), p. 9.

## 37

# Empire

JANE BOWNAS AND RENA JACKSON

In June 1883, Hardy signed a lease for the land on which Max Gate was to be built, marking a final return to Dorchester and his childhood environs. In July, his essay 'The Dorsetshire Labourer', on the perceived decline of the rural labourer, appeared in *Longman's Magazine*. July also saw the publication of Sir John Seeley's *The Expansion of England*, with its famous remark that 'We seem, as it were, to have conquered and peopled half the world in a fit of absence of mind.'[1] The two moments appear to be antithetical: the one inward, domestic, backward-looking, and the other a conscious attempt to identify the purpose of English history, onward and outward towards the Greater England. But an opposition of this kind should not encourage a reading of Hardy's life and works as impervious to empire. This article offers a brief history of empire and its rationale during Hardy's writing career from 1870 until the Great War, considers intrusions of empire upon Hardy's life, and reflects on how the imperial finds expression in his novels and early war poems.

Hardy's first publications appeared at the beginning of an era defined by its 'conscious' imperialism.[2] Prior to the 1870s, the British Empire comprised the white settler colonies in Canada, Australasia and South Africa, India, the West Indies, and a number of coastal enclaves and naval stations scattered along the main trade routes, and could be seen as a manifestation of her power and strength. In the 1870s and 1880s, however, setbacks in her foreign relations began to threaten her position in the world. British world supremacy had been based on a kind of natural monopoly of influence and power outside Europe. This monopoly was slowly being eroded by conflict in Egypt over the opening and control of the Suez Canal in 1869, the growing presence and interests of the Russians in central Asia and of the Germans in Africa, trade depression, the Anglo-Irish conflict and the works of anarchists in London.

These events led to Britain's 'enclosure' of certain areas where she had had free reign before. As Porter notes, '"Spheres of influence" could no longer be taken for granted: they had to be marked out on the map.'[3] Policies were increasingly based not only on seeking to maintain control, but also on being seen to do so. But with formal expansion there was also a contracting of the old, informal empire, as Britain's political influence in areas like Persia and Turkey and commercial predominance in places like Africa and the Pacific was receding: 'Consequently the expansion of the British empire in the 1880s was a reflection not so much of Britain's growing power in the world as of her slow decline, or at least the anticipation of it.'[4] Signs of enervation were often expressed in reluctance to cede power to native governments, Parliament's rejection of the Home Rule Bill for Ireland in 1886 being one such example. From the 1880s, Britain felt threatened by the situation in South Africa and feared that the Boers were taking control of valuable gold and diamond resources. The wars that followed may be seen as the last great effort to exert imperial power: 'a war between a European colonial power and a European-descended people for control of land that had originally been inhabited by African peoples.'[5]

By the last decades of the nineteenth century, Britain's rule over a quarter of the globe and a fifth of its population was everywhere visible within the domestic space, evident in imported foreign objects, materials used in the manufacturing industry, household goods bearing logos associated with overseas ventures, ideologically saturated printed and visual materials, textual and iconic representations in popular and juvenile fiction, newspapers and magazines, paintings, drawings, prints and photographs, religious tracts, exhibitions, music-hall turns and theatrical spectacles.[6] But by the Diamond Jubilee in 1897, both political and moral anxiety were making themselves felt beneath the display of power. In his *Imperialism* (1902), after the end of the Second Anglo-Boer War, J. A. Hobson commented on the corrupting impacts of imperial power: 'the spirit of Imperialism poisons the springs of democracy in the mind and character of the people.'[7]

Hardy's life records various encounters with empire as, increasingly, national events took on the character of imperial ones. The opening of the Great London Exhibition in 1862 'influenced him [Hardy] in the choice of a date for his migration' to London to pursue a career in architecture (*LW*: 40). This exposition had numerous colonial exhibits, and was one of a number of world and colonial fairs to take place in the late Victorian era, with ever growing emphasis on orientalist style and commercial appeal.[8] At a reception during Queen Victoria's Golden Jubilee in 1887, Hardy came directly face to face with the spectacle of empire, observing how one Indian dignitary in his 'mass of jewels and white turban', the 'Anniwalia of Kapurthala', remained aloof from 'the babble and gaiety' of the celebrations (*LW*: 210). Earlier, in the 1850s, he had witnessed less brilliant reminders of empire in its early nineteenth-century embodiment. When the practice of transportation to Australia stopped in the 1850s, Dorset was brought face to face with its substitute, as convicts were placed in purpose-built prisons in Portland and forced to do hard labour.[9] Hardy learned more about the defunct transportation regimes when his return to Dorchester in 1883 led to his full and deliberate immersion in early nineteenth-century chronicles of Dorset.

Unlike many English writers associated with the wider reaches of empire – Trollope, Rider Haggard, Kipling, Conrad, Forster, and Orwell among them – Hardy was never physically present within colonies beyond the British Isles. His overseas travels were limited to Ireland and the Continent. His knowledge of Britain's colonial transactions further afield was mediated and refracted through the accounts, written or oral, formal or informal, of those who could speak from within empire's 'native' cultures and geographies. One class of empire pundits included a widely travelled social and cultural elite, often members of the colonial establishment and with strong links to London. It was here that Hardy encountered Kipling in 1890, probably for the first time, when Kipling 'told curious details of Indian life' (*LW*: 236). Kipling's own meteoric rise to popularity in the 1890s can be credited to the way in which his intimate knowledge of India comes to bear on his works. In 1902, it was Hardy's turn to offer curious details of the changing lives of rural labourers in the English countryside to Rider Haggard (*LW*: 335–7). The latter's rich record of entanglement with empire includes hoisting the British flag over the Boer republic of Transvaal during Britain's annexation of it in 1877, serving as a peripatetic Registrar of Transvaal's High Court and, later, writing African romances.[10] Perhaps most importantly, Hardy also spent time in the company of George, later Lord Curzon, part of the powerful aristocratic elite that ruled Britain and the Empire in the century following the defeat of Napoleon. Viceroy of India from 1899 to 1905, Curzon was the epitome of the 'Orientalist' – though his policies during the Indian famine of 1899–1900 did little to alleviate its effects. In his Romanes lecture, 'Frontiers' (1907), he exhorted Britain's young men to 'march forth, strong in the faith of their ancestors' to carry out the work of 'Empire'.[11] Towards the end of his career as a novelist, Hardy also forged links with household names in the countryside, including the Pitt-Rivers family, famed for their ethnological and archaeological collections, and a rich source of information about empire.

On the opposite end of the social spectrum, but also reporting from within colonial geographies, were those relatives and friends of Hardy who emigrated to settlement colonies in pursuit of a better socioeconomic life, often with less than glowing outcomes to report. Hardy's fellow apprentice in Dorchester, Henry Bastow, who left for Tasmania, was disillusioned about making a name for himself as surveyor and architect. Poverty at home drove away, on separate occasions, two of Hardy's Puddletown cousins, Emma and Martha Sparks, to Australia with their respective families – Emma dying of poor health just one month after her arrival. The illegitimate child of Horace Moule, Hardy's close friend and mentor, was also alleged to have been brought up and eventually hanged in Australia.[12]

Hardy's attitudes to empire up until the outbreak of the Second Boer War are difficult to recover. On the subject of Irish Home Rule, he was ambiguous at the best of times: 'it was a staring dilemma … Policy for England required that it should not be granted; humanity to Ireland that it should' (*LW*: 185). His *Literary Notebooks*, however, offer some understanding of how empire is accessed and birthed into consciousness, with the proximity or contiguity principle influencing the selection of materials and the processing of their content. An abridged quotation from an article titled 'Macaulay' by John Morley, in the *Fortnightly Review* in April 1876, reads: 'The cosmopolitan or international idea which such teachers as Cobden have tried to impress on our stubborn islanders w^d. have found in Macaulay pointblank opposition' (*LN* I: 45: Hardy's underlining). Morley, whom Hardy liked and admired (and an avowed Home

Ruler), became a lens through which he viewed midcentury arguments for free trade and reduction of military and naval armaments within empire. The 'stubborn islanders', caught between the imagined altercations of two bigwigs, must have quietly appealed to him. The rationale of propinquity is also evident in a quotation from the article 'The Next Centenary of Australia' from *The Spectator* (January 1888), around the time Hardy started writing notes for *Jude the Obscure*. Here he clearly shows greater interest in the evolving identity of settler Australians – who may turn out to be more congenial than their American counterparts, with a greater 'appreciation for beauty' and a closer relationship with Europe – than he does in the fate of Aborigines, who 'will be but a memory in a century or two' (*LN* I: 228).

Hardy's domestic, circumscribed awareness of empire finds similar scope in his rural imaginary. White settlement colonies, particularly Canada and Australia[13] – featuring, for example, in *The Mayor of Casterbridge* and *Jude the Obscure* – are receptacles for agricultural emigrants and tend to take pride of place in Hardy's version of empire. These colonies throw up adversity, even death, or end in return to Wessex. The continent of Africa, most instantiations of which occur in *Two on a Tower*, is a province of adventure, exploration and plunder reserved for or powered by the titled and moneyed classes; it is also the only novel in which a meeting between English gentry and a local native is recounted. Africa, as suggested by a passing reference in *Tess of the d'Urbervilles*, is also the target of mission work. Mercenaries and entrepreneurs, such as those in *A Laodicean*, have business prospects extending to territories in South America and California. Artisans and militia, as in *A Pair of Blue Eyes* and *A Laodicean*, spend time in India; Stephen Smith can achieve more and faster success in Bombay than he could hope for in Britain. The links between class and empire, as Hardy knew them in life, are clearly reflected in the population distribution of migrants throughout Hardy's empire and the kinds of subplots bound up with them.

The encounter with empire that impinged most directly on Hardy and provoked a more personal and direct response was the outbreak of the Second Anglo-Boer War. In October 1899, he was at Southampton Docks watching the troop ships depart for South Africa: ships that over the course of the war would carry thousands of troops, including boys like Drummer Hodge, 'Fresh from his Wessex home' (*CP*: 91). The poem 'Embarcation', written as a result of this experience, expresses vividly the feelings hinted at in poems he wrote as a result of his and Emma's visit to Rome some years previously. In Rome, he had contemplated the decaying ruins of a previous empire and mused on the fleeting nature of imperial power. In Southampton he remembered how the Roman legions and other invading armies had landed on the same shores from which the British battalions were now leaving to invade foreign lands, and laments that at 'this late stage of thought, and pact, and code' armies are still sent 'To argue in the selfsame bloody mode' (*CP*: 86).

The sentiments expressed here were repeated in letters written in the autumn of 1899 and throughout 1900 to Florence Henniker, whose soldier husband was one of those he had watched embark. In a letter dated 11 October 1899, Hardy writes: 'I constantly deplore the fact that "civilised" nations have not learnt some more excellent and apostolic way of settling disputes than the old and barbarous one, after all these centuries' (*CL* II: 232), and on 19 December 1899: 'this Imperial idea is, I fear, leading us into strange waters' (*CL* II: 241). What seem to have been Hardy's views on the war were echoed by Emma in a letter to Rebekah Owen, dated 27 December 1899: 'the battles will be on a huge scale, that's certain – and a terrible ending it will all have. But the Boers fight for homes and liberties – we fight for the Transvaal Funds, diamonds and gold! … Why should not Africa be free, as is America?'[14] Despite her evident anti-imperial stance, Emma assumes a white European population at the fore. The rights at stake here are those of white settlers – Boers, like Americans – to their own newfound territories.

Support for the war amongst the general population was reinforced by popular culture, with music hall songs and newspapers leading to an increase in jingoism, patriotism and unquestioning support for the imperial project. Kipling's anti-Boer poem 'The Absent-Minded Beggar' helped manipulate public opinion and raise money for the troops. Henry Nevinson, the essayist and journalist who visited Max Gate in 1906, reported Hardy as saying that 'he liked Kipling very much as a companion, and thought he would have been a very great writer if the Imperialists had not got hold of him' (*IR*: 79). Swinburne's poem, 'The Transvaal', published in *The Times* (October 1899) was still more jingoistic and aggressively patriotic than Kipling, ending with the line 'Strike, England, and strike home'. George Gissing wrote an article criticising the poem; Hardy congratulated him for doing so.[15]

Hardy's poems stand out for their opposition to jingoistic and imperial outpourings. In a letter to Henniker, he notes, '[M]y Soldiers' Wives' Song finishes up my war effusions, of which I am happy to say that not a single one is Jingo or Imperial – a fatal defect according to the judgment of the British majority at present, I dare say' (*CL* II: 277). In his discussion of Hardy's poem, 'At the War Office, London', James Whitehead posits that he would have met with considerable social disapproval for expressing antiimperialistic views in his Boer War 'effusions'. This poem was originally published in January 1900, in the first issue of the *The Sphere*, a magazine which claimed to be politically neutral and was edited by Hardy's friend Clement Shorter. However, in its launch statement the magazine pledged 'loyalty to Queen and Empire' and expressed a 'profound sense of the infinite power for good of Great and Greater Britain'. As Whitehead points out, 'neutrality does not accommodate questioning of the raison-d'être of Empire' and Hardy's poem would have provided the 'only critical note in relation to Empire, sounded in the midst of a fanfare of imperial propaganda'.[16]

As over the subject of Home Rule for Ireland, Hardy displayed some ambiguity with respect to the war. This may have stemmed from anxieties that antiimperialism might be interpreted as anti-patriotism. His innate patriotism thus occasionally appears to have stunted opportunities to vocalise objections to Britain's role in South Africa. A letter to Florence Henniker in October 1900 argues that 'the external policy of the Tories is mostly *smarter*, (Heaven forbid that I should say *better*, in a moral sense) than that of the Liberals [...] You must play the game as other nations play it, and they will not play it humanely. At home you may give your humanity free play' (*CL* II: 270; Hardy's emphasis). Perhaps it was only in his verse, as Hardy himself noted in a memo in 1896, that he could express 'ideas and emotions which run counter to the inert crystallised opinion ... which the vast body of men have vested interests in supporting' (*LW*: 302).

In his verse drama *The Dynasts*, published in the years after the Boer War, Hardy offered parallels between the empire-building activities of Napoleon and those of Britain. Early in the drama the English Parliament is described by the Spirit of the Years as 'insular, empiric, un-ideal', and after the defeat of Napoleon, 'Europe's wormy dynasties re-robe / Themselves in their old gilt, to dazzle anew the globe!'[17] Six years after its completion, *The Dynasts*, with its realistic treatment of the suffering and chaos caused by large-scale warfare resulting from the expansionist ambitions of participating nations, was found to be extremely relevant. The Great War of 1914–18 was 'a war for the preservation of the empire, in the sense that if Britain had lost she could not have retained her empire'.[18] Shortly before the outbreak of war, Hardy wrote the poem 'His Country', in which he makes a plea for an alternative form of patriotism, which is not narrow and jingoistic and which recognises the common humanity of people worldwide (*CP*: 539). 'Empery's insatiate lust of power' was to shatter any such hope ('In Time of Wars and Tumults', *CP*: 543).

NOTES

1 John Seeley, *The Expansion of England* (Boston: Roberts Brothers, 1883), p. 8. Seeley argues that just as in the eighteenth century 'the history of England [was] not in England but in America and Asia' (p. 9), so too its future history will be in its overseas possessions.

2 During Hardy's career as novelist, Britain assumed direct or indirect control of Egypt, the Sudan, tracts of East, West, South, and Central Africa (in total, roughly a third of the continent), Malaya, North Borneo, Upper Burma, territories bordering on Afghanistan, Kuwait, Bahrein, Cyprus, the New Territories and a number of islands in the Pacific.

3 Bernard Porter, *The Lion's Share: A Short History of British Imperialism 1850–2004*, 4th edition (Harlow: Pearson Education, 2004), pp. 120–2.

4 Ibid., p. 122.

5 Paula M. Krebs, *Gender, Race, and the Writing of Empire: Public Discourse and the Boer War* (Cambridge: Cambridge University Press, 1999), pp. 35–6.

6 See Benita Parry, *Postcolonial Studies: A Materialist Critique* (London and New York: Routledge, 2004; repr. 2005), p. 113.

7 J. A. Hobson, *Imperialism: A Study*, revised edition (London: Unwin Hyman, 1938), p. 150.

8 See John M. MacKenzie, *Propaganda and Empire: The Manipulation of British Public Opinion, 1880–1960* (Manchester: Manchester University Press, 1984), pp. 96–120.

9 See Robert Gittings, *Young Thomas Hardy* (London: Heinemann, 1975), p. 23.

10 On Rider Haggard's and Kipling's contexts of writing, see Gail Ching-Liang Low, *White Skins/ Black Masks: Representation and Colonialism* (London: Routledge, 1996), pp. 1–9.

11 George Curzon, *Frontiers* (Oxford: Clarendon Press, 1907), p. 57.

12 See Gittings, *Young Thomas Hardy*, pp. 55, 144 and 185.

13 Canada acquired Dominion status (i.e., a self-governing territory acknowledging the British Crown) in 1867 and Australia in 1901, followed by New Zealand (1907), South Africa (1910) and the Irish Free State (1922).

14 Michael Millgate, ed., *Letters of Emma and Florence Hardy* (Oxford: Oxford University Press, 1996), p. 19.

15 Michael Millgate, *Thomas Hardy: A Biography Revisited* (Oxford: Oxford University Press, 2004), p. 370.

16 James S. Whitehead, Commentary on 'At the War Office, London', *The Poetry of Thomas Hardy*, Sara Haslam, ed., CD-ROM (Chester College of H.E., 2001).

17 Thomas Hardy, *The Dynasts* I, Act I, Sc. 3 (*CPW* IV: 46); *The Dynasts* III, Act VII, Sc. 8 (*CPW* V: 247).

18 Porter, *The Lion's Share*, p. 228.

## 38

# Hardy, Militarism, and War

### GLEN WICKENS

Recent criticism has begun to notice the doubling of perspectives in many of Hardy's war poems and to emphasize their dialogic, even polyphonic quality. This essay will continue the work of reappraisal by examining Hardy's war poetry and its reiterated theme of militarism in the context of a generic tradition long associated with multiple voices and perspectives – Menippean satire.[1] Since this kind of writing generally emerges during times of historical crisis, war constitutes one of its major themes. Much of the complexity of Hardy's poetic response to the crisis of war depends on the heterogeneous features it shares in common with Menippean satire, especially the conflicting voices, reduced laughter, and a concern with the ideological issues of the day and with events both great and small. If one of the most enduring traits of the menippea takes us back to the old idea of satire as a 'medley' or 'mixed plate', Hardy's poems about the coming of world war, the conflict itself, and its aftermath have a great deal more on their plate than can be explained in terms of a darkening vision.

Hardy may have been in 'no mood … to publish humour or irony' (*LW*: 396) when the First World War began but he did go on to include satires of circumstance such as 'The Dead and the Living One' in his 'Poems of War and Patriotism' (1917). The larger problem of war's 'specious' policy of 'evasion, code, and pact' takes the form of betrayal in the private sphere of love where the 'cry' of the living woman provokes the 'laugh' of the dead one (*CPW* II: 298, 302). In another ballad of 'some weirdness' (*LW*: 402), 'The Sea Fight', Hardy does not offer a straightforward celebration of a Wessex hero when recalling the death of his friend, Captain Prowse, at the battle of Jutland (31 May 1916). The poem begins on the high plane with the 'grand' *Queen Mary* sinking and the captain dying 'as heroes do' but irony quickly dismantles the cliché of the captain bravely going down with his ship when the 'we' who know him admit that they 'More really ... view him' now than when he was alive. The dead captain 'More really lives' and 'moves with men' when imagined to be part of a carnival collective, his spirit 'Gaily' roaming the ocean's deep with 'comrades' (*CPW* III: 126–7), not subordinates. Laughter survives the war in Hardy's poetry, even if at times it is reduced to bitter irony. We do not have to read 'Christmas: 1924' as his 'sombre' and 'final reading of the movement of history'.[2] The epigrammatic lines have the structure of a joke and one that, in typical Menippean fashion, includes the speaker. Hardy saves the final satirical blow for the second couplet where the end rhyme of 'mass' and 'poison-gas' (*CPW* III: 256) links the failure of religion to bring peace over time to the failure of gas to bring victory in the space of the static Western Front.

Written just four months before hostilities began, 'Channel Firing' sets the tone for much of Hardy's war poetry while representing the problem of militarism in serio-comical form. We hear its satirical laughter when God joins a Lucianic dialogue of the dead about the meaning of the sound that awakens them. Almost a classical menippea in miniature, 'Channel Firing' has its own strange mixture of elements: the graveside humour in the midst of fear, the fantastic speaking situation combined with naturalistic details (the sounds and movements of animals), the loud guns turned into a parody of the Judgment Day, colloquial expressions interspersed with formal, even archaic diction. The grotesquely funny up/down movement, skeletons sitting upright in their coffins only to lie down again, reflects a topsy-turvy world where the way things are (and have been) nullifies the way things should be. Like the broken chancel window that cannot withstand the reverberations from the gun fire, Christianity seems as helpless as the dead to prevent nations from making "'Red war yet redder'".

God enters the dialogue by way of a joke, in the same line as the drooling cow, then proceeds to overturn Christian tradition. He, not Gabriel, will blow the trumpet but not now; then again, he may never blow it. Freed from any high and serious meaning, the Judgment Day can be postponed or cancelled altogether as God becomes a comically ambivalent and hesitant speaker. He passes judgment but the worst he imagines by way of punishment evokes the typical carnivalized nether world of the menippea: the war mongers would have had "'to scour / Hell's floor for so much threatening"'. Reassured and no longer bound to any earthly obligations, the dead respond with a carnival frankness and familiarity. Parson Thirdly wishes he had "'stuck to pipes and beer'" and another speaker raises the ultimate question for which there is no collective answer, wondering if the world will ever be saner. Although 'many a skeleton shook his head' (*CPW* II: 10), many is not all, so some hope, however forlorn, continues.

From a generic standpoint, 'Channel Firing' does more than direct our attention to the dialogic style and equivocal tone of much of Hardy's war poetry. Like the 'journalistic' genre of antiquity, 'Channel Firing' also represents its subject in a zone of contact with the open-ended present. To recover this historical context, we may go back to Kaiser Wilhelm II's farewell speech to England following Queen Victoria's funeral in 1901: 'We ought to form an Anglo-German alliance, you to keep the seas while we would be responsible for the land; with such an alliance, not a mouse could stir in Europe without our permission, and the nations would, in time, come to see the necessity of reducing their armaments.'[3] Just thirteen years later, the sounds of rearmament are so frightening in 'Channel Firing' that an English mouse not only stirs but lets drop the altar crumb, as if its very survival were at stake. Through the attitude of the personified guns, the one collective voice in the poem, and the carefully chosen place names, Hardy evokes two problems of the intervening years that helped precipitate the war: the arming of Europe and the militarism that accompanied it.

When the Kaiser gave his speech about the future, almost no one in England worried about gunnery, let alone its practice in the Channel. The situation changed after Jackie Fisher, a leading proponent of improved naval gunnery, became First Sea Lord in 1904. Convinced that war with Germany was inevitable, Fisher began to concentrate the Fleet in home waters and supervised the design and construction of the *Dreadnought* (launched in 1906), the battleship that revolutionized naval warfare and whose twelve inch guns Hardy saw when he went on board in December 1910 while it was lying at Portland Roads (*LW*: 381). The building of the *Dreadnought* came as a response to the Kaiser's decision to build a powerful battle fleet to rival England's and assert Germany's role as a new world power. In the winter of 1904–5, a kind of naval panic swept England, with the press warning of an expanding High Seas

Fleet and alleged German invasion plans. The North Sea soon became the site of a mad naval arms race.

While the guns in 'Channel Firing' happen to be naval, they serve in metonymic fashion to suggest the arsenal Europe had become by 1914. Germany initiated a general land armaments race in 1912 following the Second Moroccan Crisis, so that the last two years before the war saw a sudden surge in army expansions throughout Europe. For Hardy, this expenditure on armaments, including the machine gun, the magazine rifle, quick-firing artillery, and huge siege guns, became a satire on civilization.

When the guns roar in 'Channel Firing', they proclaim their 'readiness to avenge' (*CPW* II: 10), a stance that recalls the way all nations invoked the 'right' of self-defence to justify their massive rearmament. During these years, the idea of a 'preventive' war also became part of military thinking in both England and Germany. Fisher and the admirals seriously considered the idea of a pre-emptive strike to destroy the German Fleet. Count Alfred von Schlieffen saw Germany's need to defend itself as excusing the violation of neutral states in his 1905 war plan that became, with some modifications, the basis for the German invasion of Belgium in 1914. With war imminent, the German government skilfully used the idea of a defensive war to persuade the Social Democratic Party to support it. Indeed all powers claimed to be fighting on the defensive in 1914.

Despite the ominous preparations for war in 'Channel Firing,' Hardy called the poem 'prophetic' only in retrospect, since he was as surprised as most of his contemporaries when the guns started firing for real (*LW*: 394). This irony can perhaps best be explained in terms of the idea of the 'impossibility' or disastrous impracticality of war in the monumental work that influenced the Tsar's decision to organize a Peace Conference at the Hague – Jean de Bloch's *The Future of War* (1898). Hardy does not mention reading the abridged English translation that appeared in 1899 but may have known something about Bloch through the work of publicists such as W. T. Stead who helped disseminate his ideas. Certainly Hardy would have appreciated Bloch's kind of meliorism, based as it is on a full look at the worst aspects of modern warfare. For Bloch there can be but two alternatives if the armed peace of Europe continues: 'slow destruction in consequence of expenditure on preparations for war, or swift destruction in the event of war – in both events convulsions in the social order.' If sanity prevails, nations will settle their disputes peacefully, a choice made more compelling by the soldier's perfection of the mechanism of slaughter. Although Bloch proved wrong about the economic impossibility of waging total war, he did predict with eerie precision what the next great war would be like: battles will take place at immense distances and over many days, the entrenched foes separated by a zone of murderous fire where 'more or less mutual extermination will ... [take] place without a definite result'.[4]

Like Hardy in 'The Sick Battle-God' (1901), Bloch sees modern warfare as having reached a stage where it can no longer be glorified or sanctified: 'the stormy military life and feverish activity of battle are no more surrounded by the aureole which once set them above the world of work.'[5] Assuming the voice of the historian, Hardy too recalls how in the past the Battle-God's 'haloes rayed the very gore, / And corpses wore his glory-gleam', but his 'gold nimb / And blazon have waned dimmer and more dim' (*CPW* I: 129–30).

Hardy and Bloch share the same ideological space, even using, in addition to the hagiographic imagery, the same metaphor of sickness to convey their thoughts about the future of war, but this space, as Paul Crook shows, 'was racked by discursive tensions'[6] and some of these find their way into 'The Sick Battle-God' as they do into Bloch's theory of deterrence. To Bloch, wars still have a future, though they will be entered with a nervousness never felt before. For Hardy, when soldiers 'do and dare' they now do so 'but tensely – pale of brow' (*CPW* I: 130). 'Yet wars arise, though zest runs cold', and Europe remains divided between those who 'rejoice' at the decline of the Battle-God and those who 'deplore' his demise. The ending of the poem has serious implications even if the Battle-God has been reduced to the laughing image of an idol 'bepatched with paint and lath'. 'The lurid Deity of heretofore' may be 'no more' but the 'one of saner nod' (*CPW* I: 131) it succumbs to might just be another version of the spirit of war, saner in the sense of no longer seeing battle as a sacred or heroic affair.

Writers opposed to the arming of Europe extended the metaphor of sickness to include the militarism in which war found its apology. 'Militarism' entered general usage in the 1860s as a derogatory term applied to Bismarck's Prussia and Napoleon III's France and, though different meanings developed, they all described a pathological state of affairs.[7] Since the idea of militarism became central to Hardy's thinking about the historical causes of the First World War, we may consider some of the meanings that inform his poetry and comments on the war. One kind of militarism Hardy invokes in 'Channel Firing' refers to a process of reciprocal armament that creates an irrational dynamic difficult to control, as emphasized by the absence of living human agency in the poem. In the *Times Literary Supplement* article 'What Is Militarism?' that Hardy read with approval in 1916 (*LW*: 403), the writer warns of the danger of catching the Prussian disease of a militarism that sees peace as a perpetual effort to avoid defeat in war. What made Prussia's militarism appear unique to Hardy could be traced back to the ideological outcome of its crushing defeats by Napoleon's armies. Hardy quotes from a Dorset man's letter, written from Berlin in 1815, on how '"Bounaparte has rendered Germany completely military"' (*LW*: 451).

Although Hardy saw the Great War as another 'dynastic struggle' with 'thousands … led to the slaughter by the ambitions of Courts & Dynasties', he reserved most of the blame for Wilhelmine Germany, at one point even describing the terrible events of 1914 as 'all wrought by the madness of one man' (*CL* V: 57) – the Kaiser. After the war began, he also saw more in Prussian militarism than armaments, attacking its glorification of war and the warrior and the political power it wielded in the interests of a ruling elite. To his mind, the atrocities in Belgium and France did not express the German nation but 'an unscrupulous military oligarchy' (*CL* V: 67). Hardy directs the invective of his poetry at the 'gangs whose glory threats and slaughter are' and at 'Empery's insatiate lust of power' (*CPW* II: 294–5). As a public poet, he may have felt pressured to write what was expected of him but he still found ways of saying what he really thought. In '"I Met a Man"', he uses the fantastic element of Menippean satire to report what a strange man claims to have heard from God's soliloquies that condemn '"All Lords of War"' in the very language of animal struggle that militarists used to justify its biological necessity: the '"gambling clans / Of human Cockers"' play with the lives of soldiers to swell their '"All-Empery plans"' *(CPW* II: 304). By 1916, it had become apparent to Hardy that the war, to borrow Alfred Vagt's words, 'had been pursued as a gamble in which no one won, in which each gambler staking his utmost in the game hoped to get the utmost out of it by wearing out his opponent first'.[8]

No one epitomized a militarism that transcended practical military objectives more than the Kaiser who, with his love of military costumes and parades, viewed his role as that of a warlord ruling by divine right. A contemporary reader might well have heard the Kaiser's voice in the jingoistic start – love of country transformed into hatred of another – of Hardy's 'England to Germany in 1914': "O England, may God punish thee!"' (*CPW* II: 291). A year before coming to the throne, Wilhelm had declared that '"One cannot have enough hatred for England"'[9] and though he would later characterize himself as an Anglophile in the infamous *Daily Telegraph* interview of 1908, his speeches remained subject to flare-ups of rage against the British. The Kaiser also saw himself as having a special relationship to God, proclaiming, for example, to the German army of the east in 1914 that '"The Spirit of the Lord has descended upon me because I am the emperor of the Germans! I am the instrument of the Almighty. I am his sword, his agent. War and death to all those who do not believe in my mission!"'[10] We can understand why Hardy invites the reader of 'In Time of "The Breaking of Nations"' to hear the quiet evocation of work and love against the threatening voice of God speaking through Jeremiah (51:20) and promising to punish and destroy Babylon. The Biblical allusion in the title makes historical sense when we remember that one blustering dynast often spoke like an Old Testament prophet.

Hardy wrote 'England to Germany in 1914' in October of that year (*LW*: 396) shortly after reading J. A. Cramb's *Germany and England* (1914). What Hardy has England say to Germany, so reasonable, friendly, and fair, can be read as a rejoinder to Cramb, a Scottish historian who assumes the voice of militant nationalism in Germany to explain and justify that country's hatred of England. While Cramb draws back from the conclusion that war is inevitable, he describes a probable future conflict in a disturbingly placid way from the point of view of a Battle-God who is far from sick: 'And one can imagine the ancient, mighty deity of all the Teutonic kindred ... looking serenely down upon the English and the Germans, locked in a death-struggle' and 'smiling upon ... the heroism of the children of Odin the War-god!'[11]

Hardy attacked Cramb as a 'dreamer' with 'an inordinate admiration for the German idea of power' as evidenced in his 'attempts to elevate the vulgar ambition of German Junkers to the height of a noble national aspiration,' adding 'that Nietzsche, [Treitschke], Cramb & all of the school … insanely regard life as a thing improvable by force to immaculate gloriousness' (*CL* V: 50). A few weeks later, in a letter to the *Manchester Guardian,* Hardy began to link the German conduct of the war with militarist thought, seeing in the destruction of Rheims cathedral a sign that a 'disastrous blight' upon Germany 'has been wrought by the writings of Nietzsche, with his exemplifiers Treitschke, Bernhardi, &c.' (*THPV*: 352).

The school of Nietzsche and his followers give '"Sly slaughter"' and the desire to '"Stab first"' (*CPW* II: 299) a moral and spiritual imperative. In Nietzsche's militarisation of Schopenhauer's Will to live, war means a new 'religion of Valour, … the glory of action, heroism, the doing of great things'.[12] Lecturing in Berlin in the 1890s, the historian Heinrich von Treitschke also preached the divine majesty of war, but in an imperialistic way, insisting that the day of reckoning with England would have to come for Germany to fulfill its sacred mission of world conquest and cultural domination. All the justifications of war come together in General Friedrich von Bernhardi's best-selling *Germany and the Next War* (1912; English translation 1914): German Idealism's exaltation of the Prussian state, Nietzsche's philosophy of power, and the belief, crudely derived from Social Darwinism, that 'Might … is the supreme right.' War is both a 'biological necessity' and a 'moral obligation',[13] without which there can be no advancement of the race.

Whether we read Cramb or Bernhardi, we find that Germany's apocalyptic struggle takes the form of a renewal of the glorious past and the deeds of the fathers such as Alaric, Charlemagne, and Frederick the Great. Imperialism and militarism usually look back through history to find a cloak of tradition to cover their new demands of power, 'the one invoking the images of Emperors long dead, the other recalling past glories of action'.[14] The last two lines of 'Channel Firing' rehearse these strategies before Hardy lifts the cloak that justifies war. As the sound of gunnery practice carries inland, we travel back across the years with the mention of Stourton Tower, erected in the eighteenth century to commemorate King

Alfred the Great's victory over the Danes in 879, and Camelot, the castle of the legendary King Arthur who, according to medieval histories and romances, defeated the invading Saxons in the early sixth century. Defending the realm has a glorious past but when the sound of the guns reaches prehistoric Stonehenge, there are no more heroic events, just a mysterious monument associated in popular tradition with human sacrifice. War means bloodshed if it means anything at all.

As the Menippean approach to Hardy suggests, 'Channel Firing' and his war poems that followed should not be read as the unmediated expression of Hardy's beliefs. As a satirist, Hardy creates voices or voice-ideas that reflect and refract the great dialogue of a Europe deeply divided about war and peace. The idea of patriotism split in two, so that Hardy could talk about a 'narrow' kind 'still upheld by Junkers and Jingoists' and a broader kind in which love of country is 'extended to the whole globe' (*CL* V: 202). But what pacifists referred to as the 'lower' or 'exclusive' type of patriotism constituted the higher type to militarists. At the start of his 'War and Patriotism' sequence of poems, Hardy represents patriotism in dialogic forms that suggest how fractured the spirit of 1914 actually was. In 'The Men Who March Away', he mimics the martial kind of patriotism but in a way that reveals its doubts.[15] In 'His Country' he uses the utopian journey so often found in the menippea to represent internationalism but the speaker's rhetorical questions, the fantastic nature of the worldwide journey, and the intertextual entanglements with *The Rime of the Ancient Mariner*, another poem with a prose gloss, a journey, and perhaps too simple moral, all work to cast doubt on the ideal of one peaceful country as a real possibility. It is precisely these multiple perspectives and complicating ironies that make Hardy the war poet worth reading. By reviving the spirit of Menippus and writing the war in different voices, Hardy not only prepared the way for the modernism of T. S. Eliot and Ezra Pound but also left one of the most varied responses to the issues and events of the Great War.

NOTES

1  Although Hardy never used the term 'Menippean', he read widely enough in his study of satire in 1890 (see *LW*: 240) to cover many writers, including Lucian, who figure prominently in retrospective

attempts to define the elusive 'genre' of Menippean satire and identify its canonical works. Much of what Mikhail Bakhtin says about the characteristics of the menippea was already available to Hardy through his careful reading (see *LN* I: 64–8) of John Addington Symonds's *Studies of the Greek Poets* (1873), which treats early Attic comedy as belonging to the serio-comical genres.

2 Harold Orel, *The Final Years of Thomas Hardy, 1912–1928* (London: Macmillan, 1976), p. 134.

3 Robert K. Massie, *Dreadnought: Britain, Germany, and the Coming of the Great War* (New York: Random House, 1991), p. 303.

4 Jean de Bloch, *The Future of War* (Boston: The World Peace Foundation, 1914), pp. 56, 29.

5 Bloch, *Future of War*, p. 353.

6 Paul Crook, *Darwinism, War and History* (Cambridge: Cambridge University Press, 1994), p. 123.

7 See Nicholas Stargardt, *The German Idea of Militarism: Radical and Socialist Critics, 1866–1914* (Cambridge: Cambridge University Press, 1994), p. 13.

8 Alfred Vagt, *A History of Militarism, Civilian and Military*, revised edition (London: Hollis Carter, 1959), p. 244.

9 John C. G. Röhl, 'The Emperor's New Clothes', in John C. G. Röhl and Nicolaus Sombart, eds., *Kaiser Wilhelm II: New Interpretations* (Cambridge: Cambridge University Press, 1982), p. 33.

10 Emilio Willems, *A Way of Life and Death: Three Centuries of Prussian Militarism* (Nashville: Vanderbilt University Press, 1986), p. 86.

11 J. A. Cramb, *Germany and England* (London: John Murray, 1914), p. 137.

12 Cramb, *Germany and England*, p. 116.

13 Freidrich von Bernhardi, *Germany and the Next War*, trans. Allen H. Powles (London: Edward Arnold, 1914), pp. 23, 18, 24. Hardy's knowledge of Treitschke and Bernhardi seems to have come from reading Cramb.

14 Vagt, *History of Militarism*, p. 15.

15 See John Paul Riquelme, 'The Modernity of Thomas Hardy's Poetry', *Cambridge Companion to Thomas Hardy*, ed. Dale Kramer (Cambridge University Press, 1999), p. 212.

## 39

# Hardy and Music

JOHN HUGHES

Recent writers on Hardy have seen to it that the topic of music has been given a comparable value to that which he granted it himself in the countless musical scenes, incidents, references, and allusions that feature throughout his work, the notebooks, the letters, and the *Life*. Further, attention to this perpetual emphasis on musical responsiveness – and its association with desire, class, community, history, family, and romance – has coincided with a broadening sense of Hardy's intellectual world. As biographers and critics have pondered the subtleties of his intricate representations of music, so these discussions have led back to those far-reaching investigations – scientific, sociological, aesthetic, philosophical – that attracted him as a reader throughout his life. So, for instance, questions of the nature of mind – of its temporal, social, or affective features; of its unconscious, affective or material conditions – emerge from any close study of Hardy's writing on music, and find themselves reprised in his notes on William James or Bergson.

As accounts of the role of music in Hardy's work commonly emphasise how it prises open the socially enforced closures of subjectivity, so they have contributed to a qualification of stubborn, received images of the author himself as identifiable with his own solitary and brooding consciousness, in both the work and life.[1] One simple illustration of music's role as a trope in this revision of the biographical context is Claire Tomalin, at the conclusion of her book, summoning as her abiding image 'the fiddler's son, with music in his blood and bone ... dancing on the stone cottage floor, outside time, oblivious, ecstatic'.[2] Tomalin's reminder implies how Hardy studies and biography neglect such a self-forgetful Hardy, where other images tend to prevail – Hardy as morbidly secretive, as consumed by marital discontent, or as an increasingly bitter iconoclast.[3] In musical episodes, the incommensurability and tension between Hardy's 'ecstatic temperament' and the unsparing, dispirited counter-tendency, often appear as the mainspring of Hardy's art. Though a Hardy speaker or narrator will ruefully exact a 'full look at the Worst' ('In Tenebris II': *CP*: 168), one can detect the traces of that formative susceptibility to pleasure so memorably evoked in the *Life*: the child dancing and listening, often over-whelmed, to the 'endless jigs, hornpipes, reels, waltzes' his father would play 'of an evening' (*LW*: 19).

Anticipating later discussions, Brian Maidment raised crucial ethnographic, as well as personal, questions about the double-bind facing Hardy as a metropolitan writer drawing on musical enthusi-asms embedded in this retreating familial and social world:

Yet how could his belief in the emotional strength and communal occasions of traditional music – the one embarrassingly personal and the other aggressively unfashionable, even archaic – be made access-ible to readers not just excluded from such performances, but entirely ignorant of their continuing existence and historical significance? [4]

Yet Hardy's tastes also became wider, eventually ranging from older music-hall songs to military bands; from quadrilles heard in the street to hymns of humble dedication loved since childhood; from Emma's piano music to concert recitals and more intimate *soirées*: from musical effects in nature, or bird-song, to visits from singing undergraduates to Max Gate. Clearly, the musical-historical trails lead off and divide in every direction, and provide one kind of map of Hardy's sensibility throughout his life. Contextually too, they provide leads for those concerned with the rise of the metropolitan music-hall, or with musicological researches into the links of music and birdsong, or with documenting or conserving (like Hardy him-self) early nineteenth-century cultures of church or folk music.

Indeed, the celebration and exploration of Hardy's own musical tastes and associations has led to musical items now being a staple of Hardy conferences, and recent work has also begun to recover Hardy's relationships with composers, many of whom visited him, like Edvard Greig, or responded to his work with pieces or set-tings.[5] Within his life-time, these included Rutland Broughton, Gerald Finzi, Gustav Holst and John Ireland, and the list continues to expand. In terms of literary criticism, too, the efflorescence of interest in Hardy and music has produced diversity.[6] Recent critics have concentrated on the musical allusions or effects of the poetry;

on music as a trope for sensibility, inspiration and pleasure; on music as a solvent for social constructions of gender and class; on music as a philosophical *topos* for antirationalist metaphysics; on music and folk-song culture.[7] Further, the significances of Hardy's musicality, and his perpetual emphasis on musical responsiveness, have interested those working within the burgeoning (and differentiated) interdisciplinary field concerned with the interfaces of nineteenth-century music, culture, and literature.[8]

This broad concentration on music in Hardy has assisted an acknowledgment of those facets of his work that associate it with the most significant explorations undertaken within nineteenth- and early-twentieth-century culture and thought. Later parts of this discussion will summarise prevalent features of Hardy's representation of musical experience – its dynamic, physical, involuntary, and collective aspects. But contextually speaking, the discussion of such characteristics leads into those works that always fascinated him, intellectually and temperamentally: for instance, the scientific or socioeconomic thinking about evolution of Charles Darwin or Herbert Spencer, or J. S. Mill's secular thoughts about individuality, society, and progress.[9] Later, there was a turn to related interests, though of a more overtly philosophical and anti-rationalist kind – the positivism of Comte, the materialism of Von Hartman, the pragmatism of James, the vitalism of Bergson, the metaphysics of the unconscious in Schopenhauer.

In this context, the reciprocal relations between Hardy's reading and writing become particularly important, in that the former can seem to be directed by abiding intellectual questions that he sought also to convey in the writing, and that can often appear to be construed in terms of musical experience. Most usefully, this allows one to consider at the level of the written texture, as it were (rather than that more familiar level of authorial pronouncement), the responsive, philosophical dimensions of Hardy's work. Further, the conceptual paradoxes of mind and temporality that drive literary-theoretical readings can easily be brought to bear here, Hardy seeming a peculiarly uncanny or untimely writer in the ways his writing on music anticipates cruxes of psychoanalytical or poststructuralist readings. So, Claire Seymour has argued that Hardy's treatment of music anticipates Freud's essay, while Gilles Deleuze offered an appreciation of Hardy's fictional characters as exemplifying his own Nietzschean philosophy of becoming. Deleuze describes them as 'packets of sensation in the raw', 'bloc[s] of variable sensations', encountering each other 'along the line of chance'.[10]

From this point of view, the poems and fiction reverberate not only with evocations of music, but with unresolved yet far-reaching ethical and metaphysical queries triggered by its strange powers. To take a brief example: in a somewhat cryptic note dated 25 June 1887, Hardy described one of the frequent concerts he attended in later years: 'At a concert at Prince's Hall I saw Souls outside Bodies' (*LW*: 209). One might suspect that what gripped Hardy initially was his erotic impression of the women, their faces and bodies self-forgetfully rapt by the effect of the music. However, his formulation of 'Souls outside Bodies' conveys an incipiently philosophical fascination that circulates provisionally around the question of how one can use words to convey the strangeness of this everyday experience: the collective entrancement and subliming of identity that crystallises in a concert hall. In Hardy's work, music is not simply outside or inside a subject, as it were, as an object of experience that might be consumed or contemplated, but is, rather, represented more as a consuming process of becoming and self-change describable in terms of its effects of conduction, resonance, reverberation. Musical experience, like music itself, is an antiphonal process of incorporation and variation, so that the ontological features of music become reproduced in the dynamic events it brings about. In this broadening metaphysical context, it no longer seems simply figurative to talk about a character's self-change in terms of ensembles, counter-point, and duration, and of quasi-musical passages of subjective variation and improvisation that transcend the centripetal logic of cognition or volition, the barriers of class, and the closures of chronological time.

Hardy's ethical and aesthetic values are also those that most decisively transmitted themselves to those influenced by him. Virginia Woolf memorably referred to his capacity to be 'taken be surprise' by an unforeseen inspiration of sensibility, so that he 'seem[s] suddenly and without ... consent to be lifted up and swept onwards', as on a 'wave', with 'a sudden quickening of power which we cannot foretell, nor ... control, a single scene breaks off from the rest'.[11] At this point, one can recall the interweaving of music, waves, movement and subjectivity, and the break with novelistic good form, in Woolf's first book, *The Voyage Out*. Similarly, one could link Hardy's scenic linking of music and unconscious desire to his influence on D. H. Lawrence, and the latter's description of Hardy's characters as perpetually bursting or struggling into being.[12] In different ways, one could trace through the *topos* of music links to other admirers, like John Cowper Powys or Marcel Proust.

For Hardy the poet, as 'Shelley's Skylark', 'The Darkling Thrush' or 'A Singer Asleep' display, the motif of music was inevitably associated with his troubled lyricism, and a sense of belatedness even more acute than that experienced by earlier post-Romantic poets. In a juvenile Tennyson poem, 'The Exile's Harp', a Byronic protagonist, echoing the psalms, takes leave from the ancestral home, and the lost, perhaps forbidden, joys of music. His gesture prefigures how far Tennysonian artifice, and self-projection, will continue to use music as a figure for displacement and grief:

> I will hang thee, my Harp, by the side of the fountain,
> On the whispering branch of the lone-waving willow.[13]

For Hardy, as for Browning's Christian speaker in 'Abt Vogler', music does not immure, but is transfiguring and mysterious, its epiphanic raptures insistently signalling for the speaker some possibility of renewal. In the rigour and depth of his manifold explorations of music, if not in matters of faith, Browning appears Hardy's great mentor.

The musical example of Browning was also, importantly, metrical, since his poetry exemplifies the tension, even division, between prosodic pattern and spoken language that Dennis Taylor has suggested is the key feature in comprehending the rhythms of Hardy's poetry, and its abrupt shifts of attention: as Taylor puts it, 'The mind may interact with rhythms of the clock, or the rhythms of music.'[14] Usually in Hardy's poetry, constitutive divisions in attitude are fundamentally a matter of sound and meter, as in 'On Stinsford Hill at Midnight', a poem in ballad meter based on a midnight incident, recorded in a note of 4 February 1894. Hardy was walking from Dorchester to Bockhampton, where he came across a salvation army girl 'almost in white on the top of Stinsford Hill, beating a tambourine and dancing', and resembling one of the 'angelic quire' fallen from the sky: 'I could hardly believe my eyes ... Not a soul was there but her and myself' (*LW*: 278). The poem characteristically translates into its metrical substance Hardy's sense of the transfigurative power of music, its power to draw out and draw on, magnetically creating new configurations of desire. Sonic features enact both the sway of music, and the conflicts it produces:[15]

> o  B   o B   O   B  o   B
> I called again: 'Come nearer; much
>      o   B  o B  o  B  [o B]
>    That kind of note I need!'
> o    B   o   b   -o-   B -o-   b
> The song kept softening, loudening on
>      o   b o  B    o  B  [o B]
>    In placid calm unheed. (*CP* 597)

In the third line, his attempt at dialogue founders on her oblivious music making. Metrically, the iambic pattern gives way there also to musical suggestiveness, as the more or less emphatic beats (b, B), and dactylic feet ('*soft*-en-ing, *loud*-en-ing') transmit the captivating effect, the diminuendos and fortissimos, of a waltz. In the last line, Hardy's attitude modulates back to a contemplative sense of the woman's enviable calm, an attitude at odds with his earlier calling out, and turbulent responsiveness. The final line ('In placid calm unheed') takes pause, its sense of an indefinitely prolonged meditative interval underscored by the calmative effect of the cadenced return to the iambic, and the low echoic pulse of an alliterative pedal point ('*so/ng*, soften*/ing* louden*/ing* /*on*, / *In* … *un*heed').

Similarly, as the poem ends, excitement and sensation pass again into an even more accentuated and pained, but composed, awareness of her heedlessness:

> 'This world is dark, and where you are,'
>    I said, 'I cannot be!'
> But still the happy one sang on,
>    And had no heed of me.

Like Wordsworth's solitary reaper, the girl sings on indefinitely regardless, her happiness and mind closed to the poem's speaker, the song passing into the virtualities of memory and poetry. And to a degree, like Wordsworth's speaker, the poet carries the song and this separateness within himself, as an enigmatic inspiration.

However, the important difference (and one which shows how far the Romantic context is internal to the poem), is how decisively the speaker ends up not sustained by the girl's song, but cast adrift by it. Its insistence in his memory is inseparable from his feeling bereft, and affectively exposed, in a circuit between hope and disappointment that the poem recapitulates, and that the speaker comes to reflect upon. Analysis of countless other poems on musical topics would similarly indicate how Hardy's modernity involved such a dynamic, disjunctive invocation of musical effects and tropes.

Biographically, musical pleasure was inseparable for Hardy from the complex inter-relations of class, community and love. As a child, the songs he sung with Lady Julia Martin fomented the overwhelming, precocious ardour he felt for her. As Claire Tomalin put it the feeling was 'one he never forgot' – perhaps because it was, naturally enough, one he could never act on.[16] Indeed, it might be as accurate to say that the passion never forgot him, since it is plausible to detect the formative effects of such unresolved yearning in the patterns of the early fiction, where the courses of romance, time and again abetted by musical incidents, breach the class barrier for Will Strong/Egbert Mayne, Gabriel Oak, Dick Dewy, and others. And, if the names of these early characters suggest a compensatory fantasy of masculine control, so too it is arguable that the dominant motif throughout Hardy's fictional career is the staging of love through a male infatuation of an essentially passive kind, predicated on social distance, and the woman's discombobulating superiority and elusiveness.[17]

This description suggests too, perhaps, how far Hardy's fiction depends also on the physical and the accidental – on chance encounters and susceptibilities in which cognitive identity gives way to passages of feeling and correspondence, outside of social precept. An example would be the young girl in 'On the Western Circuit' who rides the steam-circus. Her paradisal air draws on the hero, Charles Raye. She is 'absolutely unconscious of everything save the act of riding: her features were rapt in an ecstatic dreaminess; for the moment she did not know her age or her history or her lineaments, much less her troubles' (*LLI*: 111). Such an imaginative responsiveness provides Hardy with his pretext, as his prose seeks expressive equivalents in the set-piece opening scene (before the plot, as is the way in the stories, ironically recoils upon desire). Unsurprisingly perhaps, as Joan Grundy was one of the first to point out, Hardy accordingly often depends on musical metaphors or traits in describing the affective individuality in his characters: Christopher shakes 'like a harp-string' in *The Hand of Ethelberta* (*HE*: 22). Farfrae's personal attractions are linked to his fascinating possession of the 'hyperborean crispness, stringency, and charm, as of a well-braced musical instrument' (*MC*: 23). Again, the Cytherea who looks up at Manston 'with parted lips at his face' after his extemporizations on the *Pastoral Symphony* during the storm, betrays a passionate reactiveness to music that she shares with almost every sympathetic character in Hardy's writing, male and female (*DR*: VIII.4). In what we might plausibly surmise as something like the original version of this scene – reworked in 'An Indiscretion in the Life of the Heiress' – it is the male figure, Egbert, who is enraptured. This time the music is the less pantheistic Handel's *Messiah*, but again Hardy's writing sympathetically threatens to come off its hinges:

The varying strains shook and bent him to themselves as a rippling brook shakes and bends a shadow. The music did not show its power by attracting his attention to its subject; it rather dropped its own libretto and took up in place of that the poem of his life and love.[18]

The sentences dilate – doubling verbs and improvising figurative and rhythmical enactments approximating to the individuating, entrancing, paradoxical power of music.

Nonetheless, in the fiction, of course, the ratios between the transports of musical susceptibility, and the constraints of society and cognition, increasingly took ironic, satiric and tragic forms. The problem in *Tess* is not that the soul cannot go out of the body, but that the body and desire have, socially speaking, nowhere to go. The plot reveals Angel as a dreamer with a harp, unable to move outside the precincts of his class identity, and becoming the implacable instrument of social precept. Pierston in *The Well-Beloved* is similarly a sardonic figure, as well as the vehicle for Hardy to satirise – both pitilessly and pitifully – the romantic readiness of earlier characters. In this novel, as in *Jude*, music is associated with the tiresomely automatic projections both of romance, and of a Romantic context now decisively superseded, with a knowing irony that both targets and employs Hardy's own Shelleyan susceptibilities.

432

NOTES

1 Michael Millgate, 'Hardy as Biographical Subject', *A Companion to Thomas Hardy*, ed. Keith Wilson (Oxford: Wiley-Blackwell, 2009), pp. 7–18.

2 Claire Tomalin, *Thomas Hardy: The Time-Torn Man* (London: Viking, 2006), p. 380.

3 On Hardy's 'ecstatic temperament' (*LW*: 19) in relation to music, see C. J. Weber, 'Thomas Hardy's Music: With a Bibliography', *Music and Letters* 21:2 (1940), pp. 172–8; F. B. Pinion, *A Hardy Companion* (London: Macmillan, 1968); and Joan Grundy, *Hardy and the Sister Arts* (London: Macmillan, 1979).

4 Brian Maidment, 'Hardy's Fiction and English Traditional Music', *Thomas Hardy Annual* IV (1986), p. 17. Hardy's social dislocation is explored also in John Lucas, *Modern English Poetry from Hardy to Hughes* (London: Batsford, 1986) and Phillip Mallett, '*Jude the Obscure*: A Farewell to Wessex', *The Thomas Hardy Journal* 11:2 (October 1995), pp. 48–59.

5 The many settings of the poetry, and the circumstances of their composition, are the focus of Susan Bell's 2008 Loughborough University PhD thesis: '*Verse Into Song': Composers and their Settings of Poems by Thomas Hardy*. See also Gillian Beer, 'The Senses of Musical Settings in Hardy's Poetry', *Thomas Hardy Journal* 22 (Autumn 2006), pp. 7–14, and Claire Seymour, '"A Song Outlasts a Dynasty": Gerald Finzi's Settings of Thomas Hardy's Poetry', *Thomas Hardy Journal* 22 (Autumn 2006), pp. 15–32.

6 Daniel Karlin discusses the poetical association of Hardy's lyricism with Romanticism in 'The Figure of the Singer in the Poetry of Thomas Hardy', *The Achievement of Thomas Hardy*, ed. Phillip Mallett (London: Macmillan, 2000), pp. 117–36. Tim Armstrong finds the poetry anticipating Adorno's concern with the commodifying technologies, the musical memory-machines, of capitalist modernity, in 'Hardy, History and Recorded Music', *Thomas Hardy and Contemporary Literary Studies*, ed. Tim Dolin and Peter Widdowson (London: Palgrave, 2004), pp. 153–66. In her piece informed by Freudian notions of the uncanny, Claire Seymour offers a useful survey of Hardy's musical affiliations: 'Hardy and Music: Uncanny Sounds', *Companion to Thomas Hardy*, ed. Wilson, pp. 223–38.

7 See John Hughes, '*Ecstatic Sound': Music and Individuality in the Work of Thomas Hardy* (Aldershot: Ashgate, 2001), and Mark Asquith, *Thomas Hardy, Metaphysics and Music* (London: Palgrave, 2005).

8 Caroline Jackson-Houlston's *'Ballads, Songs and Snatches': The Appropriation of Folk Song and Popular Culture in British 19th-Century Realist Prose* (Aldershot: Ashgate, 1999) documents how Hardy's representation of ballad and folk song was bound up with his awareness of its vulnerability to social change, and sentimentalizing commodification. See also Delia Da Sousa Correa's *George Eliot, Music and Victorian Culture* (London: Palgrave, 2002) and (as editor) *'Phrase and Subject': Studies in Literature and Music* (Oxford: Legenda, 2006). Phyllis Welliver explores the cultural, as well as literary, significance of music in two books, and an edited collection: *Women Musicians in Victorian Fiction, 1860–1900* (Aldershot: Ashgate, 2000); *The Musical Crowd in English Fiction, 1840–1910: Class, Culture and Nation* (London: Palgrave, 2006); and (as editor) *The Figure of Music in Nineteenth-Century British Poetry* (Aldershot: Ashgate, 2005). Nicky Losseff and Sophie Fuller's volume, *The Idea of Music in Victorian Fiction*, explores a host of canonical and noncanonical fiction writers (Aldershot: Ashgate, 2004). Ashgate's 'Music in Nineteenth-Century Britain' series and interdisciplinary journal, *Nineteenth-Century Music Review*, similarly reveal the growth of the field.

9 See Gillian Beer, *Darwin's Plots* (Cambridge: Cambridge University Press, 2000); Angelique Richardson, 'Hardy and Biology', *Thomas Hardy: Texts and Contexts*, ed. Phillip Mallett (Basingstoke: Palgrave, 2002), pp. 156–79; George Levine, 'Hardy and Darwin: An Enchanting Hardy?', ed. Wilson, *Companion to Thomas Hardy*, pp. 36–53; and Phillip Mallett, 'Hardy and Philosophy', *Companion to Thomas Hardy*, ed., Wilson, pp. 21–35.

10 Gilles Deleuze and Claire Parnet, *Dialogues*, trans. Hugh Tomlinson and Barbara Habberjam (London: Athlone Press, 1987), p. 40.

11 Virginia Woolf, 'Thomas Hardy's Novels', *The Common Reader* (London: Hogarth, 1959), p. 247.

12 D. H. Lawrence, 'Study of Thomas Hardy', *D. H. Lawrence: Selected Literary Criticism*, ed. Anthony Beal (London: Heinemann, 1973), p. 167.

13 Alfred Tennyson, *The Poems of Tennyson*, ed. Christopher Ricks (London: Longman, 1969), p. 85.

14 Dennis Taylor, *Hardy's Metres and Victorian Prosody* (Oxford: Clarendon Press, 1988), p. 7.

15 Thomas Carper and Derek Attridge, *Meter and Meaning* (London: Routledge, 2003), p. 147: **B** beat [emphasized syllable], **b** beat [unemphasized syllable], **[B]** virtual beat [no syllable] (perceived at the end of trimeter lines, as in ballad stanzas), **o**

offbeat [unemphasized syllable], **O** offbeat [emphasized syllable], **-o-** double offbeat [two unemphasized syllables], **[o]** virtual offbeat [no syllable, perceived offbeat], **ô** implied offbeat [no syllable, necessary rhythmical pause}, **~o~** triple offbeat [three unemphasized syllables], (exceedingly rare in stricter metrical styles)

16  Tomalin, *The Time-Torn Man*, p. 27.

17  As Penny Boumelha puts it, Hardy's 'eroticization' of 'cross-class romance' is 'almost obsessive': 'The Patriarchy of Class: *Under the Greenwood Tree, Far from the Madding Crowd, The Woodlanders*', *The Cambridge Companion to Thomas Hardy*, ed. Dale Kramer (Cambridge: Cambridge University Press, 1999), p. 132.

18  'An Indiscretion in the Life of an Heiress', *The Excluded and Collaborative Stories*, ed. Pamela Dalziel (Clarendon Press: Oxford, 1992), p. 128.

# 40

# Thomas Hardy and the Visual Arts

### JANE THOMAS

Thomas Hardy is a highly visual author. His novels and stories are enriched with passages of stunning description which interrupt the plot to provide moments of aesthetic stasis. References to painting and drawing, sculpture and, less prominently, photography, add nuance to his descriptions of people, places and affect. His range includes Dutch Realism, Impressionism, the Pre-Raphaelites, the Venetian Renaissance, Expressionists and Symbolists, French Realists and landscape painters. Drawing and painting from nature from an early age, he was versed in the techniques of draughtsmanship and read journals such as *The Illustrated Magazine of Art*. He timed his arrival in London to coincide with the opening of the Great Exhibition of 1862, which featured a huge gallery of national and international art which he visited two or three times a week (*LW*: 40). He also visited the National Gallery (where he concentrated 'for twenty minutes after lunch' on one master at a time); Prince Albert's 'Brompton Boilers' at South Kensington, housing many of the best paintings and artefacts from the 1851 Great Exhibition Museum; and the Royal Academy, where he later attended private viewings and annual dinners.

More avant-garde venues included the Dudley and the Grosvenor Galleries (he attended the latter's Summer Exhibition in June 1878, less than a year after it opened) where he would have seen paintings by Burne-Jones, Albert Moore, Whistler and other artists shunned by the more conservative Royal Academy. He read and took notes from Ruskin's *Modern Painters* and from influential writing on art and aesthetics by Pater and John Addington Symonds. In 1863, he contemplated a career as an art critic and began a notebook on 'Schools of Painting' (*LW*: 47).[1] He and Emma visited galleries and museums in Italy, Holland, Paris, and Luxembourg. He knew Whistler, Burne-Jones, Alfred Parsons, Thomas Woolner, and Simeon Solomon; he was a frequent visitor to the studios of Richard Henry Park, G. F. Watts, and Hamo Thornycroft and to the home of Alma-Tadema (*LW*: 216).

Hardy's narrative technique is informed by ideas from painting. He regularly employs terms such as 'line', 'perspective', 'profile', 'foreground', 'background', and 'middle distance'. In *Tess* the narrator describes the Vale of Blackmoor as it might appear to one of the many landscape painters who had yet to visit it, the atmosphere 'languorous' and 'so tinged with azure that what artists call the middle-distance partakes also of that hue, while the horizon beyond is of the deepest ultramarine' (*Tess*: 2).[2] He was impressed by the immediacy of visual art, particularly its ability to communicate sensational images. In May 1888 he describes Gabriel Guay's *The Death of Jezebel* as 'a horrible tragedy, and justly so, telling its story in a flash' (*LW*: 217). Hardy uses a similar technique to describe the deaths of Jude and Sue's children, where the reader is encouraged to visualize the back of the door on which their bodies hang (*Jude*: VI.2). At the Royal Academy he noted the effect of suggestion in Jean Léon Gérôme's *Jerusalem* or *Consummatum est Jerusalem* (1867) where 'The *shadows only* of the three crucified ones are seen' (*LW*: 79) and his decision to *suggest* another 'consummatum' – Tess's execution – by the black flag 'moving slowly up the staff, and extend[ing] itself upon the breeze' may owe its origin to Gérôme's 'fine conception'.

Hardy's pictorialism is evidence of his auto didacticism and uneasy relationship with Realism, which he dismissed somewhat baldly as concerned with things 'copied or reported inventorily', and thus 'not Art', which involved 'a disproportioning – (i.e. distorting, throwing out of proportion) – of realities' in order to highlight what really matters (*LW*: 239). He proposed a new form of creative address to the world to encourage a deeper and more focussed engagement than mere 'observation' would allow, and deploys a set of highly stylised devices which refer to works of art, artists, techniques and the subtle organisation of space, light effects and perspectives combined with emblematic or symbolic elements in a manner comparable to a painting or sculpture. This is not simply to illustrate or ornament the narrative but subtly to communicate visual effects, ideas, sentiments and emotions.

Bullen and Taylor both note how Hardy invokes painting 'associatively rather than referentially', rarely using ekphrasis.[3] For Lloyd

Fernando, this 'rhetoric of painting' lends his novels a preconceived air of 'static vividness' that detracts from their narrative power.[4] For Bullen, however, it is part of Hardy's developing style as a novelist, evidence of a struggle between 'the comfort and the solace of the permanent or unchanging', and 'the destructive power of 'becoming''. The passage of time, change and decay infuses his novels with melancholy. Moments of stasis – when the narrative is briefly fixed in a tableau, a set piece or a detailed visualisation of a landscape or character – are Hardy's way of making the world stand still at a felicitous moment: not 'happy' or 'fulfilled', perhaps, but strikingly apt or aesthetically satisfying, so that life briefly exhibits 'the spherical completeness of perfect art' (*LW*: 177). A character or landscape is temporarily abstracted from the forces of chance and change, highlighting with some poignancy the recognition that each moment carries within it the impulse of its own dissolution. They are 'moments of vision' in every sense: the products of contemplative observation reproduced in pictorial form, and evidence of Hardy's ability to imbue even the most mundane of objects and events with deep significance.[5]

In May 1863 Hardy noted that the Dutch School 'owes none of its fame to dignity of subject'.[6] The sub-title of *Under the Greenwood Tree: A Rural Painting of the Dutch School* (1872) suggests that from the start he was more interested in aesthetics and textuality than realism. Unlike George Eliot, he establishes a dialogue between Realism and reality, Art and life.[7] Allusions to Dutch Realism don't simply justify his focus on 'common people' or underline the 'reality' or 'truthfulness' of his portrayal of rural life. The self-conscious 'framing' of his characters in doorways, windows and the spaces of domestic architecture points more to artfulness than 'truth', suggesting the isolation, enclosure and elevation of selected elements of a scene in a border or case, and drawing attention to the construction and the structure of a novel as a work of art, not a reflection of life. Hardy's novel presented his readers with images of a class of people about whom they knew very little except under the generic term 'Hodge', yet could recognise from the walls of fashionable galleries. Ruth Bernard Yeazell reminds us that the images of daily life in these paintings were extremely selective, and to evoke them 'in phrases like "the Dutch School" ... was inevitably to conjure with a particular set of formulae and conventions'.[8]

438

Like the artist, the lover selects and elevates. The first presentation of Fancy Day as 'a young girl famed as a picture by the window
architrave, and unconsciously illuminating her countenance to a
vivid brightness by a candle she held in her left hand, close to her
face' may suggest Godfried Schalcken's *Young Girl with a Candle*
to the reader, but to Dick and his companions she is 'a spiritual
vision' (*UGT*: I.5). Elevating or idealising themselves, or the object
of their affection, and then mistaking that subjective vision for the
objective truth is one of the many tragic errors Hardy's lovers make
in their attempts to solve the 'immortal puzzle' of human sexual
relationships (Preface to *The Woodlanders*).

Hardy borrows techniques from the Pre-Raphaelites to illustrate
this: there are echoes of Rossetti's *The Blessed Damozel* in this 'vision'
of Fancy Day. The earlier Pre-Raphaelite painters, including Millais
and Holman Hunt, George Frederic Watts, Evelyn de Morgan,
and, in particular, Edward Burne-Jones emphasised the beauty of
the human form in their ethereal depictions of scenes of life, love
and loss from Medieval, Greek, and Arthurian myth and legend.
After his visit to the Grosvenor Gallery's Summer Exhibition in
1878 Hardy wrote: 'Seemed to have left flesh behind, and entered a
world of soul' (*LW*: 124). The *Times* critic of *The Return of the Native*
referred to Hardy's 'Grosvenor Gallery' style, and the character of
Eustacia Vye is '"composed" of elements from Pater's account of the
*Mona Lisa*, Rossetti's fatal Venus, and Reynolds's aristocratic dei-
ties'.[9] Although it is unlikely that Hardy saw Rossetti's paintings
he knew his sonnets and the type of beauty fashionable at the time.
With her luxuriant hair restrained only by 'a thin fillet of black vel-
vet', her languid melancholy, the lines of her lips and each corner of
her mouth 'as clearly cut as the point of a spear' (*RN* I:7), Eustacia
resembles a Rossetti heroine such as *Venus* or *Proserpine* (1874)
imprisoned in Hades and yearning for the skies of Enna, or a figure
from a Burne-Jones painting such as *Laus Veneris*, first shown at
the Grosvenor Gallery in 1877, or *The Beguiling of Merlin* exhibited
the following year.[10] Her dream of dancing with a man in silver
armour who removes his casque to kiss her in 'an iridescent hollow,
arched with rainbows' (*RN*: II.3) – who will rescue her from hea-
thenish Egdon – is straight from Burne-Jones's canvasses: in his
early painting of *St George* (1873–7), the subject of the Mummer's
play in which Eustacia plays a surreptitious part on Christmas Eve,

the armoured knight's shield bears an image of a maiden caught in the coils of a dragon. The narrator is ironic at Eustacia's expense, drawing telling comparisons between her romantic and tragic conceptions of herself and the prosaic realities of her surroundings. Celestial imperiousness, 'love, wrath, and fervour, had proved to be somewhat thrown away on netherward Egdon' (*RN*: I.7). Nowhere are they more completely wasted than on Clym Yeobright, whose response to descriptions of this proud Tartarean beauty is, 'Do you think she would like to teach children'? (*RN*: III.2).

If Eustacia is keen to emphasise her unearthly qualities to her earthly lover, Tess Durbeyfield desires exactly the reverse. In the misty, early morning milking fields of Talbothays Angel sees Tess as a 'visionary essence of woman', calling her 'Artemis, Demeter, and other fanciful names, half-teasingly, which she did not like because she did not understand them. "Call me Tess," she would say askance; and he did' (*Tess*: 20). Hardy's most sustained indictment of the masculine idealisation of ordinary women appears in *The Well-Beloved* (1897) whose central character Jocelyn Pierston is a sculptor of the Pre-Raphaelite school.[11]

The distinction between idealization and a subjective point of view is an important one for Hardy as it marks the borderline between an idiosyncratic and a deluded mode of regard. 'Art' involved the subtle re-visioning of the material world in order to reveal a deeper 'truth' that might be otherwise 'overlooked' (*LW*: 239). Careful and deliberate selection, editing and ordering revealed a pattern, or patterns, which might not be obvious to the casual viewer. The artist was a 'seer' capable of profound spiritual insight, whose role was not to represent the material world but to interpret it. Hardy noted in June 1882 that 'in life the seer should watch that pattern among general things which his idiosyncrasy moves him to observe, and describe that alone. This is, quite accurately, a going to Nature, yet the result is no mere photograph, but purely the product of the writer's own mind' (*LW*: 158). The groundwork should be 'a precise transcript of ordinary life' (and here Hardy is firmly in the realist tradition), but the elements that compose the design should be 'uncommon' (but not too 'unlikely') so as to stimulate the interest and engagement of the reader, and the mode of perception, and its communication, should offer new perspectives and revelations (*LW*: 154).

In January 1886 Hardy wrote: 'My art is to intensify the expression of things, as is done by Crivelli, Bellini, &c. so that the heart and inner meaning is made vividly visible' (*LW*: 183). Egdon Heath expresses 'the moods of the more thinking among mankind' (*RN*: I.1), and in *The Woodlanders* the natural world of Hintock Wood is an expression of Schopenhauer's *Wille*, the blind incessant impulse or 'Unfulfilled Intention, which makes life what it is': 'The leaf was deformed, the curve was crippled, the taper was interrupted; the lichen ate the vigour of the stalk, and the ivy slowly strangled to death the promising sapling.' (*W*: 7) He also sought to intensify the *impression* of things: subduing physical forms to their 'visible essences' (*LW*: 183). In 1881, confined to bed with internal bleeding, he pondered how to combine the accurate reproduction of natural forms with a more penetrative vision: 'seeing into the *heart of a thing* (as rain, wind, for instance)' to produce a different kind of realism (*LW*: 151). In the 'Conclusion' to *Studies in the History of the Renaissance* (1873) Pater suggests that a 'clear, perpetual outline' is simply an image or grouping of elemental forces which in reality 'pass out beyond' the momentary coherence of form. When we reflect more deeply on the 'flood of external objects' that seems to compose experience 'they are dissipated ... the cohesive force seems suspended like some trick of magic; each object is loosed into a group of impressions – colour, odour, texture – in the mind of the observer' that is more real than the immediate material world.

The artist who most famously saw into the heart of things was J. M. W. Turner, whose work underwent a dramatic shift towards the end of his life, leading many of his critics to accuse him of insanity. Ruskin praised Turner's ability to capture fugitive atmospheric effects and devoted much of *Modern Painters* to his later work. Hardy may have come to Turner through Ruskin, or at the 1862 International Exhibition or the National Gallery. In January 1889 he was particularly impressed with Turner's watercolours as landscapes '*plus* a man's soul'. Instead of objects modified by light, Turner painted '*light as modified by objects*' (*LW*: 225). 'Scenic' accuracy is sacrificed in order to present the 'mystery' of Nature. Unlike his near contemporary Richard Bonnington, Turner seemed to paint the deeper underlying reality of a scene: 'what are sometimes called abstract imaginings' (*LW*: 192).[12] Hardy imagines Turner asking himself: 'What pictorial drug can I dose man with, which shall affect his eyes somewhat in the manner of this reality which I cannot carry to him?' (*LW*: 226)

Hardy's comparison of the effect of Turner's paintings to an hallucinogenic drug, opening the doors of perception, is fascinating. Turner's attempts to capture the effects of sunlight on mist had a demonstrable effect on one of Hardy's most atmospheric novels. The yellow luminosity of the early morning October mist lighting up the ridge of the vale of Tess's birth, a symbolic barrier between her past innocent self and her present; the mingling of her hopes with the sunshine in 'an ideal photosphere' (*Tess*: 16); the 'spectral, half-compounded, aqueous light' of the open mead or its 'mixed, singular, luminous gloom' (*Tess*: 20), and the 'highly-charged mental atmosphere' surrounding her on the morning of her wedding – a 'condition of mind, wherein she felt glorified by an irradiation not her own, like the Angel whom St John saw in the sun' (*Tess*: 33) – suggest not only Turner's fugitive atmospheric effects, but how those effects communicate subtle moods and sensations.

Hardy notes Palgrave's contention that 'Landscape ... can only move us much when the spectator's soul feels that the artists soul [*sic*] is speaking through the forms & colours of his canvas. This was the secret of our gᵗ. landsᵗˢ. from Gainsb. to Turner' (*LN* I: 195). A *Times* review of Edmund Gosse's memoir of the landscape painter Cecil Gordon Lawson declares the perennial struggle in art as between the 'realist' and the 'poetical' school of painting: the 'realist' school is characterised by 'the endeavour of the artist ... to forget himself in what he sees' while the artist of the 'poetic' school 'transfuse[s] all the external world with his own thought & emotion' (*LN* I: 153). This personal, subjective, emotional response to experience drew Hardy to the work of Turner and the Impressionists on whom Turner had such an influence, leading to his insistence that a novel is 'an impression', not 'an argument'. The term 'impression' is another complex one for Hardy. It describes the impossibility of accurate and total representation of the material world, and also that which has a profound effect on an artist or writer: what he *chooses* to represent on his canvas or in his pages.

At the Winter Exhibition at the 'Society of British Arts' in December 1886 Hardy noted the strength and good technique of the 'impressionist school' and what he understood to be its principle: 'what you carry away with you from a scene is the true feature to grasp; or in other words, *what appeals to your own individual eye and heart in particular* amid much that does not so appeal, and which you therefore omit to record.' This, he surmises, 'is even more suggestive in the direction of literature than in that of art' (*LW*: 191). Art could only ever be 'approximate' rather than 'exact' (*LW*: 169) and therefore the role of the artist was to reveal something other than material realities. In January 1887 he wrote:

The much-decried, mad, late-Turner rendering is now necessary to create my interest. The exact truth as to material fact ceases to be of importance in Art – it is a student's style – the style of a period when the mind is serene and unawakened to the tragical mysteries of life; when it does not bring anything to the object that coalesces with and translates the qualities that are already there. (*LW*: 192)

Hardy distinguishes between two conceptions of truth: the objective, photographic 'truth' of realism, and the subjective, more painterly truth of art.[13] However, he is keen to stress that there is no such thing as a universal truth underlying appearances, which the artist perceives and then reveals to a discerning viewer, finding in Kant corroboration that 'all known or knowable objects' exist only in relation to a 'conscious subject' and therefore cannot be regarded as 'things in themselves' (*LN* II: 94).

Hardy's notion of 'patterning' applies not just to what he calls his 'idiosyncratic mode of regard'; his particular political and philosophical reading of human and animal existence in nineteenth-century rural England. It points to something that Wilde developed as a central proposition of fin-de-siècle aestheticism. 'On the Decay of Lying' insists that great Art provides models of particular excellence that Life, driven by the urge to find distinctive modes of expression, imitates.[14] Our appreciation and understanding of the vast dazzle of experience is shaped by those who find patterns that communicate with and move us. We then discover echoes of those patterns, which help us to structure the chaos of existence into meaningful forms which take on the aspect of 'truths'. In the same month that 'The Decay of Lying' was published, Hardy concluded that art was 'the secret of how to produce by a false thing the effect of a true' (*LW*: 226), reflecting Wilde's notion that Art is the 'telling of beautiful untrue things'. His phrase 'the effect of a true' recognises both the contingent, subjective nature of artistic truth and how our sense of what is true depends upon whether or not we recognise or connect with what art reveals.

Hardy's regular visits to galleries in London and Paris and his familiarity with art journals, guide books and reviews in the periodical press of the time showed him how artists came into and went out of fashion, but he was drawn to schools of art and artists whose practice and subject matter seemed most nearly to reflect his own. Art offered him a language other than the purely verbal to structure his imagination and avoid the 'word-painting' he so abhorred. In Hardy's 'moments of vision' – particularly those that owe their power and poignancy to the visual arts – the process of 'becoming' is briefly transmuted into something akin to Virginia Woolf's 'moments of being' when 'a pattern is revealed behind the cotton wool'.[15] Woolf's characters experience rapture in this moment; Hardy's moments of vision have more poignancy. A dominant 'pattern' for Hardy was the inevitable process of change, insecurity, and confusion resulting in wrong or misguided choices or the depredations of chance and time. The momentary stilling of his characters into living tableaux gives depth and resonance to their experiences and holds them, briefly, in a suspension from which they must move into sadness, separation and even death. Hardy's recasting or reordering of experience into recognisable visual forms, demonstrates what Wilde called Life's 'imitative instinct'; the ways in which the energy of life finds expression in and through the agency of art.

NOTES

1 See *The Personal Notebooks of Thomas Hardy*, ed. Richard Taylor (London and Basingstoke: Macmillan, 1978), pp. 105–14.
2 See J. B. Bullen, *The Expressive Eye: Fiction and Perception in the Work of Thomas Hardy* (Oxford: Clarendon Press, 1986), pp. 7–10.
3 *Personal Notebooks*, p. xix.
4 Lloyd Fernando, 'Thomas Hardy's Rhetoric of Painting', *Review of English Literature* 6 (October 1965), p. 68.
5 Bullen, *The Expressive Eye*, p. 255.
6 *Personal Notebooks*, p. 112
7 Chapter 17 of *Adam Bede* responded to Ruskin's castigation of the Dutch school for its low subject matter and 'evil effect' on the public mind; see *George Eliot: Selected Writing*, ed. Rosemary Ashton (Oxford: Oxford University Press, 1992), p. 248.

8  Ruth Bernard Yeazell, *Art of the Everyday* (Princeton: Princeton University Press, 2008), p. 18.
9  Bullen, *The Expressive Eye*, p. 107.
10 Paintings in the 1878 exhibition included Burne-Jones's *The Love Song (Le Chant d'Amour)* and *Laus Veneris*, and Whistler's *Thames – Nocturne in Blue and Silver*.
11 Jane Thomas, ed., Thomas Hardy's *The Well-Beloved* with *The Pursuit of the Well-Beloved* (Ware: Wordsworth, 2000), pp. ix–xxvii.
12 Emma Hardy owned a landscape painting attributed to Bonnington (1801–28), given her by the sculptor Thomas Woolner.
13 In *A Laodicean* Hardy acknowledges that even photographs cannot be depended upon to give a 'true' image of their subject.
14 Oscar Wilde, 'The Decay of Lying: a Dialogue', *Nineteenth Century* 25 (January–June 1889), pp. 35–56.
15 Virginia Woolf, 'A Sketch of the Past', *Moments of Being*, ed. Jeanne Schulkind, 2nd edition (London: Hogarth Press, 1985), p. 72.

PART V

# Legacies

# 41

# Lawrence's Hardy

MICHAEL HERBERT

Hardy and Lawrence have an unusual relationship in that each is a shaping influence on the writings of the other. Whereas Hardy's influence on Lawrence is direct and well attested,[1] the younger man's influence is not on Hardy himself but on how aspects of his novels came to be discussed, after both men were dead, in the light (and sometimes the shadow) cast by Lawrence's *Study of Thomas Hardy*.[2] Written in 1914 but not published until 1936, the *Study* from the first seemed, even to its author, to be 'about anything but Thomas Hardy',[3] becoming later a kind of personal manifesto or confession, 'mostly philosophicalish, slightly about Hardy'.[4] This exuberant slant, together with more humorous teasing of himself, Hardy, and the reader, is maintained in the work, but if it were in fact only marginally about Hardy, it could not have had the impact it has had on subsequent readings of Hardy's novels. Although the *Study* is central to the study of Lawrence himself, including as it does 'philosophicalish' and other material closer to his own concerns than to those of his ostensible subject, much of it is focused directly and – for all its subtlety – straightforwardly on the fictional characters of a predecessor he admires, shares much fellow-feeling with, and could be said, simply, to love. Perhaps partly because of these strongly positive emotions, Lawrence is easily disappointed by what he considers failures of the beloved author; but it is the positive that inspired him to produce by far his longest piece of criticism on a single literary figure.

It could have been much longer. As Lawrence asserts at the start of his third chapter, 'This is supposed to be a book about the people in Thomas Hardy's novels. But if one wrote everything they give rise to it would fill the Judgement Book' (*Study* 20). Homing in on the people, the characters, with the immediate recognition that the topics raised are impossibly numerous, is typical. It gives the *Study*, for all its grand generalisation and 'philosophicalish' speculation (much of it, for some readers, more obfuscating than illuminating), an essentially concrete, *un*abstract, human and humane base from which to launch the various flights of critical arrows, some missing their target (or aiming at what seems to be the wrong target), but many scoring a bull's-eye.

The 'human' aspects that most obviously come to mind are those connected with characterisation, and here the *Study* has been profoundly influential in its psychological approach, which turned upside down many conventional responses – especially conventionally moral ones.[5] No longer is the apparent malevolence of 'fate' the prime interest, or 'pessimism', or 'improbable' coincidence. The focus instead is on the importance of Hardy as an explorer of the world of the unconscious, before the word was used for that submerged Freudian iceberg of which characters' external qualities of appearance and 'personality' and possessions and class and social relations are merely the visible tip. The visible tip is what conventional novelists present; in Hardy, the interest lies in what is of essence in the characters, which Lawrence memorably terms 'explosive':

Nowhere, except perhaps in Jude, is there the slightest development of personal action in the characters: it is all explosive. Jude, however, does see more or less what he is doing, and act from choice. He is more consecutive. The rest explode out of the convention. They are people each with a real, vital, potential self, even the apparently wishy-washy heroines of the earlier books, and this self suddenly bursts the shell of manner and convention and commonplace opinion, and acts independently, absurdly, without mental knowledge or acquiescence. (*Study*: 20)

The case is made challengingly, and sounds overstated: it would be difficult to sustain the notion of there being only one Hardy character who has any 'development of personal action', without considerably restricting the definition of these terms; likewise, it seems improbable that 'all' these characters explode, even if discussion is confined to the main ones. But Lawrence helps his case by reference to each novel in turn, with considerable detail in the analysis of the major later ones, and while there can be argument about his mode of utterance, typically forceful and unacademic, as about particulars and terminology, there can be no doubting the significant impact of his reading in this one aspect alone. For when the psychology of characters, rather than 'fate', is taken as the explanation for so much that seems improbable in Hardy's novels, readers can learn from Lawrence that the coincidences and accidents are probably not coincidental and accidental but determined psychologically, often as a result of unconscious desire and other motivations unrecognised by the characters themselves. Furthermore, it is usually from these inner compulsions that the tragedy springs, when their inner tensions and turmoil lead characters to explode into seemingly inexplicable actions, for which they must pay, as they have flouted the conventions. It is a measure of Lawrence's achievement that it does not seem an overstatement to call him the midwife of a new Hardy, one who is studied psychologically.

Lawrence's psychological insights in the *Study* have, then, virtually singlehandedly instigated a change from a Victorian to a twentieth-century approach to Hardy. All subsequent readings have inevitably taken Lawrence's into account, implicitly or explicitly. But wholehearted approbation is not essential: other critics can and do take issue with the *Study* on points of detail as well as larger arguments, without demoting its historical or literary critical significance. For even the widely admired psychological dimension of the *Study* can bring in its train some problematic interpretations that have duly attracted disagreement. This is particularly the case when Lawrence appears to be reviewing Hardy's characters in the light of his own, who are moulded by their predecessors, as well as moving on from them, in several ways, especially psychosexual ones. The danger is all too obvious: the critic can come up with rationales for characters remote from the evidence presented by their creator. While we can invoke the intentional fallacy to allow the critic to suggest what the text is saying, as opposed to what the author thought it was saying, there are times when Lawrence appears to be admonishing Hardy for not being Lawrence. This seems to confirm the commonly held belief that critics write more about themselves than their subjects, as one great writer is analysed here by another with a number of similar artistic aims, which goes beyond that other widely held belief, that a later writer of genius inevitably alters our reading of what came before. And the alterations effected by Lawrence, as a critic as well as a creative writer (and he is both in the *Study*), spring from his seeing Hardy's essentially tragic characters in the kind of relationships that he is himself most interested in: relationships with one another and with themselves as individuals seeking fulfilment, with polarised personalities and moralities, loves and sexualities, with what Lawrence liked to call the spirit of place, and with the microcosmic community as well as the macrocosmic universe. Mostly, as it happens, these interests largely overlap with those of Hardy, also a novelist endeavouring – among other less-Lawrentian things, but certainly also including these Lawrentian things – to present his characters, insofar as the age allowed, in intimate sexual relationships and with acute psychological understanding. It is this psychology of characters, more overtly sexualised, that Lawrence not only develops as his own signature tune but also naturally identifies, and identifies with, in looking back to his predecessor's novels.

When Lawrence moves to the outside rather than internal forces operating on Hardy's characters, he fixes on landscape rather than fate as the prime means of placing their tragedies. Starting with *The Return of the Native*, he finds the setting gives the fiction a real tragic power:

> This is a constant revelation in Hardy's novels: that there exists a great background, vital and vivid, which matters more than the people who move upon it [...]
> This is the wonder of Hardy's novels, and gives them their beauty. The vast, unexplored morality of life itself ... and in its midst goes on the little human morality play [...]
> And this is the quality Hardy shares with the great writers, Shakespeare or Sophocles or Tolstoi, this setting behind the small action of his protagonists the terrific action of unfathomed nature, setting a smaller system of morality ... within the vast, uncomprehended and incomprehensible morality of nature or of life itself, surpassing human consciousness. (*Study*: 28–9)

In the course of his recognition of the importance of the 'great background' in Hardy, putting forward what is not only the first but remains the most eloquent, coherent and persuasive exposition of the topic, Lawrence advances to a significant addition in the idea of two kinds of morality, that of the little human characters versus that of the tremendous natural backdrop of Wessex. The latter is usually seen as amoral or nonmoral, if not, as Lawrence says

'we' call it, immoral. There is no contradiction, of course, in rejecting moralistic for psychological analysis of Hardy's characters yet
remaining a writer and critic who discusses morality as extensively
here as anywhere, but at this point Lawrence moves to a comparative downgrading of Hardy that has proved controversial. It
is actually a downgrading of Tolstoy as well as Hardy, set against
Shakespeare and Sophocles: Lawrence alleges that the latter have
their characters transgress the greater morality of nature or, indeed,
fate; the former, on the other hand, merely transgress the lesser
human morality of society's mechanical rules.

It is not clear why this 'lesser' tragedy of individuals versus society must make for lesser art, although Lawrence repeatedly asserts
this as if it were self-evident, declaring that Hardy's characters
(and Tolstoy's) should have fought against and not succumbed to
mere social pressure: he even wonders whether the situation of
these characters is properly tragic at all, as opposed to painful,
since 'they were not at war with God, only with Society' (*Study*:
30). This is an odd position to take when Lawrence's own characters, no matter that he and they talk about their relation to the
cosmos, are even more modern than Hardy's in being defined by so
much social and especially class conflict, and in so many personal
and especially sexual ways that could be said not only to go further
than Hardy's but also to be further from any Shakespearean or
Sophoclean battle with destiny or fate, gods or God. Could Hardy
or Lawrence plausibly not have had their 'lesser' kinds of modern
tragedy in their novels and still be regarded as major writers of
modern fiction? It seems unlikely.

There is a related controversial assertion – not quite so odd –
raised in the *Study*: Hardy's morality or 'metaphysic' is at war with
his art. Because he believes (again like Tolstoy) the Law must
always overcome Love, Hardy makes

clumsy efforts to push events into line with his theory of being, and to
make calamity fall on those who represent the principle of Love. He
does it exceedingly badly, and owing to this effort his form is execrable
in the extreme.

His feeling, his instinct, his sensuous understanding is, however,
apart from his metaphysic, very great and deep, deeper than that perhaps of any other English novelist. (*Study*: 93)

Typically, the trashing of Hardy's philosophy and form is immediately followed by veneration of his feeling, instinct, and 'sensuous understanding' – the very oppositions commonplace in critics of Lawrence. The characters in both writers who 'represent the principle of Love' are those who break out of the conventional mould, live passionately, and are called 'aristocrats' in the *Study*. Tess is the preeminent example here, with even her much-debated passivity beautifully seen as born from 'self-acceptance, a true aristocratic quality, amounting almost to self-indifference' (*Study* 95). Lawrence is like Hardy in championing such characters, but he is disappointed that Hardy allows his aristocrats – including Eustacia, Tess, Jude, and Sue – to be cowed and then destroyed by lesser mortals and lesser moralities.

These criticisms of Hardy's 'merely' societal tragic victims who are inartistically forced to give in when they should have been made to fight and overcome because of their individualistic 'greater light' (*Study*: 30) have been neatly answered by Phillip Mallett in relation to *Jude the Obscure* (and *Anna Karenina*), and could be extended to Lawrence's view of other Hardy novels:

Sue and Jude (or Anna and Vronsky) ought to have won, to have come through: 'they were not at war with God, only with Society'. But this is to suppose that 'society' is one identifiable target, as it were 'out there', separate from the characters; what Hardy suggests is that the values of the society are not 'out there', distinct from the consciousness of Jude and Sue, but permeate their language and their being. This point is central to our understanding of the novel. However bracing Lawrence's energy in repudiating his society, we need to recognise that Hardy's vision of his characters' relation to society is entirely different: less romantic, but perhaps more persuasive. There is no rainbow vision, no world elsewhere, for Jude and Sue.[6]

Lawrence is certainly 'bracing' in his own rejection of society in his novels and other works, but readers of his *Study of Thomas Hardy* need to be alert to the limitations of its vision as well as its refreshing originality and energy. And when he gets onto the issues where he can be reconciled, as it were, with Hardy, as in their shared vision of tragedy as not death or disaster so much as something to be endured, to be gone through with, Lawrence can be more enlightening than startling, more judiciously on target than daz-zlingly all over the place.

It is, as so often, a matter of balance. One remarkable aspect of Lawrence's blind spots, or gaps in the picture, is that they are often not only at precisely the points at which his own novels either take the matter further (when Hardy's perceived timidity or other limitation comes under attack, as shown above) or are very close to his predecessor's (when he is liable to shy away, perhaps under some anxiety of influence, or for modesty, as shown below), but also match these blanks and omissions with extraordinarily resonant original perceptions. This matching of the 'blind' and the 'perceptive' is supported (without the use of these terms) by the way in which Mark Kinkead-Weekes sees a similar balance in, say, Lawrence's criticism of *The Return of the Native*:

Of course this is Lawrence's *Return of the Native* rather than Hardy's [...] It ignores the many-sidedness of Hardy's vision and the curiously shifting relation between the author and the fiction. It produces an Eustacia too tragically heightened and released from ironies, a reddleman too reduced from enigmatic suggestiveness, an Egdon too much a Lawrentian life-force to be faithful to Hardy's multiple view of the heath and its inhabitants. Yet the deep structure Lawrence sees is there, significantly so; and the analysis of Clym is in many respects sharper than Hardy's own Victorian uncertainty about his hero.[7]

Clym in *The Return of the Native* is indeed given a sharp analysis, but perhaps the most notable feature of it is not how much but how little it deals with what is plainly closest to Lawrence's own concerns: given all the links with *Sons and Lovers*, and particularly the relationship between the heroes and their mothers, to have no reference at this point to Clym's unconscious or 'Oedipal' relationship with Mrs Yeobright is surprising. Surely this of all places is the one in which Lawrence could have contributed most to the study of Hardy, the place in which his experience by 1914, as a person and as a novelist, was most acutely relevant? Yet he does not take this opportunity. In commenting only that Clym's remorse over her 'does not ring true', being conventional and 'exaggerated by the push of tradition' (*Study*: 24), and for once ignoring any deeper psychological possibilities of the kind that are his regular fare,

Lawrence seems to be sidestepping the issue, perhaps because this time he recognised (maybe unconsciously, which would be deliciously apt) that it is *too* close to his own work. There is no such barrier of influence or modesty or whatever it might be when it comes to Tess and the others, and the penetration of Lawrence's psychological vision here indeed cuts through to a new diagnosis of the essential bases of Hardy's characters and themes.

Perhaps, though, the more subtle parallel with *Sons and Lovers* is not *The Return of the Native* but *Jude the Obscure*, as Richard Swigg has cogently suggested, among many other things in his careful tracing of the multifarious links between Hardy and Lawrence:

*Jude* ... becomes a tragedy under Lawrence's arrangement because the two principles, Law and Love, are confused. At first it seems like another *Sons and Lovers* with Jude in the place of Paul Morel. A man seeks fulfilment, awakening, in the blood and spirit, but he cannot find a woman who has both qualities in equal measure. He can find a spiritual bride in Sue (or Miriam) and a sensual bride in Arabella (or Clara), but not the two together in one woman [...] Arabella is good for [Jude], Lawrence thinks, because she scorns the mental form of his desires [...] and diverts him back on the right course. But although she gives him physical consummation, she is spiritually impotent, self-gratifying, and Jude, with his sensual manhood gained, must pass on to Sue for his spiritual and mental awakening.[8]

Such connections among the *Study* and the novels of both Hardy and Lawrence powerfully demonstrate the many different threads brought into play by Lawrence's creative as much as critical rereadings and rewritings of Hardy.

Hardy ends with *Jude*; Lawrence ends with Sue. It is often noticed that Lawrence was the first to point out that *Jude* is a reverse image of *Tess*, with all the ramifications this implies. This is not something that can be easily argued against, so some critics resistant to the *Study* prefer to focus on what they see as objectionable in his response to Sue, which allegedly sees her primarily not only as an embodiment of a sexual problem – 'She was born with the vital female atrophied in her' (*Study*: 108) – but as merely a part of Jude's experience rather than having her own independent existence. This is not, however, the whole story. What Lawrence concludes his commentary on *Jude* with is Sue not as conundrum or consort but as someone special:

Sue had a being, special and beautiful. Why must not Jude recognise it in all its specialty? [...] Why must it be assumed that Sue is an 'ordinary' woman – as if such a thing existed. Why must she feel ashamed if she is special? (*Study*: 122)

Movingly, Lawrence, left wondering why there was no place for Sue, posits reverence for life as the means of giving her a place that does not yet exist. There could hardly be a stronger testament to his own 'feminist' credentials.

Lawrence's thoughtful provoking of thought in readers of Hardy is intensely valuable in itself, whether it leads, in different aspects, to rejection or qualification or grateful recognition and acceptance of a hitherto unnoticed or unformulated truthfulness of observation. The range and acuity of his insights make them not only superb analytical achievements in themselves but also a means of inspiring – whether by arousing opposition or endorsement – further exploration and analysis by readers of Hardy's novels. Because of this, the *Study* remains as relevant a context for students of Hardy (as well as Lawrence) in the twenty-first century as it was in the twentieth. Lawrence's Hardy is by no means the only Hardy, but remains the most individual, idiosyncratically insightful, and influential response to 'the people in Thomas Hardy's novels'.

### NOTES

1 See, for example: John Alcorn, *The Nature Novel from Hardy to Lawrence* (London and Basingstoke: Macmillan, 1977), especially ch. 5, 'Hardy and Lawrence', pp. 78–89; Peter J. Casagrande, *Hardy's Influence on the Modern Novel* (Basingstoke and London: Macmillan, 1987), especially ch. 2, '"Now it Remains": Hardy and D. H. Lawrence', pp. 32–61; Terry R. Wright, 'Hardy's Heirs: D. H. Lawrence and John Cowper Powys', *A Companion to Thomas Hardy*, ed. Keith Wilson (Oxford: Wiley-Blackwell, 2009), pp. 465–78. Such assessments of Hardy's influence on Lawrence invariably also include mention of the latter's views on the former – the subject of the present chapter.

2 *Study of Thomas Hardy and Other Essays*, ed. Bruce Steele (Cambridge: Cambridge University Press, 1985): cited in the text as *Study*.

3 *The Letters of D. H. Lawrence,* vol. II, ed. George T. Zytaruk and James T. Boulton (Cambridge: Cambridge University Press, 1982), p. 212.

4 Ibid., p. 292.

5 The change from Victorian moralistic to twentieth-century psychological readings is lucidly traced by Robert Langbaum, *Thomas Hardy in Our Time* (Basingstoke and London: Macmillan, 1995), pp. 1–26.

6 Phillip Mallett, 'Sexual Ideology and Narrative Form in *Jude the Obscure*', *English* 38 (1989), p. 217.

7 Mark Kinkead-Weekes, 'Lawrence on Hardy', *Thomas Hardy After Fifty Years*, ed. L. St. J. Butler (London and Basingstoke: Macmillan, 1977), p. 93.

8 *Lawrence, Hardy, and American Literature* (London: Oxford University Press, 1972), p. 77.

# 42

# Larkin's Hardy

JOHN OSBORNE

Philip Larkin's vaunted admiration for the poetry of Thomas Hardy is a relation of betrayal as well as fidelity. Indeed, the reductive orthodoxy from which both poets need releasing is one for which Larkin is held responsible in his editing of *The Oxford Book of Twentieth-Century English Verse* (1973).[1] Disenchanted reviewers pointed out that where Eliot was allocated only nine poems, Hardy got twenty-seven, Kipling thirteen, Betjeman twelve, Graves eleven, Edward Thomas nine, Housman and de la Mare eight apiece. By allocating Hardy more poems than anyone else in an apparently anti-Modernist context, Larkin unintentionally ensured that their names would thereafter be linked as agents of reaction. In the very year of the anthology, Donald Davie's *Thomas Hardy and British Poetry* proposed that 'Hardy's engaging modesty and his decent liberalism represent a crucial selling short of the poetic vocation', while Larkin offered a 'poetry of lowered sights and patiently diminished expectations'. Fifteen years later, Ken Edwards bemoaned the fact that 'no longer does the establishment revile modernism in poetry; it simply ignores it. The models to follow once again are Hardy and Larkin.' As recently as 2004 Randall Stevenson declared in *The Last of England?* that 'Hardy's wan wistfulness and brooding regret for the past added to his appeal for Movement writers ... backward-looking in theme as well as style.'[2]

One way to broach the unfairness of the foregoing is recall the status quo at the time of Larkin's intervention. In his polemical *New Bearings in English Poetry* (1932), F. R. Leavis found only Hopkins, Eliot and Pound worthy of individual chapters. Four years later, in the *Faber Book of Modern Verse*, Michael Roberts declared the triumph of Hopkins, Yeats, Pound, Eliot, Wallace Stevens, Hart Crane, Auden, and Dylan Thomas. Equally great but less experimental poets like Hardy, Housman, Kipling, Edward Thomas, and Robert Frost were expunged from the record. When Donald Hall revised the anthology in 1965 he added poets old (William Carlos Williams, MacDiarmid, David Jones) and new (Olson, Berryman, Lowell, Thom Gunn, Hughes, Plath, Geoffrey Hill) but maintained the embargo on Hardy, Frost, Edward Thomas and company.

Larkin's Oxford anthology was an attempt to redress the balance: the Modernists would be demoted, cosmopolites would make room for a return of the native, Hardy would zoom from zero to hero. However, as Larkin candidly admitted, the 'English line' failed to provide the hoped-for neglected masterpieces, obliging him to acknowledge the superiority of the Modernists: 'the worst thing about the Georgians as a class was that their language was stale. It was Eliot and Yeats, and perhaps even Pound, who sharpened up the language.'[3] If we return to the anthology with this reluctant admission in mind and count not the poems but the actual space allocated, these are the poets best represented: Eliot with twenty-nine pages; Hardy and Auden with twenty-four each; Yeats, twenty-one; Kipling, nineteen; Betjeman, eighteen; Bunting, eleven; Dylan Thomas, ten and a half; D. H. Lawrence, ten; MacNeice, nine. Hardy might have appeared as captain of the home team in the battle against the international brigade; in practice he keeps company with Eliot, Yeats, and Auden, the only contributors to merit over twenty pages apiece, and must perforce be redefined as one of the moderns.

Regarding Larkin's specific choices, Phillip Mallett has made two pertinent points: first, 'the poems come from the full chronological range of Hardy's work'; and, second, the 'selection looks idiosyncratic'.[4] The reasons for both points may be one and the same: that Larkin was promoting the virtues of Hardy's entire *oeuvre* against the consensual view that only one poem in ten is worthwhile, the masterpieces being concentrated in the years 1912–13 following the death of the poet's first wife. Two further paradoxes are entailed. First, largely excluding the 1912–13 elegies from his anthology, Larkin scants Hardy's most personal poems, those that might be thought to reward a biographical interpretation, and thereby brings him closer to the Modernist theory of impersonality, which we associate with Eliot, Joyce, and Pound. As Eliot put it in 'Tradition and the Individual Talent' (1919), 'poetry … is not the expression of personality, but an escape from personality'.[5] This is a note Hardy struck twenty years earlier in the introduction to *Wessex Poems*

(1898) and repeated down the years, as in the preface to *Time's Laughingstocks* (1909): 'the sense of disconnection, particularly in respect of those lyrics penned in the first person, will be immaterial when it is borne in mind that they are to be regarded, in the main, as dramatic monologues by different characters'(*CP*: 190). This is the Hardy that Larkin honours by including so few poems whose narrators are ascertainably authorial ('After a Journey', 'He Never Expected Much') and so many narrated by autonomous 'characters': loyal female lovers ('She, to Him'), heartless male seducers ('I Need Not Go'), promiscuous young women ('The Ruined Maid'), grave-yard skeletons ('Channel Firing'), cemetery plants ('Voices from Things Growing in a Churchyard'), and so on.

The second paradox is that although Larkin's selection sports its fair share of the quaint and clumsy usages for which Hardy is known, earnests of his being old-fashioned, the chosen poems discontinuously unfold an ideology that is decidedly modern. God is either absent ('The Oxen') or indifferent, perhaps even malign ('The Convergence of the Twain'). The human condition is consequently characterized by existential alienation ('In Tenebris, II'). The most palpable index of the absurdity of our position in the universe is a view of death as annulment ('Thoughts of Phena', 'Where the Picnic Was', 'The Sunshade'), the only afterlife that awaits us being a vegetal return to the natural cycle ('Voices from Things Growing in a Churchyard'). Granted the brevity of life and the finality of death, allowing social conventions to diminish appreciation of our earthly span is reprehensible: war, with its accompanying patriot-isms, is folly ('Channel Firing'); the church is no longer a site of religious belief but of the this-worldly rites of music, sexual attrac-tion ('A Church Romance') and burial ('During Wind and Rain'); marital propriety is often destructive ('The Newcomer's Wife'), whereas those who lead sexually scandalous lives have more fun than the respectable ('The Ruined Maid', 'The Mound'). Nature can be consolatory in its beauty ('If It's Ever Spring Again') and its mystery ('The Year's Awakening'), the poems affirming respect for other forms of animal life ('Snow in the Suburbs'). This does not alter the fact that our journey to the grave is experienced as the opposite of a welcome return to Mother Nature's embrace. Rather, time's relentlessness renders ironical our hopes and expectations. The best we can hope for is to see through our delusions – to be one of Larkin's *less deceived* – and thereby make our peace with the littleness of life ('He Never Expected Much').

None of this is to deny the shock of the new when turning from Larkin's Hardy to Larkin's Eliot. The earliest Eliot poem in the Oxford anthology, 'The Love Song of J. Alfred Prufrock', completed in 1911, already makes existing poetic registers, including Hardy's, look antique. However, what Larkin's selections as insistently document is that at the level of belief, as opposed to style, Eliot's is the more reactionary development. From the estrangement of 'Prufrock' and the nihilism of *The Waste Land* (though that poem ends with the sound of thunder, promising spiritually regenerative rain) via the agonized Christian rebirth of 'Journey of the Magi' and *Murder in the Cathedral* (excerpts) to the luminously transcendental 'Little Gidding', Eliot is shown zealously striding forward into the pre-Nietzschean past. At the ideological level, Hardy is more Modernist than Modernists like Eliot; where they retreated from the nuclear crisis of modernity, the death of God, he, like his admirer Larkin, kept faith with his lack of faith.

It was likely, wrote Eliot, that 'poets in our civilization, as it exists at present, must be *difficult*'.[6] Larkin's favourite debating ploy was to oppose the pleasure principle to this Modernist concept of difficulty: 'The poetry I've enjoyed has been the kind of poetry you'd associate with me, Hardy pre-eminently ... people who accept the forms they have inherited but use them to express their own content.'[7] One Modernist 'technique' he was particularly scathing about was literary allusion, as the need for explication can only appeal to academics and will be experienced by lay readers as intimidating and obscure. The example of Hardy is the opposite: 'When I came to Hardy it was with a sense of relief that I didn't have to try and jack myself up to a concept of poetry that lay outside my own life – this is perhaps what I felt Yeats was trying to make me do.'[8]

There is something disingenuous about this argument. Even if we agree (as a growing minority of revisionist critics would not) that Hardy's poems avoid the dense allusiveness of an Eliot, the description of him as one of the poets 'who accept the forms they have inherited' itself implies an art characterized by citation. Hymn tunes, ballad metres, sonnets, quatrains, nursery rhymes, refrains – these and other staples of the English tradition are not timeless and unbounded, they are historically and culturally embedded. To use them is to orientate the new text in relation to previous ones; in other words, to allude.

Despite this obvious truth, it has become a critical commonplace to regard Hardy's and Larkin's eschewal of citation as an aspect of their anti-Modernism. W. E. Williams introduced his *Thomas Hardy: A Selection of Poems* (1960) by defining Hardy's *oeuvre* as uniquely free from influence or echo:

One of the favourite occupations of a certain kind of scholar is to detect the 'influences' revealed by a writer's work, to ferret out the clues which show how and where he assimilated other styles into his own. As C. Day Lewis has so aptly said: 'Influence-spotters don't have a very happy time with him.' Hardy's poems, like his novels, derive from his own nature, experience, and integrity, and it is this characteristic which makes his testimony so personal and so moving.[9]

A. T. Tolley, a leading player in the Larkin debate, is equally adamant that 'there is little use of inter-texuality (conscious or unconscious) in Larkin's work: the reference to other literatures as a dimension of understanding ... was anathema to him.'[10] This is an orthodoxy that cannot withstand so much as a glance at the contents pages of the two poets, their respective titles suggesting a musical as well as a temperamental affinity. Consider Hardy's 'Prologue' (Larkin's 'Prologue'), 'First Sight of Her and After' ('First Sight'), 'On a Midsummer Eve' ('Midsummer Night'), 'Memory and I' ('I Remember, I Remember'), 'Going and Staying' ('Arrivals, Departures'), 'The Going' ('Going'), 'On the Departure Platform' ('One man walking a deserted platform'), 'At the Railway Station, Upway' ('Autobiography at an Air-Station'), 'Departure' ('Poetry of Departures'), 'She, I, and They' ('Mother, Summer, I'), 'Winter Night in Woodland' ('Winter Nocturne'), 'The Man Who Forgot' ('Forget What Did'), 'He Resolves to Say No More' ('The Poet's Last Poem') and 'Epilogue' ('Epilogue').

As with the titles, so with the poems, many Larkin pieces directly invoking a Hardy prototype. The first two verses of 'In Sherborne Abbey' lurk behind the arras of 'An Arundel Tomb'. 'Skin' is shadowed by Hardy's 'I Look Into My Glass' ('I look into my glass, / And view my wasting skin': *CP*: 81). 'The Oxen', which Larkin included in his Oxford anthology, underwrites the close of 'Climbing the hill within the deafening wind'. The celebrated ending of 'Toads Revisited' ('Give me your arm, old toad, / Help me down Cemetery Road') is modelled on the first of Hardy's 1866 'She, to Him' sequence ('Will you not grant to old affection's claim / The hand of friendship down Life's sunless hill?'[11] Various of Hardy's train journey poems capture the frame-by-frame succession of views from a carriage window, as in 'Faintheart in a Railway Train', in a manner that may have left an imprint upon 'The Whitsun Weddings'. 'The Selfsame Song' meditates on birds in a manner akin to Larkin's 'The Trees', the last line of which ('Begin afresh, afresh, afresh') was anticipated by Hardy's 'Song to an Old Burden' ('Shall I then joy anew anew anew').[12]

It is a token of Larkin's high regard that he sometimes used a Hardy echo to challenge a citation from another author incorporated in the same poem. Sidney's *Astrophel and Stella* supplies the title of 'Sad Steps' but Larkin deflates that source in the spirit of Hardy's 'Shut Out That Moon' and 'I Looked Up from My Writing'. 'The Mower' invokes four poems of that name by Andrew Marvell, but draws its tone and substance from the third verse of Hardy's 'Afterwards'. 'This Be the Verse' plucks its title from Robert Louis Stevenson's 'Requiem' only to savagely undercut that sentimental elegy with strophes modelled on Hardy's 'Epitaph for a Pessimist'. Time and again, Hardy's manner and music are administered as 'correctives' to the more inflated rhetoric of earlier masters. Far from using Hardy as a portal into the past, as critics like Samuel Hynes have claimed, Larkin uses him as a litmus test in subjecting 'the tradition' to the acids of modernity.[13]

In those instances where Larkin uses Hardy as an antidote to other authors, the argument of the poem is conducted through a contention of citations in a manner much more in keeping with Modernist aesthetics than with Larkin's own propaganda: 'Poems don't come from other poems, they come from being oneself in life.'[14] This fidelity through betrayal is replicated at the thematic level, Larkin referencing Hardy at the expense of others while refusing to be subservient to the master's views. One way we can explore this and simultaneously offer a refreshment of the Larkin debate is by pursuing Hardy's unremarked influence upon the poem 'Aubade'.

Andrew Motion suggests that 'Aubade' was stalled until the poet's mother died on 17 November 1977 and provided the impetus to finish the work.[15] The truth is less oedipal, more text-centred, more indebted to Hardy. The first three verses were written in 1974 and the poem then set aside incomplete. Larkin resumed work on it on 18 May 1977 – *six months before his mother's death* – in response to a request for a poem commemorating the fiftieth anniversary of Hardy's death. Contrary to the biographical consensus, it was Hardy's death half a century earlier, rather than Eva Larkin's death half a year hence, that released Larkin's writer's block and allowed him to complete his last masterpiece.

In his introduction to the Faber cassette recording of 'Aubade', Larkin implies that even the subject of his poem was inspired by Hardy:

In 1871 Thomas Hardy wrote in his notebook: 'Dawn. Lying just after waking. The sad possibilities of the future are more vivid than at any other time.' I've always found this true. And there came a time when it seemed more sensible to get up and write about it, rather than lie there worrying. The result was this poem, 'Aubade'.[16]

Moreover, behind Larkin's strong lines one feels the pressure of a dozen Hardy poems on the interlinked themes of insomnia, pre dawn intimations of mortality and the slow resumption of everyday life at sunrise – a pressure that sometimes breaks surface to form a distinct echo or allusion. 'Aubade' begins by specifying the hour ('Waking at four') and ends by describing the in-creeping dawn ('Slowly light strengthens') in language strikingly close to the opening lines of 'Four in the Morning': 'At four this day of June I rise: / The dawn-light strengthens steadily' (*CP*: 714). The drabness of Larkin's dawn ('The sky is white as clay, with no sun') is anticipated in 'Haunting Fingers': 'the morning sky grew greyer, / And day crawled in' (*CP*: 592). Larkin's undermining of the lovers motif of the traditional aubade, *eros* succumbing to *thanatos* ('Unresting death a whole day nearer now'), is shared with Hardy's 'The New Dawn's Business' in which the narrator asks: 'What are you doing outside my walls, / O Dawn of another day? ... / And your face so deedily grey?' The dawn replies with a list of that day's 'odd jobs', most of them decidedly grim: 'I show a light for killing the man / Who lives not far from you, / ... And for earthing a corpse or two' (*CP*: 835). Again, the terminal self-questioning of Hardy's 'I looked back' ('I shall a last time see / This picture; when will that time be?') is reprised in the anxiety of the narrator of 'Aubade' pondering 'how / And where and when I shall myself die'.[17]

Here we face another instance of fidelity spiced with betrayal, for in adapting Hardy to his purpose Larkin edits him from an agnostic into an atheist. 'Aubade' is categorical that religion is bogus ('That vast moth-eaten musical brocade / Created to pretend we never die') and death final ('the total emptiness for ever, / The sure extinction that we travel to'), while the God concept is so redundant as not to merit mention. Hardy, by contrast, defined himself as an agnostic and rationalized his shift from novelist to poet as a means to make apparent to hostile opinion his distance from atheism (*LW*: 302). His poems repeatedly attempt to de-anthropomorphize and de-Christianize God:

> 'O we are waiting for one called God,' said they,
> '(Though by some the Will, or Force, or Laws;
> And, vaguely, by some, the Ultimate Cause)'
>
> (*CP*: 513)

The welter of signifiers conveys how belief in God has come unstuck but not, as in Larkin, its total abandonment. Similarly, Larkin's allusions, like his Oxford anthology, conveniently ignore those Hardy poems in which ghosts retain such powers as to posit a life after death. The anthology finds room for 'After a Journey', whose 'voiceless ghost' may be read as a metaphor for the haunting of the bereaved by memories of a lost loved one; but not for 'I Travel as a Phantom Now', 'The Dead Man Walking', 'Ah, Are You Digging on my Grave?' or 'The Levelled Churchyard' (in which the dead voice the fear that their identities will be jumbled together in a graveyard clearance, as though humans posthumously retain an holistic sense of self). Every great writer invents his or her own ancestry: Larkin's Hardy is Hardy revised and expurgated to late twentieth-century taste.

For half a century critics have recycled the stereotype of Larkin as the High Priest of Miserabilism. Detractors like Scupham (for whom Larkin is 'the melancholic mouse-trap maker of Hull') are able to claim that any positives in his verse are drained of life by a swarm of qualifiers, negative prefixes and suffixes.[18] Limiting ourselves for the sake of brevity to vocables prefixed with *un-*, we can quickly discover examples that are indisputably negative in meaning: unworkable, unswept, uninformed, unsatisfactory, unrecommended, untruthful and untruth. However, just as numerous are cases of *what might have been* in which the negativity may be attributed to free will rather than to deterministic forces and may therefore have been otherwise: 'my childhood was unspent'; 'Unchilded and unwifed'; 'the unraised hand calm, / The apple unbitten in the palm'; 'love unused, in unsaid words'; 'unshared friends and unwalked ways'. Other such usages shade towards the positive end of the emotional spectrum, describing conditions of tranquillity: undisturbed, undriven, unhurried, unforced, untried, untroubled, untalkative, unriven, 'the soul unjostled, / The pocket unpicked'. Yet more positive are those words that express energy (unresting) or freedom (unbarred, unfenced, unhindered) or opportunity (potential is 'unlimited'). Outright positives include: unfakable, unlosable, unspoilt, undiminished, unfingermarked, unmolesting; expressions such as 'set unchangeably in order', 'blindingly undiminished' and 'unvariably lovely there' increasing their powers of affirmation by incorporating (so as to negate) a hint of the negative.[19] When one remembers that there are approximately one hundred and fifty different *un-* words in Larkin's *Collected Poems* (and nearly fifty with the suffix *-less*), the view of his diction as unvaryingly desolate and desolating seems absurd: he gets a broader emotional range out of negatively prefixed words than do most poets from the open dictionary. At the same time, the combination in single vocables of positive and negative inflections serves to place that emotional content in an historically specific, post-Nietzschean universe stripped of transcendentals. All of this, Larkin learned from Hardy.

Larkin was adamant that Hardy is 'not a transcendental writer, he's not a Yeats, he's not an Eliot; his subjects are men, the life of men, time and the passing of time, love and the fading of love'.[20] Larkin dates his admiration to 'the morning I first read "Thoughts of Phena At News of Her Death"', a poem that combines the commonplace 'unease' with the arresting 'Disennoble' and the altogether remarkable 'unsight' (*CP*: 62). Elsewhere Hardy offers 'the unslumbering sea' (compare with Larkin's 'unhindered moon'); 'why unblooms the best hope ever sown?'; 'I, unknowing you'; 'I sang that song in summer, / All unforeknowingly'; 'time untouched me'; 'The whole day long I unfulfil'; and, in the heartrending 'Tess's Lament', 'I'd have my life unbe'.[21] In my opinion Larkin was drawn to Hardy less for his Englishness, as many commentators claim, than for a fidelity to doubt encapsulated in this fixation with negative prefixes. And this is central to their joint bequest to poets of the new millennium.

Consider the case of Carol Ann Duffy, who differs from Hardy and Larkin in so many ways: as woman, parent, Poet Laureate, unabashed bisexual – for she too must betray as well as emulate if she is not to be lost in their vapour trails. Duffy's latest collection, *Rapture* (2005), a love poem in fifty-two parts, consciously duets with Larkin: the title piece echoes 'High Windows'; 'Bridgewater Hall' descants on 'Broadcast'; and the last movement of 'Wintering' invokes 'Morning At Last'. Hardy's presence may be indirect but is still palpable: the third line of 'Spring' ('rain's mantra of reprieve, reprieve, reprieve') echoes the last line of Larkin's 'The Trees' which we have already seen to be indebted to Hardy's 'Song to an Old Burden'. More pertinently, as the love affair charted in the book begins to unravel so the *un-* words accumulate: six in the short 'Grief'; four uses of 'unloving' in the poem of that name; while in the last stanza of the last poem, 'Over', the beloved's name is described as 'a key, unlocking all the dark'.[22] If behind these Duffy poems one hears the distant reverberation of, say, Larkin's 'Talking in Bed', anterior to them all one senses a generalized debt to such Hardy poems as 'The Going' in which a sequence of *un-* words provides the poem, vertebra by vertebra, with its hidden backbone (Unmoved, unknowing, unrolled, Unchangeable), the effect of which becomes fully apparent only in the very last words:

> O you could not know
> That such swift fleeing
> No soul foreseeing –
> Not even I – would undo me so!
> (*CP*: 339)

This is the Hardy I have tried to delineate in this essay: the one who realizes that once God is removed as transcendental guarantor, all hierarchies are undone and all discourses relativized; the one who even as he gestures towards region, tribe and indigeneity, remains unhoused from any concept of home or belonging; the one whose example is of active use to poets as different and as considerable as Larkin and Duffy; the one in whose works, so often regarded as backward-looking and quaint, the future keeps breaking through.

NOTES

1 Philip Larkin, ed., *The Oxford Book of Twentieth-Century English Verse* (Oxford: Oxford University Press, 1973).

2 Donald Davie, *Thomas Hardy and British Poetry* (London: Kegan Paul, 1973), pp. 40, 71; Ken Edwards, *The New British Poetry, 1968–88*, ed. Gillian Allnutt and others (London: Paladin, 1988), p. 265; Randall Stevenson, *The Last of England?: The Oxford Literary History, vol. XII, 1960–2000* (Oxford: Oxford University Press, 2004), p. 171.

3 Philip Larkin, *Further Requirements: Interviews, Broadcasts, Statements and Book Reviews, 1952–1985*, ed. Anthony Thwaite (London: Faber, 2001), p. 97.

4 Phillip Mallett, 'Seamus Heaney's Larkin, Philip Larkin's Hardy', *Rivista di Studi Vittoriani* 26 (2011), p. 85.

5 *T. S. Eliot: Selected Prose*, ed. John Hayward (Harmondsworth: Penguin Books, 1963), p. 29.

6 'The Metaphysical Poets', ibid., p. 112.

7 Larkin, *Further Requirements*, p. 19.

8 Ibid., p. 54.

9 W. E. Williams, ed., *Thomas Hardy: A Selection of Poems* (Harmondsworth: Penguin Books, 1960), p. 15.

10 A. T. Tolley, *My Proper Ground: A Study of the Work of Philip Larkin and its Development* (Edinburgh: Edinburgh University Press, 1991), p. 177.

11 Philip Larkin, *Collected Poems*, ed. Anthony Thwaite (London: Marvell and Faber, 1988) p. 148; Hardy, *CP*: 115.

12 Larkin, *Collected Poems*, p. 166; Hardy, *CP*: 830.

13 Samuel Hynes, ed., *Thomas Hardy, Selected Poems* (Oxford: Oxford University Press, 1996), p. xxii.

14 Larkin, *Further Requirements*, p. 54.

15 Andrew Motion, *Philip Larkin: A Writer's Life* (London, Faber, 1993).

16 *Douglas Dunn and Philip Larkin: Faber Poetry Cassette* (London: Faber, 1984).

17 Larkin, *Collected Poems*, pp. 208–9; *CP*: 913.

18 Peter Scupham, 'A Caucus-race', *Phoenix* 11/12 (Autumn–Winter, 1973–4), p. 174.

19 Larkin, *Collected Poems*, pp. 81, 195, 125, 31, 50, 40, 113, 106, 72.

20  Philip Larkin, *Required Writing: Miscellaneous Pieces, 1955–1982* (London: Faber, 1983), p. 175.

21  Larkin, *Required Writing*, pp. 29–30; *CP*: 323, 9, 235, 577, 578, 579, 177.

22  Carol Ann Duffy, *Rapture* (London: Picador, 2005), pp. 55, 62.

## 43

# Hardy on Film

ROGER WEBSTER

The relationship between Hardy's novels and film has received considerable critical attention: as early as 1922, six years before Hardy's death, Joseph Warren Beach considered his writing as being like a 'movie'.[1] More recently, in his introduction to Hardy's epic poem *The Dynasts*, John Wain notes 'The presiding eye is that of the film camera […] *The Dynasts* is neither a poem, nor a play, nor a story. It is a shooting script.'[2] In 'Thomas Hardy as Cinematic Novelist' David Lodge identifies narrative techniques which antic-ipate methods developed in film, especially the presentation of scenes as if viewed through a camera lens.[3] Lodge argues that it is not just the techniques of visualisation which have parallels with cinema, but also the lack of an authoritative omniscience in the narrator's voice: Its neutrality or disinterestedness is akin to a film scene without a voiceover. By the time Lodge's essay was published in 1981, there had been two recent major feature film adaptations of Hardy's novels, John Schlesinger's *Far from the Madding Crowd* (1967) and Roman Polanski's *Tess* (1979), and with the number of adaptations since then, especially for television, the way in which we read Hardy is increasingly coloured by cinematic awareness: for many readers, their first encounters with his fiction may well be through screen versions. Of Hardy's fourteen published nov-els, at least nine have been adapted for screen and of these several have had successive versions, most notably *Tess of the d'Urbervilles* (1891);[4] there have also been screen adaptations of Hardy's short stories, mainly for television. The first film versions were pro-duced during Hardy's lifetime: in 1913 in America of *Tess of the d'Urbervilles,* followed by *Far from the Madding Crowd* (1874) in 1915 and *The Mayor of Casterbridge* (1886) in 1921, both British, and another American version of *Tess* in 1924. Hardy was aware of these productions, especially of *Tess*, and expressed concerns about the first, disliking its American qualities. The second version was also American but much of it was filmed on location in Dorset, which apparently pleased Hardy, although the historical setting was moved to the 1920s and he never saw it.

Hardy's fictional writing has strong visual qualities, which draw in particular on painting, arguably anticipate cinema and lend themselves well to screen adaptation. He had a profound interest in and knowledge of painting, both classical and contemporary; his novels contain many references to art by mainly Italian and Dutch painters but also, particularly in his later writing, to Turner. The allusions to painting are complemented by his use of a number of techniques that might be described as painterly: framing, lighting and colour effects, chiaroscuro, and scenes which are distinctive in terms of landscape or portraiture. The relationship between painting and cinema has been discussed in more general critical approaches as well as specifically with regard to Hardy, including the influence of Turner, whose later paintings have a kinetic or indeed with hindsight a cinematic quality.[5] While writing *The Woodlanders* Hardy wrote in his journal:

I don't want to see landscapes, i.e., scenic paintings of them, because I don't want to see the original realities [...] The much decried, mad, late-Turner rendering is now necessary to create my interest. (*LW*: 192)

A couple of years later he admired Turner's water colours, paintings of '*light as modified by objects*', and mentions his experimental 'strange mixtures', singling out oil paintings such as 'Rain, Steam and Speed' and 'Snowstorm and a Steamboat' which unlike his more static early works foreground dynamic movement (*LW*: 225–6). The emphasis on and development of the visual in Hardy's fiction can be seen as a parallel to Turner's development from traditional classical subject matter and techniques to the 'mad, late-Turner rendering'; Hardy's shift from the pastoral stasis of *Under the Greenwood Tree* (1872), interestingly subtitled as 'A Rural Painting of the Dutch School', to the tensions of the increasingly mobile, shifting plots and texture of the later novels brings his writing closer to cinema as well as to painting.

*A Pair of Blue Eyes* (1873) offers an example of cinematic technique in Hardy's novels. It is an early work, not yet on screen, though recognising its 'cinematically vivid descriptions' David Lodge had a plan to adapt it.[6] The scene at the beginning of chapter 22 involves

Knight clinging to a cliff whilst Elfride, the heroine, attempts to rescue him from above by making an improvised rope from her undergarments. The intense visualisation of the scene ranges from the panoramic and long-shot effect of Knight hanging on the cliff, to close-up descriptions of details of the landscape, in particular of a trilobite fossil embedded in the cliff face which seems to regard him. Much of the episode's significance is generated not only by Knight's thoughts on his predicament, but also by the visual dynamics, equivalent to cinematic montage, which suggest his situation in both immediate and more universal historical terms: not so much a narrative voice as a camera lens implying significance. To quote John Wain again, 'The cinema by-passes language and talks to us directly in images, so that these images take on symbolic force.'[7]

Recent feature film adaptations have turned to what are usually considered Hardy's major novels, and indeed have contributed significantly to the creation of a Hardy 'canon', shaping which texts are classified as his major and minor novels.[8] Although they lend themselves well to cinematic treatment, a film version of a novel is itself an autonomous text and should not necessarily be judged on how faithful it is to the original text.[9] John Schlesinger's *Far from the Madding Crowd*, released in 1967, set the tone for a number of adaptations in terms of cinematography, sound score, rural setting and pastoral tone. In plot and physical setting it follows the novel closely, especially in its evocations of nineteenth-century rural landscape. Where it departs from the novel and employs cinematic licence, the techniques employed enhance significant themes and moments of experience. For example, after Bathsheba has sent Boldwood an anonymous valentine card, in the film he stares obsessively at the teasing words 'Marry Me' written on it. At the end of the scene the camera moves to a close-up shot of two clocks ticking relentlessly and the heads of Boldwood's two dogs following him in unison: the detailed shot works as an unspoken narratorial comment on the situation. In the novel, only a single clock is briefly mentioned, but there is an extended narratorial comment on Boldwood's situation: the expanded film shot provides a significant cinematic equivalent. A later scene, in which Joseph Poorgrass returns from the Casterbridge workhouse with Fanny Robin's coffin, is shot with a distorting lens technique to provide Joseph's blurred drunken perspective. In the novel, Gabriel finds Joseph the worse for drink at an inn and drives him back, but there is little emphasis on the journey: the cinematic licence again enhances the narrative, anticipating by optical distortions the emotional disturbances to come, as well as providing a note of humour. The film is more faithful to the novel by not slavishly mirroring it.

Schlesinger's production creates an interesting blend: the representation of historical verisimilitude as nineteenth-century Wessex/Dorset, shot largely on location with impressive cinematography by Nicholas Roeg, combined with a 1960s tone. Bathsheba is played by Julie Christie, the iconic female face of the 'swinging sixties', having starred in films such as *Darling* (1965) and *Dr Zhivago* (1965), the first also directed by Schlesinger; Terence Stamp, with his Zapata moustache, who plays Sergeant Troy, and had appeared in a number of 1960s films, notably *The Collector* (1965) and *Modesty Blaise* (1966), anticipates the album cover of the Beatles' *Sergeant Pepper's Lonely Hearts Club Band* in the same year as the film. There is a general, if not strongly foregrounded, alternative 'pop' feel to the film with its rural imagery, folksy music, and Alan Bates's shepherd's garb reminiscent of the Carnaby Street Afghan coats: as if *The Incredible String Band* meets Thomas Hardy in Wessex instead of Woodstock. Schlesinger's film offers a historically displaced version of pastoral and of a potential organic community, which is very much a product of the *zeitgeist*. Combined with these qualities is the larger theme of 'Englishness', which the film is both the product of and a contributor to: that is, the ideological formation of English national identity and culture which becomes prominent in the early twentieth century. A particular feature of Englishness is the pastoral myth associated with the 'organic' community;[10] William Empson defined pastoral as 'putting the complex into the simple'[11] and although Hardy's title for the novel can be seen as an ironic antidote to simplified urban perspectives on the rural scene,[12] Schlesinger's film tends to affirm a pastoral vision of social cohesion temporarily disturbed by the intrusion of Sergeant Troy.

Roman Polanski's *Tess* was the next major feature-film adaptation, and again, although attempting faithfulness to the novel in a number of ways, it has certain contemporary features and allusions. It was shot largely in Brittany and Normandy as equivalents to

Dorset, to avoid the extradition agreement between Britain and the United States, where Polanski was wanted for sex with an underage girl; even a nineteenth-century version of Stonehenge was constructed in France. There are fortuitous parallels between Polanski's biography and the novel's narrative: alienation and exile, seduction and rape, crime and punishment. Polanski has also said that he was drawn to the novel by his first wife Sharon Tate, who was murdered in 1969 by Charles Manson's sect, and to whom the film is dedicated: again there are potential parallels around the sacrificial victim theme. The characters are played by less well-known actors than in *Far from the Madding Crowd* and the film lacks modish qualities, although Natassja Kinski who plays Tess in her first major film is the daughter of Klaus Kinski, the celebrated German actor and director; Peter Firth plays Angel Clare, and Leigh Lawson, Alec d'Urberville. The running time is around three hours dependent on version, considerably longer than the norm for feature films, and its striking visual qualities won an Oscar for the cinematographer Geoffrey Unsworth, who died during its making, together with Ghislain Cloquet who took over. The film was commercially successful but met with mixed critical acclaim.[13]

Although Polanski's *Tess* shares the emphasis on landscape and visual effects with Schlesinger's *Far from the Madding Crowd*, it avoids clichéd pastoralism and modish allusions, focusing on the character of Tess. The landscape and environment tend to act as an illuminating backdrop rather than dynamic and contradictory forces that combine to destroy her, although there are some notable exceptions such as the threshing machine scene and the period at Flintcomb-Ash. As Peter Widdowson argues, the film is in the mould of Polanski's 'fascination with psychological disturbance, violence, and destructive sexuality as motifs',[14] previously explored in films such as *Repulsion* (1965) or *Rosemary's Baby* (1968), although the narrative does not offer the potential for, nor does Polanski attempt to represent, these areas in depth. Rather, the character of Tess becomes a dehistoricised figure of alienation, an existential character who has more in common with Sarah Woodruff, the heroine of John Fowles's *The French Lieutenant's Woman* (1967). What the film foregrounds most strongly is Tess's dilemma as a figure of romantic tragedy, rather than someone trapped by the social and economic forces and contradictions of 'environment': class, gender, religion, and modernity. This is not to diminish the film, nor to suggest it fails as a reproduction of the novel: it avoids the trap of attempting slavish faithfulness and of being too strongly located within the climate of its moment of production. It also offers a less idealised treatment of community and representation of Englishness than Schlesinger's *Far from the Madding Crowd*.

There have been several screen productions of *Tess of the d'Urbervilles* for television following Polanski's film, the most notable being the 2008 BBC adaptation broadcast directed by David Blair. The total running time of the four episodes is four hours, allowing extended screenplay and emphasis on the depiction of landscape and setting, both to powerful effect. David Nicholls's screenplay provides depth and detail, for example in the attention given early in the adaptation to Alec d'Urberville's relationship with his mother and the depiction of his domestic setting. At the conclusion, Nicholls indulges in some screen licence, of which Hardy might well have approved, introducing flashback scenes just prior to Tess's execution, where the opening May-Day dancing episode is reenacted through her imagination and she now dances with Angel Clare. The cinematography is again impressive: the production was shot in 35mm format as opposed to the more usual Super 16mm for television, which provides greater picture quality and potential for panorama and detail. Shot largely in Dorset, Wiltshire, and Gloucestershire, the environment inevitably feels more indigenous than does Polanski's *Tess*. The overall visual tone is closer to Turner's watercolours than the stronger hues reminiscent of his dynamic oil paintings in both Schlesinger's *Far from the Madding Crowd* and Polanski's *Tess*.

The adaptation is frequently more naturalistic (apparently actors were prohibited from wearing make-up throughout filming) and compared to many of the more chocolate-box television adaptations of nineteenth-century novels in recent decades has a washed-out, visceral feel. The character performances are strong although largely from relatively unknown actors, in particular Gemma Arterton's Tess, who in contrast to Kinski provides a dynamic and ambivalent presence alternating between passive victim and active protagonist. Alec d'Urberville, played by Hans Matheson, is less Leigh Lawson's dashing cad and more an amoral nouveau-riche figure linked to changing class and wealth structures, who threatens Tess not just sexually but economically. The scene in which Tess visits Angel's parents during his absence abroad and her hardships at Flintcomb-Ash provides a good contrast between the two versions. The wider conspiring forces of religion and class determining Tess's predicament are thoughtfully emphasised in the BBC production, unlike Polanski's more concentrated focus on the emotional impact and interplay of character. Finally, the music scores of the two versions are significant: Polanski, in keeping with the richer colour palette, employs stirring music reminiscent of Elgar or Vaughan Williams, whereas Rob Lane's score for Blair's production is more plangent and elegiac, complementing the visual tones and avoiding the richer overtones of a musical rural Englishness.

The next feature film of a Hardy novel, following Polanski's *Tess*, is Michael Winterbottom's *Jude* (1996), a joint English and American production also broadcast on television. It is immediately striking for the shift from monochrome in its early scenes set around Marygreen to full colour as Jude moves to Christminster. This is not an entirely original technique but very appropriate to the novel:[15] Hardy's use of the colour spectrum across his novels changes considerably, from the varied intense hues and emphasis on colour terminology in novels such as *Far from the Madding Crowd*, *The Woodlanders* (1887), and *Tess* to the more subdued and restricted tones of *The Return of the Native* (1878) and in particular *Jude the Obscure* (1896). The shift from monochrome to colour early in *Jude*, combined with exaggerated camera perspectives, evokes the novel's opening scenes: as Paul Niemeyer remarks, Winterbottom 'uses his locations to create a sense of barrenness and dislocation. If anything, this *seems* like what a film of *Jude the Obscure* should look like.'[16] Indeed *Jude* is a very painterly film, with allusions to Turner, Italian and Dutch classical art, and possibly Manet and French Impressionism, which complement the novel's visual qualities and references and acknowledge Hardy's strong interest in art.[17]

Winterbottom's *Jude* departs significantly from the literary text in a number of ways; with a running time of 122 minutes there is an obvious need for selectivity and compression. In an interesting comparison between the film and the BBC's 1971 adaptation directed by Hugh David, which has a running time of 262 minutes, Robert Schweik argues that although superficially David's version is more 'faithful' to the literary text, Winterbottom's film captures more of the essential qualities and significance of the novel by deviating imaginatively from it.[18] The pig-killing episode is a very good example: in David's version the scene is rendered largely through dialogue between Jude and Arabella, combined with the pig's squeals, whereas in Winterbottom's we see the gory slaughtering and then a series of butchering shots interspersed with Jude trying to study before wandering off into a bleak landscape, conveying poignantly through sequencing and juxtaposition Jude's dilemma and the contradictions in which he is trapped. Both versions depart from the novel's narrative, but Winterbottom's is more inventive and generates a more complex and profound set of meanings. The film *Jude* suggests that by not slavishly following the novel, the screen version may come closer to the literary experience while retaining cinematic autonomy and integrity.

The final feature film to consider here is *The Claim* (2000), a version of *The Mayor of Casterbridge*, again directed by Michael Winterbottom. As the departure from the novel's title indicates, it does not attempt to offer a direct adaptation or invite comparison; the only acknowledgement to the novel is in the closing titles. Set in 1860s California during the Gold Rush, it was filmed on location in Canada and America; the screenplay is by Frank Cottrell Boyce, and it is difficult to view in direct relation to the novel, raising the question of how far adaptation can be stretched. The displacement in geographical if not historical setting frees the audience from viewing the film with reference to the novel, but as in Winterbottom's *Jude*, though in a yet more indirect way, there are significant and powerful parallels with the novel. At the level of character and plot, there is considerable mirroring: the equivalent to Michael Henchard is Daniel Dillon, played by Peter Mullen, who has become in effect the owner-ruler of a town named 'Kingdom Come', developed from the wealth of the claim to a mining stake he acquired in exchange for his wife and child, the former played by Natassja Kinski. The pivotal figure in the novel, Donald Farfrae, is represented by Donald Dalglish, played by Wes Bentley, the Pacific Railway's Chief Engineer who like Farfrae personifies new technology and a threat to the established order, again with a suggestion of Scottishness in his name. The narrative involves Dalglish befriending Dillon, while the proposed railway which Dillon desires eventually has to by-pass Kingdom Come for geographical reasons, thus threatening its existence. Concurrently Dillon's former wife Elena, who is terminally ill, returns with her daughter Hope to find Dillon; Dalglish befriends and eventually marries Hope.

The mechanics of the plot work very well in the transposed environment, and 'environment' in a Hardyesque sense is key to an initially less obvious but stronger parallel with and relationship to the novel. The remote American setting constructs a minimal and elemental backdrop which complements the skeletal plot of the film. Although it lacks the subtle and weblike structures of the landscapes and communities of the Wessex novels, a combination of social and natural forces ultimately conspires to determine events beyond Dillon's seeming omnipotence. The historical context reduces human transactions to the cash-nexus: almost every interchange and relationship is determined by gold or money, which are foregrounded throughout. Dillon can only express emotion, especially guilt, through materialism; at the centre of the plot is the revelation, through flashback, of the fundamental transaction which has led to great wealth and power but loss of wife, child, and feeling. Dillon's hubris is the major developing theme of the film, as is Henchard's in the novel, and it is a neat literary conceit that early in the film a character recites the end of Shelley's 'Ozymandias' (1818) in Dillon's presence. The film avoids a conventional treatment of the novel, in effect defamiliarising Hardy, removing characters and plot from the Wessex setting that characterises every novel to a greater or lesser extent and virtually every adaptation, but by doing so focuses on and distils individual actions and their relationship to wider social, historical and natural forces in ways which relate closely to the novel.

To conclude, screen versions of Hardy's fiction can offer more than versions of literary texts in a different medium, or a more accessible way into Hardy's novels and short stories. They can stand as major cinematic works in their own right: directors of the calibre of Schlesinger, Polanski and Winterbottom are not interested in offering mere filmic imitations of Hardy's novels. To view these films without having read the novels they are based on does not necessarily diminish the film experience. On the other hand, it is testament to Hardy's enduring power and influence as a writer that great directors are drawn to his works, and equally that their films can and do provide illuminating, highly creative perspectives on and extensions of Hardy's fiction.

NOTES

1 Joseph Warren Beach, *The Technique of Thomas Hardy* (Chicago: University of Chicago Press, 1920), p. 134. The title 'Movie' is also given to his chapter on *The Mayor of Casterbridge* and *The Woodlanders*.

2 John Wain, 'Introduction' to Thomas Hardy, *The Dynasts* (London: Macmillan, 1965), p. x.

3 David Lodge, 'Thomas Hardy as Cinematic Novelist', *Working with Structuralism* (London: Routledge and Kegan Paul, 1981).

4 For the most recent filmography of screen adaptations see T. R. Wright, ed., *Thomas Hardy on Screen* (Cambridge: Cambridge University Press, 2005), pp. 196–201. There is a detailed filmography in Paul J. Niemeyer, *Seeing Hardy: Film and Television Adaptations of the Fiction of Thomas Hardy* (Jefferson, N.C.: McFarland, 2003), pp. 247–66.

5 See for example Roger Webster, 'From Painting to Cinema: Visual Elements in Hardy's Fiction', *Hardy on Screen*, ed. Wright, pp. 20–36.

6 David Lodge, quoted in 'On the Home Front', *The Guardian*, 13 June 2009, Features and Reviews, p. 2.

7 John Wain, 'Introduction' to *The Dynasts*, p. xiii.

8 For a discussion, see Peter Widdowson, *Hardy in History: A Study in Literary Sociology* (London: Routledge, 1989), pp. 11–76.

9 For a discussion of the relationship between film and literature, see James Naremore, ed., *Film Adaptation* (London: Athlone Press 2000); Keith Cohen, *Film and Fiction: The Dynamics of Exchange* (New Haven, Conn.: Yale University Press, 1979); Robert Giddings and Erica Sheena, eds., *The Classic Novel: From Page to Screen* (Manchester: Manchester University Press, 2000).

10 See Raymond Williams, *The Country and the City* (London: Chatto and Windus, 1973) for an extended discussion of literary depictions of rural society and the idea of the organic community.

11 William Empson, *Some Versions of Pastoral* (London: Chatto and Windus, 1935), p. 22.

12 The title alludes ironically to the line, 'Far from the madding crowd's ignoble strife', in Thomas Gray's 'Elegy Written in a Country Churchyard' (1751).

13 See Widdowson, *Hardy in History*, pp. 116–17.

14  Ibid., p. 115.
15  For example, Victor Fleming's *The Wizard of Oz* (1939), or more recently Woody Allen's *The Purple Rose of Cairo* (1985) and Kenneth Branagh's *Dead Again* (1991). In the history of cinematography, initially the use or insertion of colour photography was considered a special effect, as opposed to the conventional use of monochrome; now the opposite seems to be the case.
16  Niemeyer, *Seeing Hardy*, p. 172
17  Roger Webster, 'From painting to cinema', *Hardy on Screen*, ed. Wright, pp. 30–4.
18  Robert Schweik, 'Adapting Hardy's *Jude the Obscure* for the Screen: A Study in Contrasts', *Hardy on Screen*, ed. Wright, pp. 183–95.

# FURTHER READING

### ABBREVIATIONS

Brantlinger and Thesing: Patrick Brantlinger and William B. Thesing, eds. *A Companion to the Victorian Novel*. Oxford: Blackwell, 2002.

Kramer: Dale Kramer, ed. *The Cambridge Companion to Thomas Hardy*. Cambridge: Cambridge University Press, 1999.

Mallett: Phillip Mallett, ed. *Advances in Thomas Hardy Studies*. London: Palgrave Macmillan, 2004.

Morgan: Rosemarie Morgan, ed. *Ashgate Research Companion to Thomas Hardy*. Aldershot: Ashgate, 2010.

Wilson: Keith Wilson, ed. *A Companion to Thomas Hardy*. Oxford: Wiley-Blackwell, 2009.

### BIBLIOGRAPHIES

Davis, W. Eugene, and Helmut E. Gerber. *Thomas Hardy: An Annotated Bibliography of Writings about Him*. De Kalb, Ill.: Northern Illinois University Press, 1973.

Davis, W. Eugene, and Helmut E. Gerber. *Thomas Hardy: An Annotated Bibliography of Writings about Him, Vol. II: 1970–1978 and Supplement for 1871–1969*. De Kalb, Ill.: Northern Illinois University Press, 1983.

Davis, W. Eugene. 'The First Hundred Years of Hardy Criticism: 1871–1971'. Morgan: 39–56.

Draper, Ronald P., and Martin Ray, eds. *An Annotated Critical Bibliography of Thomas Hardy*. London and New York: Macmillan, 1989.

Pettit, Charles P. C. 'Hardy Bibliographies'. Morgan: 23–38.

Purdy, Richard Little. *Thomas Hardy: A Bibliographical Study*. Oxford: Clarendon Press, 1954.

Purdy, Richard Little. *Thomas Hardy: A Bibliographical Study*. Introduction and Supplement by Charles P. C. Pettit. London: The British Library, and New Castle, Del.: Oak Knoll Press, 2002.

LIFE, LETTERS, AND NOTEBOOKS

Beatty, C. J. P., ed. *The Architectural Notebook of Thomas Hardy.* Dorchester: Dorset Natural History and Archaeological Society, 1966.

Björk, Lennart A., ed. *The Literary Notebooks of Thomas Hardy.* 2 vols. London: Macmillan, 1985.

Dalziel, Pamela, and Michael Millgate, eds. *Thomas Hardy's 'Studies, Specimens &c.' Notebook.* Oxford: Clarendon Press, 1994.

Dalziel, Pamela, and Michael Millgate, eds. *Thomas Hardy's 'Poetical Matter' Notebook.* Oxford: Oxford University Press, 2009.

Greenslade, William, ed. *Thomas Hardy's 'Facts' Notebook: A Critical Edition.* Aldershot: Ashgate, 2004.

Hardy, Evelyn, and Frank B. Pinion, eds. *One Rare Fair Woman: Thomas Hardy's Letters to Florence Henniker, 1893–1922.* London: Macmillan, 1972.

Millgate, Michael, ed. *The Life and Work of Thomas Hardy, by Thomas Hardy.* London: Macmillan, 1984.

Millgate, Michael, ed. *Thomas Hardy's Public Voice: The Essays, Speeches, and Miscellaneous Prose.* Oxford: Clarendon Press, 2001.

Orel, Harold, ed. *Thomas Hardy's Personal Writings.* New York: St. Martin's Press, 1990.

Pettit, Charles P. C. 'Hardy Archives'. Morgan: 57–68.

Purdy, Richard Little, and Michael Millgate, eds. *The Collected Letters of Thomas Hardy.* 7 vols. Oxford: Clarendon Press, 1978–88.

Taylor, Richard H., ed. *The Personal Notebooks of Thomas Hardy.* London: Macmillan, 1979.

BIOGRAPHY

Amigoni, David. *Victorian Biography: Intellectuals and the Ordering of Discourse.* Hemel Hempstead: Harvester Wheatsheaf, 1993.

Brennecke, Ernest. *The Life of Thomas Hardy.* New York: Greenberg, 1925.

Broughton, Trev Lynn. *Men of Letters, Writing Lives: Masculinity and Literary Auto/biography in the Late Victorian Period.* London: Routledge, 1999.

Bullen, J. B. 'The Buried Life: A New Edition of F. E. Hardy's "Biography"'. *Thomas Hardy Annual* 5 (1987): 187–96.

Cox, J. Stevens, ed. *Thomas Hardy: Materials for a Study of His Life, Times and Works.* 2 vols. Guernsey: Toucan Press, 1968–71.

Deacon, Lois, and Terry Coleman. *Providence and Mr. Hardy.* London: Hutchinson, 1966.

Dolin, Tim. 'The Early Life and Later Years of Thomas Hardy: An Argument for a New Edition'. *Review of English Studies* 58 (2007): 698–714.

Gibson, James. *Thomas Hardy: A Literary Life*. London: Macmillan, 1996.

Gibson, James, ed. *Thomas Hardy: Interviews and Recollections*. London: Macmillan, 1999.

Gittings, Robert. *Young Thomas Hardy*. London: Heinemann, 1975.

Gittings, Robert. *The Older Hardy*. London: Heinemann, 1978.

Gittings, Robert, and Jo Manton. *The Second Mrs Hardy*. London: Heinemann, 1979.

Hands, Timothy. *Thomas Hardy: Distracted Preacher? Hardy's Religious Biography and Its Influence on His Novels*. London: Macmillan, 1989.

Hardy, Emma. *Some Recollections*, ed. Evelyn Hardy and Robert Gittings. London: Oxford University Press, 1961.

Hardy, Evelyn. *Thomas Hardy: A Critical Biography*. London: The Hogarth Press, 1954.

Hardy, Florence Emily. *The Early Life of Thomas Hardy, 1840–1891*. London: Macmillan, 1928.

Hardy, Florence Emily. *The Later Years of Thomas Hardy, 1892–1928*. London: Macmillan, 1930.

Hedgcock, Frank A. *Thomas Hardy: penseur et artiste*. Paris: Librairie Hachette, 1911.

Johnson, S. R. 'Thomas Hardy the Obscure: Hardy's Final Fiction'. *English Literature in Transition* 35:3 (1992): 300–8.

Kay-Robinson, Denys. *The First Mrs Thomas Hardy*. London: Macmillan, 1979.

Mallett, Phillip. 'Hardy and the Biographers'. Morgan: 465–83.

Millgate, Michael. *Testamentary Acts: Browning, Tennyson, James, Hardy*. Oxford: Clarendon Press, 1992.

Millgate, Michael. 'Thomas Hardy: The Biographical Sources'. Kramer: 1–18.

Millgate, Michael. *Thomas Hardy: A Biography Revisited*. Oxford: Oxford University Press, 2004.

Millgate, Michael. 'Hardy as Biographical Subject'. Wilson: 7–18.

Orel, Harold. *The Final Years of Thomas Hardy, 1912–1928*. London: Macmillan, 1976.

Orel, Harold. *The Unknown Thomas Hardy: Lesser-Known Aspects of Hardy's Life and Career*. London: Macmillan, 1987.

Neill, Edward. *The Secret Life of Thomas Hardy: 'Retaliatory Fiction'*. Aldershot: Ashgate, 2004.

Newey, Vincent, and Philip Shaw, eds. *Mortal Pages, Literary Lives: Studies in Nineteenth Century Autobiography*. Aldershot: Scolar Press, 1996.

Peterson, Linda. *Victorian Autobiography: The Tradition of Self-Interpretation*. New Haven, Conn.: Yale University Press, 1986.

Pite, Ralph. *Thomas Hardy: The Guarded Life*. London: Picador, 2006.

Ray, Martin, ed. *Thomas Hardy Remembered*. Aldershot: Ashgate, 2007.

Seymour-Smith, Martin. *Hardy*. London: Bloomsbury, 1994.

Taylor, Richard H., ed. *Emma Hardy Diaries*. Manchester: Carcanet New Press, 1985.

Tomalin, Claire. *Thomas Hardy: The Time-Torn Man*. London: Penguin Viking, 2006.

Turner, Paul. *The Life of Thomas Hardy*. Oxford: Blackwell, 1998.

Weber, Carl. *Hardy of Wessex: His Life and Literary Career*. New York: Columbia University Press, 1940.

Weber, Carl. *Hardy and the Lady from Madison Square*. Waterville, Me.: Colby College Press, 1952.

### COMPOSITION, PUBLICATION, AND RECEPTION

Altick, Richard. *The English Common Reader: A Social History of the Mass Reading Public, 1800–1900*. Chicago: University of Chicago Press, 1957.

Blake, Andrew. *Reading Victorian Fiction: The Cultural Context and Ideological Content of the Nineteenth-Century Novel*. London: Macmillan, 1989.

Chase, Mary Ellen. *Thomas Hardy: From Serial to Novel*. Minneapolis: University of Minnesota Press, 1927.

Dalziel, Pamela. *Thomas Hardy: The Excluded and Collaborative Stories*. Oxford: Clarendon Press, 1992.

Dalziel, Pamela. 'Exploiting the Poor Man: The Genesis of Hardy's *Desperate Remedies*'. *Journal of English and Germanic Philology* 94:2 (1995): 220–32.

Feltes, N. N. *Modes of Production of Victorian Novels*. Chicago: Chicago University Press, 1986.

Gatrell, Simon. *Hardy the Creator: A Textual Biography*. Oxford: Clarendon Press, 1988.

Griest, Guinevere L. *Mudie's Circulating Library and the Victorian Novel*. Bloomington: Indiana University Press, 1970.

Ingham, Patricia. 'The Evolution of *Jude the Obscure*'. *Review of English Studies* 27 (1976): 27–37, 159–69.

Jordan, John O., and Robert L. Patten, eds. *Literature in the Marketplace: Nineteenth-Century British Publishing and Reading Practices*. Cambridge: Cambridge University Press, 1995.

Keating, Peter J. *The Haunted Study: A Social History of the English Novel, 1875–1914*. London: Secker & Warburg, 1989.

Kramer, Dale. 'Revisions and Vision: Thomas Hardy's *The Woodlanders*'. *Bulletin of the New York Public Library* 75 (1971): 195–230, 248–82.

Laird, John Tudor. *The Shaping of 'Tess of the d'Urbervilles'*. Oxford: Clarendon Press, 1975.

Law, Graham. *Serializing Fiction in the Victorian Press*. London: Palgrave, 2000.

Morgan, Rosemarie. *Cancelled Words: Rediscovering Thomas Hardy*. London and New York: Routledge, 1992.

Paterson, John. *The Making of 'The Return of the Native'*. Berkeley and Los Angeles: University of California Press, 1963.

Ray, Martin. *Thomas Hardy: A Textual Study of the Short Stories*. Aldershot: Ashgate, 1997.

Sutherland, John. *Victorian Fiction: Writers, Publishers, Readers*. London: Palgrave Macmillan, 2006.

Waller, Philip. *Writers, Readers and Reputations: Literary Life in Britain 1870–1918*. Oxford: Oxford University Press, 2006.

Widdowson, Peter. *Hardy in History: A Study in Literary Sociology*. London: Routledge, 1989.

Winfield, Christine. 'The Manuscript of Hardy's *The Mayor of Casterbridge*'. *Papers of the Bibliographical Society of America* 67 (1973): 37–58.

Wright, T. R. *Hardy and His Readers*. London: Macmillan, 2003.

CRITICAL RESPONSES I: 1870–1970

Abercrombie, Lascelles. *Thomas Hardy: A Critical Study*. London: Secker, 1912.

Beach, Joseph Warren. *The Technique of Thomas Hardy*. Chicago: University of Chicago Press, 1922.

Brown, Douglas. *Thomas Hardy*. London: Longmans, Green, 1954.

Cecil, David. *Hardy the Novelist: An Essay in Criticism*. London: Constable, 1943.

Chew, Samuel C. *Thomas Hardy, Poet and Novelist*. New York: Knopf, 1921.

Cox, R. G., ed. *Thomas Hardy: The Critical Heritage*. London: Routledge & Kegan Paul, 1970.

Clarke, Graham, ed. *Thomas Hardy: Critical Assessments*. 4 vols. Volume I: *The Contemporary Response*. Mountfield: Helm Information, 1993.

Elliott, A. P. *Fatalism in the Works of Thomas Hardy*. Philadelphia: University of Pennsylvania Press, 1935.

Guérard, Albert. *Thomas Hardy: The Novels and Stories*. Cambridge, Mass.: Harvard University Press, 1949.

Holloway, John. *The Victorian Sage: Studies in Argument*. London: Macmillan, 1953.

Hopkins, R. Thurston. *Thomas Hardy's Dorset*. London: Cecil Palmer, 1922.

Howe, Irving. *Thomas Hardy*. New York: Macmillan, 1967.

Johnson, Lionel. *The Art of Thomas Hardy*. New York: Russell & Russell, 1894.

Kettle, Arnold. *Hardy the Novelist*. Swansea: University of Swansea, 1967.

Lerner, Laurence, and John Holmstrom, eds. *Thomas Hardy and His Readers: A Selection of Contemporary Reviews*. London: Barnes and Noble, 1968.

McDowall, Arthur. *Thomas Hardy: A Critical Study*. London: Faber and Faber, 1931.

Morrell, Roy. *Thomas Hardy: The Will and the Way*. Kuala Lumpur: University of Malaysia Press, 1965.

Rutland, William R. *Thomas Hardy: A Study of His Writings and Their Background*. Oxford: Basil Blackwell, 1938.

Southern Review 6: *Hardy Centennial Issue*. Baton Rouge: Louisiana State University Press, 1940.

Symons, Arthur. *A Study of Thomas Hardy*. London: Chas. J. Sawyer, 1927.

Webster, Harvey Curtis. *On a Darkling Plain: The Art and Thought of Thomas Hardy*. Cambridge: Cambridge University Press, 1947.

Wing, George. *Thomas Hardy*. New York: Grove Press, 1963.

CRITICAL RESPONSES II: 1970 TO THE PRESENT

Bayley, John. *An Essay on Hardy*. Cambridge: Cambridge University Press, 1978.

Boumelha, Penny. *Thomas Hardy and Women: Sexual Ideology and Narrative Form*. Brighton: Harvester Press, 1982.

Brooks, Jean R. *Thomas Hardy: The Poetic Structure*. London: Elek Books, 1971.

Butler, Lance St J., ed. *Thomas Hardy After Fifty Years*. Macmillan: London, 1977.

Butler, Lance St J., ed. *Alternative Hardy*. Macmillan: London, 1989.

Casagrande, Peter. *Unity in Hardy's Novels: 'Repetitive Symmetries'*. London: Macmillan, 1982.

Casagrande, Peter. *Hardy's Influence on the Modern Novel*. London: Macmillan, 1987.

Clarke, Graham, ed. *Thomas Hardy: Critical Assessments of Writers in English*. 4 vols. Mountfield, East Sussex: Helm Information, 1993.

Daleski, H. M. *Thomas Hardy and Paradoxes of Love*. Columbia: University of Missouri Press, 1997.

Dolin, Tim, and Peter Widdowson, eds. *Thomas Hardy and Contemporary Literary Studies*. London: Palgrave Macmillan, 2004.

Draper, Ronald P., ed. *Hardy: The Tragic Novels*. London: Macmillan, 1975; rev. ed. 1991.

Dutta, Shanta. *Ambivalence in Hardy: A Study of His Attitude to Women*. London: Macmillan Press, 2000.

Ebbatson, Roger. *The Evolutionary Self: Hardy, Forster, Lawrence*. Brighton: Harvester Press, 1982.

Elvy, Margaret. *Sexing Hardy: Thomas Hardy and Feminism*. London: Crescent Moon, 1998.

Enstice, Andrew. *Thomas Hardy: Landscapes of the Mind*. London: Macmillan, 1979.

Fincham, Tony. *Hardy the Physician: Medical Aspects of the Wessex Tradition*. London: Palgrave Macmillan, 2008.

Fisher, Joe. *The Hidden Hardy*. London: Macmillan, 1992.

Garson, Marjorie. *Hardy's Fables of Integrity: Woman, Body, Text*. Oxford: Clarendon Press, 1991.

Gatrell, Simon. *Thomas Hardy and the Proper Study of Mankind*. London: Macmillan, 1993.

Gilmartin, Sophie. *Ancestry and Narrative in Nineteenth-Century British Literature: Blood Relations from Edgeworth to Hardy*. Cambridge: Cambridge University Press, 1998.

Giordano Jr. Frank R. *'I'd Have My Life Unbe': Thomas Hardy's Self-Destructive Characters*. Alabama: University of Alabama Press, 1984.

Goode, John. *Thomas Hardy: The Offensive Truth*. Oxford: Blackwell, 1988.

Greenslade, William. *Degeneration, Culture and the Novel 1880–1940*. Cambridge: Cambridge University Press, 1994.

Gregor, Ian. *The Great Web: The Form of Hardy's Major Fiction*. London: Faber and Faber, 1974.

Hardy, Barbara. *Thomas Hardy: Imagining Imagination: Hardy's Poetry and Fiction*. London: Athlone Press, 2000.

Higonnet, Margaret R., ed. *The Sense of Sex: Feminist Perspectives on Thomas Hardy*. Urbana: University of Illinois Press, 1993.

Hornback, Bert. *The Metaphor of Chance: Vision and Technique in the Works of Thomas Hardy*. Athens: Ohio University Press, 1971.

Hyman, Virginia. *Ethical Perspectives in the Novels of Thomas* Hardy. Harmondsworth: Penguin, 1985.

Ingham, Patricia. *Thomas Hardy: A Feminist Reading*. Hemel Hempstead: Harvester, 1989.

Ingham, Patricia. *Thomas Hardy*. Oxford: Oxford University Press, 2003.

Irwin, Michael. *Reading Hardy's Landscapes*. London: Palgrave Macmillan, 2000.

Jedzerewski, Jan. *Thomas Hardy and the Church*. London: Macmillan, 1996.

Johnson, Bruce. *True Correspondence: A Phenomenology of Hardy's Novels*. Gainesville: University Presses of Florida, 1983.

Kramer, Dale, ed. *Critical Approaches to the Fiction of Thomas Hardy*. London: Macmillan, 1979.

Langbaum, Robert. *Thomas Hardy in Our Time*. London: Macmillan, 1995.

Larson, Jill. *Ethics and Narrative in the English Novel, 1880–1914*. Cambridge: Cambridge University Press, 2001.

Lock, Charles. *Thomas Hardy: Criticism in Focus*. London: Bristol Classical, 1992.

Mallett, Phillip V., and Ronald P. Draper, eds. *A Spacious Vision: Essays on Thomas Hardy*. Penzance: Patten Press, 1994

Mallett, Phillip, ed. *The Achievement of Thomas Hardy*. London: Macmillan, 2000.

Mallett, Phillip, ed. *Thomas Hardy: Texts and Contexts*. London: Macmillan, 2002.

Meisel, Perry. *Thomas Hardy: The Return of the Repressed*. New Haven, Conn.: Yale University Press, 1972.

Miller, J. Hillis. *Thomas Hardy: Distance and Desire*. Cambridge, Mass.: Harvard University Press, 1970.

Miller, J. Hillis. *Fiction and Repetition: Seven English Novels*. Cambridge, Mass.: Harvard University Press, 1982.

Miller, J. Hillis. *Topographies*. Stanford, Calif,: Stanford University Press, 1995.

Millgate, Michael. *Thomas Hardy: His Career as a Novelist*. London: Bodley Head, 1971.

Moore, Kevin Z. *The Descent of the Imagination: Postromantic Culture in the Later Novels of Thomas Hardy*. New York: New York University Press, 1990.

Morgan, Rosemarie. *Women and Sexuality in the Novels of Thomas Hardy*. London: Routledge, 1988.

O'Toole, Tess. *Genealogy and Fiction in Thomas Hardy: Family Lineage and Narrative Line*. London: Macmillan, 1997.

Page, Norman, ed. *Thomas Hardy: The Writer and His Background*. London: Bell & Hyman, 1980.

Pettit, Charles P. C., ed. *New Perspectives on Thomas Hardy*. London: Macmillan, 1994.

Pettit, Charles P. C., ed. *Reading Thomas Hardy*. London: Macmillan, 1998.

Salter, C. H. *Good Little Thomas Hardy*. New York: Barnes & Noble, 1981.

Sherman, G. W. *The Pessimism of Thomas Hardy: A Social Study*. Madison, N.J.: Fairleigh Dickinson University Press, 1976.

Smith, Anne, ed. *The Novels of Thomas Hardy*. New York: Barnes and Noble, 1979.

Sumner, Rosemary. *Thomas Hardy: Psychological Novelist*. London: Macmillan, 1981.

Sumner, Rosemary. *A Route to Modernism: Hardy, Lawrence, Woolf*. London: Macmillan, 2000.

Swigg, Richard. *Lawrence, Hardy and American Literature*. Oxford: Oxford University Press, 1972.

Taylor, Richard H. *The Neglected Hardy: Thomas Hardy's Lesser Novels*. London: Macmillan, 1982.

Thomas, Jane. *Thomas Hardy, Femininity and Dissent: Reassessing the 'Minor' Novels*. London: Macmillan, 1999.

White, R. J. *Thomas Hardy and History*. New York: Harper and Row, 1974.

Widdowson, Peter. *On Thomas Hardy: Late Essays and Earlier*. London: Macmillan, 1998.

Wolfreys, Julian. *Thomas Hardy*. London: Palgrave Macmillan, 2009.

Wotton, George. *Thomas Hardy: Towards a Materialist Criticism*. Dublin: Gill & Macmillan, 1985.

Wright, T. R. *Hardy and the Erotic*. London: Macmillan, 1989.

CRITICAL RESPONSES III: POETRY AND *THE DYNASTS*

Armstrong, Tim. *Haunted Hardy: Poetry, History, Memory*. London: Palgrave Macmillan, 2000.

Bailey, J. O. *Thomas Hardy and the Cosmic Mind: A New Reading of 'The Dynasts'*. Chapel Hill: University of North Carolina Press, 1956.

Bailey, J. O. *The Poetry of Thomas Hardy: A Handbook and Commentary*. Chapel Hill: University of North Carolina Press, 1970.

Buckler, William. *The Poetry of Thomas Hardy: A Study in Art and Ideas*. New York: New York University Press, 1983.

Clements, Patricia, and Juliet Grindle, eds. *The Poetry of Thomas Hardy*. New York: Barnes and Noble, 1980.

Davie, Donald. *Thomas Hardy and British Poetry*. London: Routledge & Kegan Paul, 1973.

Davie, Donald, ed. *Agenda: Thomas Hardy Special Issue* 10 (Autumn–Winter 1972).

Dean, Susan. *Hardy's Poetic Vision in 'The Dynasts': The Diorama of a Dream*. Princeton, N.J.: Princeton University Press, 1977.

Gibson, James, and Trevor Johnson, eds. *Thomas Hardy: Poems*. London: Macmillan, 1979.

Giordano Jr., Frank R., ed. 'The Poetry of Thomas Hardy: A Commemorative Issue'. *Victorian Poetry* 17:1 and 2 (1975).

Green, Brian. *Hardy's Lyrics: Pearls of Pity*. London: Macmillan, 1996.

Hynes, Samuel. *The Pattern of Hardy's Poetry*. Chapel Hill: University of North Carolina Press, 1961.

Johnson, Trevor. *A Critical Introduction to the Poems of Thomas Hardy*. London: Macmillan, 1991.

Lucas, John. *Modern English Poetry from Hardy to Hughes*. London: Batsford, 1986.

Marsden, Kenneth. *The Poems of Thomas Hardy: A Critical Introduction*. Oxford: Oxford University Press, 1969.

Maynard, Katherine Kearney. *Thomas Hardy's Tragic Poetry: The Lyrics and 'The Dynasts'*. Iowa City: University of Iowa Press, 1991.

Orel, Harold. *Thomas Hardy's Epic-Drama: A Study of 'The Dynasts'*. Lawrence: University of Kansas Press, 1963.

Orel, Harold. *Critical Essays on Thomas Hardy's Poetry*. New York: G. K. Hall, 1995.

Pandey, R. K. *Human Concerns in the Poetry of Thomas Hardy*. New Delhi: Mahaveer and Sons, 2007.

Paulin, Tom. *Thomas Hardy: The Poetry of Perception*. London: Macmillan, 1975.

Ray, Martin, ed. *The Poetry of Thomas Hardy: Contemporary Reviews*. London: Palgrave Macmillan, 2004.

Richardson, James. *Thomas Hardy: The Poetry of Necessity*. Chicago: University of Chicago Press, 1977.

Taylor, Dennis. *Hardy's Poetry, 1860–1928*. London: Macmillan, 1981.

Taylor, Dennis. *Hardy's Metres and Victorian Prosody*. Oxford: Clarendon Press, 1988.

Taylor, Dennis. 'The Chronology of Hardy's Poetry'. *Victorian Poetry* 37 (1999): 1–58.

Ward, John Powell. *The English Line*. London: Palgrave Macmillan, 1991.

Ward, John Powell. *Thomas Hardy's Poetry*. Buckingham: Open University Press, 1992.

Wickens, Glen. G. *Thomas Hardy: Monism and the Critical Tradition: The One and the Many in 'The Dynasts'*. Toronto: University of Toronto Press, 2002.

Wright, Walter. *The Shaping of 'The Dynasts'*. Lincoln: University of Nebraska Press, 1967.

Zietlow, Paul. *Moments of Vision: The Poetry of Thomas Hardy*. Cambridge, Mass.: Harvard University Press, 1974.

### GENRE: REALISM, TRAGEDY, AND THE SHORT STORY

Belsey, Catherine. *Critical Practice*. London: Methuen, 1980.

Benjamin, Walter. 'The Storyteller: Reflections on the Works of Nikolai Leskov'. *Illuminations: Essays and Reflections*, ed. Hannah Arendt. London: Jonathan Cape: 83–110.

Brady, Kristin. *The Short Stories of Thomas Hardy: Tales of Past and Present*. London: Macmillan, 1982.

Byerly, Alison. *Realism, Representation and the Arts in Nineteenth-Century Literature*. Cambridge: Cambridge University Press, 1997.

Caserio, Robert L. *Plot, Story, and the Novel: From Dickens and Poe to the Modern Period*. Princeton, N.J.: Princeton University Press, 1979.

Childers, Joseph W. 'Victorian Theories of the Novel'. Brantlinger and Thesing: 406–23.

Correa, Delia de Sousa, ed. *The Nineteenth-Century Novel: Realisms*. London: Routledge, 2000.

Dentith, Simon. *A Rhetoric of the Real: Studies in Post-Enlightenment Writing from 1790 to the Present*. Hemel Hempstead: Harvester, 1990.

Gilmartin, Sophie, and Rod Mengham. *Thomas Hardy's Shorter Fiction: A Critical Study*. Edinburgh: Edinburgh University Press, 2007.

Hanson, Clare. *Short Stories and Short Fictions, 1880–1980*. London: Macmillan, 1984.

Keen, Suzanne. *Victorian Renovations of the Novel: Narrative Annexes and the Boundaries of Representation*. Cambridge: Cambridge University Press, 1998.

King, Jeanette. *Tragedy in the Victorian Novel: Theory and Practice in the Novels of George Eliot, Thomas Hardy and Henry James*. Cambridge University Press, 1978.

Kramer, Dale. *Thomas Hardy: The Forms of Tragedy*. London: Macmillan, 1975.

Kramer, Dale. 'Hardy: The Driftiness of Tragedy'. Morgan: 371–85.

Levine, George. *The Realistic Imagination: English Fiction from Frankenstein to Lady Chatterley*. Chicago: University of Chicago Press, 1981.

Levine, George, ed. *Realism and Representation: Essays on the Problem of Realism in Relation to Science, Literature and Culture*. Madison: University of Wisconsin Press, 1993.

Liggins, Emma, Andrew Maunder, and Ruth Robbins. *The British Short Story*. London: Palgrave Macmillan, 2010.

Newton, K. M. *Modern Literature and the Tragic*. Edinburgh: Edinburgh University Press, 2008.

Orel, Harold. *The Victorian Short Story*. Cambridge: Cambridge University Press, 1986.

Poole, Adrian. *Tragedy: A Very Short Introduction*. Oxford: Oxford University Press, 2005.

Reilly, Jim. *Shadowtime: History and Representation in Hardy, Conrad and George Eliot*. London: Routledge, 1993.

Shaw, Valerie. *The Short Story: A Critical Introduction*. London: Longman, 1983.

Steiner, George. *The Death of Tragedy*. London: Faber and Faber, 1961.

Trotter, David. *Cooking with Mud: The Idea of Mess in Nineteenth-Century Art and Fiction*. Oxford: Oxford University Press, 2000.

Walder, Dennis, ed. *The Realist Novel*. London: Routledge/Open University Press, 1996.

Widdowson, Peter. "'… into the hands of pure-minded English girls": Hardy's Short Stories and the Late Victorian Literary Marketplace'. Wilson: 364–77.

CLASS, EDUCATION, AND RURAL SOCIETY

Birch, Dinah. *Our Victorian Education*. Oxford: Blackwell, 2008.

Cooper, Andrew. 'Voicing the Language of Literature: Jude's Obscured Labor'. *Victorian Literature and Culture* 28:2 (2000): 391–410.

Dentith, Simon. *Society and Cultural Forms in Nineteenth Century England*. London: Macmillan, 1998.

DeVine, Christine. *Class in Turn-of-the-Century Novels of Gissing, James, Hardy and Wells.* Aldershot: Ashgate, 2005.

Ebbatson, Roger. *Hardy: The Margin of the Unexpressed.* Sheffield: Sheffield Academic Press, 1993.

Ebbatson, Roger. 'Hardy and Class'. Mallett: 111–34.

Ebbatson, Roger. '"A Thickness of Wall": Hardy and Class'. Wilson: 162–77.

Gagnier, Regenia. 'Money, the Economy, and Social Class'. Brantlinger and Thesing: 48–66.

Harrison, J. F. C. *Late Victorian Britain, 1875–1901.* London: Fontana, 1990.

Haggard, H. Rider. *Rural England: Being an Account of Agricultural and Social Researches Carried Out in the Years 1901 [and] 1902.* 2 vols. London: Longmans, 1902.

Horn, Pamela. *Education in Rural England, 1800–1914.* Dublin: Gill and Macmillan, 1978.

Howkins, Alun. *Reshaping Rural England: A Social History, 1850–1925.* London: Harper Collins Academic, 1991.

Ingham, Patricia. *The Language of Gender and Class: Transformation in the Victorian Novel.* London: Routledge, 1996.

Jann, Rosemary. 'Hardy's Rustics and the Construction of Class'. *Victorian Literature and Culture* 28:2 (2000): 411–25.

Keith, W. J. *Regions of the Imagination: The Development of British Rural Fiction.* Toronto: University of Toronto Press, 1988.

Kerr, Barbara. *Bound to the Soil: A Social History of Dorset.* Wakefield: EP Publishing, 1975.

Lawson, John, and Harold Silver. *A Social History of Education in England.* London: Methuen, 1973.

Lucas, John. *The Literature of Change: Studies in the Nineteenth-Century Provincial Novel.* Brighton: Harvester Press, 1977.

Mattisson, Jane. *Knowledge and Survival in the Novels of Thomas Hardy.* Lund: Lund University, 2002.

McKibbin, Ross. *The Ideologies of Class: Social Relations in Britain 1880–1950.* Oxford: Clarendon Press, 1990.

Mingay, G. E., ed. *The Victorian Countryside.* 2 vols. London: Routledge & Kegan Paul, 1971.

Payne, Christiana. *Toil and Plenty: Images of the Agricultural Landscape in England, 1780–1890.* New Haven, Conn.: Yale University Press, 1993.

Phillipps, K. C. *Language and Class in Victorian England.* Oxford: Oxford University Press, 1984.

Pite, Ralph. *Hardy's Geography: Wessex and the Regional Novel.* London: Palgrave Macmillan, 2002.

Plietzsch, Birgit. *The Novels of Thomas Hardy as a Product of Nineteenth-Century Social, Economic and Cultural Change.* Berlin: Tenea, 2003.

Radford, Andrew. *Mapping the Wessex Novel: Landscape, History and the Parochial in British Literature, 1870–1940.* London: Continuum, 2010.

Reeder, David A., ed. *Educating Our Masters.* Leicester: Leicester University Press, 1980.

Robbins, Ruth, and Julian Wolfreys, eds. *Victorian Identities: Social and Cultural Formations in Victorian Literature.* Basingstoke: Macmillan, 1996.

Rose, Jonathan. 'Education, Literacy, and the Victorian Reader'. Brantlinger and Thesing: 31–47.

Scott, Patrick, and Pauline Fletcher, eds. *Culture and Education in Victorian England.* London: Bucknell University Press, 1990.

Smith, D. *Conflict and Compromise: Class Formation in English Society, 1830–1914.* London: Routledge & Kegan Paul, 1982.

Snell, K. D. M. *Annals of the Labouring Poor: Social Change and Agrarian England, 1600–1900.* Cambridge: Cambridge University Press, 1987.

Snell, K. D. M., ed. *The Regional Novel in Britain and Ireland 1800–1990.* Cambridge: Cambridge University Press, 1998.

Stephens, W. B. *Education in Britain, 1750–1914.* New York: St Martins Press, 1998.

Thompson, F. M. L. *The Rise of Respectable Society: A Social History of Victorian Britain, 1830–1900.* London: Fontana, 1988.

Wiener, Martin J. *English Culture and the Decline of the Industrial Spirit, 1850–1980.* 2nd edition, Cambridge: Cambridge University Press, 2004.

Williams, Raymond. *The Country and the City.* London: Chatto and Windus, 1973.

NATION AND CITY, WAR AND EMPIRE

Ackroyd, Peter. *London: The Biography.* London: Chatto and Windus, 2000.

Anderson, Benedict. *Imagined Communities: Reflections on the Origin and Spread of Nationalism.* London: Verso, 1983.

Attridge, Steve. *Nationalism, Imperialism and Identity in Late Victorian Culture.* London: Palgrave Macmillan, 2003.

Bivona, Daniel. *British Imperial Literature, 1870–1940: Writing and the Administration of Empire.* Cambridge: Cambridge University Press, 1998.

Brantlinger, Patrick. *Rule of Darkness: British Literature and Imperialism, 1830–1914.* Ithaca and London: Cornell University Press, 1988.

Coleman, B. I., ed. *The Idea of the City in Nineteenth-Century Britain.* London: Routledge & Kegan Paul, 1973.

Colls, Robert, and Philip Dodd, eds. *Englishness: Politics and Culture, 1880–1920.* London: Croom Helm, 1986.

David, Deirdre. 'Empire, Race, and the Victorian Novel'. Brantlinger and Thesing: 84–100.

David, Saul. *Victoria's Wars: The Rise of Empire.* London: Penguin, 2007.

Dentith, Simon. *Epic and Empire in Nineteenth-Century Britain.* Cambridge: Cambridge University Press, 2006.

Dyos, H. J., and Michael Wolff, eds. *The Victorian City: Images and Realities.* 2 vols. London: Routledge & Kegan Paul, 1973.

Ebbatson, Roger. *An Imaginary England: Nation, Landscape and Literature, 1840–1920.* Aldershot: Ashgate, 2005.

Eldridge, C. C. *Victorian Imperialism.* London: Hodder and Stoughton, 1978.

Eldridge, C. C. *The Imperial Experience: From Carlyle to Forster.* London: Palgrave Macmillan, 1996.

Gervais, David. *Literary Englands: Versions of Englishness in Modern Writing.* Cambridge: Cambridge University Press, 1993.

Hobson, J. A. *Imperialism: A Study.* London: Nisbet, 1902.

Nead, Lynda. *Victorian Babylon: People, Streets and Images in Nineteenth-Century London.* New Haven, Conn.: Yale University Press, 2000.

Pakenham, Thomas. *The Boer War.* London: Weidenfeld & Nicolson, 1979.

Parrinder, Patrick. *Nation and Novel: The English Novel from Its Origins to the Present Day.* Oxford: Oxford University Press, 2006.

Porter, Bernard. *The Lion's Share: A Short History of British Imperialism 1850–2004.* 4th edition; Harlow: Pearson Education, 2004.

Porter, Roy, ed. *Myths of the English.* London: Polity Press, 1993.

Said, Edward. *Culture and Imperialism.* London: Chatto and Windus, 1993.

Sheppard, Francis. *London 1808–1870: The Infernal Wen.* London: Secker and Warburg, 1971.

Tidrick, Kathryn. *Empire & the English Character.* London and New York: Tauris, 1990.

Whitehead, James S. 'Hardy and Englishness'. Mallett: 203–28.

MARRIAGE, THE NEW WOMAN, AND MASCULINITY

Adams, James Eli. *Dandies and Desert Saints: Styles of Victorian Manhood.* Ithaca, N.Y.: Cornell University Press, 1995.

Ardis, Ann L. *New Women, New Novels: Feminism and Early Modernism.* New Brunswick, N.Y.: Rutgers University Press, 1990.

Bland, Lucy. *Banishing the Beast: Sexuality and the Early Feminists.* London: Penguin, 1995.

Danahay, Martin. *Gender at Work in Victorian Culture: Literature, Art and Masculinity.* Aldershot: Ashgate, 2005.

Dellamora, Richard. *Masculine Desire: The Sexual Politics of Victorian Aestheticism.* Chapel Hill: University of North Carolina Press, 1990.

Devereux, Joanna. *Patriarchy and Its Discontents: Sexual Politics in Selected Novels and Stories of Thomas Hardy.* London: Routledge, 2003.

Dowling, Linda. *Hellenism and Homosexuality in Victorian Oxford.* Ithaca, N.Y.: Cornell University Press, 1994.

Federico, Annette. *Masculine Identity in Hardy and Gissing.* Rutherford, N.Y.: Fairleigh Dickinson University Press, 1991.

Fernando, Lloyd. *'New Women' in the Late Victorian Novel.* State College, Penn.: Pennsylvania State University Press, 1977.

Heilmann, Ann, ed. *The Late Victorian Marriage Question.* 5 vols. London: Routledge Thoemmes, 1998.

Heilmann, Ann. *New Woman Strategies: Sarah Grand, Olive Schreiner, Mona Caird.* Manchester: Manchester University Press, 2004.

Hollis, Patricia. *Women in Public: The Women's Movement, 1850–1900.* London: George Allen & Unwin, 1979.

Horstman, Allen. *Victorian Divorce.* London: Croom Helm, 1985.

Jeffreys, Sheila. *The Spinster and Her Enemies: Feminism and Sexuality, 1880–1930.* London: Pandora Press, 1985.

Langland, Elizabeth. *Nobody's Angels: Middle Class Women and Domestic Ideology in Victorian Culture.* Ithaca, N.Y.: Cornell University Press, 1995.

Ledger, Sally. *The New Woman: Fiction and Feminism at the Fin de Siècle.* Manchester University Press, 1997.

McLaren, Angus. *The Trials of Masculinity: Policing Sexual Boundaries, 1870–1930.* Chicago: University of Chicago Press, 1997.

Mallett, Phillip. 'Women and Marriage in Victorian Society'. *Marriage and Property*, ed. Elizabeth M. Craik. Aberdeen: Aberdeen University Press, 1984: 159–89.

Mallett, Phillip. 'Hardy and Masculinity: *A Pair of Blue Eyes* and *Jude the Obscure*'. Morgan: 387–402.

Mason, Michael. *The Making of Victorian Sexuality.* Oxford: Oxford University Press, 1994.

Mason, Michael. *The Making of Victorian Sexual Attitudes.* Oxford: Oxford University Press, 1994.

Poovey, Mary. *Uneven Developments: The Ideological Work of Gender in Mid-Victorian England.* Chicago: University of Chicago Press, 1988.

Richardson, Angelique, and Chris Willis, eds. *The New Woman in Fiction and Fact: Fin-de-Siècle Feminisms.* London: Palgrave Macmillan, 2001.

Roper, Michael, and John Tosh, eds. *Manful Assertions: Masculinities in Britain Since 1800.* London: Routledge, 1991.

Russet, Cynthia Eagle. *Sexual Science: The Victorian Construction of Womanhood.* Cambridge, Mass.: Harvard University Press, 1989.

Sedgwick, Eve Kosofsky. *Between Men: English Literature and Male Homosocial Desire.* New York: Columbia University Press, 1985

Shanley, Mary Lyndon. *Feminism, Marriage, and the Law in Victorian England.* Princeton, N.J.: Princeton University Press, 1989.

Showalter, Elaine. *Sexual Anarchy: Gender and Culture at the Fin de Siècle.* London: Bloomsbury, 1991.

Tosh, John. *Manliness and Masculinities in Nineteenth-Century Britain: Essays on Gender, Family and Empire.* London: Pearson Education, 2005.

Tosh, John. *A Man's Place: Masculinity and the Middle-Class Home in Victorian England.* New Haven, Conn.: Yale University Press, 2007.

Vance, Norman. *The Sinews of the Spirit: The Ideal of Christian Manliness in Victorian Literature and Religious Thought.* Cambridge: Cambridge University Press, 1985.

Weeks, Jeffrey. *Sex, Politics and Society: The Regulation of Sexuality Since 1800.* London: Longman, 1981.

### SCIENCE AND CULTURE

Amigoni, David. *Colonies, Cults and Evolution: Literature, Science and Culture in Nineteenth-Century Writing.* Cambridge: Cambridge University Press, 2007.

Beer, Gillian. *Darwin's Plots: Evolutionary Narrative in Darwin, George Eliot and Nineteenth-Century Fiction.* 3rd edition; Cambridge: Cambridge University Press, 2009.

Beer, Gillian. *Open Fields: Science in Cultural Encounter.* Oxford: Clarendon Press, 1996.

Bowler, Peter J. *Evolution: The History of an Idea.* 4th edition; Berkeley: University of California Press, 2009.

Carroll, Joseph. *Literary Darwinism: Evolution, Human Nature, and Literature.* London: Routledge, 2004.

Christie, John, and Sally Shuttleworth, eds. *Nature Transfigured: Science and Literature 1700–1900*. Manchester: Manchester University Press, 1989.

Clarke, G. W., ed. *Rediscovering Hellenism: The Hellenic Inheritance and the English Imagination*. Cambridge: Cambridge University Press, 1989.

Collini, Stefan. *Public Moralists: Political Thought and Intellectual Life in Britain 1850–1930*. Oxford: Clarendon Press, 1991.

Cosslett, Tess. *The 'Scientific Movement' and Victorian Literature*. Brighton: Harvester Press, 1982.

Dale, Peter Allan. *In Pursuit of a Scientific Culture: Science, Art and Society in the Victorian Age*. Madison: University of Wisconsin Press, 1989.

Dowson, Gowan. *Darwin, Literature and Victorian Respectability*. Cambridge: Cambridge University Press, 2007.

Gilmour, Robin. *The Victorian Period: The Intellectual and Cultural Context of English Literature, 1830–1890*. London: Longman, 1993.

Glendening, John. *The Evolutionary Imagination in Late Victoirian Novels*. Aldershot: Ashgate, 2007.

Gossin, Pamela. *Thomas Hardy's Novel Universe: Astronomy, Cosmology and Gender in the Post-Darwinian World*. Aldershot: Ashgate, 2007.

Heyck, T. W. *The Transformation of Intellectual Life in Victorian England*. London: Croom Helm, 1982.

Janet Oppenheim, '*Shattered Nerves': Doctors, Patients and Depression in the Nineteenth Century*. Oxford: Oxford University Press 1991.

Jenkyns, Richard. *The Victorians and Ancient Greece*. Cambridge, Mass.: Harvard University Press, 1980.

Levine, George, ed. *One Culture: Essays in Science and Literature*. Madison: University of Wisconsin Press, 1987.

Levine, George. *Darwin and the Novelists: Patterns of Science in Victorian Fiction*. Chicago: University of Chicago Press, 1988.

Luckhurst, Roger, and Justine McDonagh, eds. *Transactions and Encounters: Science and Culture in the Nineteenth Century*. Manchester: Manchester University Press, 2002.

Morton, Peter. *The Vital Science: Biology and the Literary Imagination, 1860–1900*. London: George Allen & Unwin, 1984.

Paradis, James, and Thomas Postlewait, eds. *Victorian Science and Victorian Values: Literary Perspectives*. New Brunswick, N.J.: Rutgers University Press, 1985.

Richardson, Angelique. *Love and Eugenics in the Late Nineteenth Century: Rational Reproduction and the New Woman.* Oxford: Oxford University Press, 2003.

Richardson, Angelique, 'Hardy and Science: A Chapter of Accidents'. Mallett: 156–80.

Rimmer, Mary. 'Hardy, Victorian Culture and Provinciality'. Mallett: 135–55.

Small, Helen, and Trudi Tate, eds. *Literature, Science, Psychoanalysis, 1830–1970.* Oxford: Oxford University Press, 2003.

Turner, Frank. *The Greek Heritage in Victorian Britain.* New Haven, Conn.: Yale University Press, 1981.

Young, Robert M. *Darwin's Metaphor: Nature's Place in Victorian Culture.* Cambridge: Cambridge University Press, 1985.

### ARCHAEOLOGY, ANTHROPOLOGY, AND LANGUAGE

Ashton, Michael. *Interpreting the Landscape: Landscape Archaeology and Local History.* London: Routledge, 1997.

Blake, N. F. *Non-Standard Language in English Literature.* London: Deutsch, 1981.

Bowler, Peter. *The Invention of Progress: The Victorians and the Past.* Oxford: Basil Blackwell, 1990.

Burrow, J. W. *A Liberal Descent: Victorian Historians and the English Past.* Cambridge: Cambridge University Press, 1981.

Chapman, Raymond. *The Language of Thomas Hardy.* London: Macmillan, 1990.

Clodd, Edward. *The Childhood of the World. A Simple Account of Man in Early Times.* London: Macmillan, 1873.

Daniel, Glynn. *A Short History of Archaeology.* London: Thames and Hudson, 1981.

Daniel, Glynn, and Colin Renfrew. *The Idea of Prehistory.* Edinburgh: Edinburgh University Press, 1988.

Desmond, Adrian. *Archetypes and Ancestors: Palaeontology in Victorian London, 1850–75.* Chicago: University of Chicago Press, 1982.

Dorson, Richard. *The British Folklorists. A History.* London: Routledge & Kegan Paul, 1968.

Dowling, Linda. 'Victorian Oxford and the Science of Language'. *Publications of the Modern Language Association* 97 (1982): 160–78.

Dowling, Linda. *Language and Decadence in the Victorian Fin de Siècle.* Princeton, N.J.: Princeton University Press, 1986.

Elliott, Ralph W. V. *Thomas Hardy's English*. Oxford: Basil Blackwell, 1984.

Firor, Ruth. *Folkways in Thomas Hardy*. Philadelphia: University of Pennsylvania Press.

Hirooka, Hideo. *Thomas Hardy's Use of Dialect*. Tokyo: Shinozaki Shorin, 1983.

Hudson, Kenneth. *A Social History of Archaeology: The British Experience*. London: Macmillan, 1981.

Ingham, Patricia. 'Thomas Hardy and the Dorset Dialect'. *Five Hundred Years of Words and Sounds*, ed. E. G. Stanley and D. Gray. Cambridge: D. S. Brewer, 1983: 84–91.

Kuklich, Henrika. *The Savage Within: The Social History of British Anthropology, 1885–1945*. Cambridge University Press, 1991.

Levine, Philippa A. *The Amateur and the Professional: Antiquarians, Archaeologists and Historians*. Cambridge: Cambridge University Press, 1986.

Page, Norman. 'Hardy and the English Language'. *Thomas Hardy: The Writer and His Background*, ed. Norman Page. London: Bell & Hyman: 151–72.

Radford, Andrew. *Thomas Hardy and the Survivals of Time*. Aldershot: Ashgate, 2003.

Stocking Jr., George W. *Victorian Anthropology*. New York: Free Press, 1987.

Taylor, Dennis. *Hardy's Literary Language and Victorian Philology*. Oxford: Clarendon Press, 1993.

Udal, John Symonds. *Dorsetshire Folklore (with a Fore-Say by William Barnes)*. 2nd edition; Guernsey: Toucan Press, 1970.

Van Riper, A. Bowdoin. *Men Among the Mammoths: Victorian Science and the Discovery of Human Prehistory*. Chicago: Chicago University Press, 1993.

Wright, Joseph, ed. *The English Dialect Dictionary*. 6 vols. Oxford University Press, 1898–1905.

Zeitler, Michael. *Representations of Culture: Thomas Hardy's Wessex and Victorian Anthropology*. New York: Peter Lang, 2007.

### PHILOSOPHY AND RELIGION

Annan, Noel, *Leslie Stephen: The Godless Victorian*. London: Weidenfeld & Nicolson, 1984.

Bebbington, D. W. *Evangelicalism in Modern Britain: A History from the 1730s to the 1980s*. London: Unwin Hyman, 1989.

Chadwick, Owen. *The Victorian Church*. 2 vols. Oxford: Oxford University Press, 1966 and 1970.

Collins, Deborah. *Thomas Hardy and His God: A Liturgy of Unbelief*. London: Macmillan, 1990.

Cosslett, Tess, ed. *Science and Religion in the Nineteenth Century*. Cambridge: Cambridge University Press, 1984.

Fraser, Hilary. 'The Victorian Novel and Religion'. Brantlinger and Thesing: 101–18.

Hilton, Boyd. *The Age of Atonement: The Influence of Evangelicalism on Social and Economic Thought, 1785–1865*. Oxford: Oxford University Press, 1992.

Himmelfarb, Gertrude. *Victorian Minds*. London: Weidenfeld & Nicolson, 1968.

Jasper, David, and T. R. Wright, eds. *The Critical Spirit and the Will to Believe: Essays in Nineteenth-Century Literature and Religion*. London: Macmillan, 1989.

Jay, Elisabeth, ed. *The Evangelical and Oxford Movements*. Cambridge: Cambridge University Press, 1983.

Lightman, Bernard. *The Origins of Agnosticism: Victorian Unbelief and the Limits of Knowledge*. Baltimore: Johns Hopkins University Press, 1987.

Mallett, Phillip. 'Hardy and Philosophy'. Wilson: 21–35.

Parsons, Gerald, ed. *Religion in Victorian Britain*. 4 vols. Manchester: Manchester University Press, 1988.

Reardon, B. M. G. *Religious Thought in the Victorian Age: A Survey from Coleridge to Gore*. London: Longman, 1980

Royle, Edward. *Radicals, Secularists, and Republicans: Popular Freethought in Britain, 1866–1915*. Manchester: Manchester University Press, 1980.

Ryan, Alan. *J. S. Mill*. London: Routledge & Kegan Paul, 1975.

Symondson, Anthony, ed. *The Victorian Crisis of Faith*. London: SPCK, 1970.

Ten, C. L., ed. *Mill's 'On Liberty': A Critical Guide*. Cambridge: Cambridge University Press, 2008.

Turner, Frank M. *Between Science and Religion: The Reaction to Scientific Naturalism in Late Victorian England*. New Haven, Conn.: Yale University Press, 1974.

Wheeler, Michael. *Death and the Future Life in Victorian Literature and Theology*. Cambridge: Cambridge University Press, 1990.

Wright, T. R. *The Religion of Humanity: The Impact of Comtean Positivism on Victorian Britain*. Cambridge: Cambridge University Press, 1986.

LAW AND CENSORSHIP

Conley, Carolyn. 'Rape and Justice in Victorian England'. *Victorian Studies* 29:4 (1986): 519–36.

Craig, Alec. *The Banned Books of England and Other Countries: A Study of the Conception of Literary Obscenity*. London: George Allen & Unwin, 1937.

Davis, William A. *Thomas Hardy and the Law: Legal Presences in Hardy's Life and Fiction*. Newark: University of Delaware Press, 2003.

Lacey, Nicola. *Women, Crime, and Literature: From Moll Flanders to Tess of the d'Urbervilles*. Oxford: Oxford University Press, 2008.

Marsh, Joss. *Word Crimes: Blasphemy, Culture, and Literature in Nineteenth-Century England*. Chicago: University of Chicago Press, 1998.

Posner, Richard A. *Law and Literature: A Misunderstood Relation*. Cambridge, Mass.: Harvard University Press, 1988.

Schramm, Jan-Melissa. *Testimony and Advocacy in Victorian Law, Literature and Theology*. Cambridge: Cambridge University Press, 2000.

Thomas, Donald. *A Long Time Burning: The History of Literary Censorship in England*. London: Routledge & Kegan Paul, 1965.

Walkowitz, Judith R. *Prostitution and Victorian Society: Women, Class, and the State*. Cambridge: Cambridge University Press, 1980.

Ward, Ian, ed. *Law and Literature: Possibilities and Perspectives*. Cambridge: Cambridge University Press, 1995.

Wiener, Martin J. *Reconstructing the Criminal: Culture, Law, and Policy in England, 1830–1914*. Cambridge: Cambridge University Press, 1989.

Williams, Melanie. *Empty Justice: One Hundred Years of Law, Literature and Philosophy*. London: Cavendish Publishing, 2002.


MUSIC, ART, FILM

Andres, Sophie. *The Pre-Raphaelite Art of the Victorian Novel: Narrative Challenges to Visual Gendered Boundaries*. Columbus: Ohio State University Press, 2005.

Asquith, Mark. *Thomas Hardy: Metaphysics and Music*. London: Palgrave Macmillan, 2005.

Beegan, Gerry. *The Mass Image: A Social History of Photomechanical Reproduction in Victorian London*. Basingstoke: Palgrave Macmillan, 2008.

Berger, Sheila. *Thomas Hardy and Visual Structures: Framing, Disruption, Process*. New York: New York University Press, 1990.

Bullen, J. B. *The Expressive Eye: Fiction and Perception in the Works of Thomas Hardy*. Oxford: Clarendon Press, 1986.

Bullen, J. B. 'Hardy and the Visual Arts'. Wilson: 210–22.

Dalziel, Pamela. 'Drawings and Withdrawings: The Vicissitudes of Thomas Hardy's *Wessex Poems*'. *Studies in Bibliography* 50 (1997): 390–400.

Giddings, Robert, Peter Selby, and Chris Wensley. *Screening the Novel: The Theory and Politics of Literary Adaptation*. London: Macmillan, 1990.

Grundy, Joan. *Hardy and the Sister Arts*. London: Macmillan, 1979.

Hughes, John. '*Ecstatic Sound': Music and Individuality in the Work of Thomas Hardy*. Aldershot: Ashgate, 2001.

Jackson, Arlene M. *Illustration and the Novels of Thomas Hardy*. Totowa, N.J.: Rowman and Littlefield, 1981.

Klein, Michael, and Parker, Gillian, eds. *The English Novel and the Movies*. New York: Ungar, 1981.

Lambourne, Lionel. *The Aesthetic Movement*. London: Phaidon, 1996.

Maas, Jeremy. *Victorian Painters*. London: Barrie & Jenkins, 1978.

Marsh, Joss, and Kamilla Elliott. 'The Victorian Novel in Film and on Television'. Brantlinger and Thesing: 458–77.

Maxwell, Richard, ed. *The Victorian Illustrated Book*. Charlottesville: University Press of Virginia, 2002.

Merrill, Linda. *A Pot of Paint: Aesthetics on Trial in 'Whistler v Ruskin'*. Washington, D.C.: Smithsonian Institution Press, 1992.

Niemeyer, Paul J. *Seeing Hardy: Film and Television Adaptations of the Fiction of Thomas Hardy*. Jefferson, N.C.: McFarland, 2003.

Seymour, Claire. 'Hardy and Music: Uncanny Sounds'. Wilson: 223–38.

Spear, Jeffrey. 'The Other Arts: Victorian Visual Culture'. Brantlinger and Thesing: 189–206.

Warner, Eric, and Graham Hough, eds. *Strangeness and Beauty: An Anthology of Aesthetic Criticism 1840–1910*. 2 vols. Cambridge University Press, 1983.

Wright, Terry, ed. *Thomas Hardy on Screen*. Cambridge: Cambridge University Press, 2005.

Yeazell, Ruth Bernard. *Art of the Everyday: Dutch Painting and the Realist Novel*. Princeton, N.J.: Princeton University Press, 2008.

# INDEX

CPSIA information can be obtained at www.ICGtesting.com
Printed in the USA
LVOW08s1338300816

502483LV00004B/161/P